다락원

TOEIC

Intensive

저자 LORI

전 LORI 어학원 원장(만점강사)
전 경성대학교 대학원 디지털디자인학과 외래교수
전 삼성 SDI, 삼성자동차, LG전자, 한진해운, 고려제강 등 기업체 출강

저서

시나공토익 FINAL 1000제 2탄 RC (길벗)
모질게 토익 이코노미 RC 1000제 (21세기 북스)
TNT TOEIC 입문 (다락원)
TNT TOEIC 기초 (다락원)
TNT TOEIC 실전연습 (다락원)
토익 정답지 모의고사 2005 (ENM 리서치)
토익 정답지 2004 (ENM 리서치)

TNT TOEIC Intensive

지은이 LORI
펴낸이 정규도
펴낸곳 (주)다락원

초판 1쇄 인쇄 2016년 4월 20일
초판 5쇄 발행 2021년 3월 23일

책임편집 노동일, 조상익
디자인 김나경, 윤현주

다락원 경기도 파주시 문발로 211
내용문의 (02)736-2031 내선 550~551
구입문의 (02)736-2031 내선 250~252
Fax (02)732-2037
출판등록 1977년 9월 16일 제406-2008-000007호

값 15,800원 (본책+해설집+MP3 CD)

ISBN 978-89-277-0916-9 18740
     978-89-277-0914-5 18740(set)

http://www.darakwon.co.kr
다락원 홈페이지를 방문하시면 상세한 출판정보와 함께 동영상
강좌, MP3 자료 등 다양한 어학 정보를 얻으실 수 있습니다.

TOEIC

Intensive

Preface

이 교재는 500점대에 머물러있는 토익 초급 학습자들이 한 달 안에 중급 레벨인 700점 이상의 점수를 받을 수 있도록 하기 위한 목적으로 만들어졌다. 만약 토익을 처음 접하거나 점수대가 400점대인 학생이라면 이 책의 전 단계에 해당하는 〈TNT TOEIC Basic Course〉편을 권한다.

필자는 실제 교육 현장에서 오랫동안 강의를 하면서 시간과 노력을 많이 들이는데도 점수를 올리지 못하는 학습자들을 보며 많이 안타까웠고, 그러한 학생들에게 도움이 되었으면 하는 바람으로 700점대의 점수를 받기 위해 반드시 알아야하는 필수 요점들만으로 교재를 구성하였다.

시중에 나와 있는 많은 기본서들은 700점대의 점수를 받기 위한 학습서로서는 LC와 RC 각각의 내용이 너무 방대하기 때문에 500점대의 점수를 받는 학습자들은 교재의 두께에 부담을 느낄 수밖에 없는 것 같다.

토익은 토익만의 문제 유형이 있기 때문에 이에 맞추어 효율적으로 학습한다면 원하는 점수를 단기간 내에 얻을 수 있다. 다시 말해, 출제 의도를 파악하지 못한 상태에서 무작정 문제만 많이 푼다고 해도 성적은 쉽게 오르지 않는다는 것이다.

이 교재는 필자의 현장 강의 경험을 바탕으로 학습자들이 빠르고 쉽게 토익 문제를 이해할 수 있도록 반드시 숙지해야 하는 파트별 빈출 중요 포인트를 유형별로 제시하였고, 이를 곧바로 적용해서 연습해 볼 수 있는 맞춤형 문제와 그 문제 풀이를 통해 심화학습이 가능하도록 하였다. 700점대 달성을 위한 내용들만으로 책을 구성했기 때문에 이에 맞추어 집중적으로 학습한다면 목표하는 점수를 금방 성취할 수 있을 것이다.

학습자들은 'LC+RC' 한 달 학습용으로 만들어진 이 책을 통해 700점대에 꼭 필요한 빈출 유형과 빈출 어휘, 빈출 표현, 빈출 구문 그리고 필수 문법사항을 정리하고, 실전 문제 유형으로 재구성된 연습문제를 통해 토익에 대한 적응력을 키워나갈 수 있을 것이다.

실력은 효율적인 학습과 꾸준한 훈련 속에서 향상되는 것이다. 문제의 정답만을 외울 것이 아니라 문제의 유형과 요점을 정확히 이해하고 전체 문맥에 주의하여 교재의 내용을 학습한다면 한 달 만에 좋은 성과를 낼 수 있을 것이라 확신한다.

LORI

Contents

 별책 정답 및 해설

What is the TOEIC?

• TOEIC이란?

TOEIC(Test of English for International Communication)은 영어를 모국어로 사용하지 않는 사람이 국제 환경에서 생활하거나 업무를 수행할 때 필요한 실용 영어 능력 수준을 평가하는 시험이다. 현재 한국과 일본은 물론 전 세계 약 60여 개 국가에서 연간 약 4백만 명 이상의 수험생들이 응시하고 있으며, 이 수험 결과는 인력 채용 및 승진, 해외 파견 근무자 선발 등 다양한 방면에 활용되고 있다.

• TOEIC 시험의 구성

구성	Part	내용		문항 수	시간	배점
Listening Comprehension	1	사진 묘사		6	45분	495점
	2	질의 응답		25		
	3	짧은 대화		39		
	4	설명문		30		
Reading Comprehension	5	단문 공란 채우기		30	75분	495점
	6	장문 공란 채우기		16		
	7	독해	단일 지문	29		
			복수 지문	25		
Total	7 Parts			200문항	120분	990점

• TOEIC 시험 출제 분야

TOEIC 시험의 목적은 일상생활과 업무 수행에 필요한 영어 능력을 평가하는 것이기 때문에 시험 출제 범위도 이를 벗어나지 않는다. 출제 범위는 일상적인 상황 이외에 비즈니스와 관련된 주제를 다루고 있기는 하지만 전문적인 지식을 묻는 수준은 아니다. 마찬가지로, 특정 국가나 문화에 대한 이해를 요구하는 문제 또한 출제되지 않는다. 구체적인 출제 범위는 아래와 같다.

Corporate Development 협력 개발	research, product development
Dining Out 외식	business and informal lunches, banquets, receptions
Entertainment 엔터테인먼트	cinema, theater, music, art, exhibitions, museums, media
Finance and Budgeting 재무·예산	banking, investments, taxes, accounting, billing
General Business 일반 업무	contracts, negotiations, mergers, marketing, sales, warranties, business planning, conferences, labor relations
Health 건강	medical insurance, visiting doctors, dentists, clinics, hospitals
Housing/Corporate Property 주택·법인 재산	construction, specifications, buying and renting, electric and gas services
Manufacturing 제조	assembly lines, plant management, quality control
Office 사무실	board meetings, committees, letters, memoranda, telephone, fax and e-mail messages, office equipment and furniture, office procedures
Personnel 인사	recruiting, hiring, retiring, salaries, promotions, job applications, job advertisements, pensions, awards
Purchasing 구매	shopping, ordering supplies, shipping, invoices
Technical Areas 기술 분야	electronics, technology, computers, laboratories and related equipment, technical specifications
Travel 여행	trains, airplanes, taxis, buses, ships, ferries, tickets, schedules, station and airport announcements, car rentals, hotels, reservations, delays and cancellations

About This Book

• PART 1 사진 묘사 •

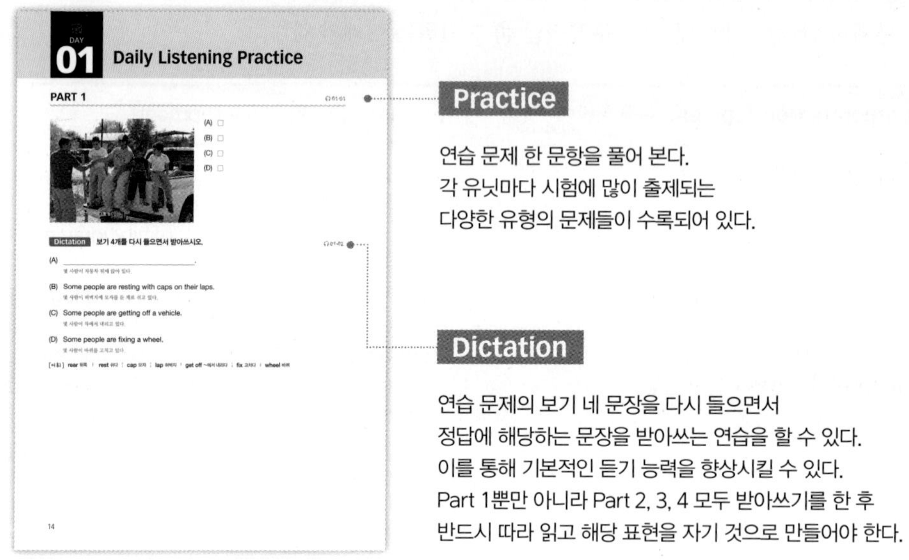

Practice

연습 문제 한 문항을 풀어 본다.
각 유닛마다 시험에 많이 출제되는
다양한 유형의 문제들이 수록되어 있다.

Dictation

연습 문제의 보기 네 문장을 다시 들으면서
정답에 해당하는 문장을 받아쓰는 연습을 할 수 있다.
이를 통해 기본적인 듣기 능력을 향상시킬 수 있다.
Part 1뿐만 아니라 Part 2, 3, 4 모두 받아쓰기를 한 후
반드시 따라 읽고 해당 표현을 자기 것으로 만들어야 한다.

• PART 2 질의 - 응답 •

Practice

각 유닛마다 네 문항의
예제를 풀어 봄으로써
해당 유형의 문제에 익숙해질 수 있다.

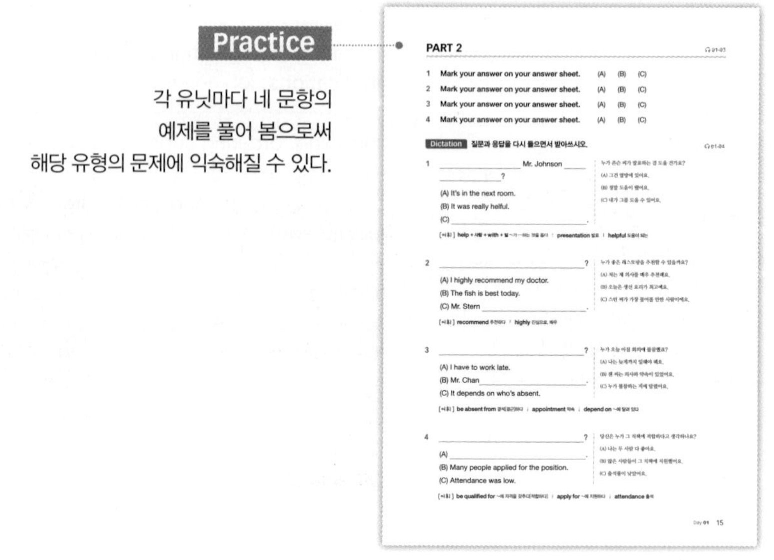

Practice

Part 3은 두 세트,
Part 4는 한 세트의
연습 문제를 풀어 볼 수
있도록 구성되어 있다.

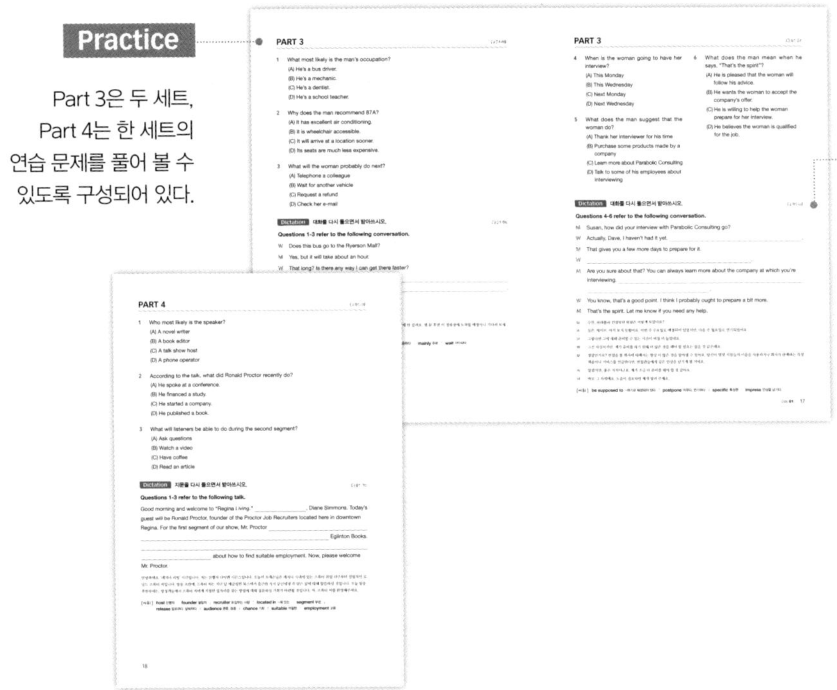

Dictation

Part 3의 경우에는
대화문을, Part 4의 경우
에는 설명문을 다시 들으
면서 빈칸을 채우는 연습
을 한다. 정답의 단서가
되는 내용들이 빈칸으로
구성되어 있다.

• ACTUAL TEST •

Practice

LC의 마지막 유닛인 Day
19·20은 Actual Test로
구성되어 있다. 실전과 똑
같은 문제를 풀어보면서
학습한 내용을 최종적으로
연습해 볼 수 있다.

About This Book

• PART 5 단문 빈칸 채우기 •

문법

각 유닛마다 시험에 많이
출제되는 다양한 유형의
문법 사항들이 수록되어 있다.

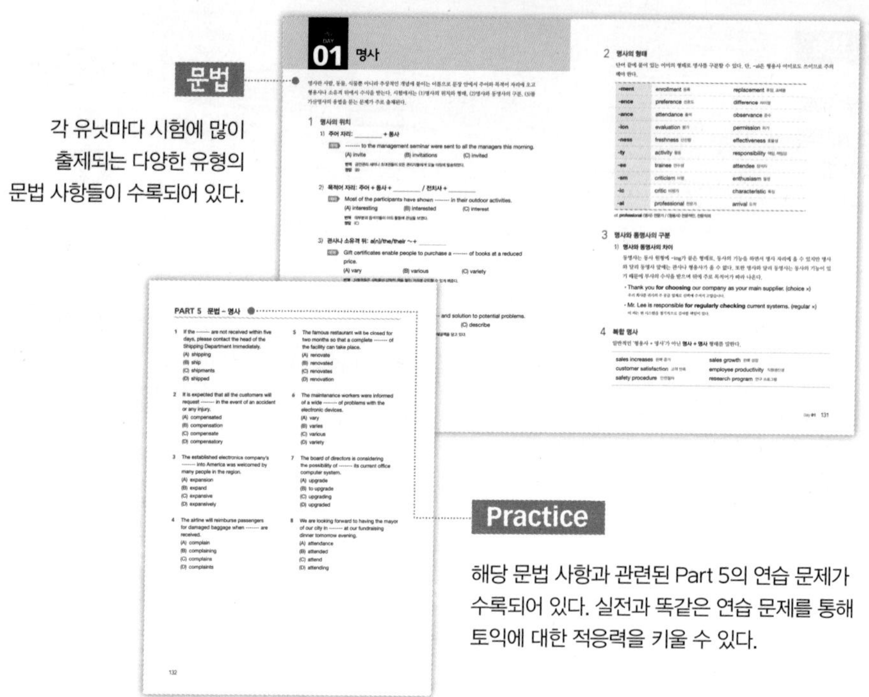

Practice

해당 문법 사항과 관련된 Part 5의 연습 문제가
수록되어 있다. 실전과 똑같은 연습 문제를 통해
토익에 대한 적응력을 키울 수 있다.

• PART 6 장문 빈칸 채우기 •

Practice

Day 1, 2, 6, 8, 11, 13, 16에는
Part 5 연습 문제와 함께
Part 6 장문 빈칸 채우기의
연습 문제가 수록되어 있다.

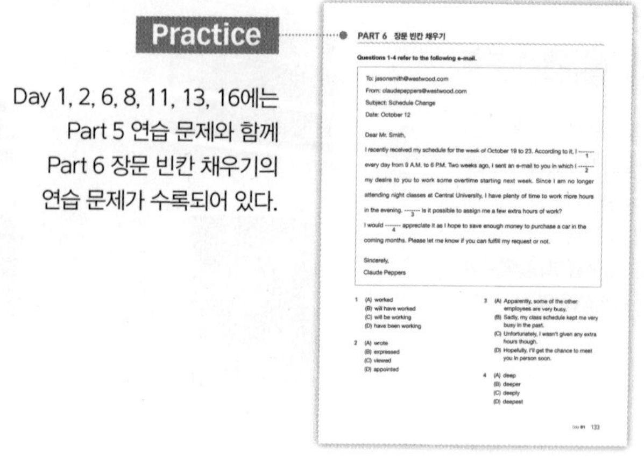

• PART 7 독해 •

단일 지문

Day 2, 4, 7, 9, 12, 14, 17에는
Part 7의 단일 지문이 수록되어 있다.
다양한 주제의 지문들을 활용한 문제들이 수록되어
있어, 실제 시험에 대한 대비를 할 수 있다.

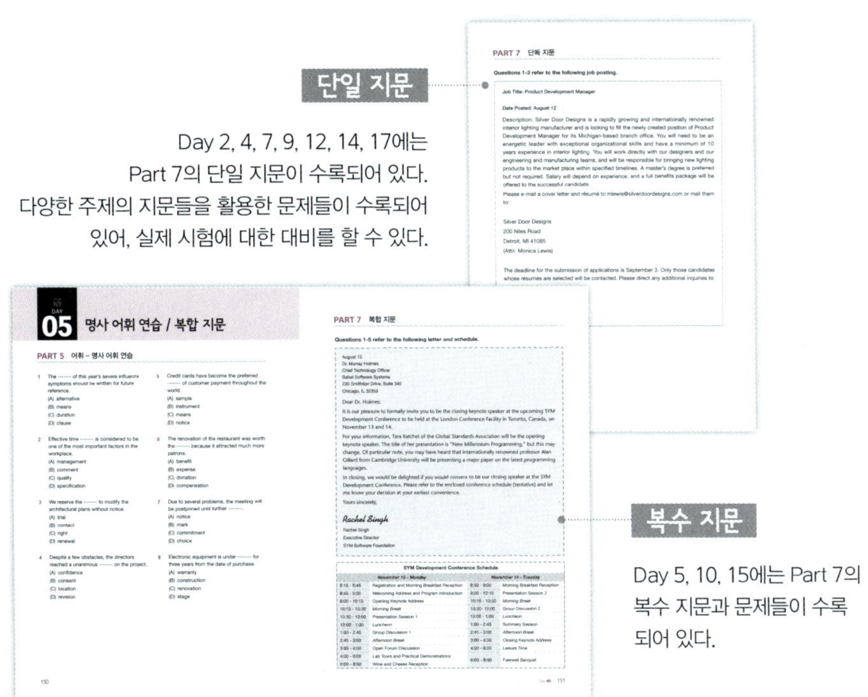

복수 지문

Day 5, 10, 15에는 Part 7의
복수 지문과 문제들이 수록
되어 있다.

• ACTUAL TEST •

Practice

RC의 마지막 유닛인 Day
19·20은 Actual Test로
구성되어 있다. 실전과 똑
같은 문제를 풀어보면서
학습한 내용을 최종적으로
연습해 볼 수 있다.

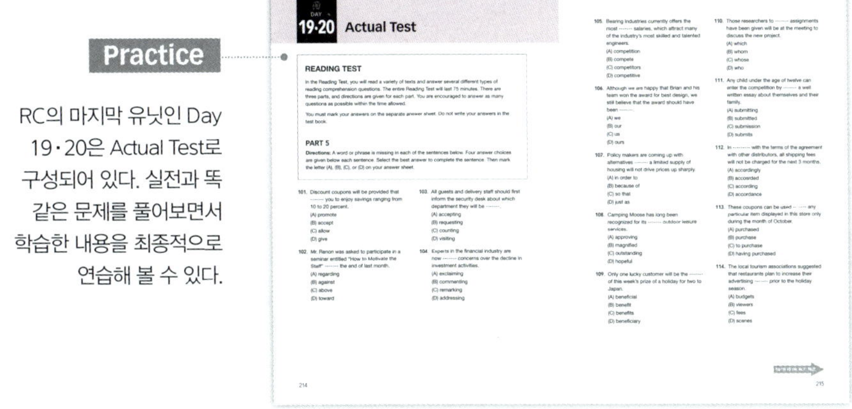

Listening
Comprehension

PART 1

(A) ☐
(B) ☐
(C) ☐
(D) ☐

Dictation   보기 4개를 다시 들으면서 받아쓰시오.

🎧 01-02

(A) _______________________________________.

몇 사람이 자동차 뒤에 앉아 있다.

(B) Some people are resting with caps on their laps.

몇 사람이 허벅지에 모자를 둔 채로 쉬고 있다.

(C) Some people are getting off a vehicle.

몇 사람이 차에서 내리고 있다.

(D) Some people are fixing a wheel.

몇 사람이 바퀴를 고치고 있다.

[어휘] rear 뒤쪽 ｜ rest 쉬다 ｜ cap 모자 ｜ lap 허벅지 ｜ get off ~에서 내리다 ｜ fix 고치다 ｜ wheel 바퀴

PART 2

1 Mark your answer on your answer sheet.   (A)   (B)   (C)

2 Mark your answer on your answer sheet.   (A)   (B)   (C)

3 Mark your answer on your answer sheet.   (A)   (B)   (C)

4 Mark your answer on your answer sheet.   (A)   (B)   (C)

Dictation 질문과 응답을 다시 들으면서 받아쓰시오.   🎧 01-04

1 ________________________ Mr. Johnson ________

________________ ?

(A) It's in the next room.

(B) It was really helful.

(C) ________________________ .

누가 존슨 씨가 발표하는 걸 도울 건가요?

(A) 그건 옆방에 있어요.

(B) 정말 도움이 됐어요.

(C) 내가 그를 도울 수 있어요.

[어휘] **help + 사람 + with + 일** ~가 …하는 것을 돕다 | **presentation** 발표 | **helpful** 도움이 되는

2 ________________________ ?

(A) I highly recommend my doctor.

(B) The fish is best today.

(C) Mr. Stern ________________ .

누가 좋은 레스토랑을 추천할 수 있을까요?

(A) 저는 제 의사를 매우 추천해요.

(B) 오늘은 생선 요리가 최고예요.

(C) 스턴 씨가 가장 물어볼 만한 사람이에요.

[어휘] **recommend** 추천하다 | **highly** 진심으로, 매우

3 ________________________ ?

(A) I have to work late.

(B) Mr. Chan ________________ .

(C) It depends on who's absent.

누가 오늘 아침 회의에 불참했죠?

(A) 나는 늦게까지 일해야 해요.

(B) 챈 씨는 의사와 약속이 있었어요.

(C) 누가 불참하는 지에 달렸어요.

[어휘] **be absent from** 결석[결근]하다 | **appointment** 약속 | **depend on** ~에 달려 있다

4 ________________________ ?

(A) ________________ .

(B) Many people applied for the position.

(C) Attendance was low.

당신은 누가 그 직책에 적합하다고 생각하나요?

(A) 나는 두 사람 다 좋아요.

(B) 많은 사람들이 그 직책에 지원했어요.

(C) 출석률이 낮았어요.

[어휘] **be qualified for** ~에 자격을 갖추다[적합하다] | **apply for** ~에 지원하다 | **attendance** 출석

PART 3

1   What most likely is the man's occupation?

(A) He's a bus driver.

(B) He's a mechanic.

(C) He's a dentist.

(D) He's a school teacher.

2   Why does the man recommend 87A?

(A) It has excellent air conditioning.

(B) It is wheelchair accessible.

(C) It will arrive at a location sooner.

(D) Its seats are much less expensive.

3   What will the woman probably do next?

(A) Telephone a colleague

(B) Wait for another vehicle

(C) Request a refund

(D) Check her e-mail

Dictation   대화를 다시 들으면서 받아쓰시오.   🎧 01-06

Questions 1-3 refer to the following conversation.

W   Does this bus go to the Ryerson Mall?

M   Yes, but it will take about an hour.

W   That long? Is there any way I can get there faster?

M   ________________________. ___________________________________

the Gardner Highway. ____.

W   이 버스가 라이어슨 몰로 가나요?

M   네, 하지만 한 시간 가량 걸려요.

W   그렇게나 오래요? 그곳에 더 빨리 갈 수 있는 방법은 없나요?

M   87A번 버스를 타세요. 주로 가드너 고속도로를 통해 가기 때문에 20분 밖에 안 걸려요. 몇 분 후면 이 정류장에 도착할 예정이니 기다려 보세요.

[어휘] **take** (시간이) 걸리다, (교통 수단을) 타다 | **fast** 빨리 | **travel** 가다, 이동하다 | **mainly** 주로 | **wait** 기다리다

4 When is the woman going to have her interview?

   (A) This Monday

   (B) This Wednesday

   (C) Next Monday

   (D) Next Wednesday

5 What does the man suggest that the woman do?

   (A) Thank her interviewer for his time

   (B) Purchase some products made by a company

   (C) Learn more about Parabolic Consulting

   (D) Talk to some of his employees about interviewing

6 What does the man mean when he says, "That's the spirit"?

   (A) He is pleased that the woman will follow his advice.

   (B) He wants the woman to accept the company's offer.

   (C) He is willing to help the woman prepare for her interview.

   (D) He believes the woman is qualified for the job.

Dictation 대화를 다시 들으면서 받아쓰시오.

🎧 01-08

Questions 4-6 refer to the following conversation.

M Susan, how did your interview with Parabolic Consulting go?

W Actually, Dave, I haven't had it yet. _______________________________.

M That gives you a few more days to prepare for it.

W _______________________________.

M Are you sure about that? You can always learn more about the company at which you're interviewing. _______________________________ _______________________________.

W You know, that's a good point. I think I probably ought to prepare a bit more.

M That's the spirit. Let me know if you need any help.

M 수잔, 파라볼라 컨설팅의 면접은 어떻게 보았나요?

W 실은, 데이브, 아직 보지 못했어요. 이번 주 수요일로 예정되어 있었지만, 다음 주 월요일로 연기되었어요.

M 그렇다면 그에 대해 준비할 수 있는 시간이 며칠 더 늘었네요.

W 그건 사실이지만, 제가 준비를 하기 위해 더 많은 것을 해야 할 필요는 없을 것 같은데요.

M 정말인가요? 면접을 볼 회사에 대해서는 항상 더 많은 것을 알아낼 수 있어요. 당신이 몇몇 직원들의 이름을 사용하거나 회사가 판매하는 특정 제품이나 서비스를 언급한다면, 면접관들에게 깊은 인상을 남기게 될 거예요.

W 알겠지만, 좋은 지적이군요. 제가 조금 더 준비를 해야 할 것 같아요.

M 바로 그 자세예요. 도움이 필요하면 제게 알려 주세요.

[어휘] **be supposed to** ~하기로 예정되어 있다 | **postpone** 미루다, 연기하다 | **specific** 특정한 | **impress** 인상을 남기다

PART 4

1 Who most likely is the speaker?

   (A) A novel writer

   (B) A book editor

   (C) A talk show host

   (D) A phone operator

2 According to the talk, what did Ronald Proctor recently do?

   (A) He spoke at a conference.

   (B) He financed a study.

   (C) He started a company.

   (D) He published a book.

3 What will listeners be able to do during the second segment?

   (A) Ask questions

   (B) Watch a video

   (C) Have coffee

   (D) Read an article

Dictation 지문을 다시 들으면서 받아쓰시오.　🎧 01-10

Questions 1-3 refer to the following talk.

Good morning and welcome to *Regina Living*. ＿＿＿＿＿＿＿＿＿＿＿＿, Diane Simmons. Today's guest will be Ronald Proctor, founder of the Proctor Job Recruiters located here in downtown Regina. For the first segment of our show, Mr. Proctor ＿＿＿＿＿＿＿＿＿＿＿＿＿＿＿＿＿＿＿＿＿＿＿＿＿＿＿＿＿＿＿ Eglinton Books.

＿＿＿＿＿＿＿＿＿＿＿＿＿＿ about how to find suitable employment. Now, please welcome Mr. Proctor.

안녕하세요, *레지나 리빙* 시간입니다. 저는 진행자 다이앤 시몬스입니다. 오늘의 초대손님은 레지나 시내에 있는 프록터 취업 리쿠루터 설립자인 로날드 프록터 씨입니다. 방송 초반에, 프록터 씨는 지난 달 에글링턴 북스에서 출간한 저서 *당신에게 꼭 맞는 일*에 대해 말씀하실 것입니다. 오늘 방송 후반부에는, 방청객들께서 프록터 씨에게 적절한 일자리를 찾는 방법에 대해 질문하실 기회가 마련될 것입니다. 자, 프록터 씨를 환영해주세요.

[어휘] **host** 진행자 | **founder** 설립자 | **recruiter** 모집하는 사람 | **located in** ~에 있는 | **segment** 부분 | **release** 발표하다, 발매하다 | **audience** 관중, 청중 | **chance** 기회 | **suitable** 적절한 | **employment** 고용

Daily Listening Practice

PART 1

🎧 02-01

(A) ☐
(B) ☐
(C) ☐
(D) ☐

Dictation 보기 4개를 다시 들으면서 받아쓰시오.

🎧 02-02

(A) Some plants are being hung from the ceiling.
식물들이 천장에 걸리는 중이다.

(B) ______________________________________.
남자들이 유니폼을 착용한 상태이다.

(C) A tablecloth is being removed.
식탁보가 치워지는 중이다.

(D) The chefs are lighting a candle.
주방장들이 촛불을 켜고 있다.

[어휘] **plants** 식물들 | **hang[-hung-hung]** 걸다 | **ceiling** 천장 | **wear** 착용하다 | **uniform** 제복 | **tablecloth** 식탁보 | **remove** 치우다, 제거하다 | **chef** 주방장 | **light** 켜다 | **candle** 촛불

1 Mark your answer on your answer sheet.　　(A)　(B)　(C)

2 Mark your answer on your answer sheet.　　(A)　(B)　(C)

3 Mark your answer on your answer sheet.　　(A)　(B)　(C)

4 Mark your answer on your answer sheet.　　(A)　(B)　(C)

Dictation　질문과 응답을 다시 들으면서 받아쓰시오.

🎧 02-04

1 __________________________________ ?

(A) My vacuum cleaner broke down.

(B) Next to the school.

(C) __________________________________ .

팩스 기계에 무슨 문제가 있어요?

(A) 내 진공청소기가 고장 났어요.

(B) 학교 옆에요.

(C) 출력이 안 돼요.

[어휘] **What's wrong with ~?** ~에 무슨 문제가 있어요? | **vacuum cleaner** 진공청소기 | **break down** 고장 나다 | **print** 인쇄[출력]하다

2 ______________________ Ms. Eden ______ ?

(A) She is hardworking.

(B) __________________________________ .

(C) She sent an e-mail.

이든 씨는 무슨 일을 합니까?

(A) 그녀는 열심히 일해요.

(B) 주로 행정 업무요.

(C) 그녀는 이메일을 보냈어요.

[어휘] **hardworking** 열심히 일하는 | **administrative** 경영의, 행정의

3 __________________________________ ?

(A) By the end of this week.

(B) Two hours and a half.

(C) __________________________________ .

우리는 몇 시에 쉬기로 되어 있나요?

(A) 이번 주 금요일까지요.

(B) 두 시간 반이요.

(C) 2시 30분에요.

[어휘] **be supposed to-V** ~하기로 되어 있다 | **take a break** 휴식하다

4 __________________________________ ?

(A) __________________________________ .

(B) The dining car is full.

(C) No, I'm not interested.

어떤 종류의 자동차를 구입했으면 하세요?

(A) 공간이 넓은 것으로요.

(B) 식당차가 꽉 찼어요.

(C) 아뇨, 관심 없어요.

[어휘] **plenty of** 많은 | **dining car** (기차의) 식당칸

PART 3

1 Who is the man?

    (A) A news reporter

    (B) A stage actor

    (C) A parking attendant

    (D) A baseball coach

2 What is the problem?

    (A) The woman's car won't start.

    (B) The front gate is locked.

    (C) The tickets are all sold out.

    (D) The facility is currently full.

3 What does the man suggest the woman do?

    (A) Try a different location

    (B) Return another day

    (C) Sit in another section

    (D) Request a full refund

Dictation 대화를 다시 들으면서 받아쓰시오. 🎧 02-06

Questions 1-3 refer to the following conversation.

M ____ .

W My two boys and I have tickets to see the baseball game here. I don't know what I'll do if I can't find a place to park.

M Oh, you must not have read the notice. ____________________________________ the St. Richard Outdoor Market.

____

________________________________ .

W Thank you very much for that information.

M 죄송하지만 이 주차장에는 빈 공간이 없습니다.

W 저와 제 두 아들은 이 야구 경기 티켓을 갖고 있어요. 주차할 곳을 찾지 못한다면 어떻게 해야 할 지 모르겠군요.

M 아, 공지를 읽지 못하셨나 보군요. 이곳에서 동쪽으로 한 블록 떨어진 곳인 세인트 리차드 야외시장 앞에 주차 공간이 좀 있어요. 시장은 오늘 이 일요일이라 문을 닫았지만 누구든 그곳 주차장을 사용할 수 있답니다.

W 좋은 정보 알려줘서 고마워요.

[**어휘**] **empty** 비어 있는 ｜ **space** 공간 ｜ **parking lot** 주차장 ｜ **place** 장소 ｜ **notice** 공지 ｜ **closed** 문을 닫은 ｜ **use** 사용하다 ｜ **information** 정보

4 What are the speakers mainly discussing?

    (A) How much to offer a job candidate

    (B) Which position they need a new employee for

    (C) The results of some interviews

    (D) When they should hire some employees

6 What will the speakers likely do next?

    (A) Decide which person to hire

    (B) Apply for some jobs at other companies

    (C) Conduct another interview

    (D) Submit their résumés

5 How does the man feel about Simon?

    (A) He was unimpressed by Simon.

    (B) He thought Simon was well prepared.

    (C) He liked how Simon answered the questions.

    (D) He believes Simon has the experience they need.

Dictation 대화를 다시 들으면서 받아쓰시오.

🎧02-08

Questions 4-6 refer to the following conversation.

W1 I thought Tony stood out more than the other two people we interviewed.

M Why do you feel that way?

W1 ____ .

W2 ____ .

M ___________________________________ . ___________________________________ . ___________________

___________________________________ .

W1 That's precisely how I feel.

W2 Well, I got a good feeling about him. I didn't really like either Tony or Marcia.

M I agree with you about Marcia but not regarding Tony.

W1   저는 면접을 본 다른 두 사람보다 토니가 더 뛰어나다고 생각했어요.

M   왜 그렇게 생각했죠?

W1   마케팅 경력이 많았고, 우리가 물어 본 질문에도 하나하나 잘 대처했고요.

W2   저도 그가 잘 했다고 생각하지만, 저는 사이먼이 고용하기에는 더 나은 인물인 것 같아요.

M   저는 반대로 느꼈어요. 저는 그로부터 전혀 깊은 인상을 받지 못했어요. 준비가 잘 된 것 같지가 않았고 몇몇 질문에는 대답을 주저하더군요.

W1   저도 똑같이 느꼈어요.

W2   음, 저는 그에 관해 좋은 인상을 받았어요. 저는 정말로 토니나 마샤는 모두 마음에 들지 않았어요.

M   마샤에 대해서는 당신과 같은 생각이지만, 토니에 관해서는 아니에요.

[어휘] **handle** 다루다, 처리하다 ǀ **opposite** 정반대의 것 ǀ **hesitate** 주저하다 ǀ **precisely** 정확히 ǀ **regarding** ~에 관해서

1   Where most likely are the listeners?

     (A) At a boarding gate

     (B) On an airplane

     (C) In the baggage claim area

     (D) At a check-in counter

2   What is mentioned about the problem?

     (A) It has been repaired.

     (B) It requires some new parts.

     (C) It will take ten minutes to fix.

     (D) It cannot be fixed right now.

3   What does the speaker mean when she says, "That's our way of saying sorry for inconveniencing you"?

     (A) The flight attendants will try to cheer up the passengers.

     (B) The captain will make up for the lost time in the air.

     (C) The airline will reimburse passengers some money.

     (D) The listeners will get some food as an apology.

Dictation   지문을 다시 들으면서 받아쓰시오.   🎧02-10

Questions 1-3 refer to the following announcement.

May I have your attention, please? I just spoke with Captain Russell, and he said that we're almost ready to depart. _______________________________

_______________________________. All they need to do _______________________________. Once they finish doing that, we'll close the doors and start taxiing to the runway. I know you're all eager to get going, so please take your seats and fasten your seatbelts. We should be in the air within the next ten minutes. On behalf of Eagle Airlines, I would like to apologize for this delay. _________

_______________________________. That's our way of saying sorry for inconveniencing you.

주목해 주시겠습니까? 저는 조금 전에 러셀 기장님과 이야기를 나누었는데, 그분께서는 출발 준비가 거의 다 되었다고 말씀하셨습니다. 정비사들이 문제를 확인했으며 모든 일을 처리하고 있습니다. 그들이 해야 할 일은 도구를 정리하는 것뿐입니다. 일을 마치는 대로, 문을 닫고 활주로로 이동하기 시작할 것입니다. 여러분 모두가 비행을 열망하고 계시다는 점을 알고 있기 때문에, 좌석에 앉아 주시고 안전벨트를 착용해 주시기 바랍니다. 앞으로 10분 후에는 하늘에 계시게 될 것입니다. 이글 항공을 대신하여, 이번 지연에 대해 사과를 드리고 싶습니다. 순항 고도에 이르는 대로, 음료와 스낵을 무료로 제공해 드리도록 하겠습니다. 불편을 끼쳐드린 점에 대해 사과를 드리고자 합니다.

[어휘] **depart** 출발하다, 떠나다 | **mechanic** 정비사 | **identify** 확인하다 | **take care of** ~을 다루다, ~을 처리하다 |
     pack up (짐을) 싸다 | **taxi** (이륙을 위해) 천천히 이동하다 | **runway** 활주로 | **be eager to** ~하기를 열망하다 |
     on behalf of ~을 대신하여 | **cruising altitude** 순항 고도

PART 1

🎧 03-01

(A) ☐

(B) ☐

(C) ☐

(D) ☐

Dictation 보기 4개를 다시 들으면서 받아쓰시오.

🎧 03-02

(A) A man is recapping a bottle.

한 남자는 병뚜껑을 닫고 있다.

(B) ___________________________________.

탁자 위에 몇몇 병들이 있다.

(C) Some bottles are lying on their sides.

몇 개의 병이 측면으로 누워 있다.

(D) A cook is chopping some vegetables.

한 요리사가 채소를 썰고 있다.

[어휘] **recap** 뚜껑을 닫다 | **lying** 놓여있는 | **on their sides** 측면으로 | **cook** 요리사 | **chop** ~을 썰다 | **vegetable** 채소

PART 2

1   Mark your answer on your answer sheet.   (A)   (B)   (C)

2   Mark your answer on your answer sheet.   (A)   (B)   (C)

3   Mark your answer on your answer sheet.   (A)   (B)   (C)

4   Mark your answer on your answer sheet.   (A)   (B)   (C)

Dictation 질문과 응답을 다시 들으면서 받아쓰시오.   🎧 03-04

1 _______________________________________?

(A) Yes, it's in the cabinet.

(B) _______________________________________.

(C) It's for my supervisor.

[어휘] **edit** 편집하다 | **proposal** 제안서 | **supervisor** 상사

언제 제안서 교정을 끝낼 수 있어요?

(A) 예, 캐비닛 안에 있어요.

(B) 내일 아침에요.

(C) 제 상관을 위한 거예요.

2 _______________________________________?

(A) For a day or two.

(B) _______________________________________.

(C) At a company in Moscow.

[어휘] **board** 이사회

토론토에서 열리는 이사회의가 언제죠?

(A) 하루나 이틀 동안이요.

(B) 아마 다음 주 초 일거예요.

(C) 모스코바에 있는 회사에서요.

3 _______________________________________?

(A) For two days.

(B) _______________________________________.

(C) We fixed it a week ago.

[어휘] **get ~ finished** ~을 끝내다 | **repair** 수리; 수리하다 | **at the latest** 늦어도 | **fix** 수리하다

당신은 언제 수리를 끝내야 하나요?

(A) 이틀 동안이요.

(B) 늦어도 내일까지요.

(C) 우리가 일주일 전에 그것을 수리했어요.

4 _______________________________________?

(A) _______________________________________.

(B) In Conference Room C.

(C) The search is still on.

[어휘] **be supposed to-V** ~하기로 되어 있다 | **session** 회의

회의를 위해 언제 모이기로 되어 있나요?

(A) 30분 후에요.

(B) 회의실 C에서요.

(C) 계속 찾고 있어요.

1   Why can't the speakers go to Bert's Diner as planned?

(A) The manager is sick.

(B) A piece of equipment is broken.

(C) Some food items were not delivered.

(D) A water pipe is leaking.

2   For whom are the speakers arranging a lunch?

(A) New employees

(B) Event participants

(C) School children

(D) Foreign investors

3   When did Wilma's Café reopen?

(A) Yesterday

(B) Last week

(C) Two weeks ago

(D) Last month

Dictation   대화를 다시 들으면서 받아쓰시오.   🎧 03-06

Questions 1-3 refer to the following conversation.

W   _____________________________ Bert's Diner _____________ . _____________

_____________________________________ .

M   Then why don't we just eat at Wilma's Café instead?

W   There are only four or five tables in that café. ________________________

_____________________________ .

M   Oh, you haven't heard about their recent expansion? They were closed for a month to allow for the addition of two more rooms. ________________________ and now have space for over 40 guests.

W   버트 식당의 사장과 방금 통화했어요. 그곳 오븐이 고장이어서 점심 준비를 할 수 없다고 하네요.

M   그렇다면 그냥 윌마 카페에서 먹는 건 어때요?

W   윌마 카페에는 테이블이 네댓 개밖에 없잖아요. 이 컨퍼런스에 참석하는 23명이 식사를 하기에는 곤란해요.

M   오, 당신은 그곳의 확장 소식을 아직 못 들으셨군요. 방 두 개를 추가하느라 한 달 간 문을 닫았었어요. 지난 주 목요일에 다시 문을 열었고, 이제 40명이 넘는 손님을 받을 공간이 된대요.

[어휘] **owner** 소유주 | **diner** 식당 | **working** 작동하는 | **prepare** 준비하다 | **instead** 대신 | **possibly** 가능하게도 | **accommodate** 수용하다 | **attend** 참석하다 | **recent** 최근의 | **expansion** 확장 | **closed** 문을 닫은 | **allow for** ~을 준비하다 | **addition** 추가 | **reopen** 다시 문을 열다 | **space** 공간

Speaker	Time
Walter Mitchell	11:00 – 12:00
Holly Morris	12:00 – 1:00
Victor Jones	1:00 – 2:00
Jane Cross	2:00 – 3:00

4 What does the woman indicate about Holly Morris?

(A) She works in the oil industry.

(B) She is an author.

(C) She attends college.

(D) She is her friend.

5 What is the man going to do next?

(A) Meet a friend from college

(B) Attend another talk

(C) Get something to eat

(D) Read a book

6 Look at the graphic. What time will the man and woman meet?

(A) At 12:00

(B) At 1:00

(C) At 2:00

(D) At 3:00

Questions 4-6 refer to the following conversation and schedule.

M　That was an excellent talk by Walter Mitchell we heard now.

W　I agree. ____. I never even considered looking at the industry the way he does.

M　You can say that again. So which speaker do you want to listen to next?

W　I'm thinking about attending the talk by Holly Morris. ____. Do you want to listen to her talk?

M　No, thanks. You go ahead and do that. ________________________________.

W　All right. When do you want to meet up again?

M　____ is Jane Cross. She's an old friend from college.

W　I wasn't aware of that. Okay, I'll see you at her talk then.

M　방금 들은 월터 미첼의 연설은 훌륭했어요.

W　동감이에요. 석유 산업에 관한 그의 통찰력이 뛰어나다고 생각했어요. 그가 보는 방식으로 그 산업을 바라 보는 것은 생각해 본 적이 없어요.

M　전적으로 동감이에요. 그러면 이다음으로 어떤 연사의 이야기를 듣고 싶은가요?

W　홀리 모리스의 강연을 듣는 것을 생각 중이에요. 저는 그녀의 책을 두어 권 읽어 보았죠. 당신도 그녀의 강연을 듣고 싶나요?

M　저는 사양할게요. 당신은 가서 들으세요. 저는 점심 식사를 하겠어요.

W　좋아요. 언제 다시 만나면 좋을까요?

M　오늘 제가 관심이 가는 다른 연사는 제인 크로스뿐에요. 그녀는 저의 오래된 대학 친구죠.

W　그 점은 제가 몰랐군요. 좋아요, 그럼 그녀의 강연에서 다시 보도록 해요.

[어휘] **excellent** 탁월한, 뛰어난　|　**insight** 통찰력　|　**brilliant** 찬란한; 명석한　|　**consider** 고려하다

PART 4

1 Where does the talk take place?
- (A) On an airplane
- (B) At an art auction
- (C) At a beach resort
- (D) On a tour bus

2 According to the speaker, what will the listeners do later in the day?
- (A) Sail along a nearby beach
- (B) Pick up new passports
- (C) Enter a foreign country
- (D) Visit a museum in San Juan

3 What does the speaker ask the listeners to do?
- (A) Ensure they have travel documents
- (B) Purchase their tickets early
- (C) Turn off their cellular phones
- (D) Pack some essential items

Dictation 지문을 다시 들으면서 받아쓰시오.　🎧03-10

Questions 1-3 refer to the following announcement.

On behalf of Jasper International Travel, ____.
We will be departing in just a few minutes. The bus will be traveling for approximately 2 hours
before ____
________________________. According to the latest weather forecast, we are in for sunny skies
all day today so you will have a lot of chances to enjoy spectacular views of the Pacific Ocean.
Before we leave, ____ as Mexican
border inspectors will be checking for these items.

재스퍼 국제 여행사를 대신해, 저희 국제 버스 투어에 오신 여러분을 환영합니다. 우리는 잠시 후에 출발하겠습니다. 이 버스로 미국과 멕시코 국경에
도착하는데 약 2시간이 걸릴 것이며, 그런 다음 멕시코의 아름다운 해변 도시인 산 후안으로 들어갈 것입니다. 최근 일기 예보에 따르면, 오늘 날씨는
종일 화창하겠다니 태평양의 장관을 즐길 기회가 많을 것입니다. 떠나기에 앞서, 멕시코 국경 검사관들이 여러분의 티켓과 여권을 검사할 것이오니,
티켓과 여권 모두를 잘 챙겨 두시기 바랍니다.

[어휘] **on behalf of** ~을 대신해 ｜ **depart** 출발하다 ｜ **approximately** 거의, 대략 ｜ **reach** 이르다, 도달하다 ｜ **border** 경계, 국경 ｜
　　　cross 건너다 ｜ **according to** ~에 따르면 ｜ **forecast** 예보 ｜ **chance** 기회 ｜ **spectacular** 장관을 이루는, 극적인 ｜
　　　leave 떠나다 ｜ **inspector** 조사관, 감독관 ｜ **check** 확인하다 ｜ **item** 물건, 제품

PART 1

🎧 04-01

(A) ☐
(B) ☐
(C) ☐
(D) ☐

Dictation 보기 4개를 다시 들으면서 받아쓰시오.　　🎧 04-02

(A) The man is handing a paper to the woman.
남자가 여자에게 종이 한 장을 건네고 있다.

(B) The woman is opening a binder.
여자가 바인더를 펼치고 있다.

(C) ________________________________.
그들이 서로 마주보고 있다.

(D) The man is positioning a piece of equipment.
남자가 장비를 배치하고 있다.

[어휘] hand 건네다 | face 마주보다 | each other 서로 | position 배치하다 | equipment 장비

PART 2

1   Mark your answer on your answer sheet.   (A)   (B)   (C)

2   Mark your answer on your answer sheet.   (A)   (B)   (C)

3   Mark your answer on your answer sheet.   (A)   (B)   (C)

4   Mark your answer on your answer sheet.   (A)   (B)   (C)

Dictation 질문과 응답을 다시 들으면서 받아쓰시오.   🎧 04-04

1 _______________________________?

(A) The park is crowded.
(B) Almost 10 hours.
(C) _______________________________.

어디에 차를 주차하세요?
(A) 공원이 붐비네요.
(B) 거의 10시간이요.
(C) 병원 뒤에요.

[어휘] **park** 주차하다 | **crowded** 붐비는, 혼잡한 | **almost** 거의 | **behind** ~뒤에

2 _______________________________?

(A) The president will make a speech.
(B) _______________________________.
(C) In the top drawer.

본사가 어디에 위치해 있어요?
(A) 사장이 연설할 거예요.
(B) 시내에요.
(C) 맨 위 서랍에요.

[어휘] **be located** 위치해 있다 | **make a speech** 연설하다 | **downtown** 시내, 중심가

3 _______________________________?

(A) _______________________________.
(B) The staples are on Mr. Parker's desk.
(C) It must be about papers.

스테플러를 어디에 보관하나요?
(A) 가장 아래 서랍에요.
(B) 스테플러 심은 파커 씨의 책상 위에 있어요.
(C) 서류들에 관한 것이 분명해요.

[어휘] **keep** 보관하다 | **drawer** 서랍

4 _______________________________?

(A) _______________________________.
(B) Between 3 and 5.
(C) Sorry, I can't remember them.

세탁소 전화번호를 어디서 알 수 있죠?
(A) 전화번호부를 찾아보세요.
(B) 3시에서 5시 사이에요.
(C) 미안해요. 그것들이 기억이 안 나네요.

[어휘] **find** 찾다 | **the number for** ~의 전화번호 | **laundry** 세탁(소) | **directory** 전화번호부 | **remember** 기억하다

1 What is happening in the conference room?

(A) Some improvements are being made.

(B) Someone is giving a presentation.

(C) Terms of a contract are being discussed.

(D) A burnt out light bulb is being changed.

2 What does the woman say about her new office chair?

(A) The back is too low.

(B) The wheels are broken.

(C) It is very comfortable.

(D) It is made of fabric.

3 What does the man want to do?

(A) Finish a report

(B) Go to an office

(C) Meet the painters

(D) Make a phone call

Dictation 대화를 다시 들으면서 받아쓰시오.   🎧 04-06

Questions 1-3 refer to the following conversation.

W Bill, what is that noise coming from inside the conference room?

M ___________________________________ . ___________________________________

___________________________________ .

W Well, any change to that ugly room would be great. My office looks much better ever since they replaced the chair and desk last week. ___________________________________ .

M I haven't been in your office since the new furniture was put in. ___________________________________

___________________________________ ?

W   빌, 회의실에서부터 들려오는 이 소음은 뭔가요?

M   그들은 마침내 보수공사를 시작했어요. 오래된 바닥 타일을 교체하고 벽과 천장을 페인트칠하고 있어요.

W   음, 그 보기 싫은 방에는 어떤 변화라도 좋을 거예요. 제 사무실은 지난주에 그들이 의자와 책상을 교체한 이후에 훨씬 좋아 보여요. 특히 가죽 의자가 매우 편안해요.

M   새 가구가 들어온 이후로 당신 사무실에 가 본 적이 없어요. 지금 당신 사무실에서 커피 한잔 할까요?

[어휘] noise 소음 | inside 안쪽 | finally 마침내 | renovation 수리 | replace 교체하다 | repaint 다시 칠하다 | ceiling 천정 | change 변화 | ugly 보기 싫은 | especially 특히 | leather 가죽의 | comfortable 편안한

4   Why is the man going to be late?

     (A) His plane is late.

     (B) He missed his train.

     (C) There is bad weather.

     (D) His car broke down.

5   What does the man request that the woman do?

     (A) Upgrade him to a better room

     (B) Cancel his reservation

     (C) Extend his stay by a day

     (D) Hold his room for him

6   What time does the last shuttle bus depart from the airport?

     (A) At 7:30

     (B) At 9:00

     (C) At 9:30

     (D) At 10:00

Dictation   대화를 다시 들으면서 받아쓰시오.   ⌒ 04-08

Questions 4-6 refer to the following conversation.

W   Good afternoon. This is the Bayside Hotel. How may I help you?

M   Hello. My name is Roger Smith. I have a reservation for today, _______________________

_______________________ .

W   We normally hold reservations until 7:30. Are you going to be coming here after that time?

M   Yes, I am. ____ , so I most

likely won't be at the hotel until 10:00. Will my reservation still be valid?

W   Since you called, ____ _______________________ .

M   That's great. Thank you very much. By the way, will the hotel shuttle bus still be running at around 9:30?

W   Sorry, but _______________________ at 9:00.

W   안녕하세요. 베이사이드 호텔입니다. 어떻게 도와 드릴까요?

M   안녕하세요. 제 이름은 로저 스미스에요. 오늘 예약을 해 두었지만, 예상보다 늦을 것 같아서요.

W   보통은 7시 30분까지 예약이 유효합니다. 그 시간 이후에 이곳으로 오실 건가요?

M   네, 그래요. 제 비행기가 두어 시간 늦게 이륙을 할 예정이어서, 아마도 10시까지는 호텔로 가지 못할 것 같아요. 그래도 제 예약이 유효할까요?

W   전화를 주셨기 때문에, 저희가 절대로 취소시키지 않겠습니다.

M   잘 되었군요. 정말 고마워요. 그건 그렇고, 호텔 셔틀 버스가 9시 30분경에도 운행을 할까요?

W   죄송하지만, 공항에서 막차가 9시에 떠나요.

[어휘] normally 보통은, 평소에는 | **hold a reservation** 예약하다, 예약을 취소시키지 않다 | **take off** 이륙하다 | **valid** 유효한 |
cancel 취소하다

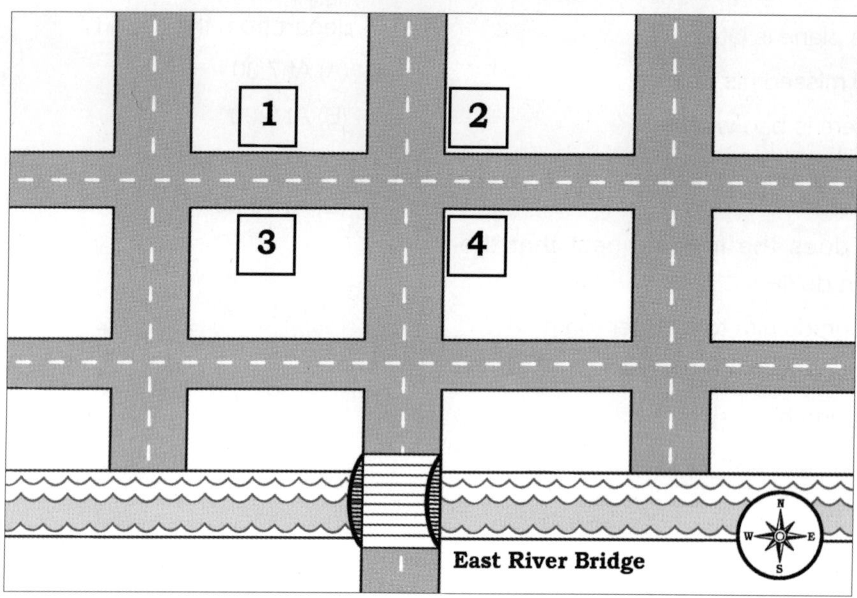

1   Why is Rick visiting the speaker's office?

   (A) To meet about a job

   (B) To give a presentation

   (C) To negotiate a contract

   (D) To make a proposal

2   What does the speaker request that Rick do?

   (A) Send him a text message when he arrives

   (B) Bring all of the necessary files with him

   (C) Call him if he cannot find the office

   (D) Wait outside as soon as he arrives

3   Look at the map. Where is the man's office located?

   (A) 1

   (B) 2

   (C) 3

   (D) 4

Questions 1-3 refer to the following message and map.

Hi, Rick. I think you might have a minor problem finding my office for today's interview ______________________________________. So why don't I give you directions here? Once you cross the East River Bridge, keep going straight for two blocks. Just so you know, you'll be heading north. At the second intersection, ______________________________________. ______________________________________. There's a parking garage on the right-hand side of the street. Park there. Then, you need to cross the street. My office is ______________________ ______________________. If you can't find it, give me a call, and ______________________________________.
See you soon. Bye.

안녕, 릭. 저는 당신이 전에 이곳 도시에 온 적이 없기 때문에 오늘 면접을 위해 제 사무실을 찾아오는데 약간의 어려움을 겪을 수도 있을 것이라고 생각해요. 그래서 제가 이곳으로 오는 길을 당신에게 알려 주는 것이 어떨까요? 이스트 리버 교를 건넌 후, 두 블록 직진하세요. 아시다시피, 당신은 북쪽을 향하고 있어요. 두 번째 교차로에 오면, 오른쪽에 주유소가 있을 거에요. 그 교차로에서 좌회전을 해야 하고, 그 다음에 반 블록을 가세요. 거리의 오른쪽에 주차장 건물이 있어요. 그곳에 주차를 하세요. 그런 다음에는, 거리를 건너세요. 제 사무실은 주차장 건물 반대편 빌딩에 있어요. 만약 찾지 못하는 경우에는, 제게 전화를 하면 제가 당신을 만나러 밖으로 나갈게요. 곧 만나요. 안녕.

[어휘] **have been to** ~에 가 본 적이 있다 ｜ **give directions** 길을 알려 주다 ｜ **head** 향하다 ｜ **intersection** 교차로 ｜ **gas station** 주유소 ｜ **parking garage** 주차장, 주차장 건물 ｜ **opposite** ~의 반대편에

PART 1

(A) ☐
(B) ☐
(C) ☐
(D) ☐

Dictation 보기 4개를 다시 들으면서 받아쓰시오.

🎧 05-02

(A) ____.

문이 계단을 마주하고 있다

(B) Bricks are being laid.

벽돌들이 쌓이고 있다.

(C) The steps are being swept.

계단에 빗질이 되는 중이다

(D) A potted plant has been placed near an entrance.

화분이 입구 근처에 놓여있다.

[어휘] **face** 마주하다 ｜ **staircase** 계단 ｜ **lay bricks** 벽돌을 쌓다 ｜ **steps** 계단 ｜ **sweep[-swept-swept]** 쓸다 ｜ **place** 놓다 ｜ **near** 근처에 ｜ **entrance** 입구

PART 2

1   Mark your answer on your answer sheet.   (A)   (B)   (C)

2   Mark your answer on your answer sheet.   (A)   (B)   (C)

3   Mark your answer on your answer sheet.   (A)   (B)   (C)

4   Mark your answer on your answer sheet.   (A)   (B)   (C)

Dictation 질문과 응답을 다시 들으면서 받아쓰시오.   🎧 05-04

1 ______________________________________ ?

(A) It will be ready tomorrow.

(B) ______________________________________ .

(C) That's right. I don't eat meat.

[어휘] **Why don't you ~?** ~하는 게 어때? | **meat** 고기

다음 토요일에 점심 먹으러 오는 게 어때요?

(A) 내일 준비될 거예요.

(B) 좋아요.

(C) 맞아요. 전 고기는 먹지 않아요.

2 ______________________________________ ?

(A) I can't remember it.

(B) Advance registration is required.

(C) ______________________________________ .

[어휘] **make reservations** 예약하다 | **in advance** 미리, 사전에 | **registration** 등록

우리 미리 예약을 해야 하지 않을까요?

(A) 기억할 수가 없어요.

(B) 사전 등록이 요구됩니다.

(C) 좋은 생각인 것 같아요.

3 ______________________________________ ?

(A) Yes, I knew that.

(B) ______________________________________ .

(C) Because you went over it.

[어휘] **look at** ~을 보다 | **go over** ~을 검토하다

귀사의 새 카탈로그를 볼 수 있을까요?

(A) 네, 저는 그것을 알고 있었어요.

(B) 제 책상 위에 있어요.

(C) 당신이 그것을 검토했기 때문이에요.

4 ______________________________________ ?

(A) Actually, it was not that good.

(B) ______________________________________ ?

(C) No, the computer is compatible.

[어휘] **manual** 사용설명서 | **compatible** 호환할 수 있는

이 컴퓨터 프로그램 사용법을 알려주시겠어요?

(A) 실은, 그렇게 좋지 않습니다.

(B) 사용설명서를 가지고 있지 않나요?

(C) 아뇨, 그 컴퓨터는 호환할 수 있어요.

1 What is the woman preparing?

(A) A report

(B) An invoice

(C) An application

(D) A book review

2 What does the man offer to do?

(A) Make a reservation

(B) Check some figures

(C) Find a phone number

(D) Deliver a document

3 Why is the woman in a hurry?

(A) She is late for a meeting.

(B) She will give a presentation.

(C) She has an appointment.

(D) She will meet a client.

Dictation 대화를 다시 들으면서 받아쓰시오.　　🎧 05-06

Questions 1-3 refer to the following conversation.

M ____?

W _________________________________. It took a little longer than I expected because some of the figures from last month's sales were somewhat strange and I had to check them with the sales manager. Now _____________________________ Mr. Jackson.

M Oh, I have a meeting with Mr. Jackson in his office in five minutes. _____________________________.

W Thanks. ____

___________________________.

M 그 보고서 작업은 잘 되어 가나요?

W 방금 끝냈어요. 예상보다 좀 오래 걸렸는데, 지난 달 판매수치 일부가 약간 이상해서 판매과장님과 확인을 해야 했거든요. 이제 잭슨 씨에게 이것을 팩스로 보내드려야 해요.

M 아, 제가 5분 뒤에 잭슨 씨의 사무실에서 그와의 회의가 있어요. 제가 가져다 드릴게요.

W 고마워요. 사실 저는 치과 약속이 있어 서둘러 나가야 하는데, 그렇게 해주시면 시간이 많이 절약되겠어요.

[어휘] **finish** 끝내다 ｜ **a little** 약간 ｜ **expect** 예상하다 ｜ **figure** 수치 ｜ **somewhat** 다소 ｜ **strange** 이상한 ｜ **actually** 실은 ｜ **rush off to** ~로 서둘러 가다 ｜ **dentist** 치과 의사 ｜ **appointment** 약속 ｜ **save** 아끼다

PART 3

4 Where are the speakers going to go?

    (A) To an interview

    (B) To a conference

    (C) To a meeting

    (D) To a seminar

5 How does the woman suggest going?

    (A) By bus

    (B) By car

    (C) By taxi

    (D) By train

6 Where will the speakers meet tomorrow?

    (A) At the woman's home

    (B) In the company's parking lot

    (C) At the bus stop

    (D) At the train station

Dictation 대화를 다시 들으면서 받아쓰시오.   🎧 05-08

Questions 4-6 refer to the following conversation with three speakers.

M1 The conference at Miller Textiles starts at 9:30 tomorrow. How shall we go there?

M2 I would like to drive there.

W That would be more comfortable, ________________________________ ?

________________________________ .

M2 You may be right. What do you believe we should do then?

W ________________________________ .

M1 I'd rather not. ____ ________________________________ .

W How about if each of us goes there individually?

M1 That won't look good if one of us is late. We want to make a good impression.

M2 Let's drive. ________________________________ at 8:00 and drive us. We'll get there in time.

M1 밀러 텍스타일스에서의 컨퍼런스가 내일 9시 30분에 시작해요. 거기까지 어떻게 갈 건가요?

M2 저는 운전을 해서 가는 것이 좋아요.

W 그렇게 하면 더 편하기는 하겠지만, 시간 내에 그곳에 도착할까요? 리치몬드의 출퇴근 교통 혼잡은 꽤 심할 수도 있거든요.

M2 당신 말이 맞을지도 몰라요. 그러면 우리가 어떻게 하는 것이 좋을까요?

W 저는 버스를 타는 것이 좋아요.

M1 저는 아니에요. 그러면 저는 상당히 불편할 거에요.

W 우리가 각각 개별적으로 그곳에 가는 것은 어떤가요?

M1 우리 중 하나가 늦는다면 좋아 보이지 않을 거에요. 우리는 좋은 인상을 남기기를 원해요.

M2 운전을 하죠. 여기 주차장에서 8시에 만나서 차를 몰고 가요. 시간 내에 그곳에 도착하게 될 거에요.

[어휘] **propose** 제안하다, 의도하다 | **inconvenient** 불편한 | **individually** 개별적으로, 각각 | **impression** 인상

1   Who most likely is the speaker?

(A) The head of maintenance

(B) A new employee in payroll

(C) The owner of a bookstore

(D) The president of a company

2   What will Donald McKenzie probably do after the talk?

(A) Deliver a bookcase

(B) Speak to his supervisor

(C) Book a hotel room

(D) Go to the fifth floor

3   Why will Nereus Robinson remain in the office?

(A) To fix the lights in the office

(B) To meet with some executives

(C) To answer the phone

(D) To finish typing a report

Dictation   지문을 다시 들으면서 받아쓰시오.   05-10

Questions 1-3 refer to the following talk.

I'll quickly run through what needs to be done this afternoon. _______________

the Sanford Conference Room _________________________________.

Donald McKenzie _________________________________. Also, elevator number 3 is not working

so Maria Fleming will phone Jackson Elevator and Escalator Services to arrange for a repair.

Finally, Cecilia Doherty and I will be fixing a bookcase in the payroll office, room 115. If you

need anything, please come and see me in payroll or you can also speak to Nereus Robinson.

Mr. Robinson _________________________________

_________________________________.

오늘 오후에 어떤 일을 해야 하는지 빠르게 훑어볼게요. 5층 샌포드 컨퍼런스 룸의 에어컨을 고쳐야 합니다. 도날드 맥킨지가 그 일을 담당할 거예요. 또, 3번 엘리베이터가 작동을 안 하니 마리아 플레밍은 잭슨 엘리베이터 앤 에스컬레이터 서비스에 전화하셔서 수리를 요청하시고요. 마지막으로, 세실리아 도허티와 저는 115호 경리부의 서가를 고칠 것입니다. 무엇이든 필요하시면, 경리부로 저를 보러 오시거나 네레우스 로빈슨에게 말씀하셔도 돼요. 로빈슨 씨는 수리 요청 전화를 더 많이 받게 될 경우를 대비해서 오후 내내 우리 사무실에 있을 겁니다.

[어휘]   quickly 빠르게 | **run through** (빨리) 살펴보다 | **fix** 고치다 | **look after** 감독하다 | **arrange** 준비하다, 마련하다 |
repair 수리, 수선 | **finally** 마지막으로 | **payroll** 경리 | **in case** (~할) 경우를 대비해서 | **receive** 받다 | **request** 요청하다

DAY 06 Daily Listening Practice

PART 1

(A) ☐
(B) ☐
(C) ☐
(D) ☐

Dictation   보기 4개를 다시 들으면서 받아쓰시오.   🎧 06-02

(A)   Branches have been piled under the park bench.
      가지들이 공원 벤치 아래에 쌓여있다.

(B)   A vendor is putting a hat on a table.
      상인이 테이블에 모자를 놓고 있다.

(C)   ____.
      통들이 테이블 위에 놓여있다.

(D)   People are looking in the same direction.
      사람들이 같은 방향을 보고 있다.

[어휘] **branch** 가지 ┃ **pile** 쌓다 ┃ **vendor** 상인 ┃ **put** 놓다 ┃ **hat** 모자 ┃ **container** 통, 용기 ┃ **rest** 놓여있다 ┃ **direction** 방향

PART 2

1 **Mark your answer on your answer sheet.**　　(A)　(B)　(C)

2 **Mark your answer on your answer sheet.**　　(A)　(B)　(C)

3 **Mark your answer on your answer sheet.**　　(A)　(B)　(C)

4 **Mark your answer on your answer sheet.**　　(A)　(B)　(C)

Dictation　질문과 응답을 다시 들으면서 받아쓰시오.　　　　🎧 06-04

1 ________________________________?

(A) It's not brief.

(B) ________________________________.

(C) Not that many.

제 서류가방 봤어요?

(A) 간략하지 않아요.

(B) 미안한데 못 봤어요.

(C) 그렇게 많지는 않아요.

[어휘] **briefcase** 서류가방 ｜ **brief** 간략한

2 ________________________________?

(A) Yes, I'll send it out.

(B) ________________________________.

(C) You will need it immediately.

제가 오늘 아침에 보낸 메모를 읽으셨나요?

(A) 예, 제가 발송할 거예요.

(B) 아뇨, 메모가 지금 막 도착했어요.

(C) 당장 그게 필요할 거예요.

[어휘] **send out** 발송하다 ｜ **get here** 도착하다 ｜ **immediately** 즉시

3 ________________________________
________________________?

(A) It must have been a city officer.

(B) I assembled it myself.

(C) ________________________________.

새 지점에 대해 뭔가 들었어요?

(A) 틀림없이 시 공무원이었을 거예요.

(B) 제가 그것을 조립했어요.

(C) 좋을 거예요.

4 ________________________________
________________________?

(A) ________________________________.

(B) Thanks, they would be helpful.

(C) They look much too tired.

그들이 건강 검진 결과를 받았나요?

(A) 못 받았다고 들었어요.

(B) 고마워요, 그들이 도움이 될 거예요.

(C) 그들은 너무 많이 지쳐 보여요.

[어휘] **physical checkup** 건강 검진 ｜ **helpful** 도움이 되는 ｜ **tired** 지친

1 What is causing the delay?

(A) Payment has not been received.

(B) A section of road is being repaired.

(C) A traffic light is not working.

(D) Some items were not delivered.

2 What is the man concerned about?

(A) Missing a plane

(B) Not having taxi fare

(C) Losing a document

(D) Not finishing a report

3 What will the speakers probably do next?

(A) Withdraw some cash

(B) Fax a document

(C) Call the airport

(D) Go outside

Dictation 대화를 다시 들으면서 받아쓰시오. 06-06

Questions 1-3 refer to the following conversation.

M   What did you learn from Golden Taxi?

W   ____ Davis Avenue and Wilcox Street. That cab coming to our office is expected to be stuck in traffic for a long time so they are sending another one here.

M   _________________________. _____________________________

_____________________________.

W   Don't worry. We will make it on time. The taxi was on Montgomery Street which is only three blocks away from our office. Why don't we just wait for it outside?

M   골든 택시에서 뭐라고 하던가요?

W   데이비스 애비뉴와 윌콕스 스트리트 코너에 있는 신호등이 고장이래요. 우리 사무실로 오던 택시는 꽤 오래 동안 교통정체에서 벗어나지 못할 것 같아 다른 차를 여기로 보내주겠대요.

M   빨리 도착했으면 좋겠네요. 우리 비행기가 2시간 뒤에 출발인데, 공항까지는 적어도 30분은 걸리니까요.

W   걱정 말아요. 우리는 제때 도착할 수 있을 거에요. 택시는 우리 사무실에서 겨우 세 블록 떨어진 몽고메리 스트리트에 있었어요. 밖에 나가 기다릴까요?

[어휘] **learn** 알게 되다, 배우다 | **broken** 고장 난 | **traffic light** 신호등 | **cab** 택시 | **be stuck in traffic** 교통 정체에 발이 묶이다 | **leave** 떠나다 | **make it on time** 제때 도착하다

Address	Description
28 Shamrock Lane	209 Aberdeen Street
45 Henry Road	4 bedrooms; 2 bathrooms
85 Davenport Avenue	3 bedrooms; 3 bathrooms
209 Aberdeen Street	4 bedrooms; 3 bathrooms

4   What is suggested about the man?

(A) He has children.

(B) He is a real estate agent.

(C) He is going to change jobs.

(D) He is a teacher.

5   When does the woman want to meet the man?

(A) At 12:00

(B) At 3:00

(C) At 4:00

(D) At 6:00

6   Look at the graphic. What is the address of the house the woman wants to show the man?

(A) 209 Aberdeen Street

(B) 45 Henry Road

(C) 28 Shamrock Lane

(D) 85 Davenport Avenue

Questions 4-6 refer to the following conversation and list.

W   Hello, Mr. Wheeler. This is Kay Kennedy calling from Top Realty.

M   Good morning, Ms. Kennedy. Do you have some good news for me?

W   I think I do. I found ____.

M   Tell me about it, please.

W   ____, so there's plenty of room for everyone. ____, and it has a large yard.

M   That sounds ideal. Do you have time to show it to us around 3:00 or 4:00?

W   ____. However, I'm available at 6:00. How does that sound?

M   Let me ask my wife first and see what she says. Then, I'll call you right back.

W   안녕하세요, 윌러 씨. 저는 탑 부동산의 케이 케네디입니다.

M   안녕하세요, 케네디 씨. 제게 좋은 소식이라도 있나요?

W   그런 것 같아요. 제가 고객님과 고객님 가족의 마음에 꼭 들만한, 정말로 멋진 주택을 찾았거든요.

M   그에 대해 제게 말씀해 주세요.

W   4개의 침실과 2개의 욕실을 갖추고 있기 때문에, 모든 사람에게 충분한 공간이 있죠. 우수한 초등학교 인근에 위치해 있으며, 커다란 마당도 가지고 있고요.

M   이상적인 것으로 들리는군요. 3시나 4시경에 저희에게 보여 줄 수 있는 시간이 있으신가요?

W   제가 사장님과의 회의에 참석해야 해서 오후에는 시간이 없어요. 하지만 6시에는 시간이 되죠. 어떻게 들리시나요?

M   먼저 제 아내에게 물어보고 그녀가 어떻게 말하는지를 볼게요. 그런 다음, 제가 다시 전화를 드리죠.

[어휘] **plenty of** 많은 ｜ **room** 방; 공간 ｜ **outstanding** 뛰어난, 우수한 ｜ **yard** 마당, 뜰 ｜ **ideal** 이상적인 ｜ **available** 이용 가능한; 만날 수 있는

1 When did the speaker report the problem?

(A) Yesterday morning

(B) Yesterday evening

(C) This morning

(D) This evening

2 What does the speaker instruct the listener to do?

(A) Speak with Mr. Driessen at once

(B) Have a broken item repaired

(C) Take care of his equipment

(D) Look after all of his experiments

3 What does the speaker mean when he says, "It is imperative that you keep your word"?

(A) The listener needs to solve the problem today.

(B) The listener should pay better attention to him.

(C) The listener has to return his phone call at once.

(D) The listener ought to contact the Maintenance Department.

Dictation 지문을 다시 들으면서 받아쓰시오. 06-10

Questions 1-3 refer to the following telephone message.

Hello, Mr. Driessen. This is Dr. Wayne Conner calling from the Cornell Laboratory. Yesterday morning, ________________________________ . ____ . Unfortunately, nobody from the Maintenance Department has arrived yet. It's already 5 in the evening, and most of us are getting ready to go home for the day. ____ .
We have many valuable pieces of equipment in here. It isn't safe to leave the door unlocked again. We can't risk ____ ________________________________ . I insist that you send someone down here to fix the problem immediately.

드리슨 씨, 안녕하세요. 저는 코넬 연구소의 웨인 코너 박사입니다. 어제 아침, 저는 당신과 전화로 연구실 문의 고장 난 잠금 장치에 대해 이야기했습니다. 당신은 문이 즉시 수리될 것이라고 제게 확언하셨습니다. 안타깝게도, 관리부의 누구도 아직 오지 않았습니다. 지금이 벌써 저녁 5시이고, 저희 대부분은 퇴근 준비를 하고 있습니다. 당신이 약속을 지키는 것이 중요합니다. 저희는 이곳에 값비싼 많은 장비들을 두고 있습니다. 또 다시 문을 잠그지 않고 놔둔다는 것은 안전하지 못한 일입니다. 저희는 도난을 당하거나 일부 장비의 운행이 중단되는 위험을 무릅쓸 수는 없습니다. 저는 당신이 문제 해결을 위해 즉시 누군가를 여기로 보내 주실 것을 요청드립니다.

[어휘] **lock** 자물쇠, 잠금 장치 ㅣ **assure** 확언하다 ㅣ **Maintenance Department** 관리부 ㅣ **go home for the day** 퇴근하다 ㅣ
imperative 긴급한, 긴요한 ㅣ **keep one's word** 약속을 지키다 ㅣ **valuable** 귀중한, 소중한 ㅣ **risk** ~할 위험을 무릅쓰다 ㅣ
interrupt 중단시키다 ㅣ **insist** 주장하다

PART 1

07-01

(A) ☐
(B) ☐
(C) ☐
(D) ☐

Dictation　보기 4개를 다시 들으면서 받아쓰시오.　　07-02

(A) _______________________________________.
   인도에 보행자가 없다.

(B) There are several houses in need of repair.
   수리가 필요한 집이 몇 채 있다.

(C) The cars on the street are parked illegally.
   거리에 차들이 불법으로 주차되어 있다.

(D) The commuters are stuck in traffic.
   통근자들이 교통체증을 겪고 있다.

[어휘] pedestrian 보행자 ｜ in need of ~이 필요한 ｜ illegally 불법적으로 ｜ be stuck in traffic 교통체증에 걸리다

PART 2

1   **Mark your answer on your answer sheet.**   (A)   (B)   (C)

2   **Mark your answer on your answer sheet.**   (A)   (B)   (C)

3   **Mark your answer on your answer sheet.**   (A)   (B)   (C)

4   **Mark your answer on your answer sheet.**   (A)   (B)   (C)

Dictation 질문과 응답을 다시 들으면서 받아쓰시오.   07-04

1 ____ ?

(A) No, the company is hiring now.

(B) About 2 months ago.

(C) ____ .

[어휘] **hire** 고용하다 ｜ **through** [수단] ~을 통해서 ｜ **recruit** 채용하다

새 직장은 어떻게 찾았나요?

(A) 아뇨, 그 회사는 지금 채용 중이에요.

(B) 대략 두 달 전에요.

(C) 직업소개소를 통해서요.

2 ____ ?

(A) ____ .

(B) When the supervisor gets back.

(C) The project has been delayed.

[어휘] **supervise** 감독하다 ｜ **supervisor** 감독관, 상관 ｜ **get back** 돌아오다 ｜ **delay** 연기하다

얼마나 오래 이 프로젝트를 감독했죠?

(A) 거의 3년 동안이요.

(B) 감독관이 돌아올 때요.

(C) 프로젝트가 연기 되었어요.

3 ____ ?

(A) ____ .

(B) To contact the supplier.

(C) It's a final draft.

[어휘] **trip to** 명사 ~행 여행 ｜ **contact** 연락하다 ｜ **draft** 초안, 도면

하노이 출장은 어땠나요?

(A) 매우 성공적이었어요.

(B) 공급업체와 연락하려고요.

(C) 그게 최종안이에요.

4 ____

Ms. Deltashi's ______________________________ ?

(A) She's doing well.

(B) ____ .

(C) She wants approval.

[어휘] **early retirement** 조기 은퇴 ｜ **approval** 승인, 허가

델타시 씨의 조기 은퇴를 어떻게 알았어요?

(A) 그녀는 잘 하고 있어요.

(B) 그녀 자신이 제게 말했어요.

(C) 그녀는 허가를 원하고 있어요.

PART 3

1 What does the woman want to do?

    (A) Apply for a credit card

    (B) Have an appliance fixed

    (C) Buy a computer

    (D) Make an appointment

2 What is the problem?

    (A) An item is not in stock.

    (B) The store will close soon.

    (C) The manager is away.

    (D) Some equipment is broken.

3 What will the woman probably do next?

    (A) Phone someone

    (B) Turn on a computer

    (C) Look for a paper

    (D) Place an order

Dictation 대화를 다시 들으면서 받아쓰시오. 07-06

Questions 1-3 refer to the following conversation.

W ____

________________________________ . ________________________

and charge them to my credit card.

M Of course, miss, but unfortunately, ________________________ .

That particular item is very popular these days.

W ________________________ ? I don't mind waiting a few days.

M Certainly. I guaranteed that it will be here by the day after tomorrow and we will contact you

as soon as it arrives.

W 귀사 웹사이트에서 신상품인 AZ-3000 컴퓨터와 BL150 프린터 광고를 봤어요. 그것들을 신용카드로 구매하고 싶습니다.

M 물론 가능하십니다. 그런데, 유감스럽게도 BL150 프린터가 현재 품절된 상태에요. 요즘 이 제품이 인기가 아주 좋아서요.

W 주문을 해 둘 수 있을까요? 며칠 기다려도 상관없어요.

M 물론입니다. 내일 모레까지는 입고될 것이 분명하니 상품이 도착하는 대로 연락 드리겠습니다.

[어휘] advertisement 광고 | brand new 신상품인 | charge (지불·대금 따위)를 청구[요구]하다 | unfortunately 유감스럽게도 | completely 완전히 | be sold out 품절되다 | at the moment 현재 | particular 특정의 | item 제품 | popular 인기가 있는 | order 주문하다 | mind ~하기를 꺼리다 | certainly 물론 | guarantee 보증하다, 장담하다 | contact 연락하다

4 What does the man say about Ron?

(A) He helped the company get a new contract.

(B) He is the company's newest employee.

(C) He is currently working at Simmons Construction.

(D) He just signed a contract with the company.

5 What will the speakers most likely do next?

(A) Fire one of their colleagues

(B) Place a call to Simmons Construction

(C) Have a meeting with Maria

(D) Continue discussing the matter

6 What does the man mean when he says, "I see your point"?

(A) The company needs to hire more employees.

(B) Ron should continue looking for new clients.

(C) The Simmons Construction project is more important.

(D) Maria would be better than Ron at the job.

Dictation 대화를 다시 들으면서 받아쓰시오.

🎧07-08

Questions 4-6 refer to the following conversation.

W Now that Simmons Construction has signed a deal with us, ____.

M I vote for Ron. He was integral to getting the contract signed.

W That's true, but I don't think he'd be a good choice as a liaison. He's never done it before, and ___________________________. _____________________________.

M I see your point. In that case, who do you think we should use?

W ____, she's proving to be a good employee.

M Okay. ____.

W 시먼스 건설이 저희와 계약을 체결했으니, 누가 그 회사와 가장 긴밀히 연락해야 할지 결정을 해야 해요.

M 저는 론에게 투표할게요. 그가 계약서의 서명을 이끌어낸 장본인이었잖아요.

W 그건 사실이지만, 저는 연락 담당자로서 그가 좋은 선택은 아닐 것으로 생각해요. 그는 전에 그와 같은 일을 해 본 적이 없고, 그의 성격은 그 일에 맞지 않아요. 저는 차라리 그에게 신규 고객을 유치하는 일을 맡길 거에요.

M 당신 뜻을 알겠어요. 그런 경우라면, 우리가 누구를 활용해야 할까요?

W 이곳에서 일을 시작한지는 얼마 되지 않았지만, 마리아는 뛰어난 직원으로 판명되고 있죠.

M 좋아요. 우리가 그녀에게 소식을 알릴 수 있도록 그녀를 이리로 부르죠.

[어휘] **sign a deal** 계약을 체결하다 | **determine** 결정하다 | **vote for** ~에게 표를 던지다, ~에게 투표하다 | **integral** 필수적인 | **liaison** 연락 담당자 | **personality** 인격, 성격 | **would rather** 차라리 ~하겠다 | **secure** 확보하다 | **even though** 비록 ~일지라도

PART 4

1   Where most likely are the listeners?

(A) At a sports event

(B) At an art auction

(C) At a training session

(D) At an awards banquet

2   In what division does Soomi Choi work?

(A) Sales

(B) Research

(C) Finance

(D) Legal

3   What will Ms. Choi probably do next?

(A) Start a meeting

(B) Give a speech

(C) Phone a colleague

(D) Finish a proposal

Dictation   지문을 다시 들으면서 받아쓰시오.   07-10

Questions 1-3 refer to the following talk.

Good evening, ladies and gentlemen. I hope you all enjoyed your lobster dinner. I will now

____, Wilcox Energy's Leader-of-the-Year Award.

____, organized and directed

a huge project that helped Wilcox secure a contract to build 85 windmills on Chatworth Island.

She also worked closely with Wilcox's finance division to secure funding for another research

project that will start in New Zealand in mid-January. _________________________________

Ms. Soomi Choi as ____.

안녕하십니까, 신사 숙녀 여러분. 여러분 모두 랍스터 요리를 맛있게 드셨기를 바랍니다. 이제 오늘 저녁의 첫 번째 상인 월콕스 에너지 사의 올해의 지도자상을 시상하겠습니다. 올해의 수상자인 연구 부서의 관리자는 월콕스가 채트워스 섬에 85개의 풍차를 건설하는 계약을 딸 수 있게 해준 엄청난 프로젝트를 구성하고 지도했습니다. 또한 그녀는 월콕스 재무부와 면밀히 협력하여 1월 중순 뉴질랜드에서 시작될 또 다른 연구 프로젝트의 자금을 확보하기도 했습니다. 이 상을 수상하고 소감을 말씀하시기 위해 단상으로 올라 오는 수미 최 씨를 모두들 큰 박수로 맞이해 주십시오.

[어휘] **present** 수여하다 | **prize** 상 | **award** 상 | **recipient** 받는 사람, 수령인 | **supervisor** 관리자 | **research** 연구, 조사 |
department 부(서) | **organize** 구성하다, 조직화하다 | **direct** 지휘하다 | **huge** 거대한 | **secure** 확보하다, 획득하다 |
contract 계약 | **windmill** 풍차 | **closely** 밀접하게, 친밀하게 | **finance** 금융, 재정 | **division** 부(서) | **funding** 자금, 기금 |
applause 박수(갈채) | **accept** 받다

PART 1

🎧 08-01

(A) ☐
(B) ☐
(C) ☐
(D) ☐

Dictation   보기 4개를 다시 들으면서 받아쓰시오.

🎧 08-02

(A) _______________________________________.
모자가 벽에 걸려있다.

(B) People are seated on opposite sides of the table.
사람들이 테이블 맞은편에 앉아 있다.

(C) A couple is arranging some flowers.
한 커플이 꽃꽂이를 하고 있다.

(D) A woman is sitting in an outdoor café.
한 여자가 야외 카페에 앉아 있다.

[어휘] **seated** 앉아 있는 | **opposite** 맞은편의 | **arrange flowers** 꽃꽂이하다 | **outdoor** 야외

PART 2

1   Mark your answer on your answer sheet.   (A)   (B)   (C)

2   Mark your answer on your answer sheet.   (A)   (B)   (C)

3   Mark your answer on your answer sheet.   (A)   (B)   (C)

4   Mark your answer on your answer sheet.   (A)   (B)   (C)

Dictation   질문과 응답을 다시 들으면서 받아쓰시오.   🎧 08-04

1 _________________________________ ?

(A) Because it's open for business.

(B) The library is close to my office.

(C) ___________________________ .

왜 오늘 도서관이 휴관인가요?

(A) 왜냐하면 그곳은 영업중이라서요.

(B) 도서관은 제 사무실과 가까워요.

(C) 국경일이라서요.

[어휘] **library** 도서관 ｜ **be open for business** 개업하다, 개장하다 ｜ **be close to** ～에 가까이 있다 ｜ **national holiday** 국경일

2 _________________________________ ?

(A) I decided yesterday.

(B) Yes, I'm going to change jobs.

(C) ___________________________ .

왜 이사하기로 결정했나요?

(A) 어제 결정했어요.

(B) 네, 직업을 바꿀 거예요.

(C) 이곳의 생활비는 너무 비싸요.

[어휘] **decide** 결정하다 ｜ **cost of living** 생활비

3 _____________ Mr. Chan _____________ __________________ ?

(A) ___________________________ .

(B) He'd appreciate your assistance.

(C) Not to him.

챈 씨가 올해 은퇴하기로 결심한 이유가 뭐죠?

(A) 잘 모르겠어요.

(B) 그는 당신 도움을 고맙게 여길 거예요.

(C) 그에게는 아니에요.

[어휘] **be determined to-V** ～하기로 마음먹다 ｜ **retire** 은퇴하다 ｜ **assistance** 도움

4 _________________________________ ?

(A) ___________________________ .

(B) They moved to Florida.

(C) They don't like the agenda.

회의가 금요일로 바뀐 이유가 뭔가요?

(A) 이사회가 수요일에 바쁘기 때문이에요.

(B) 그들은 플로리다로 이사갔어요.

(C) 그들은 그 안건을 좋아하지 않아요.

[어휘] **be moved to** ～로 바뀌다 ｜ **agenda** 안건

1 Who is the woman probably speaking to?

(A) A bank manager

(B) A travel agent

(C) A fabric supplier

(D) A store clerk

2 Why is the woman calling?

(A) To ask about fixing an appliance

(B) To cancel an appointment

(C) To discuss a billing error

(D) To ask about business hours

3 What does the man offer the woman?

(A) Speedy delivery

(B) Lower prices

(C) Free classes

(D) In-home maintenance

Dictation 대화를 다시 들으면서 받아쓰시오.　　08-06

Questions 1-3 refer to the following conversation.

M　Good afternoon. Jackson's Household Appliance. ________________________ ?

W　Yes, I purchased a microwave from you yesterday afternoon, but, for some reason, ________ ________________. ________________________ ?

M　Certainly. If you bring it in along with your receipt, one of our technicians can repair it right here in our store, or, if you prefer, ________________________ .

W　Well, my son has the car right now, so I can't go to your store. Please send someone over.

M　안녕하세요. 잭슨 가전제품점입니다. 무엇을 도와 드릴까요?

W　네, 제가 어제 오후에 그곳에서 전자레인지를 샀는데, 어찌된 일인지 작동하지 않아요. 고쳐줄 수 있으세요?

M　물론입니다. 영수증과 함께 제품을 가지고 오시면, 저희 기술자가 매장에서 바로 수리해 드리거나, 원하시면, 저희가 고객님 댁으로 사람을 보내드릴 수도 있습니다.

W　음, 지금 아들이 차를 가지고 있어서 매장으로 갈 수가 없어요. 사람을 보내주세요.

[어휘] **purchase** 구입하다 ┃ **microwave** 전자레인지 ┃ **reason** 이유 ┃ **work** 작동하다 ┃ **fix** 고치다 ┃ **receipt** 영수증 ┃ **technician** 기술자 ┃ **repair** 수리하다 ┃ **prefer** 선택하다

PART 3

4 What are the speakers mainly discussing?

(A) When a conference is going to be held

(B) What will be discussed at a conference

(C) Where a conference will be this year

(D) Who is going to attend a conference

5 Where will this year's event be held?

(A) In Dallas

(B) In Denver

(C) In Nashville

(D) In New Orleans

6 Who is going to go to the event?

(A) Bob

(B) Mr. Mason

(C) Mary

(D) Jim

Dictation 대화를 다시 들으면서 받아쓰시오. 08-08

Questions 4-6 refer to the following conversation with three speakers.

W Jim said that the annual marketing conference in New Orleans is going to be held next month. Do you know who's going?

M1 Mr. Mason informed me ________________________ .

M2 Are you aware of who the other two are?

M1 One is David Hampton. And ________________________ .

W I'd love to go. Several of my clients from Dallas and Nashville will be there, ________________________
________________________ .

M1 Are you interested in going, too, Bob?

M2 Yes, ________________________ in Denver last year, so I don't mind if Mary goes instead of me.

W That's very considerate of you, Bob.

W 짐이 말하기를, 올해 뉴올리언스에서의 마케팅 컨퍼런스가 다음 달에 열릴 것이라고 하더군요. 누가 갈 건지 알고 있나요?

M1 메이슨 씨가 저와 다른 두 명을 보낼 것이라고 제게 알려 주셨어요.

M2 나머지 두 명이 누구인지 알고 있나요?

M1 한 명은 데이비드 햄프턴이에요. 그리고 다른 한 명은 제가 선택을 해야 해요.

W 제가 가고 싶어요. 댈러스와 내슈빌의 고객 중 몇 명도 그곳에 올 것이라서, 제가 그 행사에 참석하는 것이 가장 좋을 것 같아요.

M1 당신도 가는 것에 관심이 있나요, 밥?

M2 네, 하지만 저는 작년 덴버에서 컨퍼런스에 참석을 했었기 때문에, 저 대신 메리가 가도 상관은 없어요.

W 배려심이 정말 깊군요, 밥.

[어휘] **annual** 연례의, 매년의 | **inform** 알리다, 고지하다 | **be aware of** ~에 대해 알다 | **ideal** 이상적인 | **considerate** 사려가 깊은

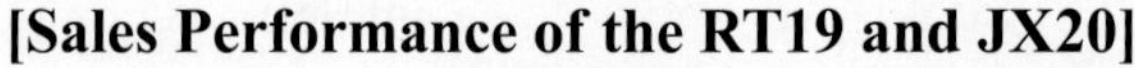

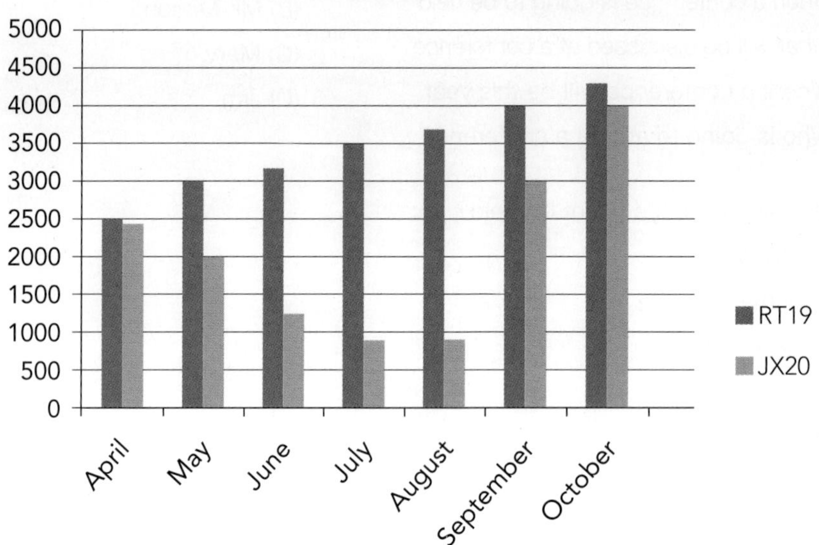

1   What does the speaker say about the RT19?

(A) It was sold at a cheaper price than the JX20.

(B) People liked the advertisements for it.

(C) It came out one month before the JX20.

(D) Customers reported positively on it.

2   What did the engineers do to the JX20?

(A) They made it with lighter materials.

(B) They fixed the problems with it.

(C) They changed its design.

(D) They added some new functions.

3   Look at the graphic. How many JX20 units were sold the first month it was rereleased?

(A) 900

(B) 2,400

(C) 3,000

(D) 4,000

Questions 1-3 refer to the following excerpt from a meeting and graph.

In April, we released two products. They are the RT19 and the JX20. As you can see from the chart, ________________________________ . ________________________________ , so they started by selling roughly the same amount the first month. However, customer feedback on the RT19 was positive while the JX20 was mostly disliked by customers. As a result, the RT19 ________________________________ ________________ . On the other hand, sales of the JX20 declined heavily. In August, we rereleased the JX20. ________________________________ ________________________ . At first, sales were flat. But in September, they started rising. Now, it's selling nearly as well as the RT19 is.

4월, 우리는 두 개의 상품을 출시했습니다. RT19과 JX20가 그것입니다. 도표에서 보실 수 있듯이, 이들은 다른 수준의 성공을 나타내고 있습니다. 우리는 두 제품 모두에 대해 막대한 광고를 진행했기 때문에, 첫 달은 거의 동일한 양으로 팔리기 시작했습니다. 하지만, RT19에 관한 고객의 반응은 긍정적이었던 반면, JX20는 대부분의 고객들이 싫어했습니다. 그 결과, 이후 여러 개월 동안 RT19은 보다 많은 제품이 판매되기 시작했습니다. 반면, JX20 판매량은 상당히 감소했습니다. 8월에, 우리는 JX20를 재출시했습니다. 우리 엔지니어들이 시스템 상의 결함을 모두 제거했고 이를 훨씬 더 우수한 제품으로 만들었습니다. 처음에는, 판매량이 일정했습니다. 하지만 11월에, 상승하기 시작했습니다. 현재, 이는 거의 RT19만큼 잘 팔리고 있습니다.

[어휘] **release** 놓아 주다; 출시하다 ｜ **advertise** 광고하다 ｜ **feedback** 피드백, 반응 ｜ **positive** 긍정적인 ｜ **decline** 쇠퇴하다, 감소하다 ｜ **rerelease** 재출시하다 ｜ **get rid of** ~을 제거하다 ｜ **flaw** 결함, 흠　**flat** 평평한

Daily Listening Practice

PART 1

🎧 09-01

(A) ☐
(B) ☐
(C) ☐
(D) ☐

Dictation 보기 4개를 다시 들으면서 받아쓰시오.

🎧 09-02

(A) A beach has been deserted.
해변이 방치되어 있다.

(B) Trees are casting shadows on the sand.
모래 위에 나무 그늘이 드리워져 있다.

(C) _________________________________.
몇몇 사람들이 물속에 있다.

(D) Rowboats are lined up at the water's edge.
조각배들이 해변을 따라 줄지어 있다.

[어휘] **desert** 버리다, 돌보지 않다 | **cast** (그림자 등을) 드리우다 | **rowboat** 노를 저어 타는 배

1	Mark your answer on your answer sheet.	(A)	(B)	(C)
2	Mark your answer on your answer sheet.	(A)	(B)	(C)
3	Mark your answer on your answer sheet.	(A)	(B)	(C)
4	Mark your answer on your answer sheet.	(A)	(B)	(C)

Dictation 질문과 응답을 다시 들으면서 받아쓰시오.　🎧 09-04

1 ____ .

(A) Well, I'm busy now.

(B) What does he look like?

(C) ________________________________ ?

곧 비가 올 것 같아요.

(A) 난 지금 바빠요.

(B) 그가 어떻게 생겼나요?

(C) 우산 갖고 왔어요?

[어휘] **look like** ~처럼 보이다 ｜ **What do/does ~ look like?** ~가 어떻게 생겼어요? ｜ **bring** 가져[데려]오다

2 ____ .

(A) The temporary secretary is really efficient.

(B) Sure, to the address.

(C) ________________________________ .

업그레이드된 모델은 정말 효율적인 것 같아요.

(A) 그 임시직 비서는 정말 유능해요.

(B) 물론, 그 주소로요.

(C) 네, 옛날 것보다 훨씬 낫군요.

[어휘] **upgraded** 기능이 향상된 ｜ **efficient** 효율적인 ｜ **temporary** 임시의 ｜ **far** 〈비교급 강조 부사〉 훨씬

3 ____
________ ____ ________ .

(A) __________ Keito ________________ .

(B) The traffic jam is terrible.

(C) It will be out tomorrow.

기계에 종이가 걸려 있어서 서류를 팩스로 보낼 수가 없어요.

(A) 케이토에게 고쳐달라고 하세요.

(B) 교통 혼잡이 심해요.

(C) 내일 발송될 거예요.

[어휘] **fax** 팩스로 보내다 ｜ **jam** 막히게 하다, 고장내다 ｜ **terrible** 지독한

4 ____ .

(A) ________________________________ .

(B) No, they caught a cold.

(C) I'm not at work.

일주일 내내 기침을 하고 있어요.

(A) 몸이 좋지 않다니 유감이네요.

(B) 아뇨, 그들은 감기에 걸렸어요.

(C) 나는 직장에 있지 않아요.

[어휘] **cough** 기침하다 ｜ **feel bad** 건강이 좋지 않다 ｜ **catch a cold** 감기에 걸리다

1 Why is the woman supposed to meet with the man?

    (A) To talk about lowering production costs

    (B) To discuss a performance review

    (C) To plan a new marketing strategy

    (D) To review last month's sales figures

2 Why does the woman want to reschedule the meeting?

    (A) She will leave town.

    (B) She didn't finish a report.

    (C) Her supervisor is not free.

    (D) She is away on vacation.

3 What time will the meeting between the two speakers take place?

    (A) At 11:00 A.M.

    (B) At 11:15 A.M.

    (C) At 1:00 P.M.

    (D) At 4:30 P.M.

Dictation 대화를 다시 들으면서 받아쓰시오.　　09-06

Questions 1-3 refer to the following conversation.

W Excuse me, Mr. Vlack, but could I please talk with you about our meeting this afternoon?

M ____

________________________________ ?

W That is correct. ____

________________________________ Dawson City. Since I have to drive there, would it

be possible to reschedule our meeting until sometime this afternoon?

M Yes, of course. ____ ?

W 죄송하지만 블랙 씨, 오늘 오후 회의에 대해 잠시 이야기할 수 있을까요?

M 당신의 최근 판매부 업무 실적에 대한 나의 평가와 관련한 11시 15분 회의 말씀이신가요?

W 맞습니다. 저는 도슨 시에서 저를 오후 1시에 만나고 싶어 하시는 잠재고객 한 분과 지금 막 전화통화를 했어요. 제가 거기까지 운전을 해야 하니 회의를 오늘 오후 중으로 조정할 수 있을까요?

M 네, 물론이죠. 저는 4시 30분에 시간이 있으니 그때 제 사무실로 오시는 게 어때요?

[어휘] **refer to** 언급하다, 관계가 있다 | **concerning** ~와 관련한 | **evaluation** 평가 | **recent** 최근의 | **division** 부서 | **correct** 정확한 | **potential** 잠재적인, 유망한 | **client** 고객 | **possible** 가능한 | **reschedule** 일정을 조정하다

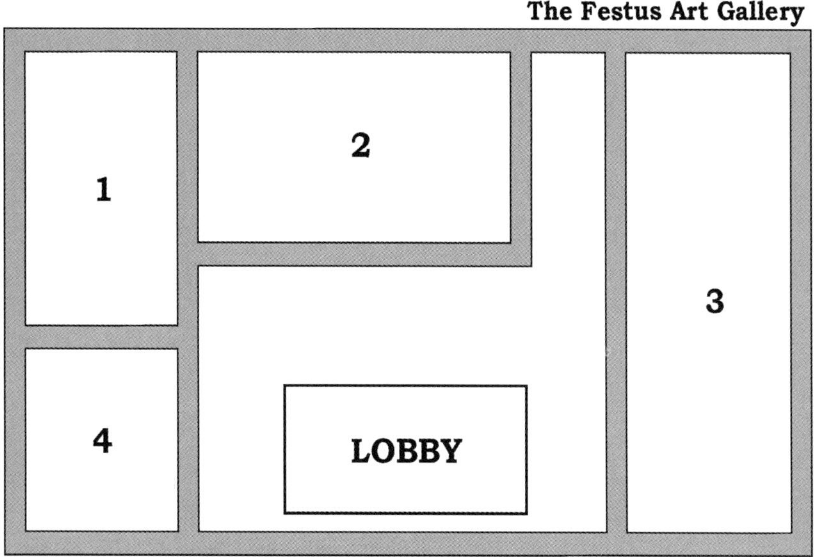

4   What does the man say about the Festus Art Gallery?

(A) He is visiting it for the first time.

(B) It has some beautiful works of art.

(C) The building has two floors.

(D) It charges too much for admission.

5   According to the woman, which exhibit is temporary?

(A) The Renaissance art exhibit

(B) The European sculpture exhibit

(C) The Chinese art exhibit

(D) The modern art exhibit

6   Look at the graphic. Where is the man going to go first?

(A) 1

(B) 2

(C) 3

(D) 4

Questions 4-6 refer to the following conversation and map.

W Welcome to the Festus Art Gallery. Can I help you with something?

M Yes, please. I've never been here before, so could you tell me where everything is?

W Of course. ______________________________. ______________________________

____.

M What's in the gallery to the left?

W ____. One contains a visiting

exhibit of Chinese art. It will only be here until next week. The second contains European

sculptures.

M Okay. Is there anything else I should see?

W Yes, if you go to the right, you can see the Renaissance art exhibit. ______________________

______________.

M Thanks for your assistance. ____ and

then look at the others.

W 페스터스 미술관에 오신 것을 환영합니다. 제가 도와 드릴까요?

M 네, 그렇게 해 주세요. 제가 전에 이곳에 와 본 적이 없어서 그런데요, 뭐가 어디에 있는지 말씀해 주실 수 있나요?

W 물론이죠. 우리는 지금 정문 로비에 있어요. 앞으로 직진하시면 현대 미술 전시관이 있어요.

M 왼쪽 화랑에는 무엇이 있나요?

W 실은 왼쪽에 두 곳의 전시장이 있어요. 한 곳에는 중국 미술 초대전이 진행 중이죠. 이곳에서는 다음 주까지만 진행될 거예요. 두 번째 전시장
에는 유럽 조각 작품들이 소장되어 있고요.

M 알겠어요. 그밖에 제가 봐야 할 다른 것들이 있을까요?

W 네, 오른쪽으로 가시면, 르네상스 미술전을 보실 수 있어요. 개인적으로 제가 가장 좋아하는 것이죠.

M 도와 주셔서 고마워요. 먼저 현대 미술전을 관람한 후, 나머지 곳들을 살펴 볼게요.

[어휘] **front lobby** 정문 로비 | **ahead of** ~의 앞에 | **display hall** 전시관 | **contain** 포함하다 | **sculpture** 조각 |
       check out 확인하다; 살펴보다

PART 4

1 Why has traffic been delayed on Montgomery Street?

(A) A traffic light is not working.

(B) Some power lines are down.

(C) A delivery truck broke down.

(D) The road is undergoing repairs.

2 What was moved to the front of Rochester Elementary School?

(A) An advertisement billboard

(B) A bus stop

(C) A newsstand

(D) A ticket office

3 What will happen on Tuesday?

(A) A bridge will be reopened.

(B) A new bus line will be added.

(C) A school will be closed.

(D) A grocery store will have a sale.

Dictation 지문을 다시 들으면서 받아쓰시오. ⌒09-10

Questions 1-3 refer to the following traffic report.

It's 11:00 and time for CKCL's local traffic update. Montgomery Street ______________ ______________ Ellis Avenue and Regent Street ______________ ______________ that were knocked down during last night's storm. Crews hope to have everything fixed no later than 2:00. Meanwhile, ______________ Melvin's Grocery ______________ Montgomery Street ______________ Rochester Elementary School on nearby Doris Avenue. Anyone who uses that bus stop should get on and get off in front of the school until further notice. Also, motorists are reminded that ______________ Armstrong Bridge ______________ .

11시, CKCL 지역 교통 방송 시간입니다. 몽고메리 스트리트의 엘리스 애비뉴와 리젠트 스트리트 구간은 간밤의 폭풍으로 쓰러진 전선들 때문에 계속 폐쇄되어 있습니다. 작업반이 모든 것을 2시까지는 고칠 수 있기를 바랍니다. 그 동안, 몽고메리 스트리트의 멜빈 식료품점 앞 버스 정거장은 인근 도리스 애비뉴의 로체스터 초등학교로 옮겨집니다. 그 정거장을 이용하실 분들은 추후 공지가있을 때까지 초등학교 앞에서 승하차 하셔야 합니다. 또한, 운전자들께 암스트롱 교각의 건설이 다음 주 월요일 저녁에 끝나게 되어, 다음 주 화요일에는 그 다리로 운행하실 수 있다는 것을 알려드립니다.

[어휘] **local** 지역의 | **traffic** 교통 | **update** 최신정보 | **continue** 계속 ~하다 | **due to** ~때문에 | **fallen** 떨어진, 쓰러진 | **power line** 송전선, 전력선 | **knock down** 때려 부수다 | **storm** 폭풍(우) | **crew** 작업반 | **fix** 고치다 | **no later than** (늦어도) ~까지 | **meanwhile** 그 동안에 | **in front of** ~의 앞의 | **grocery** 식료(품) | **elementary school** 초등학교 | **nearby** 인근의 | **get on** ~에 타다 | **get off** ~에서 내리다 | **until further notice** 다음 통지가 있을 때까지 | **motorist** 운전자 | **remind** 상기시키다 | **construction** 건설 | **expect** 기대하다, 예상하다 | **complete** 완료하다 | **mean** 뜻하다, 의미하다

Daily Listening Practice

PART 1

(A) ☐
(B) ☐
(C) ☐
(D) ☐

Dictation　보기 4개를 다시 들으면서 받아쓰시오.　🎧 10-02

(A)　She's washing some glasses.
　　여자가 유리잔들을 세척하고 있다.

(B)　She is repositioning a machine.
　　여자가 기계의 위치를 옮기고 있다.

(C)　She's putting on her glasses.
　　여자는 안경을 쓰는 중이다.

(D)　______________________________________.
　　여자가 기계 앞에 서 있다.

[어휘] **reposition** 위치를 옮기다　|　**put on** 착용하다, 입다

PART 2

1 Mark your answer on your answer sheet.   (A)   (B)   (C)

2 Mark your answer on your answer sheet.   (A)   (B)   (C)

3 Mark your answer on your answer sheet.   (A)   (B)   (C)

4 Mark your answer on your answer sheet.   (A)   (B)   (C)

Dictation 질문과 응답을 다시 들으면서 받아쓰시오.   🎧 10-04

1 ________________________________?

(A) ________________________________.

(B) The corner office belongs to the manager.

(C) Much better, thank you.

책상을 코너에 놓는 게 좋나요, 아니면 창문 근처가 낫나요?

(A) 어느 쪽이든 좋아요.

(B) 코너에 있는 사무실은 매니저 사무실이예요.

(C) 훨씬 낫네요, 고마워요.

[어휘] **prefer** 보다 좋아하다 | **belong to** ~의 것이다 | **much** 〈비교급 강조부사〉 훨씬

2 ________________________________?

(A) ________________________________.

(B) We were on the same train.

(C) Yes, I gave it back.

기차를 타는 게 좋나요, 아니면 비행기가 좋나요?

(A) 비행기가 더 나아요.

(B) 우리는 같은 기차에 탔었어요.

(C) 네, 그것을 돌려줬어요.

[어휘] **would rather** ~하고 싶다 | **fly** 비행기를 타다

3 ________________________________ Julia?

(A) The boss didn't mention it.

(B) It's a different kind of report.

(C) ________________________________.

이 보고서를 타이핑 해줄 수 있나요, 아니면 줄리아에게 부탁할까요?

(A) 사장님은 그것에 대해 언급하지 않았어요.

(B) 다른 종류의 보고서예요.

(C) 점심 후에 시간이 있어요.

[어휘] **type** 타이프 치다 | **mention** 언급하다 | **kind** 종류 | **have time** 시간이 나다

4 ________________________________?

(A) They can choose it.

(B) ________________________________.

(C) Windows will be installed soon.

여기 안쪽에 앉기를 원하세요, 아니면 저쪽 창가를 원하세요?

(A) 그들은 그것을 선택할 수 있어요.

(B) 우린 신선한 공기가 필요해요.

(C) 창문들이 곧 설치될 거예요.

[어휘] **inside** 안쪽에 | **choose** 선택하다 | **install** 설치하다

1 Why is the man calling?

    (A) To transfer some money

    (B) To schedule some tests

    (C) To talk to a specialist

    (D) To order a product

2 What does the man need to do?

    (A) Apply for insurance

    (B) Go to a bank

    (C) Phone another clinic

    (D) Complete a form

3 What does the man ask the woman to do?

    (A) Send a document by mail

    (B) Cancel an appointment

    (C) E-mail him a form

    (D) Purchase a fax machine

Dictation 대화를 다시 들으면서 받아쓰시오.　🎧 10-06

Questions 1-3 refer to the following conversation.

W   Good afternoon, King Street Health Clinic. Janice speaking.

M   Hello. __________________________________. __________________

__________________________? __________________________________?

W   Yes, sir, we provide allergy testing. When you arrive for the tests, __________________

__________________________ indicating your known reactions to foods, dusts, and other

substances. We could either send you the form as an e-mail attachment, or we could mail

it. Which do you prefer, sir?

M   My printer is out of ink, so you had better __________________________________.

W   안녕하세요. 킹 스트리트 헬스 클리닉의 제니스입니다.

M   여보세요, 제가 알레르기 검사를 요구하는 직장에 지원하려고 해서요. 그 병원에서 검사를 하나요? 그렇다면 다음 주에 검사 받을 수 있나요?

W   네, 고객님. 저희 병원에서도 알레르기 검사를 합니다. 검사 받으러 오실 때 환자분께서 음식이나 먼지, 그리고 기타 물질에 대해 알고 계셨던 반응을 저희 양식에 적어 오셔서 의사 선생님께 제출하셔야 합니다. 양식은 이메일로 첨부해 드리거나 우편으로 보내 드릴 수 있습니다. 어떤 방법이 편하시겠어요?

M   프린터 잉크가 다 떨어져서, 보통우편으로 보내주시는 편이 낫겠습니다.

[어휘] **clinic** 병원 ｜ **apply for** 신청하다 ｜ **require** 요구하다 ｜ **allergy** 알레르기 ｜ **provide** 제공하다 ｜ **indicate** 나타내다 ｜ **reaction** 반응 ｜ **dust** 먼지 ｜ **substance** 물질 ｜ **attachment** 첨부 ｜ **prefer** 선호하다 ｜ **regular mail** 보통우편

4 What are the speakers mostly discussing?

    (A) A meeting with a new client

    (B) The replacement of some furniture

    (C) How some of their clients think of them

    (D) The redesign of the entire office

5 When would the man like the woman to complete his request?

    (A) By lunch

    (B) By this afternoon

    (C) By this evening

    (D) By tomorrow morning

6 What is the woman going to do this afternoon?

    (A) Attend a meeting

    (B) Look through some catalogs

    (C) Order some new items

    (D) Visit a furniture store

Dictation 대화를 다시 들으면서 받아쓰시오.　　🎧 10-08

Questions 4-6 refer to the following conversation.

M We need to replace some of the desks and chairs here.

W What's the matter with them? I think they're pretty comfortable.

M They look old and tattered, and ____.
They reflect badly on us as a whole.

W I see. ____?

M Why don't you find a few items that look nice and then show them to me? ________________
____ before I make a final decision.

W All right. I'll get to work on it as soon as I can.

M Do you think ____?

W I doubt it. I've got a meeting at Ferris Metals that will last most of the afternoon.

M　이곳 책상과 의자를 재배치해야 해요.

W　문제라도 있나요? 저는 꽤 편하다고 생각하는데요.

M　낡고 망가진 것처럼 보이고, 몇몇 방문객들은 그에 대해 부정적인 언급을 하고 있어요. 전체적으로 우리에게 부정적인 인식을 가져다 주죠.

W　알겠어요. 그러면 제가 가구를 새로 주문하기를 원하나요?

M　좋아 보이는 것들을 몇 개 찾아서 저한테 보여 주는 것이 어떨까요? 최종 결정을 내리기 전에 전체 비용이 어느 정도 들지 알아야 해서요.

W　좋아요. 가능한 빨리 그 일을 시작하도록 할게요.

M　오늘 저녁까지 당신이 선택한 것을 제게 보내 줄 수 있을까요?

W　힘들 것 같은데요. 페리스 금속에서 오후 시간 대부분 동안 진행될 회의가 있거든요.

[어휘] **replace** 재배치하다 ｜ **comfortable** 편안한 ｜ **tattered** 낡은, 누더기가 된 ｜ **comment** 논평하다 ｜ **negatively** 부정적으로 ｜
reflect badly on ~에게 부정적인 인식을 하게 만들다 ｜ **as a whole** 전체적으로 ｜ **final decision** 최종 결정

PART 4

1 What does the speaker suggest about the personal trainers?

(A) They teach members in small groups.

(B) They focus on developing people's muscles.

(C) They listen to the people they work with.

(D) They must be paid extra for training sessions.

2 What is true about the Lowell Health Club?

(A) New members can sign up on its Web site.

(B) It has three locations throughout the city.

(C) The gym only closes on national holidays.

(D) People can join up for a discounted price.

3 What does the speaker mean when he says, "It requires effort on your part"?

(A) People need to work out to lose weight.

(B) People must make an effort to contact the gym.

(C) People need to be honest with the trainers.

(D) People need to work hard to become more skilled.

Dictation 지문을 다시 들으면서 받아쓰시오. 🎧 10-10

Questions 1-3 refer to the following advertisement.

Now that the holiday season is over, many of you have probably put on some extra pounds. There's no need to be alarmed though. Simply sign up for a membership at the Lowell Health Club. ____

___________________. By showing up at the gym at least three times a week, you'll start getting slimmer immediately. But remember that working out isn't easy. It requires effort on your part. Still, ____. Call 509-4305 to find out about our special membership offer that will save you money. Or visit us at 56 Pecan Avenue. We're open

____.

휴가철이 끝났기 때문에, 여러분 중 많은 분들께서는 아마도 몸무게가 증가하셨을 것입니다. 하지만 놀라실 필요는 없습니다. 로웰 헬스 클럽에 가입만 하십시오. 저희의 개인 트레이너들이 여러분과 이야기를 나누고 체중을 감량할 수 있는 최선의 방법을 알려 드릴 것입니다. 일주일에 최소 3번만 체육관에 나오신다면, 여러분들은 즉시 날씬해지기 시작할 것입니다. 하지만 운동은 쉽지 않다는 점을 기억해 주십시오. 여러분들의 노력이 필요합니다. 하지만, 저희는 여러분들이 운동을 시작하여 날씬한 혹은 근육질의 몸매를 만들 수 있도록 도와 드릴 수 있습니다. 509-4305로 전화하셔서 비용을 절약할 수 있는, 회원 가입을 위한 특별 조건을 알아 보십시오. 혹은 피컨 가 56번지로 가로 저희를 찾아 주십시오. 저희는 연중 매일 24시간 문을 열고 있습니다.

[어휘] **holiday season** 휴가철, 연휴 | **probably** 아마 | **put on extra pounds** 살이 찌다 | **alarm** 놀라게 하다, 경고하다 |
trainer 트레이너 | **determine** 결정하다; 알아내다 | **lose weight** 살을 빼다 | **muscular** 근육의, 근육질의

11 Daily Listening Practice

PART 1

🎧 11-01

(A) ☐
(B) ☐
(C) ☐
(D) ☐

Dictation 보기 4개를 다시 들으면서 받아쓰시오.

🎧 11-02

(A) _________________________________.
　　도자기가 책 위에 놓여있다.

(B) A stack of books has been set on a shelf.
　　책 한 무더기가 선반에 놓여있다.

(C) A rack is being adjusted.
　　격자 선반이 조절되고 있다.

(D) A book is wrapped in cloths.
　　책이 천에 싸여있다.

[어휘] **pottery** 도자기(류) ｜ **a stack of** 한 무더기의 ｜ **rack** 격자 선반 ｜ **adjust** 조절하다 ｜ **wrap** 싸다 ｜ **cloths** 천

PART 2

1 **Mark your answer on your answer sheet.** (A) (B) (C)

2 **Mark your answer on your answer sheet.** (A) (B) (C)

3 **Mark your answer on your answer sheet.** (A) (B) (C)

4 **Mark your answer on your answer sheet.** (A) (B) (C)

Dictation 질문과 응답을 다시 들으면서 받아쓰시오. 🎧 11-04

1 _______________________________________
   _______________________ ?

언제 이 비행기가 공항에 도착하는지 아세요?

(A) It's a clear day.

(A) 날이 맑아요.

(B) There was a mechanical problem.

(B) 기술적인 문제가 있었어요.

(C) _______________________________________ .

(C) 일정을 확인해볼게요.

[어휘] **mechanical** 기술적인

2 _______________________________________
   _______________________ ?

서류정리함 열쇠들이 어디 있는지 아세요?

(A) Just to Mr. Thompson.

(A) 그냥 톰슨 씨에게요.

(B) _______________ Mr. Baker's _______ .

(B) 베이커 씨 책상 위에 놔뒀어요.

(C) Files are being updated.

(C) 파일이 업데이트되고 있어요.

3 _______________ Mr. Delco _______________ ?

델코 씨가 왜 회의를 소집했는지 아세요?

(A) _______________________________________ .

(A) 새 직원을 소개하기 위한 것 같아요.

(B) That can save us some money.

(B) 그렇게 하면 우리가 돈을 조금 절약할 수 있어요.

(C) You called her the other day.

(C) 일전에 당신이 그녀에게 전화했었어요.

[어휘] **call a meeting** 회의를 소집하다 | **the other day** 며칠 전에

4 _______________________________________ ?

누가 그 공석의 후임이 될지 아세요?

(A) This is the only one you have.

(A) 이게 당신이 가진 것 전부예요.

(B) What place did you vacate?

(B) 어디를 비웠죠?

(C) _______________________________________ .

(C) 아직 결정이 나지 않았어요.

[어휘] **fill** 채우다, 후임이 되다 | **vacant** 비어 있는 | **vacate** 비우다

1 What are the speakers mainly discussing?

   (A) A customer

   (B) A partner

   (C) A fax machine

   (D) A graph

2 When is the meeting with the finance head?

   (A) This morning

   (B) This afternoon

   (C) Tomorrow morning

   (D) Tomorrow afternoon

3 What will the speakers probably do?

   (A) Meet a potential client

   (B) Have a lunch meeting

   (C) Fax a quarterly report

   (D) Reschedule an appointment

Dictation 대화를 다시 들으면서 받아쓰시오.　🎧 11-06

Questions 1-3 refer to the following conversation.

W1 Ms. Drummond, ____? I need

   to discuss those figures with you ____.

W2 Yes, Ms. Boyce. I e-mailed it to you about half an hour ago.

W1 Oh, I see. I haven't had a chance to check my inbox yet. I'll go take a look at it now. It's

   11:45 now, so ____? 10 minutes is

   more than enough time to review the graph.

W2 Certainly, Ms. Boyce. I'll see you at noon.

W1 드럼몬드 씨, 지난 달 판매 실적 그래프를 갖고 있나요? 1시 30분에 있을 재무부장과의 회의 전에, 당신과 매출액에 대해 논의할 게 있어요.

W2 네, 보이스 씨. 30분 전쯤에 그래프를 이메일로 보내드렸어요.

W1 아, 그랬군요. 이메일 수신함을 확인할 틈이 없었어요. 지금 가서 확인해 볼게요. 지금이 11시 45분이니까 점심을 먹으면서 판매 실적에 대해 이야기하는 게 어때요? 도표 검토는 10분이면 충분할 거예요.

W2 좋습니다. 보이스 씨. 12시에 뵐게요.

[어휘] **graph** 그래프 | **sale** 판매실적, 매출액 | **discuss** 논의하다, 토론하다 | **figure** 숫자, 총액 | **finance** 재정의, 재무의 |
   check 확인하다 | **inbox** 수신함 | **over lunch** 점심 식사를 하면서

4 When is the company going to relocate?

(A) This week

(B) In one month

(C) Six months from now

(D) Next year

6 How does the man feel about moving?

(A) He is fine with moving.

(B) He is worried about buying a house.

(C) He does not want to move his family.

(D) He thinks it will be too expensive.

5 What is suggested by the speakers?

(A) Their company is located in Portland.

(B) None of them owns a car.

(C) They visit Seattle on business.

(D) They are currently looking for work.

Dictation 대화를 다시 들으면서 받아쓰시오.　　🎧 11-08

Questions 4-6 refer to the following conversation with three speakers.

M　_______________________________ that we're going to be relocating soon.

W1　It's not simply a rumor. It's going to happen sometime next month.

M　How do you know that?

W1　Mr. Carlyle asked me how I felt about moving to Seattle. I asked him why, and then he told me.

W2　So we're really going to be moving there? _______________________________ from Portland.

M　If we relocate to Seattle, we'll all have to move.

W1　I'm not willing to do that, so _______________________________. I don't want to move my family to another city.

M　_______________________, so it doesn't bother me too much. But _______________________________

_______________________________.

W2　That's a good point.

M　우리가 곧 이전을 하게 될 것이라는 소문이 돌고 있더군요.

W1　단순한 소문이 아니에요. 다음 달에 일어날 일이죠.

M　어떻게 알고 있나요?

W1　칼라일 씨께서 제게 시애틀로의 이전에 대해 어떻게 생각하는지 물어 보셨어요. 제가 그분께 이유를 여쭤보니, 말씀을 해 주시더군요.

W2　그러면 우리가 정말로 그곳으로 이전할 것인가요? 그곳은 포틀랜드에서 차로 3시간 거리에요.

M　우리가 시애틀로 이전을 하면, 우리 모두 이사를 가야 할 거에요.

W1　저는 그렇게 하고 싶지 않기 때문에, 다른 일자리를 찾아야 할 것 같네요. 제 가족들이 다른 도시로 이사를 가는 것은 원치 않거든요.

M　저는 아직 미혼이기 때문에, 제게는 큰 걸림돌이 되지 않아요. 하지만 생활비가 이곳보다 더 높을 것이라고 생각해요.

W2　좋은 지적이군요.

[어휘] **rumor** 소문, 루머 ｜ **relocate** 이전하다, 이동하다 ｜ **be willing to** 기꺼이 ~하다 ｜ **single** 단 하나의; 미혼의 ｜ **bother** 괴롭히다

PART 4

1 Why is the speaker giving this talk?

    (A) To introduce new staff members

    (B) To announce a raise in pay

    (C) To appoint a regional manager

    (D) To explain a system change

2 What should employees get from their supervisors?

    (A) A new ID

    (B) A new computer

    (C) An application form

    (D) A subway map

3 Why would an employee most likely go to general affairs?

    (A) To cancel a meeting

    (B) To obtain some instructions

    (C) To schedule an appointment

    (D) To collect a work schedule

Dictation 지문을 다시 들으면서 받아쓰시오.   🎧 11-10

Questions 1-3 refer to the following talk.

Please have a seat. This meeting will be very quick. ________________________, Dawson Equipment

________________. At the end of a shift, each person must enter his or her new employee ID number and hours in one of the computers located in room 107. The new system will keep track of your hours and adjust your wages accordingly. Please be sure to enter your information every day. ________________

________________. If you experience any difficulties, please see either Ms. Yuri Nakamura or Frederick Simmons in general affairs. ________________________________.

착석해 주시기 바랍니다. 이번 회의는 매우 짧을 것입니다. 다 아시겠지만, 도슨 이큅먼트는 내일부터 새로운 급료 지불 시스템을 적용하므로 여러분은 바뀌는 적용법을 알고 있어야 합니다. 교대 근무시간이 끝나면, 각 직원은 107호실에 설치된 컴퓨터에 새로운 직원 ID 번호와 시간을 입력해야 합니다. 새로운 시스템은 근무시간을 기록해서 그에 따라 여러분의 급료를 책정할 것입니다. 여러분의 정보를 매일 입력해 주셔야 함을 꼭 기억하시기 바랍니다. 여러분의 새 ID는 나갈 때 여러분의 팀장한테서 받으시면 됩니다. 문제가 생기면 총무부의 유리 나카무라나 프레데릭 시몬스를 찾으시기 바랍니다. 그들이 여러분의 정보 입력 방법에 대해 간편한 몇 가지 조처 목록을 만들어 두었습니다.

[어휘] **payroll** 급료 지불 명부 | **shift** (교대제의) 근무 시간 | **enter** 입력하다 | **located in** ~에 위치한 | **keep track of** 기록하다 | **adjust** 조절하다, 정산하다 | **wage** 급료 | **accordingly** 그에 따라, 그에 상응하게 | **pick up** 찾아가다 | **supervisor** 팀장 | **experience** 겪다, 경험하다 | **difficulty** 어려움, 고초 | **general affairs** 총무부 | **input** 입력하다

Daily Listening Practice

PART 1

🎧 12-01

(A) ☐
(B) ☐
(C) ☐
(D) ☐

Dictation　보기 4개를 다시 들으면서 받아쓰시오.

🎧 12-02

(A)　Kitchen utensils are scattered on the floor.
주방기구들이 바닥에 흩어져 있다.

(B)　The door of the refrigerator has been opened.
냉장고 문이 열려 있다.

(C)　People are seated around the table.
사람들은 식탁에 둘러앉아 있다.

(D)　________________________________.
의자들이 실내에 놓여 있다.

[어휘] **kitchen utensils** 주방기구들　|　**scattered** 흩어져있는　|　**refrigerator** 냉장고　|　**be seated** 앉아 있다

PART 2

1 Mark your answer on your answer sheet. (A) (B) (C)

2 Mark your answer on your answer sheet. (A) (B) (C)

3 Mark your answer on your answer sheet. (A) (B) (C)

4 Mark your answer on your answer sheet. (A) (B) (C)

Dictation 질문과 응답을 다시 들으면서 받아쓰시오. 🎧 12-04

1 ________________________________ ?

(A) She's not working now.

(B) He went to the second floor.

(C) ________________________________ ?

[어휘] **vending machine** 자판기 | **at the end of** ~끝에

이 층에는 자판기가 없나요?

(A) 그녀는 지금 근무 중이 아니에요.

(B) 그는 이층에 갔어요.

(C) 있어요, 복도 끝에요.

2 ________________________________ ?

(A) No, it's the same one.

(B) ________________________________ ?

(C) I thought it was not necessary.

[어휘] **too ~ to-V** …하기에는 너무 ~하다 | **necessary** 필수적인

스웨터를 입기엔 날씨가 너무 따뜻하지 않나요?

(A) 아뇨, 똑같은 거예요.

(B) 여기 안이 춥다고 생각하지 않으세요?

(C) 내 생각에 필요하지 않았어요.

3 ________________________________ ?

(A) Yes, she's a new arrival.

(B) All right, then.

(C) ________________________________ .

[어휘] **equipment** 장비 | **arrival** 도착, 도착자

장비가 아직 도착하지 않았나요?

(A) 예, 그녀는 새로 온 분이에요.

(B) 그렇다면 괜찮아요.

(C) 아직 안 온 것 같아요.

4 __________ Ms. Becker ________________________

________________________ ?

(A) Submit it in writing.

(B) That's what I've been told.

(C) ________________________________ .

[어휘] **notify A of B** A에게 B에 대해 알리다 | **cancellation** 취소 | **in writing** 서면으로

베커 씨가 당신에게 취소에 대해 알리지 않았나요?

(A) 서면으로 제출하세요.

(B) 그것이 제가 들은 얘기입니다.

(C) 아뇨, 전혀 못 들었어요.

1 Where does the conversation most likely occur?

(A) At a ferry dock

(B) At a bus station

(C) At an airport

(D) At a subway station

2 What does the man want to know?

(A) A gate number

(B) The type of vehicle

(C) An arrival time

(D) The price of a ticket

3 What does the woman suggest the man do?

(A) Exchange his ticket

(B) Put a tag on his suitcase

(C) Leave sometime tomorrow

(D) Wait for the boarding call

Dictation 대화를 다시 들으면서 받아쓰시오.

🎧 12-06

Questions 1-3 refer to the following conversation.

M Could you help me for a minute? ________________________ St. Richard __________

____ .

W They usually post that information on the board but you're right, it's not there. Let me check our main schedule in this book here. Is that an express bus?

M No, it isn't.

W According to this, it's coach number 1436 and ________________________________ .

____ .

M 잠시 도와주실 수 있으세요? 저는 2시 30분 발 세인트 리차드 행 버스를 탈 예정인데, 어떤 탑승구로 가야 할 지 잘 모르겠어요.

W 보통은 안내판에 정보가 나타나는데, 말씀대로 보이지 않는군요. 여기 이 책에 적혀 있는 주요 일정을 한번 살펴볼게요. 고속버스인가요?

M 아닙니다.

W 이 책대로라면, 그 버스는 1436번이고 10번 출구에서 출발합니다. 탑승시간이 되면 기사님이 안내를 할 것이니 저쪽 탑승구 주변의 의자에 앉아 계시는 게 좋을 것 같네요.

[어휘] **boarding gate** 탑승구 ǀ **usually** 보통은, 일반적으로 ǀ **board** 게시판, 탑승하다 ǀ **according to** ~에 따르면 ǀ **coach** 버스 ǀ
depart 출발하다 ǀ **make an announcement** 공지하다 ǀ **suggest** 제안하다 ǀ **have a seat** 자리에 앉다

City	Distance
Milton	5km
Springfield	75km
Jackson	180km
Watertown	302km

4   What are the speakers mainly discussing?

(A) How much longer they need to drive

(B) Where they should put gas in their car

(C) What they are going to do in Milton

(D) What they should eat for lunch

5   What did the speakers do one hour ago?

(A) They had some food.

(B) They left their home.

(C) They visited a friend.

(D) They went shopping.

6   Look at the graphic. What is the distance to the speakers' final destination?

(A) 5km

(B) 75km

(C) 180km

(D) 302km

Questions 4-6 refer to the following conversation and road sign.

M　We're about to arrive at the exit for Milton. ____________________

____________________ ?

W　No, that's all right. We had lunch an hour ago, so I'm not hungry now. You're not already getting hungry again, are you?

M　No, I'm not. However, ____________________ Jackson without filling up the car with gas.

W　____________________ ? We're not about to run out, are we?

M　No, don't worry about that. We've got about half a tank left.

W　How about stopping for gas at Springfield? ____________________

____________________ .

M　That should be all right. We can probably make it there in the next hour or so.

M　밀턴으로 빠지는 출구에 곧 도착할 거에요. 옆길로 들어서서 정차를 할 건가요?

W　아니오, 괜찮아요. 한 시간 전에 점심을 먹어서, 지금은 배가 고프지 않군요. 당신도 벌써 다시 배가 고픈 것은 아니죠, 그런가요?

M　아니오, 배가 고프지는 않아요. 하지만, 우리가 차에 기름을 채우지 않고서 잭슨까지 계속 갈 수 있을 것이라고는 생각하지 않아요.

W　지금 남아 있는 기름이 얼마나 되죠? 곧 떨어지지는 않겠죠, 그렇지 않나요?

M　아니오, 그에 대해서는 걱정하지 말아요. 연료통의 약 반 정도가 채워져 있거든요.

W　스프링필드의 주유소에서 정차하는 것이 어떨까요? 그때쯤에는 아마도 무언가를 먹고 싶어질 수도 있고요.

M　괜찮을 것 같군요. 아마도 한 시간 정도 후에 그곳에 도착할 수 있을 거에요.

[**어휘**] **be about to** 막 ~하려고 하다　|　**take a turnoff** 옆길로 들어서다　|　**all the way** 계속, 쭉　|　**fill up** (기름 등을) 채우다　|　**gas** 가솔린　|　**run out** 소진되다, 다 써버리다

Radio Station	Format
95.5 WDNG	sports; music
102.7 WMRT	news; talk shows
99.3 WPTR	foreign language programming
101.7 WCOB	education; news

1   Who is Brett Hampton?

   (A) A radio host

   (B) A university professor

   (C) A writer

   (D) A news reporter

2   What will listeners hear next?

   (A) A news program

   (B) An advertisement

   (C) An interview

   (D) A weather update

3   Look at the graphic. On which radio station is this announcement being aired?

   (A) WMRT

   (B) WCOB

   (C) WDNG

   (D) WPTR

Questions 1-3 refer to the following announcement and chart.

Thank you all for tuning in to tonight's program. I hope you had a great time listening to Dr. Ramsey talk about ____. I know I had lots of fun interviewing him. Be sure to listen to tomorrow's show. We're going to have a special guest. It's local author Brett Hampton. He's going to chat with us about his latest novel, ________

________________________. ____,

and then Steve Isaacs will be on next with his show, *The Steve Isaacs Hour*. He'll recap all of the local and state news of the day. ____, so be sure to listen to Steve's take on them.

오늘 밤의 프로그램에 주파수를 맞춰 주신 모든 분들께 감사를 드립니다. 지역 대학에서 진행 중인 램지 박사의 혁신적인 연구 이야기를 들으시면서 멋진 시간을 보내셨기를 바랍니다. 저도 그분을 인터뷰하면서 매우 재미있었습니다. 내일 쇼도 잊지 말고 들어 주십시오. 특별 게스트를 모실 예정입니다. 바로 지역 작가인 브렛 햄프턴입니다. 그는 그의 최신 소설에 관해 우리와 이야기를 나눌 것인데, 이 소설은 베스트셀러 목록에서 순위가 급등하고 있습니다. 이제 짧은 광고 방송을 들은 후, 다음 순서로서 스티브 아이삭스가 자신의 쇼인 *더 스티브 아이삭스 아워*와 함께 자리로 올 것입니다. 그는 오늘 하루 동안의 모든 지역 뉴스 및 주 뉴스를 간략히 알려 드릴 것입니다. 오늘 주목할만한 사건이 몇 가지 있었기 때문에, 잊지 말고 그에 관한 스티브의 의견을 들어 주십시오.

[어휘] **tune in to** ~으로 주파수를 맞추다 ｜ **innovative** 혁신적인 ｜ **chat with** ~와 이야기를 나누다 ｜ **latest** 최신의 ｜ **shoot up** 급등하다 ｜ **commercial break** 광고, 광고 시간 ｜ **recap** 개요를 말하다 ｜ **noteworthy** 주목할만한

Daily Listening Practice

PART 1

(A) ☐

(B) ☐

(C) ☐

(D) ☐

Dictation 보기 4개를 다시 들으면서 받아쓰시오.

🎧 13-02

(A) He is falling over a rock.

남자는 돌에 걸려 넘어지고 있다.

(B) _______________________________________.

남자는 손을 깍지 끼고 있다.

(C) He is bending his neck.

남자는 고개를 숙이고 있다.

(D) He is lifting a candle.

남자는 양초를 들어 올리고 있다.

[어휘] **fall over** ~에 걸려 넘어지다 ┃ **rock** 바위, 돌 ┃ **fold one's hands** 깍지를 끼다 ┃ **bend one's neck** 고개를 숙이다 ┃ **lift** ~을 올리다 ┃ **candle** 양초

PART 2

1   **Mark your answer on your answer sheet.**   (A)   (B)   (C)

2   **Mark your answer on your answer sheet.**   (A)   (B)   (C)

3   **Mark your answer on your answer sheet.**   (A)   (B)   (C)

4   **Mark your answer on your answer sheet.**   (A)   (B)   (C)

Dictation   질문과 응답을 다시 들으면서 받아쓰시오.   🎧 13-04

1 ____________________________________ ?

영업부의 공석에 지원하고 싶으세요?

(A) ____________________________________ ?

(A) 아뇨, 그 자리에 관심 없어요.

(B) Yes, it does.

(B) 네, 그것은 그래요.

(C) There are many vacant rooms.

(C) 많은 빈 방들이 있어요.

[어휘] **apply for** ~에 지원하다 | **vacancy** 공석 | **vacant** 비어 있는

2 ____________________________________ ?

당신은 회의에 참석할 수 있나요?

(A) The meeting will last for 30 minutes.

(A) 회의는 30분 동안 지속될 거예요.

(B) ____________________________________ .

(B) 예, 그렇게 할 계획이에요.

(C) That's true.

(C) 그건 사실이에요.

[어휘] **last for** ~동안 지속되다 | **plan on** 계획을 세우다

3 ____________________________________ ?

이 비용 제안서에 관해 좀 도와주시겠어요?

(A) Projected costs are a million dollars.

(A) 예상 비용은 백만 달러입니다.

(B) She worked hard on them.

(B) 그녀는 그것들에 관해 열심히 일했어요.

(C) ____________________________________ .

(C) 물론, 오후 내내 시간이 있어요.

[어휘] **proposal** 제안 | **projected** 예상되는 | **work on** ~을 작업하다

4 ____________________________________ ?

지금 바로 이 두 장에 서명해야 하나요?

(A) Sorry, I will turn it down.

(A) 죄송하지만 거절하겠어요.

(B) ____________________________________ .

(B) 즉시 그것들이 필요해요.

(C) You had some help.

(C) 당신은 도움을 좀 받았죠.

[어휘] **sign** 서명하다 | **turn down** 거절하다

PART 3

1 What are the speakers mainly discussing?

    (A) A problem with an order

    (B) A conference schedule

    (C) A marketing strategy

    (D) An increase in salary

2 When is the awards dinner?

    (A) Monday

    (B) Tuesday

    (C) Wednesday

    (D) Friday

3 What does the woman say she will do?

    (A) Review a contract

    (B) Repair a microphone

    (C) Submit an application

    (D) Call a supplier

Dictation 대화를 다시 들으면서 받아쓰시오.　🎧 13-06

Questions 1-3 refer to the following conversation.

M Wendy, ____
George AV Supplies? It's been almost three weeks, and they are still not here.

W I know, Jack. I called yesterday. Apparently, a lot of equipment was damaged during the
transport, but they know that __________________________________, and they guarantee
that we will have the mikes by then.

M But I don't want to leave this until the last minute. Tell them to have the microphones here
by 3:00 on Wednesday, or we will take our business elsewhere.

W All right. ____.

M 웬디, 우리가 조지 AV 장비에 주문한 무선 마이크는 어떻게 된거죠? 거의 3주가 다 되어 가는데도 도착하지 않네요.

W 저도 알고 있어요. 잭. 어제 전화해 봤는데, 운송 중에 많은 장비가 고장 난 것 같아요. 하지만 그들도 시상식 만찬이 금요일 저녁이라는 것을
아니까, 그때까지 마이크를 확실히 보내준다고 했습니다.

M 하지만 이 문제를 시상식 직전까지 남겨 두고 싶지 않아요. 그 쪽에 전화해서 수요일 3시까지 마이크를 보내달라고 하고, 그렇지 않으면 다른
업체를 알아보겠다고 전하세요.

W 네. 지금 바로 전화해서 우리의 입장을 확실히 이해시키겠습니다.

[어휘] **cordless microphone** 무선 마이크 ┃ **phone** 전화하다 ┃ **apparently** 분명히 ┃ **damaged** 손상된 ┃ **transport** 수송, 운송 ┃
guarantee 보장하다 ┃ **last minute** 마지막 순간 ┃ **elsewhere** 다른 곳에 ┃ **make sure** 확실하게 하다 ┃ **position** 입장, 처지

PART 3

4 Why does the woman want to return the blouse?

    (A) She dislikes the design.

    (B) It doesn't fit her well enough.

    (C) She dislikes the color.

    (D) There are some stains on it.

5 What does the man ask the woman to do?

    (A) Fill out a form

    (B) Select a new item

    (C) Speak with the manager

    (D) Go to a counter

6 What does the woman mean when she says, "I'm afraid not"?

    (A) She forgot to bring the receipt.

    (B) She does not want to make an exchange.

    (C) There is nothing in the store she wants.

    (D) She cannot remember when she bought the item.

Dictation 대화를 다시 들으면서 받아쓰시오.　　🎧 13-08

Questions 4-6 refer to the following conversation.

W Excuse me. I purchased this blouse here three days ago, ________________________

________.

M What's the matter with it? Didn't you get the right size?

W It fits perfectly, but ________________________. Take a look at them here.

M I'm very sorry about that. If you prefer, you can simply exchange it ________________________

________________________. Would you prefer that?

W I'm afraid not. ________________________.

M Sure. If you'll follow me to the checkout counter, I can process the return for you. Oh, ________________________, didn't you? You can't return anything without one.

W Yes, I've got it here in my bag.

W 실례합니다. 저는 3일 전에 이곳에서 이 블라우스를 구입했는데, 돈을 돌려 받고 싶어요.

M 문제가 무엇인가요? 사이즈가 맞지 않았나요?

W 꼭 맞았지만, 옷에 두어 개의 얼룩이 있어요. 여기를 봐 주세요.

M 그에 대해서는 정말로 죄송합니다. 원하시면, 완벽한 상태의 다른 블라우스로 교환을 하실 수도 있어요. 그렇게 하시겠어요?

W 아니요. 차라리 돈을 돌려 받을게요.

M 알겠습니다. 저를 따라 계산대로 오시면, 제가 환불 절차를 진행해 드릴게요. 오, 영수증을 가지고 오셨죠, 그렇지 않나요? 영수증이 없으면 어떤 것도 환불을 받으실 수 없어요.

W 네, 여기 제 가방에 가지고 왔어요.

[어휘] **perfectly** 완벽하게 | **stain** 얼룩 | **would rather** 차라리 ~하겠다 | **checkout counter** 계산대 | **process** 처리하다 | **receipt** 영수증

PART 4

1 What does the message give information about?

(A) A party room

(B) An organization's office

(C) A jewelry store

(D) A candy shop

2 What time does the office open on Fridays?

(A) At 9 A.M.

(B) At 9:25 A.M.

(C) At 1 P.M.

(D) At 5 P.M.

3 How can a caller reach a specific person on the staff?

(A) Wait for the beep

(B) Request general information

(C) Press number 2

(D) Leave a message

Dictation 지문을 다시 들으면서 받아쓰시오.　🎧 13-10

Questions 1-3 refer to the following recorded message.

_______________________________ Green Alliance. If you are seeking general information, please press 1. If you know ______________ ______________, press 2 for a list of extensions. Our office is open _______________________________. If you wish to leave a message in our general mailbox, please wait for the beep. Our address is 29 Diamond Drive, suite 301; visitors are welcome _______________________________.

그린 얼라이언스에 전화 주셔서 감사합니다. 종합 정보를 원하시면, 1번을 누르세요. 통화하시려는 상대방을 아시면 2번을 눌러서 내선번호 목록을 참조하세요. 저희의 영업시간은 월요일부터 금요일 9시부터 5시까지입니다. 저희 우편함에 메시지를 남기려면, 삐 소리를 기다리세요. 주소는 다이아몬드 드라이브 29번지 301호이며, 영업시간에는 방문객들을 환영합니다.

[어휘] **seek** 찾다 ｜ **party** (전화의) 상대방 ｜ **extension** 내선번호 ｜ **normal** 정상의 ｜ **business hours** 업무시간

Daily Listening Practice

PART 1

🎧 14-01

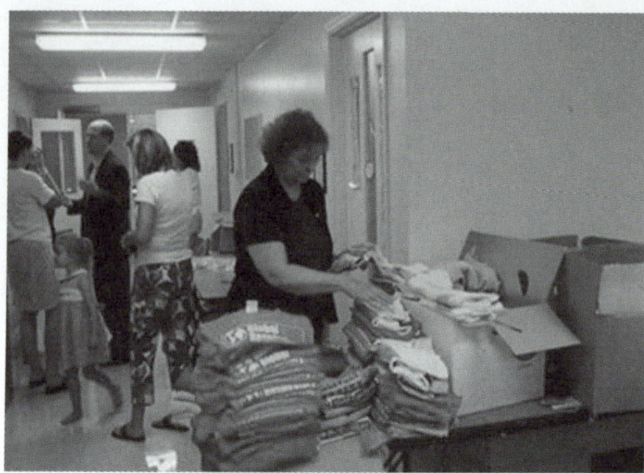

(A) ☐
(B) ☐
(C) ☐
(D) ☐

Dictation 보기 4개를 다시 들으면서 받아쓰시오.

🎧 14-02

(A) Various items are on sale.

다양한 물건들이 할인 판매 중이다.

(B) A woman is removing some laundry.

한 여자가 빨래를 꺼내고 있다.

(C) ___________________________________.

옷들이 쌓여 있다.

(D) They are turning on the lamps.

그들이 전등을 켜고 있다.

[어휘] **various** 다양한 | **on sale** 할인 중인 | **remove** 제거하다, 옮기다 | **laundry** 세탁물 | **pile up** ~을 쌓다

PART 2

1   Mark your answer on your answer sheet.   (A)   (B)   (C)
2   Mark your answer on your answer sheet.   (A)   (B)   (C)
3   Mark your answer on your answer sheet.   (A)   (B)   (C)
4   Mark your answer on your answer sheet.   (A)   (B)   (C)

Dictation   질문과 응답을 다시 들으면서 받아쓰시오.   🎧 14-04

1   ___________________________ ?

(A) Actually, it tastes a little sour.

(B) ___________________________ .

(C) The rest are by the door.

쉬고 나니 몸이 좀 나아졌나요?

(A) 사실, 약간 시큼한 맛이 나네요.

(B) 당연하지요, 훨씬 나아졌어요.

(C) 나머지 사람들은 문 옆에 있어요.

[어휘] **feel better** 더 나아지다 | **rest** 휴식; 쉬다 | **taste sour** 시큼한 맛이 나다

2   ___________________________ ?

(A) ___________________________ .

(B) It opens early on Monday.

(C) She's folding chairs.

여분의 폴더를 가지고 있는 사람 있나요?

(A) 내 것을 빌려 가세요.

(B) 월요일 일찍 문을 열어요.

(C) 그녀가 의자들을 접고 있어요.

[어휘] **extra** 여분의 | **borrow** 빌리다 | **fold** 접다

3   ___________________________ ?

(A) Yes, the views are great.

(B) ___________________________ .

(C) Let's meet at his office.

송장들을 가져오는 걸 잊으셨나요?

(A) 예, 전망이 훌륭하군요.

(B) 아뇨, 가져왔어요.

(C) 그의 사무실에서 만나요.

[어휘] **forget** 잊다 | **invoice** 송장 | **view** 전망; 보다

4   ___________________________
___________________________ ?

(A) It's not necessary to leave early.

(B) ___________________________ .

(C) The author is a friend of ours.

우리가 일찍 나가고 싶으면 허가가 필요한가요?

(A) 일찍 나갈 필요는 없어요.

(B) 물론이에요. 매니저한테 말하세요.

(C) 그 작가는 우리 친구예요.

[어휘] **authorization** 허가 | **necessary** 필요한 | **author** 작가

1 What is the woman looking for?

(A) Her employer's office

(B) Her new office

(C) The auditorium

(D) A parking lot

2 Where is the man probably going?

(A) The new employee orientation

(B) Headquarters

(C) Bob's office

(D) Lost and Found

3 How long has the man worked for the company?

(A) 1 year

(B) 2 years

(C) 3 years

(D) 4 years

Dictation 대화를 다시 들으면서 받아쓰시오.   🎧 14-06

Questions 1-3 refer to the following conversation.

M You look a bit lost. Do you need some help?

W Yes, ________________________________ . ________________________________ ,

but I can't seem to find it. I thought it was somewhere around here.

M ____ .

I was lost just like you. Follow me. ________________________ . Nice to you meet you.

I'm Bob, Bob Kendal from Personnel.

M 길을 잃으신 것 같군요. 도와드릴까요?

W 예, 저는 신입사원 오리엔테이션 때문에 왔어요. 강당에서 열릴 거라고 했는데 못 찾겠어요. 여기 근처 어디인 것 같은데요.

M 2년 전 이 회사에 처음 왔을 때의 저를 생각나게 하네요. 저도 당신처럼 길을 잃었었죠. 따라오세요. 저도 그곳에 가거든요. 만나서 반가워요. 저는 인사부에 있는 밥, 밥 켄달이에요.

[어휘] **lost** 길 잃은 | **auditorium** 강당 | **remind A of B** A에게 B를 생각나게 하다

4 What is going to happen at 12:30?

    (A) Ms. Jackson will arrive at the office.

    (B) Some computers will be delivered.

    (C) An overseas client will make a phone call.

    (D) A meeting will be held.

5 What does the woman say she will do?

    (A) Call the delivery company

    (B) Remain in the office during lunch

    (C) Meet with Ms. Jackson

    (D) Upgrade her computer

6 How will the woman eat lunch?

    (A) She brought some food from home.

    (B) She will eat at the cafeteria.

    (C) She will order food from a deli.

    (D) She will visit a nearby restaurant.

Dictation 대화를 다시 들으면서 받아쓰시오.　🎧 14-08

Questions 4-6 refer to the following conversation with three speakers.

W Do you know when the new computers are arriving?

M1 I got a call from the store. They should be here around 12:30.

M2 _______________________________ . Who's going to sign for them?

W I guess I can stay in the office. ____ .

M1 Thanks a lot, Karen. I'd volunteer, but I'm meeting Ms. Jackson from Tempe Partners for lunch today.

W Don't mention it, Steve. I need to get some work done, ____ .

M2 Did you bring anything from home? Or ____

_______________________ ?

W I appreciate the offer, but ____ .

  Someone from there will bring my sandwich up here.

W　새 컴퓨터가 언제 도착할 것인지 알고 있나요?

M1　제가 매장으로부터 전화를 받았어요. 12시 30분경에는 이곳에 도착할 거예요.

M2　하지만 그때는 점심 시간이잖아요. 누가 서명을 할 건가요?

W　제가 사무실에 남아 있을 수 있을 거예요. 저로서는 배달원이 도착할 때까지 기다리는 것이 상관없어요.

M1　정말 고마워요, 카렌. 제가 하고 싶지만, 저는 오늘 점심에 템피 파트너스의 잭슨 씨와 만날 것이라서요.

W　별말씀을요, 스티브. 마쳐야 할 일들이 몇 개 있어서, 저는 책상에서 점심을 먹을 거예요.

M2　집에서 무언가를 가지고 왔나요? 아니면 제가 구내식당에서 무언가를 가져다 줄까요?

W　제안은 고맙지만, 아래층 식품점에 무언가를 주문할 거예요. 그곳 사람이 이곳으로 샌드위치를 가져다 줄 거예요.

[어휘] **deliveryman** 배달부, 배달원 | **volunteer** 자원하다, 자발적으로 하다 | **offer** 제안, 제의 | **deli** 조제 식품점 | **downstairs** 아래층에

PART 4

1 According to the speaker, what did Watson Technology do?

(A) Sign a contract to purchase some items

(B) Invest money in the company

(C) Show a display of its newest technology

(D) Request additional funding

2 What does the speaker tell the listeners to do?

(A) Propose some new projects

(B) Spend their money carefully

(C) Submit new budget proposals

(D) Get in touch with Watson Technology

3 What does the speaker mean when she says, "After all, we'd like everyone to share in the wealth"?

(A) Each department will receive additional funding.

(B) The company has lots of money to spend any way it wants.

(C) The value of the company's stock is rising.

(D) All of the employees are going to get bonuses

Dictation 지문을 다시 들으면서 받아쓰시오.　🎧 14-10

Questions 1-3 refer to the following excerpt from a meeting.

I'm pleased to announce we've secured some new investment. The group from Watson Technology was ____. They were particularly intrigued with some of our newest projects. For that reason, we signed a deal that will provide us with $10 million in funding. ____________________________ to the R&D Department so that we can continue work on our projects. ____________________________________ to our other departments. After all, ____________________________________. Here's what you should do: Send me revised budgets for your departments. Focus only on what you absolutely must have. We don't want a single dollar to be wasted. I expect e-mails from everyone no later than 10 tomorrow morning.

몇 가지 신규 투자를 유치하게 되었다는 점을 알리게 되어 기쁘게 생각합니다. 왓슨 테크놀로지는 지난 주에 그들이 보았던 것에 깊은 인상을 받았습니다. 그들은 특히 우리의 새로운 프로젝트들에 대해서 호기심을 나타냈습니다. 그러한 이유로, 우리는 1천만 달러의 자금을 제공받게 될 거래를 성사시켰습니다. 대부분의 자금은 그러한 프로젝트를 계속 진행하기 위해 연구개발부로 돌아가게 될 것입니다. 하지만 일부 자금은 다른 부서에도 배정될 것입니다. 어쨌거나, 우리는 모든 사람들이 재원을 공유하기를 원합니다. 여러분들께서 하셔야 할 일을 알려 드리겠습니다: 여러분 부서의 수정 예산안을 저에게 보내 주십시오. 반드시 필요한 것에만 초점을 맞추어야 합니다. 단 1달러도 낭비되기를 원하지 않습니다. 저는 늦어도 내일 아침 10시까지 모든 분들로부터 이메일을 전송받기를 바랍니다.

[어휘] **secure** 확보하다 | **investment** 투자 | **particularly** 특히 | **intrigue** 호기심을 갖게 하다 | **deal** 거래 | **funding** 자금; 자금을 대다 | **budget** 예산; 예산을 세우다 | **share** 공유하다 | **wealth** 부 | **revise** 수정하다, 개정하다 | **absolutely** 절대적으로

15 Daily Listening Practice

PART 1

15-01

(A) ☐
(B) ☐
(C) ☐
(D) ☐

Dictation 보기 4개를 다시 들으면서 받아쓰시오. 15-02

(A) The wall is completely bare.
벽이 텅 비어 있다.

(B) A cloth is covering a round table.
식탁보가 원형 탁자를 덮고 있다.

(C) The entrance is undergoing repairs.
입구는 수리 중이다.

(D) ___________________ ______________.
몇몇 좌석에 사람이 앉아 있다.

[어휘] **bare** 텅 빈, 세간이 없는 ｜ **entrance** 입구, 현관 ｜ **undergo** 겪다, 받다 ｜ **repairs** 수선, 복구 작업 ｜ **occupied** 좌석이 차있는

PART 2

1   **Mark your answer on your answer sheet.**   (A)   (B)   (C)

2   **Mark your answer on your answer sheet.**   (A)   (B)   (C)

3   **Mark your answer on your answer sheet.**   (A)   (B)   (C)

4   **Mark your answer on your answer sheet.**   (A)   (B)   (C)

Dictation   질문과 응답을 다시 들으면서 받아쓰시오.   🎧 15-04

1 ______________________________ ?

(A) Yes, I turned it off.

(B) ______________________________ .

(C) There are a few works on the wall.

곧 휴가죠, 그렇지 않나요?

(A) 네, 제가 껐어요.

(B) 그럼요, 5시에 출발해요.

(C) 벽에 몇몇 작품들이 걸려있어요.

[어휘] **off work** 일을 쉬는 | **turn off** 끄다 | **absolutely** 절대적으로, 전적으로

2 ______________________________ ?

(A) ______________________________ .

(B) Yes, she hired a new agency.

(C) In half an hour.

당신은 임시 비서를 고용했죠, 아닌가요?

(A) 예, 그녀는 이틀 전에 시작했어요.

(B) 예, 그녀는 새 대행사를 고용했어요.

(C) 30분 후에요.

[어휘] **temporary** 임시의 | **agency** 대행사, 대리점

3 ______________________________ ?

(A) We are seated on the bench.

(B) ______________________________ .

(C) No, they didn't see it.

그들은 테라스에 앉고 싶어하죠, 그렇지 않나요?

(A) 우리는 벤치에 앉아 있어요.

(B) 네, 그렇습니다.

(C) 아뇨, 그들은 그것을 못 봤어요.

[어휘] **patio** 파티오, 테라스 | **be seated** 앉다 | **absolutely** 절대적으로

4 ______________________________ ?

(A) What a marvelous book!

(B) ______________________________ .

(C) The registration process is complex.

워크숍에 등록해야죠, 안 그래요?

(A) 정말 훌륭한 책이네요!

(B) 네, 그래야 해요.

(C) 등록 과정이 복잡해요.

[어휘] **register for** ~에 등록하다 | **marvelous** 멋진, 훌륭한 | **registration** 등록 | **process** 과정

PART 3

1 Where does the conversation take place?

    (A) At a museum

    (B) In a train station

    (C) On a street corner

    (D) At a supermarket

2 What does the woman ask about?

    (A) A newly opened exhibit

    (B) A discount for students

    (C) The regular business hours

    (D) Employment opportunities

3 What does the man suggest?

    (A) Completing some forms

    (B) Visiting an art gallery

    (C) Purchasing a membership

    (D) Checking a map

Dictation 대화를 다시 들으면서 받아쓰시오. 🎧 15-06

Questions 1-3 refer to the following conversation.

W ____ _______________

___________________________ .

M Yes, that is correct. I just need to see your university ID.

W I'm a history major at Emerson University. Here's my ID.

M ___________________________________ the Layton Museum _________, usually once or twice a month. If you plan to do that, ____ ? You will save even more on the regular admission price. This pamphlet explains all your options.

W 저희 교수님들 중 한 분께 들었는데, 대학생들은 일반 입장료에서 40퍼센트를 할인 받을 수 있다고요?

M 네, 그렇습니다. 대학교 학생증만 보여 주시면 됩니다.

W 저는 에머슨 대학교에서 역사를 전공하고 있어요. 여기 학생증이 있습니다.

M 역사에 관심이 높은 많은 사람들이 레이튼 박물관에 자주 오지요. 보통 한 달에 한 두 번이요. 학생도 그러고 싶으시다면 회원이 되시는 건 어떠세요? 일반 입장료에서 더 많은 금액을 할인 받을 수 있어요. 이 팜플릿에 여러 옵션이 적혀 있어요.

[어휘] **entitle** 자격을 주다 | **regular** 일반적인 | **admission** 입장 | **correct** 옳은, 정확한 | **major** 전공(자) | **enthusiast** 열중하는 사람 | **often** 종종 | **usually** 일반적으로 | **consider** 고려하다 | **save** 절약하다 | **explain** 설명하다 | **option** 선택권

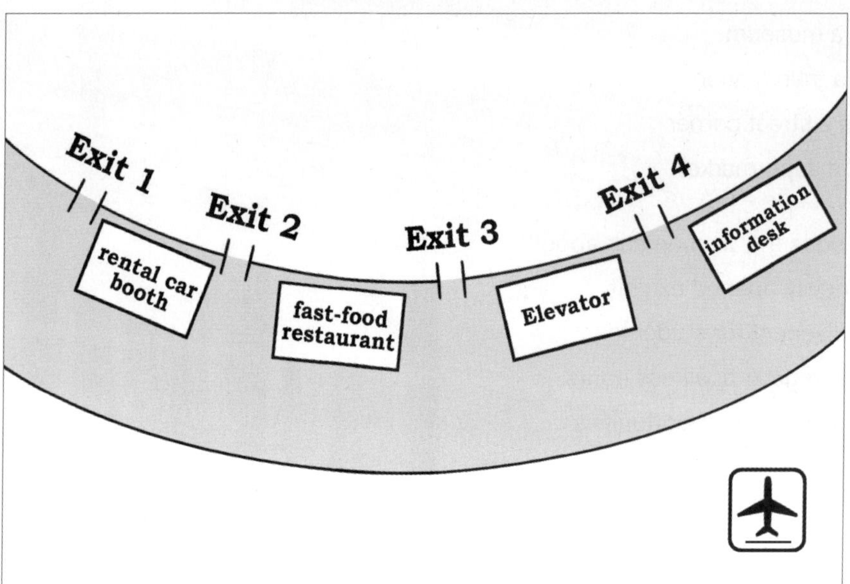

4   Where most likely are the speakers?

(A) At a hotel

(B) At a bus stop

(C) At an airport

(D) At a train station

5   What does the man suggest to the woman?

(A) Her reservation has been canceled.

(B) Her bus is going to leave soon.

(C) She must pay money to take the bus.

(D) She needs to rent a car.

6   Look at the graphic. Which exit should the woman take?

(A) Exit 1

(B) Exit 2

(C) Exit 3

(D) Exit 4

Questions 4-6 refer to the following conversation and map.

W Pardon me, but could you give me some assistance, please?

M Yes, how may I be of service?

W I flew in from Paris, and ____.
However, I'm not sure where to go.

M Could you tell me the name of your hotel, please?

W Yes, hold on a moment . . . I've got a reservation at the Crown Hotel.

M ____. ________________________________
________________________________. ________________________________. You'll see a
sign posted for the hotel's shuttle bus.

W Great. Do you know how often the bus leaves?

M ____, and it's five to eleven right
now. You'd better hurry.

W 실례지만, 저를 도와 주실 수 있으신가요?

M 네, 어떻게 도와 드릴까요?

W 저는 파리에서 비행기를 타고 왔는데, 호텔까지 셔틀 버스를 타야 해요. 하지만, 어디로 가야 할지 모르겠어요.

M 호텔 이름을 알려 주시겠어요?

W 네, 잠시만요⋯ 크라운 호텔에 예약이 되어 있어요.

M 직진을 해서 엘리베이터와 패스트푸드점을 지나치세요. 렌터카 부스까지 계속 가시고요. 그런 다음, 그곳을 지나쳐서 문밖으로 나가세요. 호텔
   셔틀 버스가 게시되어 있는 표지판을 보게 될 거에요.

W 그렇군요. 버스가 얼마나 자주 출발하는지 아시나요?

M 한 시간에 한 번 정시마다 출발하는데, 지금이 11시 5분전이군요. 서두르시는 것이 좋겠어요.

[어휘] booth 부스 | sign 표지판 | post 게시하다 | at the top of the hour 정시마다 | had better ~하는 편이 낫다

PART 4

1 Who most likely is Ms. Ricketts?

(A) A writer

(B) A consultant

(C) A machinist

(D) A clerk

2 What is the purpose of the message?

(A) To provide directions

(B) To give details of a strike

(C) To report a problem

(D) To request an interview

3 What most likely is *The Dryden Star*?

(A) A TV drama

(B) A newspaper

(C) A textbook

(D) A romance novel

Dictation 지문을 다시 들으면서 받아쓰시오.   🎧 15-10

Questions 1-3 refer to the following telephone message.

Good afternoon Ms. Ricketts. My name is Cara Noland and I'm phoning from *Writer's Monthly*.

____.

We are looking for someone to write a regular column on practical writing tips. In your résumé, you indicated that ____ Delbert Auto _________________________________ *The Dryden Star*. Both our editor and I were truly impressed with that article. We will be interviewing applicants this Wednesday between 1:00 and 6:00. ____ at 416-9837.

안녕하세요, 리케츠 씨. 제 이름은 카라 놀란드이며 *라이터스 먼슬리* 소속입니다. 저희에게 원고를 제공하시는 데 관심 있으시다며 귀하의 이력서를 보내주셨지요. 저희는 실질적인 글쓰기 요령에 관한 정기 칼럼을 쓰실 분을 찾고 있습니다. 이력서에는 귀하께서 델버트 오토 사의 지금까지 계속되고 있는 파업에 관해 드라이든 스타 일면 기사를 쓰셨다고 되어 있더군요. 편집자와 저는 그 기사를 무척 인상 깊게 보았습니다. 이번 주 수요일 1시부터 6시까지 지원자들을 면접할 예정입니다. 귀하와도 인터뷰를 했으면 하니, 여전히 관심이 있으시다면, 가능한 한 빨리 416-9837로 전화 주시기 바랍니다.

[어휘] résumé 이력서 | indicate 가리키다, 나타내다 | be interested in ~에 관심 있다 | look for ~을 찾다 | regular 정기의, 규칙적인 | practical 실질적인 | tip 요령 | ongoing 계속 진행 중인 | strike 파업 | auto 자동차 | appear 나오다, 발간되다 | truly 진심으로 | be impressed with ~에 감동하다, 깊은 인상을 받다 | article 기사 | applicant 지원자

16 Daily Listening Practice

PART 1

16-01

(A) ☐
(B) ☐
(C) ☐
(D) ☐

Dictation 보기 4개를 다시 들으면서 받아쓰시오.

16-02

(A) They're standing in the alleyway.
그들은 골목길에 서 있다.

(B) They're seated at various places.
그들은 여러 곳에 앉아 있다.

(C) ___________________________.
그들은 무리 지어 달리고 있다.

(D) They're wearing the same uniforms.
그들은 똑같은 유니폼을 입고 있다.

[어휘] **alleyway** 골목길 | **seated** 앉아 있는 | **various** 다양한 | **in a group** 무리를 지어 | **the same** 똑같은

1   Mark your answer on your answer sheet.   (A)   (B)   (C)

2   Mark your answer on your answer sheet.   (A)   (B)   (C)

3   Mark your answer on your answer sheet.   (A)   (B)   (C)

4   Mark your answer on your answer sheet.   (A)   (B)   (C)

Dictation   질문과 응답을 다시 들으면서 받아쓰시오.

🎧 16-04

1 _________________________________ ?

(A) The meeting lasted for an hour.

(B) _________________________________ .

(C) It's in the next room.

식당에서 만나는 게 어때요?
(A) 회의는 한 시간 동안 계속됐어요.
(B) 좋은 생각이에요.
(C) 그것은 옆방에 있어요.

[어휘] **cafeteria** 간이식당 ǀ **last for** ~동안 지속되다

2 _________________________________ Moriko?

(A) _________________________________ .

(B) The last speaker was excellent.

(C) As soon as she gets back.

언제 모리코에게 마지막으로 전화했나요?
(A) 일주일 전에요.
(B) 마지막 연설자는 훌륭했어요.
(C) 그녀가 돌아오자마자요.

[어휘] **last** 마지막(으로) ǀ **excellent** 뛰어난 ǀ **as soon as** ~하자마자 ǀ **get back** 돌아오다

3 Ms. Ito _________________________________ ?

(A) The speaker is my associate.

(B) Usually between 10 and 12.

(C) _________________________________ .

이토 씨가 인상적인 연설을 했어요, 그렇지 않나요?
(A) 그 연사는 내 동료예요.
(B) 보통 10에서 12 사이로요.
(C) 네, 저도 매우 재미있게 들었어요.

[어휘] **impressive** 인상적인 ǀ **give a speech** 연설하다 ǀ **associate** 동료

4 _________________________________ ?

(A) I need to see a doctor.

(B) _________________________________ .

(C) It was a long meeting.

나머지 서류들을 가져와야 하지 않나요?
(A) 의사에게 가봐야 해요.
(B) 맞아요, 제가 그것들을 가져 올게요.
(C) 긴 회의였어요.

[어휘] **bring** 가져가다 ǀ **see a doctor** 의사를 만나다, 진찰받다

1 Where most likely does the conversation take place?

(A) In a fire station

(B) In a pharmacy

(C) In a hospital

(D) In an airport

2 What is the man's concern?

(A) He may miss a connecting flight.

(B) He is unable to locate his luggage.

(C) He doesn't remember a fax number.

(D) He forgot to transfer some funds.

3 Where does the woman suggest that the man go?

(A) To the nearest bookstore

(B) To a tourist information center

(C) To the customer service desk

(D) To the building's main entrance

Dictation 대화를 다시 들으면서 받아쓰시오.　🎧 16-06

Questions 1-3 refer to the following conversation.

M　Excuse me. ____________________ Raleigh Air ____________________ .
____________________ .

W　Are you sure this is the right place? Raleigh has several flights daily from London to Birmingham.

M　But I was on fight number 609 and that's the same number on that board.

W　I see. ____________________
____________________ . ____________________ .

M　실례합니다. 저는 런던에서 출발한 랠라이 항공기에 탑승했었습니다. 제가 부친 큰 여행가방을 가지러 왔는데, 어디에도 보이지 않는군요.

W　짐을 찾는 곳이 여기인 것이 확실한가요? 랠라이 항공은 런던에서 버밍엄까지 매일 여러 대의 비행기를 운행하거든요.

M　저는 609 항공편에 탑승했는데, 저 게시판에 나오는 번호와 같습니다.

W　그렇군요. 저쪽 커피숍을 지나가시면 오른편에 고객 서비스 데스크가 보이실 겁니다. 그곳에서 당신을 도와드릴 수 있을 거예요.

[어휘] **pick up** (물건 등을) 가지고 가다 ｜ **suitcase** 여행가방 ｜ **check** (짐을) 부치다 ｜ **right** 옳은 ｜ **place** 장소 ｜ **several** 여러 개의 ｜
same 같은 ｜ **board** 게시판

PART 3

4   Where are the speakers?

    (A) At a hotel

    (B) At a bus station

    (C) At an airport

    (D) At a train station

5   What does the woman ask the man to give her?

    (A) His credit card

    (B) His ticket

    (C) His reservation form

    (D) His itinerary

6   What does the man mean when he says, "This must be my lucky day"?

    (A) He will get to his destination on time.

    (B) His reservation will not be canceled.

    (C) He is pleased with his upgrade.

    (D) His ticket is still valid.

Dictation   대화를 다시 들으면서 받아쓰시오.   🎧 16-08

Questions 4-6 refer to the following conversation.

M   Hello. I had a seat on Flight 47, _________________________________. The person at the gate told me to come here and speak with you.

W   I'm very sorry about the cancelation. Is Dallas _________________________?

M   No, it's not. I'm supposed to change flights there and then go to Phoenix.

W   In that case, _________________________________, I can get you on a direct flight to Phoenix.

M   I'll take it. What do I need to do?

W   Let me see your ticket, please. I have to make a few changes to it, and then I can get you a seat. _________________________.

M   This must be my lucky day. Thanks a lot.

M   안녕하세요. 저는 47 비행기편의 좌석을 예약했는데, 2분 전에 취소가 되었어요. 게이트에 있는 사람이 제게 이곳으로 와서 당신과 이야기를 하라고 하더군요.

W   취소가 된 점에 대해서는 정말로 죄송합니다. 오늘의 최종 목적지가 댈러스인가요?

M   아니오, 그렇지 않아요. 그곳에서 비행기를 바꾸어 탄 후에 피닉스로 갈 예정이죠.

W   그런 경우라면, 두어 시간 기다려도 괜찮으시면, 피닉스로 가는 직항편을 타도록 해 드릴 수 있어요.

M   그렇게 할게요. 제가 어떻게 하면 되나요?

W   제게 티켓을 보여 주세요. 제가 티켓에 몇 가지 사항을 변경시킨 후에 좌석을 드릴 수 있어요. 또한 비즈니스석으로 업그레이드를 해 드릴게요.

M   운이 좋은 날이군요. 정말 고마워요.

[어휘] **cancelation** 취소 | **final destination** 최종 목적지 | **change flights** 비행기를 바꾸어 타다 | **direct** 직접의 | **lucky** 운이 좋은

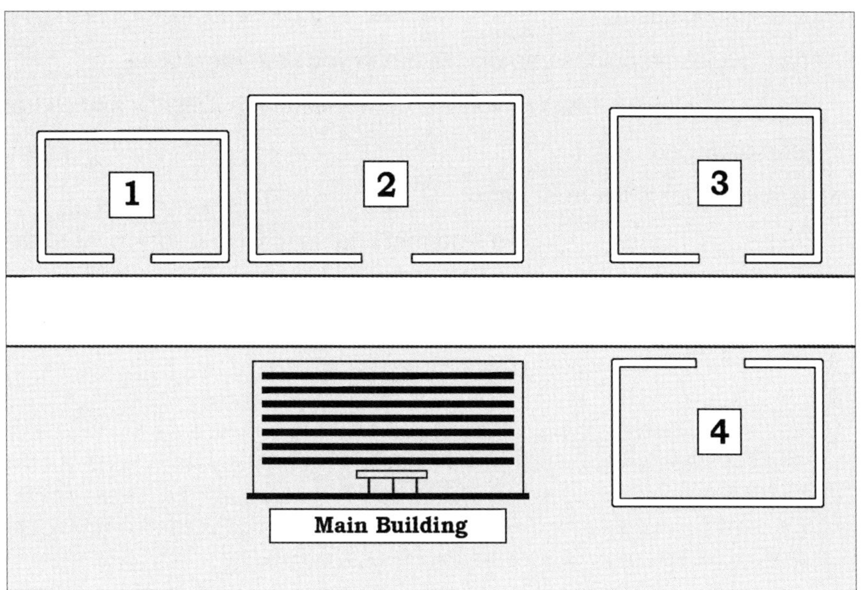

1 Who most likely are the listeners?

(A) New employees

(B) Security guards

(C) Factory workers

(D) Company executives

2 When will the listeners get their security passes?

(A) In a few minutes

(B) After lunch

(C) At the end of the day

(D) Tomorrow morning

3 Look at the graphic . Where is the company parking lot?

(A) 1

(B) 2

(C) 3

(D) 4

Questions 1-3 refer to the following except from a talk and map.

Now that your orientation session is finished, we need to tour the facilities. We're going to go everywhere today, but let me point some places out to you first. Right now, _______________________

_______________________. Most of you will be working here. Directly across from the main building is the company parking lot. _______________________ when you arrive. To the left of the parking lot is the front gate. _______________________

_______________________. We'll do that after lunch. Now, look over to the right. Do you see those two huge buildings? Those are our primary factories. The one on the left runs 24 hours a day _______________________. Let's visit the one on the left first.

오리엔테이션이 끝났으므로, 시설을 견학해야 합니다. 우리는 오늘 모든 곳을 돌아다닐 것이지만, 먼저 몇몇 장소들을 여러분들께 알려 드리도록 하겠습니다. 현재, 우리는 본관 앞에 서 있습니다. 여러분 대부분이 이곳에서 근무를 하게 될 것입니다. 본관 바로 맞은편에는 회사 주차장이 있습니다. 도착을 하시면 차량은 그곳에 주차하셔야 합니다. 주차장 왼쪽으로는 정문이 있습니다. 구역 내로 입장을 허가받기에 앞서, 보안증을 받으셔야 합니다. 점심 식사 후에 그 일을 할 것입니다. 자, 오른쪽을 봐 주십시오. 저 커다란 건물 두 채가 보이시나요? 그것은 주 공장입니다. 왼쪽에 있는 것은 하루 24시간 가동이 되는 반면, 오른쪽에 있는 것은 16시간 운영됩니다. 먼저 왼쪽 건물을 방문해 봅시다.

[**어휘**] **orientation session** 오리엔테이션 | **facility** 시설 | **point out** 지적하다 | **vehicle** 차량 | **security pass** 보안증, 출입증 | **primary** 주된, 주요한

Daily Listening Practice

PART 1

🎧 17-01

(A) ☐
(B) ☐
(C) ☐
(D) ☐

Dictation 보기 4개를 다시 들으면서 받아쓰시오.

🎧 17-02

(A) One man is reaching for a knob.
한 남자가 손잡이를 향해 손을 뻗고 있다.

(B) There is a fountain next to the men.
남자들 옆에 식수대가 있다.

(C) The men are reviewing applications.
남자들은 신청서를 검토하고 있다.

(D) _______________________________________.
자료들이 탁자 위에 가지런히 놓여 있다.

[어휘] **reach for** ~을 잡으려 손을 뻗다 ｜ **a knob** (문, 서랍 등의) 손잡이 ｜ **fountain** 식수대, 분수대 ｜ **review** ~을 검토하다 ｜ **application** 신청서 ｜ **material** 자료, 재료 ｜ **arranged** 정돈된

PART 2

1   **Mark your answer on your answer sheet.**   (A)   (B)   (C)

2   **Mark your answer on your answer sheet.**   (A)   (B)   (C)

3   **Mark your answer on your answer sheet.**   (A)   (B)   (C)

4   **Mark your answer on your answer sheet.**   (A)   (B)   (C)

Dictation   질문과 응답을 다시 들으면서 받아쓰시오.   🎧 17-04

1 _______________________________________?

(A) She's one of our clients.

(B) To the theater.

(C) _____________________________________.

[어휘] **take A out** A와 외출하다 | **plant manager** 공장장

누가 오늘밤 고객들을 데리고 갈 거죠?

(A) 그녀는 우리 고객들 중 한 명이에요.

(B) 극장으로요.

(C) 공장장이요.

2 _______________________________________?

(A) We saw her in the stairway.

(B) It's a dangerous habit.

(C) _____________________________________.

[어휘] **steep** 경사진 | **stairway** 계단 | **dangerous** 위험한 | **take** 타다

계단이 경사가 급해요. 그렇지 않나요?

(A) 우리가 계단에서 그녀를 봤어요.

(B) 위험한 습관이에요.

(C) 그래서 저는 항상 엘리베이터를 타지요.

3 _________________________ Sara _____________?

(A) Yes, he does.

(B) _____________________________________.

(C) I think you can make it.

[어휘] **invite A to B** A를 B에 초대하다 | **make it** 제때에 오다, 해내다

너희 파티에 새라를 초대하는 게 어때?

(A) 그래, 그는 그래.

(B) 이미 초대했어.

(C) 너는 제시간에 올 수 있을 거야.

4 _______________________________________

_______________________?

(A) The library is always crowded.

(B) I recommend walking.

(C) _____________________________________?

[어휘] **crowded** 붐비는 | **recommend V-ing** ~하는 걸 추천하다 | **suggestion** 제안

도서관을 일요일에도 열어야 한다고 생각하지 않니?

(A) 그 도서관은 항상 붐벼.

(B) 산책을 해봐.

(C) 네가 그 제안을 해보는 게 어때?

PART 3

1 What are the speakers discussing?

(A) An upcoming conference

(B) A job opportunity

(C) A statistical error

(D) A computer problem

2 What does the man probably do?

(A) Auto assembly

(B) Modeling

(C) Data research

(D) Legal consulting

3 What will the man do next?

(A) Register for a conference

(B) Organize a meeting

(C) Research a corporation

(D) Put in some overtime

Dictation 대화를 다시 들으면서 받아쓰시오.　🎧 17-06

Questions 1-3 refer to the following conversation.

W John, ____?

M I haven't had a chance yet, Angela. Things have been really hectic lately. Just look at all these papers on my desk. I think the ad you clipped from the newspaper for me is somewhere in this pile. Do you recall any of the job details?

W Well, Hansen Research ___________________________________. ____ except you can earn a lot more money at Hansen's because it's the second biggest company in our industry.

M But that could also mean I will have to work lots and lots of hours. ______________________________________. ____.

W 　존, 제가 지난 주에 말했던 일자리에 이력서 제출했나요?

M 　아직 그럴 틈이 없었어요, 안젤라. 최근에 정말 정신 없이 바빴거든요. 제 책상 위에 놓인 이 종이들 좀 봐요. 당신이 신문에서 오려준 광고도 이 종이더미 속 어딘가에 있을 거예요. 그 자리에 대해 어떤 거라도 생각나는 거 있으세요?

W 　음, 한센 연구소에서 자료 분석자를 찾고 있어요. 한센은 우리 업계에서 두 번째로 큰 기업이니까 그곳에서 돈을 더 많이 받게 된다는 점만 빼면, 이곳에서 하는 일과 완전히 같아요.

M 　하지만 그 말은 훨씬 더 많은 시간 동안 근무해야만 한다는 의미일 수도 있죠. 이력서를 제출하기 전에 정보가 더 필요하겠어요. 우선 한센 웹 사이트에서 내용을 읽어봐야겠어요.

[**어휘**] **send in** ~을 제출하다 ｜ **hectic** 몹시 바쁜 ｜ **lately** 최근에 ｜ **clip** 오려내다 ｜ **pile** 더미 ｜ **recall** 상기하다 ｜ **look for** ~을 찾다

4 What will the man do tonight?

    (A) Stay late at the office

    (B) Have dinner at a restaurant

    (C) Look at a property by the waterfront

    (D) Finish writing a report

5 What does the man want to know?

    (A) The best way to get to his destination

    (B) How the food at Pacino's is

    (C) Where he can take the bus

    (D) How the prices at a restaurant are

6 What will Cheryl do next?

    (A) Have lunch with the man

    (B) Attend her next meeting

    (C) Write down some directions

    (D) Take public transportation

Dictation 대화를 다시 들으면서 받아쓰시오.　🎧 17-08

Questions 4-6 refer to the following conversation with three speakers.

M　I've got to visit Pacino's for a dinner meeting tonight. _________________________?

W1　Are you talking about the restaurant down by the waterfront?

M　Yes, that's the place I am visiting.

W1　I've never been there, _________________________________. How about you, Cheryl?

W2　You're in luck, Dave. I had lunch there two days ago.

M　Do you think I should drive or take a bus there?

W2　The bus stop is more than three blocks away, so _________________________________.

M　So I should drive there, right?

W2　That's right. _________________________________. Do either of you have a pen I can borrow?

W　저는 오늘밤 저녁 모임을 위해 파치노스를 방문해야 해요. 두 분 중에 그곳에 어떻게 가는지 아시는 분이 있나요?

W1　해안가에 있는 식당을 이야기하고 있는 건가요?

W　네, 그곳이 바로 제가 방문하려고 하는 곳이죠.

W1　저는 그곳에 가본 적이 없지만, 그에 관해서는 좋은 이야기를 많이 들었어요. 당신은 어떤가요, 셰릴?

W2　운이 좋군요, 데이브. 제가 이틀 전에 그곳에서 점심을 먹었거든요.

W　제가 그곳으로 차를 몰고 가야 할까요, 아니면 버스를 타고 가야 할까요?

W2　버스 정류장이 세 블록 이상 떨어져 있기 때문에, 대중 교통은 피하라고 충고하고 싶군요.

W　그러면 그곳까지 차를 몰고 가야겠네요, 그렇죠?

W2　맞아요. 당신을 위해 길을 그려 드릴게요. 혹시 두 분 중 제가 빌릴만한 펜을 가지고 있는 분이 있나요?

[어휘] have got to ~해야 한다 ｜ **waterfront** 해안가 ｜ **public transportation** 대중 교통 ｜ **write down** 쓰다, 적다

1 What is the main purpose of the announcement?

(A) To provide details of Lois McMillan's exhibit

(B) To report some personal missing items

(C) To announce the closing of a gallery

(D) To mention a special in the gift shop

2 What are listeners instructed to do?

(A) Fill out a membership application form

(B) Check their e-mails for upcoming events

(C) Talk to the manager about problems

(D) Collect belongings before they leave

3 What will happen next month?

(A) An exhibit will commence.

(B) Some lectures will be given.

(C) A new wing will be constructed.

(D) Renovations will be done.

Dictation 지문을 다시 들으면서 받아쓰시오. 🎧 17-10

Questions 1-3 refer to the following announcement.

Attention all visitors. _______________________
the Alfred Holmes Gallery _______________________. Our gift shop, however, just inside
the main entrance, will not close for another 30 minutes. _______________________
_______________________. We would
also like to remind you that _______________________, Landscape
Watercolors by Lois McMillan, _______________________.
Coupons for that exhibit are available just outside our gift shop. Once more, our exhibition halls
will close in 15 minutes.

모든 방문객들께 알립니다. 알프레드 홈즈 갤러리 1층 및 2층 전시장의 관람 시간이 15분 후면 끝납니다. 하지만, 정문 바로 안쪽에 있는 선물매장은
30분 더 영업합니다. 전시장에 처음 들어오실 때 맡기셨던 코트나 기타 물건들을 꼭 챙기시기 바랍니다. 그리고 저희 새로운 전시인 로이스 맥밀란의
풍경 수채화전 개막이 다음 달 첫 번째 월요일에 시작된다는 점도 알려드리고 싶습니다. 이 전시를 위한 쿠폰은 선물매장 밖에서 구하실 수 있습니다.
다시 한번 말씀 드립니다. 저희 전시장은 15분 후에 닫습니다.

[**어휘**] **exhibition/exhibit** 전시 | **entrance** 입구 | **item** 물건, 제품 | **check** (소지품을) 맡기다 | **enter** 들어가다 | **remind**
상기시키다 | **be scheduled to** ~할 예정이다 | **available** 입수할 수 있는, 이용할 수 있는

PART 1

🎧 18-01

(A) ☐

(B) ☐

(C) ☐

(D) ☐

Dictation 보기 4개를 다시 들으면서 받아쓰시오.

🎧 18-02

(A) Some items are lying near a cash register.
몇몇 물품들이 금전등록기 근처에 놓여 있다.

(B) ___________________________________.
용기들이 전시를 위해 채워져 있다.

(C) A piece of glass is being measured.
유리 치수를 재는 중이다.

(D) A meal is being put into a plastic bag.
식사가 비닐봉지에 넣어지고 있다.

[어휘] lying 놓여있는 ｜ cash register 금전등록기 ｜ container 그릇, 용기 ｜ filled 채워져 있는 ｜ measure 치수를 재다 ｜ meal 식사 ｜
plastic bag 비닐봉지

PART 2

1 Mark your answer on your answer sheet.　　(A)　(B)　(C)

2 Mark your answer on your answer sheet.　　(A)　(B)　(C)

3 Mark your answer on your answer sheet.　　(A)　(B)　(C)

4 Mark your answer on your answer sheet.　　(A)　(B)　(C)

Dictation 질문과 응답을 다시 들으면서 받아쓰시오.　　🎧 18-04

1 ____?

(A) I want to work today.

(B) We're scheduled to arrive at 7.

(C) ____________________. ____________________.

걷는 게 나을까요, 아니면 버스를 타는 게 나을까요?

(A) 저는 오늘 일하고 싶어요.

(B) 우린 7시에 도착할 예정이에요.

(C) 걸어요. 우리는 운동이 필요해요.

[어휘] **would rather** ~하고 싶다 | **be scheduled to-V** ~할 예정이다 | **could use** 필요하다

2 ____?

(A) He takes the subway.

(B) Carl ____________________________________.

(C) By the end of the day.

이 송장을 누구에게 제출해야 하나요?

(A) 그는 지하철을 탑니다.

(B) 칼이 주로 그 일을 처리해요.

(C) 오늘까지예요.

[어휘] **submit A to B** A를 B에게 제출하다 | **invoice** 송장 | **take care of** 처리하다

3 ________________ Dr. Sanchez, __ ________ ?

(A) ________ - ________________________.

(B) I'll check out right away.

(C) Yes, he's my relative.

산체스 박사님이시죠, 아닌가요?

(A) 아뇨, 저는 그의 동료입니다.

(B) 곧 퇴실할 겁니다.

(C) 예, 그는 제 친척이에요.

[어휘] **colleague** 동료 | **check out** 체크아웃하다, 퇴실하다 | **relative** 친척

4 ____?

(A) Over an hour.

(B) ____________________________________.

(C) She hasn't received any response.

교육은 언제 끝나게 되죠?

(A) 한 시간 동안이요.

(B) 늦어도 목요일이요.

(C) 그녀는 어떤 답변도 받지 못했어요.

[어휘] **training session** 교육 | **at the latest** 늦어도 | **response** 응답

1 Why is the woman calling?

    (A) She wants the man to make some extra copies.

    (B) She needs a 30% discount.

    (C) Her copy machine is out of paper.

    (D) Her printer has to be fixed.

2 When will the print order be ready?

    (A) At 3 P.M.

    (B) At 3:30 P.M.

    (C) In 2 hours

    (D) In 5 hours

3 Who is going to pick up the print order?

    (A) The woman

    (B) Katherine

    (C) Dr. McArthur

    (D) Vanessa

Dictation 대화를 다시 들으면서 받아쓰시오.　🎧 18-06

Questions 1-3 refer to the following conversation.

W　Hello. This is Katherine from Dr. McArthur's office. ____ .

M　Hi, Katherine. We're kind of backed up due to technical problems at the moment, so it depends on when you'd like to pick up your order.

W　I have to run an errand right now, so ______________ Vanessa ______________ .

M　Let me see. ______________ . That should be plenty of time. ______________ ______________ .

W　여보세요. 맥아서 박사 연구실의 캐서린입니다. 저희 인쇄 주문에 30부를 추가할 수 있는지 알아보려고 전화 드렸어요.

M　안녕하세요, 캐서린 씨. 지금 기계적인 문제들로 작업이 약간 밀려서 언제 주문한 것을 가져가실지에 달렸어요.

W　저는 지금 심부름을 가야 해서 바네사가 5시에 들르게 할게요.

M　어디 보자. 지금이 3시이군요. 시간은 충분하겠네요. 그때까지 준비해 놓을게요.

[**어휘**] **back up** 밀리다, 정체하다 ｜ **run an errand** 심부름 가다 ｜ **come by** 들르다 ｜ **plenty of** 많은

Diana Thompson
Pickup: Friday, 11:30 A.M.

Chocolate Cupcakes	20
Jelly Donuts	12
Fudge Brownies	24
Oatmeal Cookies	30

4 Why is the woman calling?

(A) To make an order

(B) To add to an order

(C) To cancel an order

(D) To postpone an order

5 What does the woman say the people coming prefer?

(A) Food made from chocolate

(B) Food with nuts in it

(C) Food with icing on it

(D) Food with fruit in it

6 Look at the graphic. Which item does the woman order extra of?

(A) Chocolate cupcakes

(B) Jelly donuts

(C) Fudge brownies

(D) Oatmeal cookies

Questions 4-6 refer to the following conversation and list.

M　Good afternoon. Rose's Bakery. How may I help you?

W　Hello. This is Diana Thompson calling. I made an order with you yesterday.

M　Yes, Ms. Thompson. I spoke with you on the phone then. What can I do for you?

W　I spoke with my boss, and he mentioned ____ ________________________. So I need to increase my order.

M　Of course. I've got your order form here in front of me. What do you need more of?

W　Well, ____, so how about ________ ________________________________?

M　Sure. ________________________________. Shall I add 12 more to the total?

W　Yes, that would be perfect. Thanks a lot.

M　안녕하세요. 로즈 베이커리입니다. 어떻게 도와 드릴까요?

W　안녕하세요. 저는 다이애나 톰슨이에요. 어제 주문을 했고요.

M　네, 톰슨 씨. 그때 제가 전화로 통화를 했죠. 어떻게 해 드릴까요?

W　제 상사와 이야기를 나누었는데, 그분께서는 우리가 계획했던 것보다 더 많은 사람들이 행사에 참석할 것이라고 언급하시더군요. 그래서 주문량을 늘려야 해요.

M　그러시군요. 여기 제 앞에 당신의 주문서가 있어요. 무엇이 더 필요하신가요?

W　음, 참석할 대부분의 사람들이 정말로 견과류를 좋아하기 때문에, 견과류가 들어간 품목들을 12개 더 추가시키는 것이 어떨까요?

M　좋습니다. 24개를 주문하셨습니다. 합계에 12개를 추가할까요?

W　네, 그러면 완벽할 것 같아요. 정말 고맙습니다.

[어휘] **mention** 언급하다, 말하다　|　**nut** 견과, 견과류　|　**dozen** 12개　|　**add** 더하다　|　**total** 합, 계

PART 4

Department	Head
R&D	Bill Morrison
Sales	Jethro Walker
Marketing	Ian Smith
Accounting	Bruce Wright

1   Why did the speaker's department go over budget?

(A) It developed a large number of new products.

(B) It bought advertisements for many games.

(C) It did not sell as many items as expected.

(D) It paid several employees large bonuses.

2   What did the speaker's department do in the second quarter?

(A) It hired some new workers.

(B) It promoted Lisa Sanders.

(C) It fired a couple of employees.

(D) It transferred three individuals.

3   Look at the graphic. Who most likely is the speaker?

(A) Bruce Wright

(B) Bill Morrison

(C) Ian Smith

(D) Jethro Walker

Questions 1-3 refer to the following excerpt from a meeting and chart.

I'd like to provide you with an update on the work my department has been doing. In the second quarter, we ran over budget by 5%. The reason was that we had a great deal of _______________ ____. The Sales Department insisted _____________ ____. We had only been planning to market 2 or 3 of our biggest games. Instead, we advertised on TV, the radio, and the Internet for all 8 releases. Fortunately, ____ _____________. Due to the extra workload, we took on three new employees. They're doing quite well. In addition, one employee, Lisa Sanders, resigned her position to move to another company.

저는 저희 부서에서 진행 중인 업무에 관해 새로운 소식을 알려 드리고자 합니다. 2분기에, 저희는 예산을 5% 정도 초과했습니다. 그 이유는 고려하지 못했던 추가적인 지출이 많았기 때문입니다. 영업부는 저희에게 새로 출시된 모든 제품에 대해 막대한 홍보를 해야 한다고 주장했습니다. 우리는 가장 중요한 2개 혹은 3개의 게임에만 마케팅을 할 계획을 세워 두었습니다. 대신, 저희는 8개의 모든 출시품에 대해 TV, 라디오, 그리고 인터넷 광고를 했습니다. 다행히도, 모든 게임에서 예상보다 높은 판매량을 보였기 때문에 저희 노력은 결실을 맺었습니다. 추가 업무로 인하여, 저희는 세 명의 신입 직원을 채용했습니다. 그들은 일을 꽤 잘하고 있습니다. 또한, 리사 샌더스라는 직원 한 명은 이직을 하기 위해 퇴사를 했습니다.

[어휘] **provide A with B** A에게 B를 제공하다 ｜ **run over** ~을 넘다, 넘치다 ｜ **account for** ~을 고려하다 ｜ **promote** 홍보하다 ｜ **release** 출시, 출시품 ｜ **market** 마케팅하다 ｜ **advertise** 광고하다 ｜ **pay off** 성과를 내다, 값을 하다 ｜ **workload** 업무량 ｜ **take on** ~을 고용하다 ｜ **resign** 사임하다

Actual Test

LISTENING TEST

In the Listening test, you will be asked to demonstrate how well you understand spoken English. The entire Listening Test will last approximately 45 minutes. There are four parts, and the directions are given for each part. You must mark your answers on the separate answer sheet. Do not write your answers in your test book.

PART 1

Directions: For each question in this part, you will hear four statements about a picture in your test book. When you hear the statements, you must select the one statement that best describes what you see in the picture. Then find the number of the question on your answer sheet and mark your answer. The statements will not be printed in your test book and will be spoken only one time.

Statement (B), "The man is signing his name." is the best description of the picture, so you should select answer (B) and mark it on your answer sheet.

1.

2.

3.

4.

GO ON TO THE NEXT PAGE

5.

6.

PART 2

Directions: You will hear a question or statement and three responses spoken in English. They will not be printed in your test book and will be spoken only one time. Select the best response to the question or statement and mark the letter (A), (B), or (C) on your answer sheet.

Example

Sample Answer

Ⓐ   Ⓑ   ●

You will hear :	Did you attend the meeting for the next project?
You will also hear :	(A) The projector is nice.
	(B) Yes, the meeting went longer than expected.
	(C) No, I had to meet a client.

The best response to the question, "Did you attend the meeting for the next project?" is choice (C), "No, I had to meet a client," so (C) is the correct answer. You should mark answer (C) on your answer sheet.

7. Mark your answer on your answer sheet.

8. Mark your answer on your answer sheet.

9. Mark your answer on your answer sheet.

10. Mark your answer on your answer sheet.

11. Mark your answer on your answer sheet.

12. Mark your answer on your answer sheet.

13. Mark your answer on your answer sheet.

14. Mark your answer on your answer sheet.

15. Mark your answer on your answer sheet.

16. Mark your answer on your answer sheet.

17. Mark your answer on your answer sheet.

18. Mark your answer on your answer sheet.

19. Mark your answer on your answer sheet.

20. Mark your answer on your answer sheet.

21. Mark your answer on your answer sheet.

22. Mark your answer on your answer sheet.

23. Mark your answer on your answer sheet.

24. Mark your answer on your answer sheet.

25. Mark your answer on your answer sheet.

26. Mark your answer on your answer sheet.

27. Mark your answer on your answer sheet.

28. Mark your answer on your answer sheet.

29. Mark your answer on your answer sheet.

30. Mark your answer on your answer sheet.

31. Mark your answer on your answer sheet.

GO ON TO THE NEXT PAGE

32. Where are the speakers?
(A) In a coffee shop
(B) In an office
(C) In a market
(D) In an apartment

33. Who did the man contact?
(A) A hotel manager
(B) A ticket agent
(C) A technician
(D) A dentist

34. What will the woman most likely do next?
(A) Call an accountant
(B) Purchase an appliance
(C) Cancel an appointment
(D) Plug in a heater

35. What does the man request?
(A) A bus ticket to Trenton
(B) An outline of a report
(C) An information booklet
(D) A ride to a conference

36. What will the speakers probably do tomorrow?
(A) Put in some overtime hours
(B) Discuss their presentations
(C) Plan a business meeting
(D) Book a table in a restaurant

37. Why is the woman taking the commuter train?
(A) Her car has a flat tire.
(B) She lost her driver's license.
(C) Driving takes too long.
(D) The bus is always late.

38. What does the woman ask about?
- (A) A lost credit card
- (B) Some car repairs
- (C) A recent order
- (D) A new address

39. What product are the speakers discussing?
- (A) Computer desks
- (B) Swivel chairs
- (C) Conference tables
- (D) Coffee makers

40. What does the man offer to do?
- (A) Consult another division
- (B) Increase the salary
- (C) Verify the phone number
- (D) Reserve a hotel room

41. What are the speakers discussing?
- (A) A charity event
- (B) A traffic accident
- (C) A conference schedule
- (D) A quarterly report

42. What might be a problem?
- (A) The bad weather
- (B) The long distance
- (C) The broken fax machine
- (D) The billing error

43. According to the woman, what will happen on Saturday?
- (A) A new hospital will open.
- (B) The summer vacation will start.
- (C) The employees will work overtime.
- (D) A pro bowler will attend the event.

44. What does the man want to do?
- (A) Book an airline ticket
- (B) Open a bank account
- (C) Purchase car insurance
- (D) Build a new house

45. What is the problem?
- (A) The ATM is out of service.
- (B) The account has been closed.
- (C) An employee is away.
- (D) The fire alarm is not working.

46. What does the woman suggest the man do?
- (A) Phone the main branch
- (B) Come back next week
- (C) Cancel the meeting
- (D) Set up an appointment

47. What is the woman looking for?
- (A) Memos
- (B) Manuals
- (C) Invoices
- (D) Résumés

48. Who is Mr. Murphy probably meeting now?
- (A) Division managers
- (B) A new sales team
- (C) Job applicants
- (D) A client

49. What does the man offer to do?
- (A) Schedule some appointments
- (B) Locate some files
- (C) Book a flight
- (D) E-mail some reports

GO ON TO THE NEXT PAGE

50. What are the speakers discussing?
    (A) A movie
    (B) A news story
    (C) A schedule change
    (D) Car problems

51. Who called the woman last night?
    (A) A police officer
    (B) An important executive
    (C) A dental assistant
    (D) A contractor

52. What will the woman probably do this afternoon?
    (A) Leave for a conference
    (B) Go to a job interview
    (C) Move into a new house
    (D) Have her car repaired

53. Where is this conversation most likely taking place?
    (A) A travel agency
    (B) A publishing company
    (C) A mortgage company
    (D) A public library

54. What does the woman give the man?
    (A) A billing statement
    (B) An application
    (C) A telephone book
    (D) A rental contract

55. What does the woman suggest that the man do?
    (A) Send a form in the mail
    (B) Pay online via credit card
    (C) Review their website
    (D) Visit another company

56. What is the speakers' company opening soon?
    (A) A branch office
    (B) An exhibition hall
    (C) A restaurant
    (D) A call center

57. How far ahead of schedule is the project?
    (A) Three days
    (B) Two weeks
    (C) A month
    (D) Two months

58. According to the woman, what needs to be done in the future?
    (A) Computer installation
    (B) Interior painting
    (C) Radio advertisements
    (D) A training orientation

59. What are the speakers discussing?
    (A) The details of a trip
    (B) The newspaper headlines
    (C) The bargains in a store
    (D) The plans for a workshop

60. What does the man suggest?
    (A) Renting tables and chairs
    (B) Rescheduling an appointment
    (C) Changing the meeting room
    (D) Repairing the copier

61. What does the woman ask for?
    (A) A subway map
    (B) A registration form
    (C) A fax number
    (D) A business address

62. What are the speakers mainly discussing?
   (A) The previous end-of-the-year party
   (B) The need to plan for a work event
   (C) The restaurant they are going to eat at
   (D) The seminar they will attend in three
      weeks

63. Where do the speakers most likely work?
   (A) At a law firm
   (B) At a restaurant
   (C) At a hotel
   (D) At an engineering company

64. What does the woman request that the
   man do?
   (A) Make some phone calls for her
   (B) Call a local hotel
   (C) Plan the entire party
   (D) Give her some information

65. Who is Mr. Steele?
   (A) The woman's boss
   (B) The speakers' colleague
   (C) A client of the woman's
   (D) A friend of Mr. Harrison's

66. What is mentioned about the Harrison
   project?
   (A) The deadline for completing it is
      approaching.
   (B) The clients are satisfied with the work
      done on it.
   (C) The work on it has gone over budget.
   (D) It is going to be postponed by a month.

67. What is the woman going to do next?
   (A) Send an e-mail to Mr. Steele
   (B) Speak with Mr. Jefferson in person
   (C) Attend a meeting with her boss
   (D) Give the men their newest assignment

Date	City
Vancouver	July 13
Seattle	July 14
San Francisco	July 15
Los Angeles	July 16

68. Why did Fred Powell call the woman?
   (A) To invite her to attend a meeting
   (B) To cancel his meeting with the man
   (C) To inform her he is going on a trip
   (D) To have the man meet him in Vancouver

69. Where is the man going to go to a
   seminar?
   (A) Los Angeles
   (B) Seattle
   (C) Vancouver
   (D) San Francisco

70. Look at the graphic. On which day does
   the man need to change his schedule?
   (A) July 13
   (B) July 14
   (C) July 15
   (D) July 16

GO ON TO THE NEXT PAGE

71. What does Markey's sell?

(A) Electronics
(B) Plants
(C) Automobiles
(D) Books

72. When will Markey's close?

(A) In 15 minutes
(B) In 30 minutes
(C) In 1 hour
(D) In 2 hours

73. Where can the special display be found?

(A) Near the store entrance
(B) Next to the elevator
(C) On the top floor
(D) In the parking garage

74. Why is the speaker calling Mr. Davidson?

(A) To advertise his services
(B) To check a delivery address
(C) To confirm some scheduled work
(D) To request some changes to a plan

75. Where does the speaker most likely work?

(A) At a bicycle store
(B) At a gardening service
(C) At a shipping company
(D) At a real estate agency

76. When will the speaker visit Mr. Davidson?

(A) At 8 A.M.
(B) At 10 A.M.
(C) At 2 P.M.
(D) At 4 P.M.

77. What is the purpose of the talk?

(A) To show appreciation for a prize

(B) To welcome the new faculty

(C) To explain a computer program

(D) To introduce the office staff

78. According to the talk, how long has the speaker worked at a university?

(A) About two years

(B) About four years

(C) About six years

(D) About eight years

79. Why does the speaker mention the Learning Foundation?

(A) It donated several textbooks.

(B) It purchased classroom items.

(C) It provided funds for the project.

(D) It gave an award to a student.

80. What is the purpose of the talk?

(A) To explain the hiring process

(B) To present a staff member

(C) To change a marketing plan

(D) To create a new division

81. What products does this company most likely sell?

(A) Automobile parts

(B) Kitchen appliances

(C) Children's clothing

(D) Camping equipment

82. According to the talk, what will Ms. Perez do for this company?

(A) Design new automobile parts

(B) Open a European branch office

(C) Draft its new products manual

(D) Help determine buyers' preferences

83. What is unusual about the current weather conditions?

(A) Heavy rain

(B) High temperatures

(C) Scattered showers

(D) Strong winds

84. What do officials at the weather bureau advise?

(A) Remaining indoors

(B) Conserving electricity

(C) Wearing a thick coat

(D) Saving water

85. When will the weather be better for outdoor activities?

(A) On Monday

(B) On Tuesday

(C) On Wednesday

(D) On Thursday

GO ON TO THE NEXT PAGE

86. Where is the audience?
    (A) In a car factory
    (B) In a folk village
    (C) In a historic home
    (D) At an art show

87. Who is Martin Drake?
    (A) A tour guide
    (B) An art collector
    (C) An architect
    (D) A painter

88. What did William Hamilton do?
    (A) He opened an art museum.
    (B) He was a school teacher.
    (C) He ran a travel agency.
    (D) He owned a shipping company.

89. Why is the speaker giving this talk?
    (A) To introduce a sales representative
    (B) To explain the interview process
    (C) To announce some key policy changes
    (D) To review the results of a research
        study

90. What do the listeners have to do?
    (A) Note impressions of each applicant
    (B) Fill out an application form
    (C) Provide details of a conference
    (D) Attend a panel discussion

91. What will the listeners do tomorrow
    morning?
    (A) Welcome a foreign client
    (B) Change the business hours
    (C) Hire a new employee
    (D) Install some new computers

92. Who is the speaker?
    (A) A buyer
    (B) An engineer
    (C) An executive
    (D) A department head

93. What does the speaker say about Bedford
    Systems?
    (A) It is not doing as well as it once was.
    (B) It is the country's largest electronics
        firm.
    (C) It is going to release some new
        products.
    (D) It just hired some new high-level
        employees.

94. What does the speaker mean when he
    says, "Let me provide you with a brief
    outline of it"?
    (A) He will talk about the company's past.
    (B) He will explain his plan for the company.
    (C) He will introduce some of the
        department heads.
    (D) He will describe the newest product.

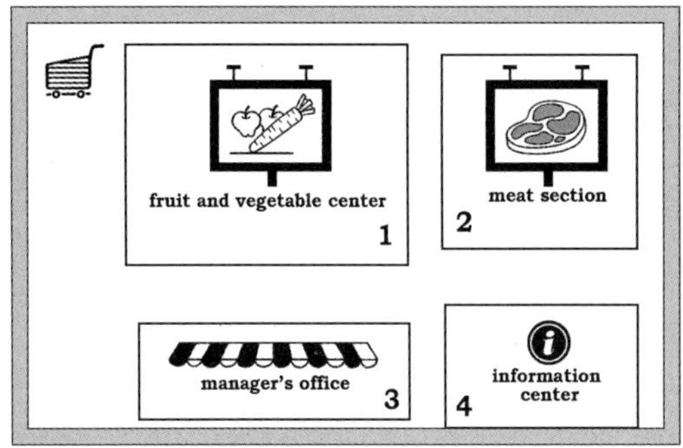

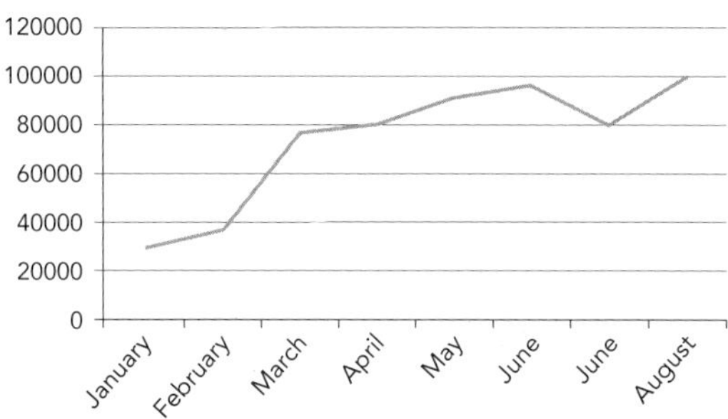

95. Where should listeners go to buy items on sale?

(A) The bakery

(B) The deli

(C) The fruit and vegetable area

(D) The electronics area

96. What does the speaker suggest that listeners do?

(A) Send e-mail

(B) Use coupons

(C) Make suggestions

(D) Go to the checkout counter

97. Look at the graphic . What section of the store is going to temporarily close?

(A) 1

(B) 2

(C) 3

(D) 4

98. What is the purpose of the talk?

(A) To describe a future plan

(B) To make a request for more funding

(C) To go over recent attendance numbers

(D) To discuss some new rides at the park

99. According to the speaker, what happened in July?

(A) Some rides closed temporarily.

(B) Attendance at the park increased.

(C) There were mostly sunny skies.

(D) Lots of new visitors came to the park.

100. Look at the graphic. In which month did the new rollercoaster open?

(A) March

(B) April

(C) June

(D) August

Reading
Comprehension

명사

명사란 사람, 동물, 식물뿐 아니라 추상적인 개념에 붙이는 이름으로 문장 안에서 주어와 목적어 자리에 오고 형용사나 소유격 뒤에서 수식을 받는다. 시험에서는 (1)명사의 위치와 형태, (2)명사와 동명사의 구분, (3)불가산명사의 용법을 묻는 문제가 주로 출제된다.

1 명사의 위치

1) 주어 자리: __________ + 동사

예제 ------- to the management seminar were sent to all the managers this morning.

(A) invite   (B) invitations   (C) invited

번역 금전관리 세미나 초대권들이 모든 관리자들에게 오늘 아침에 발송되었다.
정답 (B)

2) 목적어 자리: 주어 + 동사 + __________ / 전치사 + __________

예제 Most of the participants have shown ------- in their outdoor activities.

(A) interesting   (B) interested   (C) interest

번역 대부분의 참석자들이 야외 활동에 관심을 보였다.
정답 (C)

3) 관사나 소유격 뒤: a(n)/the/their ~ + __________

예제 Gift certificates enable people to purchase a ------- of books at a reduced price.

(A) vary   (B) various   (C) variety

번역 상품권들은 사람들이 다양한 책을 할인 가격에 구입할 수 있게 해준다.
정답 (C)

4) 형용사 뒤: 형용사 + __________

예제 The summary contains a detailed ------- and solution to potential problems.

(A) description   (B) described   (C) describe

번역 그 요약서는 발생할 수 있는 문제에 대한 자세한 설명과 해결책을 담고 있다.
정답 (A)

2 명사의 형태

단어 끝에 붙어 있는 어미의 형태로 명사를 구분할 수 있다. 단, –al은 형용사 어미로도 쓰이므로 주의해야 한다.

-ment	enrollment 등록	replacement 후임, 교체품	
-ence	preference 선호도	difference 차이점	
-ance	attendance 출석	observance 준수	
-ion	evaluation 평가	permission 허가	
-ness	freshness 신선함	effectiveness 효율성	
-ty	activity 활동	responsibility 책임, 책임감	
-ee	trainee 연수생	attendee 참석자	
-sm	criticism 비평	enthusiasm 열정	
-ic	critic 비평가	characteristic 특징	
-al	professional 전문가	arrival 도착	

cf. **professional** 〈명사〉 전문가 / 〈형용사〉 전문적인, 전문직의

3 명사와 동명사의 구분

1) 명사와 동명사의 차이

동명사는 동사 원형에 –ing가 붙은 형태로, 동사의 기능을 하면서 명사 자리에 올 수 있지만 명사와 달리 동명사 앞에는 관사나 형용사가 올 수 없다. 또한 명사와 달리 동명사는 동사의 기능이 있기 때문에 부사의 수식을 받으며 뒤에 주로 목적어가 따라 나온다.

- Thank you **for choosing** our company as your main supplier. (choice ×)
  우리 회사를 귀사의 주 공급 업체로 선택에 주셔서 고맙습니다.

- Mr. Lee is responsible **for regularly checking** current systems. (regular ×)
  이 씨는 현 시스템을 정기적으로 검사할 책임이 있다.

4 복합 명사

일반적인 '형용사 + 명사'가 아닌 **명사 + 명사** 형태를 말한다.

sales increases 판매 증가	sales growth 판매 성장
customer satisfaction 고객 만족	employee productivity 직원생산성
safety procedure 안전절차	research program 연구 프로그램

1 If the ------- are not received within five days, please contact the head of the Shipping Department immediately.
(A) shipping
(B) ship
(C) shipments
(D) shipped

2 It is expected that all the customers will request ------- in the event of an accident or any injury.
(A) compensated
(B) compensation
(C) compensate
(D) compensatory

3 The established electronics company's ------- into America was welcomed by many people in the region.
(A) expansion
(B) expand
(C) expansive
(D) expansively

4 The airline will reimburse passengers for damaged baggage when ------- are received.
(A) complain
(B) complaining
(C) complains
(D) complaints

5 The famous restaurant will be closed for two months so that a complete ------- of the facility can take place.
(A) renovate
(B) renovated
(C) renovates
(D) renovation

6 The maintenance workers were informed of a wide ------- of problems with the electronic devices.
(A) vary
(B) varies
(C) various
(D) variety

7 The board of directors is considering the possibility of ------- its current office computer system.
(A) upgrade
(B) to upgrade
(C) upgrading
(D) upgraded

8 We are looking forward to having the mayor of our city in ------- at our fundraising dinner tomorrow evening.
(A) attendance
(B) attended
(C) attend
(D) attending

Questions 1-4 refer to the following e-mail.

To: jasonsmith@westwood.com

From: claudepeppers@westwood.com

Subject: Schedule Change

Date: October 12

Dear Mr. Smith,

I recently received my schedule for the week of October 19 to 23. According to it, I ------- **1** every day from 9 A.M. to 6 P.M. Two weeks ago, I sent an e-mail to you in which I ------- **2** my desire to you to work some overtime starting next week. Since I am no longer attending night classes at Central University, I have plenty of time to work more hours in the evening. ------- **3** Is it possible to assign me a few extra hours of work?

I would ------- **4** appreciate it as I hope to save enough money to purchase a car in the coming months. Please let me know if you can fulfill my request or not.

Sincerely,

Claude Peppers

---

1 (A) worked
   (B) will have worked
   (C) will be working
   (D) have been working

2 (A) wrote
   (B) expressed
   (C) viewed
   (D) appointed

3 (A) Apparently, some of the other employees are very busy.
   (B) Sadly, my class schedule kept me very busy in the past.
   (C) Unfortunately, I wasn't given any extra hours though.
   (D) Hopefully, I'll get the chance to meet you in person soon.

4 (A) deep
   (B) deeper
   (C) deeply
   (D) deepest

DAY 02 형용사

형용사는 명사의 성질이나 상태를 나타내는 품사로 be동사 뒤에서 주어의 상태를 설명하거나 명사 앞에서 해당 명사를 직접 수식하는 데 쓰인다. 우선 형용사의 위치와 형태를 알아야 하고 기본적인 형용사 형태 외에 현재분사형(V-ing)과 과거분사형(V-ed)으로 된 형용사 어휘도 따로 외워둬야 한다.

1 형용사의 위치

1) 명사 앞에서 명사를 수식한다.

예제 Staff members were satisfied with ------- sales figures that were announced last week.

(A) impress   (B) impression   (C) impressive

번역 직원들은 지난주에 발표된 인상적인 판매 수치에 대해 만족해했다.
정답 (C)

2) be동사나 be동사 상당어구 뒤에서 주어의 상태를 설명한다.

▸ be, remain + ____________ ~인 상태로 있다
▸ become, get + ____________ ~한 상태가 되다
▸ seem, look, appear + ____________ 상태가 ~인 것 같다

예제 1 We are having trouble handling bulky products because the storage space is -------.

(A) limit   (B) limiting   (C) limited

번역 보관 장소가 제한되어 있기 때문에 우리는 부피가 큰 제품을 다루는데 힘들어하고 있다.
정답 (C)

예제 2 The production department members seem ------- to work night shifts because of increased orders.

(A) readily   (B) ready   (C) readiness

번역 생산 부서 직원들은 주문 물량의 증가로 밤 근무를 할 준비가 된 것 같다.
정답 (B)

3) 목적어 뒤에서 목적어를 보충 설명한다.

- The goal of our internship program is to **make** interns **suitable** for the required position.
  우리 인턴쉽 프로그램의 목적은 인턴들을 요구된 직책에 적합하게 만드는 것이다.

- We have made a lot of efforts to **keep** customers **satisfied** with our products and service.
  우리는 고객들이 우리의 제품과 서비스에 계속 만족하도록 노력했다.

- The sales representative **found** the noisy customers in the corner shop.
  외판원은 모퉁이 가게에서 시끄러운 고객들을 발견했다.
- The sales representative **found** the noisy customers **very satisfied**.
  외판원은 시끄러운 고객들이 만족해 한다고 생각했다.

- The advertising company **considered** some applicants for the position.
  그 광고회사는 그 공석에 몇몇 응시자들을 고려했다.
- The advertising company **considered** its new advertisements **effective and powerful**.
  그 광고회사는 새 광고가 효과적이고 강력하다고 여겼다.

2 형용사의 형태

-ic	strategic 전략의	dramatic 극적인
-ous	numerous 많은, 다수의	serious 심각한
-ful	successful 성공적인	powerful 강력한
-ble	stable 안정된	compatible 호환이 되는
-ry	necessary 필수적인	temporary 임시의
-ent / -ant	fluent 유창한	significant 중요한, 상당한
-ive	persuasive 설득력 있는	representative 반영하는
-al	experimental 실험적인	critical 비판적인
명사+ly	friendly 친절한	timely 시기 적절한 / costly 비싼
	likely 가능성 있는	quarterly 분기의

3 자주 나오는 형용사

1) 현재분사형 형용사 (V–ing)

promising results 좋은 결과
growing company 성장하고 있는 회사
disappointing sales figures 실망스러운 매출액
remaining equipment 남아있는 장비

2) 과거분사형 형용사 (V–ed)

damaged merchandise 손상된 상품
finished products 완성된 제품
detailed information 자세한 정보
confirmed reservation 확인된 예약
limited number 제한된 숫자
guided tour 가이드가 수행하는 투어

1 All the visitors to the power plant must wear ------- clothing provided when entering the laboratory.
(A) protect
(B) protection
(C) protective
(D) protecting

2 As your application still remains -------, we will not be able to process your paperwork properly.
(A) incompletely
(B) incomplete
(C) incompletion
(D) to complete

3 The serious financial problems have become ------- since more funds were added last quarter.
(A) managing
(B) manageable
(C) manage
(D) manageably

4 It is ------- that all the forms should be filled out correctly prior to entering the reception room.
(A) advice
(B) advisor
(C) advise
(D) advisable

5 The new management is expected to announce its ------- growth plans in the foreseeable future.
(A) strategy
(B) strategic
(C) strategically
(D) strategize

6 The government announced that it was ------- to lower interest rates to boost the economy.
(A) ready
(B) readier
(C) readily
(D) readiness

7 According to the report, the Jacktown Fabric Corporation posted ------- profits last quarter.
(A) impress
(B) to impress
(C) impressed
(D) impressive

8 Management found recent sales figures too -------, so they are planning to improve the quality of our products.
(A) disappoint
(B) disappointed
(C) disappointing
(D) disappointment

PART 7 단독 지문

Questions 1-3 refer to the following job posting.

Job Title: Product Development Manager

Date Posted: August 12

Description: Silver Door Designs is a rapidly growing and internationally renowned interior lighting manufacturer and is looking to fill the newly created position of Product Development Manager for its Michigan-based branch office. You will need to be an energetic leader with exceptional organizational skills and have a minimum of 10 years experience in interior lighting. You will work directly with our designers and our engineering and manufacturing teams, and will be responsible for bringing new lighting products to the market place within specified timelines. A master's degree is preferred but not required. Salary will depend on experience, and a full benefits package will be offered to the successful candidate.

Please e-mail a cover letter and résumé to mlewis@silverdoordesigns.com or mail them to:

Silver Door Designs

200 Niles Road

Detroit, MI 41085

(Attn: Monica Lewis)

The deadline for the submission of applications is September 3. Only those candidates whose résumés are selected will be contacted. Please direct any additional inquiries to:

Ms. Monica Lewis
Phone: (269) 456-8673
Fax: (269) 456-2245

1   What is a necessary requirement for the
    applicant?
    (A) A master's degree
    (B) Fluency in a second language
    (C) Excellent organizational ability
    (D) Technological certifications

2   What duty will the successful candidate be
    responsible for?
    (A) Training new designers for the company
    (B) Creating new products within a limited
        time
    (C) Leading an overseas manufacturing
        team
    (D) Working with large engineering
        companies

3   What can be inferred about the hiring
    process?
    (A) Two letters of reference should be
        submitted.
    (B) Applicants should make a brief
        presentation.
    (C) There will be both written and oral tests.
    (D) Unsuccessful applicants will not be
        contacted.

부사는 문장에서 꼭 필요한 품사는 아니다. 하지만 동사, 형용사, 다른 부사, 전치사구 또는 문장을 꾸며주기 때문에 가장 많이 등장하는 품사 중 하나이다. 시험에서는 부사의 적절한 위치를 고르거나 적절한 부사를 고르는 어휘 문제가 많이 출제된다.

1 부사의 위치

1) 형용사 앞에서 형용사의 의미를 더해준다: _________ + 형용사

- **Heavily** discounted rates appealed to both customers and travel agencies.
  상당히 할인된 가격이 고객과 여행사 둘 다에게 매력적이었다.

2) 동사 앞에서 동사의 의미를 보충해준다: 주어 + _________ + 동사

- All the team members **unanimously** agreed that Mr. Chan worked most productively.
  모든 동료들은 챈 씨가 가장 생산적으로 일했었다는 것에 만장일치로 동의했다.

3) 자동사를 뒤에서 수식해준다: 자동사 + _________

- Speakers need to speak **clearly** to the audience.
  연사들은 청중에게 명확하게 연설할 필요가 있다.

4) 목적어 뒤에서 동사를 수식해준다: 주어 + 타동사 + 목적어 + _________

- The mobile phone company will release a new model **shortly**.
  그 휴대폰 회사는 새로운 사양을 곧 출시할 것이다.

5) 수동태 앞 또는 뒤에서 p.p.를 수식해준다: be + _________ + p.p. + _________

- Please make sure that the office doors are **securely** locked before you leave.
  나가기 전에 사무실 문들이 안전하게 잠겨 있는지 확인하세요.

6) V –ing 형태의 형용사, 진행형, 동명사를 앞에서 수식해준다: _________ + V–ing

- The president is capable of **easily** solving financial problems.
  그 사장은 제정적인 문제를 쉽게 해결할 수 있다.

7) 현재완료 have p.p. 사이에서 p.p.를 수식해준다: have + _________ + p.p.

- Members have **specifically** discussed new regulations.
  회원들은 새로운 규정들을 구체적으로 토론하고 있다.

2 혼동하기 쉬운 부사 형태

late 형 늦은 / 부 늦게	lately 최근에
hard 형 어려운 / 부 열심히	hardly 거의 ~하지 않다
high 형 높은 / 부 높게	highly 매우
ready 형 준비된 / 부 미리, 신속히	readily 손쉽게
fair 형 정당한 / 부 정당하게	fairly 매우
full 형 꽉 찬 / 부 충분히	fully 완전히
near 형 가까운 / 부 가까이	nearly 거의
close 형 가까운, 빽빽한 / 부 가까이에, 빽빽하게	closely 자세히
wide 형 넓은 / 부 넓게	widely 널리
just 형 올바른, 공정한 / 부 바로, 막	justly 공정하게

3 특이한 부사

once 한때는

- Ms. Lee was **once** an efficient financial analyst.
  이 씨는 한 때 유능한 재무 분석가였다.

otherwise 다른 식으로

- Don't revise the details unless you are **otherwise** directed by your supervisor.
  상사에게서 달리 지시 받지 않으면 세부사항을 수정하지 말라.

PART 5 문법 – 부사

1 The CEO ------- decided to hold a party honoring employees who have been with the company for over 20 years.

(A) final

(B) finally

(C) finalize

(D) finalist

2 Employees tend to rely ------- on their supervisors in case there is an unexpected emergency.

(A) heavy

(B) heavily

(C) heaviness

(D) heavier

3 It is ------- recommended that all the tenants comply with the newly established regulations.

(A) strong

(B) strength

(C) strengthen

(D) strongly

4 The new employee has ------- impressed her supervisor with her positive attitude and commitment.

(A) consist

(B) consistent

(C) consisted

(D) consistently

5 The Arden Odea is one of the most ------- located convention sites in the province.

(A) convenience

(B) convenient

(C) conveniences

(D) conveniently

6 An aggressive advertising campaign for a ------- anticipated new movie is expected to be launched next week.

(A) highly

(B) height

(C) high

(D) heighten

7 The Human Resources Department Manager responded ------- to suggestions by the employees.

(A) position

(B) positive

(C) positively

(D) positioning

8 Carson Organization is ------- claiming to be the most reliable source of information on U.S. economic policy.

(A) repeat

(B) repeated

(C) repetitive

(D) repeatedly

Questions 1-4 refer to the following advertisement.

Enjoy the Fine Life at Patricio's

Patricio's is the newest ski resort to open around Pine Mountain. ------- at the foot of the mountain, Patricio's is the place you should visit on your next vacation. We have 120 rooms, all of ------- are richly furnished. Every room has a great view of the local area.

Patricio's is the perfect spot to start your day of skiing since the ski lift to the top of the mountain is fewer than 50 meters away from our front entrance. So ski all day long and then come back to Patricio's ------- dinner in our four-star restaurant. Or relax with a drink or two at Sandy's, the bar located right next to the lobby. To celebrate our grand opening, all rooms and ski lessons are being offered at 50% off for the next two months. ------- Stay at Patricio's, and you'll have the best vacation ever.

---

1 (A) Locate
   (B) Locating
   (C) Location
   (D) Located

2 (A) whom
   (B) which
   (C) what
   (D) that

3 (A) enjoying
   (B) enjoy
   (C) will enjoy
   (D) to enjoy

4 (A) Call 904-4344 for more details.
   (B) You'll love the food we serve here.
   (C) Our skating instructors are the best.
   (D) Look out the windows at the magnificent views.

DAY 04 문장의 형식과 동사의 종류

1 1형식: 주어 + 자동사 + (부사) / 주어 + 자동사 + (전치사 + 명사)

자동사는 목적어 없이도 스스로 완벽하게 동사 역할을 하는 동사로, 목적어를 쓰려면 전치사가 있어야 하는 동사이다.

- **I go.** (주어 + 자동사)
  나는 간다.

- Brian Snyder **worked hard**. (주어 + 자동사 + 부사)
  브라이언 스나이더는 열심히 일했다.

- **I go to the library** on weekends. (주어 + 자동사 + 전치사 + 명사)
  나는 주말마다 도서관에 간다.

- Brian Snyder **worked hard on the project**. (주어 + 자동사 + 부사 + 전치사 + 명사)
  브라이언 스나이더는 그 프로젝트에 관여하여 열심히 일했다.

자주 나오는 자동사 + 전치사 표현

participate in ~에 참여하다	talk about ~에 관해 이야기하다	apply for ~에 지원하다, 신청하다
listen to ~을 듣다	respond to ~에 응답하다	speak to ~에게 말을 걸다
react to ~에 반응하다		

2 2형식: 주어 + be동사 + 형용사/명사

자동사 중에는 주어를 보충 설명해 주는 보어(형용사, 명사)가 필요한 불완전 자동사들이 있다. be동사와 be동사 상당어구가 여기에 속한다.

be동사 ~이다

- Security guards **were alert** during the football match.
  경비원들은 축구 경기 동안 경계 태세로 있었다.

look/seem/appear ~처럼 보이다

- The managers **looked exhausted**.
  매니저들이 피곤해 보였다.

remain/stay/keep ~인 상태이다

- The office **remains unoccupied**.
  그 사무실은 비어 있었다.

get/become ~이 되다

- They **became accustomed** to the work environment.
  그들은 업무 환경에 익숙해졌다.

feel/taste/sound ~하게 느껴지다/맛이 나다/들리다

- The idea **sounds good**.
  그 아이디어가 좋은 것 같다.

3 3형식: 주어 + 타동사 + 목적어

타동사는 목적어를 취하는 동사이며 목적어는 동사가 나타내는 행위의 대상이다. 타동사의 목적어가 될 수 있는 말로는 명사, 대명사, 동명사(V-ing), that절이 있다.

- The managers are **discussing the terms** of the contract.
  매니저들이 계약 조건을 논의하고 있다.
- The owner of the restaurant **considered extending** its store hours.
  식당 주인은 상점시간 연장을 고려했다.
- The bill **shows that** we have consumed too much electricity this month.
  청구서가 이번 달에 너무 많은 전기를 소모했다는 것을 보여준다.

4 4형식: 주어 + 수여동사 + 간접목적어 + 직접목적어

타동사 가운데 목적어를 두 개 쓸 수 있는 동사를 '수여동사'라고 부른다. 수여동사는 기본적으로 '~에게(간접목적어) …을(직접목적어) 주다'는 의미를 나타내는 동사들이고 대개 전치사 to를 써서 간접목적어와 직접목적어의 위치를 바꾸기도 한다.

The director **will offer <u>an outstanding salesperson</u> <u>an annual paid leave</u>**.
간접목적어   직접목적어

→ The director **will offer <u>an annual paid leave</u>** to **<u>an outstanding salesperson</u>**.
직접목적어   간접목적어

이사는 우수 판매원에게 연차휴가를 제공할 것이다.

자주 나오는 수여동사

give 주다	offer 제공하다	grant 주다	award 수여하다
bring 가져오다	send 보내다	lend 빌려주다	present 제시하다

5 5형식: 주어 + 타동사 + 목적어 + 보어

불완전 타동사는 목적어 다음에 목적어의 상태를 설명하는 목적보어가 오는 동사들이다. 목적보어로는 목적어와 동격을 나타내는 명사, 목적어의 상태를 나타내는 형용사, 목적어의 행위를 나타내는 부정사가 올 수 있다.

- People **call me Lucy**.
  사람들은 나를 루시라 부른다.

- His speech **made the audience encouraged**.
  그의 연설은 청중이 고무되도록 만들었다.

1 In case there is an emergency, such as a natural disaster, it is wise to ------- calm and act accordingly.
(A) help
(B) find
(C) discuss
(D) remain

2 Dr. Armstrong is expected to give a lecture on how to --------- illnesses effectively and easily.
(A) shift
(B) respond
(C) acquaint
(D) diagnose

3 The committee will ------- whether or not to take immediate action on the mismanagement.
(A) discuss
(B) contribute
(C) notify
(D) inform

4 His subordinate, Ms. Edwin, ------- why she couldn't make it to the meeting on time.
(A) told
(B) talked
(C) explained
(D) sent

5 The finance company has a good reputation among business people for ------- them start-up costs.
(A) borrowing
(B) emerging
(C) loaning
(D) renting

6 One of my colleagues offered to ------- me some tips so that I can use the support program.
(A) proceed
(B) give
(C) feature
(D) approve

7 The company is going to ------- Mr. Zioba the head of the inspection team at the beginning of next month.
(A) express
(B) agree
(C) name
(D) reserve

8 In order to ------- a table, you had better call the restaurant in advance.
(A) reserve
(B) grant
(C) connect
(D) invest

PART 7 단독 지문

Questions 1-4 refer to the following text message chain.

Johnson, Erica	5:04 P.M.

Do you know who's giving the opening speech at tomorrow's orientation session?

Wilson, Tina	5:05 P.M.

I'm pretty sure that it's Ralph Summers.

Johnson, Erica	5:05 P.M.

Impossible. He's in Austria meeting with the people from Semex.

Wilson, Tina	5:06 P.M.

I wasn't aware of that. Let me talk to my supervisor.

Johnson, Erica	5:06 P.M.

Take your time.

Wilson, Tina	5:11 P.M.

Mr. Waterman said that Julie Jenkins is going to do it. According to him, this will be her first time to speak to the new trainees. So he made a request.

Johnson, Erica	5:11 P.M.

What does he want?

Wilson, Tina	5:13 P.M.

He'd like you to meet her to go over what she needs to discuss since you've done this before on a couple of occasions.

Johnson, Erica	5:14 P.M.

Is he kidding? The workday is nearly complete, and the session starts at 8:30 A.M. tomorrow.

Wilson, Tina	5:16 P.M.

That's what I told him. But he wants you to lend her a hand. He said he'd really appreciate your assistance.

Johnson, Erica	5:17 P.M.

Okay. I'll drop by her office in a bit. But I'm not going to meet my own deadline, so he needs to explain why to Ms. Trammel.

1   Who most likely is Ralph Summers?
    (A) An Austrian businessman
    (B) A Semex employee
    (C) A colleague of Ms. Johnson's
    (D) Ms. Wilson's supervisor

2   What does Mr. Waterman request that Ms. Johnson do?
    (A) Attend the orientation session
    (B) Give some help to Julie Jenkins
    (C) Stay late after work
    (D) Submit her work to Ms. Trammel

3   At 5:16 P.M., what does Ms. Wilson mean when she writes, "That's what I told him"?
    (A) She agrees with Ms. Johnson.
    (B) She already talked to her supervisor.
    (C) She can do the presentation herself.
    (D) She needs some more assistance.

4   What does Ms. Johnson say she will do?
    (A) Call her supervisor
    (B) Meet her deadline
    (C) Visit a coworker
    (D) Speak with Ms. Trammel

명사 어휘 연습 / 복합 지문

PART 5 어휘 – 명사 어휘 연습

1 The ------- of this year's severe influenza symptoms should be written for future reference.
(A) alternative
(B) means
(C) duration
(D) clause

2 Effective time ------- is considered to be one of the most important factors in the workplace.
(A) management
(B) comment
(C) quality
(D) specification

3 We reserve the ------- to modify the architectural plans without notice.
(A) trial
(B) contact
(C) right
(D) renewal

4 Despite a few obstacles, the directors reached a unanimous ------- on the project.
(A) confidence
(B) consent
(C) location
(D) revision

5 Credit cards have become the preferred ------- of customer payment throughout the world.
(A) sample
(B) instrument
(C) means
(D) notice

6 The renovation of the restaurant was worth the ------- because it attracted much more patrons.
(A) benefit
(B) expense
(C) donation
(D) compensation

7 Due to several problems, the meeting will be postponed until further -------.
(A) notice
(B) mark
(C) commitment
(D) choice

8 Electronic equipment is under ------- for three years from the date of purchase.
(A) warranty
(B) construction
(C) renovation
(D) stage

PART 7 복합 지문

Questions 1-5 refer to the following letter and schedule.

August 15

Dr. Murray Holmes

Chief Technology Officer

Babel Software Systems

230 Smithson Drive, Suite 340

Chicago, IL 32353

Dear Dr. Holmes:

It is our pleasure to formally invite you to be the closing keynote speaker at the upcoming SYM Development Conference to be held at the London Conference Facility in Toronto, Canada, on November 13 and 14.

For your information, Tara Ratchet of the Global Standards Association will be the opening keynote speaker. The title of her presentation is "New Millennium Programming," but this may change. Of particular note, you may have heard that internationally renowned professor Alan Gillard from Cambridge University will be presenting a major paper on the latest programming languages.

In closing, we would be delighted if you would consent to be our closing speaker at the SYM Development Conference. Please refer to the enclosed conference schedule (tentative) and let me know your decision at your earliest convenience.

Yours sincerely,

Rachel Singh

Rachel Singh

Executive Director

SYM Software Foundation

SYM Development Conference Schedule			
November 13 - Monday		**November 14 - Tuesday**	
8:15 - 8:45	Registration and Morning Breakfast Reception	8:30 - 9:00	Morning Breakfast Reception
8:45 - 9:00	Welcoming Address and Program Introduction	9:00 - 10:15	Presentation Session 2
9:00 - 10:15	Opening Keynote Address	10:15 - 10:30	*Morning Break*
10:15 - 10:30	*Morning Break*	10:30- 12:00	Group Discussion 2
10:30 - 12:00	Presentation Session 1	12:00 - 1:00	*Luncheon*
12:00 - 1:00	*Luncheon*	1:00 - 2:45	Summary Session
1:00 - 2:45	Group Discussion 1	2:45 - 3:00	*Afternoon Break*
2:45 - 3:00	*Afternoon Break*	3:00 - 4:30	Closing Keynote Address
3:00 - 4:00	Open Forum Discussion	4:00 - 6:00	Leisure Time
4:00 - 6:00	Lab Tours and Practical Demonstrations	6:00 - 9:00	Farewell Banquet
6:00 - 8:00	Wine and Cheese Reception		

1 What is the purpose of the letter?
   (A) To ask for a speech at the event
   (B) To announce a schedule change
   (C) To promote a new model
   (D) To get feedback about the conference

2 In the letter, the word "formally" in paragraph 1, line 1, is closest in meaning to
   (A) tentatively
   (B) officially
   (C) cordially
   (D) reluctantly

3 What can be inferred about Tara Ratchet?
   (A) She is a specialist in computer design.
   (B) She will be making an address on Monday.
   (C) She is responsible for organizing the conference.
   (D) She changed her appointment to Tuesday.

4 According to the letter, what is special about the conference this year?
   (A) It is being held in the United Kingdom.
   (B) Some government officials are attending.
   (C) A famous academic will be a speaker.
   (D) There will be a fundraising event.

5 What is scheduled on Monday at 7 P.M.?
   (A) Group Discussion
   (B) Summary Session
   (C) Wine and Cheese Reception
   (D) Farewell Banquet

Questions 6-10 refer to the following advertisement, invoice, and letter.

Mario's Catering
Let Us Cater Your Next Party

From June 1 to August 31:

- Take 25% off all of our special summer packages. This includes our sandwich platters, barbecue plates, and seafood specials.

- Get a free cake of your choice whenever you spend more than $500 on a single event.

- Receive free delivery and free next-day pickup of used dishes, utensils, and cooking equipment with any order that includes 2 or more main dishes.

Call 809-3033 or visit our Web site at www.marioscatering.com to place an order. Orders made at least one week in advance are guaranteed. Add 20% to all orders made fewer than 48 hours prior to the event.

Mario's Catering
548 W. Main Street
New York, NY
809-3033

Customer Name: *Naomi Washington*
Address: *3423 18th Street, Brooklyn, NY*
Telephone Number: *833-2024*
E-Mail Address: *nwashington@homemail.com*

Order Date: *June 20*
Order Type: [ ] pickup [✔] delivery to *404 25th Avenue, Brooklyn*
Date: *July 1*   **Time** *11:30 A.M.*

Product	Quantity	Price
Beef BBQ Plate	4	$320
Summer Sandwich Platter	3	$210
Deluxe Dessert Tray	2	$120
Iced Tea (5 Gallons)	2	$40
	Subtotal	$700
	Tax	$42
	Total	$742

Instructions: *Selected chocolate cake with vanilla icing as free dessert. Go between 10:00 A.M. and 11:00 A.M. on July 2 to retrieve all used items.*

July 3

Dear Mr. Fermi,

My name is Naomi Washington. Your establishment was one of the caterers at my company's annual picnic on July 1. This is the fourth year in a row we've hired you to provide food at the event. Unfortunately, it may be the last time we ever do so.

The food was excellent as always. The same cannot be said for the service provided by your employees. To begin with, the free dessert we should have received never arrived. When I asked Carl, who delivered it, he claimed not to know about it despite the fact that the order was written on the invoice. In addition, the next day, nobody from your establishment returned to pick up the dishes and other items until 4:00 in the afternoon. The person who came was rude and failed to apologize for coming at that time.

I must admit that I was shocked by their behavior. So was everyone else at the company. Until we receive a guarantee that nothing like this will ever happen again, Thompson Plastics will no longer do business with your establishment.

Regards,
Naomi Washington

6 Which of the following is NOT mentioned in the advertisement?
(A) Orders can be made online or by telephone.
(B) Free delivery is provided for all orders during summer.
(C) Customers must pay more for some orders.
(D) Items sold for the summer season are being discounted.

7 When was the order placed?
(A) On June 1
(B) On June 20
(C) On July 1
(D) On July 3

8 What is true about the order?
(A) It qualifies for free delivery.
(B) It was made over the telephone.
(C) It will be picked up by Ms. Washington.
(D) It includes two types of drinks.

9 What is the purpose of the letter?
(A) To demand a refund
(B) To request an apology
(C) To express displeasure
(D) To ask for a rebate

10 What did Ms. Washington NOT receive?
(A) Summer sandwich platters
(B) Beef BBQ plates
(C) A cake
(D) Cooking equipment

조동사와 여러 가지 타동사

조동사는 동사를 도와서 미래, 추측, 능력, 허가, 의무 따위를 나타낸다. 조동사는 항상 동사 앞에 오며 조동사 다음에는 동사원형을 써야 한다. 또한 타동사 가운데는 to부정사(to-V)나 동명사(V-ing)만 목적어로 취하는 동사들이 있는데 이 동사들은 따로 외워두어야 한다.

1 조동사 + 동사원형

주어 +
- will 의지/추측: ~할 것이다, ~일 것이다
- can 능력/허가: ~할 수 있다
- may 허가/추측: ~해도 된다, ~일 수도 있다
- should 당위: 마땅히 ~해야 한다
- must 의무: ~하지 않으면 안 된다

+ V 〈능동〉 / be p.p. 〈수동〉

1) 자동사가 올 경우: 조동사 + 자동사 + 부사[전치사 + 명사]

예제 The mechanic told me that my car would not ------- properly without a regular check up.

(A) functions　　　　(B) function　　　　(C) be functioned

번역 정비사는 내 차가 정기적인 검사를 받지 않으면 제 기능을 못할 것이라 말했다.
정답 (B)

2) 타동사가 올 경우: 조동사 + 타동사 + 명사

예제 The collaboration of the two brands can ------- their commercial value.

(A) increased　　　　(B) be increased　　　　(C) increase

번역 두 브랜드의 합작은 그들의 상업 가치를 높일 수 있다.
정답 (C)

3) 타동사인데 목적어가 없는 경우: 조동사 + be p.p. + 부사[전치사 + 명사]

예제 All the lights in this facility should ------- off after completing the experiment.

(A) turn　　　　(B) turns　　　　(C) be turned

번역 이 건물에 있는 모든 전등은 실험이 끝난 후에 소등되어야 한다.
정답 (C)

2 목적어로 to부정사를 쓰는 타동사

목적어로 to부정사(to-V)를 쓰는 타동사들은 대개 소망, 계획, 결심, 합의, 거절 등 미래의 의미가 담겨 있다. 또한 to부정사와 의미상 주어의 관계가 수동이면 to be p.p.형태를 써야 한다.

1) 의미상 주어와의 관계가 능동일 경우

> **예제** They are planning ------- the careers of their members by providing more useful materials.
>
> (A) enhanced　　　　　(B) to enhance　　　　　(C) enhances
>
> **번역** 그들은 보다 유용한 자료를 제공하여 회원들의 경력을 계발시키는 것을 계획하고 있다.
> **정답** (B)

2) 의미상 주어와의 관계가 수동일 경우

> **예제** The agreement failed ------- because some of the clauses were not negotiable.
>
> (A) reaching　　　　　(B) to reach　　　　　(C) to be reached
>
> **번역** 몇 가지 조항이 협상 불가였기 때문에 합의 도출에 실패했다.
> **정답** (C)

to-V를 목적어로 취하는 빈출 동사

tend to-V ~하는 경향이 있다	hope to-V ~하기를 희망하다
plan to-V ~할 계획이다	agree to-V ~하는 데 동의하다
decide to-V ~하기로 결정하다	fail to-V ~하는 데 실패하다, ~하지 못하다
refuse to-V ~하기를 거절하다	hesitate to-V ~을 주저하다

3 목적어로 동명사를 쓰는 타동사

동명사(V-ing)를 목적어로 쓰는 동사들은 시작, 지속, 종결, 취향, 제안 따위를 나타낸다. 또한 동명사도 동사의 성질을 가지고 있기 때문에 의미상 주어와 동명사가 수동 관계이면 being p.p.형태를 써야 한다.

1) 의미상 주어와의 관계가 능동일 경우

> **예제** Small and medium-sized companies try to avoid ------- with international companies.
>
> (A) to compete　　　　　(B) compete　　　　　(C) competing
>
> **번역** 중소기업들은 국제적인 기업들과의 경쟁을 피하기 위해 애쓴다.
> **정답** (C)

2) 의미상 주어와의 관계가 수동일 경우

> **예제** The passengers enjoyed ------- well by the crew during their cruise.
>
> (A) to treat   (B) being treated   (C) to be treated
>
> **번역** 승객들은 선상 여행 동안 직원들의 친절한 접대를 즐겼다.
> **정답** (B)

V-ing를 목적어로 취하는 빈출 동사

enjoy 즐기다	finish 끝내다	mind 꺼려하다	include 포함하다
avoid 피하다	postpone 연기하다	consider 고려하다	discontinue 중단하다
suggest 제안하다	recommend 추천하다		

4 to부정사를 목적보어로 쓰는 타동사

1) 주어 + 타동사 + 목적어 + to-V

요청: ask, require, request
허용: allow, enable
설득: encourage, invite, persuade, convince
강요: force, compel, urge

> **예제** Internet technologies encourage people ------- quick opinions.
>
> (A) form   (B) forming   (C) to form
>
> **번역** 인터넷 기술은 사람들이 신속한 여론을 형성하도록 촉진한다.
> **정답** (C)

2) 주어 + 타동사 + 목적어 + to be p.p.

> **예제** Our representatives want the problem -------.
>
> (A) to be handled   (B) to handle   (C) handle
>
> **번역** 우리 직원들은 그 문제가 처리되기를 원한다.
> **정답** (A)

5 let/help + 목적어 + 동사원형

let은 '~하게 하다'란 뜻으로 목적어 다음에 동사원형을 쓰고, help는 목적어 뒤에 to부정사나 동사원형이 나온다. 목적어가 생략되어 「help+(목적어)+(to)+동사원형」 형태로도 쓴다.

- Let the staff **know** as soon as you get the data.
  자료를 얻는 즉시 직원들에게 알려 주세요.

- The new policy will help the unemployment rate **decrease** gradually.
  새 정책이 실업률을 점진적으로 줄이는데 도움이 될 것이다.

6 그 밖의 동명사 관용구

spend money [time] V-ing ~하는 데 돈[시간]을 쓰다

have difficulty [trouble/a hard time] V-ing ~하는 데 어려움을 겪다

look forward to V-ing ~하기를 고대하다

be accustomed [used] to V-ing ~하는 데 익숙하다

be committed to V-ing ~하는 데 헌신하다

1 Our company is struggling ------- international investment in the construction project.

(A) receiving
(B) to receive
(C) received
(D) receives

2 As a result of rising costs, we are advised to consider ------- this cheaper supply contract.

(A) negotiate
(B) negotiated
(C) negotiating
(D) to negotiate

3 Our company must ------- stricter regulations on dress codes to improve our corporate image.

(A) establish
(B) establishing
(C) establishes
(D) to establish

4 The managers are not likely ------- us to transfer data to others since they are confidential.

(A) permits
(B) to permit
(C) permission
(D) permit

5 Please let your supervisor ------- immediately when you have to take a leave of absence.

(A) know
(B) to know
(C) known
(D) have known

6 The consultant tried to help people ------- the simplest and most effective solution to the housing problems.

(A) find
(B) finding
(C) found
(D) founded

7 The Mayes Corporation plans ------- its profits by using cheaper materials in the future.

(A) increasingly
(B) increasing
(C) to increase
(D) increases

8 The new shopping district is expected ------- thousands of customers from neighboring cities.

(A) attraction
(B) attractive
(C) to attract
(D) attract

Questions 1-4 refer to the following letter.

September 9

Dear Ms. Wilkinson,

Thank you so much for your assistance during the summer. Because of you, my time as an intern at McGregor Industries was ------- fun and educational. When I first started, you made me feel comfortable and really taught me a lot. I was worried I was going to be stuck making copies for everyone. ------- You gave me a number of projects to work on. Thanks to my time there this summer, I have decided that I want to ------- a career in the robotics industry. I've enrolled in a couple of robotics classes for my last year at my school. I intend to focus intently on them. And I'll likely ------- for a full-time job at McGregor after I graduate next spring. Again, thank you very much for everything.

Sincerely,

Lloyd Bannister

1 (A) each
(B) both
(C) ever
(D) such

2 (A) It's something I really enjoy doing.
(B) I shouldn't have been concerned though.
(C) There was not much for me to do there.
(D) Some employees were difficult to work with.

3 (A) follow
(B) propose
(C) pursue
(D) consider

4 (A) apply
(B) relate
(C) enroll
(D) register

동사의 시제

시제 문제는 대개 시간을 나타내는 부사가 문장의 시제를 결정하기 때문에 시간 부사를 외워두면 간단히 해결할 수 있다.

1 과거 시제

과거의 어떤 시점에 일어난 일을 나타내며 과거를 나타내는 시간 부사로는 ago, previously, the other day, recently, last week[month/year] 등이 있다.

- The number of recruitments from the marketing team **increased** sharply last month.
  마케팅팀 채용숫자가 지난달에 급격히 증가했다.

2 현재 시제

반복되는 습관이나 현재 일어나는 일이나 상태를 말할 때 쓰고, 함께 쓰는 시간 부사로는 currently, presently, usually 등이 있다.

- Our company usually **ships** the books to the client upon receiving the payment.
  일반적으로 우리 회사는 결제되는 대로 바로 고객에게 책을 발송한다.

3 현재완료 시제

과거의 일이 현재까지 영향을 줄 때 쓰는 시제로 「since + 과거 시점」, 「in[for/over] the last[past] + 기간」이 오면 현재완료 시제(have p.p.)를 쓴다.

- The team **has worked** very hard since last week's employee evaluation meeting.
  지난주 직원평가 회의 이후 그 팀은 매우 열심히 일해 왔다.
- Unfortunately, our sales volume **has** consistently **declined** over the past few months.
  유감스럽게도 지난 몇 달 동안 판매량이 계속해서 감소했다.

4 미래 시제

미래에 일어날 일을 나타내는 시제이고 soon, tomorrow, next, in + 기간, coming month 등이 오면 미래 시제(will + 동사원형)를 쓴다.

- The director **will announce** the names of the major contributors to the project next week.
  부장이 프로젝트에 기여한 주요 공로자 명단을 다음 주에 발표할 것이다.

5 미래완료 시제

현재 일어나고 있는 일이 미래 어느 시점까지 연결되어 계속되는 것을 나타내며 will have p.p.의 형태를 취한다. 대개 미래 시점을 나타내는 부사구나 기간을 나타내는 부사구가 따라 나온다.

- By 2020, he **will have worked** as the head of the marketing department for fifteen years.
  2020년이면 그는 마케팅부서의 부장으로 15년 동안 일하는 것이다.

6 주절과 종속절의 시제 일치

종속절의 시제는 주절의 시제를 따라야 한다. 주절이 현재이면 종속절에는 현재, 과거, 미래 시제가 다 나올 수 있지만, 주절이 과거이면 종속절에는 과거나 과거완료 시제가 나와야 한다.

- When I **visited** the consultant, he **was consulting** with another client.
  내가 컨설턴트를 방문했을 때 그는 다른 고객과 상담 중이었다.

7 시제 불일치

1) 시간과 조건의 부사절에서는 현재 시제로 미래를 나타낸다.

when + 주어 + 동사 ~할 때	by the time + 주어 + 동사 ~할 무렵이면
before + 주어 + 동사 ~하기 전에	after + 주어 + 동사 ~한 후에
as soon as + 주어 + 동사 ~하자마자	as long as + 주어 + 동사 ~하는 한/~라면

- We **will** not be able to resume normal operations **before** the electrical power **is** restored.
  전력이 복구되기 전에는 정상적인 조업을 재개할 수 없을 것이다.
- We **will** commence the meeting **as soon as** team members **return** from their lunch break.
  우리는 팀원들이 점심시간에서 돌아오자마자 미팅을 시작할 것이다.

2) **종속절의 조동사 should 생략**

주절에 주장, 제안, 요구 동사가 오거나 필수, 의무, 중요성을 나타내는 형용사가 올 때 that절의 동사는 시제나 인칭에 상관없이 동사원형이 온다. 이때 동사원형 앞에는 조동사 should가 생략된 것이다.

동사	형용사
insist 주장하다	important 중요한
suggest, propose, recommend 제안하다	essential/necessary 필수적인
require, request, ask, demand 요청하다	imperative 강제적인
	mandatory 의무적인

- The department head **requested** that each employee (should) **read** all the instructions carefully.

  부서장은 각각의 직원이 지시사항을 주의 깊게 읽을 것을 요구했다.

- It is **necessary** that equal opportunities (should) **be** offered to small businesses.

  동등한 기회가 중소기업들에게 제공되어야 한다.

PART 5   문법 – 동사의 시제

1   The company was looking for highly
motivated people when it ------- its branch
offices.
(A) expands
(B) will expand
(C) expanded
(D) was expanded

2   The board of directors ------- an engineering
company to oversee the progress of the
construction work last month.
(A) has selected
(B) will select
(C) selected
(D) will be selected

3   The investment's success ------- on the
stability of the real estate market over the
next few years.
(A) depended
(B) depend
(C) has depended
(D) will depend

4   It is necessary that we ------- our
presentation so that it can focus more on
our company's achievements.
(A) modifying
(B) modified
(C) to modify
(D) modify

5   It ------- necessary to double the production
quota by next year to keep up with the
market demand.
(A) is
(B) was
(C) had been
(D) will be

6   Before committee members -------
evidence, regulations will probably be
established.
(A) present
(B) will present
(C) presented
(D) has presented

7   There ------- an enormous effort by the
company to increase its share of the market
over the past few years.
(A) are
(B) was
(C) has been
(D) is

8   Since Mr. Benson was named as the head
of the department, he ------- no progress.
(A) made
(B) has made
(C) makes
(D) will make

Questions 1-4 refer to the following advertisement.

West Richmond Garden Center

West Richmond Garden Center is proud to be an award-winning garden and landscaping company that has been serving the residents of Virginia for over half a century. As the largest and most complete garden center in the entire region, West Richmond Garden Center truly has everything for your gardening and landscaping needs.

West Richmond Garden Center is a family-owned business with a team of over 200 employees who are dedicated to providing customers with friendly service. Moreover, to help you garden easily and successfully, we offer expert gardening advice from a team of qualified professionals, who are always happy to assist you.

Take advantage of this week's special 20% discount on customized fertilizers to keep your plants, trees and flowers looking their best. Although all plants can benefit from fertilizer, it is best to use a product intended specifically for the unique needs of the plant that you are feeding. It might be helpful to consult with our staff to determine which fertilizer best suits your needs.

So we invite you to stop by our convenient location at 120 Sutherland Avenue in Fairfax and discover the many pleasures of gardening.

Hours of Operation (Summer):
Monday to Saturday from 8:00 A.M. to 9:00 P.M.
Sunday from 9:00 A.M. to 2:00 P.M.

Our hours do change seasonally and on certain holidays. Pleasecall 703-523-6256 for specific holiday hours.

1   What is special about West Richmond Garden Center?
   (A) It uses cutting-edge technology.
   (B) It is recommended by well-known florists.
   (C) It provides special classes for children.
   (D) It has more than 50 years of history.

2   What is NOT true about West Richmond Garden Center?
   (A) It is the biggest in the area.
   (B) It is owned by the city.
   (C) It is usually open all week.
   (D) It employs gardening experts.

3   What is mentioned about fertilizer?
   (A) It is available in two different sizes.
   (B) Consultation with an expert is necessary before use.
   (C) Different plants need different types of fertilizers.
   (D) It is half of its regular price this week only.

4   According to the advertisement, why would someone call the number provided?
   (A) To place a special order
   (B) To learn about business hours
   (C) To arrange for delivery
   (D) To receive gardening advice

수동태

태(voice)는 동사의 동작의 방향을 나타내는 문법 사항이다. 능동태는 행위자가 주어이고 대상이 목적어라서 동작의 방향이 주어에서 목적어로 향하는데 반해, 수동태는 대상이 주어이고 행위자는 동사 뒤에 나오기 때문에 동작의 방향이 능동태와 반대이다.

1 능동태 vs. 수동태

1) 능동태: 행위자 + 타동사 + 대상 (~가 …을 한다)

- **Mr. Lieu will submit progress reports** to his supervisor next week.

  행위자(주어)　　　타동사　　　　대상(목적어)

  류 씨는 다음 주에 그의 상사에게 진척 보고서를 제출할 것이다.

2) 수동태: 대상 + be p.p. + 행위자 (~가 …에게 ~되다/당하다)

- **Progress reports will be submitted** to his supervisor tomorrow **by Mr. Lieu**.

  대상(주어)　　　　　　　be p.p.　　　　　　　　　　　　　　　　행위자(by + 명사)

  진척 보고서가 류 씨에 의해 다음 주에 그의 상사에게 제출될 것이다.

2 수동태를 만드는 방법

1단계 능동태의 목적어를 수동태의 주어 자리로 옮긴다.

2단계 동사 형태를 be + 과거분사(p.p.)로 바꾼다.

3단계 일반적으로 by 뒤의 행위자는 의미 전달에 중요하지 않기 때문에 생략된다.

- We will **hold** a meeting tomorrow. 〈능동태〉　우리는 내일 회의를 열 것이다.

  → A meeting will **be held** (by us) tomorrow. 〈수동태〉　회의는 내일 열릴 것이다.

3 목적어가 없는 문장은 수동태를 만들 수 없다.

목적어가 있는 타동사 문장만 수동태로 바꿀 수 있기 때문에 목적어가 없는 자동사는 수동형(be + p.p.)으로 만들 수 없다.

- An accident **was happened**. (✕) → An accident **happened**. (○)
- The shipment will **be arrived** soon. (✕) → The shipment will **arrive** soon. (○)

| arrive 도착하다 | appear 나타나다 | emerge 등장하다 | proceed 진행되다 |
| happen / occur / take place / arise (일이) 발생하다, 일어나다 | | | |

4 수동태 동사의 형태와 시제

시제	동사의 형태	예시	의미
현재	is/are p.p.	is/are reduced	감소되다
과거	was/were p.p.	was/were reduced	감소되었다
현재완료	has/have been p.p.	has/have been reduced	감소되어 왔다
과거완료	had been p.p.	had been reduced	감소되어 왔었다
미래	will be p.p.	will be reduced	감소될 것이다

5 By 이외의 전치사를 쓰는 수동태 표현

be concerned **about** ~에 대해 걱정하다

be equipped **with** ~로 갖춰지다   be filled **with** ~로 가득 차다
be pleased **with** ~로 기뻐하다   be satisfied **with** ~에 만족하다

be devoted **to** ~에 헌신하다   be dedicated **to** ~에 전념하다
be committed **to** ~에 헌신하다   be sent **to** ~로 보내지다
be forwarded **to** ~로 보내지다

be composed **of** ~로 구성되다   be made **of** ~로 만들어지다

be engaged **in** ~에 참여하다   be involved **in** ~에 관련되다
be interested **in** ~에 흥미를 갖다

6 수동태 문장에서 be p.p. 뒤에 오는 동사 형태는 to-V이다.

- We **expect** all laboratory assistants **to** benefit from the training program. 〈능동태〉
  우리는 모든 실험실 조교들이 그 훈련 프로그램의 혜택을 받을 것이라 기대한다.

- All laboratory assistants **are expected** (by us) **to** benefit from the training program.
  〈수동태〉

  실험실의 모든 조교들은 그 훈련 프로그램의 혜택을 볼 것으로 기대 받고 있다.

1 One of the most difficult problems ------- whenever we try to achieve goals.

(A) arise

(B) arises

(C) is arisen

(D) are arisen

2 High Tech, Inc. is ------- relatively higher profits than other companies in the same industry.

(A) generate

(B) generating

(C) to generate

(D) generated

3 Your letter of March 10 regarding publication rights ------- to the proper department for immediate action.

(A) forward

(B) was forwarded

(C) has forwarded

(D) will forward

4 Please be aware that the old computers will ------- with new ones by the end of the fiscal year.

(A) replacing

(B) replaces

(C) be replaced

(D) be replacing

5 Most of the experts are familiar with the issue that ------- in the merger.

(A) is involved

(B) has involved

(C) are involved

(D) have involved

6 Analysts were ------- to present evidence that companies would experience an economic upturn.

(A) please

(B) pleased

(C) pleasing

(D) pleasant

7 All the files have to be promptly ------- to enhance the accuracy of the records.

(A) submit

(B) submitting

(C) to submit

(D) submitted

8 There is a trend that recently more students ------- in internships to obtain better jobs.

(A) were participated

(B) will be participated

(C) participates

(D) have been participating

Questions 1-4 refer to the following e-mail.

To: Catherine Jones <catherine_j@personalmail.com>

From: Customer Service <customerservice@weston.com>

Subject: Your Complaint

Dear Ms. Jones,

We received your e-mail on August 11 and looked into the matter about which you complained. For some reason, you received two ------- products rather than the two <u>1</u> separate items which you ordered.

We apologize for this mistake. We just mailed ------- item (item number ER430A) that <u>2</u> you did not receive. It was sent by express mail and should arrive within two business days. You may keep the other item that we sent ------- error. And we would like to give <u>3</u> you $20 off the next online order you make with us. Just enter the coupon code "SUMMER SURPRISE" when you are about to check out. ------- <u>4</u>

Sincerely,

Winston Phiiips, Customer Service Representative, Weston, Inc.

1 (A) damaged
   (B) used
   (C) identical
   (D) sample

2 (A) another
   (B) each other
   (C) the other
   (D) some others

3 (A) in
   (B) on
   (C) with
   (D) at

4 (A) You can use the coupon on our Web site or at the store.
   (B) Please inform us if there are any problems with the items we're sending.
   (C) Thank you very much for placing another order with us.
   (D) We hope you are satisfied with how we are handling this.

대명사

대명사는 말 그대로 명사를 대신해서 쓰는 말이기 때문에 앞에 나온 명사와 성(gender), 수(number), 격 (case)을 일치시켜야 한다. 특히, 격과 관련하여 대명사는 문장에서 어떤 구실을 하느냐에 따라 형태가 바뀐다.

1 대명사의 격 일치

주어 위치에는 주격, 명사 앞에는 소유격, 타동사와 전치사 뒤에는 목적격이 온다.

수	인칭	주격	소유격	목적격	소유대명사	재귀대명사
단수	1인칭	I	my	me	mine	myself
	2인칭	you	your	you	yours	yourself
	3인칭	he	his	him	his	himself
		she	her	hers	hers	herself
		it	its	it	–	itself
복수	1인칭	we	our	us	ours	ourselves
	2인칭	you	your	you	yours	yourselves
	3인칭	they	their	them	theirs	themselves

1) 주격

- Because **the laptops** are reasonably priced, **they** will be sold out quickly.
  그 노트북들은 가격이 저렴하기 때문에 곧 다 팔릴 것이다.

2) 소유격

- It is **your** responsibility to oversee the progress of the project.
  프로젝트의 진행과정을 감독하는 것이 귀하의 책무입니다.

3) 목적격

- Because Mr. Knight is scheduled to give a lecture, I have to help **him**.
  나이트 씨가 강의할 예정이어서 나는 그를 도와줘야 한다.

2 소유대명사와 이중소유격

1) 소유대명사

소유대명사는「소유격 + 명사」의 구실을 하기 때문에 그 뒤에 명사가 따라올 수 없다.

- Your cell phone has satisfactory features, but **mine** does not.
  너의 핸드폰은 만족스런 기능들을 갖추었는데 내 것은 그렇지 않다.

2) 이중소유격과 소유격을 강조하는 own

- Ms. Bolt visited a colleague of **hers** in New York while she was on a business trip.
  볼트 씨는 출장 동안 뉴욕에 있는 그녀의 동료를 만났다.
- I wasn't able to use the Internet this morning with **my own** computer.
  오늘 아침에 내 컴퓨터로는 인터넷 사용을 할 수 없었다

3 강조 용법 (생략 가능)

주어나 목적어를 강조하는 데 쓰인다. 문장 끝이나 강조하고 싶은 명사 가까이에 쓰고 재귀대명사의 강조용법의 특징은 생략이 가능하다는 것이다.

- Mr. Williams made some mistakes **himself** on the estimate proposal.
  윌리엄스 씨 자신이 견적 제안서에 약간의 실수를 했다.
- She **herself** answered the phone since other members were in a meeting.
  다른 직원들이 미팅 중이었기 때문에 그녀 자신이 전화를 받았다.

4 재귀대명사의 관용적 용법

> **by oneself = alone = on one's own** 혼자서, ~끼리

- Mr. Brown had to make a crucial decision **by himself**.
  브라운 씨는 혼자서 중대한 결정을 해야 했다.
- The interns arranged all the refreshments for the workshop **by themselves**.
  인턴들은 워크숍을 위한 다과를 그들끼리 준비했다.

5 반복되는 명사를 대신하는 지시대명사 that of / those of

앞에 나온 명사의 반복을 피하기 위해서 of 앞에 오는 단수 명사를 받을 때는 that을, 복수 명사를 받을 때는 those로 표시한다. of 앞에 오는 명사를 대명사로 쓸 때는 this/these/it을 쓸 수 없다.

- **The summer** of Japan is similar to **that** of our country.
  일본의 여름은 우리나라의 여름과 비슷하다.
- **The ideas** of the rival company seem as good as **those** of our company.
  경쟁사의 아이디어들은 우리 회사의 아이디어만큼 좋은 것 같다.

1 The chamber of commerce helps local businesses easily resolve ------- problems.
(A) they
(B) their
(C) them
(D) themselves

2 If the goods do not meet your satisfaction, you can return ------- within thirty days for a full refund.
(A) it
(B) them
(C) him
(D) yourselves

3 The two managers volunteered to deal with those technical problems by -------.
(A) themselves
(B) them
(C) they
(D) their

4 The opening of the new shopping complex will be held on Monday, and the mayor ------- will attend the party, too.
(A) he
(B) him
(C) his
(D) himself

5 I have worked with Mr. Lee for years and have found ------- to be dedicated and diligent.
(A) he
(B) him
(C) his
(D) himself

6 It's not possible for Stephanie to finish this statistical analysis ------- by the end of the day.
(A) alone
(B) by alone
(C) by them
(D) by themselves

7 After you complete the enclosed survey, please send ------- responses to us within five working days.
(A) you
(B) your
(C) yours
(D) yourself

8 Because advances in the quality were impressive, this year's sales were as good as ------- in the year 2014.
(A) that
(B) they
(C) it
(D) those

Questions 1-5 refer to the following article.

Maryville (September 10) – All the beaches in Maryville have officially closed for the summer. According to the city's mayor, Sheldon Arlington, more visitors than ever went to the four beaches this year. --[1]-- This helped the restaurants, hotels, travel agencies, and other businesses involved in the travel industry be highly profitable.

"We spent a great amount of money fixing our infrastructure over the past three years," commented Mr. Arlington. "We believe we have the best facilities anywhere within a 100-mile radius. I think that has a great deal to do with our attracting so many visitors this summer."

--[2]-- While it normally rains around 25 days from June 1 to August 31, Maryville only recorded 15 rainy days during that time. Those extra clear days were therefore money in the bank for the city's tourism industry. --[3]--

Mr. Arlington indicated that the city plans to keep improving its facilities with the objective of becoming the premier beach location in the entire state. --[4]-- He stated that several parking lots will be enlarged next month, and construction on a new golf course will begin in January. Those should both help the city attract even more visitors in the future.

---

1 According to the article, what has Maryville done to attract more tourists?

(A) Opened more restaurants
(B) Provided tax breaks to companies
(C) Improved its infrastructure
(D) Heavily promoted its beaches

2 What is going to happen in Maryville next year?

(A) There will be an election for mayor.
(B) A golf course will be built.
(C) The beaches will be cleaned up.
(D) Parking lots will be made larger.

3 In which of the positions marked [1], [2], [3], and [4] does the following sentence best belong?

"The city was also fortunate to get sunny weather for most of the summer season."

(A) [1]
(B) [2]
(C) [3]
(D) [4]

형용사 어휘 연습 / 복합 지문

PART 5 어휘 – 형용사 어휘 연습

1 Your membership fees are four days -------,
so you are advised to pay soon.

(A) overdue
(B) permanent
(C) ample
(D) devoted

2 It is important to develop ------- marketing
tools in order to increase our sales.

(A) official
(B) interested
(C) unused
(D) valuable

3 The Digital Corporation announced -------
profits at the end of the year.

(A) intense
(B) refundable
(C) impressive
(D) alternative

4 Next year's employment prospects look
more ------- than this year's.

(A) promising
(B) applicable
(C) obtained
(D) convenient

5 People are becoming ------- of the
importance of a healthy diet and exercises.

(A) optimistic
(B) temporary
(C) courteous
(D) aware

6 The workers are now under ------- pressure
because of their tight schedules.

(A) disappointing
(B) mounting
(C) declining
(D) delinquent

7 If you have any trouble with your car, you'd
better visit an ------- car dealership.

(A) unstable
(B) authorized
(C) final
(D) lasting

8 Eliminating unnecessary overhead
expenses can be ------- to our company
and customers.

(A) deliberate
(B) financial
(C) possible
(D) beneficial

PART 7 복합 지문

Questions 1-5 refer to the following e-mails.

To: customersvc@highseas.com
From: Anne Ryding <aryding@techgear.com>
Re: King of the High Seas Cruise

Hello,

I recently took a cruise on your ship called King of the High Seas. It was one of the most disappointing experiences in my life.

First, the food was terrible. I tried to order a steak one day and what I got looked more like a hamburger. Several times the food we were served was cold. The worst thing is that my husband got food poisoning on the first day so for the first half of our cruise he wasn't able to enjoy anything.

Once my husband was finally feeling better, he wanted to use some of the facilities. He was really looking forward to the hot tubs on the top deck. When we went to go use it though, it had an "out of order" sign on it. He wanted to use the pool instead, but he was told that it was only for kids. And our room wasn't much better. It was MUCH smaller than the brochure made it look and it smelled funny.

I will never go on a cruise with your company again.

Anne Ryding

To: Anne Ryding <aryding@techgear.com>
From: customersvc@highseas.com
Re: Re: King of the High Seas Cruise

Hello, Ms. Ryding.

Thank you for taking the time to write us about your experience on the King of the High Seas. Although we have been rated the top cruise company for the Caribbean ten years in a row by Cruise World magazine, there are still times when people have bad experiences. I have spoken directly with some of the staff members about your experience and they were very apologetic. We will do everything we can to fix the problems you noticed with our cruise.

To show our regret for your experience, I would like to offer you fifty percent off on your next cruise. You will automatically be raised to first class treatment with a suite rather than a regular room. This offer is valid for the next year on any ship that you choose. Please remember to use your discount code, which is 5684509, and present it with a photo ID.

Again I'm very sorry to hear about your experience but I hope that your next cruise will make it better.

Thanks again,
Lynn Shan

1 What is the main purpose of Ms. Ryding's e-mail?
   (A) To ask for a change in an itinerary
   (B) To complain about the service
   (C) To inquire about a cruise package
   (D) To thank Lynn for a wonderful cruise

2 What is true about King of the High Seas?
   (A) Its professional staff members are all certified.
   (B) It is offering reduced prices to loyal customers.
   (C) It has facilities exclusively for kids.
   (D) It grows fruits and vegetables on board.

3 What does Lynn Shan mention about the business?
   (A) It was established a decade ago.
   (B) It will hire more security guards.
   (C) It has been selected as a top company for years.
   (D) It will soon travel to international locations.

4 What did Lynn Shan most likely tell the staff?
   (A) They are doing a very good job.
   (B) Cold meals were served to the customer.
   (C) They should help the doctor on board sometimes.
   (D) They should send an e-mail to Anne Ryding.

5 What information does Lynn Shan NOT give to Anne Ryding?
   (A) Type of room available
   (B) Her phone number
   (C) Valid period on a discount
   (D) Special code

Questions 6-10 refer to the following letter and e-mails.

September 5

Dear Mr. Kirby,

I am writing this letter to inform you of my intention to resign from my position as senior director of the R&D Department as of September 30. As you are well aware, I have been contemplating retiring for the past couple of years. I have finally decided that now is the time to leave so that I can spend more time with my family, particularly my grandchildren.

I would like to thank you for everything you have done for me over the past three decades. It's been an honor and a privilege to work at Dansby Chemicals. During my time here, I've been a part of an outstanding team, and I feel like we have made many positive contributions.

I realize you are going to initiate a search for my replacement. However, I strongly urge you to consider Jack Wharton for the job. Even though he has been here for merely two years, he has excelled during that time. He is not only an outstanding scientist, but he also possesses excellent people skills.

Sincerely,
Wayne Rogers

To: Melanie Hamilton <m_hamilton@atlanticindustrial.com>
From: Jessica Steele <jessica@dansbychemicals.com>
Subject: Interview
Date: September 15

Dear Ms. Hamilton,

The job search committee at Dansby Chemicals has reviewed your résumé and determined that you are the leading candidate for the position of senior director of the R&D Department. We are particularly interested in the fact that you own seven patents, which indicates the quality of your research ability.

We would like you to come here to interview for the position. We understand that you are busy at your current job, so how about having the interview on Saturday, September 19? We realize that this is short notice since you will have to fly from Albany to Baltimore. We have taken the liberty of reserving first-class tickets for you and your husband on Friday, September 18. Please see the attached itinerary. It contains both your travel plans and information about the hotel you will be staying at. If you agree to come, a driver will pick you and your husband up at the airport.

Since time is short, would you please respond to this e-mail as soon as possible so that we can confirm you will be coming? Everyone on the search committee is looking forward to meeting you.

Sincerely,

Jessica Steele
Vice President, Dansby Chemicals

To: David Kirby <davidk@dansbychemicals.com>
From: Jessica Steele <jessica@dansbychemicals.com>
Subject: R&D Dept. Position
Date: September 21

David,

As you instructed, we offered Melanie Hamilton the position as soon as her interview concluded since she was such a strong candidate. She requested a couple of days to consider our offer because she didn't want to make a decision without her husband present.

She just sent me an e-mail, and I've got some bad news. She has decided to stay in the Albany area. She mentioned that she really wanted to take the job, but she didn't want to relocate since both of her children are in high school. She stated, however, that she would be amenable to changing jobs in three years when her daughter starts attending college.

Since Ms. Hamilton won't be working with us, why don't we go with Wayne's original suggestion? He's clearly the second-best candidate for the job, and we know what kind of work he'll do. What do you think?

Melanie

6   Why did Mr. Rogers write the letter?
(A) To apply for an open position
(B) To indicate that he is quitting his job
(C) To nominate a colleague for an award
(D) To promote a new project he is doing

7   According to the first e-mail, what is true about Ms. Hamilton?
(A) She lives in the Baltimore area.
(B) She works in her company's R&D Department.
(C) She is highly qualified for the job at Dansby Chemicals.
(D) She just received a patent on one of her inventions.

8   What does Ms. Steele request that Ms. Hamilton do?
(A) Call her by the end of the day
(B) Make her own travel arrangements
(C) Drive to Baltimore this coming weekend
(D) Give a swift answer to her e-mail

9   In the second e-mail, the word "relocate" in paragraph 2, line 3 is closest in meaning to
(A) move
(B) research
(C) change
(D) attempt

10 What does Ms. Steele suggest that Mr. Kirby do?
(A) Encourage Mr. Rogers to remain on the job
(B) Hire Mr. Wharton for the open position
(C) Offer Ms. Hamilton a higher starting salary
(D) Fly to Albany to speak with Ms. Hamilton personally

DAY 11 접속사

접속사는 문장 처음이나 중간에 와서 독립된 두 문장을 하나로 연결해 준다. 접속사 가운데는 의미상 문장 첫머리에 나오지 못하는 접속사도 있기 때문에 구분해서 외워둬야 한다.

1 상관접속사

짝을 이뤄 함께 붙어 다니는 접속사를 상관접속사라고 한다. 한쪽에 나온 접속사를 보고 나머지를 찾아낸다.

both A and B A와 B 둘 다	not A but B A가 아니라 B
either A or B A나 B 둘 중 하나	neither A nor B A와 B 둘 다 아닌
not only A but (also) B A 뿐만 아니라 B도	B as well as A A 뿐만 아니라 B도

- The house is **both** inexpensive **and** convenient. 그 집은 싸고 편리하다.
  - A: 형용사　　　B: 형용사

- He goes shopping **either** by bus **or** on foot. 그는 버스로 또는 걸어서 쇼핑하러 간다.
  - A: 전치사구　B: 전치사구

- **Not only** will he play well, **but also** he will study hard. 그는 잘 놀 뿐만 아니라 공부도 열심히 할 것이다.
  - A: 문장　　　　　　　B: 문장

2 인과관계를 나타내는 접속사

1) 이유를 나타내는 접속사: because/as/since/now that + 주어 + 동사

이들 접속사는 이유를 나타내는 부사절을 이끌며 문장 처음에 올 수도 있고 중간에 올 수도 있다. 주절에는 결과를 나타내는 내용이 나온다.

- **Because** the response from customers was satisfactory, my team was happy.

  = My team was happy **because** the response from customers was satisfactory.
  고객들의 반응이 만족스러워서 저희 팀은 행복했습니다.

2) 이유를 나타내는 전치사: because of/due to/on account of/as a result of/
thanks to/owing to + 명사

- **Due to** an unexpected business trip, I can't attend the staff meeting tomorrow.
  예상치 못한 출장 때문에 저는 내일 직원회의에 참석할 수가 없어요.

3) 결과를 나타내는 접속사 및 접속부사: so/therefore/consequently/thus

결과를 나타내는 접속사 및 접속부사는 '그래서, 그러므로, 그리하여'라는 뜻으로 앞에 나온 사건
의 결과를 보여준다. 이때 접속부사는 세미콜론(;)과 함께 문장 중간에 오거나 두 개의 독립된 문장
사이에 놓일 수도 있다.

- The bank refused to approve Ethan's application for a loan, **so** he got into trouble.
  은행은 에단의 융자금 신청을 거절했다. 그래서 그는 어려움에 빠졌다.

3 상반 관계를 나타내는 접속사

1) 양보를 나타내는 접속사: although/though/even though/even if + 주어 + 동사

- **Although** there was a mechanical problem, the train arrived on time.
- = The train arrived on time, **although** there was a mechanical problem.
  기계적인 결함이 있었지만 기차는 정각에 도착했다.

2) 양보를 나타내는 전치사: in spite of/despite + (동)명사

- Current surveys indicate a strong preference for luxury cars **despite** the economic downturn.
  최근의 조사는 경기하락에도 불구하고 호화차량에 대한 강한 선호도를 보여준다.

> **the fact that ~ 앞에는 전치사가 온다.**

- **Despite the fact that** our company has become internationally successful, it still has some problems.
  우리 회사는 세계적으로 성공했다는 사실에도 불구하고 여전히 몇몇 문제들을 가지고 있다.

3) 대조·역접을 나타내는 접속부사: yet/nevertheless/nonetheless/however

- I expressed my intention regarding the project; however, it was completely ignored.
  프로젝트에 관한 내 의도를 표현했지만 완전히 무시되었다.

4 목적을 나타내는 접속사

so that 주어 + (조)동사: '~할 수 있도록, ~하기 위한'이라는 뜻이며, 동사를 받을 때는 'in order to V,
so as to V'의 형태로 출제된다.

- You should confirm a revised itinerary **so that** you will not miss the flight.
  당신은 항공기를 놓치지 않기 위해서 수정된 일정표를 확인해야 합니다.

5   결과를 나타내는 접속사

so + 형용사/부사 + that 절

- Mr. Keller is **so** efficient **that** he deserves a promotion to the managerial position.
  → be동사가 쓰였으므로 so 뒤에 형용사를 쓴다.
  켈러 씨는 매우 능률적이기 때문에 관리직 승진을 받을 자격이 된다.

- He spoke **so** hesitantly **that** nobody paid any attention.
  → 일반동사가 쓰였으므로 so 뒤에 부사를 쓴다.
  그가 너무 주저하며 이야기했기 때문에 아무도 집중하지 않았다.

such + a + 형용사 + 명사 + that 절

- The outdoor activity was **such a great success that** we decided to provide it once again.
  → such 뒤에 오는 명사가 불가산이면 관사가 오지 않는다.
  야외 활동이 너무나 성공적이어서 우리는 야외 활동을 한 번 더 마련하기로 결정했다.

6   조건을 나타내는 접속사

in case + 주어 + 동사 (= in the event that + 주어 + 동사: 만약 ~할 경우에는)

- Your absence will be allowed **in case** there is an emergency.
  긴급 상황이 발생할 경우에는 결근이 허용될 것입니다.

in case of + 명사 (= in the event of + 명사: 만약 ~인 경우에는)

- We will notify staff immediately **in case of** changes in plans.
  계획에 수정이 있을 경우 우리는 즉시 직원들에게 알릴 것입니다.

unless + 주어 + 동사 (= if ~not: 만약 ~이 아니라면)

- I won't pay **unless** you deliver the goods to us immediately.
  즉시 제품을 배달해주지 않으면 나는 대금을 지불하지 않을 것입니다.

1 I will participate in the workshop on behalf of my boss ------- he asked me to.
(A) because of
(B) because
(C) although
(D) despite

2 ------- power maintenance in the building, service will be interrupted from 3 to 5 o'clock on Friday.
(A) Not only
(B) Despite
(C) Due to
(D) If

3 The central bank will maintain its existing policy ------- it causes higher interest rates and a number of bankruptcies.
(A) in spite of
(B) both
(C) even if
(D) in case of

4 It was announced that neither insufficient support ------- a lack of commitment is a factor in declining sales.
(A) so
(B) but
(C) yet
(D) nor

5 ------- measures are taken, traffic congestion will get even worse in no time.
(A) Also
(B) Unless
(C) Therefore
(D) Nevertheless

6 The controversial report included both strict reforms ------- the layoffs of temporary workers.
(A) or
(B) but
(C) and
(D) nor

7 Considerable profits were obtained ------- losses from serious flood damage in the region.
(A) regarding
(B) despite
(C) but
(D) although

8 ------- lower prices, more potential customers will be able to buy the property.
(A) Owing to
(B) As much as
(C) Whether
(D) In case

Questions 1-4 refer to the following article.

Carson City (April 11) – At a press conference on April 10, a spokesman for local business Peterson Silver made a stunning ------- (1). One month ago, Peterson Silver discovered a new ------- (2) of silver in Nevada. At the present time, the location of the mine is being kept a secret. According to the spokesman, it could be the largest source of silver ever found in the country. Peterson Silver estimates the area contains at least 500 million ounces of silver. ------- (3) It is also planning to hire more than 200 new employees. Carson City has been suffering economically for the past few years. Most of the jobs ------- (4) to go to residents of Carson City, which should help improve the local economy.

1 (A) announced
  (B) announcer
  (C) announcement
  (D) announcing

2 (A) supplier
  (B) foundation
  (C) source
  (D) mountain

3 (A) The company is now acquiring the equipment needed to run such a large mine.
  (B) Miners from around the country are currently heading to the location of the deposit.
  (C) The company has silver mines in several places around the entire country.
  (D) CEO Brandon Stewart was just appointed to his job at Peterson Silver last month.

4 (A) expect
  (B) have expected
  (C) are expected
  (D) will expect

두 문장을 연결할 때 분사구문을 이용하면 보다 간결한 표현을 만들 수 있다. 분사구문을 만드는 방법은 다음과 같다. ① 접속사를 생략한다. ② 주어가 일치할 경우 접속사 문장의 주어를 생략한다. ③ 시제가 같을 경우는 접속사절의 동사를 V-ing, 접속사절의 시제가 앞 설 경우는 having + p.p.형태로 바꾼다. 단, being이나 having been은 생략할 수 있다.

1 분사구문의 형태

- **When he turned the light on**, he was surprised to find her in the office. 〈부사절〉
  → **Turning the light on**, he was surprised to find her in the office. 〈분사구문〉
  불을 켰을 때 그는 사무실에 있는 그녀를 보고 놀랐다.

2 분사구문 만들기

원래 문장	**As I reviewed** the reports, I **asked** my secretary to revise the mistakes.
① 접속사를 생략한다.	**As I reviewed** the reports, I **asked** my secretary to revise the mistakes.
② 주어가 일치할 경우 접속사절의 주어를 생략한다.	**As~~I~~ reviewed** the reports, I **asked** my secretary to revise the mistakes.
③ 시제가 같을 경우는 접속사절의 동사를 V-ing 형태로 바꾼다.	원래 문장의 reviewed와 주절의 asked가 모두 과거 시제로 시제가 같음. **As~~I~~ reviewed(→ reviewing)** the reports, I **asked** my secretary to revise the mistakes.
완성된 분사구문	**Reviewing** the reports, I asked my secretary to revise the mistakes. 나는 보고서를 검토하면서 비서에게 실수를 수정하라고 요청했다.

3 분사구문에서 접속사의 의미를 강조할 때

접속사를 생략했을 때 의미가 불분명해질 경우에는 의미를 분명히 하기 위해 접속사를 살려둔다. 대표적인 접속사로 '때'를 나타내는 when(ever), while, '가정'을 나타내는 if, unless, once, '대조'를 나타내는 although, though 등이 있다.

When ~할 때

- **When you are preparing** estimates, don't forget to include service charges.
  → **When** (being) **preparing** estimates, don't forget to include service charges.
  계산서를 준비하실 때 봉사료를 포함시키는 것을 잊지 마세요.

While ~동안에

- Workers should wear protective equipment **while they are working** at the construction site.

  → Workers should wear protective equipment **while** (being) **working** at the construction site.

  작업자들은 건설 현장에서 일하는 동안 보호 장비를 착용해야 한다.

- **While they were on duty**, they were advised not to use their mobile phones.

  → **While** (being) **on duty**, they were advised not to use their mobile phones.

  근무 중에 그들은 이동 전화를 사용할 수가 없었다.

If ~라면

- We are going to conduct a thorough survey **if it is necessary**.

  → We are going to conduct a thorough survey **if necessary**.

  필요하다면 철저한 조사를 할 것이다.

  cf) 위 예문과 같이 부사절의 주어가 비인칭 주어 it 또는 일반적인 사람인 경우, 부사절에서 주어와 be동사를 생략한다.

Unless ~하지 않는다면

- You have to pay within thirty days **unless it is stated otherwise on your bill**.

  → You have to pay within thirty days **unless stated otherwise on your bill**.

  청구서에 달리 언급 되어진 바가 없다면, 30일 이내에 지불해야 한다.

Although 비록 ~는 아니라도 해도

- Employees are advised to attend the teamwork seminar **although it is not mandatory**.

  → Employees are advised to attend the teamwork seminar **although not mandatory**.

  의무적인 것은 아니지만 직원들은 팀워크 세미나에 참여해 주세요.

4 분사구문의 관용 표현

as planned 계획한 바대로	as discussed 논의된 바대로
as indicated 지시된 대로	considering 명사 / that 절 ~을 고려하면

- **As discussed** at the previous meeting, we offered the reimbursement for our mistakes.

  이전 회의에서 논의된 대로 우리의 잘못에 대해 배상금을 지불했다.

1 ------- buying a computer, you are encouraged to compare prices and product quality.
(A) Whether
(B) When
(C) That
(D) Unless

2 Children are not allowed to enter the reception hall ------- accompanied by adults.
(A) although
(B) before
(C) without
(D) unless

3 ------- that there are many potential workers, we do not need to worry for a few years.
(A) Consider
(B) Considered
(C) Considering
(D) Consideration

4 ------- near the tourist attraction, the ACE Hotel is very attractive to tourists.
(A) Location
(B) To locate
(C) Locating
(D) Located

5 When ------- the applications, the personnel manager's main focus was on the candidates' experience in software design.
(A) review
(B) reviews
(C) reviewing
(D) reviewed

6 All of the participants are required to follow the safety regulations as -------.
(A) direct
(B) directed
(C) to direct
(D) is directing

7 We have become one of the most famous travel companies, ------- the best service ever.
(A) provide
(B) provides
(C) provided
(D) providing

8 ------- received the overseas training, we learned how to accommodate different cultures.
(A) Have
(B) Has
(C) Had
(D) Having

Questions 1-2 refer to the following e-mail.

To: Derek Gently <derek_gently@virginia.edu>
From: Doug Adams <d.adams@soluspharm.net>
Date: June 11
Subject: Business Advisory Board Invitation

Dear Professor Gently:

An individual with your experience and insights in the pharmaceutical industry would be the perfect person to help me determine the future direction of my company, Solus Pharmaceuticals. Therefore, I'm pleased to invite you to become a member of my company's Business Advisory Board.

The Business Advisory Board will meet quarterly, with each meeting consisting of a two-hour discussion followed by a luncheon. Of course, I will cover any expenses you have from attending advisory board meetings and also give $2,500 directly to you or to a charity of your choice.

Thank you for taking the time to consider being a part of Solus Pharmaceuticals Business Advisory Board. I'm available to discuss any questions you may have. You can reach me by phone at (416) 545-3256. I look forward to your reply.

Sincerely,

Doug Adams, CEO
Solus Pharmaceuticals, Inc.

1 What is the purpose of the e-mail?
   (A) To introduce a new medicine
   (B) To ask for a price estimate
   (C) To offer an advisory position
   (D) To arrange a board meeting

2 What can be inferred about the Business Advisory Board?
   (A) It meets regularly four times a year.
   (B) Its annual membership fee is $2,500.
   (C) It agrees with the increase in product price.
   (D) Its members don't need any experience.

DAY 13 관계대명사

관계대명사는 절과 절을 연결하는 접속사의 역할과 함께 앞에 나오는 명사, 즉 선행사를 대신하는 대명사 역할을 동시에 한다. 이때 관계대명사가 이끄는 관계사절은 앞에 나온 선행사를 꾸며주는 형용사 구실을 한다.

1 관계대명사의 역할

관계대명사는 문장에서 접속사와 대명사 역할을 동시에 하며 형용사절을 이끈다.

접속사 역할	두 문장을 하나로 연결한다. 쉽게는 and의 역할을 한다고 생각하면 된다.
대명사 역할	앞 문장에 나온 명사를 대신 받는다. 관계대명사도 대명사이기 때문에 사람과 사물을 구분하고 주격, 목적격, 소유격을 구분해서 쓴다.

- We will hire a person **and he** has exceptional communicating skills.
  → We will hire a person **who** has exceptional communicating skills.
  우리는 우수한 의사소통 능력을 가진 사람을 고용할 것이다.

2 관계대명사의 종류

선행사	주격	소유격	목적격
사람	who	whose	whom
사물	which	whose	which
사람 / 사물	that	–	that

1) 주격 관계대명사

관계대명사가 문장에서 주어 역할을 할 경우 선행사가 사람이면 who, 사물이면 which를 쓴다. 관계대명사 that은 사람과 사물 둘 다에 쓸 수 있다.

명사 + **who/which/that** + 동사

- I assisted my supervisor. + The supervisor was in charge of calculating yearly revenue.
  → I assisted my supervisor **and he** was in charge of calculating yearly revenue.
  → I assisted my supervisor **who** was in charge of calculating yearly revenue.
  나는 연 세입 계산을 담당하고 있는 상사를 도왔다.

- The company hired a law firm. + The firm specializes in environmental issues.

  → The company hired a law firm **and it** specializes in environmental issues.

  → The company hired a law firm **which** specializes in environmental issues.
  그 회사는 환경 문제를 전문으로 하는 법률 사무소에 업무를 의뢰했다.

> **those who ~ ~하는 사람들**

those는 일반적인 사람들, 즉 those people who에서 people을 생략한 형태이다. those who 뒤에는 항상 복수동사가 온다.

- **Those who** are unable to attend the first training session should report to the manager.
  첫 번째 교육에 참가하지 못한 사람들은 매니저에게 보고해야 한다.

2) 소유격 관계대명사

앞에 선행사가 있고 뒤따라 명사가 나오면 사람·사물에 관계없이 소유격 관계대명사는 whose를 쓴다.

> **명사 + whose + 명사**

- Companies prefer candidates· + The candidates' capabilities are suited for them.

  → Companies prefer candidates **and their** capabilities are suited for them.

  → Companies prefer candidates **whose** capabilities are suited for them.
  회사들은 그들에게 적합한 능력을 가진 후보자들을 선호한다.
- Please review the document. + The document's cover is red.

  → Please review the document **and its** cover is red.

  → Please review the document **whose** cover is red.
  빨간색 표지의 문서를 재검토해 주세요.

3) 목적격 관계대명사

목적격 관계대명사 whom, which, that 뒤에는 목적어가 없는 문장이 오며, 관계대명사 목적격은 생략가능하다. 그러나 전치사 다음에 오는 목적격 관계대명사는 생략할 수도, that을 쓸 수도 없다.

> **명사 + (whom/which/that) + 주어 + 타동사**
> **명사 + (whom/which/that) + 주어 + 동사 + 전치사**
> **명사 + 전치사 + whom/which + 주어 + 동사**

- I organized all the files. + I need it for tomorrow's conference.

  → I organized all the files **and** I need **it** for tomorrow's conference.

  → I organized all the files **(which/that)** I need for tomorrow's conference.
  나는 내일 컨퍼런스에 필요한 모든 자료들을 정리했다.

- I finally got a job. + I was looking for the job.

  → I finally got a job **and** I was looking for it.

  → I finally got a job **(which/that)** I was looking for.

  → I finally got a job **for which** I was looking.
  찾고 있던 직업을 마침내 얻었다.

4) 선행사를 포함하는 관계대명사 what

관계대명사 what은 the thing which와 같은 뜻이다. 그 자체에 선행사를 포함하고 있기 때문에 시험에서 동사 다음에 밑줄이 올 경우 what을 먼저 생각해야 한다. 단, 관계사절이기 때문에 what을 포함한 문장 안에 주어 또는 목적어가 없어야 한다. 관계대명사 what이 이끄는 절은 명사 역할을 하기 때문에 주어나 목적어 자리에 올 수 있다.

- **The thing which** Mr. Smith is doing will contribute to the success of the project.

  → **What** Mr. Smith is doing will contribute to the success of the project. (주어 자리)
  스미스 씨가 하고 있는 일이 프로젝트 성공에 기여할 것이다.

- I didn't understand **the thing which** she was talking about.

  → I didn't understand **what** she was talking about. (목적어 자리)
  나는 그녀가 말했던 것을 이해 못했다.

3 관계사절의 성·수 일치

관계사절 안에서도 성·수 일치 문제가 다뤄진다. 주격 관계대명사 뒤에 오는 동사의 수는 선행사의 수에 일치시킨다.

> 선행사(단수) + 주격 관계대명사 + 3인칭 단수동사(is, was, 일반동사+(e)s)
> 선행사(복수) + 주격 관계대명사 + 복수동사(are, were, 일반동사 원형)

- We implemented a new system **that measures** employees' achievements.
  우리는 직원들의 성과를 측정할 새로운 시스템을 시행했다.

- We are discussing the defective parts **that need** to be replaced quickly.
  빨리 교체되어야할 결함이 있는 부품들을 논의하고 있다.

1 If managers ------- have time fill in for sick employees, they will be respected.

(A) who
(B) whoever
(C) whose
(D) which

2 We have several people ------- train the professionals on site every day to deal with problems.

(A) who
(B) whether
(C) which
(D) what

3 Please ensure that you have to return merchandise ------- has defects within a week of purchase.

(A) there
(B) who
(C) when
(D) that

4 Most of the applicants were put on the waiting list for the positions for ----   they signed up.

(A) which
(B) that
(C) who
(D) what

5 The names of the candidates ------- qualifications are suitable for the job will be posted tomorrow.

(A) that
(B) which
(C) who
(D) whose

6 ------- who want to reduce their unnecessary expenses are advised to read Ms. Parker's recent book.

(A) That
(B) Those
(C) Everyone
(D) Anybody

7 Temporary workers get paid on a weekly basis, ------- is common in most work places.

(A) who
(B) where
(C) which
(D) that

8 Tazan Narration Ltd. conslsts of seven employees, all of ------- are under the age of 30.

(A) what
(B) them
(C) this
(D) whom

Questions 1-4 refer to the following e-mail.

TO: Linda Chu <lindachu@perryfinancial.com>

FROM: Tom Rogers <t_rogers@davisconsulting.com>

SUBJECT: Speaking Date

Dear Ms. Chu,

Thank you for the offer to visit your company and to give a presentation to your ------- **1**.

I would be more than pleased to speak to the people at your company about the precious metals market. Unfortunately, I am ------- **2** on the date you requested. I'm going to be out of the country from November 6-10. When I return, I have appointments all day long on the 11th. ------- **3** You requested that I speak from 11 A.M. until noon on the 7th. How about visiting your company at that time on either the 12th or 13th instead? If that time is unacceptable, please inform me when you ------- **4** me there.

Regards,

Tom Rogers

Davis Consulting

---

1 (A) clients
(B) colleagues
(C) friends
(D) members

2 (A) unavailable
(B) approved
(C) free
(D) unapproachable

3 (A) Moreover, I am unaware of where your company is.
(B) Apparently, I'm going to be out of the office on that day.
(C) Consequently, I can be at your firm precisely when you want.
(D) However, my calendar is currently empty the next two days.

4 (A) like
(B) will like
(C) would like
(D) will be liking

DAY 14 「주격 관계대명사 + be동사」의 생략

접속사에서 「주어 + be동사」를 동시에 생략하듯이 「주격 관계대명사 + be동사」를 생략할 수 있다. 주격 관계대명사만 생략하는 것은 불가능하다. 요즘은 형용사 어휘 문제도 「주격 관계대명사 + be동사」를 생략한 후의 형태에서 출제되기 때문에 생략 구조를 이해하지 못하면 어휘 문제를 잡기 힘들다. 또한 이 구조를 파악해야만 성·수 일치 문제도 풀 수 있다.

1 선행사 + (주격 관계대명사 + be동사) + 형용사

- This tourist map will be very helpful to those who are less familiar with this city.

  → This tourist map will be very helpful to those **less familiar with this city**.

  이 여행자 지도는 이 도시를 잘 모르는 사람들에게 도움이 될 것이다.

- The vehicle that is known for its outstanding performance is selling well.

  → The vehicle **known for its outstanding performance** is selling well.

  뛰어난 성능으로 알려진 그 차량은 잘 팔리고 있다.

2 선행사 + (주격 관계대명사 + be동사) + V-ing

선행사가 능동적으로 '~하다'라는 뜻일 때 현재분사(V-ing)를 쓴다.

> **동사가 타동사일 때: 선행사 + __________ + 명사**

- Due to unexpected delays, which are causing problems, they seem upset now.

  → Due to unexpected delays **causing problems**, they seem upset now.

  문제를 야기시키는 예상치 못한 지연 때문에 그들은 당황한 것 같다.

> **동사가 자동사일 때: 선행사 + __________ + 전치사 + 명사/부사**

- People who are participating in the trade fair will get valuable lessons.

  → People **participating in the trade fair** will get valuable lessons.

  무역박람회에 참석하는 사람들은 값진 교훈을 얻을 것이다.

3 선행사 + (주격 관계대명사 + be동사) + p.p.

선행사가 수동적으로 '~되어지다'라는 뜻일 때 과거분사(p.p.)를 쓴다.

선행사 + __________ + 전치사 + 명사

- Orders **which are received on weekends** will be processed on the next business day.

  → Orders **received on weekends** will be processed on the next business day.
  주말에 접수된 주문은 다음 영업일에 처리될 것이다.

선행사 + __________ + 부사

- The door **that was installed yesterday** is now securely closed.

  → The door **installed yesterday** is now securely closed.
  어제 설치된 문은 안전하게 닫혀 있다.

1　The company policy ------- the use of electronic devices at work has been announced.
(A) prohibit
(B) prohibited
(C) prohibiting
(D) for prohibit

2　The most visited museum ------- within walking distance of my place is well known for its extensive collections.
(A) locates
(B) location
(C) locate
(D) located

3　The company newsletter ------- on the last week of every month contains useful information.
(A) publish
(B) published
(C) publishing
(D) publish

4　Mr. Ford was appointed to head the committee ------- on the educational reform project.
(A) work
(B) works
(C) worked
(D) working

5　The vice president ------- to travel to Southeast Asia on business had to cancel the trip because of strike by airlines.
(A) schedule
(B) schedules
(C) scheduled
(D) scheduling

6　We really apologize for any inconvenience ------- by poor service and employee negligence.
(A) cause
(B) causing
(C) caused
(D) causes

7　Everyone ------- in the charity activity donated clothes and money to people in need.
(A) involve
(B) involving
(C) involved
(D) involvement

8　If you have experience ------- any technical problem, contact us promptly for assistance.
(A) encounter
(B) encountering
(C) encountered
(D) to encounter

Questions 1-4 refer to the following letter.

March 21

To the Owner,

My name is Heather Myers. I've been eating at your establishment since 2005 and go there with my husband at least once a month. On March 18, we had dinner there at around 6:30.

Dinner was superb, just like every other meal we have had at Golden Times. --[1]-- But the service provided by John, one of your servers, was even better. John remembered us from the previous time we visited. --[2]-- He also took our orders, which were a bit complicated, down perfectly, so we got our meals exactly how we wanted them. John constantly checked on us to make sure we were enjoying our dinner and to ask if we needed anything. --[3]--

The best part, however, came while we were in the parking lot. We were about to get into our car to return home when John came running out. Apparently, my husband had forgotten his wallet. John found it and returned it to him. --[4]-- He wouldn't even accept the $20 my husband offered him.

I thought you might like to know about what a great employee John is. I hope he stays at your restaurant for a long time, and I definitely will request that he be our server whenever we dine there.

Sincerely,
Heather Myers

---

1 What is the purpose of the letter?
(A) To describe an unpleasant event
(B) To request an apology
(C) To praise an employee
(D) To compliment a meal

2 What is suggested by Ms. Myers?
(A) She dislikes eating dinner at her home.
(B) She intends to visit Golden Times in the future.
(C) She has had John as a waiter several times.
(D) She likes the low prices at Golden Times.

3 In which of the positions marked [1], [2], [3], and [4] does the following sentence best belong?
"As a result, he knew exactly what drinks we wanted."
(A) [1]
(B) [2]
(C) [3]
(D) [4]

타동사 어휘 연습 / 복합 지문

PART 5 어휘 – 타동사 어휘 연습

1 Employees should ------- all their travel expenses and report to Financial Department.
(A) verify
(B) renew
(C) display
(D) compile

2 The expansion will ------- us to offer more customers even better services.
(A) demonstrate
(B) enable
(C) prohibit
(D) compare

3 Eastern Construction wants to ------- the progress of the planned construction project.
(A) implement
(B) oversee
(C) assist
(D) surpass

4 We do not ------- any responsibility for valuables lost outdoors.
(A) leave
(B) remind
(C) resume
(D) accept

5 This seminar has been designed to ------- concerns about joint ventures.
(A) hesitate
(B) alleviate
(C) deteriorate
(D) exceed

6 Shipping vegetables in the refrigerated container helps ------- their freshness.
(A) retain
(B) purchase
(C) undergo
(D) diversify

7 The report shows that road constructions ------- the extensive development of the economy.
(A) relocate
(B) respond
(C) influence
(D) dilute

8 Most organizations held a series of events to ------- funds for their research projects.
(A) adopt
(B) raise
(C) inform
(D) attribute

Questions 1-5 refer to the following e-mails.

TO: Joseph Cohn <josephcohn@northstarfood.com>
FROM: Calvin Masters <cmasters@sdaa-con.com>
SUBJECT: Californian Agricultural Conference Sponsorship

Dear Mr. Cohn,

On behalf of the San Diego Agricultural Association(SDAA), I would like to express our sincerest gratitude for North Star Food's registration in this year's Californian Agricultural Conference to be held this year from October 10 to 12.

As your company's chief marketing executive, you know the Californian Agricultural Conference brings together California's leading agricultural producers and retailers in one location. This is also an ideal opportunity for participating companies to sponsor different elements of the conference.

Accordingly, the SDAA would like to invite your company to become a sponsor of this year's conference. The following sponsorship levels and benefits are open for your company's participation:

Bronze Sponsor - $1,000
• Listed as a Bronze Sponsor in the conference program.
• Acknowledgement during the final banquet

Silver Sponsor - $1,500
• All the benefits of a Bronze Sponsor
• Allowed to insert your company's brochures in the conference packages

Gold Sponsor - $2,500
• All the benefits of a Silver Sponsor
• Use of all presentation rooms

Please contact me at (914) 324-5353 or e-mail me at cmasters@sdaa-con.com for additional details and to arrange your sponsorship.

Thank you again for your participation in this year's Californian Agricultural Conference.

Sincerely,

Calvin Masters
Conference Coordinator
Californian Agricultural Conference

TO: Calvin Masters <cmasters@sdaa-con.com>
FROM: Joseph Cohn <josephcohn@northstarfood.com>
SUBJECT: RE: Californian Agricultural Conference Sponsorship

Dear Mr. Masters,

After careful consideration, it is a pleasure to inform you that North Star Food has decided to become a Silver Sponsor of the Californian Agricultural Conference. As you mentioned in your message, this is an ideal opportunity to promote the North Star brand among industry participants, and we do not want to miss this chance.

If you could provide payment details for sponsorship, I would be grateful. I will be out of the office all next week, so please forward this information to my assistant, David Adams (T: 914-252-8329, E-mail: dadams@northstarfood.com).

Best regards,

Joseph Cohn

---

1   Why did Calvin Masters write to Joseph Cohn?
   (A) To confirm registration for the sponsorship
   (B) To announce the best sponsor company
   (C) To encourage others to help small companies
   (D) To introduce a sponsorship opportunity

2   What does Calvin Masters imply about the conference?
   (A) Attendance has been growing over the past few years.
   (B) It is attended by important industry representatives.
   (C) The cost of operating the conference is very high.
   (D) Several famous guest speakers will participate.

3   What benefit does a Silver Sponsor have that a Bronze Sponsor does not?
   (A) It is listed in the main conference program.
   (B) It can distribute brochures to conference participants.
   (C) It can use all the presentation rooms.
   (D) It can deliver an address during the final banquet.

4   What fee will North Star Food pay for its level of sponsorship?
   (A) $1,000
   (B) $1,500
   (C) $2,000
   (D) $2,500

5   What information will David Adams get from Mr. Masters?
   (A) Details on how to pay for sponsorship
   (B) Directions to the conference center
   (C) Lists of available accommodations
   (D) Profiles of attending guest speakers

Questions 6-10 refer to the following announcement, form, and e-mail.

Society of Mechanical Engineers to Hold Conference in Minneapolis

At its most recent meeting, the Society of Mechanical Engineers (SME) voted to hold its annual conference in Minneapolis, Minnesota. The conference is going to be held from March 10-12. As usual, there will be numerous events, including seminars, speeches, workshops, and an international job fair. There will also be numerous opportunities for individuals to read their own research papers. For more information about the conference and how to become a part of it, visit our Web site at www.sme.org. Several local hotels and rental car companies as well as a couple of national airlines have agreed to offer discounts of up to 40% to attendees. The full list of those companies is available on the Web site. Attendance at the conference will cost $50 for members of the SME and $120 for nonmembers. Preregistration is not necessary as tickets can be purchased at the door. We look forward to seeing all of our members—and many other individuals—at the coming event.

Society of Mechanical Engineers
Annual Conference
Registration Form

Name: *Peter Dawson*

E-Mail Address: *petedawson@arlingtonconstruction.com*

Telephone Number: *(205) 402-5648*

SME Status: [✔] member   [ ] nonmember

Membership Number: *59430*

Registration Fee: [✔] paid   [ ] not paid

Payment Method: [ ] cash   [✔] check   [ ] credit card

Expected Days of Attendance: [✔] March 10   [✔] March 11   [✔] March 12

Do you require assistance reserving a hotel? [ ] yes   [✔] no

Do you require assistance reserving a vehicle? [ ] yes   [✔] no

To: undisclosed recipients
From: haroldsmith@sme.org
Subject: SME Conference
Date: March 5

Dear SME Member,

It is with great regret that I must inform you all that next week's conference has been canceled. The recent inclement weather in the Minneapolis area caused a great amount of damage to the Minneapolis Civic Center, which was to be the site of the conference. Yesterday, city engineers examined the building and determined it had suffered damage to its structural integrity. As such, no more events are permitted in the building until it is repaired.

We had anticipated that something like this might happen, so we tried to find an alternate venue both in Minneapolis and also in nearby St. Paul. Sadly, every place we looked at is booked.

Everyone who paid to register for the conference will be reimbursed no later than March 15. If you need assistance getting a refund on a hotel, vehicle, or airplane reservation, please contact us.

If enough members express a willingness to attend another event in the summer, we will schedule one then. Please respond to this e-mail and inform us if and when you have time in the summer.

Once again, we at the SME would like to apologize for this unfortunate event.

Sincerely,

Harold Smith, President, SME

---

6 What is suggested about the conference?

(A) It has been held in previous years.

(B) Few SME nonmembers attend it.

(C) It is a profitable event for the SME.

(D) It is held in Minneapolis each year.

7 What will NOT be held at the conference?

(A) Workshops

(B) A job fair

(C) Seminars

(D) A trade show

8 How much did Mr. Dawson pay to register for the conference?

(A) $40

(B) $50

(C) $100

(D) $120

9 What is the purpose of the e-mail?

(A) To explain why the conference is moving to another city

(B) To announce the cancelation of the conference

(C) To state that the conference has been postponed

(D) To mention that refunds will not be provided

10 What does Mr. Smith request that people do?

(A) Tell him if they can go to a conference later in the year

(B) Suggest alternate venues for the conference

(C) Request reimbursement on their registration fees

(D) Go to the event that is being held in St. Paul

수량형용사와 수 일치

수량형용사는 명사 앞에서 '많은 ~', '적은 ~'와 같이 명사의 수나 양을 나타내는 형용사를 말한다. 기본적으로 수를 나타내는 형용사는 셀 수 있는 명사와 함께 쓰고 양을 나타내는 형용사는 셀 수 없는 명사와 함께 쓴다. 또한 주어가 단수냐, 복수냐에 따라 동사의 형태를 주어에 일치시켜야 한다. 특히, 주어가 3인칭 단수이면 현재형 동사에는 −(e)s가 붙는다.

1 수량형용사

1) 셀 수 있는 명사 앞에만 쓰는 수량형용사

every/another/one/each/this/that + 단수 명사 + 단수 동사

- **Every** employer **has** to have specific plans to exceed the target.
  모든 고용주는 목표를 초과하려면 구체적인 계획을 가져야 한다.
- **Another** computer system failure **was** detected.
  다른 컴퓨터 시스템 결함이 발견되었다.

all/other/many/several/these/those + 복수 명사 + 복수 동사

- **All** the names of exceptional employees **were** posted on the board.
  뛰어난 직원들의 이름 모두가 게시판에 게시되었다.
- **Other** employees **are** impressed with her work experience.
  다른 직원들은 그녀의 업무경험에 만족한다.

2) 셀 수 없는 명사 앞에만 쓰는 수량형용사

much/a little/little/a great deal of/a large amount of + 단수 명사 + 단수 동사

- **Much** equipment in the laboratory **is** fragile so you should be careful.
  실험실의 많은 장비들이 깨지기 쉬우니 조심해야 한다.

3) **a few/few와 a little/little의 차이점**

a few와 few는 셀 수 있는 명사의 복수형 앞에 쓰이고, a little과 little은 셀 수 없는 명사 앞에서
명사를 수식한다. a few나 a little은 '약간 있다'는 긍정의 뜻을 나타내지만 관사 a가 없이 few나
little이 되면 '거의 없다'는 부정의 뜻이 된다.

- Due to **a few** defects, we have to recall the products.
  몇몇 결함 때문에 그 제품들을 회수해야 한다.

- **Few** employees attended the training session last week.
  지난 주 연수에 참석한 직원이 거의 없었다.

- I've been able to save **a little** money.
  저는 약간의 돈을 절약할 수 있었어요.

- I was so busy that I had **little** time to proofread the manuscript.
  나는 너무 바빠서 원고 교정 볼 시간이 거의 없었다.

2 수 일치

1) **주어가 단수일 때 동사의 형태**

be동사 - is, was

- The restaurant near the lake **was** built approximately 5 years ago.
  호숫가 레스토랑은 약 5년 전에 지어졌다.

일반동사·동사원형 + (e)s

- Mr. Park, a financial expert, **expects** an economic crisis to occur in the coming
  years.
  재정 전문가 박 씨는 경제위기가 몇 년 후에 일어날 것이라 예상한다.

2) **주어가 복수일 때 동사의 형태**

be동사 - are, were

- Serious objections **are** anticipated.
  심각한 반대가 예상된다.

일반동사 – 동사원형

- Managers **stress** the effects of working overtime.
  관리자들은 초과 근무의 효과를 강조한다.

3) 동명사(V-ing)가 주어일 때 동사의 형태

> 동명사 + (목적어) + 단수 동사

- Renewing passports **is** expected to take a long time.
  여권 갱신은 시간이 오래 걸릴 것으로 예상된다.

4) There is 단수 명사 vs. There are 복수 명사

> **There is** + 단수 명사

- There **is a list** of speakers for next week's committee meeting.
  다음 주 위원회 미팅 연설자들 목록이 있다.

> **There are** + 복수 명사

- There **are many revisions** in the architectural plan for the new store.
  새 가게 건축 도면에 많은 수정 사항이 있다.

5) The number of 복수 명사 vs. A number of 복수 명사

> **The number of** 복수 명사 + 단수 동사: ～의 수

- **The number of** loan applications **has** risen steadily over the last few years.
  지난 몇 년 동안 대출 신청 숫자가 꾸준히 증가했다.

> **A number of** 복수 명사 + 복수 동사: 많은 ～

- **A number of** diners **were** pleased with the chef's new menu.
  많은 손님들이 주방장의 새 메뉴에 만족해 했다.

1 After moving to the office, I began to experience ------- malfunctions on my computer.

(A) a little
(B) much
(C) a few
(D) every

2 Please be aware that ------- measures must be implemented in order to prevent possible defects.

(A) all
(B) every
(C) much
(D) almost

3 Several ------- designed our new computer systems to suit the needs of their company.

(A) research
(B) researching
(C) researcher
(D) researchers

4 A few sales representatives ------- gathered in the lobby to watch the product demonstration.

(A) has
(B) is
(C) have
(D) was

5 A number of employees ------- part in the intensive training sessions which are provided by the company.

(A) has taken
(B) have taken
(C) takes
(D) is taken

6 The supervisor's knowledge of the procedures ------- him to help his staff resolve any serious technical problems.

(A) enable
(B) enables
(C) enabling
(D) to enable

7 When Mr. William's research ------- were finally published last week, he looked very delighted.

(A) result
(B) resulting
(C) results
(D) resulted

8 ------- a high level of expertise in related fields is required in order to be considered for the position.

(A) Demonstrate
(B) Demonstrated
(C) Demonstrating
(D) Will demonstrate

Questions 1-4 refer to the following notice.

Reading Bridge Closed for Repairs

-------(1) The bridge was damaged on October 8 when a barge collided with it. Several parts of the bridge, including one of its supports, suffered extensive amounts of damage. The bridge has been -------(2) unsafe for traffic. Repair work on the bridge will begin on October 12. It is expected to take at least one month to complete. During that time, drivers must seek -------(3) ways to cross the West River. Both the Hampton Bridge and the Silver Bridge are located nearby. Drivers are -------(4) to use them or other bridges until the Reading Bridge reopens. For questions regarding the Reading Bridge, call 423-3030 during regular business hours.

1
(A) The Reading Bridge will be repaired next month.
(B) The Reading Bridge has been closed.
(C) Traffic is moving steadily on the Reading Bridge.
(D) Tolls are being charged for the Reading Bridge.

2
(A) spoken
(B) declared
(C) stated
(D) announced

3
(A) alternately
(B) alternated
(C) alternate
(D) alternates

4
(A) urged
(B) approved
(C) assisted
(D) informed

비교급과 최상급

형용사와 부사의 비교급은 두 가지 대상을 비교할 때 쓰고 최상급은 셋 이상의 대상을 비교할 때 쓴다. 비교 방식에 따라 원급 비교(~만큼 …하다), 비교급 비교(~보다 더 …하다), 최상급 비교(가장 …하다)로 구분된다.

1 원급 비교

두 비교 대상이 동등한 상태임을 나타내며 형태는 「as + 원급 형용사/부사 + as」(~만큼 …한)이다. be 동사 상당어구 다음에 오는 as ~ as 사이에는 형용사가 오고, 수동태나 완전한 문장 다음에 오는 as ~ as 사이에는 부사가 온다.

- The designs of SD's athletic clothing are not **as diverse as** ours. (be동사 다음)
  SD사의 스포츠 의류 디자인은 우리 것만큼 다양하지 않다.

- Please send us your samples **as quickly as** possible. (완전한 문장 다음)
  되도록 빨리 귀사의 견본품을 보내 주십시오.

> as __________ as 사이에 명사가 들어가는 경우

수량을 나타내는 many와 much는 원급 비교에 쓰일 때 「as + much/many + 명사 + as」(~만큼 많은)의 형태로 항상 명사와 같이 붙어 다닌다.

- Please collect **as much information as** you can. 가능하면 많은 정보를 수집하세요.

2 비교급 비교

비교급을 이용한 비교는 두 비교 대상의 차이를 나타낼 때 쓰며 '~보다 더 …하다'로 해석한다. 형태는 「형용사/부사의 비교급 + than」이다. 1음절이거나 −y로 끝나는 2음절 형용사와 부사는 −er을 붙여서 비교급을 만들고 그밖에 2음절 이상인 형용사와 부사는 앞에 more를 붙여서 비교급을 만든다.

- Foter Enterprise's first quarter profits were **higher than** originally expected.
  포터 엔터프라이즈 사의 1/4분기 수익이 원래 예상보다 높았다.

- Graty's new appliances seem **more attractive than** the old ones.
  그래티 사의 새 가전제품들은 이전 것들보다 더 괜찮아 보인다.

1) more/less '~ 보다 더 많은/적은'을 뜻하는 비교

'~보다 더 …한' 이라는 표현은 more를 쓰지만 '~보다 덜 …한'은 「less + 원급」을 써서 나타낸다.

- Our policy is **more[less] effective than** theirs.
  우리의 정책이 그들의 정책보다 더[덜] 효과적이다.

2) The + 비교급을 쓰는 경우

기본적으로 비교급에는 the를 쓰지 않지만 다음과 같은 경우에는 비교급에도 the를 붙인다.

> **the** 비교급 + **of the two** 복수명사

비교 대상이 둘임을 나타내는 of the two(둘 중에서)가 명시되어 있을 때 비교급 앞에 the를 붙인다.

- Mr. Parker looked **the more** qualified **of the two** candidates.
  파커 씨가 그 두 명의 응시자 중에서 더 적격인 것으로 보였다.

> **the** + 비교급 + 주어 + 동사 ~, **the** + 비교급 + 주어 + 동사 ~

'~하면 할수록 더 …하다'라는 뜻으로 비교급이 쌍을 이루어 다니며 각 비교급 앞에 the를 쓴다. 형용사의 비교급을 쓸지 부사의 비교급을 쓸지는 동사에 의해 결정된다. be동사일 때는 형용사 비교급, 일반동사일 때는 부사 비교급이 온다.

- **The more** we use the new software program, **the more** satisfied we are.
  새 프로그램을 더 많이 사용할수록 우리는 더 많이 만족한다.

3) 비교급 강조 부사: even, much, far, a lot

- Many sectors of business experienced **much higher** profits this year.
  올해 많은 사업 부분에서 훨씬 높은 수익을 냈다.

4) 라틴계 비교

라틴어에서 유래한 −or로 끝나는 비교급들은 전치사 than 대신 to를 쓴다.

> prior to ~보다 먼저   superior to ~보다 우수한   inferior to ~보다 열등한

3 최상급 비교

최상급은 '가장 …하다'라는 뜻을 나타내며 비교 대상의 범위가 셋 이상일 때 쓴다. 1음절이거나 −y로 끝나는 2음절 형용사는 −est, 2음절 이상인 형용사는 앞에 most를 붙여서 최상급을 만든다. 최상급 형용사 앞에는 반드시 정관사 the나 소유격이 온다.

1) 비교 범위 한정의 예

- NewT Weekly is the most reliable source for trends **of all** the magazines.
  NewT 위클리는 동향을 알 수 있는 가장 신뢰할만한 자료이다.   모든 잡지들 중에서

  that I have **ever** read.
  내가 읽은 것들 중에서

  in our city. 우리 도시에서

1 This new computer is ------- than the old one that we purchased a few years ago.
(A) most efficient
(B) more efficient
(C) efficiently
(D) efficient

2 We are proud that our products have been the ------- of any available products on the market.
(A) good
(B) better
(C) best
(D) well

3 This project is ------- assignment that our department has ever undertaken.
(A) most challenging
(B) challenged
(C) the most challenging
(D) more challenging

4 The harder it is to repay, the ------- banks suffer serious losses.
(A) most
(B) many
(C) a little
(D) more

5 I think the suggestion Mr. Kim gave a week ago is by far ------- one.
(A) good
(B) the best
(C) better
(D) the better

6 Ms. Chan was one of the ------- outstanding employees in monitoring the department budget.
(A) more
(B) much
(C) less
(D) most

7 Reimbursement will be paid as ------- as possible in order to avoid any criticism.
(A) quick
(B) quicker
(C) quickly
(D) quickest

8 It is likely that hazardous road conditions prevent driving from becoming ------- easier.
(A) very
(B) so
(C) too
(D) far

Questions 1-3 refer to the following article.

LZR-Tech Issues Largest Recall in Company History

LZR-Tech issued a country-wide recall on one of its most popular models of lawn mowers. Company representatives are recalling all purchased LZR-Tech A32 lawn mowers obtained from the months of May through August of this year.

According to the press release issued by the company, the A32 models were manufactured with unapproved components. The mistake, believed to be confined to the Detroit LZR-Tech factory, occurred as a result of mislabeled parts. Since that particular factory also manufactures various overseas brands, the oversight caused A32 models manufactured in May through August to be fitted with larger gas tanks than required.

Company representatives claim that the A32 models are not of any risk to public safety, but in an effort to improve customer service, the models will be recalled. Customers who have purchased an A32 model during the above mentioned time frame are asked to visit the company's website and submit a claim along with the machine's serial number. LZR-Tech will offer a newer replacement regardless of the condition of the currently owned defective item and they estimate that delivery will take approximately 7 days following the claim.

1 What is mentioned about LZR-Tech A32?
(A) It is manufactured in Detroit.
(B) It is a recently developed product.
(C) It will no longer be available for purchase.
(D) It will be recalled regardless of the time of purchase.

2 Why is the A32 model being recalled?
(A) It is the wrong color.
(B) It was made with incorrect parts.
(C) It is dangerous to use.
(D) It contains harmful chemicals.

3 What should customers have ready?
(A) A model number
(B) A proof of purchase
(C) An instruction manual
(D) A serial number

18 전치사

1 In / At / On

in	넓은 장소	**in** the world 세계에서
	분야	the decline **in** its population 인구의 감소
	시간 (~후에)	The meeting will be **in** 10 minutes. 10분 후에 회의가 있다.
	관용어구	**in** writing 서면으로 **in** detail 세부적으로 **in** person 직접, 몸소 **in** particular 특히
at	구체적인 장소	**at** the train station 기차역에서
	구체적인 시점	**at** 5:20 5시 20분에 **at** the end of this year 연말에 **at** the beginning of this year 연초에
	관용어구	**at** all times 항상 **at** least 적어도 **at** first 처음에는
on	표면	**on** the desk 책상 위에
	특정일/요일	**on** August 23 8월 23일에 **on** Tuesday 화요일에
	관용어구	**on** the rise 상승세인 **on** sale 할인중인 **on** business[vacation/leave] 업무로[휴가차] We spend donations **on** building houses for the homeless. 우리는 기부금을 집 없는 사람들을 위해 집을 짓는 데 쓴다.

2 Within / From / By

within	~이내에 ~안에	**within** 30 days of purchase 구매일로부터 30일 안에 **within** our organizations 조직 내에서
from	시작점	**from** the parking lot to work 주차장에서 직장까지 * from A to B: A 부터 B까지
	억제, 원인, 이탈	refrain **from** using cellular phones 휴대폰 사용을 자제하다 benefit **from** his experience 그의 경험으로부터 혜택을 받다 be absent **from** class 수업에 결석하다
	관용어구	**distinguish** our products **from** those of another company 우리 제품과 다른 회사의 제품을 구분하다 **prevent** the road **from** being slippery 도로가 미끄러워지는 것을 막다
by	수단	**by** train 기차로 (수단의 by는 관사와 같이 쓰지 않는다.) written **by** hand 손으로 쓰여진 **by** credit card 신용카드로 **by** adopting the policy 그 정책을 채택함으로써
	완료 (~까지)	submit the reason for turning down the offer **by** March 3 제안을 거절하는 이유를 3월 3일까지 제출하다
	관용어구	**by** chance 우연히 reduce the cost **by** 5% 5%만큼 비용을 삭감하다 (차이)

3 For / Throughout / Through

for	기간 (~동안)	**for** ten years = **for** a decade 10년 동안
for	목적지	leave **for** the island 섬으로 떠나다 be bound **for** Chicago 시카고 행이다
	관용어구	**for** free 무료로 **for** sale 판매용으로 be known **for** ~로 유명하다 **for** commercial purposes 상업적인 목적으로

throughout	~동안, 내내	**throughout** the year 1년 내내 **throughout** the last quarter 지난 분기 내내
	~전체에서	**throughout** the world[region/province] 세계[지역] 전역에서

through	~을 관통해서	pass **through** the forest 숲을 관통해서 지나가다
	수단	**through** the use of a Personal Digital Assistant 휴대용 정보 단말기 사용을 통해

4 After / Before / Except / 기타

after	전치사	**after**(= following) its publication 출판 후에 * after가 전치사로 쓰일 때는 following과 바꿔 쓸 수 있다.
	접속사	**after** the news was announced 뉴스가 발표된 후에 * after가 접속사로 쓰일 때는 following으로 바꿔 쓸 수 없다.

before	전치사	**before** the date 그 날짜 전에 * before가 전치사로 쓰일 때는 prior to와 바꿔 쓸 수 있다.
	접속사	**before** the morning meeting started 아침 회의가 시작되기 전에 * before가 접속사로 쓰일 때는 prior to로 바꿔 쓸 수 없다.

except	~을 제외하고	**except** an emergency 응급 사태를 제외하고

기타 관용어구	in combination with ~와 함께 in conjunction with ~와 함께 interfere with 방해하다 in accordance with ~에 따라 be compatible with ~와 호환이 되다, 어울리다

READING TEST

In the Reading Test, you will read a variety of texts and answer several different types of reading comprehension questions. The entire Reading Test will last 75 minutes. There are three parts, and directions are given for each part. You are encouraged to answer as many questions as possible within the time allowed.

You must mark your answers on the separate answer sheet. Do not write your answers in the test book.

PART 5

Directions: A word or phrase is missing in each of the sentences below. Four answer choices are given below each sentence. Select the best answer to complete the sentence. Then mark the letter (A), (B), (C), or (D) on your answer sheet.

101. Discount coupons will be provided that ------- you to enjoy savings ranging from 10 to 20 percent.

(A) promote
(B) accept
(C) allow
(D) give

102. Mr. Renon was asked to participate in a seminar entitled "How to Motivate the Staff" ------- the end of last month.

(A) regarding
(B) against
(C) above
(D) toward

103. All guests and delivery staff should first inform the security desk about which department they will be -------.

(A) accepting
(B) requesting
(C) counting
(D) visiting

104. Experts in the financial industry are now ------- concerns over the decline in investment activities.

(A) exclaiming
(B) commenting
(C) remarking
(D) addressing

105. Bearing Industries currently offers the most ------- salaries, which attract many of the industry's most skilled and talented engineers.
(A) competition
(B) compete
(C) competitors
(D) competitive

106. Although we are happy that Brian and his team won the award for best design, we still believe that the award should have been -------.
(A) we
(B) our
(C) us
(D) ours

107. Policy makers are coming up with alternatives ------- a limited supply of housing will not drive prices up sharply.
(A) in order to
(B) because of
(C) so that
(D) just as

108. Camping Moose has long been recognized for its ------- outdoor leisure services.
(A) approving
(B) magnified
(C) outstanding
(D) hopeful

109. Only one lucky customer will be the ------- of this week's prize of a holiday for two to Japan.
(A) beneficial
(B) benefit
(C) benefits
(D) beneficiary

110. Those researchers to ------- assignments have been given will be at the meeting to discuss the new project.
(A) which
(B) whom
(C) whose
(D) who

111. Any child under the age of twelve can enter the competition by ------- a well written essay about themselves and their family.
(A) submitting
(B) submitted
(C) submission
(D) submits

112. In --------- with the terms of the agreement with other distributors, all shipping fees will not be charged for the next 3 months.
(A) accordingly
(B) accosrded
(C) according
(D) accordance

113. These coupons can be used ------- any particular item displayed in this store only during the month of October.
(A) purchased
(B) purchase
(C) to purchase
(D) having purchased

114. The local tourism associations suggested that restaurants plan to increase their advertising ------- prior to the holiday season.
(A) budgets
(B) viewers
(C) fees
(D) scenes

GO ON TO THE NEXT PAGE

115. I would like to assure you that there are several ways to promote ------- services to prospective customers.

(A) mine

(B) your

(C) theirs

(D) us

116. ------- those with outstanding job performance ratings will be considered for the promotion.

(A) Almost

(B) Only

(C) Entirely

(D) Neither

117. Most companies have regulations that ------- how much they should spend on advertising for a year.

(A) determine

(B) determining

(C) determines

(D) determiner

118. Mr. Brent is waiting for an ------- about the estimated delivery and installation date from the supplier of the new computers.

(A) invoice

(B) analyst

(C) expectation

(D) update

119. After looking through all the resumes, we ------- separated the applicants with potential from those that did not meet all the requirements for the position.

(A) apparently

(B) carefully

(C) cordially

(D) aggressively

120. Most employees thought that Ms. Chin's argument in favor of using a different agency to plan the conference was very -------.

(A) persuasive

(B) persuaded

(C) persuade

(D) persuasion

121. This manual provides ------- on how to operate your new microwave oven properly.

(A) instruct

(B) instructor

(C) instructions

(D) instructional

122. We should employ a new accountant as soon as possible before the situation becomes -------.

(A) criticism

(B) critical

(C) critic

(D) critically

123. The staff at this tourism center often receive compliments on their ------- of local attractions from visitors.

(A) familiarity

(B) exhibition

(C) agreement

(D) knowledge

124. Competent and -------, Maggie Brown was an obvious choice to replace Mark as chairperson of the committee following his retirement.

(A) efficiency

(B) efficiently

(C) efficiencies

(D) efficient

125. The software company's technical service
will be ------- throughout the remainder of
the week due to unexpected problems.
(A) refrained
(B) understood
(C) unavailable
(D) affordable

126. We've tried to improve the speed with
which we serve the food in our restaurant,
but we continue to receive ------- from
customers.
(A) complaints
(B) complaining
(C) complaint
(D) complained

127. These gift vouchers are to be used
------- for the purpose of buying yourself a
new CD player for your car.
(A) sole
(B) soloist
(C) soleness
(D) solely

128. The bus company is ------- that it shares
any responsibility for the accident on Main
Street last Monday evening.
(A) splitting
(B) denying
(C) pleading
(D) granting

129. ------- much you try to avoid speaking
about this month's low sales figures, you
will need an explanation for the meeting
with the sales manager this afternoon.
(A) Moreover
(B) Because
(C) Still
(D) However

130. I think that Sharon prefers to work -------
herself, but unfortunately this project will
only succeed if each person on the team
fulfills his or her role.
(A) by
(B) in
(C) to
(D) with

GO ON TO THE NEXT PAGE

Questions 131-134 refer to the following advertisement.

Visit Holly's Flowers

Holly's Flowers, located at 59 Southern Avenue, sells the best and freshest flowers in the city. We have all kinds of flowers, ------- from roses, carnations, and lilies to exotic
131.
orchids from foreign lands. We sell flowers individually and in bunches. Speak to one of our sales staff members about the reason you're getting flowers, and they'll let you know which types of flowers are -------. We sell vases along with our flowers, and we
132.
wreaths and other floral arrangements, too.

Since spring is here, there are lots of special events, including graduations and marriages, in many people's lives. Don't ruin these ------- by purchasing wilted, inferior
133.
flowers just because you got them for a bargain price. -------
134.

131. (A) range
    (B) ranged
    (C) are ranged
    (D) ranging

132. (A) comparable
    (B) disposable
    (C) viable
    (D) appropriate

133. (A) occasional
    (B) occasions
    (C) occasionally
    (D) occasioned

134. (A) Instead, pay a bit more but get the highest quality at Holly's Flowers.
    (B) Thank you for shopping at Holly's Flowers for the past fifteen years.
    (C) And remember to give the code listed above to get a big discount.
    (D) Apparently, these flowers are popular with many shoppers nowadays.

Vice President Walton to Retire

This morning, Jessica Walton informed CEO Stanton that she intends to retire at the end of the month. Ms. Walton has ------- a job as the president of Jackson **135.** Manufacturing, which is located in Manchester, England. We wish Ms. Walton all the best as she travels across the ocean ------- a new chapter in her life. We would also **136.** like to thank Ms. Walton for her 23 years of service here at Doubleton. She has been a valuable ------- for the company, and we are going to miss her greatly. A farewell party **137.** is going to be held for Ms. Walton before she departs. ------- In the meantime, a search **138.** committee for a new vice president will be formed. Anyone interested in applying for the job should get in touch with Robert Penske at extension 506.

135. (A) applied
(B) requested
(C) transferred
(D) accepted

136. (A) begins
(B) to begin
(C) having begun
(D) will begin

137. (A) asset
(B) equipment
(C) talent
(D) strength

138. (A) She appreciated the gifts she was given.
(B) Submit your applications by the end of the month.
(C) Ms. Walton expected to see everyone there.
(D) The details of that event will be posted later.

GO ON TO THE NEXT PAGE

From: Enrico Romano

To: All Accounting Department Staff Members

Subject: Errors

Date: February 10

It has been brought to my attention that a large number of errors have been made by accountants in the past month. These include mistakes made on employee paychecks and also on contracts that we have ------- with other companies.
139.

These mistakes are unacceptable and must stop. From now on, all numbers must be double-checked by supervisors until they are confirmed. While this ------- extra hours
140.
of work, it is something that must be done to ensure that we do everything correctly.

------- If you must work overtime, then that is what you will do. Each of you must also
141.
attend some remedial accounting classes that will be held starting on February 21.

The classes are -------, and failure to take them will result in your employment being
142.
terminated.

139. (A) hired
(B) registered
(C) employed
(D) signed

140. (A) will require
(B) has required
(C) was requiring
(D) may be required

141. (A) I still expect all assignments to be completed on time.
(B) You can come to work at nine and leave at six every day.
(C) I'm very pleased with how most of you have been performing.
(D) The time of the daily meeting has been changed to four today.

142. (A) immediate
(B) mandatory
(C) extensive
(D) elective

To: <customerservice@deluxecard.com>

From <geraldsellers@mymail.com>

Re: Fraudulent Charge

Date: April 26

Dear Sir/Madam,

My name is Gerald Sellers. I recently received my Deluxe Card statement for the month of April and was incredibly ------- when I opened it. On April 2 and April 5, I was **143.** charged $500 on each date for a cash advance. I have absolutely no idea ------- these **144.** two charges are as I have never gotten a cash advance from my credit card.

I have attached a copy of the bill with the charges I am contesting circled. I ask that you please remove them from my bill since I am not responsible for them.------- **145.** It appears as though someone has obtained my credit card number and is using it without my knowledge. I would appreciate you ------- me a new card as soon as you **146.** can.

Sincerely,

Gerald Sellers

143. (A) pleased
   (B) shocked
   (C) impressed
   (D) reserved

144. (A) how
   (B) where
   (C) what
   (D) which

145. (A) In addition, please cancel that credit card immediately.
   (B) I will submit my payment within the next three days.
   (C) I still intend to use the credit card that I have been issued.
   (D) Would it be possible to have my credit limit increased?

146. (A) will issue
   (B) issued
   (C) issuing
   (D) have issued

GO ON TO THE NEXT PAGE

PART 7

Directions: In this part you will read a selection of texts, such as magazine and newspaper articles, letters, and advertisements. Each text is followed by several questions. Select the best answer for each question and mark the letter (A), (B), (C), or (D) on your answer sheet.

Questions 147-148 refer to the following notice.

Attention: All Employees

All employees must wash their hands and arms before beginning work and after using the toilet. This includes food preparers, dishwashers, servers, and anyone else who has contact with food, food utensils, or food equipment. As a general rule, bare hand contact with ready-to-eat food (e.g. sandwiches, salads, fruit, bread, etc.) should be avoided by all employees. This can be done through the use of utensils such as tongs, tissues, forks, scoops, or gloves. Food preparers may touch ready-to-eat food with their bare hands when necessary provided they strictly adhere to the hand-washing requirements. Servers are specifically prohibited from touching ready-to-eat food with their bare hands. Let's keep our workplace clean and safe!

147. Where would one most likely see this notice?

(A) In a health club
(B) In a supermarket
(C) In a hospital
(D) In a restaurant

148. What are servers not allowed to do?

(A) Enter the washroom after 7
(B) Touch food with their hands
(C) Use fragrance-free soaps
(D) Visit the workplace when off-duty

Murray, Aaron   2:55 P.M.

Hi, Carol. Where are you? The interviews are set to begin in 5 minutes.

Chapman, Carol   2:55 P.M.

I'm still waiting outside Mr. Jefferson's office. He hasn't had a chance to speak with me yet.

Murray, Aaron   2:56 P.M.

Wasn't your appointment with him for 2:30? What's going on?

Chapman, Carol   2:56 P.M.

His secretary said he's having a teleconference with a new client in Russia. She doesn't know when he'll be done.

Murray, Aaron   2:57 P.M.

Can you reschedule that meeting and talk to him later?

Chapman, Carol   2:58 P.M.

Sorry, but it's crucial that I speak with him immediately. You'd better go ahead without me.

Murray, Aaron   2:59 P.M.

Okay. But please come down as soon as you can. We've got several people to interview this afternoon.

---

149. What does Mr. Murray request that Ms. Chapman do?

(A) Speak with the client in Russia

(B) Make an appointment with Mr. Jefferson

(C) Visit his office for an interview

(D) Meet Mr. Jefferson at a later time

150. At 2:58 P.M., what does Ms. Chapman mean when she writes, "You'd better go ahead without me"?

(A) Mr. Murray should start the interviews without her.

(B) Mr. Murray should talk to Mr. Jefferson by himself.

(C) Mr. Murray should make the arrangements alone.

(D) Mr. Murray should go to lunch with everyone else.

GO ON TO THE NEXT PAGE

Negotiate Successfully

Ensure that you have top-notch negotiating skills

Negotiation is your opportunity to demonstrate your commitment (and our company's) to long-term relationships to maximize value for both parties. Good negotiation skills can increase the level of trust and credibility you have with your customers. The following checklist provides key preparation points for your next negotiation.

✓ Do not begin negotiations unless you've had the opportunity fully to present your proposition to the customer.

✓ Be certain you're dealing with a person with the authority to negotiate and make decisions.

✓ Know in advance at what point the agreement is no longer beneficial to you and our company and be prepared to walk away.

✓ Be prepared to be patient.

Of course, these are just the basics. If you sign up for our free educational seminar, you will have the opportunity to learn a great deal more about the art of negotiation. Call Tim in Human Resources (ext. 5646) and reserve your space now.

---

151. What does the notice say is a benefit of good negotiation skills?

(A) Finding a quicker solution for a problem

(B) Purchasing raw materials inexpensively

(C) Distributing products to wider areas

(D) Earning more trust from customers

152. What is NOT mentioned as a part of preparing for a negotiation?

(A) Ensure you are dealing with the right person.

(B) Make sure you arrive early.

(C) Know when to end the negotiations.

(D) Do not rush the process.

153. What should people do if they want to learn more?

(A) Call a staff member

(B) Visit an academy

(C) Go to a website

(D) Read a brochure

To: All Department Heads
From: Lisa Irvington, HR Department
Subject: Performance Reviews
Date: October 4

I'd like to remind everyone that the performance reviews for your employees need to be submitted no later than this Friday, October 8 at 5:00 P.M. All of them should refer only to the work done by the employees during the third quarter of this year. --[1]--

Since a couple of you are doing this for the first time, let me explain the process in brief. You should have already received the forms for your employees. You need to fill out the blanks on each form. --[2]-- They need to be handwritten rather than typed. Simply give your honest opinion of how each individual performed his or her duties during the months of July, August, and September. If a person did something notable, be sure to include it in the comments section at the bottom. Finally, there is a new question on this form. It asks if you believe that the employee should be retained or let go. --[3]--

If you have any questions regarding the forms, my office door is always open. Or just call me at extension 34, and I'll do my best to answer any inquiries you have. --[4]-- But please don't wait for the last minute this as I'm going to be in meetings all day on Friday and won't be able to respond to questions immediately.

154. What is NOT mentioned about the performance evaluations?

(A) They are for only a part of the year.

(B) They should be written by hand.

(C) They must indicate if employees should receive raises.

(D) They require the people writing them to make comments.

155. According to the memo, what is Ms. Irvington going to do on October 8?

(A) Pass out some forms

(B) Attend some meetings

(C) Submit her evaluations

(D) Process the forms

156. In which of the positions marked [1], [2], [3], and [4] does the following sentence best belong?

"Should you choose the latter option, you must provide a written explanation of your position."

(A) [1]

(B) [2]

(C) [3]

(D) [4]

GO ON TO THE NEXT PAGE

2015 International News Media Conference Event Program

Presentation Schedule for September 15

Presentation Topic	Presenter	Biographical Note	Venue
Freedom of the Press in the Middle East	Sa-id Albazzaz	Publisher & Editor-in-Chief, Azzaman Daily Newspaper, Iraq	Diamond Hall (2nd Floor)
Opportunities in the New Digital Media	Terry Pedersen	Executive Director of VG Multimedia, Norway	Ruby Hall (3rd Floor)
The Tabloid Boom: Opportunity or Threat?	Ake Lunde	Senior Editor of Berlingske Tidende, Denmark	Emerald Room (2nd Floor)
Photojournalism and New Visual Strategies	Jean Mounier	Head of Photography, Agence France Presse, France	Sapphire Room (1st Floor)

157. Where would this information most likely be found?

(A) On a news company's website

(B) In a university textbook

(C) On a school bulletin board

(D) n a conference information package

158. Which speaker works with photographs?

(A) Sa-id Albazzaz

(B) Jean Mounier

(C) Terry Pedersen

(D) Ake Lunde

159. Where will Terry Pedersen be making his presentation?

(A) Ruby Hall

(B) Sapphire Room

(C) Diamond Hall

(D) Emerald Room

Goldberg rejoins Generex as senior VP

Herbert Goldberg will join Generex Video in the position of senior vice president effective December 14. With responsibility for all of Generex Video's activities, Goldberg will report to Lance Brown, the CEO of the Generex Entertainment Corporation. He will be based in Los Angeles.

Goldberg originally joined Generex Video in 1997 and served as director of sales before moving to the VIP Entertainment Group, where he was the VP of International Sales. Upon his return to Generex Video, he will take over responsibilities for the home video division and will also inherit the responsibilities of senior sales VP from George Seinfeld, who departs the company on December 10.

Several other Generex executives have chosen to leave the company during the recent period of restructuring, including Marketing VP Susan Hewitt and Investor Relations VP Daniel Lim.

160. What can be inferred about Herbert Goldberg?

(A) He is the company's youngest CEO.

(B) He is responsible for a new division.

(C) He previously worked for Generex.

(D) He has won several industry awards.

161. Who is NOT known to be leaving the company soon?

(A) Daniel Lim

(B) Susan Hewitt

(C) George Seinfeld

(D) Lance Brown

GO ON TO THE NEXT PAGE

Notice to all patients:

You have rights under federal laws that ensure the protection of your health information.

- **You can ask to get a copy of your medical records.**

  In most cases, copies must be given to you within 15 days. You may have to pay for the cost of copying and mailing if you make such a request.

- **You can make corrections to your health information.**

  You can ask to change any wrong information in your file or add information to your file if it is incomplete. In most cases, the file should be changed within 30 days of your request.

- **You can control how your health information is used.**

  In general, your health information cannot be used or shared with third parties unless you give your permission by signing a specific authorization form.

This is a brief summary of the protection provided under federal health privacy law. You can learn more about your rights by visiting www.hhs.gov/privacyinfo.

162. What is the purpose of this notice?
- (A) To remind patients about insurance requirements
- (B) To request copies of medical records
- (C) To inform people about their rights
- (D) To announce changes in government policy

163. How could others access your personal information?
- (A) They must ask you to sign a form.
- (B) They must contact your employer.
- (C) They should visit a government office.
- (D) They should write a letter.

164. According to the notice, where can one receive additional information?
- (A) In a brochure
- (B) Through consultation
- (C) On a website
- (D) In a seminar

To: Jerry Armstrong <jerrya@castawaytours.com>
From: Helen Ambler <helenambler@homemail.com>
Subject: Thank You
Date: August 23

Dear Mr. Armstrong,

My husband and I recently returned home from the trip you booked for us last month. Thank you very much for everything you did. We had the time of our lives on that trip, and it was thanks to you and your staff at Castaway Tours. --[1]--

When you first proposed that we rent a car and drive through parts of Italy, I thought it was a terrible idea. However, my husband convinced me that you must have known what you were talking about, so I went along with it. --[2]-- I must admit that both of you were correct; it was incredible. Rather than flying from Venice to Florence to Rome, by driving, we got to see so much of the country. --[3]-- While going to each city, we took the opportunity to explore several small towns and lesser-known historical sites. We even had some of the best food I've ever eaten in a tiny village around seventy kilometers north of Rome.

We're already thinking about taking another trip to Europe since we had such a great time on this one. We can't decide between Spain and Hungary. --[4]-- We'll have time for two weeks of traveling in late December and early January. When you have a chance, give me a call, and my husband and I will visit your office to discuss the matter.

Helen Ambler

165. Why did Ms. Ambler write the e-mail?
(A) To apologize for her previous behavior
(B) To thank Mr. Armstrong for his contributions
(C) To request a refund from her recent trip
(D) To discuss a payment she made

166. According to Ms. Ambler, what is true about her trip?
(A) She visited more than one country.
(B) She traveled with her entire family.
(C) She stayed in hotels in small villages.
(D) She enjoyed how she traveled during it.

167. In which of the positions marked [1], [2], [3], and [4] does the following sentence best belong?

"I know you've been to each place, so which do you prefer?"

(A) [1]
(B) [2]
(C) [3]
(D) [4]

To Helen Sparks <h.sparks@freemail.com>
From Margaret Poole <clarkalbert@caresociety.com>
Subject Membership Info
Date March 15

Dear Ms. Sparks,

Thank you for your inquiry regarding membership in the Cancer Research Society. We are pleased to send you a Cancer Research Society membership application.

There has never been a better time to join the Cancer Research Society, the world's largest organization of scientists dedicated to the treatment and ultimate cure of cancer. Your membership includes an automatic subscription to Cancer Research Quarterly and The Journal of Health Online, providers of the latest research news and state-of-the-art features. Membership also provides eligibility for various grants and awards from the Cancer Research Society as well as discounts on additional scientific journal subscriptions.

Attached is additional information on the society's programs and services along with an application form and membership payment form. Please refer to the attached fact sheet for further details on membership categories and advantages. Remember that your curriculum vitae must accompany your application. If applying for student membership, proof of enrollment in a degree-granting institution is also required.

Again, thank you for your interest in the Cancer Research Society.

Sincerely,

Margaret Poole
Membership Director

168. Why was the e-mail sent to Ms. Sparks?

    (A) She joined a medical organization.

    (B) She subscribed to an online journal.

    (C) She requested some information.

    (D) She submitted an application.

169. What is NOT an advantage joining the Cancer Research Society?

    (A) The obtainment of an honorary degree

    (B) Discounts on some scientific journals

    (C) Free access to an Internet journal

    (D) Consideration for financial benefits

170. What information is included in the fact sheet?

    (A) Membership types and benefits

    (B) Recent medical research results

    (C) Details about an international conference

    (D) Lists of major medical publications

171. What additional document should Ms. Sparks submit?

    (A) A résumé

    (B) A degree

    (C) A research article

    (D) A medical report

GO ON TO THE NEXT PAGE

Questions 172-175 refer to the following text message chain.

Morris, Chris   11:22 A.M.

Susan, how are the preparations for today's luncheon going?

Anderson, Susan   11:23 A.M.

Pretty well. Bob and George both arrived and are helping me set up the chairs and tables.

Morris, Chris   11:25 A.M.

Good. I told them to see if you needed any assistance. I'm glad they're being of use to you.

Anderson, Susan   11:25 A.M.

Yeah, everything should be ready within the next ten minutes.

Morris, Chris   11:26 A.M.

What about the food? Has everything gotten there?

Anderson, Susan   11:28 A.M.

The people from Julie's Catering just came in. They're bringing the food into the room right now. Should we set it out on the tables?

Morris, Chris   11:30 A.M.

We might as well. It's close enough to lunchtime. Has the cake arrived yet?

Anderson, Susan   11:30 A.M.

What cake?

Morris, Chris   11:31 A.M.

The one we ordered from Baked Delights. Somebody was supposed to drop it off no later than 11. It should be somewhere in the room.

Anderson, Susan   11:34 A.M.

Sorry, Chris, but there isn't a cake anywhere. I don't know anything about it. Why don't you take care of it?

Morris, Chris   11:36 A.M.

I guess I'd better. I'll have to ask Percy for the contact information. He's the one who ordered it.

172. Why did Mr. Morris contact Ms. Anderson?

   (A) To ask her for some advice

   (B) To request some assistance

   (C) To receive a progress report

   (D) To tell her to make an order

173. What does Mr. Morris indicate about Bob and George?

   (A) They are two new employees.

   (B) Both of them work for a catering company.

   (C) He asked them to provide some help.

   (D) They are employed by Baked Delights.

174. At 11:34 A.M., what does Ms. Anderson mean when she writes, "Why don't you take care of it"?

   (A) She doesn't have time to fulfill Mr. Morris's request.

   (B) Mr. Morris should visit her immediately.

   (C) Mr. Morris needs to call Baked Delights.

   (D) She is going to continue setting up for the luncheon.

175. What will Mr. Morris most likely do next?

   (A) Purchase a cake

   (B) Speak with a colleague

   (C) Call Julie's Catering

   (D) Contact Bob and George

Danielle Bates
502 Tacoma Avenue
Seattle, WA 98104

Dear Ms. Bates,

Thank you for your reservation request of May 2. It is a pleasure to inform you that your seat reservations for the May 27 performance of Swan Lake have been confirmed and that two tickets (Section B1) are enclosed with this letter. Please ensure that the tickets are in line with your reservation request.

As you know, the National Dance Theater of Seattle celebrates its fiftieth anniversary this year. Over the decades, we have focused on offering superior performances on a par with troupes around the world in both ballet and contemporary dance. This season, we are proud to offer both classic ballets and contemporary works. We have developed a total of 34 ballets, including full-length ballets such as Cinderella, the Nutcracker, and Esmeralda. By offering these diverse experiences, we are able to create enriching programs that meet the wide range of requests we receive from our audiences.

If you would like to change your reservation, please call me at 555-3853, e-mail me at dschulenberg@ndts.com, or visit our ticket office on the main level of the theater building. Thank you again for your interest in our performances. We look forward to seeing you at the National Dance Theater of Seattle.

Sincerely,

Diane Schulenburg

Diane Schulenburg

To: Diane Schulenburg <dschulenberg@ndts.com>
From: Danielle Bates <dbather88@freshmail.com>
Subject: Ticket Exchange
Date: May 9

Dear Ms. Schulenburg,

Thank you for sending my tickets to me. If possible, would I be able to exchange these tickets for the same performance on May 25? Also, I would like to request one additional ticket. I have a friend who will be visiting me that day from out of town, and that particular ballet is her favorite. Please let me know if it is possible to exchange the tickets. I look forward to your reply.

Sincerely,

Danielle Bates

176. What is the purpose of the letter?
   (A) To make ticket reservations
   (B) To describe a new ballet
   (C) To respond to a request
   (D) To announce program changes

177. What is NOT mentioned as a way of changing reservations?
   (A) Sending a fax
   (B) E-mailing the representative
   (C) Visiting an office
   (D) Calling the representative

178. In the letter, the word "focused" in paragraph 2, line 2, is closest in meaning to
   (A) concentrated
   (B) enhanced
   (C) reflected
   (D) viewed

179. What is the favorite ballet of Danielle Bates's friend?
   (A) Cinderella
   (B) The Nutcracker
   (C) Swan Lake
   (D) Esmeralda

180. When would Mr. Bates like to see the play?
   (A) May 2
   (B) May 9
   (C) May 25
   (D) May 27

GO ON TO THE NEXT PAGE

Albert Young, Sparc Incorporated's longtime chief technology officer, will retire this July. Young, now 61, is a 30-year veteran of Sparc. Most recently, he worked as the leader of Sparc's successful expansion into Asian markets. For 18 of his 30 years at the multinational computer chip maker, Young was devoted to the development of cutting-edge technologies. As the head of the Sparc's technology and design division, Young oversaw the development of several new chip designs, including Sparc's newest Integra series. Industry experts attribute building a strong foundation for Sparc, which now dominates global chip markets, to Young and his dedication to the advancement of global computer industry will be recognized at an award ceremony to be held in San Diego on May 4.

"Albert has been a key contributor to Sparc's success over the years, and we wish him well in retirement," said Sparc CEO Richard Beretta in a statement. Young's last day will be July 5.

The San Diego Chamber of Commerce
cordially invites

Terrance Kent, CEO of Thames Construction, Ltd.

to its 23rd Annual Global Business Leaders Awards Ceremony
being held to honor the remarkable accomplishments of
international business leaders and pioneers
at Marquis Hotel, 333 West Harbor Drive, San Diego
on May 4 at 7:30 P.M.

Dress code is formal; cocktails and dinner will be served.
Please RSVP to Larry Ganders at l.ganders@sdcc.org.

181. What is the purpose of the article?
   (A) To inform people about a new product
   (B) To announce a retirement
   (C) To describe a marketing plan
   (D) To review employee performance

182. In what role did Mr. Young spend most of his career?
   (A) Market expansion
   (B) Development
   (C) Production
   (D) Accounting

183. In the article, the word "oversaw" in paragraph 1, line 6, is closest in meaning to
   (A) supervised
   (B) glanced
   (C) reviewed
   (D) overlooked

184. What will Mr. Young probably do at the Marquis Hotel?
   (A) Deliver a presentation
   (B) Announce a new product
   (C) Host a dinner event
   (D) Receive an award

185. Who is Terrance Kent?
   (A) A chamber representative
   (B) A company CEO
   (C) A hotel manager
   (D) A chip designer

GO ON TO THE NEXT PAGE

Evaluation Form
Gerald's Burgers

We at Gerald's Burgers strive to provide our customers with the best possible food and service. Please take a moment to answer the questions in this survey. When you complete it, submit it to the manager on duty. You will receive a coupon for a free regular fries or onion rings valid on your next visit to Gerald's Burgers.

At Gerald's Burgers, how is the...	Excellent	Good	Bad	Poor
At Gerald's Burgers, how is the...		✓		
freshness of the food	✓			
price of the food	✓			
quality of the service				✓
speed of the service			✓	

Comments: *I come to Gerald's Burgers with my family once a week. You can't beat the prices here. The food isn't bad either. But the service has been getting worse these days. The restaurant we usually visit isn't very clean either. We may start going to Happy Burgers soon. Tina Weatherly*

To Tim Bales <timbales@geraldsburgers.com>
From Lisa Cantwell <lisac@geraldsburgers.com>
Re Customer Evaluations
Date August 12

Tim,

Have you seen the results of the survey we ran during the month of July? Judy sent me the numbers ten minutes ago, and they're stunning. We aren't doing nearly as well as we had thought. And I think I've found the reasons why our revenues declined in both the first and second quarters of the year.

Overall, we got high grades for the price of our food. We already knew that we sell the cheapest burgers in the country though. But in restaurant after restaurant in every state we have stores in, we got terrible marks for the service that we provide. Many comments focused upon how poorly our employees treat our customers and how slowly they do their jobs. And there were numerous unsolicited comments about how dirty our restaurants are.

I'm putting you in charge of a committee to come up with some new guidelines for our stores. Our franchise owners are going to be contacting us soon, and we must have answers for them immediately. I need something from you no later than this Friday.

Lisa

186. According to the evaluation, what is indicated about the customer?

(A) She thinks the prices at Gerald's Burgers are high.

(B) She visits Happy Burgers each week.

(C) She is dissatisfied with the service at Gerald's Burgers.

(D) She thinks that Happy Burgers has dirty restaurants.

187. In the e-mail, the word "marks" in paragraph 2, line 3 is closest in meaning to

(A) results

(B) offers

(C) comments

(D) responses

188. What does Ms. Cantwell ask Mr. Bales to do?

(A) Contact some leading franchise owners

(B) Speak with some customers at the restaurant

(C) Lead a group dedicated to fixing the problems

(D) Meet her in her office on Friday

189. Which complaint about Gerald's Burgers do the new rules NOT address?

(A) The cleanliness of the restaurants

(B) The service the employees provide

(C) Customer-employee relations

(D) The speed that the employees work

190. What does Ms. Cantwell mention in the memo?

(A) Employees may lose their jobs for not following the rules.

(B) She will hold a meeting at headquarters on August 31.

(C) No more changes will be made at the company.

(D) Gerald's Burgers will open some new stores soon.

GO ON TO THE NEXT PAGE

Richmond (April 17) – Stanley Lawrence, the mayor of Richmond, announced at a press conference that he hopes to encourage businesses to come to the city. He stated that the city of Richmond would provide tax incentives to any business hiring ten or more local residents to full-time positions. Taxes in Richmond are higher than in most cities in the state. Mr. Lawrence aims to change that in the future though.

Mr. Lawrence also mentioned that companies looking to set up shop in Richmond won't have to deal with bureaucratic red tape. He intends to streamline the process of establishing a business and getting the necessary licenses and zoning permits. This is something about which many businesses and private individuals have loudly complained in recent years.

Finally, the mayor said that any land owned by the city would be sold at below-market prices to companies signing agreements to open shops or businesses in Richmond. The city owns a large amount of land in the downtown area, and some of it is in highly desirable locations. At the present time, the land is unused, but if Mr. Lawrence has his way, it will be sold off and built upon soon.

Apply for a job at Wilson Construction, Richmond's best construction firm.

There is a construction boom going on in Richmond these days, and you can be a part of it. Wilson Construction is now hiring. Here is a small sample of the jobs available.

Construction Worker: 2 years of experience required. Must be able to follow instructions and to work well with a team. Paid by the hour. Can earn overtime. Salary determined by experience.

Receptionist: No experience necessary. Can be trained for the job. Must have a pleasant personality. Duties include greeting visitors, answering phone calls, and taking messages. Should have good personal skills. Full-time position.

Carpenter: 5 years of experience required. Must be able to pass a basic test at the interview. A sharp eye for detail is required. Full-time position. Salary plus the opportunity to earn overtime and performance bonuses.

Truck Driver: Must have a commercial driver's license. Must have a clean driving record with no accidents. Full-time position. Must be 18 or older. No experience needed.

Visit our Web site (www.wilsonconstruction.com) and apply for these and other jobs. Get started on your career in the construction industry.

May 24

Dear Mr. Corinth,

Mr. Robertson and I were both highly impressed with you at the interview you did on May 22. We would like you to know that you passed the skills test with a grade that was the highest of all the job applicants. As a result, we would like to offer you a job at Wilson Construction.

Should you accept our offer, you can start working as soon as tomorrow. In fact, I would prefer that. We have numerous projects going on and need all the manpower we can get. You can contact me at 405-6586 with your response during regular business hours.

As for your salary, you will start at $55,000 a year. You will be paid overtime at the rate of $34 an hour. Any bonuses you earn will depend upon the quality of the work that you do and the speed that the project is completed.

I'm looking forward to hearing a positive response from you.

Sincerely,

Jeffrey Wilson
Owner, Wilson Construction

---

191. According to the article, what is true about Mr. Lawrence?

(A) He was just elected mayor of Richmond.

(B) He is a business owner in Richmond.

(C) He hopes to attract companies to Richmond.

(D) He has lived in Richmond his entire life.

192. In the article, the word "streamline" in paragraph 2, line 2 is closest in meaning to

(A) reduce

(B) examine

(C) consider

(D) simplify

193. What is NOT mentioned about the receptionist position?

(A) The person will talk on the telephone at work.

(B) It will involve full-time work.

(C) The person doing it does not need experience.

(D) Knowledge of a foreign language is desired.

194. For which position did Mr. Corinth apply?

(A) Carpenter

(B) Truck driver

(C) Receptionist

(D) Construction worker

195. When would Mr. Wilson like for Mr. Corinth to start working?

(A) On April 17

(B) On May 24

(C) On May 25

(D) On June 1

The Murray Institute
One-Day Seminar on Global Marketing
Saturday, October 12

Time	Instructor	Title
9:00 A.M. – 10:40 A.M	Roger Jackson	Legal Aspects of Global Marketing
11:00 A.M. – 12:00 P.M.	Jason Laurel	How to Market Your Firm Abroad
1:00 P.M. – 2:20 P.M.	Andrea Carter	Social Media and Global Marketing
2:30 P.M. – 4:20 P.M.	Marcus Liu	Advertising on TV in Foreign Countries
4:30 P.M. – 6:00 P.M.	Kate McDowell	Making a Profit in Another Country

All the instructors are well-known and respected in their fields. There are only 150 seats available, so make your reservation today. Visit www.murrayinstitute.com or call 609-4400 for more information. The fee for the course is $250. Sorry, but no refunds are provided.

To: All Staff, Marketing Department
From: Gloria Myers
Re: Murray Institute Seminar
Date: September 29

I recently became aware that the Murray Institute is going to be holding a seminar on global marketing a couple of weeks from now. Since we opened our first stores abroad this year, I feel that we probably have a lot to learn by attending this seminar. Please take a look at the schedule, which I have attached to this memo. If any of the lectures interest you, then I strongly suggest that you attend the seminar.

I spoke with Rod Grover in the administration office, and he said the company will cover the registration fee for everyone in the Marketing Department who wants to attend. However, I called the Murray Institute, and the person there told me that there are only 20 spaces remaining. So if you're interested in attending, let me know no later than 5:00 this evening. I'm going to call and make the reservations then. I'm planning to attend, and I hope that those of you involved in our ventures in Italy, India, and Russia will, too.

Dear Ms. Myers,

This is Stewart Morris from the Marketing Department. Thank you very much for informing me about the upcoming seminar being sponsored by the Murray Institute. I have been to three of their special events in the past, but I was unaware of this one. I looked at the schedule and am interested in attending. I would love to hear Andrea Carter speak.

I would like for you to make a reservation for me. However, I need to inform you that I will not be able to attend the last lecture. I am scheduled to fly to Moscow, Russia, at 8:00 P.M., so I have to leave for the airport no later than 5:00. Will it be a problem if I fail to see Ms. McDowell speak? If it's not an issue, please make a reservation for me for the event.

Sincerely,
Stewart Morris

196. What is NOT true about the seminar?

(A) It features lecturers that are known to others.

(B) It is going to last for one day.

(C) It has a limited number of seats.

(D) It can only be registered for online.

197. What is the purpose of the memo?

(A) To inform employees about a seminar

(B) To insist that employees attend an event

(C) To promote the company's upcoming seminar

(D) To encourage employees to focus on marketing

198. What does Ms. Myers request that people do?

(A) Get a brochure from her office

(B) Give her a registration form

(C) Contact her about attending the event

(D) Pay the registration fee in advance

199. What is the title of the lecture Mr. Morris wants to attend?

(A) Social Media and Global Marketing

(B) How to Market Your Firm Abroad

(C) Making a Profit in Another Country

(D) Advertising on TV in Foreign Countries

200. What is suggested about Mr. Morris?

(A) He is going to Russia on company business.

(B) He sometimes gives lectures on marketing.

(C) He has met Ms. McDowell in the past.

(D) He frequently travels to other countries.

Memo

Memo

Memo

20일 만에
끝내는
신(新)토익
훈련법

Third Edition
TNT
TOEIC
LORI 지음

Intensive

해설집

다락원

해설집

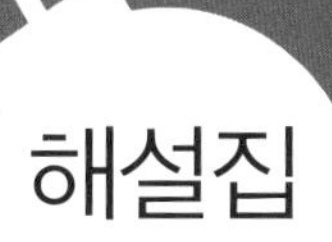

Listening Comprehension

PART 1

[정답] (A)

(A) Some people are sitting on the rear of a car.
(B) Some people are resting with caps on their laps.
(C) Some people are getting off a vehicle.
(D) Some people are fixing a wheel.

[해설]

복수 인물 사진이 제시될 때는 공통된 '동작이나 상태'가 주로 정답이 된다. 공통적인 동작 즉, 자동차 뒷부분에 앉아 있는 모습(sitting on the rear of a car)을 표현한 (A)가 정답이 된다. (B)는 허벅지 위에 모자(with caps on their laps)가 보이지 않고, (C)는 내리는 중(getting off)인 동작도 보이지 않고 (D)의 경우, 고치는(fixing) 모습이 아니므로 정답이 될 수 없다.

PART 2

1 (C)   **2** (C)   **3** (B)   **4** (A)

1

Who will help Mr. Johnson with his presentation?
(A) It's in the next room.
(B) It was really helpful.
(C) I can help him.

[해설]

'누가'를 묻는 Who 의문문은 주로 '이름, 회사, 부서, 단체명, 인칭 대명사' 등이 정답이 되기 때문에, 인칭대명사 I로 응답한 (C)가 정답이다. (A)는 장소를 묻는 Where에 대한 응답이고 (B)는 상태를 묻는 How에 대한 응답이다.

2

Who can recommend a good restaurant?
(A) I highly recommend my doctor.
(B) The fish is best today.
(C) Mr. Stern is the best person to ask.

[해설]

Who 의문문에 대해 이름 Mr. Stern으로 응답한 (C)가 정답이 된다. (A)는 질문에 나온 recommend를 반복한 함정이고, (B)는 restaurant이란 단어에 연상되는 fish를 써서 오답을 유도하고 있다.

3

Who was absent from this morning's meeting?
(A) I have to work late.
(B) Mr. Chan had an appointment with the doctor.
(C) It depends on who's absent.

[해설]

의문사 Who를 포함한 키워드 absent를 듣고 핵심 포인트 '누가 결석했는지'를 파악해야한다. 누가에 대해서 Mr. Chan으로, 과거 시제로 물었으니 과거로 응답한 (B)가 정답이 된다. (A)는 질문과 대답의 연관성이 전혀 없고, (C)는 질문에 나온 who's absent를 그대로 반복한 함정이다.

4

Who do you think is qualified for the position?
(A) I like them both.
(B) Many people applied for the position.
(C) Attendance was low.

[해설]

Who 의문문에 대해 인칭 대명사 them으로 응답한 (A)가 정답이 된다. (B)는 질문에 나온 for the position을 반복한 오답 유도 문장이고, (C)는 Who에 대한 대답이 아니다.

PART 3

1 (A)   **2** (C)   **3** (B)   **4** (C)   **5** (C)   **6** (A)

Questions 1-3 refer to the following conversation.

> W   Does this bus go to the Ryerson Mall?
> M   Yes, but it will take about an hour.
> W   That long? Is there any way I can get there faster?
> M   You should take bus 87A. It takes only 20 minutes because it travels mainly on the Gardner Highway. It will be here at this stop in a few minutes so please wait.

1

[번역]

남자의 직업은 무엇이겠는가?
(A) 그는 버스 기사이다.
(B) 그는 기계공이다.
(C) 그는 치과의사이다.
(D) 그는 학교 선생님이다.

[해설]

대화의 전반적인 내용 및 상황 파악을 전제로 풀어야 하는 문제이다. 여자는 남자에게 버스가 특정 장소에 가는지, 더 빠른 노선은 없는지 질문하고, 남자는 이에 대해 답변하고 있으므로 남자는 버스 운전기사로 유추할 수 있다.

[어휘]

occupation 직업 ｜ mechanic 기계공 ｜ dentist 치과의사

2

[번역]

남자는 왜 87A번을 권하는가?
(A) 에어컨이 잘 작동한다.
(B) 휠체어를 타고 탑승할 수 있다.
(C) 어떤 장소에 더 빨리 도착할 것이다.
(D) 요금이 훨씬 저렴하다.

[해설]

라이어슨 몰로 가는 더 빠른 노선은 없냐는 여자의 질문에 남자는 You should take bus 87A. It takes only 20 minutes because it travels mainly on the Gardner Highway라고 답변한다. 남자가 운행하는 버스는 1시간이 걸리는데 반해 87A는 20분이면 된다고 하므로 (C)가 정답이다.

[어휘]

recommend 추천하다 | excellent 훌륭한 | accessible 접근이 용이한 | arrive 도착하다 | location 장소 | soon 곧, 빠른 시일 내에 | seat 좌석 | expensive 비싼

3

[번역]

여자는 아마도 다음에 무엇을 할 것인가?
(A) 동료에게 전화를 한다.
(B) 다른 차량을 기다린다.
(C) 환불을 요청한다.
(D) 이메일을 확인한다.

[해설]

남자는 87A라는 노선을 안내해 준 뒤, It will be here at this stop in a few minutes so please wait이라고 여자에게 말한다. 그러므로 좀 더 빨리 특정 장소에 도착하기를 원하는 여자는 남자의 권유에 따를 것임을 유추할 수 있다. 그러므로 정답은 (B)가 된다.

[어휘]

probably 아마도 | colleague 동료 | vehicle 차량 | request 요청하다 | refund 환불

Questions 4-6 refer to the following conversation.

> M Susan, how did your interview with Parabolic Consulting go?
> W Actually, Dave, I haven't had it yet. It was supposed to be this Wednesday, but it got postponed until next Monday.
> M That gives you a few more days to prepare for it.
> W That's true, but I don't think I need to do too much more to get ready.
> M Are you sure about that? You can always learn more about the company at which you're interviewing. If you use the names of some employees or mention specific products or services it sells, you'll impress the interviewers.
> W You know, that's a good point. I think I probably ought to prepare a bit more.
> M That's the spirit. Let me know if you need any help.

4

[번역]

여자는 언제 면접을 볼 예정인가?
(A) 이번 주 월요일
(B) 이번 주 수요일
(C) 다음 주 월요일
(D) 다음 주 수요일

[해설]

여자의 면접은 원래 이번 주 수요일이었지만, 다음 주 월요일로 연기되었다.

5

[번역]

남자는 여자가 무엇을 할 것을 제안하는가?
(A) 시간을 내 준 것에 대해 면접관에게 고마워한다
(B) 회사에서 만든 제품을 구입한다
(C) 파라볼라 컨설팅에 대해 더 알아본다
(D) 면접에 관해 그의 직원들과 이야기한다

[해설]

You can always learn more about the company at which you're interviewing.이라는 남자의 조언에서 정답의 단서를 찾을 수 있다. 남자는 여자에게 면접을 볼 회사에 대해 더 많이 알아보라고 충고하고 있다.

6

[번역]

남자가 "That's the spirit"이라고 말할 때 남자는 무엇을 의미하는가?
(A) 그는 여자가 자신의 충고를 따르겠다는 말에 기뻐한다.
(B) 그는 여자가 회사의 제안을 받아들이기를 원한다.
(C) 그는 기꺼이 여자의 면접 준비를 도우려고 한다.
(D) 그는 여자에게 그 일자리에 지원할 자격이 있다고 믿는다.

[해설]

That's the spirit.은 직역하면 '바로 그 자세야' 혹은 '바로 그 정신이야'라는 의미인데, 실질적으로는 '잘하고 있다'는 격려의 뜻을 나타낸다.

[어휘]

be willing to 기꺼이 ~하다 | qualified for ~에 대한 자격을 갖춘

PART 4

1 (C)　**2** (D)　**3** (A)

Questions 1-3 refer to the following talk.

> Good morning and welcome to *Regina Living*. I'm your host, Diane Simmons. Today's guest will be Ronald Proctor, founder of the Proctor Job Recruiters located here in downtown Regina. For the first segment of our show, Mr. Proctor will be talking about his book, *The Best Job for You*, which was released just last month by Eglinton Books. During the last segment of today's show, members of the

1

[번역]

화자는 누구겠는가?
(A) 소설 작가
(B) 도서 편집자
(C) 토크쇼 진행자
(D) 전화 교환원

[해설]

첫 문장에서 '레지나 리빙' 시간이라고 한 뒤 바로 이어 I'm your host,
Diane Simmons라며 본인을 진행자라고 밝히므로 (C)가 정답이 된다.

[어휘]

novel 소설 │ editor 편집자 │ operator (전화)교환원

2

[번역]

담화에 따르면, 로날드 프록터는 최근 무엇을 했는가?
(A) 컨퍼런스에서 연설했다.
(B) 연구에 투자했다.
(C) 회사를 열었다.
(D) 책을 출판했다.

[해설]

'로날드 프록터의 최근'이 문제의 핵심 어구임을 감안하고 담화를 듣
도록 한다. 중반부의 Mr. Proctor will be talking about his book, *The
Best Job for You*, which was released just last month by Eglinton
Books를 통해 최근에(recently) 저서가 출간되었음을 알 수 있다. 따라
서 (D)가 정답이다.

[어휘]

recently 최근 │ finance 자금을 대다 │ publish 출판하다

3

[번역]

청중은 후반부에 무엇을 할 수 있는가?
(A) 질문을 한다.
(B) 비디오를 본다.
(C) 커피를 마신다.
(D) 기사를 읽는다.

[해설]

문제의 핵심 어구 'during the second segment'에 유의해 담화를 들으
면, 후반부의 During the last segment of today's show, members of
the audience will have a chance to ask Mr. Proctor questions에서 정
답 (A)를 찾을 수 있다.

[어휘]

have 먹다, 마시다 │ article 기사

PART 1

[정답] (B)

(A) Some plants are being hung
　　from the ceiling.
(B) The men are wearing
　　uniforms.
(C) A tablecloth is being
　　removed.
(D) The chefs are lighting a
　　candle.

[해설]

2인 사진이 제시될 때는 두 사람의 공통점을 나타내는 서술부에 집중
해야 한다. 두 사람이 유니폼을 입은 상태(wearing uniforms)를 표현한
(B)가 정답이 된다. 사물이 주어인데 사람의 동작을 나타내는 현재진행
형 (be + −ing)으로 표현한 (A)와 (C)는 불가하다. 사진에서 초(candle)
가 보이지 않으므로 (D) 또한 정답이 아니다.

PART 2

1 (C)　　**2** (B)　　**3** (C)　　**4** (A)

1

What's wrong with the fax machine?
(A) My vacuum cleaner broke down.
(B) Next to the school.
(C) It won't print.

[해설]

의문사 What이 주어이고 is가 따라 나올 때는 축약되어 What's로 표현
되므로 우선 발음에 익숙해져야 하고 그 다음 나오는 형용사를 잘 들
어야 한다. '팩스기에 뭐가 문제냐'라는 질문에 '출력이 안 된다'고 답한
(C)가 정답이 된다. (A)는 진공청소기에 대한 이야기이고, (B)는 의문
사 Where에 대한 응답이다.

2

What kind of work does Ms. Eden do?
(A) She is hardworking.
(B) Mostly administrative work.
(C) She sent an e-mail.

[해설]

What 다음에 kind라는 명사가 나오므로 '종류'를 묻는 문제이다. 따라
서 Ms. Eden이 하는 일의 종류가 행정 업무임을 밝힌 (B)가 정답이 된
다. (A)는 질문의 work와 발음이 비슷한 hardworking을 이용한 오답
유도 문장이고, (C)는 시제나 내용이 질문과 어울리지 않는다.

3

What time are we supposed to take a break?
(A) By the end of this week.
(B) Two hours and a half.
(C) At two thirty.

[해설]

의문문이 What time '몇 시' 즉 '시각'을 묻는 문제이므로 정확한 시각을 나타낸 (C)가 정답이 된다. (A)는 시점을 묻는 When(언제)~?에 대한 응답이고, (B)는 기간을 나타내는 How long(얼마나 오래)~?에 대한 응답이므로 답이 될 수 없다.

4

What type of car do you want to buy?
(A) Something with plenty of space.
(B) The dining car is full.
(C) No, I'm not interested.

[해설]

What 다음에 type이라는 명사가 나오므로 '어떤 종류'를 묻는 문제이다. 어떤 종류를 묻는 질문에 대한 정답으로 'something + 수식어(~한 어떤 것)'가 자주 출제되며 정답으로는 (A)가 알맞다. (B)는 질문의 car를 반복한 함정이고, (C)는 의문사 의문문에 No로 대답했으므로 불가하다.

PART 3

1 (C)　**2** (D)　**3** (A)　**4** (C)　**5** (A)　**6** (A)

Questions 1-3 refer to the following conversation.

> M　I am sorry but there aren't any empty spaces in this parking lot.
> W　My two boys and I have tickets to see the baseball game here. I don't know what I'll do if I can't find a place to park.
> M　Oh, you must not have read the notice. There are some empty parking spaces just one block east of here in front of the St. Richard Outdoor Market. That market is closed today because it's Sunday, but anybody can use the parking lot.
> W　Thank you very much for that information.

1
[번역]

남자는 누구인가?
(A) 뉴스 리포터
(B) 무대 배우
(C) 주차요원
(D) 야구 코치

[해설]

남자는 I am sorry but there aren't any empty spaces in this parking lot이라는 말로 대화를 시작하고 있다. 방문객에게 주차장 상황에 대해 알려주고 있으므로 (C)가 답임을 알 수 있다.

[어휘]

stage 무대 ｜ attendant 종업원, 안내인

2
[번역]

무엇이 문제인가?

(A) 여자의 차에 시동이 걸리지 않는다.
(B) 정문이 잠겨있다.
(C) 표가 매진되었다.
(D) 시설이 현재 꽉 찼다.

[해설]

남자의 말 I am sorry but there aren't any empty spaces in this parking lot에서 또 다시 단서가 제시되므로, 대화를 듣기 전에 미리 문제를 읽어 두고 주요 정보를 놓치지 않도록 주의해서 풀어야 한다. 주차 공간이 없다는 말을 full이라는 단어로 묘사한 (D)가 답이 된다.

[어휘]

locked 잠긴 ｜ be sold out 매진되다 ｜ facility 시설 ｜ currently 현재 ｜ full 꽉 찬

3
[번역]

남자는 여자에게 무엇을 하라고 제안하는가?
(A) 다른 장소에 가 본다.
(B) 다른 날 다시 온다.
(C) 다른 섹션에 앉는다.
(D) 전액 환불을 요청한다.

[해설]

제안 사항은 주로 대화의 후반부에서 제시된다는 점을 유념하고 대화를 들어보자. 남자는 There are some empty parking spaces just one block east of here in front of the St. Richard Outdoor Market ~ anybody can use the parking lot이라고 말하며 차를 주차할 수 있는 다른 장소를 알려준다. 그러므로 정답은 (A)가 된다.

[어휘]

try 시도해 보다 ｜ different 다른 ｜ location 장소 ｜ return 돌아오다 ｜ section 구획 ｜ request 요청하다 ｜ full 전체의 ｜ refund 환불

Questions 4-6 refer to the following conversation with three speakers.

> W1　I thought Tony stood out more than the other two people we interviewed.
> M　Why do you feel that way?
> W1　He's got a lot of experience in marketing, and he handled every single question that we asked well.
> W2　I thought he did a good job, but I believe Simon would be a better person to hire.
> M　I felt the opposite. I wasn't impressed with him at all. He didn't seem well prepared and hesitated when answering some questions.
> W1　That's precisely how I feel.
> W2　Well, I got a good feeling about him. I didn't really like either Tony or Marcia.
> M　I agree with you about Marcia but not regarding Tony.

4
[번역]

화자들은 주로 무엇에 관해 이야기하고 있는가?
(A) 입사 지원자에게 얼마를 제시해야 하는지

(B) 어떤 직위에 신입 사원이 필요한지
(C) 인터뷰 결과
(D) 언제 직원을 고용해야 하는지

[해설]

대화 첫 부분의 the other two people we interviewed라는 어구를 통해
정답을 유추할 수 있다. 이후에도 세 사람은 면접을 본 세 명에 대해 각
자의 의견을 피력하고 있으므로 정답은 (C)이다.

[어휘]

job candidate 입사 지원자

5

[번역]

남자는 사이먼을 어떻게 생각하는가?
(A) 그는 사이먼의 행동에 대해 깊은 인상을 받지 못했다.
(B) 그는 사이먼이 준비가 잘 되어 있었다고 생각했다.
(C) 그는 사이먼이 질문에 대답한 방식이 마음에 들었다.
(D) 그는 사이먼이 필요한 경력을 갖추고 있다고 생각했다.

[해설]

사이먼이 고용하기에 나은 인물이라는 여자2의 말에 남자는 반대 의견
을 제시하면서 I wasn't impressed with him at all.라고 말한다. 따라서
남자는 사이먼에게 깊은 인상을 받지 못했다.

6

[번역]

화자들은 다음에 무엇을 할 것 같은가?
(A) 어떤 사람을 고용할지 결정한다
(B) 다른 회사의 일자리에 지원한다
(C) 다른 면접을 실시한다
(D) 이력서를 제출한다

[해설]

면접을 본 세 명의 입사 지원자의 장단점에 대해 이야기하고 있으므로
결국에는 누구를 채용할 것인지를 결정할 것이다.

PART 4

1 (B) 2 (A) 3 (D)

Questions 1-3 refer to the following announcement.

May I have your attention, please? I just spoke with
Captain Russell, and he said that we're almost ready
to depart. The mechanics have identified the problem
and taken care of everything. All they need to do
is pack up their tools. Once they finish doing that,
we'll close the doors and start taxiing to the runway.
I know you're all eager to get going, so please take
your seats and fasten your seatbelts. We should be
in the air within the next ten minutes. On behalf of
Eagle Airlines, I would like to apologize for this delay.
As soon as we reach our cruising altitude, we'll start
handing out free drinks and snacks. That's our way
of saying sorry for inconveniencing you.

1

[번역]

화자들은 어디에 있는 것 같은가?
(A) 탑승 게이트에
(B) 비행기에
(C) 수화물 찾는 곳에
(D) 탑승 수속대에

[해설]

Captain(기장), Airlines(항공사)와 같은 단어나 start taxiing to the
runway, as soon as we reach our cruising altitude와 같은 표현에 주의
하면 이 안내방송은 기내에서 이루어지고 있는 것임을 알 수 있다.

[어휘]

boarding gate 탑승 게이트 | baggage claim area 수화물 찾는 곳 |
check-in counter 탑승 수속대, 체크인 카운터

2

[번역]

문제에 대해 무엇이 언급되고 있는가?
(A) 수리되었다.
(B) 새 부품이 필요하다.
(C) 수리하는데 10분이 걸릴 것이다.
(D) 지금 당장 수리할 수가 없다.

[해설]

All they need to do is pack up their tools.(해야 할 일은 도구를 챙기는
것뿐이다.)라는 말을 통해 문제가 모두 해결되었음을 알 수 있다.

[어휘]

part 부분; 부품

3

[번역]

여자가 "That's our way of saying sorry for inconveniencing you"라
고 말했을 때, 여자는 무엇을 의미하는가?
(A) 승무원들이 승객들의 기분을 북돋으려고 할 것이다.
(B) 공중에서 기장이 잃어버린 시간을 만회해 줄 것이다.
(C) 항공사가 승객들에게 돈으로 보상을 해 줄 것이다.
(D) 청자들은 사과의 표시로 음식을 받게 될 것이다.

[해설]

앞 문장에서 무료로 음료와 간식을 제공하겠다고 말한 후, "불편을 끼
쳐 드린 것에 대한 저희의 사과 방식이다"라고 그 이유를 밝히고 있다.
따라서 정답은 (D)이다.

[어휘]

flight attendant (비행기) 승무원 | cheer up 기분을 북돋다 | make
up for ~을 만회하다, ~을 보충하다 | reimburse 변제하다, 보상하다 |
apology 사과, 사죄

PART 1

[정답] (B)

(A) A man is recapping a bottle.
(B) There are some bottles on the table.
(C) Some bottles are lying on their sides.
(D) A cook is chopping some vegetables.

[해설]

보기의 주어가 다양하므로 각각의 주어 및 서술어가 사진과 일치하는지 주의해서 들어야 한다. 병들이 탁자 위에 놓여 있는 모습을 표현한 (B)가 정답이다. (A)와 (C)는 사진 속에 등장하는 bottle을 이용하고 있지만 남자가 병뚜껑을 닫는 모습(recapping)도, 병들이 엎어져 있는 모습(lying on their sides)도 아니다. (D)는 사진과 관련이 없는 문장이다.

PART 2

1 (B) **2** (B) **3** (B) **4** (A)

1

When can you finish editing the proposal?
(A) Yes, it's in the cabinet.
(B) Tomorrow morning.
(C) It's for my supervisor.

[해설]

의문사 When(언제)은 '때'를 묻는 질문이므로 '내일 아침'이라는 시점을 제시한 (B)가 정답이 된다. (A)는 의문사 의문문에 yes/no로 대답했고 (C)는 시점을 묻는 질문과 관계없는 응답이므로 모두 정답이 될 수 없다.

2

When is the board meeting in Toronto?
(A) For a day or two.
(B) Probably early next week.
(C) At a company in Moscow.

[해설]

시점을 묻는 의문사 When에 대한 정답은 '다음 주 초'라는 내용의 (B)가 된다. (A)는 기간을 묻는 의문사 How long~?에 대한 응답이고 (C)는 장소를 묻는 Where에 알맞은 응답이므로 정답이 될 수 없다.

3

When do you have to get the repairs finished?
(A) For two days.
(B) By tomorrow at the latest.
(C) We fixed it a week ago.

[해설]

When 의문문으로 수리가 '언제' 끝나는지 묻는 질문에 늦어도 내일까지는 끝난다고 답한 (B)가 정답이다. (A)는 기간을 묻는 How long~?에 대한 응답이고 (C)는 질문과 시제가 어울리지 않는다.

4

When are we supposed to meet for the session?
(A) In half an hour.
(B) In Conference Room C.
(C) The search is still on.

[해설]

시점을 묻는 의문사 When에 가장 적절하게 응답한 문장은 '30분 후에'라고 응답한 (A)이다. (B)는 장소를 묻는 의문사 Where에 대한 응답이고, (C)는 질문과 동떨어진 내용이므로 정답으로 불가하다.

PART 3

1 (B) **2** (B) **3** (B) **4** (B) **5** (C) **6** (C)

Questions 1-3 refer to the following conversation.

W I just spoke to the owner of Bert's Diner on the phone. Their oven is not working so they can't prepare lunch.

M Then why don't we just eat at Wilma's Café instead?

W There are only four or five tables in that café. They can't possibly accommodate the 23 people attending this conference.

M Oh, you haven't heard about their recent expansion? They were closed for a month to allow for the addition of two more rooms. They reopened last Thursday and now have space for over 40 guests.

1

[번역]

화자들은 왜 계획대로 버트 식당에 갈 수 없는가?
(A) 매니저가 아프다.
(B) 장비가 하나 고장이다.
(C) 일부 식품이 배달되지 않았다.
(D) 수도관 하나가 물이 샌다.

[해설]

질문의 핵심 어구인 Bert's Diner가 언급되는 부분을 잘 들어 보아야 한다. 여자는 I just spoke to the owner of Bert's Diner on the phone. Their oven is not working so they can't prepare lunch라며 버트 식당이 영업을 할 수 없는 이유를 설명하고 있으므로 oven이라는 하나의 기기를 a piece of equipment로 표현한 (B)가 답이 된다. 참고로, equipment는 불가산명사이기 때문에 an equipment나 equipments로 쓰지 않는다는 점을 알아두자.

[어휘]

as planned 계획대로 | equipment 장비 | broken 고장 난 | item 제품 | deliver 배달하다 | leak (물이) 새다

2

[번역]

화자들은 누구를 위해 점심을 준비하고 있는가?
(A) 신입사원들

(B) 행사 참석자들
(C) 학교 아이들
(D) 외국 투자가들

[해설]

여자는 윌마 카페로 가자는 남자의 말에 반대하며 They can't possibly accommodate the 23 people attending this conference라는 이유를 제시한다. people attending this conference를 적절히 paraphrasing한 (B)가 답이 된다.

[어휘]

arrange 마련하다, 준비하다 | participant 참석자 | investor 투자가

3
[번역]

윌마 카페는 언제 다시 영업을 시작했는가?
(A) 어제
(B) 지난주
(C) 2주 전
(D) 지난달

[해설]

마지막 대화문 중 They reopened last Thursday에서 말하는 They는 윌마 카페를 의미하므로 정답은 (B)가 된다.

Questions 4-6 refer to the following conversation and schedule.

> M That was an excellent talk by Walter Mitchell we heard now.
> W I agree. I thought his insights on the oil industry were brilliant. I never even considered looking at the industry the way he does.
> M You can say that again. So which speaker do you want to listen to next?
> W I'm thinking about attending the talk by Holly Morris. I've read a couple of her books. Do you want to listen to her talk?
> M No, thanks. You go ahead and do that. I'm going to get some lunch.
> W All right. When do you want to meet up again?
> M The only other speaker I'm interested in hearing today is Jane Cross. She's an old friend from college.
> W I wasn't aware of that. Okay, I'll see you at her talk then.

4
[번역]

여자는 홀리 모리스에 대해 무엇을 암시하는가?
(A) 그녀는 석유 업계에서 일한다
(B) 그녀는 작가이다.
(C) 그녀는 대학에 다닌다.
(D) 그녀는 그녀의 친구이다.

[해설]

여자는 홀리 모리스의 강연을 생각 중이라고 말한 후, I've read a couple of her books.라고 언급한다. 이를 통해 그녀는 작가라는 사실을 알 수 있으므로 정답은 (B)이다.

5
[번역]

남자는 다음에 무엇을 할 것인가?
(A) 대학 친구를 만난다
(B) 다른 연설을 듣는다
(C) 식사를 한다
(D) 책을 읽는다

[해설]

강연을 듣자는 여자의 제안에 남자는 거절의 뜻을 전하면서 I'm going to get some lunch.라고 말한다. 따라서 남자는 강연을 듣지 않고 점심 식사를 하러 갈 것이다.

6
[번역]

도표를 보아라. 남자와 여자는 몇 시에 만날 것인가?
(A) 12시에
(B) 1시에
(C) 2시에
(D) 3시에

[해설]

대화의 후반부에서 남자와 여자는 제인 크로스의 강연에서 다시 만나게 될 것이라는 점을 알 수 있다. 일정표에 제인 크로스의 강연은 2시에서 3시까지 진행된다고 나타나 있으므로 두 사람이 만나게 될 시각은 2시가 된다.

PART 4

1 (D)   2 (C)   3 (A)

Questions 1-3 refer to the following announcement.

> On behalf of Jasper International Travel, I'd like to welcome you to our international bus tour. We will be departing in just a few minutes. The bus will be traveling for approximately 2 hours before we reach the US-Mexico border and cross into the beautiful beachside city of San Juan, Mexico. According to the latest weather forecast, we are in for sunny skies all day today so you will have a lot of chances to enjoy spectacular views of the Pacific Ocean. Before we leave, please be sure that you have both your ticket and passport as Mexican border inspectors will be checking for these items.

1

[번역]

본 담화는 어디에서 이루어지는가?
(A) 비행기에서
(B) 미술품 경매장에서
(C) 해안 리조트에서
(D) 관광 버스에서

[해설]

첫 문장의 I'd like to welcome you to our international bus tour에서 결정적인 단서(international bus tour)를 들을 수 있다. 따라서 (D)가 정답이 된다.

[어휘]

auction 경매 ┃ resort 휴양지

2

[번역]

화자에 따르면, 청중은 오늘 무엇을 할 것인가?
(A) 가까운 해안을 항해한다.
(B) 새 여권들을 받는다.
(C) 외국에 들어간다.
(D) 산 후안의 박물관을 방문한다.

[해설]

중반부에서 대략적으로 소요되는 시간을 언급한 뒤 we reach the US-Mexico border and cross into the beautiful beachside city of San Juan, Mexico라며 미국 멕시코 국경을 넘어 멕시코의 해안 도시로 갈 것이라고 구체적인 일정을 덧붙이므로 가장 적절한 것은 Mexico를 foreign country라 바꿔 표현한 (C)가 된다. 버스로 두 시간 걸려 해안 도시로 가기 때문에 sail(항해한다)이라고 제시한 (A)를 정답으로 고르지 않도록 주의해야 한다.

[어휘]

sail 항해하다

3

[번역]

화자는 청중에게 어떻게 해달라고 요청하는가?
(A) 여행 서류들을 확실히 챙겨라.
(B) 티켓을 일찍 구입하라.
(C) 휴대전화 전원을 꺼라.
(D) 중요한 소지품들을 포장하라.

[해설]

화자의 요청 및 제안 사항은 대체로 담화의 후반부에서 확인할 수 있다는 점을 유념하자. 마지막 문장에서 please be sure that you have both your ticket and passport라며 '티켓 및 여권'을 잘 챙기라고 당부하고 있다. 이 두 서류를 travel documents로 표현한 (A)가 정답이다.

[어휘]

ensure 확실하게 하다, 보증하다 ┃ document 서류 ┃ purchase 구입하다, 사다 ┃ turn off (전원을) 끄다 ┃ pack 포장하다, (짐을) 꾸리다 ┃ essential 필수의, 없어서는 안 될

PART 1

[정답] (C)

(A) The man is handing a paper to the woman.
(B) The woman is opening a binder.
(C) They are facing each other.
(D) The man is positioning a piece of equipment.

[해설]

두 사람의 공통점을 나타내는 '동작이나 상태'를 facing each other(서로 마주보고 있다)라고 표현한 (C)가 정답이 된다. (A)의 서류를 건네는(handing a paper) 모습도, (B)에서 언급된 바인더를 펼치는(opening a binder)모습도, 그리고 (D)에서 언급된 배치하고 있는(positioning)모습도 보이지 않는다.

PART 2

1 (C)   2 (B)   3 (A)   4 (A)

1

Where do you park your car?
(A) The park is crowded.
(B) Almost 10 hours.
(C) Behind the hospital.

[해설]

Where 의문문은 장소를 묻는 의문사이므로 '전치사 + 장소'가 주로 정답이 된다. 전치사 behind + 장소로 대답한 (C)가 정답이다. (A)는 다의어인 park를 이용한 함정이고, (B)는 How long에 대한 응답이다.

2

Where is the home office located?
(A) The president will make a speech.
(B) In the downtown area.
(C) In the top drawer.

[해설]

장소와 관련된 Where을 사용해 본사의 위치를 묻는 문제이므로 구체적 장소를 제시한 (B)가 정답이다. (A)는 Who(누가)에 대한 응답이고, (C)는 질문의 주어 home office(본사)와 어울리지 않는다.

3

Where do you keep the staplers?
(A) In the bottom drawer.
(B) The staples are on Mr. Parker's desk.
(C) It must be about papers.

[해설]

Where 의문문에 구체적 장소(서랍 안)로 답한 (A)가 정답이다. (B)는 staplers와 발음이 유사한 staples를 사용해서 오답을 유도하는 문장이고, (C)는 무엇에 관한 것이냐는 질문에 대한 응답이다.

4

Where can I find the number for the laundry?
(A) Try the directory.
(B) Between 3 and 5.
(C) Sorry, I can't remember them.

[해설]

장소를 묻는 Where 의문문에 대해 구체적 장소를 제시하지 않고 '~을 확인해라'는 의미로 try나 check로 시작되는 구문으로 답할 수 있다. 따라서 '전화번호부를 찾아보라'는 (A)가 정답이 된다. (B)는 시간/수를 묻는 질문에 대한 응답이고 (C)는 them이 무엇인지 알 수가 없다.

PART 3

1 (A) **2** (C) **3** (B) **4** (A) **5** (D) **6** (B)

Questions 1-3 refer to the following conversation.

> W Bill, what is that noise coming from inside the conference room?
>
> M They finally started renovations. They're replacing the old floor tiles and repainting the walls and ceiling.
>
> W Well, any change to that ugly room would be great. My office looks much better ever since they replaced the chair and desk last week. Especially, the leather office chair is so comfortable.
>
> M I haven't been in your office since the new furniture was put in. Why don't we have a cup of coffee in your office now?

1
[번역]

회의실에서는 어떤 일이 벌어지고 있는가?
(A) 어떠한 개선이 진행되고 있다.
(B) 누군가 발표를 하고 있다.
(C) 계약서 조항들이 논의되고 있다.
(D) 수명이 다한 전구가 교체되고 있다.

[해설]

여자가 회의실에서부터 들려오는 소음의 정체가 무엇인지 묻자 남자는 They finally started renovations. They're replacing the old floor tiles and repainting the walls and ceiling이라고 대답한다. renovations를 improvements로 표현한 (A)가 정답이다.

[어휘]

improvement 개선 | presentation 발표 | term 조항 | contract 계약 (서) | bulb 전구

2
[번역]

여자는 새 사무실 의자에 대해 뭐라고 말하는가?
(A) 등받이가 너무 낮다.
(B) 바퀴가 부러졌다.
(C) 매우 편안하다.

(D) 천으로 만들어졌다.

[해설]

문제의 핵심 어구인 new office chair가 언급되는 부분을 잘 들어 보아야 한다. 여자는 Especially, the leather office chair is so comfortable이라고 말하고 있으므로 (C)가 정답임을 알 수 있다.

[어휘]

wheel 바퀴 | broken 고장 난, 부러진 | fabric 직물

3
[번역]

남자가 하고 싶어 하는 것은 무엇인가?
(A) 보고서를 끝낸다.
(B) 어떤 사무실에 간다.
(C) 페인트 공들을 만난다.
(D) 전화를 건다.

[해설]

남자가 원하는 사항을 묻고 있으므로 남자의 말에서 단서를 찾을 수 있으리라 예상할 수 있다. 남자의 마지막 대화문 Why don't we have a cup of coffee in your office now?에서 여자의 사무실에 가 보고 싶어 한다는 것을 알 수 있으므로 (B)가 답이 된다.

[어휘]

finish 끝내다 | painter 페인트 공

Questions 4-6 refer to the following conversation.

> W Good afternoon. This is the Bayside Hotel. How may I help you?
>
> M Hello. My name is Roger Smith. I have a reservation for today, but I'm going to arrive later than expected.
>
> W We normally hold reservations until 7:30. Are you going to be coming here after that time?
>
> M Yes, I am. My plane is going to take off a couple of hours late, so I most likely won't be at the hotel until 10:00. Will my reservation still be valid?
>
> W Since you called, we'll be sure not to cancel it.
>
> M That's great. Thank you very much. By the way, will the hotel shuttle bus still be running at around 9:30?
>
> W Sorry, but the last one leaves the airport at 9:00.

4
[번역]

남자는 왜 늦을 것인가?
(A) 그의 비행기가 연착되었다.
(B) 기차를 놓쳤다.
(C) 날씨가 좋지 않다.
(D) 그의 차가 고장이 났다.

[해설]

My plane is going to take off a couple of hours late라는 부분에서 비행기 연착으로 남자가 늦게 도착할 것이라는 점을 알 수 있다.

5

[번역]

남자는 여자가 무엇을 할 것을 요청하는가?

(A) 객실을 업그레이드한다

(B) 예약을 취소한다

(C) 숙박을 하루 연장한다

(D) 객실을 잡아 둔다

[해설]

Will my reservation still be valid?라는 질문을 통해, 남자는 자신이 예약한 방을 취소시키지 말 것을 요청하고 있다. 따라서 정답은 (D)이다.

[어휘]

upgrade 업그레이드하다 | extend 늘이다, 확장하다 | stay 체류

6

[번역]

마지막 셔틀 버스는 공항에서 몇 시에 출발하는가?

(A) 7시 30분

(B) 9시

(C) 9시 30분

(D) 10시

[해설]

여자의 마지막 말, Sorry, but the last one leaves the airport at 9:00.에서 막차는 9시에 출발한다는 것을 알 수 있다.

PART 4

1 (A)   **2** (C)   **3** (C)

Questions 1-3 refer to the following message and map.

> Hi, Rick. I think you might have a minor problem finding my office for today's interview <u>since you've never been to the city before</u>. So why don't I give you directions here? Once you cross the East River Bridge, keep going straight for two blocks. Just so you know, you'll be heading north. At the second intersection, <u>there will be a gas station on your right. You need to turn left at that intersection and then drive half a block</u>. There's a parking garage on the right-hand side of the street. Park there. Then, you need to cross the street. My office is <u>in the building opposite the parking garage</u>. If you can't find it, give me a call, and <u>I'll go outside to meet you</u>. See you soon. Bye.

1

[번역]

릭은 왜 화자의 사무실을 방문하려고 하는가?

(A) 일자리 때문에 만나기 위해

(B) 발표를 하기 위해

(C) 계약에 관한 협상을 하기 위해

(D) 제안을 하기 위해

[해설]

릭이 화자를 방문하려는 이유는 메시지 첫 부분의 for today's interview라는 전치사구에서 확인할 수 있다.

[어휘]

negotiate 협상하다 | make a proposal 제안하다

2

[번역]

화자는 릭이 무엇을 할 것을 요청하는가?

(A) 도착하면 그에게 문자 메시지를 보낸다

(B) 필요한 모든 파일을 가지고 온다

(C) 사무실을 찾지 못하면 그에게 전화를 한다

(D) 도착하는 대로 밖에서 기다린다

[해설]

메시지 후반부의 If you can't find it, give me a call, and I'll go outside to meet you.에서 정답을 확인할 수 있다. 릭에게 요청하는 사항은 위치를 찾지 못하는 경우 전화를 하라는 것이다.

3

[번역]

지도를 보아라. 남자의 사무실은 어디에 위치해 있는가?

(A) 1

(B) 2

(C) 3

(D) 4

[해설]

이스트 리버 교를 건너 두 블록 직진한 후, 좌회전해서 반 블록 오라고 했다. 따라서 정답은 1과 3 중 하나인데, 오른편에 있는 것이 주차장이라고 했으니 정답은 그 맞은 편에 있는 3이다. 참고로 2와 4 중의 하나는 주유소이다.

DAY 05 Daily Listening Practice   p.36

PART 1

[정답] (A)

(A) The door faces the staircase.

(B) Bricks are being laid.

(C) The steps are being swept.

(D) A potted plant has been placed near an entrance.

[해설]

사물만 나오는 사진에는 다양한 명사어휘와 동사 형태가 제시되므로 주의해야 한다. 특히 수동태 진행형(be + being + p.p.:~되는 중이다)과 수동 완료형(have + been + p.p.:~된 상태이다)의 해석에 유의해야

한다. 사람이 보이지 않기 때문에 사람의 동작을 나타내는 수동태 진행형을 사용한 (B)와 (C)는 오답이며 (D)는 화분(potted plant)이 보이지 않는다. 따라서 정답은 (A)이다.

PART 2

1 (B) 2 (C) 3 (B) 4 (B)

1

Why don't you come over for lunch next Saturday?
(A) It will be ready tomorrow.
(B) That sounds good.
(C) That's right. I don't eat meat.

[해설]

제안을 나타내는 Why don't you ~? Why don't we ~?에 적합한 응답은 받아들이거나 거절하는 답변을 골라야 하기 때문에 정답은 (B)이다. (A)는 When(언제)에 대한 응답이고 (C)는 질문과 어울리지 않는 응답이다.

2

Shouldn't we make reservations in advance?
(A) I can't remember it.
(B) Advance registration is required.
(C) That sounds like a great idea.

[해설]

Shouldn't we ~?(~해야 하지 않나요?)는 제안을 나타내는 표현이므로 여기에 동의하는 (C)가 정답이 된다. (A)는 질문에 어울리지 않는 응답이고 (B)는 질문의 advance를 반복해서 혼동을 주는 함정이므로 주의해야 한다.

3

Could I look at your new catalog?
(A) Yes, I knew that.
(B) It's on my desk.
(C) Because you went over it.

[해설]

새 카탈로그를 보여 달라는 요청에 대해 카탈로그가 위치한 장소를 알려주면서 긍정적인 답변을 한 (B)가 정답이 된다. (A)는 질문과 연관성이 없고 (C)는 Why질문에 대한 응답이다.

4

Can you tell me how to use this computer program?
(A) Actually, it was not that good.
(B) Don't you have the manual?
(C) No, the computer is compatible.

[해설]

Can you ~?를 사용해 컴퓨터 사용법을 알려달라는 요청에 대해 직접 매뉴얼을 찾아보라는 의미로 '매뉴얼을 가지고 있지 않냐'고 묻는 (B)가 정답이다. (A)는 질문과 어울리지 않는 응답이고 (C)는 질문의 computer를 반복해 혼동을 유발하고 있다.

PART 3

1 (A) 2 (D) 3 (C) 4 (B) 5 (A) 6 (B)

Questions 1-3 refer to the following conversation.

M   How are you doing with that report?
W   I just finished it. It took a little longer than I expected because some of the figures from last month's sales were somewhat strange and I had to check them with the sales manager. Now I have to fax it to Mr. Jackson.
M   Oh, I have a meeting with Mr. Jackson in his office in five minutes. I'll give it to him.
W   Thanks. I actually have to rush off to a dentist appointment and that will save me time.

1

[번역]

여자는 무엇을 준비하고 있는가?
(A) 보고서
(B) 송장
(C) 신청서
(D) 도서 서평

[해설]

남자는 How are you doing with that report?라고 여자에게 묻고 있으며, 이에 대해 여자는 I just finished it이라고 대답하고 있으므로 답은 (A)가 된다.

[어휘]

invoice 송장, 인보이스 | application 신청서 | review 검토, 비평

2

[번역]

남자는 무엇을 해주겠다고 하는가?
(A) 예약을 한다.
(B) 수치를 확인한다.
(C) 전화번호를 찾는다.
(D) 서류를 배달한다.

[해설]

여자가 I have to fax it to Mr. Jackson이라며 보고서(it)를 잭슨 씨에게 팩스로 보내야 된다고 하자, 남자는 곧 잭슨 씨를 직접 만날 거라면서 I'll give it to him이라고 말한다. 즉 서류를 전달해 주겠다고 하고 있으니 이를 deliver라는 동사를 사용해 묘사한 (D)가 답이 된다.

[어휘]

deliver 배달하다 | document 서류

3

[번역]

여자는 왜 바쁜가?
(A) 회의에 늦었다.
(B) 발표를 해야 한다.
(C) 약속이 있다.

(D) 고객을 만난다.

[해설]

be in a hurry는 '바쁘다, 급하게 움직이다'라는 뜻임을 익혀두자. 여자의 마지막 말 I actually have to rush off to a dentist appointment and that will save me time에 사용된 rush off to는 '~로 급히 가다'라는 의미이므로, 이 문장에서 답을 찾을 수 있음을 알 수 있다. dentist appointment에 가야 한다고 말하고 있으므로 답은 (C)가 된다.

Questions 4-6 refer to the following conversation with three speakers.

> M1 The conference at Miller Textiles starts at 9:30 tomorrow. How shall we go there?
>
> M2 I would like to drive there.
>
> W   That would be more comfortable, but will we arrive there in time? Rush-hour traffic can get pretty bad in Richmond.
>
> M2 You may be right. What do you believe we should do then?
>
> W   I'm in favor of taking the bus.
>
> M1 I'd rather not. That would be pretty inconvenient for me.
>
> W   How about if each of us goes there individually?
>
> M1 That won't look good if one of us is late. We want to make a good impression.
>
> M2 Let's drive. I'll meet you in the parking lot here at 8:00 and drive us. We'll get there in time.

4

[번역]

화자들은 어디로 갈 것인가?
(A) 면접장
(B) 컨퍼런스장
(C) 회의실
(D) 세미나실

[해설]

화자들은 밀러 텍스타일(Miller Textiles)의 컨퍼런스장까지 어떻게 갈 것인지를 논의하고 있다.

5

[번역]

여자는 어떻게 가자고 제안하는가?
(A) 버스로
(B) 자동차로
(C) 택시로
(D) 기차로

[해설]

여자는 차를 몰고 가자는 제안에 교통 체증의 이유를 들며 반대 의사를 표시한 후 I'm in favor of taking the bus.라고 말한다. 따라서 여자는 버스를 타고 갈 것을 주장한다.

6

[번역]

화자들은 내일 어디에서 만날 것인가?
(A) 여자의 집에서
(B) 회사의 주차장에서
(C) 버스 정류장에서
(D) 기차역에서

[해설]

대화의 마지막 부분에서 남자2는 '주차장에서 만나자고(I'll meet you in the parking lot here)' 말한다. 따라서 정답은 (B)이다.

PART 4

1 (A)   **2** (D)   **3** (C)

Questions 1-3 refer to the following talk.

> I'll quickly run through what needs to be done this afternoon. The air conditioner in the Sanford Conference Room on the 5th floor needs to be fixed. Donald McKenzie will look after that. Also, elevator number 3 is not working so Maria Fleming will phone Jackson Elevator and Escalator Services to arrange for a repair. Finally, Cecilia Doherty and I will be fixing a bookcase in the payroll office, room 115. If you need anything, please come and see me in payroll or you can also speak to Nereus Robinson. Mr. Robinson will be here in our office all afternoon in case we receive more phone calls requesting repairs.

1

[번역]

화자는 누구이겠는가?
(A) 관리부장
(B) 경리부 신입사원
(C) 서점 소유주
(D) 회사 사장

[해설]

전반적인 맥락을 주의 깊게 들으면, 본 담화에서 화자는 몇 가지 일을 사람들에게 배정하고 있는데 그 일들이 대체로 에어컨 수리, 엘리베이터 수리, 서가 수리로 압축할 수 있으므로 화자의 직책으로 가장 알맞은 것은 (A)이다.

[어휘]

head 수석, 장 | maintenance 유지 관리, 보수 | owner 소유주

2

[번역]

본 담화 후에 도날드 맥킨지는 아마도 무엇을 할 것인가?
(A) 책꽂이를 배달한다.
(B) 상사에게 말한다.
(C) 호텔 객실을 예약한다.
(D) 5층으로 간다.

전반부에서 Donald McKenzie will look after that이라며 도날드 맥킨지가 그 일을 맡을 것이라고 한 부분의 바로 앞에서 5층의 에어컨 수리 사안이 언급되었다(The air conditioner in the Sanford Conference Room on the 5th floor needs to be fixed). 따라서 (D)가 정답이 된다. 이처럼 이미 지나간 문장이 결정적인 단서가 되는 문제가 자주 출제되므로 각 문장 간의 흐름을 짚어가면서 각각의 지시대명사가 지칭하는 바를 파악하는 훈련을 평소에 해두자.

[어휘]

deliver 배송하다 | supervisor 관리자, 상사 | book 예약하다

3

[번역]

네레우스 로빈슨은 왜 사무실에 남아 있을 것인가?

(A) 사무실 조명을 고치기 위해서

(B) 몇몇 임원들과 만나기 위해서

(C) 전화를 받기 위해서

(D) 보고서 타이핑을 마치기 위해서

[해설]

질문의 핵심 어구인 'Nereus Robinson'에 유념해 담화를 들으면, 마지막 문장 Mr. Robinson will be here in our office all afternoon in case we receive more phone calls requesting repairs에서 수리 요청 전화가 더 올 경우를 대비해 오후 내내 사무실에 있을 것이라고 하므로 (C)가 정답이 된다.

[어휘]

remain 남다 | executive 임원, 이사 | finish 마치다

DAY 06 Daily Listening Practice p.41

PART 1

[정답] (C)

(A) Branches have been piled under the park bench.
(B) A vendor is putting a hat on a table.
(C) Containers are resting on a table.
(D) People are looking in the same direction.

[해설]

복수 인물들이 나오는 사진이라도 배경이나 사물에 대해 묘사한 문장이 정답이 되는 경우도 있으니 반드시 문장을 끝까지 듣고 사진과 일치하는 문장을 골라야 한다. 사진과 일치하는 문장은 (C)이고 사물이 주어일 때 resting은 '놓여있다'라고 해석하는 것을 유념해야한다.

PART 2

1 (B) **2** (B) **3** (C) **4** (A)

1

Have you seen my briefcase?
(A) It's not brief.
(B) Sorry, I haven't.
(C) Not that many.

[해설]

Have you ~? '당신은 ~ 했나요?' 라는 현재완료 질문에 현재완료로 대답한 (B)가 정답이다. (A)는 질문의 briefcase(서류가방)와 발음이 비슷한 brief(간략한)로 혼동을 유발하는 문장이고, (C)는 질문에 대한 응답으로 적절치 않다.

2

Have you read the memo I sent out this morning?
(A) Yes, I'll send it out.
(B) No, it just got here.
(C) You will need it immediately.

[해설]

메모가 방금 도착해서 아직 읽지 못했다는 내용의 (B)가 정답이다. (A)는 Yes답변은 가능하지만, 다음 문장이 send out을 반복해서 혼동을 유발하고 있고, (C)는 You로 물었는데 You로 응답한 것이 어색하다.

3

Have you heard anything about the new branch office?
(A) It must have been a city officer.
(B) I assembled it myself.
(C) It's supposed to be great.

[해설]

'새 지점에 대해 뭔가 들었습니까?'라는 질문에 '좋을 거예요'라는 답변이 가장 자연스럽기 때문에 정답은 (C)이다. (A)는 office와 비슷한 발음의 officer로 혼동을 유발하고 있고, (B)는 '내가 그것을 조립했다'란 뜻이므로 질문과 무관한 내용이다.

4

Have they gotten the results of their physical checkups?
(A) I heard they haven't.
(B) Thanks, they would be helpful.
(C) They look much too tired.

[해설]

'그들(they)이 건강검진 결과를 받았나요?'라는 질문이므로 '못 받았다고 들었다'라고 하는 (A)가 정답이 된다. (B)의 경우 고맙다는 응답이 어색하고, (C)의 피곤해 보인다는 응답 역시 어색하다.

PART 3

1 (C) **2** (A) **3** (D) **4** (A) **5** (D) **6** (B)

Questions 1-3 refer to the following conversation.

M What did you learn from Golden Taxi?
W There is a broken traffic light at the corner of Davis Avenue and Wilcox Street. That cab coming to our office is expected to be stuck in

들어 보아야 한다. 여자는 Why don't we just wait for it outside?라고
제안하고 있으며, 콜택시도 가까운 위치에 있으므로, 화자들은 택시를
타기 위해 바깥으로 나갈 것임을 유추할 수 있다.

[어휘]

probably 아마도 | withdraw 인출하다 | cash 현금

Questions 4-6 refer to the following conversation and list.

W Hello, Mr. Wheeler. This is Kay Kennedy calling from Top Realty.

M Good morning, Ms. Kennedy. Do you have some good news for me?

W I think I do. I found a really nice house that you and your family will love.

M Tell me about it, please.

W It's got four bedrooms and two bathrooms, so there's plenty of room for everyone. It's located near an outstanding elementary school, and it has a large yard.

M That sounds ideal. Do you have time to show it to us around 3:00 or 4:00?

W I'm not free in the afternoon because I've got to attend a meeting with my boss. However, I'm available at 6:00. How does that sound?

M Let me ask my wife first and see what she says. Then, I'll call you right back.

1

[번역]

무엇이 지연을 일으키고 있는가?

(A) 결제가 되지 않았다.

(B) 도로의 한 구획이 복구되고 있다.

(C) 신호등이 고장이다.

(D) 일부 물품이 배송되지 않았다.

[해설]

대화문의 앞부분만 듣고는 대화의 상황이 쉽게 파악되지 않는 내용이
기 때문에 주의를 기울여야 한다. 화자들은 콜택시를 기다리고 있는데,
콜택시가 아직 오지 않은 이유와 택시 회사 측의 해결방안 등이 제시되
고 있다. 특히, 여자의 말 There is a broken traffic light at the corner
of Davis Avenue and Wilcox Street에서 택시가 지연되고 있는 이유를
알 수 있다.

[어휘]

cause 일으키다, 야기하다 | delay 지체, 지연 | payment 지불 | receive
받다 | section 구획 | repair 수리하다

2

[번역]

남자는 무엇에 대해 걱정하고 있는가?

(A) 비행기를 놓치는 것

(B) 택시 요금이 없는 것

(C) 서류를 잃어버리는 것

(D) 보고서를 완성하지 못하는 것

[해설]

남자는 택시가 빨리 와야 할 텐데(I hope it gets here soon)라고 하면
서 그 이유로 Our plane leaves in 2 hours and it will take at least 30
minutes to get to the airport를 제시한다. 그러므로 남자가 걱정하는
이유는 (A)가 된다.

[어휘]

miss 놓치다 | fare 요금 | lose 잃어버리다 | document 서류

3

[번역]

아마도 화자들은 다음으로 무엇을 할 것인가?

(A) 현금을 인출한다.

(B) 서류를 팩스로 보낸다.

(C) 공항에 전화한다.

(D) 바깥으로 나간다.

[해설]

대화가 끝난 후에 이어질 행동에 대해 묻고 있으므로 대화 후반부를 잘

4

[번역]

남자에 관해 무엇이 암시되는가?

(A) 그에게는 아이들이 있다.

(B) 그는 부동산 중개업자이다.

(C) 그는 직업을 바꿀 것이다.

(D) 그는 교사이다.

[해설]

여자는 자신이 찾은 주택의 장점 중 하나가 '우수한 초등학교 인근에
위치해 있다(located near an outstanding elementary school)'는 점이
라고 말한다. 이를 통해 화자에게는 아이가 있음을 추측할 수 있으므로
정답은 (A)이다.

[어휘]

real estate agent 부동산 중개업자, 부동산 중개업소 직원

5

[번역]

여자는 남자를 언제 만나고 싶어하는가?

(A) 12시

(B) 3시

(C) 4시

(D) 6시

[해설]

3시와 4시경에 만나자는 남자의 제안에 여자는 회의가 있다는 이유로

거절을 한 후, I'm available at 6:00.라고 말하면서 6시 만남에 관한 의견을 남자에게 되묻고 있다.

6

[번역]

도표를 보아라. 여자가 남자에게 보여 주고자 하는 주택의 주소는 무엇인가?

(A) 애버딘 가 209번지

(B) 헨리 로 45번지

(C) 샬록 로 28번지

(D) 데번포트 가 85번지

[해설]

주택에 관한 여자의 설명 중 four bedrooms and two bathrooms라는 표현을 들어야 풀 수 있는 문제이다. 도표에서 4개의 침실과 2개의 욕실을 가진 주택을 찾으면 된다.

PART 4

1 (A)   2 (B)   3 (A)

Questions 1-3 refer to the following telephone message.

> Hello, Mr. Driessen. This is Dr. Wayne Conner calling from the Cornell Laboratory. Yesterday morning, I called and spoke with you about the broken lock on the door to the lab. You assured me that the door would be fixed immediately. Unfortunately, nobody from the Maintenance Department has arrived yet. It's already 5 in the evening, and most of us are getting ready to go home for the day. It is imperative that you keep your word. We have many valuable pieces of equipment in here. It isn't safe to leave the door unlocked again. We can't risk having anything taken or having some of our experiments interrupted. I insist that you send someone down here to fix the problem immediately.

1

[번역]

화자는 언제 문제를 보고했는가?

(A) 어제 아침

(B) 어제 저녁

(C) 오늘 아침

(D) 오늘 저녁

[해설]

메시지 초반부의 Yesterday morning, I called and spoke with you about the broken lock on the door to the lab.에서 화자는 어제 아침에 문제를 제기했다는 점을 알 수 있다.

2

[번역]

화자는 청자에게 무엇을 할 것을 지시하는가?

(A) 즉시 드리슨 씨와 이야기한다

(B) 고장 난 물품을 수리한다

(C) 장비를 관리한다

(D) 모든 장비를 살펴본다

[해설]

화자는 마지막 문장에서 '수리를 위해 사람을 보내달라(you send someone down here to fix the problem immediately)'고 요청하고 있다. 따라서 정답은 (B)이다.

[어휘]

at once 즉시, 당장 | **take care of** ~을 돌보다 | **look after** ~을 돌보다

3

[번역]

남자가 "It is imperative that you keep your word"라고 말했을 때, 남자는 무엇을 의미하는가?

(A) 청자가 문제를 오늘 해결해야 한다.

(B) 청자는 그의 말에 더 많은 주의를 기울여야 한다.

(C) 청자는 즉시 그에게 회신 전화를 해야 한다.

(D) 청자는 관리부에 연락해야 한다.

[해설]

keep one's work는 '약속을 지키다'라는 뜻이다. 여기에서 '약속'이란 즉시 문제를 해결해 주겠다는 청자의 약속을 가리키므로 정답은 (A)가 된다.

[어휘]

pay attention to ~에 주의를 기울이다, ~에 주목하다 | **return one's phone** ~에게 회신 전화를 하다

DAY 07 Daily Listening Practice   p.47

PART 1

[정답] (A)

(A) There are no pedestrians on the sidewalk.

(B) There are several houses in need of repair.

(C) The cars on the street are parked illegally.

(D) The commuters are stuck in traffic.

[해설]

(B)는 집들이 보이기는 하지만 수리가 필요한지(in need of repair) 알 수 없고 (C)는 차들이 주차되어 있으나 불법인지(illegally) 알 수 없다. (D)에서 언급된 통근자(commuters)도 교통체증(stuck in traffic)도 사진에 보이지 않는다. 따라서 정답은 (A) '인도에 보행자가 없다'이다.

PART 2

1 (C)   2 (A)   3 (A)   4 (B)

1

How did you find your new job?
(A) No, the company is hiring now.
(B) About 2 months ago.
(C) Through a recruiting agency.

[해설]

의문사 How는 다양한 것을 물을 수 있는데, How do/did you ~?는 방법, 수단을 묻는 표현이므로 수단, 방법을 나타내는 전치사 through를 써서 응답한 (C)가 정답이 된다. (A)는 의문사 의문문에 yes/no로 대답했기 때문에 불가하고, (B)는 When 질문에 대한 응답이다.

2

How long have you supervised this project?
(A) For nearly 3 years.
(B) When the supervisor gets back.
(C) The project has been delayed.

[해설]

How long ~?은 '얼마나 오래'라는 기간을 묻는 문제이므로 '거의 3년 동안'이라 응답한 (A)가 정답이 된다. (B)의 When(언제)은 '시점'을 나타내기 때문에 불가하고 (C)는 질문의 project를 반복한 함정이다.

3

How was your business trip to Hanoi?
(A) Very successful.
(B) To contact the supplier.
(C) It's a final draft.

[해설]

의문사 How 뒤에 be동사가 오면 주로 '의견이나 평가'를 묻는 표현이기 때문에, '괜찮다/안 좋다' 등의 응답이 정답이 되므로 답은 (A)가 된다. (B)의 '~하기 위해'라는 의미로 해석되는 to부정사는 이유나 목적을 묻는 Why에 대한 응답이고, (C)는 질문과 어울리지 않는 응답이다.

4

How did you know about Ms. Deltashi's early retirement?
(A) She's doing well.
(B) She told me herself.
(C) She wants approval.

[해설]

How do/did you ~?는 방법, 수단을 묻는 표현이므로 '그녀에게서 직접 들었다'라고 응답한 (B)가 정답이 된다. (A)는 안부를 묻는 How is she doing?에 알맞은 응답이며 (C)는 질문과 어울리지 않는 응답이다.

PART 3

1 (C) **2** (A) **3** (D) **4** (A) **5** (C) **6** (B)

Questions 1-3 refer to the following conversation.

W <u>I saw an advertisement on your website for a brand new AZ-3000 computer and BL150 printer. I'd like to get them</u> and charge them to my credit card.

M Of course, miss, but unfortunately, <u>the BL150 is completely sold out at the moment</u>. That particular item is very popular these days.

W <u>Could I order one?</u> I don't mind waiting a few days.

M Certainly. I guaranteed that it will be here by the day after tomorrow and we will contact you as soon as it arrives.

1

[번역]

여자는 무엇을 하고 싶어 하는가?
(A) 신용카드 신청
(B) 가전제품 수리
(C) 컴퓨터 구입
(D) 약속 잡기

[해설]

여자는 I saw an advertisement on your website for a brand new AZ-3000 computer and BL150 printer라는 말로 대화를 시작한 후 I'd like to get them이라고 덧붙인다. 이때 get은 buy, purchase와 같은 의미로 사용되었으므로 (C)가 답이 된다.

[어휘]

apply for ~을 신청하다 | appliance 가전제품 | fix 수리하다, 고치다 | make an appointment 약속을 잡다

2

[번역]

무엇이 문제인가?
(A) 한 제품의 재고가 없다.
(B) 매장이 곧 문을 닫는다.
(C) 매니저가 자리에 없다.
(D) 어떤 장비가 고장이다.

[해설]

but과 같은 역접 접속사 뒤에는 정답의 단서가 자주 제시된다. 남자의 말 but unfortunately, the BL150 is completely sold out at the moment에서 제품이 품절된 상태임을 알 수 있는데, be sold out이 be not in stock으로 표현된 (A)가 정답이다.

[어휘]

be in stock 재고가 있는 | equipment 장비

3

[번역]

여자는 다음으로 무엇을 하겠는가?
(A) 누군가에게 전화를 건다.
(B) 컴퓨터 전원을 켠다.
(C) 신문을 찾는다.
(D) 주문을 한다.

[해설]

제품의 재고가 없다는 말에도 불구하고 여자는 Could I order one?이라고 하며 제품이 도착할 때까지 기다리겠다고 말했으며, 남자는 그렇게 할 것을 권유한다. 그러므로 본 대화 다음에 이어질 상황으로 알맞은 것은 (D)가 된다.

[어휘]

probably 아마도 | place an order 주문하다

Questions 4-6 refer to the following conversation.

> W Now that Simmons Construction has signed a deal with us, we need to determine who should work the closest with the company.
>
> M I vote for Ron. He was integral to getting the contract signed.
>
> W That's true, but I don't think he'd be a good choice as a liaison. He's never done it before, and his personality isn't right for the job. I'd much rather have him work on trying to secure new clients for us.
>
> M I see your point. In that case, who do you think we should use?
>
> W Even though Maria just started working here, she's proving to be a good employee.
>
> M Okay. Let's get her in here so that we can tell her the news.

4
[번역]

남자는 론에 대해 무엇을 말하는가?
(A) 그는 회사가 새로운 계약을 성사시키는데 도움을 주었다.
(B) 그는 회사에서 가장 최근에 들어온 직원이다.
(C) 그는 시먼스 건설에서 일한다.
(D) 그는 회사와 얼마 전에 계약을 체결했다.

[해설]

He was integral to getting the contract signed.라는 남자의 말을 통해 론이 거래를 성사시키는데 중요한 역할을 했음을 알 수 있다.

5
[번역]

화자들은 다음에 무엇을 할 것 같은가?
(A) 직원 중 한 명을 해고한다.
(B) 시먼스 건설에 전화를 한다.
(C) 마리아와 만난다.
(D) 문제에 대해 계속 이야기한다.

[해설]

대화의 마지막 부분에서 남자는 Let's get her in here so that we can tell her the news.라고 말하면서 마리아라는 사람을 부르자고 제안한다. 따라서 정답은 (C)이다.

[어휘]

fire 해고하다 | colleague 동료, 동료 직원 | place a call to ~에 전화하다

6
[번역]

남자가 "I see your point"라고 말할 때 그는 무엇을 의미하는가?
(A) 회사는 더 많은 직원을 고용해야 한다.

(B) 론은 새로운 고객을 계속 찾아야 한다.
(C) 시먼스 건설 프로젝트가 더 중요하다.
(D) 그 일은 마리아가 론보다 잘 할 것이다.

[해설]

I see your point는 '당신 말의 취지를 알겠다'라는 뜻으로, 여기에서는 '론에게 신규 고객을 유치하는 일을 맡기는 것이 나을 것이다'라는 여자의 의견에 남자가 동의를 표하기 위해 사용되었다. 따라서 정답은 (B)이다.

PART 4

1 (D) **2** (B) **3** (B)

Questions 1-3 refer to the following talk.

> Good evening, ladies and gentlemen. I hope you all enjoyed your lobster dinner. I will now present the first prize of the evening, Wilcox Energy's Leader-of-the-Year Award. This year's recipient, a supervisor in the research department, organized and directed a huge project that helped Wilcox secure a contract to build 85 windmills on Chatworth Island. She also worked closely with Wilcox's finance division to secure funding for another research project that will start in New Zealand in mid-January. Let's have a big round of applause for Ms. Soomi Choi as she comes up to accept this award and talk about her story.

1
[번역]

청중은 어디에 있겠는가?
(A) 스포츠 행사장
(B) 미술품 경매장
(C) 교육 세션
(D) 시상식 연회

[해설]

전반부에서 청중을 향해 인사를 하면서, 식사(dinner)를 즐기셨기 바란다고 한 뒤, 오늘 저녁의 첫 번째 상을 수여하겠다(present the first prize of the evening)고 하므로 가장 적절한 것은 (D)이다.

[어휘]

event 행사 | auction 경매 | training 교육, 훈련 | banquet 연회

2
[번역]

수미 최는 어느 부서에 근무하는가?
(A) 판매
(B) 연구
(C) 금융
(D) 법률

[해설]

본 담화는 시상식에서 이루어지는 것이며 수상자를 단상으로 부르기 전에 그 인물의 성과를 소개하는 것을 주요 내용으로 하고 있음을 간과

해야 보다 수월하게 해결할 수 있다. 전반부에서 This year's recipient, a supervisor in the research department라며 올해 수상자는 '연구부' 사람이라 하고, 후반부에서는 큰 박수를 보내자며 수미 최를 언급(Let's have a big round of applause for Ms. Soomi Choi)한다. 따라서 (B)가 정답이 된다.

[어휘]

legal 법률의

3

[번역]

최 씨는 아마도 다음에 무엇을 하겠는가?
(A) 회의를 시작한다.
(B) 연설한다.
(C) 동료에게 전화한다.
(D) 제안서를 마친다.

[해설]

'do next?'로 끝나는 문제에 대한 결정적인 단서는 대체로 마지막에서 찾을 수 있다는 점을 유념하자. 마지막 문장 중 she comes up to accept this award and talk about her story를 통해 단상으로 올라와 상을 받고 소감을 말할 것임을 유추할 수 있으므로 정답은 (B)이다.

[어휘]

probably 아마도 | colleague 동료 | finish 끝내다 | proposal 제안
(서)

DAY 08 Daily Listening Practice   p.52

PART 1

[정답] (A)

(A) Hats are hanging on the wall.
(B) People are seated on opposite sides of the table.
(C) A couple is arranging some flowers.
(D) A woman is sitting in an outdoor café.

[해설]

(B)는 테이블 맞은편(on opposite sides of the table)에 앉은 사람이 보이지 않고, (C)는 꽃꽂이를 하고 있는 동작(arranging some flowers)도 사진에서 보이지 않기 때문에 불가하다. (D)의 경우, 사진은 실내(indoor)이기 때문에 정답이 될 수 없다. 따라서 모자가 벽에 걸려있다고 한 (A)가 정답이다.

PART 2

1 (C) **2** (C) **3** (A) **4** (A)

1

Why is the library closed today?
(A) Because it's open for business.
(B) The library is close to my office.
(C) It's a national holiday.

[해설]

도서관이 휴관하는 이유를 '국경일이다'라고 말한 (C)가 정답이 된다. (A)의 경우, because가 나오지만 질문과 어울리지 않는 응답이고, (C)는 질문의 library 반복과 closed와 비슷한 발음 close를 제시해서 오답을 유도하는 문장이다.

2

Why did you decide to move?
(A) I decided yesterday.
(B) Yes, I'm going to change jobs.
(C) The cost of living is too expensive here.

[해설]

Why 의문문으로 이사 가는 이유를 묻는 질문에 '이곳의 생활비는 비싸다'고 응답한 (C)가 정답이다. (A)는 When(언제)에 대한 응답이며 질문의 decide를 반복해 오답을 유도하고 있고 (B)는 의문사 의문문에 yes/no로 대답했기 때문에 정답이 될 수 없다.

3

Why was Mr. Chan determined to retire this year?
(A) I have no idea.
(B) He'd appreciate your assistance.
(C) Not to him.

[해설]

'왜 챈 씨가 은퇴를 결정했냐?'는 질문에 '모르겠어요'라고 응답한 (A)가 정답이 된다. (B) '그가 고맙게 여길 것이다'와 (C) '그에게는 아니다'란 답변은 질문에 어울리지 않는다.

4

Why has the meeting been moved to Friday?
(A) Because the board is busy on Wednesday.
(B) They moved to Florida.
(C) They don't like the agenda.

[해설]

'회의가 금요일로 바뀐 이유'를 묻는 질문에 because를 사용해 '이사회가 수요일에 바쁘다'라고 이유를 설명한 (A)가 정답이다. (B)는 질문의 moved to Friday와 발음이 비슷한 moved to Florida로 오답을 유도하고 있고, (C)는 meeting과 관련된 의미 연상 단어 agenda로 오답을 유도하고 있다.

PART 3

1 (D) **2** (A) **3** (D) **4** (D) **5** (D) **6** (C)

Questions 1-3 refer to the following conversation.

> M   Good afternoon. Jackson's Household Appliances. May I help you?
>
> W   Yes, I purchased a microwave from you yesterday afternoon, but, for some reason, it's not working. Can you fix it?

M Certainly. If you bring it in along with your receipt, one of our technicians can repair it right here in our store, or, if you prefer, <u>we could send someone to your home.</u>

W Well, my son has the car right now, so I can't go to your store. Please send someone over.

Questions 4-6 refer to the following conversation with three speakers.

W Jim said that the annual marketing conference in New Orleans is going to be held next month. Do you know who's going?

M1 Mr. Mason informed me <u>that he's sending me and two other people.</u>

M2 Are you aware of who the other two are?

M1 One is David Hampton. And <u>I get to choose the other one.</u>

W I'd love to go. Several of my clients from Dallas and Nashville will be there, <u>so it would be ideal for me to attend the event.</u>

M1 Are you interested in going, too, Bob?

M2 Yes, <u>but I attended a conference</u> in Denver last year, so I don't mind if Mary goes instead of me.

W That's very considerate of you, Bob.

1

[번역]

여자는 누구에게 이야기하고 있겠는가?

(A) 은행 지점장

(B) 여행사 직원

(C) 직물 공급업자

(D) 매장 점원

[해설]

여자의 대화 상대, 즉 남자에 대한 질문이므로 남자의 말에 집중한다. 남자는 첫 대화문 Jackson's Household Appliances. May I help you? 에서 남자가 가전 제품점에서 일한다는 것을 유추할 수 있으므로 정답은 (D)가 된다.

2

[번역]

여자가 전화한 까닭은 무엇인가?

(A) 가전제품 수리에 대해 문의하기 위해

(B) 약속을 취소하기 위해

(C) 계산 착오에 대해 논의하기 위해

(D) 영업시간을 문의하기 위해

[해설]

여자는 어제 그 상점에서 전자레인지를 샀다고 한 후, it's not working. Can you fix it?이라며 제품이 작동되지 않는데 고칠 수 있는지 물었다. 따라서 정답은 (A)이다.

[어휘]

cancel 취소하다 | appointment 약속 | discuss 논의하다 | billing 계산서 작성

3

[번역]

남자는 여자에게 무엇을 해 주겠다고 제안하는가?

(A) 빠른 배송

(B) 더 저렴한 가격

(C) 무료 강좌

(D) 방문 수리

[해설]

남자의 말에 집중해야 해결할 수 있는 문제이다. 남자의 두 번째 대화문 we could send someone to your home에서 여자의 집으로 사람을 보낼 수 있다는 내용이 나오므로 정답은 (D)이다.

[어휘]

speedy 빠른 | class 수업 | maintenance 정비, 보수

4

[번역]

화자들은 주로 무엇에 관해 논의하는가?

(A) 컨퍼런스가 언제 개최되는지

(B) 컨퍼런스에서 무엇이 논의될 것인지

(C) 올해 컨퍼런스가 어디에서 열릴 것인지

(D) 누가 컨퍼런스에 참석할 것인지

[해설]

뉴올리언스에서 열리는 마케팅 컨퍼런스에 참석할 사람에 대해 논의하고 있다.

5

[번역]

올해 행사는 어디에서 열릴 것인가?

(A) 댈러스

(B) 덴버

(C) 내슈빌

(D) 뉴올리언스

[해설]

대화 초반의 여자의 말을 통해 컨퍼런스는 뉴올리언스에서 열릴 것이라는 점을 알 수 있다. 참고로 (A)의 댈러스와 (C)의 내슈빌은 여자의 고객이 있는 곳이고, (B)의 덴버는 작년에 컨퍼런스가 열렸던 곳이다.

6

[번역]

누가 행사에 갈 것인가?

(A) 밥

(B) 메이슨 씨

(C) 메리

(D) 짐

[해설]

대화 후반부의 남자2의 말, I don't mind if Mary goes instead of me에서 화자 중 메리가 컨퍼런스에 가게 될 것임을 예상할 수 있다. 따라서

정답은 (C)이다. 참고로 (B)는 컨퍼런스 참석자를 지명한 화자들의 상사일 것으로 추측되며, (A)의 밥은 남자2의 이름이다.

PART 4

1 (D) **2** (B) **3** (A)

Questions 1-3 refer to the following excerpt from a meeting and graph.

> In April, we released two products. They are the RT19 and the JX20. As you can see from the chart, <u>they have had different levels of success</u>. <u>We advertised both of them a great amount</u>, so they started by selling roughly the same amount the first month. However, customer feedback on the RT19 was positive while the JX20 was mostly disliked by customers. As a result, the RT19 <u>began selling many more products in the following months</u>. On the other hand, sales of the JX20 declined heavily. In August, we rereleased the JX20. <u>Our engineers got rid of all the flaws in the system and made it a much better product</u>. At first, sales were flat. But in September, they started rising. Now, it's selling nearly as well as the RT19 is.

1

[번역]

화자는 RT19에 관해 무엇을 말하는가?
(A) JX20보다 낮은 가격에 판매되었다.
(B) 사람들은 그에 관한 광고를 좋아했다.
(C) JX20보다 한 달 앞서 출시되었다.
(D) 고객들은 그에 관해 긍정적인 반응을 보였다.

[해설]

담화 중반부의 customer feedback on the RT19 was positive라는 부분에서 RT19에 관한 고객들의 반응이 긍정적이었다는 사실을 알 수 있다.

2

[번역]

엔지니어들은 JX20에 관해 무엇을 했는가?
(A) 보다 가벼운 재료로 만들었다.
(B) 문제점을 해결했다.
(C) 디자인을 변경했다.
(D) 새로운 기능을 추가했다.

[해설]

담화 후반부에 엔지니어들이 '시스템 내의 결점을 제거해서(got rid of all the flaws in the system)' 이를 더 우수한 제품으로 만들었다는 언급을 찾아볼 수 있다.

[어휘]

material 재료, 자료 | add 더하다 | function 기능

3

[번역]

그래프를 보아라. JX20은 재출시된 첫 달에 몇 개가 판매되었는가?
(A) 900
(B) 2,400
(C) 3,000
(D) 4,000

[해설]

JX20이 재출시된 달은 August(8월)이라고 했으므로 8월의 JX20의 판매 수치를 확인하면 정답을 쉽게 찾을 수 있다.

DAY **09** Daily Listening Practice p.58

PART 1

[정답] (C)

(A) A beach has been deserted.
(B) Trees are casting shadows on the sand.
(C) Some people are in the water.
(D) Rowboats are lined up at the water's edge.

[해설]

사진에 많은 사람이 보이기 때문에 (A)에서 언급된 '방치된(deserted)' 것이 아니며, (B)에서 언급된 그늘(shadows)이 보이지 않고, (D)의 보트들(rowboats)이 보이지 않으므로 정답이 될 수 없다. 따라서 '사람들이 물속에 있다'라고 표현한 (C)가 정답이 된다.

PART 2

1 (C) **2** (C) **3** (A) **4** (A)

1

It looks like it's going to rain soon.
(A) Well, I'm busy now.
(B) What does he look like?
(C) Did you bring your umbrella?

[해설]

의문사 없이 평서문으로 말해도 상황을 유추해서 적절한 응답을 선택해야 한다. 제안이나 추가 질문을 하는 문장이 정답이 되는 경우가 많은데 '비가 올 것 같다'는 말에 '우산을 가져왔는지' 추가 질문을 한 (C)가 정답이 된다. (A)는 질문과 어울리지 않는 응답이며, (B)는 look like를 반복해 오답을 유도하는 문장이다.

2

I think the upgraded model is really efficient.
(A) The temporary secretary is really efficient.
(B) Sure, to the address.
(C) Yes, far better than the old one.

[해설]

'업그레이드된 모델이 효율적'이라는 상대의 의견에 '옛날 것보다 훨씬 낫다'라고 동의하는 (C)가 정답이 된다. (A)는 really efficient를 반복해 오답을 유도하는 문장이고, (B) '물론이죠, 그 주소로(보내주세요)'는 질문에 어울리지 않는 응답이다.

3

I can't fax any documents since the machine is jammed.
(A) Ask Keito to fix it.
(B) The traffic jam is terrible.
(C) It will be out tomorrow.

[해설]

'팩스기에 문제가 생겨서 서류를 보낼 수 없다'는 상대의 말에 '케이토에게 고쳐달라고 부탁해라'라는 해결책을 제안한 (A)가 정답이 된다. (B)는 질문의 jammed와 발음이 비슷한 jam을 이용한 함정이고, (C) '내일 나올 것이다'란 답변은 적절한 응답이 아니다.

4

I have been coughing all week.
(A) Sorry to hear that you are feeling bad.
(B) No, they caught a cold.
(C) I'm not at work.

[해설]

'일주일 내내 기침을 했다'는 상대의 말에 유감을 표한 (A)가 정답이 된다. (B)는 coughing(기침하고 있다)에서 연상되는 caught a cold(감기에 걸렸다)를 이용해 오답을 유도하고 있다. (C)의 '직장에 있지 않다'라는 답변은 적절한 응답이 아니다.

PART 3

1 (B)　**2** (A)　**3** (D)　**4** (A)　**5** (C)　**6** (B)

Questions 1-3 refer to the following conversation.

> W　Excuse me, Mr. Vlack, but could I please talk with you about our meeting this afternoon?
> M　Are you referring to our 11:15 meeting concerning my evaluation of your recent work in the sales division?
> W　That is correct. I was just speaking to a potential client on the phone who would like to meet me this afternoon at 1:00 in Dawson City. Since I have to drive there, would it be possible to reschedule our meeting until sometime this afternoon?
> M　Yes, of course. I'm free at 4:30 so why don't you come by my office then?

1

[번역]

여자는 왜 남자를 만나야 하는가?
(A) 생산 비용을 낮추는 것에 대해 얘기하려고
(B) 업무 평가를 논의하려고
(C) 새로운 마케팅 전략을 계획하려고
(D) 지난 날 판매 수치를 검토하려고

[해설]

여자가 '회의에 대해 잠시 얘기 나눌 수 있냐'고 남자에게 묻자 남자는 Are you referring to our 11:15 meeting concerning my evaluation of your recent work in the sales division?이라며 그 회의가 구체적으로 무엇에 관한 것인지 확인해 준다. 이 문장의 evaluation이 review로, recent work이 performance로 표현되어 있는 (B)가 답이 된다.

[어휘]

be supposed to ~해야 한다 ｜ lower 낮추다 ｜ production 생산 ｜ cost 비용 ｜ discuss 논의하다 ｜ performance 성과, 성적 ｜ review 검토, 검토하다 ｜ plan 계획하다 ｜ strategy 전략 ｜ figure 수치

2

[번역]

여자는 왜 회의 일정을 조정하고 싶어 하는가?
(A) 시외로 갈 것이다.
(B) 보고서를 마치지 못했다.
(C) 자신의 상사가 바쁘다.
(D) 휴가 중이다.

[해설]

여자는 I was just speaking to a potential client on the phone who would like to meet me this afternoon at 1:00 in Dawson City라는 말로 회의 일정을 조정하고 싶은 이유를 설명하고 있는데, Dawson City라는 지명을 언급한 것으로 보아 이곳은 현재 화자가 위치해 있는 지역이 아니라는 것을 알 수 있다. 그러므로 이를 '다른 지방으로 가다'라는 의미의 leave town으로 표현한 (A)가 답이 된다.

[어휘]

leave 떠나다 ｜ supervisor 상사 ｜ vacation 휴가

3

[번역]

두 화자 간의 회의는 몇 시에 열릴 것인가?
(A) 오전 11시
(B) 오전 11시 15분
(C) 오후 1시
(D) 오후 4시 30분

[해설]

회의 일정을 조정하고자 하는 여자의 바람에 대해 남자는 대화의 마지막에서 I'm free at 4:30 so why don't you come by my office then?이라고 대안을 제시한다. 그러므로 정답은 (D)가 된다.

[어휘]

take place (일, 사건 등이) 일어나다

Questions 4-6 refer to the following conversation and map.

> W　Welcome to the Festus Art Gallery. Can I help you with something?
> M　Yes, please. I've never been here before, so could you tell me where everything is?

W Of course. <u>We're standing in the front lobby now.</u>
   <u>Straight ahead of us is our exhibit of modern art.</u>
M What's in the gallery to the left?
W <u>There are actually two display halls to the left.</u>
   One contains a visiting exhibit of Chinese art.
   It will only be here until next week. The second
   contains European sculptures.
M Okay. Is there anything else I should see?
W Yes, if you go to the right, you can see the
   Renaissance art exhibit. <u>It's my personal favorite.</u>
M Thanks for your assistance. <u>I'll check out the</u>
   <u>modern art exhibit first</u> and then look at the
   others.

4

[번역]

남자는 페스터스 미술관에 대해 무엇을 말하는가?

(A) 그는 그곳 방문이 처음이다.
(B) 멋진 예술 작품들이 소장되어 있다.
(C) 건물이 2층으로 되어 있다.
(D) 입장료가 너무 비싸다.

[해설]

남자는 여자에게 도움을 청하면서 I've never been here before라고 말한다. 이를 통해 남자는 전에 이곳에 온 적이 없음을 알 수 있다.

[어휘]

for the first time 처음으로 ┃ charge (요금 등을) 부과하다 ┃ admission 허가; 입장

5

[번역]

여자에 의하면, 어떤 전시가 비상설 전시인가?

(A) 르네상스 미술전
(B) 유럽 조각 작품전
(C) 중국 미술전
(D) 현대 미술전

[해설]

visiting exhibit of Chinese art라는 표현에서 visiting(초대전의)이라는 단어에 유의하면 중국 미술전이 일시적으로 진행되고 있다는 사실을 알 수 있다. 또한 It will only be here until next week.라는 문장을 통해서도 중국 미술전이 비상설 전시라는 점을 확인할 수 있다.

6

[번역]

도표를 보아라. 남자는 먼저 어디로 갈 것인가?

(A) 1
(B) 2
(C) 3
(D) 4

[해설]

대화의 마지막 부분에서 남자는 현대 미술전을 먼저 관람할 것이라고 말한다. 여자의 말을 통해 현대 미술전은 로비 앞에서 진행되고 있음을 알 수 있으므로 남자가 갈 곳은 2이다.

PART 4

1 (B)　**2** (B)　**3** (A)

Questions 1-3 refer to the following traffic report.

> It's 11:00 and time for CKCL's local traffic update.
> Montgomery Street <u>continues to be closed between</u>
> Ellis Avenue and Regent Street <u>due to some fallen</u>
> <u>power lines</u> that were knocked down during last
> night's storm. Crews hope to have everything fixed
> no later than 2:00. Meanwhile, <u>the bus stop in front</u>
> <u>of</u> Melvin's Grocery <u>on</u> Montgomery Street <u>has</u>
> <u>been moved to</u> Rochester Elementary School on
> nearby Doris Avenue. Anyone who uses that bus
> stop should get on and get off in front of the school
> until further notice. Also, motorists are reminded that
> <u>construction of the</u> Armstrong Bridge <u>is expected</u>
> <u>to be completed by next Monday evening, which</u>
> <u>means that you will be able to drive on the bridge</u>
> <u>next Tuesday.</u>

1

[번역]

몽고메리 스트리트의 교통이 왜 정체되었는가?

(A) 교통 신호등이 작동하지 않아서
(B) 전선이 쓰러져서
(C) 배송 트럭이 고장 나서
(D) 도로가 수리 중이어서

[해설]

'몽고메리 스트리트의 정체 이유'가 문제의 핵심임을 간파하고 담화를 듣도록 한다. 전반부의 Montgomery Street continues to be closed between Ellis Avenue and Regent Street due to some fallen power lines에서 '쓰러진 전선 때문에' 계속 통제되고 있다는 내용이 나오므로 (B)가 정답이 된다.

[어휘]

delay 지연시키다, 지체시키다 ┃ delivery 배송, 배달 ┃ break down 고장 나다 ┃ undergo 겪다, 경험하다 ┃ repair 수리, 수선

2

[번역]

로체스터 초등학교 앞으로 무엇이 옮겨졌는가?

(A) 광고판
(B) 버스 정거장
(C) 신문 가판대
(D) 매표소

[해설]

문제의 핵심 어구 'Rochester Elementary School'에 유념하자. 중반부에서 the bus stop in front of Melvin's Grocery on Montgomery Street has been moved to Rochester Elementary School이라며 식료품점 앞에 있던 버스 정거장이 로체스터 초등학교로 쪽으로 옮겨졌다고 했으므로 (B)가 정답이다.

3

[번역]

화요일에 어떤 일이 생길 것인가?
(A) 다리가 다시 개통 될 것이다.
(B) 새로운 버스노선이 추가될 것이다.
(C) 학교가 휴교할 것이다.
(D) 식료품점에서 할인 판매할 것이다.

[해설]

후반부의 construction of the Armstrong Bridge is expected to be
completed by next Monday evening, which means that you will be
able to drive on the bridge next Tuesday에서 암스트롱 다리 공사가
다음주 월요일에 끝나니 화요일부터 그곳으로 운전할 수 있게 된다고
한다. 따라서 정답은 (A)가 된다.

DAY 10 Daily Listening Practice p.64

PART 1

[정답] (D)

(A) She's washing some glasses.
(B) She is repositioning a machine.
(C) She's putting on her glasses.
(D) She's standing in front of a
    machine.

[해설]

1인 사진일 때는 인물의 동작을 나타내는 동사를 집중해서 들어야 한
다. 기계 앞에 서 있다고 묘사한 (D)가 정답이 된다. 오답을 유도하는
문제로 자주 출제되는 put on(착용하는 동작)과 wear(착용한 상태)을
구분해서 숙지해야 한다. 제시된 사진은 안경을 착용한 상태(wearing)
이므로 (C) putting on은 불가하다.

PART 2

 1 (A)   2 (A)   3 (C)   4 (B)

1

Would you prefer a desk in the corner or near the
window?
(A) Either is good.
(B) The corner office belongs to the manager.
(C) Much better, thank you.

[해설]

'A or B 중 하나'를 선택하는 의문문 문제이다. '둘 중 어느 것이나 괜찮
다'라고 한 (A)가 정답이 된다. (B)는 질문의 corner를 반복한 오답 유
도 문장이고, '훨씬 낫다'라는 의미의 (C)는 질문에 어울리지 않는다.

2

Would you rather take the train or a plane?
(A) I prefer to fly.
(B) We were on the same train.
(C) Yes, I gave it back.

[해설]

'기차와 비행기 중 어느 것을 탈지' 묻는 질문에 비행기를 택한 (A)가
정답이다. (B)는 질문의 train을 반복한 오답 유도 문장이고 시제와 내
용도 질문과 어울리지 않는다. 선택 의문문에서는 yes/no로 대답하지
않으므로 (C)는 정답이 아니다.

3

Can you type this report, or should I ask Julia?
(A) The boss didn't mention it.
(B) It's a different kind of report.
(C) I'll have time after lunch.

[해설]

'보고서 타이핑을 쳐 줄 수 있는지 다른 이에게 부탁해야하는지'를 묻는
질문에 나온 단어를 직접적으로 사용하지 않고 '점심 후에 시간이 있
다'로 표현한 (C)가 정답이다. (A)는 질문과 연관이 없고, (B)는 질문의
report를 반복해 오답을 유도하고 있다.

4

Do you want to sit here inside or over there by the
window?
(A) They can choose it.
(B) We need fresh air.
(C) Windows will be installed soon.

[해설]

'안쪽에 앉고 싶은지 창가에 앉고 싶은지' 묻는 질문에 '창가에 앉고 싶
다'는 표현을 We need fresh air로 바꿔서 표현한 (B)가 정답이다. you
로 질문하면 I나 we로 답해야하므로 (A)는 정답이 아니다. (C)는 질문
의 window를 반복해 오답을 유도하고 있다.

PART 3

 1 (B)   2 (D)   3 (A)   4 (B)   5 (C)   6 (A)

Questions 1-3 refer to the following conversation.

W Good afternoon, King Street Health Clinic. Janice
   speaking.
M Hello. I'm applying for a job that requires allergy
   testing. Do you do that at your clinic? And, if so,
   can I get it done next week?
W Yes, sir, we provide allergy testing. When you
   arrive for the tests, you have to give a form to the
   doctor indicating your known reactions to foods,

dusts, and other substances. We could either send you the form as an e-mail attachment, or we could mail it. Which do you prefer, sir?

M   My printer is out of ink, so you had better <u>send it by regular mail</u>.

1

[번역]

남자가 전화를 하고 있는 이유는 무엇인가?

(A) 송금하기 위해

(B) 검사 날짜를 잡기 위해

(C) 전문가와 상담하기 위해

(D) 상품을 주문하기 위해

[해설]

남자의 행동에 대한 질문이므로, 남자의 말에 집중하자. 남자의 첫 대화문 I'm applying for a job that requires allergy testing. ~ can I get it done next week?에서 다음 주에 알레르기 검사를 받을 수 있느냐는 내용이 나온다. 따라서 정답은 (B)이다.

[어휘]

transfer 이체하다 ｜ specialist 전문가 ｜ order 주문하다 ｜ product 상품

2

[번역]

남자는 무엇을 해야 하는가?

(A) 보험을 신청한다.

(B) 은행에 간다.

(C) 다른 병원에 전화한다.

(D) 양식을 작성한다.

[해설]

남자가 해야 할 일은 여자가 알려 주는 내용에서 힌트를 얻을 수 있다. 여자의 두 번째 대화문 you have to give a form to the doctor에서 의사에게 서류를 제출해야 한다는 내용이 나오므로 정답은 (D)이다.

[어휘]

insurance 보험 ｜ phone 전화하다 ｜ complete 끝내다

3

[번역]

남자는 여자에게 무엇을 해달라고 요청하는가?

(A) 우편으로 서류를 보내달라고

(B) 약속을 취소하라고

(C) 양식을 이메일로 보내라고

(D) 팩스기를 구입하라고

[해설]

남자의 말에서 힌트를 찾을 수 있는 문제이다. send it by regular mail에 보통우편으로 서류를 보내달라는 내용이 나온다. 따라서 정답은 (A)이다.

[어휘]

cancel 취소하다 ｜ appointment 약속 ｜ purchase 구입하다

Questions 4-6 refer to the following conversation.

M   We need to replace some of the desks and chairs here.

W   What's the matter with them? I think they're pretty comfortable.

M   They look old and tattered, and <u>several visitors have commented negatively on them</u>. They reflect badly on us as a whole.

W   I see. <u>Would you like me to order some new furniture then?</u>

M   Why don't you find a few items that look nice and then show them to me? <u>I need to see how much everything will cost</u> before I make a final decision.

W   All right. I'll get to work on it as soon as I can.

M   Do you think <u>you can send me your choices by this evening</u>?

W   I doubt it. I've got a meeting at Ferris Metals that will last most of the afternoon.

4

[번역]

화자들은 주로 무엇에 대해 논의하는가?

(A) 새로운 고객과의 만남

(B) 가구 교체

(C) 고객 중 일부가 그들에 대해 어떻게 생각하는지

(D) 사무실 전체의 리디자인

[해설]

남자의 첫 번째 말인 replace some of the desks and chairs에서 정답의 단서를 찾을 수 있다. 이후에도 남자와 여자는 가구 주문에 관해 이야기한다.

[어휘]

replacement 교체 ｜ redesign 다시 디자인하다; 재설계

5

[번역]

남자는 언제 여자가 자신의 요구를 들어 주기를 원하는가?

(A) 점심 시간까지

(B) 오늘 오후까지

(C) 오늘 저녁까지

(D) 내일 오전까지

[해설]

대화 후반부의 남자의 말, Do you think you can send me your choices by this evening?에서 남자는 자신의 요청 사항이 오늘 저녁까지 실행되기를 원한다고 언급한다.

6

[번역]

여자는 오늘 오후에 무엇을 할 것인가?

(A) 회의에 참석한다

(B) 카탈로그를 살펴본다

(C) 새로운 제품을 주문한다
(D) 가구 매장에 방문한다

[해설]

여자의 마지막 말, I've got a meeting at Ferris Metals that will last most of the afternoon.에서 여자는 페리시 금속에서의 회의에 참석할 것임을 알 수 있다.

PART 4

1 (C)　**2** (D)　**3** (A)

Questions 1-3 refer to the following advertisement.

> Now that the holiday season is over, many of you have probably put on some extra pounds. There's no need to be alarmed though. Simply sign up for a membership at the Lowell Health Club. <u>Our personal trainers will talk with you to determine the best way for you to lose weight.</u> By showing up at the gym at least three times a week, you'll start getting slimmer immediately. But remember that working out isn't easy. It requires effort on your part. Still, <u>we can get you started and help you develop a thin or muscular body.</u> Call 509-4305 to find out about our special membership offer that will save you money. Or visit us at 56 Pecan Avenue. We're open <u>twenty-four hours a day every day of the year.</u>

1

[번역]

화자는 개인 트레이너에 대해 무엇을 암시하는가?
(A) 그들은 소규모로 회원들을 가르친다.
(B) 그들은 근육을 키우는 일에 집중한다.
(C) 그들은 함께 운동하는 사람들의 말에 귀를 기울인다.
(D) 그들은 교육 과정에 대해 추가 수당을 받아야 한다.

[해설]

Our personal trainers will talk with you to determine the best way for you to lose weight.라는 문장에서 개인 트레이너들은 상담을 통해 체중 감량 방식을 알려 준다는 점을 추측할 수 있다. 따라서 정답은 (C)이다.

[어휘]

focus on ~에 집중하다, ~에 초점을 맞추다 | muscle 근육 | training session 교육, 교육 과정

2

[번역]

로웰 헬스 클럽에 관해 사실인 것은 무엇인가?
(A) 신규 회원은 웹사이트에서 등록을 해야 한다.
(B) 시내에 세 곳이 있다.
(C) 체육관은 국경일에만 문을 닫는다.
(D) 사람들은 할인 가격으로 가입을 할 수 있다.

[해설]

담화 후반부에 화자는 '할인 가격(special membership offer that will save you money)'을 안내하고 있다.

3

[번역]

화자가 "It requires effort on your part"라고 말했을 때, 그는 무엇을 의미하는가?
(A) 체중을 감량하기 위해서는 운동을 해야 한다.
(B) 체육관에 연락하기 위해서는 수고를 해야 한다.
(C) 트레이너한테 솔직하게 말해야 한다.
(D) 보다 숙달되려면 열심히 운동해야 한다.

[해설]

여기서 주어인 it은 working out(운동)을 가리키며, 주어진 문장을 직역하면 '그것은 당신 측에서의 노력을 필요로 한다'라는 뜻이다. 따라서 이 말은 곧 '운동은 힘들기 때문에 본인 스스로의 노력이 필요하다'라는 의미로, 보기 중에서는 (A)가 이러한 취지의 의미에 가장 부합된다.

[어휘]

make an effort to ~하기 위해 노력하다 | honest 정직한 | skilled 숙련된

DAY 11 Daily Listening Practice　p.69

PART 1

[정답] (A)

(A) Pottery has been placed on a book.
(B) A stack of books has been set on a shelf.
(C) A rack is being adjusted.
(D) A book is wrapped in cloths.

[해설]

(B)는 책이 쌓여(a stack of books) 있지 않기 때문에 오답이고 (C)처럼 인물이 없는 사진에서 현재 진행형 수동태(be + being + p.p.)를 사용한 경우는 거의 오답이다. (D)는 사진에 천(cloths)이 보이지 않는다. 따라서 정답은 머그잔(mug)을 도자기(pottery)로 표현한 (A)가 정답이 된다.

PART 2

1 (C)　**2** (B)　**3** (A)　**4** (C)

1

Do you know when this plane arrives at the airport?
(A) It's a clear day.
(B) There was a mechanical problem.
(C) Let me check the schedule.

[해설]

'언제 비행기가 공항에 도착하는지 아느냐?'를 묻는 질문에 '일정을 확인해보겠다'고 응답한 (C)가 정답이다. (A)는 날씨를 묻는 질문에 대한 응답이고, (B)는 이유를 묻는 Why 의문문에 나올 수 있는 대답이다.

2

Do you know where the keys to the filing cabinet are?
(A) Just to Mr. Thompson.
(B) I left them on Mr. Baker's desk.
(C) Files are being updated

[해설]

'열쇠들이 어디 있는지 아느냐?'는 질문에 '베이커 씨 책상에 놔뒀다'라고 응답한 (B)가 정답이 된다. (A)의 경우, 질문이 '있다'는 뜻의 be동사(are)로 묻고 있기 때문에 '~에게'를 뜻하는 방향 전치사 to가 어색하다. (C)는 질문의 filing과 발음이 비슷한 file을 이용한 오답 유도 문장이다.

3

Do you know why Mr. Delco has called this meeting?
(A) To introduce a new employee, I think.
(B) That can save us some money.
(C) You called her the other day.

[해설]

'왜 델코 씨가 회의 소집을 했는지 아느냐?'는 질문에 '~하기 위해서'라는 의미의 to부정사를 써서 적절히 대답한 (A)가 정답이다. (B)는 질문과 관계없는 응답이고 (C)는 질문의 called를 반복한 오답유도 문장이다.

4

Do you know who's filling the vacant position?
(A) This is the only one you have.
(B) What place did you vacate?
(C) The decision hasn't been made yet.

[해설]

'누가 공석의 후임이 될지 아느냐?'는 질문에 '아직 결정이 안됐다'라고 응답한 (C)가 정답이다. (A)는 질문과 어울리지 않는 대답이고, (B)는 질문의 vacant(공석인)와 비슷한 발음 vacate(비우다)로 혼동을 유발하고 있나.

PART 3

1 (D) **2** (B) **3** (B) **4** (B) **5** (A) **6** (A)

Questions 1-3 refer to the following conversation.

W1 Ms. Drummond, <u>do you have that graph showing last month's sales</u>? I need to discuss those figures with you <u>before meeting with the finance head at 1:30</u>.

W2 Yes, Ms. Boyce. I e-mailed it to you about half an hour ago.

W1 Oh, I see. I haven't had a chance to check my inbox yet. I'll go take a look at it now. It's 11:45

now, so <u>why don't we talk about those figures over lunch?</u> 10 minutes is more than enough time to review the graph.

W2 Certainly, Ms. Boyce. I'll see you at noon.

1

[번역]

화자들은 주로 무엇에 대해 이야기하고 있는가?
(A) 고객
(B) 동업자
(C) 팩스기
(D) 그래프

[해설]

지난 달 판매 실적 그래프를 갖고 있느냐(do you have that graph showing last month's sales?)는 첫 번째 대화 내용에서 (D)가 정답임을 알 수 있다.

2

[번역]

재무부장과의 미팅은 언제인가?
(A) 오늘 오전
(B) 오늘 오후
(C) 내일 오전
(D) 내일 오후

[해설]

첫 대화문 before meeting with the finance head at 1:30에서 정답이 (B)임을 알 수 있다.

3

[번역]

화자들은 아마도 무엇을 하겠는가?
(A) 잠재고객을 만난다.
(B) 점심식사를 하면서 회의를 한다.
(C) 분기 보고서를 팩스로 보낸다.
(D) 약속 시간을 다시 정한다.

[해설]

대화가 끝난 후의 상황에 대한 단서는 주로 마지막 대화문에 나온다. Why don't we talk about those figures over lunch?라고 했으므로 점심을 먹으며 회의할 것임을 알 수 있다. 정답은 (B)이다.

[어휘]

potential 잠재의 | client 고객 | quarterly 분기의 | appointment 약속

Questions 4-6 refer to the following conversation with three speakers.

M <u>There's a rumor going around</u> that we're going to be relocating soon.

W1 It's not simply a rumor. It's going to happen sometime next month.

M　How do you know that?

W1　Mr. Carlyle asked me how I felt about moving to Seattle. I asked him why, and then he told me.

W2　So we're really going to be moving there? That's a three-hour drive from Portland.

M　If we relocate to Seattle, we'll all have to move.

W1　I'm not willing to do that, so I'll have to find another job. I don't want to move my family to another city.

M　I'm still single, so it doesn't bother me too much. But I believe the cost of living is higher than it is here.

W2　That's a good point.

4

[번역]

회사는 언제 이전을 할 것인가?

(A) 이번 주

(B) 한 달 내에

(C) 지금부터 6개월 후에

(D) 내년에

[해설]

남자가 회사의 이전 소식에 대해 이야기하지 여자1은 그것이 사실이라고 답하면서, It's going to happen sometime next month.라고 말한다. 따라서 회사의 이전은 다음 달에 이루어질 일이다.

5

[번역]

화자들에 의해 무엇이 암시되는가?

(A) 그들의 회사는 포틀랜드에 위치해 있다.

(B) 그들 중 누구도 차를 소유하고 있지 않다.

(C) 그들은 사업차 시애틀을 방문할 것이다.

(D) 그들은 현재 일자리를 찾아보고 있다.

[해설]

시애틀로의 이전 소식을 접하자 여자2는 That's a three-hour drive from Portland.라고 말한다. 따라서 화자들이 현재 근무 중인 회사는 포틀랜드에 위치해 있음을 추측할 수 있다.

6

[번역]

남자는 이전에 대해 어떻게 생각하는가?

(A) 그에게는 이전이 괜찮다.

(B) 그는 집을 구매하는 것을 걱정하고 있다.

(C) 그는 가족이 이사가는 것을 원하지 않는다.

(D) 그는 그것이 너무 비쌀 것이라고 생각한다.

[해설]

남자의 마지막 말에서 남자는 회사의 이전을 크게 반대하지 않는다는 점을 알 수 있다.

1 (D)　**2** (A)　**3** (B)

Questions 1-3 refer to the following talk.

Please have a seat. This meeting will be very quick. As you are aware, Dawson Equipment will be using a different payroll system from tomorrow, so you need to know how it will work. At the end of a shift, each person must enter his or her new employee ID number and hours in one of the computers located in room 107. The new system will keep track of your hours and adjust your wages accordingly. Please be sure to enter your information every day. You can pick up your new ID from your supervisor on your way out. If you experience any difficulties, please see either Ms. Yuri Nakamura or Frederick Simmons in general affairs. They have created a list of simple steps on how to input your information.

1

[번역]

화자가 이 이야기를 하는 까닭은?

(A) 새 직원을 소개하기 위해

(B) 급료 인상을 알리기 위해

(C) 지점장을 임명하기 위해

(D) 시스템 변경 내용을 설명하기 위해

[해설]

주제를 묻는 전반부형 문제이다. As you are aware, Dawson Equipment will be using a different payroll system from tomorrow, so you need to know how it will work에서 내일부터 새로 바뀔 급료 체계를 알아둬야 한다는 내용이 나온다.

[어휘]

raise 인상, 상승 ｜ appoint 임명[지명]하다 ｜ regional 지역의

2

[번역]

직원들이 팀장에게서 받을 것은 무엇인가?

(A) 새 신분증

(B) 새 컴퓨터

(C) 지원서 양식

(D) 지하철 노선도

[해설]

문제의 핵심 어구 supervisor에 유념해서 듣다 보면, 후반부의 You can pick up your new ID from your supervisor on your way out에서 새 신분증(ID)을 받게 된다는 내용이 나온다.

3

[번역]

직원이 왜 총무부에 가게 될 것 같은가?

(A) 회의를 취소하기 위해

(B) 설명서를 얻기 위해

(C) 약속 일정을 잡기 위해

(D) 근무 일정표를 가지러 가기 위해

[해설]

문제의 핵심 어구 general affairs에 집중해 들으면, 후반부의 If you experience any difficulties, please see either Ms. Yuri Nakamura or Mr. Frederick Simmons in general affairs 바로 다음 문장에서 정보 입력 방법에 대한 조처 목록을 만들어 두었다고 한다. 즉 '조처 목록을 가져가라'는 말이므로 '조처 목록'을 설명서(instructions)로 바꿔 표현한 (B)가 정답이 된다.

[어휘]

obtain 얻다, 획득하다 | collect 모으다, 가지러 가다

DAY 12 Daily Listening Practice   p.74

PART 1

[정답] (D)

(A) Kitchen utensils are scattered on the floor.
(B) The door of the refrigerator has been opened.
(C) People are seated around the table.
(D) The chairs have been placed in the room.

[해설]

사물만 등장하는 사진이므로 (C)는 People만 듣고도 정답에서 제외할 수 있다. (A)는 바닥에 흩어져 있다(scattered on the floor)가 사진에 보이지 않고, (B)는 문이 열린 상태(has been opened)가 아니므로 오답이다. 결국 의자들이 실내에 놓여 있다고 묘사한 (D)가 정답이 된다.

PART 2

1 (C)   2 (B)   3 (C)   4 (C)

1

Isn't there a vending machine on this floor?
(A) She's not working now.
(B) He went to the second floor.
(C) Yes, at the end of the hall.

[해설]

부정의문문의 의미는 일반의문문과 같기 때문에 의문문의 not을 해석에서 신경 쓸 필요가 없다. 그래서 '하면' Yes이고 '아니면' No이다. 따라서 '자판기가 있습니까?'라는 질문에 '네, 홀 끝에요'라고 한 (C)가 정답이다. (B)는 질문의 floor를 반복해서 오답을 유도하고 있다.

2

Isn't it too warm to wear a sweater?
(A) No, it's the same one.

(B) Don't you think it's cold in here?
(C) I thought it was not necessary.

[해설]

'스웨터를 입기에 너무 따뜻하죠?'라는 질문에 가장 어울리는 답변은 '여기 안이 춥지 않나요?'라고 반문하는 형태로 반대 의견을 표현한 (B)이다. (A)의 '그것과 똑같다'는 응답은 질문과 어울리지 않고, (C)는 시제가 질문과 어울리지 않는다.

3

Hasn't the equipment arrived yet?
(A) Yes, she's a new arrival.
(B) All right, then.
(C) Not yet, I guess.

[해설]

'장비가 도착했나요?'라는 질문에 '아직'이라고 대답한 (C)가 정답이다. (A)는 질문의 arrived와 발음이 비슷한 arrival을 이용한 오답 유도 문장이고 (B)는 질문과 연관성이 없다.

4

Didn't Ms. Becker notify you of the cancellation?
(A) Submit it in writing.
(B) That's what I've been told.
(C) No, I haven't heard anything.

[해설]

'베커 씨가 당신에게 알렸죠?'라는 질문에 가장 어울리는 답변은 '아직 어떤 것도 못 들었다'고 대답한 (C)이다. (A)는 질문과 무관한 응답이고, (B)의 '그것이 제가 들은 내용입니다'는 응답은 질문과 어울리지 않는다.

PART 3

1 (B)   2 (A)   3 (D)   4 (B)   5 (A)   6 (C)

Questions 1-3 refer to the following conversation.

M Could you help me for a minute? I am taking a bus to St. Richard at 2:30 but I don't know which boarding gate to go to.

W They usually post that information on the board but you're right, it's not there. Let me check our main schedule in this book here. Is that an express bus?

M No, it isn't.

W According to this, it's coach number 1436 and will be departing from gate 10. I'm sure the driver will make an announcement when it is time to board so I suggest that you have a seat over there near the gate.

1

[번역]

대화는 어디에서 일어나고 있겠는가?
(A) 페리 부두

(B) 버스 터미널
(C) 공항
(D) 지하철 역

[해설]

남자는 여자에게 도움을 청하면서 I am taking a bus to St. Richard at 2:30 but I don't know which boarding gate to go to라고 말하는데, 버스를 탑승할 탑승구가 있을만한 장소는 보기 중 (B)이다.

[어휘]

ferry 페리, 연락선 | dock 부두 | subway 지하철

2

[번역]

남자는 무엇을 알고 싶어 하는가?
(A) 탑승구 번호
(B) 차량의 종류
(C) 도착 시간
(D) 표 가격

[해설]

남자의 말 I don't know which boarding gate to go to에서 '어떤 탑승구인지 모른다'고 말한다. 그리고 여자는 후반부에서 ~ will be departing from gate 10이라며 남자가 모른다고 말한 정보를 알려 준다. 그러므로 정답은 (A)가 된다.

[어휘]

vehicle 차량 | arrival 도착

3

[번역]

여자는 남자에게 무엇을 하라고 제안하는가?
(A) 표를 바꾼다.
(B) 자신의 가방에 이름표를 붙인다.
(C) 내일 떠난다.
(D) 탑승 안내를 기다린다.

[해설]

'제안'과 관련된 문제는 주로 대화의 후반부에서 정답의 단서를 찾을 수 있다는 점에 유의하자. 여자의 마지막 대화문인 I'm sure the driver will make an announcement when it is time to board so I suggest that you have a seat over there near the gate를 종합하면 탑승 안내가 있을 때까지 앉아서 기다리라는 것이다. 이 대화문에 문제의 핵심 어구인 suggest가 포함되어 있지만, 정답과 관련된 내용은 그 단어가 제시되기 전에 언급되므로 전체 문장을 잘 이해하고 문제를 풀어야 한다.

[어휘]

suggest 제안하다 | tag 꼬리표, 짐표 | boarding call 탑승 안내

Questions 4-6 refer to the following conversation and road sign.

> M We're about to arrive at the exit for Milton. <u>Do you want to take the turnoff and stop for anything?</u>
> W No, that's all right. We had lunch an hour ago, so I'm not hungry now. You're not already getting hungry again, are you?
> M No, I'm not. However, <u>I don't think we'll make it all the way to</u> Jackson without filling up the car with gas.
> W <u>How much gas do we have left right now?</u> We're not about to run out, are we?
> M No, don't worry about that. We've got about half a tank left.
> W How about stopping for gas at Springfield? <u>We'll probably want to get something to eat by then as well.</u>
> M That should be all right. We can probably make it there in the next hour or so.

4

[번역]

화자들은 주로 무엇에 대해 논의하는가?
(A) 얼마나 더 운전을 해야 하는지
(B) 어디에서 주유를 해야 하는지
(C) 밀턴에서 무엇을 할 것인지
(D) 점심으로 무엇을 먹을 것인지

[해설]

주유를 하기 위해 어디에서 정차를 하는 것이 좋을지 논의하고 있다.

5

[번역]

화자들은 한 시간 전에 무엇을 했는가?
(A) 음식을 먹었다.
(B) 집을 떠났다.
(C) 친구를 방문했다.
(D) 쇼핑을 했다.

[해설]

여자의 We had lunch an hour ago, so I'm not hungry now.라는 말에서 화자들은 한 시간 전에 식사를 했음을 알 수 있다.

6

[번역]

도표를 보아라. 화자들의 최종 목적지까지 거리가 얼마인가?
(A) 5킬로미터
(B) 75킬로미터
(C) 180킬로미터
(D) 302킬로미터

[해설]

대화 중반부에서 남자는 However, I don't think we'll make it all the way to Jackson without filling up the car with gas.라고 말한다. 이를 통해 화자들의 최종 목적지는 잭슨이라는 점을 알 수 있으며 도표에 이 곳까지의 거리는 180km로 나타나 있다.

1 (C) **2** (B) **3** (A)

Questions 1-3 refer to the following announcement and chart.

> Thank you all for tuning in to tonight's program. I hope you had a great time listening to Dr. Ramsey talk about <u>the innovative work he's doing at the local university</u>. I know I had lots of fun interviewing him. Be sure to listen to tomorrow's show. We're going to have a special guest. It's local author Brett Hampton. He's going to chat with us about his latest novel, <u>which is shooting up the bestseller charts.</u> <u>We're going to take a short commercial break now,</u> and then Steve Isaacs will be on next with his show, *The Steve Isaacs Hour*. He'll recap all of the local and state news of the day. <u>There were several noteworthy events today,</u> so be sure to listen to Steve's take on them.

1
[번역]

브렛 햄프턴은 누구인가?
(A) 라디오 진행자
(B) 대학 교수
(C) 작가
(D) 뉴스 리포터

[해설]

화자는 브렛 햄프턴을 local author(지역 작가)로 소개하고 있고, 그가 라디오 방송에서 '자신의 최신 소설(his latest novel)'에 대해 이야기할 예정이라고 말한다.

[어휘]

host 진행자

2
[번역]

청자들은 다음에 무엇을 듣게 될 것인가?
(A) 뉴스 프로그램
(B) 광고
(C) 인터뷰
(D) 날씨 정보

[해설]

담화 후반부에 화자가 We're going to take a short commercial break now라고 했으므로 바로 이다음에는 광고가 이어질 것이다. *더 스티브 아이삭스 아워(The Steve Isaacs Hour)*라는 뉴스 프로그램은 광고 이후에 듣게 될 것이다.

3
[번역]

그래프를 보아라. 이 방송은 어떤 라디오 방송국에서 이루어지고 있는가?

(A) WMRT
(B) WCOB
(C) WDNG
(D) WPTR

[해설]

라디오 방송에서 안내된 내용을 종합해 보면, 첫째 지역 대학 교수와의 인터뷰가 이루어졌고, 둘째 지역 작가와의 인터뷰가 예정되어 있으며, 그리고 마지막으로 곧 뉴스가 방송될 것이라는 점을 알 수 있다. 이러한 포맷은 도표 상 news와 talk shows에 해당되는 것이므로 정답은 (A)이다.

DAY **13** Daily Listening Practice p.81

PART 1

[정답] (B)

(A) He is falling over a rock.
(B) He is folding his hands.
(C) He is bending his neck.
(D) He is lifting a candle.

[해설]

1인 사진이므로 인물의 동작을 나타내는 서술부를 집중해서 들어야 한다. 손을 깍지 끼고 있는 모습을 folding his hands로 묘사한 (B)가 정답이다. (A)의 넘어지는(falling)모습도, (C)의 구부리는(bending)모습도, (D)의 들어올리는(lifting)모습도 보이지 않으므로 오답이다.

PART 2

1 (A) **2** (B) **3** (C) **4** (B)

1

Would you like to apply for the vacancy in sales?
(A) No, I'm not interested in the job.
(B) Yes, it does.
(C) There are many vacant rooms.

[해설]

일반 의문문은 질문의 키워드인 동사를 잘 들어야 한다. '지원하고 싶나?'는 질문에 '그 일에 관심 없다'고 답한 (A)가 정답이다. (B)의 경우, 대답의 주어(it)가 질문의 주어(you)와 어울리지 않고, (C)는 질문의 vacancy(공석)와 발음이 비슷한 vacant(빈)를 이용한 오답이다.

2

Will you be able to come to the meeting?
(A) The meeting will last for 30 minutes.
(B) Yes, I'm planning on it.
(C) That's true.

[해설]

질문의 키워드인 동사에 주의해서 해석해보면, '올 수 있냐?'는 질문에 '그렇게 할 계획이다'라고 답한 (B)가 정답이 된다. (A)는 질문의 the meeting을 반복한 오답 유도 문장이고, (C)는 질문과 무관한 답변이다.

3

Could you help me with this cost proposal?
(A) Projected costs are a million dollars.
(B) She worked hard on them.
(C) Sure, I'm free all afternoon.

[**해설**]

'도와줄 수 있느냐?'는 질문에 '물론이죠, 오후 내내 시간이 있어요'라고 응답한 (C)가 정답이다. (A)는 질문의 cost를 반복한 오답 유도 문장이고, (B)의 경우, you로 물은 질문에 she로 응답하는 것은 적절치 않다.

4

Should I sign these two pages right now?
(A) Sorry, I will turn it down.
(B) We need them immediately.
(C) You had some help.

[**해설**]

'지금 바로 이 두 장에 서명해야 하느냐?'는 질문에 yes/no로 답하지는 않았지만 '서류들이 즉시 필요하다'라고 응답한 (B)가 정답이다. (A) 답변의 주어 I도 목적격 대명사 it도 질문의 two pages(복수)와 어울리지 않고, (C)는 질문과 무관한 답변이다.

PART 3

1 (A) **2** (D) **3** (D) **4** (D) **5** (D) **6** (B)

Questions 1-3 refer to the following conversation.

> M Wendy, what's going on with the cordless microphones we ordered from George AV Supplies? It's been almost three weeks, and they are still not here.
> W I know, Jack. I called yesterday. Apparently, a lot of equipment was damaged during the transport, but they know that our awards dinner is Friday evening, and they guarantee that we will have the mikes by then.
> M But I don't want to leave this until the last minute. Tell them to have the microphones here by 3:00 on Wednesday, or we will take our business elsewhere.
> W All right. I'll phone right now and make sure they understand our position.

1

[**번역**]

화자들은 주로 무엇에 대해 이야기하고 있는가?
(A) 주문 관련 문제
(B) 컨퍼런스 일정
(C) 마케팅 전략
(D) 봉급 인상

[**해설**]

남자의 첫 대화문 what's going on with the cordless microphones we ordered from George AV Supplies?에서 주문한 무선 마이크가 어떻게 되었냐는 내용이 나오므로 정답은 (A)이다.

[**어휘**]

schedule 일정 ｜ strategy 전략 ｜ increase 인상, 증대 ｜ salary 봉급, 급료

2

[**번역**]

시상식 만찬은 언제인가?
(A) 월요일
(B) 화요일
(C) 수요일
(D) 금요일

[**해설**]

여자의 첫 대화문 중 our awards dinner is Friday evening에서 정답이 (D)임을 알 수 있다. (C)는 남자가 주문품을 받아야 하는 마감일로 다시 정한 요일이다.

3

[**번역**]

여자는 무엇을 하겠다고 말하는가?
(A) 계약서를 검토한다.
(B) 마이크를 수리한다.
(C) 신청서를 제출한다.
(D) 공급업체에 전화한다.

[**해설**]

대화 후의 상황을 묻는 질문으로, 여자의 마지막 대화문 I'll phone right now and make sure they understand our position에서 업체에 전화를 걸어 입장을 확실히 하겠다는 내용이 나온다. 따라서 정답은 (D)이다.

[**어휘**]

review 검토하다 ｜ contract 계약서 ｜ repair 수리하다 ｜ submit 제출하다 ｜ application 신청서, 지원서 ｜ supplier 공급자

Questions 4-6 refer to the following conversation.

> W Excuse me. I purchased this blouse here three days ago, but I'd like to get my money back.
> M What's the matter with it? Didn't you get the right size?
> W It fits perfectly, but there are a couple of stains on it. Take a look at them here.
> M I'm very sorry about that. If you prefer, you can simply exchange it for another blouse that is in perfect condition. Would you prefer that?
> W I'm afraid not. I would rather have my money back.
> M Sure. If you'll follow me to the checkout counter, I can process the return for you. Oh, you brought the receipt, didn't you? You can't return anything without one.
> W Yes, I've got it here in my bag.

4

[번역]

여자는 왜 블라우스를 반품하고 싶어하는가?

(A) 디자인이 마음에 들지 않는다.

(B) 그녀에게 잘 맞지 않는다.

(C) 색상이 마음에 들지 않는다.

(D) 옷에 얼룩이 있다.

[해설]

환불하려는 이유를 묻는 남자의 질문에 여자는 there are a couple of stains on it이라고 답한다. 따라서 정답은 (D)이다.

5

[번역]

남자는 여자가 무엇을 할 것을 요청하는가?

(A) 양식을 작성한다

(B) 새로운 제품을 선택한다

(C) 매니저와 이야기한다

(D) 카운터로 간다

[해설]

If you'll follow me to the checkout counter, I can process the return for you.라는 말로 남자는 여자에게 카운터로 갈 것을 요청하고 있다.

6

[번역]

여자가 "I'm afraid not"이라고 말할 때 그녀는 무엇을 의미하는가?

(A) 그녀는 영수증을 가지고 와야 한다는 것을 잊었다.

(B) 그녀는 교환을 원하지 않는다.

(C) 매장에는 그녀가 원하는 것이 없다.

(D) 그녀는 언제 제품을 구입했는지 기억하지 못한다.

[해설]

I'm afraid not.은 남자의 Would you prefer that?에 대한 대답으로서 I'm afraid I would not prefer that.을 줄여 쓴 말이다. 따라서 여기에서는 교환을 원하지 않고 환불을 원한다는 의미로 사용되었다.

PART 4

1 (B)　**2** (A)　**3** (C)

Questions 1-3 refer to the following recorded message.

Thank you for calling the Green Alliance. If you are seeking general information, please press 1. If you know the party you want to reach, press 2 for a list of extensions. Our office is open from 9 to 5, Monday through Friday. If you wish to leave a message in our general mailbox, please wait for the beep. Our address is 29 Diamond Drive, suite 301; visitors are welcome during normal business hours.

1

[번역]

이 메시지는 무엇에 대한 정보를 제공하는가?

(A) 파티 룸

(B) 조직체의 사무실

(C) 보석가게

(D) 사탕가게

[해설]

Thank you for calling the Green Alliance에서 '조직체 또는 회사'에 전화한 것을 유추할 수 있으므로 (B)가 정답이 된다.

2

[번역]

금요일은 몇 시에 문을 여는가?

(A) 오전 9시

(B) 오전 9시 25분

(C) 오후 1시

(D) 오후 5시

[해설]

Our office is open from 9 to 5, Monday to Friday(월요일부터 금요일까지 9시부터 5시까지 열려 있음)에서 (A)가 정답임을 알 수 있다.

3

[번역]

전화를 건 사람은 특정인에게 어떻게 연결될 수 있는가?

(A) 신호음을 기다린다.

(B) 종합 정보를 요청한다.

(C) 2번을 누른다.

(D) 메시지를 남긴다.

[해설]

If you know the party whom you want to reach, press 2 for a list of extensions(연락하려는 상대방을 알면 2번을 누를 것)이라고 했으므로 (C)가 답이다.

[어휘]

specific 특정한 ｜ beep 삐 소리

PART 1

[정답] (C)

(A) Various items are on sale.

(B) A woman is removing some laundry.

(C) Some clothes are piled up.

(D) They are turning on the lamps.

PART 2

1 (B) **2** (A) **3** (B) **4** (B)

1

Do you feel better after getting some rest?
(A) Actually, it tastes a little sour.
(B) Of course, far better.
(C) The rest are by the door.

[해설]
'쉬고 나서 몸이 나아졌느냐?'는 질문에 '물론이죠, 훨씬 나아졌어요'
라고 응답한 (B)가 정답이다. (A)는 질문과 무관한 내용이고 (C)는 다
의어 rest로 혼동을 주고 있다. 질문에서는 rest가 '휴식'이란 의미로 쓰
였으나, (C)에서는 '나머지'로 쓰였다.

2

Does anyone have an extra folder?
(A) You can borrow mine.
(B) It opens early on Monday.
(C) She's folding chairs.

[해설]
'누가 여분의 폴더를 가지고 있느냐?'는 질문에 가장 적절한 응답은 '제
것을 빌리세요'라고 한 (A)이다. 여기서 mine은 my extra folder를 가
리키고 있다. (B)는 질문과 무관한 내용이고, (C)는 질문의 folder와 발
음이 비슷한 folding을 이용한 오답유도 문장이다.

3

Did you forget to bring the invoices?
(A) Yes, the views are great.
(B) No, I have them with me.
(C) Let's meet at his office.

[해설]
'송장 가져오는 것을 잊었나요?'란 질문에 적절한 응답은 '아뇨, 가져왔
어요'라고 한 (B)이다. (A)와 (C)는 질문과 무관한 내용이다.

4

Do we need authorization if we hope to leave early?
(A) It's not necessary to leave early.
(B) Of course. Talk to your manager.
(C) The author is a friend of ours.

[해설]
'허가가 필요한가?'를 묻는 질문에 적절한 응답은 '물론이죠, 매니저에
게 말하세요'라고 한 (B)이다. (A)는 질문에 나오는 leave early(빨리 나
가다)를 반복해서 오답을 유도하는 문장이고, (C)는 질문과 어울리지
않는 응답이다.

PART 3

1 (C) **2** (A) **3** (B) **4** (B) **5** (B) **6** (C)

Questions 1-3 refer to the following conversation.

M You look a bit lost. Do you need some help?
W Yes, I'm here for the new employee orientation.
   It's going to be held in the auditorium, but I can't
   seem to find it. I thought it was somewhere
   around here.
M You remind me of myself two years ago when
   I first came to this company. I was lost just like
   you. Follow me. I'm going there, too. Nice to you
   meet you. I'm Bob, Bob Kendal from Personnel.

1

[번역]
여자가 찾고 있는 것은?
(A) 고용주의 사무실
(B) 그녀의 새 사무실
(C) 강당
(D) 주차장

[해설]
여자의 첫 대화문 It's going to be held in the auditorium, but I can't
seem to find it에서 여자가 찾고 있는 것이 강당임을 알 수 있기 때문에
정답은 (C)이다.

2

[번역]
남자는 아마도 어디에 가는 중이겠는가?
(A) 신입사원 오리엔테이션
(B) 본사
(C) 밥의 사무실
(D) 분실물 센터

[해설]
남자의 두 번째 대화문 I'm going there, too에서 남자 역시 신입사원
오리엔테이션 장소인 강당에 가는 것을 알 수 있으므로 정답은 (A)이
다.

3

[번역]
남자는 회사에서 얼마나 오랫동안 근무해 왔는가?
(A) 1년
(B) 2년
(C) 3년
(D) 4년

[해설]
You remind me of myself two years ago, when I first came to this
company에서 남자가 2년 전에 입사했음을 알 수 있다.

Questions 4-6 refer to the following conversation with three speakers.

> W Do you know when the new computers are arriving?
>
> M1 I got a call from the store. They should be here around 12:30.
>
> M2 But we'll be at lunch then. Who's going to sign for them?
>
> W I guess I can stay in the office. I don't mind waiting for the deliveryman to arrive.
>
> M1 Thanks a lot, Karen. I'd volunteer, but I'm meeting Ms. Jackson from Tempe Partners for lunch today.
>
> W Don't mention it, Steve. I need to get some work done, so I'll have lunch at my desk.
>
> M2 Did you bring anything from home? Or would you like me to get you something from the cafeteria?
>
> W I appreciate the offer, but I'll just order something from the deli downstairs. Someone from there will bring my sandwich up here.

4

[번역]

12시 30분에 어떤 일이 일어날 것인가?
(A) 잭슨 씨가 사무실에 도착할 것이다.
(B) 컴퓨터가 배달될 것이다.
(C) 해외 고객이 전화를 할 것이다.
(D) 회의가 열릴 것이다.

[해설]

컴퓨터의 도착 시간을 묻는 질문에 남자1이 They should be here around 12:30.라고 답하고 있으므로 12시 30분에는 컴퓨터가 배달될 것임을 알 수 있다.

[어휘]

overseas 해외의 | make a phone call 전화하다

5

[번역]

여자는 자신이 무엇을 할 것이라고 말하는가?
(A) 택배 회사에 전화를 한다
(B) 점심 시간에 사무실에 남아 있는다
(C) 잭슨 씨와 만난다
(D) 컴퓨터를 업그레이드한다

[해설]

점심 시간에 컴퓨터가 배달될 것이라는 이야기를 듣고 여자는 I guess I can stay in the office.라고 말한다. 따라서 그녀가 사무실에 남아서 컴퓨터를 받게 될 것이므로 정답은 (B)이다. (C)는 남자1이 하게 될 일이다.

6

[번역]

여자는 점심을 어떻게 먹을 것인가?

(A) 집에서 음식을 가지고 왔다.
(B) 구내 식당에서 식사를 할 것이다.
(C) 식품점에서 음식을 주문할 것이다.
(D) 인근 식당에 갈 것이다.

[해설]

대화의 마지막 부분에서 여자는 I'll just order something from the deli downstairs라고 말한다.

[어휘]

nearby 근처의, 인근의

PART 4

   1 (B)   **2** (C)   **3** (A)

Questions 1-3 refer to the following excerpt from a meeting.

> I'm pleased to announce we've secured some new investment. The group from Watson Technology was impressed by what they saw last week. They were particularly intrigued with some of our newest projects. For that reason, we signed a deal that will provide us with $10 million in funding. Most of the money is going to the R&D Department so that we can continue work on our projects. But we're also going to budget some funds to our other departments. After all, we'd like everyone to share in the wealth. Here's what you should do: Send me revised budgets for your departments. Focus only on what you absolutely must have. We don't want a single dollar to be wasted. I expect e-mails from everyone no later than 10 tomorrow morning.

1

[번역]

화자에 의하면, 왓슨 테크놀로지는 무엇을 했는가?
(A) 몇몇 제품을 구입하기 위한 계약을 체결했다
(B) 회사에 투자를 했다
(C) 최신 기술을 보여 주었다
(D) 추가 자금 지원을 요청했다

[해설]

담화 초반부에 화자는 '신규 투자(new investment)'를 유치했다고 전한 후, For that reason, we signed a deal that will provide us with $10 million in funding.에서 구체적인 투자 내용을 언급하고 있다.

[어휘]

purchase 구입하다 | additional 추가의, 추가적인

2

[번역]

화자는 청자들에게 무엇을 하라고 말하는가?
(A) 새로운 프로젝트를 제안한다
(B) 자금을 주의 깊게 쓴다

(C) 새로운 예산안을 제출한다
(D) 왓슨 테크놀로지와 연락을 취한다

[해설]

화자의 요청 사항은 Here's what you should do: 이후의 문장들에서 확인할 수 있다. 화자는 예산안을 수정해서 자신에게 보낼 것을 청자들에게 요청하고 있다.

[어휘]

get in touch with ~와 연락을 취하다

3

[번역]

화자가 "After all, we'd like everyone to share in the wealth"라고 말했을 때, 그녀는 무엇을 의미하는가?
(A) 모든 부서들은 추가적인 자금을 받게 될 것이다.
(B) 회사는 원한다면 어떤 식으로도 사용할 수 있는 돈을 가지고 있다.
(C) 회사의 주식 가치가 상승하고 있다.
(D) 모든 직원들은 보너스를 받게 될 것이다.

[해설]

화자는 투자로 유입된 자금이 우선적으로 연구개발부를 위해 쓰일 것이지만, 다른 부서에게도 돌아갈 것이라고 말한 후, After all, we'd like everyone to share in the wealth.라고 말한다. 이를 통해 화자가 의미하는 바는 모든 부서들이 투자 자금을 공유하도록 하겠다는 것임을 알 수 있다.

<table><tr><td>DAY 15</td><td>Daily Listening Practice</td><td>p.91</td></tr></table>

PART 1

[정답] (D)

(A) The wall is completely bare.
(B) A cloth is covering a round table.
(C) The entrance is undergoing repairs.
(D) Some seats are occupied.

[해설]

복수 인물 사진으로 사람들이 자리에 앉아 있는 상황을 seats are occupied로 묘사한 (D)가 정답이다. (A)의 bare는 '텅 빈, 세간이 없는'이란 뜻인데 벽에 램프와 액자가 걸려있기 때문에 정답이 될 수 없고 사진에 등장하지 않는 사물(cloth, round table)을 이용한 (B) 역시 오답이며, 입구가 수리되는 상황도 사진에서 볼 수 없으므로 (C)도 오답이다.

PART 2

1 (B)   2 (A)   3 (B)   4 (B)

1

You're off work in a while, aren't you?
(A) Yes, I turned it off.
(B) Absolutely, I'm leaving at 5.
(C) There are a few works on the wall.

[해설]

질문에 나오는 off work(휴가인)의 표현을 모르면 답하기 힘든 문제이다. '5시에 떠난다'고 응답한 (B)가 정답이다. (A)의 turn off는 가전제품 따위를 끈다는 뜻이고, (C)의 works는 '작품'을 뜻하는 말이다.

2

You hired a temporary secretary, didn't you?
(A) Yes, she started 2 days ago.
(B) Yes, she hired a new agency.
(C) In half an hour.

[해설]

'임시 비서를 고용했죠?'란 질문에 가장 적절한 응답은 '이틀 전에 시작했다'고 대답한 (A)이다. (B) 질문의 hired를 반복해서 오답을 유도한 문장이다. (C)는 When 의문사 질문에 가능한 응답이다.

3

They prefer to sit on the patio, don't they?
(A) We are seated on the bench.
(B) Absolutely, they do.
(C) No, they didn't see it.

[해설]

'그들이 테라스에 앉고 싶어하죠?'라는 질문에 '네, 그렇습니다'라고 대답한 (B)가 정답이다. (A)는 질문의 주어 they와 선택지의 주어 We가 어울리지 않는다. (C)는 질문의 sit과 발음이 비슷한 see it으로 혼동을 유발하는 문장이다.

4

We have to register for the workshop, don't we?
(A) What a marvelous book!
(B) Yes, we do.
(C) The registration process is complex.

[해설]

'워크숍에 등록해야죠?'라는 질문에 가장 적절한 응답은 '네, 그래야죠'라고 한 (B)이다. (A)는 질문과 무관한 응답이고, (C)는 질문의 register와 비슷한 registration을 이용한 함정이다.

PART 3

1 (A)   2 (B)   3 (C)   3 (C)   4 (B)   5 (A)

Questions 1-3 refer to the following conversation.

W I heard from one of my professors that university students are entitled to 40 percent off the regular admission price.

M Yes, that is correct. I just need to see your university ID.

W I'm a history major at Emerson University. Here's my ID.

M Many history enthusiasts come to the Layton Museum often, usually once or twice a month. If you plan to do that, would you consider becoming a member? You will save even more on the regular admission price. This pamphlet explains all your options.

1

[번역]

본 대화는 어디에서 이루어지는가?
(A) 박물관에서
(B) 기차 역에서
(C) 길모퉁이에서
(D) 슈퍼마켓에서

[해설]

여자의 첫 번째 대화문 중 university students are entitled to 40 percent off the regular admission price에서 '입장료'와 관계된 곳임을 알 수 있어 (A)가 답일 것이라 예측해 볼 수 있는데, 대화 후반부의 남자의 말 Many history enthusiasts come to the Layton Museum often에서 이는 더욱 확실해 진다. 그러므로 정답은 (A)이다.

[어휘]

take place (일이) 일어나다

2

[번역]

여자는 무엇에 대해 묻는가?
(A) 새로 시작한 전시
(B) 학생 할인
(C) 전규 영업시간
(D) 취업 기회

[해설]

여자는 I heard from one of my professors that university students are entitled to 40 percent off the regular admission price라는 말로 대화를 시작하고 있는데, 이 문장의 핵심을 가장 잘 표현한 것은 (B)이다.

[어휘]

exhibit 전시 ｜ business hours 영업시간 ｜ employment 채용 ｜ opportunity 기회

3

[번역]

남자는 무엇을 하라고 제안하는가?
(A) 몇몇 서류를 작성하는 것
(B) 미술 갤러리에 방문하는 것
(C) 회원권을 구매하는 것
(D) 지도를 확인하는 것

[해설]

suggest, offer, recommend 등이 사용된 문제는 주로 대화 후반부에서 단서를 찾을 수 있다. 남자의 마지막 대화문 중 would you consider becoming a member?에서 (C)가 정답임을 알 수 있다.

[어휘]

suggest 제안하다 ｜ complete 완성하다 ｜ purchase 구입하다

Questions 4-6 refer to the following conversation and map.

W Pardon me, but could you give me some assistance, please?
M Yes, how may I be of service?
W I flew in from Paris, and I need to take the shuttle bus to my hotel. However, I'm not sure where to go.
M Could you tell me the name of your hotel, please?
W Yes, hold on a moment . . . I've got a reservation at the Crown Hotel.
M Walk straight past the elevator and fast-food restaurant. Keep going until you get to the rental car booth. Then, go out the doors past it. You'll see a sign posted for the hotel's shuttle bus.
W Great. Do you know how often the bus leaves?
M It departs once an hour at the top of the hour, and it's five to eleven right now. You'd better hurry.

4

[번역]

화자들은 어디에 있는 것 같은가?
(A) 호텔에
(B) 버스 정류장에
(C) 공항에
(D) 기차역에

[해설]

I flew in from Paris라는 여자의 말에서 여자는 비행기로 타고 왔음을 알 수 있다. 또한 호텔 셔틀 버스는 주로 공항과 호텔간에 운행된다는 사실을 통해서도 화자들이 공항에 있음을 알 수 있다.

5

[번역]

남자는 여자에게 무엇을 암시하는가?
(A) 여자의 예약이 취소되었다.
(B) 그녀의 버스가 곧 출발할 것이다.
(C) 그녀는 버스를 타기 위해 요금을 지불해야 한다.
(D) 그녀는 차를 빌려야 한다.

[해설]

남자는 버스가 정시마다 출발하는데 현재 시각이 5분전 11시이라고 밝힌 후, You'd better hurry.라고 말한다. 즉, 버스가 곧 출발할 것이므로 여자에게 서두를 것을 권하고 있다.

6

[번역]

지도를 보아라. 여자는 어느 출구로 나가야 하는가?
(A) 1번 출구
(B) 2번 출구
(C) 3번 출구
(D) 4번 출구

남자는 여자에게 엘리베이터와 패스트푸드점을 지나쳐 렌터카 부스까지 간 다음에 '렌터카 부스를 지나쳐 밖으로 나가라(go out the doors past it)'고 말한다. 따라서 지도상 렌터카 부스 옆에 있는 Exit 1이 정답이다.

PART 4

1 (A) **2** (D) **3** (B)

Questions 1-3 refer to the following telephone message.

> Good afternoon Ms. Ricketts. My name is Cara Noland and I'm phoning from *Writer's Monthly*. You e-mailed us your résumé indicating that you are interested in writing for us. We are looking for someone to write a regular column on practical writing tips. In your résumé, you indicated that your story on the ongoing strike at Delbert Auto appeared as a front page story in *The Dryden Star*. Both our editor and I were truly impressed with that article. We will be interviewing applicants this Wednesday between 1:00 and 6:00. We would like to interview you as well so, if you are still interested, please call me back as soon as possible at 416-9837.

1

[번역]

리케츠 씨는 누구이겠는가?
(A) 저자
(B) 컨설턴트
(C) 기술자
(D) 점원

[해설]

문제의 핵심 어구 'Ms. Ricketts'가 본 메시지의 수신자(you)임을 간파해야 보다 수월하게 해결할 수 있다. 전반부의 You e-mailed us your résumé indicating that you are interested in writing for us를 통해 '글 쓰는 것'에 관심 있어서 리케츠 씨가 화자 측에 이력서를 보낸 상황임을 알 수 있으므로 가장 적절한 것은 (A)이다.

[어휘]

machinist 기술자, 수리공 | clerk 점원

2

[번역]

본 메시지의 목적은 무엇인가?
(A) 길을 알려주기 위해서
(B) 파업에 관한 세부사항을 알려주기 위해서
(C) 문제를 알리기 위해서
(D) 인터뷰를 요청하기 위해서

[해설]

이력서를 잘 받았고 몇몇 지원자들을 곧 인터뷰할 예정인데 같이 면접하고 싶으니 관심 있으면 연락 달라(We would like to interview you

as well so, if you are still interested, please call me back as soon as possible at 416-9837)는 맥락으로 볼 때 (D)가 정답이 된다. 메시지의 목적에 대한 결정적인 단서는 대체로 전반부에서 나오지만 이처럼 전체적인 맥락을 파악해야 해결할 수 있는 유형의 문제도 출제되니 유의하자.

[어휘]

provide 제공하다 | directions 길안내 | detail 세부사항 | report 알리다, 보고하다 | request 요청하다

3

[번역]

드라이든 스타는 무엇이겠는가?
(A) TV 드라마
(B) 신문
(C) 교과서
(D) 연애 소설

[해설]

문제의 핵심 어구 'The Dryden Star'에 유의해 담화를 듣자. 중반부의 your story on the ongoing strike at Delbert Auto appeared as a front page story in *The Dryden Star*에서 '파업에 관한 이야기가 일면에 실리는' 매체임을 알 수 있다. 따라서 (B)가 정답이 된다.

[어휘]

textbook 교과서

DAY 16 Daily Listening Practice p.97

PART 1

[정답] (C)

(A) They're standing in the alleyway.
(B) They're seated at various places.
(C) They're running in a group.
(D) They're wearing the same uniforms.

[해설]

보기의 주어가 모두 They로 시작하는 복수 인물사진이므로 동작을 묘사한 서술부에 집중해서 답을 선택해야 한다. 따라서 줄을 맞춰 달리고 있는 모습을 running in a group으로 표현한 (C)가 정답이다. 사진에서는 (A)에서 언급된 골목길(alleyway)이 보이지 않고, 사람들이 앉아 있는(seated)것도 아니므로 (B) 역시 정답이 아니다. 한 명이 다른 유니폼을 입고 있으므로 (D) 역시 바른 설명이 아니다.

PART 2

1 (B) **2** (A) **3** (C) **4** (B)

1

Why don't we meet in the cafeteria?

(A) The meeting lasted for an hour.
(B) That's a great idea.
(C) It's in the next room.

[해설]

'~하는 게 어때?'라는 상대방의 제안(why don't we ~?)에 '좋은 생각이다'라고 답한 (B)가 정답이다. (A)는 질문의 meet과 발음이 유사한 meeting을 이용한 오답 함정이고, (C)는 장소를 묻는 Where 질문에 적합한 응답이다.

2

When did you last speak to Moriko?
(A) A week ago.
(B) The last speaker was excellent.
(C) As soon as she gets back.

[해설]

과거 시제로 때(When)를 묻는 질문에 (A)가 과거 시점으로 적절히 답하고 있다. (B)는 질문의 last speak와 비슷한 발음 last speaker를 이용한 오답 유도 문장이다. (C)는 질문의 주어 you에 she로 대답할 순 없다.

3

Ms. Ito gave an impressive speech, didn't she?
(A) The speaker is my associate.
(B) Usually between 10 and 12.
(C) Yes, I enjoyed it very much.

[해설]

'이토 씨가 인상적인 연설을 했죠?'란 질문에 적절한 응답은 '매우 재미있게 들었어요'라고 한 (C)이다. (A)는 질문의 speech와 발음이 비슷한 speaker를 이용한 함정이고, (B)는 질문과 무관한 대답이다.

4

Don't you have to bring the other documents?
(A) I need to see a doctor.
(B) Yes, I'll take them with me.
(C) It was a long meeting.

[해설]

'다른 서류들(other documents)을 가져와야 하지 않느냐?'는 질문에 서류(them)를 가져오겠다고 답한 (B)가 적절하다. (A)는 documents와 혼동해서 들을 수 있는 doctor을 써서 오답을 유도하고 있다. (C)는 질문과 무관한 대답이다.

PART 3

1 (D) **2** (B) **3** (C) **4** (C) **5** (B) **6** (C)

Questions 1-3 refer to the following conversation.

M Excuse me. I was on a Raleigh Air flight from London. I came here to pick up a big suitcase that I had checked but I don't see it anywhere.
W Are you sure this is the right place? Raleigh has several flights daily from London to Birmingham.
M But I was on fight number 609 and that's the same number on that board.

W I see. If you walk just past that coffee shop, you will see the customer service desk on your right. I'm sure they will be able to help you.

1

[번역]

이 대화는 어디에서 이루어지고 있겠는가?
(A) 소방서
(B) 약국
(C) 병원
(D) 공항

[해설]

남자의 말 I was on a Raleigh Air flight from London. I came here to pick up a big suitcase that I had checked을 종합하면, 그는 런던에서부터 비행기를 타고 와서 이제 짐을 찾으려고 하고 있음을 알 수 있다. 그러므로 정답은 (D)가 된다.

[어휘]

pharmacy 약국

2

[번역]

남자의 걱정은 무엇인가?
(A) 연결편 항공을 놓칠 수도 있다.
(B) 자신의 짐을 찾을 수가 없다.
(C) 팩스 번호를 기억할 수 없다.
(D) 돈을 송금하는 것을 잊어버렸다.

[해설]

남자는 짐을 찾으러 왔지만 but I don't see it anywhere라며 그것을 찾을 수가 없다고 한다. 그러므로 '위치, 장소 등을 알아내다'라는 의미의 동사 locate를 사용하여 '자신의 짐 위치를 찾을 수 없다'고 한 (B)가 정답이다.

[어휘]

concern 걱정 ┃ miss 놓치다 ┃ connecting flight 연결편 비행기 ┃ unable ~할 수 없는 ┃ locate ~의 위치를 알아내다 ┃ luggage 짐, 수하물 ┃ transfer 송금하다 ┃ fund 자금

3

[번역]

여자는 남자에게 어디로 가라고 제안하는가?
(A) 가까운 서점
(B) 여행객 정보 센터
(C) 고객 서비스 데스크
(D) 건물의 정문

[해설]

'제안'과 관련된 문제이므로 마지막 부분을 잘 들어 보아야 한다. 여자는 If you walk just pass that coffee shop, you will see the customer service desk on your right. I'm sure they will be able to help you라며 고객 서비스 데스크에 가면 도움을 구할 수 있을 것이라고 말하므로 정답은 (C)이다.

[어휘]

tourist 여행객 ┃ entrance 출입구

Questions 4-6 refer to the following conversation.

> **M** Hello. I had a seat on Flight 47, <u>but it got canceled a couple of minutes ago</u>. The person at the gate told me to come here and speak with you.
>
> **W** I'm very sorry about the cancelation. Is Dallas <u>your final destination today</u>?
>
> **M** No, it's not. I'm supposed to change flights there and then go to Phoenix.
>
> **W** In that case, <u>if you don't mind waiting a couple of hours</u>, I can get you on a direct flight to Phoenix.
>
> **M** I'll take it. What do I need to do?
>
> **W** Let me see your ticket, please. I have to make a few changes to it, and then I can get you a seat. <u>I'm also upgrading you to business class.</u>
>
> **M** This must be my lucky day. Thanks a lot.

4
[번역]

화자들은 어디에 있는가?
(A) 호텔에
(B) 버스 정류장에
(C) 공항에
(D) 기차역에

[해설]

flight, business class와 같은 표현을 통해 화자들은 공항에 있음을 알 수 있다.

5
[번역]

여자는 남자에게 무엇을 줄 것을 요청하는가?
(A) 신용 카드
(B) 티켓
(C) 예약증
(D) 여행 일정

[해설]

여자는 Let me see your ticket, please.라고 말하면서 남자에게 티켓을 보여 달라고 부탁한다. 따라서 정답은 (B)이다.

[어휘]

itinerary 여행 일정(표)

6
[번역]

남자가 "This must be my lucky day"이라고 말할 때 그는 무엇을 의미하는가?
(A) 그는 제때에 목적지에 도착하게 될 것이다.
(B) 그의 예약은 취소되지 않을 것이다.
(C) 그는 업그레이드에 의해 기뻐한다.
(D) 그의 티켓이 여전히 유효하다.

[해설]

I'm also upgrading you to business class.에 대한 반응이다. 남자는 이 말을 통해 비즈니스석으로의 좌석 업그레이드에 대한 기쁨을 나타내고 있다.

[어휘]

get to ~에 도달하다, ~에 도착하다 | valid 유효한, 효력이 있는

PART 4

1 (A)　**2** (B)　**3** (B)

Questions 1-3 refer to the following except from a talk and map.

> Now that your orientation session is finished, we need to tour the facilities. We're going to go everywhere today, but let me point some places out to you first. Right now, <u>we're standing in front of the main building</u>. Most of you will be working here. Directly across from the main building is the company parking lot. <u>You need to park your vehicles there</u> when you arrive. To the left of the parking lot is the front gate. <u>You must get a security pass before you'll be allowed onto the premises</u>. We'll do that after lunch. Now, look over to the right. Do you see those two huge buildings? Those are our primary factories. The one on the left runs 24 hours a day <u>while the one on the right has 16-hour shifts</u>. Let's visit the one on the left first.

1
[번역]

청자들은 누구인 것 같은가?
(A) 신입 직원
(B) 경비원
(C) 공장 노동자
(D) 회사 중역

[해설]

오리엔테이션 이후에 회사 시설들을 안내하고 있다. 또한 Most of you will be working here.라는 언급을 통해서도 청자들이 신입 직원일 것이라는 점을 추측할 수 있다.

[어휘]

security guard 경비원, 보안 요원 | executive 중역, 임원

2
[번역]

청자들은 언제 보안증을 얻게 될 것인가?
(A) 몇 분 후에
(B) 점심 식사 후에
(C) 일과가 끝날 때
(D) 내일 오전에

화자는 출입을 위해서는 보안증을 발급받아야 한다고 말한 후, We'll do that after lunch.라고 언급한다. 따라서 정답은 (B)이다.

3

[번역]

지도를 보아라. 회사 주차장은 어디에 있는가?

(A) 1
(B) 2
(C) 3
(D) 4

[해설]

Directly across from the main building is the company parking lot.이라는 문장을 통해 주차장은 본관 맞은 편에 있다는 사실을 알 수 있다.

DAY 17 Daily Listening Practice　p.103

PART 1

[정답] (D)

(A) One man is reaching for a knob.
(B) There is a fountain next to the men.
(C) The men are reviewing applications.
(D) Some materials are arranged on the table.

[해설]

탁자 위에 자료들이 가지런히 놓여있는 모습을 묘사한 (D)가 정답이다. 사진 속에 보이지 않는 knob(손잡이, 쥐는 부분), fountain(분수, 식수대), reviewing(검토 중인)을 제시한 (A)와 (B) 그리고 (C)는 답이 될 수 없다.

PART 2

1 (C)　**2** (C)　**3** (B)　**4** (C)

1

Who's taking the clients out tonight?
(A) She's one of our clients.
(B) To the theater.
(C) The plant manager.

[해설]

의문사 Who(누가) 질문에 대해 직책으로 응답한 (C)가 정답이다. (A)는 질문의 clients를 반복해 오답을 유도하고 있다. (B)는 장소를 묻는 질문에 대한 응답이다.

2

The stairs are steep, aren't they?
(A) We saw her in the stairway.
(B) It's a dangerous habit.
(C) That's why I always take the elevator.

[해설]

'계단이 가파르다'는 상대의 말에 '그래서 저는 항상 엘리베이터를 타지요'라고 답한 (C)가 정답이다. (A)는 질문의 stairs와 뜻이 같은 stairway를 사용해 오답을 유도하고, (B)에서 언급된 stairs(계단)와 habit(습관)은 연관이 없다.

3

Why don't you invite Sara to your party?
(A) Yes, he does.
(B) We already have.
(C) I think you can make it.

[해설]

'파티에 새라를 초대하는게 어때?'라는 제안에 '이미 초청했다'고 대답한 (B)가 정답이다. We already have invited Sara to our party에서 invited이하가 생략된 구조이다. (A)의 경우, 의문사 의문에 yes로 대답할 수 없다. (C)는 '당신'이 초대하는 게 어떠냐는 질문에 '당신'이 제시간에 올 수 있다는 말이 어색하다.

4

Don't you think the library should be open even on Sunday?
(A) The library is always crowded.
(B) I recommend walking.
(C) Why don't you make that suggestion?

[해설]

'일요일에도 도서관을 열어야 한다고 생각하지 않냐?'며 동의를 구하는 질문에 '네가 그 제안을 하는 게 어때?'라고 제안한 (C)가 정답이다. (A)는 질문의 library를 반복한 오답 함정이고, (B)는 질문과 무관한 내용이다.

PART 3

1 (B)　**2** (C)　**3** (C)　**4** (B)　**5** (A)　**6** (C)

Questions 1-3 refer to the following conversation.

> W John, did you send in your résumé for that position I mentioned last week?
> M I haven't had a chance yet, Angela. Things have been really hectic lately. Just look at all these papers on my desk. I think the ad you clipped from the newspaper for me is somewhere in this pile. Do you recall any of the job details?
> W Well, Hansen Research is looking for a data analyst. That's exactly what you do here except you can earn a lot more money at Hansen's because it's the second biggest company in our industry.

M But that could also mean I will have to work lots and lots of hours. <u>I need more information before submitting my résumé. I'll start by reading through Hansen's website.</u>

Questions 4-6 refer to the following conversation with three speakers.

M I've got to visit Pacino's for a dinner meeting tonight. <u>Do either of you know how to get there?</u>

W1 Are you talking about the restaurant down by the waterfront?

M Yes, that's the place I am visiting.

W1 I've never been there, <u>but I've heard lots of good things about it.</u> How about you, Cheryl?

W2 You're in luck, Dave. I had lunch there two days ago.

M Do you think I should drive or take a bus there?

W2 The bus stop is more than three blocks away, so <u>I'd advise against taking public transportation.</u>

M So I should drive there, right?

W2 That's right. <u>Let me write down the directions for you.</u> Do either of you have a pen I can borrow?

1

[번역]

화자들은 무엇에 대해 이야기하고 있는가?

(A) 다가오는 컨퍼런스

(B) 채용 기회

(C) 통계 오류

(D) 컴퓨터 문제

[해설]

여자의 첫 대화문 did you send in your résumé for that position I mentioned last week?에서 지난 주에 언급했던 일자리에 이력서를 냈는지 확인하는 내용으로 보아, 이 문제의 정답은 (B)이다.

[어휘]

upcoming 다가오는, 미래의 | opportunity 기회 | statistical 통계(학)의

2

[번역]

남자는 아마도 어떤 일을 하는 것 같은가?

(A) 자동차 조립

(B) 모델

(C) 자료 조사

(D) 법률 자문

[해설]

여자의 두 번째 대화문 Hansen Research is looking for a data analyst. That's exactly what you do here에서 한센 연구소에서 자료 분석가를 구하는데 업무 내용은 남자가 현재 회사에서 하는 일과 똑같다고 하므로 정답은 (C)이다.

[어휘]

auto 자동차 | legal 법률과 관련된

3

[번역]

남자는 이어서 무엇을 하겠는가?

(A) 컨퍼런스 참가 신청을 한다.

(B) 회의를 기획한다.

(C) 어떤 회사에 대해 조사한다.

(D) 야근을 한다.

[해설]

미래 행위에 대한 질문의 단서는 마지막 대화문에서 찾을 수 있다. I need more information ~ by reading through Hansen's website에서 정보가 더 필요해서 한센의 웹사이트를 살펴 보겠다는 내용이 나오므로 정답은 (C)이다.

[어휘]

resister for 신청하다 | organize 조직하다 | corporation 법인 | overtime 초과근무

4

[번역]

남자는 오늘밤에 무엇을 할 것인가?

(A) 늦게까지 사무실에 남아 있는다

(B) 식당에서 저녁을 먹는다

(C) 해안가의 부동산을 살펴본다

(D) 보고서 작성을 끝낸다

[해설]

대화의 첫 부분에서 남자는 오늘밤 '저녁 모임(dinner meeting)'을 위해 파치노스(Pacino's)라는 식당에 가야 한다고 말한다. 따라서 정답은 (B)이다.

[어휘]

stay late 늦게까지 남아 있다 | property 재산, 부동산

5

[번역]

남자는 무엇을 알고 싶어하는가?

(A) 목적지에 갈 수 있는 가장 좋은 길

(B) 파치노스의 음식이 어떤지

(C) 그가 어디에서 버스를 탈 수 있는지

(D) 식당의 가격이 어느 정도인지

[해설]

대화 초반부에서 남자는 Do either of you know how to get there?라고 묻고 있다. 또한 이후에도 차를 몰고 가는 것이 좋은지, 아니면 버스를 타는 것이 좋은지에 대한 의견을 구하고 있으므로 정답은 (A)이다.

[어휘]

destination 목적지

6

[번역]

셰릴은 다음에 무엇을 할 것인가?

(A) 남자와 점심을 먹는다

(B) 다음 회의에 참석한다

(C) 길을 그려 준다
(D) 대중 교통을 이용한다

[해설]

대화 마지막 부분의 Let me write down the directions for you.라는 말에서 그녀는 남자에게 길을 그려 줄 것임을 알 수 있다.

PART 4

1 (C)　**2** (D)　**3** (A)

Questions 1-3 refer to the following announcement.

> Attention all visitors. The exhibition halls on the first and second floor of the Alfred Holmes Gallery will close in 15 minutes. Our gift shop, however, just inside the main entrance, will not close for another 30 minutes. Please don't forget to pick up your coat or any other items that you may have checked when you first entered the gallery. We would also like to remind you that the opening of our brand new exhibit, Landscape Watercolors by Lois McMillan, is scheduled to start on the first Monday of next month. Coupons for that exhibit are available just outside our gift shop. Once more, our exhibition halls will close in 15 minutes.

1

[번역]

본 안내의 주요 목적은 무엇인가?
(A) 로이스 맥밀란의 전시에 관한 세부사항을 제공하기 위해서
(B) 개인 분실물에 대해 알리기 위해서
(C) 갤러리 관람종료에 대해 안내하기 위해서
(D) 선물매장의 특가행사를 언급하기 위해서

[해설]

담화의 주요 목적에 대한 단서는 대체로 전반부에서 찾을 수 있다는 점을 유념하자. 첫 마디로 방문객들의 주목을 끌고서, The exhibition halls on the first and second floor of the Alfred Holmes Gallery will close in 15 minutes라며 15분 후에 갤러리를 닫는다고 하므로 (C)가 정답이 된다. 나머지 보기들은 각각 담화 중에 언급된 '로이스 맥밀란 전시', '개인 소지품', '신물매장'을 이용해 혼동을 준다.

[어휘]

provide 제공하다 ｜ detail 세부사항 ｜ report 알리다 ｜ personal 개인의 ｜ missing 잃어버린 ｜ announce 발표하다 ｜ mention 언급하다

2

[번역]

청중은 어떻게 하라는 지시를 받는가?
(A) 회원 신청서를 작성하라.
(B) 곧 있을 행사들을 위해 이메일을 확인하라.
(C) 문제에 대해서는 매니저에게 이야기하라.
(D) 떠나기 전에 소지품을 챙겨라.

[해설]

화자의 요청 사항을 찾는 것이므로 'Please 동사원형' 이나 'We'd like you to ~' 구문에 집중해야 한다. 중반부에서 Please don't forget to pick up your coat or any other items that you may have checked when you first entered the gallery에서 갤러리에 들어올 때 맡겼던 것들을 챙기라고 당부하므로 coat or any other items를 belongings(소지품)로 표현한 (D)가 정답이다. 본 문장의 check가 '(소지품 따위를) 맡기다'란 의미로 쓰였다는 점도 참고로 알아두자.

[어휘]

fill out 작성하다 ｜ application 신청(서) ｜ form 서식 ｜ check 확인하다 ｜ upcoming 곧 있을, 다가오는 ｜ event 행사 ｜ belongings 소유물

3

[번역]

다음 달에 어떤 일이 일어날 것인가?
(A) 전시가 하나 시작될 것이다.
(B) 몇몇 강의들이 진행될 것이다.
(C) 새 동(棟)이 건설될 것이다.
(D) 개조작업들이 진행될 것이다.

[해설]

문제의 핵심 어구 'next month'에 유의해 담화를 듣도록 한다. 후반부의 the opening of our brand new exhibit, Landscape Watercolors by Lois McMillan, is scheduled to start on the first Monday of next month를 통해 새 전시가 시작된다는 것을 알 수 있다. 따라서 정답은 (A)이다.

[어휘]

commence 시작되다 ｜ lecture 강연 ｜ wing (건물 본관 한쪽으로 돌출되게 지은) 동(棟), 부속 건물 ｜ construct 건설하다 ｜ renovation 개조

DAY 18 Daily Listening Practice　p.108

PART 1

[정답] (B)

(A) Some items are lying near a cash register.
(B) Containers have been filled for a display.
(C) A piece of glass is being measured.
(D) A meal is being put into a plastic bag.

[해설]

사물만 나오는 사진에는 다양한 명사와 동사가 나오므로 사진에 보이지 않는 단어를 소거해 나가야한다. (A)에서 언급된 cash register(금전등록기), (C)의 measure(측정하다), (D)의 plastic bag(비닐봉지)이 사진에 보이지 않는다. 따라서 정답은 (B)이다.

PART 2

1 (C)　**2** (B)　**3** (A)　**4** (B)

1

Would you rather walk or take a bus?

(A) I want to work today.

(B) We're scheduled to arrive at 7.

(C) Let's walk. We could use the exercise.

[해설]

'걷거나 버스 타는 것' 중 걷기를 택한 (C)가 정답이다. 여기서 could use가 '필요하다'라는 뜻임에 유의해야 한다. (A) 질문의 walk와 발음이 비슷한 work를 이용해 오답을 유도하고 있다. (B)는 질문과 무관한 내용이다.

2

Who should I submit this invoice to?

(A) He takes the subway.

(B) Carl usually takes care of it.

(C) By the end of the day.

[해설]

Who 질문에 이름 Carl을 주어로 써서 '칼이 보통 그 일을 처리해요'라고 답한 (B)가 정답이다. (A)는 질문과 무관한 내용이고, (C)는 When 의문문에 적절한 대답이다.

3

You are Dr. Sanchez, aren't you?

(A) No, I'm a colleague of his.

(B) I'll check out right away.

(C) Yes, he's my relative.

[해설]

'산체스 박사님이죠?'란 질문에 적절한 응답은 '아뇨, 저는 그의 동료입니다'라고 한 (A)이다. (B)는 질문과 무관한 응답이다. (C)의 Yes(네, 제가 산체스 박사입니다)와 he's my relative(그는 나의 친척입니다)는 앞 뒤가 어울리지 않는 대답이다.

4

When will the training session be completed?

(A) Over an hour.

(B) Thursday at the latest.

(C) She hasn't received any response.

[해설]

'언제'를 묻는 When 의문사 질문에 특정 요일로 응답한 (B)가 정답이 된다. (A)는 '얼마나 오래'를 묻는 How long ~?에 적합한 응답이고, (C)는 질문과 무관한 응답이다.

PART 3

1 (A)   2 (C)   3 (D)   4 (B)   5 (B)   6 (C)

Questions 1-3 refer to the following conversation.

W Hello. This is Katherine from Dr. McArthur's office. I'm calling to see if we can add 30 more copies to our print order.

M Hi, Katherine. We're kind of backed up due to technical problems at the moment, so it depends

on when you'd like to pick up your order.

W I have to run an errand right now, so I'll have Vanessa come by at 5 P.M.

M Let me see. It's 3 P.M. now. That should plenty of time. I'll have it ready by then.

1

[번역]

여자가 전화한 이유는?

(A) 남자가 추가 복사를 해주기를 바란다.

(B) 30% 할인을 원한다.

(C) 그녀의 복사기는 종이가 떨어졌다.

(D) 인쇄기를 수리해야 한다.

[해설]

여자가 I'm calling to see if we can add 30 more copies ~라며 전화 건 목적을 말하고 있다.

[어휘]

extra 추가의, 가외의

2

[번역]

주문한 인쇄물은 언제 준비되는가?

(A) 오후 3시에

(B) 오후 3시 30분에

(C) 2시간 후에

(D) 5시간 후에

[해설]

지금은 오후 3시이고(It's 3 P.M. now) 여자는 사람을 보내어 5시경(at 5 P.M.)에 인쇄물을 찾아가겠다고 했고 남자가 그때까지 준비해 두겠다(I'll have it ready by then.)고 했다. 따라서 지금부터 2시간 후에 인쇄물이 준비될 것임을 예상할 수 있으므로 (C)가 정답이다.

3

[번역]

주문한 인쇄물을 누가 찾으러 갈 것인가?

(A) 여자

(B) 캐서린

(C) 맥아서 박사

(D) 바네사

[해설]

여자는 심부름 때문에 바빠서 바네사를 대신 보낼 것(I'll have Vanessa come by at 5 P.M.)이라고 했으므로 (D)가 정답이다.

Questions 4-6 refer to the following conversation and list.

M Good afternoon. Rose's Bakery. How may I help you?

W Hello. This is Diana Thompson calling. I made an order with you yesterday.

M Yes, Ms. Thompson. I spoke with you on the phone then. What can I do for you?

W I spoke with my boss, and he mentioned <u>that</u> <u>more people will be attending the event than we</u> <u>had planned</u>. So I need to increase my order.

M Of course. I've got your order form here in front of me. What do you need more of?

W Well, <u>most of the people coming really love nuts</u>, so how about <u>adding another dozen of the items</u> <u>with nuts in them</u>?

M Sure. <u>You ordered two dozen of them</u>. Shall I add 12 more to the total?

W Yes, that would be perfect. Thanks a lot.

4

[번역]

여자는 왜 전화를 하는가?

(A) 주문을 하기 위해

(B) 추가 주문을 하기 위해

(C) 주문을 취소하기 위해

(D) 주문을 연기시키기 위해

[해설]

여자는 행사에 올 사람이 예상보다 많을 것이라는 점을 언급한 후, 남자에게 So I need to increase my order.라고 말한다. 따라서 여자가 전화한 이유는 추가 주문을 하기 위해서이다.

5

[번역]

여자는 참석할 사람들이 무엇을 좋아한다고 말하는가?

(A) 초콜릿으로 만들어진 음식

(B) 견과류가 들어 있는 음식

(C) 설탕 가루가 뿌려진 음식

(D) 과일이 들어 있는 음식

[해설]

most of the people coming really love nuts라는 여자의 말에서 행사에 참석할 사람들은 견과류 음식을 좋아할 것이라는 점을 확인할 수 있다. 따라서 정답은 (B)이다.

[어휘]

icing 당의, 설탕 가루

6

[번역]

도표를 보아라. 여자는 어떤 제품을 추가로 주문하는가?

(A) 초콜릿 컵케이크

(B) 젤리 도넛

(C) 퍼지 브라우니

(D) 오트밀 쿠키

[해설]

남자의 마지막 말 중 You ordered two dozen of them.에서 24개를 구입한 제품이 견과류 음식임을 짐작할 수 있다. 도표에서 24개를 구입한 제품은 퍼지 브라우니(Fudge Brownies)로 나타나 있으므로 (C)가 정답이다.

1 (B)   **2** (A)   **3** (C)

Questions 1-3 refer to the following excerpt from a meeting and chart.

I'd like to provide you with an update on the work my department has been doing. In the second quarter, we ran over budget by 5%. The reason was that we had a great deal of <u>additional spending which we had</u> <u>not accounted for</u>. The Sales Department insisted <u>that we heavily promote all of our new releases</u>. We had only been planning to market 2 or 3 of our biggest games. Instead, we advertised on TV, the radio, and the Internet for all 8 releases. Fortunately, <u>our efforts paid off since every game reported sales</u> <u>that were higher than expected</u>. Due to the extra workload, we took on three new employees. They're doing quite well. In addition, one employee, Lisa Sanders, resigned her position to move to another company.

1

[번역]

화자의 부서는 왜 예산을 초과했는가?

(A) 다수의 신제품을 개발했다.

(B) 많은 게임에 대한 광고를 했다.

(C) 예상보다 많은 제품을 판매하지 못했다.

(D) 몇몇 직원들에게 많은 보너스를 지급했다.

[해설]

화자는 예산 초과의 이유로 additional spending을 언급하면서, 이러한 '추가 지출'은 계획보다 많은 게임에 대한 홍보를 하기 위해 이루어졌음을 설명하고 있다. 따라서 정답은 (B)이다.

[어휘]

develop 개발하다 | buy an advertisement 광고면을 사다, 광고하다

2

[번역]

화자의 부서는 2분기에 무엇을 했는가?

(A) 신입 직원을 고용했다.

(B) 리사 샌더스를 승진시켰다.

(C) 두 명의 직원을 해고했다.

(D) 세 명의 직원을 전근시켰다.

[해설]

담화의 후반부에 '3명의 신입 직원을 고용했다(we took on three new employees)'는 언급이 있으므로 정답은 (A)이다. 참고로 리사 샌더스는 자발적으로 퇴사를 한 인물이다.

[어휘]

fire 해고하다 | transfer 전근하다, 전근시키다

3

[번역]

도표를 보아라. 화자는 누구인 것 같은가?

(A) 브루스 라이트

(B) 빌 모리슨

(C) 이안 스미스

(D) 제쓰로 워커

[해설]

promote, market, advertise 등과 같은 단어에 유의하면 화자는 마케팅부 소속이라는 점을 알 수 있다. 도표에서 마케팅 부서의 장은 (C) 이안 스미스로 나타나 있다.

DAY **19-20** Actual Test

p.115

[정답]

1 (B)	2 (C)	3 (D)	4 (C)	5 (B)
6 (B)	7 (B)	8 (A)	9 (B)	10 (C)
11 (C)	12 (A)	13 (C)	14 (B)	15 (A)
16 (A)	17 (B)	18 (C)	19 (B)	20 (C)
21 (A)	22 (A)	23 (C)	24 (A)	25 (B)
26 (B)	27 (A)	28 (C)	29 (A)	30 (B)
31 (B)	32 (B)	33 (C)	34 (D)	35 (D)
36 (B)	37 (C)	38 (C)	39 (C)	40 (A)
41 (A)	42 (B)	43 (D)	44 (B)	45 (C)
46 (D)	47 (D)	48 (D)	49 (B)	50 (C)
51 (D)	52 (C)	53 (C)	54 (D)	55 (A)
56 (D)	57 (C)	58 (D)	59 (D)	60 (A)
61 (D)	62 (B)	63 (A)	64 (D)	65 (C)
66 (B)	67 (C)	68 (C)	69 (A)	70 (B)
71 (D)	72 (B)	73 (A)	74 (C)	75 (B)
76 (B)	77 (A)	78 (D)	79 (C)	80 (B)
81 (B)	82 (D)	83 (B)	84 (B)	85 (B)
86 (C)	87 (A)	88 (D)	89 (B)	90 (A)
91 (C)	92 (C)	93 (A)	94 (B)	95 (C)
96 (A)	97 (D)	98 (C)	99 (A)	100 (A)

PART 1

1

(A) She is bending over.

(B) She is using a vending machine.

(C) She is leaning against the wall.

(D) She is receiving some change.

[번역]

(A) 여자는 허리를 굽히고 있다.

(B) 여자는 자판기를 이용하고 있다.

(C) 여자는 벽에 기대고 있다.

(D) 여자는 거스름돈을 받고 있다.

[해설]

여자가 자판기에 돈을 넣고 있는 장면을 '자판기를 이용하고 있다 (using a vending machine)'고 묘사한 (B)가 정답이다. 오답이지만 동작을 묘사하는 bend over, lean against와 같은 표현들은 자주 등장하므로 익혀 두어야 한다.

[어휘]

bend over 구부리다 | vending machine 자판기 | lean against ~에 기대다 | change 동전

2

(A) The man is painting a roof.

(B) The man is sketching on a canvas.

(C) The man is facing the wall.

(D) The man is looking around the house.

[번역]

(A) 남자는 지붕에 페인트칠을 하고 있다.

(B) 남자는 캔버스에 밑그림을 그리고 있다.

(C) 남자는 벽을 향해 있다.

(D) 남자는 집을 둘러보고 있다.

[해설]

1인 사진이므로 동작을 묘사하는 서술부에 집중해 들었을 때, 남자가 벽을 향하고 있는 모습을 facing the wall로 표현한 (C)가 정답이다. (A)와 (B)는 각각 painting, sketching 까지만 듣고 정답으로 생각할 수 있으나 사진에 없는 roof와 canvas가 목적어로 사용되었기 때문에 오답이다.

[어휘]

roof 지붕 | sketch 스케치하다 | canvas 화포, 캔버스 | look around 둘러보다

3

(A) The picnic table is being set.

(B) Some people are sitting on the grass.

(C) The chairs are all occupied.

(D) Some people are relaxing outside.

[번역]

(A) 피크닉 테이블이 설치되고 있다.

(B) 몇 사람이 잔디 위에 앉아 있다.

(C) 의자가 전부 차 있다.

(D) 몇 사람이 밖에서 휴식을 취하고 있다.

[해설]

복수 인물 사진으로 뚜렷한 특징을 찾을 수 없을 경우에는 소거법을 이용해 정답에 접근해야 한다. 사진에 등장하지 않는 picnic table을 언급

한 (A)는 오답이고, 사람들이 잔디에 앉아 있다고 표현한 (B) 또한 그림과 다르다. (C) 모든(all) 의자에 사람들이 앉아 있다고 했기 때문에 정답이 될 수 없다. 따라서 몇몇 사람들이 야외에 있는 모습을 relaxing outside로 표현한 (D)가 정답이 된다.

[어휘]

set the table 탁자를 설치하다 ｜ occupy (자리, 장소를) 차지하다 ｜ relax 휴식을 취하다

4

(A) One woman is taking off her glasses.
(B) One woman is clearing the desk.
(C) One woman is holding a document.
(D) One woman is wrapping an item.

[번역]

(A) 한 여자는 자신의 안경을 벗고 있다.
(B) 한 여자는 책상을 치우고 있다.
(C) 한 여자는 서류를 들고 있다.
(D) 한 여자는 물건을 포장하고 있다.

[해설]

2인 사진이지만 보기의 주어가 모두 One woman이므로 동작을 나타내는 서술부에 집중해야한다. 한 여성이 종이를 들고 있는 모습을 holding a document로 표현한 (C)가 정답이 된다. 오답으로 사용되었지만 각 보기에 사용된 동사들(take off, clear, wrap)은 자주 출제되므로 그 의미를 익혀두도록 한다.

[어휘]

take off ~을 벗다 ｜ clear 치우다 ｜ hold 들다, 잡다 ｜ document 서류, 문서 ｜ wrap ~을 포장하다 ｜ item 물건

5

(A) The carpet is being vacuumed.
(B) There is a cabinet near the wall.
(C) Some seats are taken.
(D) Some stools are stacked up.

[번역]

(A) 카펫을 진공청소기로 청소하고 있다.
(B) 벽 쪽에 진열장이 있다.
(C) 몇 좌석이 차 있다.
(D) 등받이가 없는 의자가 쌓여 있다.

[해설]

사물만 등장하는 사진이므로 사람 동작을 나타내는 현재 진행형(is + being)의 (A)는 정답이 될 수 없다. seats are taken은 '좌석이 차 있다'는 의미인데 사람이 등장하지 않으므로 (C)도 정답이 될 수 없다. (D)의 stools 역시 사진에서 찾아 볼 수 없다. 따라서 벽 쪽에 진열장이 있다고 표현한 (B)가 정답이 된다.

[어휘]

vacuum 진공 청소하다 ｜ seat 좌석 ｜ stool (등받이가 없는) 의자 ｜ stack ~을 쌓아 올리다

6

(A) The centerpiece is being placed on the table.
(B) There is a plant behind the furniture.
(C) The rug is being cleaned.
(D) The picture frame is being hung.

[번역]

(A) 중앙 장식물이 탁자 위에 놓여지고 있다.
(B) 가구 뒤에 화분이 있다.
(C) 깔개를 청소하고 있다.
(D) 그림 액자를 걸고 있다.

[해설]

사물만 등장하는 사진이기 때문에 사람의 동작을 표현하는 현재진행수동태(is being p.p.)로 묘사된 (A), (C), (D)는 오답이다. 따라서 정답은 소파(sofa, couch)뒤에 나무가 있는 모습을 가구(furniture)라는 단어를 써서 표현한 (B)가 정답이다.

[어휘]

centerpiece 중앙 장식물 ｜ place ~에 놓다 ｜ plant 식물 ｜ frame 액자 ｜ hang ~을 걸다

7

When are you having your job interview?
(A) Until Saturday.
(B) Next Monday.
(C) At the company headquarters.

[번역]

당신은 언제 구직 면접을 하나요?
(A) 토요일까지요.
(B) 다음주 월요일에요.
(C) 회사의 본사에서요.

[해설]

의문사 When(언제)을 이용해 '언제 구직 면접을 받는지'를 묻는 질문에 특정요일(Monday)로 응답한 (B)가 정답이다. (A)는 Saturday라는 특정일이 언급되지만 상태나 상황의 계속을 나타내는 전치사 Until(~까지)이 함께 쓰였으므로 오답이다. 질문의 현재 진행형(are having)은 가까운 미래를 의미한다.

[어휘]

job interview 구직 면접[인터뷰] ｜ headquarters 본사

8

Did you apply for the position I mentioned before?
(A) I need more information before applying.
(B) For several reasons.
(C) I have had enough.

[번역]

제가 전에 말했던 직책에 지원하셨어요?
(A) 지원하기 전에 정보가 더 필요해요.

(B) 몇 가지 이유 때문에요.

(C) 배불리 먹었어요.

[해설]

'전에 말했던 직책에 지원했는지'를 묻는 질문에 가장 적절한 응답은 '지원하기 전에 정보가 더 필요하다'면서 지원하지 않았음을 시사하는 (A)이다. (B) '몇 가지 이유 때문에'와 (C) '배불리 먹었어요'는 지원 여부와는 어울리지 않는 답변이다.

[어휘]

apply for ~에 지원하다 | position 일자리, 직책 | mention ~에 대해 언급하다

9

Why is Robert looking for last month's sales figures?

(A) Since he left the office early.

(B) He has a meeting with the accounting manager.

(C) He is an important figure in this town.

[번역]

로버트는 왜 지난달 판매 수치를 찾고 있죠?

(A) 그가 일찍 퇴근을 해서요.

(B) 그는 회계부장과 회의가 있어요.

(C) 그는 이 마을에서 중요한 인물이에요.

[해설]

'왜 로버트가 지난달 판매 수치를 찾고 있는지'를 묻는 질문에 이유를 나타내는 접속사 because를 생략한 채 '그가 회계 부장과 회의를 할 것'이라고 말한 (B)가 정답이다. Since만을 듣고 성급하게 (A)를 정답으로 선택해서는 안 된다. (C)는 figures(수치)를 반복 사용한 함정이니 혼동하지 않도록 유의해야 한다. 선택지에서는 '인물'이란 뜻으로 쓰였다.

[어휘]

look for ~을 찾다 | sale 판매 | figure 수치, 인물 | leave ~을 떠나다 | accounting 회계

10

How long will you stay in Shanghai?

(A) Down here on the right.

(B) At 9 A.M.

(C) A couple of weeks.

[번역]

당신은 상하이에 얼마나 오래 머물 예정인가요?

(A) 이 아래 오른쪽에요.

(B) 오전 9시에요.

(C) 2주 동안이요.

[해설]

How long은 '얼마나 오래'라는 뜻으로 기간을 묻는 표현이기 때문에 '2주'라는 답변을 한 (C)가 정답이다. (A)는 장소를 묻는 Where에 적합한 대답이고 (B)는 기간이 아니라 때를 묻는 When, What time 등의 질문에 더 어울리는 대답이다.

[어휘]

stay ~에 머물다 | a couple of 둘의, 두 개의

11

Can I open the window to ventilate the room?

(A) Turn down the heat.

(B) Near the door.

(C) Sure, it's quite stuffy in here.

[번역]

방을 환기시키기 위해 창을 열어도 될까요?

(A) 온도를 낮추세요.

(B) 문 근처에요.

(C) 물론이죠, 이 안이 좀 답답하군요.

[해설]

Can I ~?는 '제가 ~해도 될까요?'라는 의미로 허가를 나타낸다. '방을 환기시키기 위해 창문을 열어도 되는지'를 묻는 질문에 허락을 나타내는 Sure로 답하고 자신도 답답한 것 같다고 부연한 (C)가 정답이다.

[어휘]

ventilate 환기시키다 | turn down ~을 끄다 | heat 난방 기구 | stuffy 숨막히는, 통풍이 나쁜

12

Do you know a lady by the name of Julie?

(A) She is my friend from high school.

(B) Yes, I've already done it.

(C) Get to the bottom of it.

[번역]

당신은 줄리라는 여성을 아나요?

(A) 그녀는 저의 고등학교 친구입니다.

(B) 네, 저는 벌써 그것을 끝냈습니다.

(C) 진상을 철저히 규명하세요.

[해설]

일반의문문 형태이며, by the name of(~라는 이름의) 표현을 사용해 '줄리라는 여성을 아는지'를 묻고 있다. 이에 대해 Yes를 생략한 채 '자신의 고등학교 친구'라고 말한 (A)가 정답이다. Yes만을 듣고 (B)를 선택하지 않도록 주의해야 한다. (C)의 Get to the bottom of는 '~의 진상을 철저히 규명하다'는 의미로, 질문에 대한 답변으로 적절치 않다.

[어휘]

bottom 바닥, 근저

13

How long is your commute?

(A) Because of a traffic jam.

(B) I usually use public transportation.

(C) Five minutes on foot.

[번역]

통근시간이 얼마나 걸리세요?

(A) 교통 체증 때문에요.

(B) 저는 보통 대중교통을 이용합니다.

(C) 걸어서 5분이요.

[해설]

How long을 이용해 '통근 시간이 얼마나 걸리는지'를 묻는 질문이다. 걸어서 5분이 걸린다며 거리(Five minutes)와 통근 방법(on foot)에 대한 정보를 동시에 제공한 (C)가 정답이다. (A)와 (B)는 질문의 commute를 듣고 연상 가능한 단어(traffic jam, public transportation)를 제시해 혼동을 유발하고 있다.

[어휘]

commute 통근하다 ┃ traffic jam 교통 정체 ┃ on foot 걸어서

14

I couldn't watch the basketball game last night because my electricity went out.
(A) At the electronics store down the street.
(B) That's too bad. It was really exciting.
(C) I was caught in traffic.

[번역]

어젯밤에 전기가 나가서 농구 경기를 볼 수 없었어요.
(A) 길 아래쪽에 있는 전자 제품 가게에서요.
(B) 그거 안됐군요. 정말 재미있었는데.
(C) 교통 체증으로 꼼짝도 못했어요.

[해설]

일반 평서문 형태는 정해진 답변을 예상할 수 없으므로 상황에 맞는 보기를 정답으로 선택해야 한다. 따라서 '그 경기가 재미있었는데 보지 못했다니 유감'이라고 말한 (B)가 정답이 된다. (A)는 질문의 electricity와 발음이 유사한 electronics를 이용해 혼동을 주고 있으니 유의하자.

[어휘]

electricity 전기 ┃ go out 나가다 ┃ be caught in traffic 교통 체증에 걸리다

15

Where should I place this vase?
(A) Near the window.
(B) All over the place.
(C) To the mountains.

[번역]

이 꽃병을 어디에 놓아야 할까요?
(A) 창가예요.
(B) 도처에요.
(C) 산으로요.

[해설]

의문사 Where를 이용해 '꽃병을 어디에 두어야 하는지' 묻고 있으므로, '창문 근처에'라고 응답한 (A)가 정답이 된다. (B)의 경우 꽃병 한 개를 '도처에' 놓을 수는 없다. (C)의 '산으로' 역시 어색하다.

[어휘]

place 놓다, 두다 ┃ vase 꽃병 ┃ all over the place 여기저기에, 도처에

16

Isn't the advertising company planning to recruit some new employees?
(A) Yes, it intends to hire at least five people.
(B) Workers of Ms. Han's ability.
(C) Headhunting is one of his most important duties.

[번역]

그 광고회사는 신입직원을 채용할 계획이 아니던가요?
(A) 네, 최소 5명을 채용하려고 해요.
(B) 한 씨 만큼의 능력을 가진 직원들이요.
(C) 인재 스카우트는 그의 가장 중요한 직무 중 하나예요.

[해설]

부정의문문은 자신이 알고 있는 정보를 상대방에게 확인하고자 할 때 쓰는 문장이기 때문에 긍정으로 해석해야 정확한 답을 잡을 수 있다. '신입 직원을 채용할 계획이냐'고 묻자 그렇다고 대답하고 나서 '최소 5명을 채용할 것'이라고 부연 설명하는 (A)가 정답이 된다. (B)는 어떤 직원을 채용할 것이냐는 질문에 적합하다.

[어휘]

plan to ~을 계획하다 ┃ recruit 모집하다 ┃ intend to ~할 작정이다 ┃ hire 고용[채용]하다 ┃ ability 능력 ┃ headhunting 인재 스카우트 ┃ duty 직무, 임무

17

What does he have to do with this matter?
(A) Take care of the budget report.
(B) He embezzled public funds.
(C) What's the matter?

[번역]

그가 이 문제와 무슨 관련이 있죠?
(A) 예산 보고서를 처리하세요.
(B) 그가 공금을 횡령했어요.
(C) 무슨 일 있어요?

[해설]

'~와 관련이 있다'라는 뜻의 have to do with를 알고 있는지가 이 문제의 핵심이다. 그가 이 문제와 무슨 관련이 있느냐고 묻자 '그가 공금을 횡령했다(그렇기 때문에 관련이 있다)'라고 대답한 (B)가 가장 적절하다. (C)는 질문의 matter를 반복 사용한 함정이다.

[어휘]

have to do with ~와 관련이 있다 ┃ matter 문제 ┃ take care of ~을 처리하다 ┃ budget 예산 ┃ embezzle (금품 등을) 횡령하다 ┃ public funds 공금

18

Didn't you say that you reserved a table at the Chinese restaurant?
(A) This was the form to sign in with.
(B) Can I have your order?
(C) I tried, but they're fully booked.

[번역]

중식당에 자리를 예약했다고 하지 않았나요?
(A) 이것이 서명하고 들어가는 양식이었어요.
(B) 주문하시겠습니까?
(C) 그러려고 했지만 예약이 꽉 찼어요.

[해설]

부정의문문이 나오면 부정어 not을 생략하고 긍정문과 같은 의미로 해석하면 질문을 보다 쉽게 이해할 수 있다. '예약했다고 말했죠?'를 묻는 질문에 '예약을 하려고 했지만 식당예약이 모두 찼다'라고 말한 (C)가 정답이 된다. (B)는 질문의 restaurant를 듣고 연상 가능한 내용이므로 혼동하지 말자.

[어휘]

reserve ~을 예약하다 ┃ form 서식 ┃ sign in 서명하고 들어가다 ┃ order 주문 ┃ fully booked 예약이 꽉 찬

19

How would you like your steak?
(A) Money is at stake.
(B) Medium rare, please.
(C) I'll call Stacy for a ride.

[번역]

스테이크를 어떻게 해드릴까요?
(A) 돈이 걸려있어요.
(B) 중간보다 조금 덜 익혀주세요.
(C) 스테이시에게 태워달라고 부탁할 거예요.

[해설]

How would you like ~?는 '~을 어떻게 해드릴까요?'라는 뜻이기 때문에 중간보다 조금 덜 익힌 정도(medium rare)로 해달라고 말한 (B)가 정답이 된다. (A)와 (C)는 질문의 steak와 발음이 유사한 stake(건 돈, 지분)와 Stacy를 사용한 발음 함정이다.

[어휘]

How would you like ~? ~을 어떻게 해드릴까요? | at stake ~이 걸려 있는

20

We should try to get there before our clients arrive.
(A) To make an appointment.
(B) He was one of the VIPs in the audience.
(C) That's what I'm saying.

[번역]

고객들이 도착하기 전에 우리가 먼저 그곳에 가 있어야 해요.
(A) 약속을 정하기 위해서요.
(B) 그는 청중석에 앉은 귀빈 중 한 명이었어요.
(C) 제가 말하려던 바예요.

[해설]

일반 평서문으로, '고객들이 도착하기 전에 먼저 가 있어야 한다'는 의견에 '자신이 말하려던 것'이라며 동의하는 (C)가 정답이 된다. (A)의 to부정사는 '~하기 위해서'란 뜻으로 Why에 대한 답으로 적합하다.

[어휘]

get to ~에 도착하다 | client 고객 VIP 귀빈 | audience 청중, 관객

21

You're going to turn this room into a study, aren't you?
(A) Yes, because it's been empty for about half a year.
(B) I'm going to the movies tonight.
(C) He changed it completely.

[번역]

이 방을 서재로 바꾸실 거지요, 그렇지요?
(A) 네, 그 방이 반년 동안 비어 있어서요.
(B) 오늘밤 영화를 보러 갈 거예요.
(C) 그는 그것을 완전히 바꾸었어요.

[해설]

aren't you?는 부가의문문으로 확인 및 동의를 구하기 위해 사용된다. '방을 서재로 바꿀 것인지'를 확인하는 것에 Yes라고 대답을 하고 '반년 정도 비어 있었다(그래서 바꾸려고 한다)'라고 설명한 (A)가 가장 적절하다. (C)는 turn의 유의어인 change를 이용해서 오답을 유도하므로 주

의해야 한다.

[어휘]

turn A into B A를 B로 바꾸다 | study 서재 | empty 빈 | change ~을 바꾸다 | completely 완전히, 확실히

22

Can you hold this paper for me while I tie my shoes?
(A) Sure, why not?
(B) What is the title of this book?
(C) I didn't think so.

[번역]

신발끈을 묶는 동안 이 서류 좀 들어주시겠어요?
(A) 물론이죠.
(B) 이 책의 제목이 뭐죠?
(C) 저는 그렇게 생각하지 않았어요.

[해설]

Can[Could, Will, Would] you ~?는 '~해 주시겠어요?'라는 뜻이며 부탁할 때 쓰는 표현이다. '신발을 묶는 동안 서류를 들어달라'는 부탁에 '안 될 것이 뭐가 있느냐'면 흔쾌히 승낙한 (A)가 정답이 된다. 정답의 why not은 '물론, 왜 안 되겠어'라는 뜻으로 상대의 부탁을 기꺼이 받아들임을 나타낸다.

[어휘]

hold 잡다, 붙들다 | paper 서류 | while ~하는 동안에 | tie one's shoes 신발끈을 매다

23

What time did you take a message from Mr. Hoben?
(A) I'm planning to do it tomorrow.
(B) 4:30 P.M. is better.
(C) At five in the afternoon.

[번역]

당신은 호벤 씨에게서 몇 시에 메시지를 받았나요?
(A) 그 일은 내일 할 예정입니다.
(B) 오후 4시 30분이 더 좋겠군요.
(C) 오후 5시에요.

[해설]

시간을 묻는 What time을 이용해 때를 묻고 있으므로 '오후 5시'라고 대답한 (C)가 정답이 된다. (B)도 시간 정보를 제공하지만 비교를 나타내는 better를 사용해 주어진 선택 사항 중 오후 4:30이 더 좋다는 의미이므로 질문에 대한 답으로는 적절치 않다.

[어휘]

take a message 메시지를 받다

24

What's all the fuss about?
(A) The vice president will arrive soon to inspect the factory.
(B) No, I'm not responsible for the failure.
(C) There's no doubt about that.

[번역]

왜 이리 야단들이죠?

(A) 부사장님이 공장 시찰을 위해 곧 도착할 예정이에요.

(B) 아니요, 저는 그 실패에 대해 책임이 없어요.

(C) 그것에 대해 의심의 여지가 없어요.

[해설]

'무슨 일 때문에 그리 야단(fuss: 소란, 야단법석)인지' 묻는 질문에 '부사장님이 곧 시찰을 올 것이다(그래서 소란스럽다)'라고 답한 (A)가 정답이 된다. (B)의 경우 의문사 의문문에 No는 불가하고, (C)'그것에 대해 의심의 여지가 없다'란 답변은 질문에 어울리지 않는다.

[어휘]

fuss 소란 | vice president 부사장 | inspect 시찰하다 | factory 공장 | be responsible for ~에 대해 책임이 있다 | failure 실패, 실수 | doubt 의심

25

You'd better turn your cell phone off during the performance.

(A) It starts in ten minutes.

(B) I already turned it off.

(C) No, in the community center.

[번역]

공연 중에 휴대폰을 꺼두는 게 좋겠어요.

(A) 10분 뒤에 시작해요.

(B) 벌써 꺼두었어요.

(C) 아니요, 시민 회관에서요.

[해설]

You'd better ~는 '당신은 ~하는 것이 좋다'는 뜻으로 상대에게 제안하거나 권유할 때 쓰는 표현이다. '공연 중에는 휴대폰을 꺼두는 것이 좋겠다'는 권유에 '이미 껐다'고 말한 (B)가 정답이 된다. (A)는 공연 시작은 언제인지를 묻는 질문에, (C)는 공연 장소를 묻는 질문에 각각 더 어울리는 대답이다.

[어휘]

turn off ~을 끄다 | performance 공연 | community 지역사회, 공동체

26

Would you prefer a round-trip or a one way ticket?

(A) Sure, I'll buy you a ticket.

(B) A return ticket, please.

(C) I prefer a single room.

[번역]

왕복표를 원하십니까, 아니면 편도를 원하십니까?

(A) 물론이죠, 제가 당신에게 표를 사줄게요.

(B) 왕복표로 주세요.

(C) 저는 1인실을 선호합니다.

[해설]

구입하려는 표가 '왕복인지 편도인지'를 묻는 선택 의문문이다. 이에 대해 '왕복표를 달라'고 말한 (B)가 정답이다. 왕복표를 뜻하는 round-trip ticket, return ticket을 익혀 두어야 한다. (A)는 질문의 ticket을 반복 사용한 함정이다. (C)의 1인실(a single room)은 호텔과 관련된 표현이지 티켓과는 어울리지 않는다.

[어휘]

prefer ~을 선호하다 | round-trip 왕복의 | one-way 편도의 | return ticket 왕복표

27

My design for a new city hall was finally accepted by the officials.

(A) I heard that. Congratulations!

(B) They're holding a reception.

(C) The legislation was passed by Congress.

[번역]

제가 디자인한 시청 신축 설계 안이 마침내 공무원들에게 승인을 받았어요.

(A) 저도 그 소식 들었어요. 축하합니다!

(B) 그들은 환영회를 열고 있어요.

(C) 그 법안은 국회에서 통과되었어요.

[해설]

일반 평서문으로 '내가 디자인한 시청 신축 설계 안이 승인 받았다'는 말에 대해 '그 소식을 들었어요. 축하해요'라고 말한 (A)가 가장 적절한 대화를 완성한다. (B) '그들은 환영회를 열고 있어요'와 (C) '그 법안이 국회에서 통과 되었어요'라는 답변은 질문과 어울리지 않는다.

[어휘]

city hall 시청 | finally 마침내 | accept ~을 승인하다 | official 공무원 | Congratulations! 축하합니다 | hold ~을 개최하다 | reception 환영파티 | legislation 법안 | pass ~을 통과하다 | Congress 국회

28

Shouldn't we change to a new materials supplier?

(A) It is one of our materials providers.

(B) We have to meet the deadline.

(C) Yes, we have so many problems with our current one.

[번역]

우리는 재료 공급업체를 새로 바꿔야 하지 않을까요?

(A) 그 업체는 우리의 재료 공급업체 중 한 곳입니다.

(B) 우리는 마감일을 맞춰야 해요.

(C) 네, 현재 거래업체와 문제가 아주 많아요

[해설]

부정의문문으로 '재료 공급업체를 바꾸어야 하지 않냐'는 상대의 제안에 긍정(Yes)을 한 후에 '현재 공급업체와는 문제가 많다'는 의견을 추가한 (C)가 정답이 된다. (A)는 supplier의 유의어인 provider를 이용해 혼동을 주고 있으며, (B) meet the deadline은 '마감일을 맞추다'라는 표현은 질문에 대한 답변으로 적절치 않다.

[어휘]

material 재료, 원료 | supplier 공급업체 | provider 공급업체 | deadline 마감일 | current 현재의

29

I'm really disappointed to hear that I have to work this weekend.

(A) Has something urgent come up?

(B) I was appointed to be his secretary.

(C) No, I haven't heard the news.

[번역]

저는 이번 주말에 일해야 한다는 소식을 듣고 정말 실망했어요.

(A) 무슨 급한 일이 생긴 거예요?
(B) 저는 그의 비서로 임명되었어요.
(C) 아뇨, 저는 그 소식 못 들었어요.

'이번 주말에 일해야 한다는 소식을 듣고 실망했다'는 말에 '무슨 급한 일이 생겼나요?'라고 되묻는 (A)가 가장 적절하다. (B)는 질문의 disappointed와 발음이 유사한 appointed를 이용한 함정이다. (C)는 만약 No가 없다면 정답이 될 수도 있겠지만, 소식을 듣고 실망했다는 말에 '아뇨'라고 답한 것은 문맥상 적절하지 못하다.

disappointed 실망한 | urgent 긴급한 | come up 생기다, 나타나다 | appoint 임명하다

30

We cannot choose a building design until Mr. Dunn reviews the proposals, can we?
(A) Even so, it was criticized harshly.
(B) No, but he asked us to give him another week.
(C) I'm not sure whether he likes it or not.

던 씨가 제안서들을 검토하기 전에는 우리가 건물 디자인을 선택할 수 없는 거지요, 그렇지요?
(A) 그렇다 하더라도 그것은 심한 비난을 받았어요.
(B) 네, 그런데 그는 일주일 더 시간을 달라고 부탁했어요.
(C) 그가 그것을 좋아하는지 싫어하는지 모르겠어요.

평서문 의문문은 특정 유형의 답변을 예상하기 쉽지 않기 때문에 정확한 해석이 필요하다. '던 씨가 기획안들을 검토하기 전까지 우리가 디자인을 선택할 수 없죠?'라는 질문에 '선택할 수 없다, 그가 (검토하는데) 일주일의 시간을 더 달라고 했다'고 답한 (B)가 가장 적절한 응답이다. (A)와 (C)는 질문에 어울리는 답변들이 아니다.

choose 선택하다 | until (부정어와 함께) ~하여 비로소 (~하다) | review 검토하다 | proposal 제안서 | criticize 비판하다 | harshly 심하게 | whether ~인지 아닌지

31

Do you know Mr. Gilman's extension?
(A) Yes, he expanded his business.
(B) Sorry, I cannot remember it right now.
(C) I left my coat in the meeting room.

길먼 씨의 내선 번호를 아세요?
(A) 네, 그는 자기 사업을 확장했습니다.
(B) 미안하지만 지금 기억이 나지 않네요.
(C) 저는 회의실에 코트를 두고 왔어요.

'길먼 씨의 내선 번호를 아느냐'고 묻는 질문에 '지금 잘 생각이 나지 않는다'라고 답한 (B)가 정답이다. (A)는 extend와 유사하게 들리는 expand를 이용한 함정이고 (C)의 '회의실에 코트를 두고 왔어요'는 질문에 어울리지 않는 답변이다.

extension 내선, 구내 전화 | expand ~을 확장하다 | business 사업, 회사 | remember ~을 기억하다 | leave ~을 두고 가다

PART 3

Questions 32-34 refer to the following conversation.

W It's freezing in here. I'd better turn up the heat.
M Don't bother. The thermostat's not working. (33) I contacted our maintenance man about it, but he's extremely busy and can't be here before 2:00. Apparently, (32)a lot of other offices in the building have the same problem.
W 2 o'clock? Well, it's only 10:30 now, (34)but, fortunately, I keep an electric heater behind the filing cabinet for this type of emergency.

W 너무 춥네요. 온도를 높여야겠어요.
M 괜한 수고하지 마세요. 온도 조절 장치가 고장이에요. 정비공에게 연락했는데, 너무 바빠서 2시 전에는 못 온대요. 건물 안 다른 사무실들도 같은 문제가 있나 봐요.
W 2시요? 음, 지금 겨우 10시 30분인데. 그렇지만 다행히도 저는 이런 비상 사태를 대비해서 서류 캐비닛 뒤에 전기 히터를 보관하고 있어요.

freezing 몹시 추운 | turn up 높이다 | bother 애쓰다 | thermostat 자동 온도 조절 장치 | contact 연락하다 | maintenance man 정비공 | extremely 몹시 | apparently 명백히 | electric heater 전기 히터 | filing 서류철 | emergency 비상 사태

32

화자들이 있는 장소는?
(A) 커피숍
(B) 사무실
(C) 시장
(D) 아파트

남자의 대화문에 나오는 a lot of other offices in the building have the same problem에서 대화의 장소는 '사무실'임을 알 수 있다. 따라서 정답은 (B)이다.

33

남자가 연락한 사람은 누구인가?
(A) 호텔 매니저
(B) 매표인
(C) 기술자
(D) 치과의사

남자의 대화문에서 I contacted our maintenance man이라는 내용이 나

오는데 'maintenance man'을 A technician으로 바꿔 표현한 (C)가 정
답이다.

34

[번역]

여자는 다음으로 무엇을 하겠는가?
(A) 회계사에게 연락한다.
(B) 기구를 산다.
(C) 약속을 취소한다.
(D) 히터를 튼다.

[해설]

여자가 다음에 할 일을 묻는 질문 단서는 마지막 대화문에서 나온다.
여자의 마지막 대화문 중 but, fortunately, I keep an electric heater
behind the filing cabinet for this type of emergency에서 유추해 볼 때
정답은 (D)이다.

[어휘]

accountant 회계사 ｜ purchase 사다 ｜ appliance 기구 ｜ cancel
취소하다 ｜ plug in 전원을 꽂다

Questions 35-37 refer to the following conversation.

> M I heard you're presenting at the software
>   development conference in Trenton tomorrow. I'm
>   speaking as well, so (35)I was wondering if I could
>   get a lift.
> W I've opted for the commuter train this time. But
>   let's go together anyway. (36)We can share our
>   presentation ideas on the way.
> M Okay. But since when did you decide to stop
>   driving?
> W Since I spoke to Susan, my neighbor, last week.
>   Susan went to Trenton daily for work only by car
>   for many years. Two months ago, however, she
>   switched to the commuter train and claims that (37)
>   her travel time has been cut in half.

[번역]

M 당신이 내일 트렌턴에서 열리는 소프트웨어 개발 컨퍼런스에서 발
   표한다고 들었어요. 저도 발표하기로 되어 있는데 당신 차를 같이
   타도 될까요?
W 전 이번에 통근 열차를 탈거예요. 그렇지만 어쨌든 같이 가요. 가
   는 길에 발표 내용을 토론할 수 있으니까요.
M 좋습니다. 그런데 운전은 언제 그만두셨어요?
W 제 이웃인 수잔과 지난주에 이야기해 본 이후로요. 수잔은 트렌턴
   으로 몇 년 동안 매일 자동차로만 출퇴근했어요. 그러다 두 달 전
   에 통근 열차로 바꾸었는데, 이동 시간이 절반으로 줄었다는 거예
   요.

[어휘]

present 발표하다 ｜ development 개발 ｜ lift 편승 ｜ opt for 선택하다 ｜
commuter train 통근 열차 ｜ neighbor 이웃 ｜ switch 바꾸다 ｜ claim
주장하다 ｜ travel time 이동 시간 ｜ cut in half 반으로 줄이다

35

[번역]

남자가 요청하는 것은 무엇인가?
(A) 트렌턴행 버스 티켓
(B) 보고서 개요
(C) 정보 책자
(D) 컨퍼런스까지의 편승

[해설]

남자의 말에 귀를 기울여 보면, 첫 대화문에서 I was wondering if I
could get a lift라며 편승 여부를 묻고 있다. a lift를 a ride로 바꾸어 표
현한 (D)가 정답이다.

[어휘]

ticket 티켓, 입장권 ｜ outline 개요 ｜ booklet 소책자 ｜ ride (차 등에)태움

36

[번역]

화자들은 내일 무엇을 하겠는가?
(A) 몇 시간 동안 초과 근무를 한다.
(B) 발표할 내용에 대해 토론한다.
(C) 회의 일정을 짠다.
(D) 식당 좌석을 예약한다.

[해설]

여자의 첫 대화문에 '가는 길에 발표할 내용을 나눌 수 있다'는 뜻의 We
can share our presentation ideas on the way가 나온다. 따라서 정답은
share ideas를 discuss로 표현한 (B)이다.

[어휘]

put in (시간, 노력을) 들이다 ｜ overtime 초과근무 ｜ discuss 논의하다 ｜
book 예약하다

37

[번역]

여자가 통근 열차를 이용하는 까닭은?
(A) 자동차 바퀴가 펑크 나서
(B) 운전 면허증을 잃어 버려서
(C) 운전 시간이 너무 오래 걸려서
(D) 버스가 항상 늦어서

[해설]

여자의 두 번째 대화문은, 이웃이 통근 열차를 이용하고부터 출퇴근 시
간이 절반으로 줄었다(her travel time has been cut in half)고 해서 자
신도 자동차 대신 통근 열차를 이용한다는 내용이다. 따라서 정답은
(C)이다.

[어휘]

flat tire 펑크난 타이어 ｜ license 면허증 ｜ take long 오래 걸리다

Questions 38-40 refer to the following conversation.

> W Hello, (38)this is Lisa Rogers at Top Investors
>   calling about order number C58-7492.
> M C58-7492? Just a minute, please, Ms. Rogers.
>   Yes, here it is. (39)We received an order late
>   Friday afternoon for seven conference-style
>   tables.

According to our records, it was processed
Monday morning and forwarded to our Shipping
Department that afternoon.

W So does that mean the tables are on the way
here?

M (40)Mr. Robert Spencer is the head of shipping.
Let me speak to him and phone you back by
1:30.

[번역]

W 여보세요, 저는 탑 인베스터스에 근무하는 리사 로저스라고 하는
데요, 주문 번호 C58-7492 때문에 전화 드렸습니다.

M C58-7492번이요? 잠시만 기다려 주세요, 로저스 씨. 네, 여기 있
네요. 지난 금요일 오후에 회의실용 테이블 7개를 주문하셨네요.
기록을 보니, 월요일 오전에 주문이 처리되었고, 그날 오후에 저희
배송팀으로 넘어갔군요.

W 그러면 테이블을 배송 중이라는 말씀이신가요?

M 로버트 스펜서 씨가 배송 팀장이십니다. 제가 그분과 얘기해 본 후
1시 30분까지 고객님께 전화 드리겠습니다.

[어휘]

order 주문 | process 가공 처리하다 | shipping 배송 | department
부(서)

38

[번역]

여자는 무엇에 대해 문의하는가?

(A) 분실한 신용카드

(B) 자동차 수리

(C) 최근 주문

(D) 새 주소

[해설]

여자의 첫 번째 대화문 중 this is Lisa Rogers at Top Investors calling
about order number C58-7492에서 전화를 건 까닭이 주문 내역 때문
이라는 것을 알 수 있다. 따라서 정답은 (C)이다.

[어휘]

lost 분실된 | repair 수리 | recent 최근 | address 주소

39

[번역]

화자들은 어떤 상품에 대해 이야기 중인가?

(A) 컴퓨터 책상

(B) 회전 의자

(C) 회의 테이블

(D) 커피 메이커

[해설]

주문 내역에 대해 문의하는 여자에게 답변하는 남자의 첫 번째 대화문
중 We received an order late Friday afternoon for seven conference-
style tables에서 주문 상품이 회의용 테이블임으로 정답은 (C)이다.

[어휘]

swivel chair 회전 의자

40

[번역]

남자는 무엇을 하겠다고 제안하는가?

(A) 다른 부서에 문의한다.

(B) 급료를 인상한다.

(C) 전화 번호를 확인한다.

(D) 호텔 객실을 예약한다.

[해설]

남자의 두 번째 대화문 Mr. Robert Spencer is the head of shipping.
Let me speak to him and phone you back by 1:30에서 배송팀이 아닌
남자가 배송팀 담당자와 이야기를 하고나서 다시 전화드리겠다고 했으
므로 배송팀(shipping)을 다른 부서(another division)로, 이야기 하다
(speak to)를 문의하다(consult)로 바꿔 표현한 (A)가 정답이 된다.

[어휘]

consult 상담하다 | increase 늘리다 | salary 급료 | verify ~이
정확한지 확인하다

Questions 41-43 refer to the following conversation.

W Why haven't you signed up for our (41)annual
company bowling tournament on Saturday?
This year, we're raising money for the Elm Street
Children's Hospital.

M Since O'Connor Bowling is closed for
renovations, I just assumed that the event will be
called off. After all, O'Connor is the only bowling
facility in town.

W But I called my friend Mark Smith, the owner of
Smith's Lanes, and he's agreed to host (41)our
charity tournament. (43)Plus, Shawn Dewitt, a
national pro, will be there. (42)I know that Smith's
is well over an hour away, but it's worth it.

[번역]

W 토요일에 열릴 사내 연례 볼링 경기에 왜 신청하지 않았어요? 올
해는 엘름 스트리트 아동 병원을 위한 모금을 할 거예요.

M 오코너 볼링장이 수리 때문에 문을 닫아서 행사가 취소될 거라 생
각했어요. 오코너가 동네에서는 유일한 볼링장이니까요.

W 그런데 제가 스미스 레인을 경영하는 친구 마크 스미스에게 전화
해서 자선 경기를 그곳에서 열기로 했어요. 게다가 국가 프로선수
인 숀 드윗도 올 예정이구요. 스미스 레인에 가려면 한 시간 넘게
걸리기는 해도, 그럴 만한 가치가 있어요.

[어휘]

sign up 신청하다 | annual 연간의 | bowling tournament 볼링 경기
| raise money 모금하다 | renovation 보수 | assume 추측하다 | be
called off 취소되다 | facility 시설 | agree 동의하다 | host 개최하다 |
charity 자선 | worth 가치가 있는

41

[번역]

화자들은 무엇에 관해 얘기하고 있는가?

(A) 자선 행사

(B) 교통 사고

(C) 회의 일정
(D) 분기 보고서

[해설]

대화를 여는 첫 문장에 나오는 annual company bowling tournament
on Saturday와 마지막 대화문에 나오는 our charity tournament를 종합
하면 '자선'을 목적으로 한 '볼링 경기'가 열릴 예정임을 알 수 있다. 따
라서 정답은 (A)이다.

[어휘]

quarterly 분기의

42

[번역]

문제가 될 수 있는 것은 무엇인가?
(A) 나쁜 날씨
(B) 장거리
(C) 고장 난 팩스기계
(D) 청구 착오

[해설]

여자의 두 번째 대화문 중 I know that Smith's is well over an hour
away에서 스미스 레인에 가려면 한 시간은 넘게 걸린다는 것을 알 수
있다. 따라서 정답은 (B)이다.

[어휘]

broken 고장 난 ｜ billing 청구서

43

[번역]

여자의 말에 따르면 토요일에 어떤 일이 있을 것인가?
(A) 새로운 병원이 개업한다.
(B) 여름휴가가 시작된다.
(C) 직원들이 초과근무를 한다.
(D) 프로 볼링선수가 행사에 참여한다.

[해설]

여자의 마지막 말 중 Plus, Shawn Dewitt, a national pro, will be there
에서 be there를 attend로 바꾸어 표현한 (D)가 정답이다.

[어휘]

work overtime 초과 근무하다 ｜ attend 참가하다

Questions 44-46 refer to the following conversation.

> M Hi, I'm opening a used bookstore in my home
> just down the street, and (44)I'd like to speak to
> someone about opening a checking account
> here.
> W (45)Ms. Susan Riley handles small business
> accounts, but she's currently away at a meeting
> in our main branch and isn't expected back till
> 3:30. Would you like to meet with her then?
> M No, that won't work. I have some painters coming
> over between 3:00 and 4:00.
> W Well, Ms. Riley is available first thing tomorrow
> morning when the bank opens at 9:30. (46)I'd be
> happy to schedule an appointment for you.

[번역]

M 안녕하세요. 저는 길 아래쪽에 있는 저희 집에서 중고 서점을 열려
고 하는데, 계좌를 개설하는 것에 대해 상담하고 싶어서요.
W 수잔 라일리 씨가 소기업 계좌 담당인데 지금은 회의 때문에 본점
에 나가 있습니다. 3시 30분까지는 못 올 거예요. 그 때 만나도 괜
찮으시겠어요?
M 안되겠네요. 3시에서 4시 사이에 페인트 공들이 오기로 해서요.
W 음, 라일리 씨는 내일 아침 은행이 문을 여는 9시 30분에는 있을
겁니다. 제가 약속 시간을 잡아드릴게요.

[어휘]

used 중고의 ｜ bookstore 서점 ｜ checking account 당좌 예금 ｜
handle 처리하다, 취급하다 ｜ currently 현재 ｜ main branch 본점 ｜
expect 예상하다 ｜ painter 페인트 공 ｜ available 이용 가능한, 바쁘지 않은

44

[번역]

남자는 무엇을 하기를 원하는가?
(A) 항공 티켓 예매
(B) 은행 계좌 개설
(C) 자동차 보험 계약
(D) 새 집 건설

[해설]

남자의 첫 번째 대화문 중 I'd like to speak to someone about opening
a checking account here에서 계좌를 개설하는 것에 대해 상담하고 싶
다는 내용이 나온다. 따라서 정답은 (B)이다. (A)의 book은 '예약하다'
는 뜻으로 쓰였으며, 대화의 유사한 발음 bookstore를 이용한 함정이
다.

[어휘]

book 예약하다 ｜ insurance 보험 ｜ build 짓다

45

[번역]

무엇이 문제인가?
(A) 현금 입출금기를 이용할 수 없다.
(B) 계좌가 해지되었다.
(C) 직원이 외출 중이다.
(D) 화재 경보기가 작동하지 않는다.

[해설]

여자의 답변 중 Ms. Susan Riley handles small business accounts, but
she's currently away at a meeting in our main branch에서 소기업 계
좌 담당자가 지금은 회의 참석 때문에 외출했다는 것을 알 수 있다. 따
라서 정답은 (C)이다.

[어휘]

ATM 현금 자동 인출기 ｜ away 자리에 없는 ｜ out of service 고장이 난 ｜
fire alarm 화재 경보(기)

46

[번역]

여자는 남자에게 무엇을 하라고 제안하는가?
(A) 본점에 전화하라.
(B) 다음 주에 다시 오라.
(C) 회의를 취소하라.
(D) 약속을 정하라.

여자의 마지막 대화문에 I'd be happy to schedule an appointment for you에서 약속을 정하자는 내용이 나온다. schedule(일정을 잡다)를 set up(정하다)으로 바꿔 표현한 (D)가 정답이다.

[어휘]

cancel 취소하다 | set up 정하다

Questions 47-49 refer to the following conversation.

> W Ted, two applicants for our summer position of office assistant have interviews at 3:00 and 3:15, but [47]I can't find their résumés anywhere. I'm sure I left that folder right here.
>
> M I think Mr. Murphy has it. He interviewed someone for the same position this morning.
>
> W I know. I phoned his office, and they said [48]he went across town to meet a client.
>
> M Well, I'm sure personnel keeps all information related to our summer employment programs. Just give me the applicants' names. [49]I'll go get their files for you.

[번역]

W 테드, 여름에 우리 사무실에서 조수로 일할 지원자 2명의 면접이 3시와 3시 15분에 있어요. 그런데 그들 이력서가 어디에 있는지 모르겠어요. 서류를 바로 여기에 둔 게 확실한데.

M 머피 씨가 갖고 있을 거예요. 오늘 아침에 같은 직책의 지원자를 면접했거든요.

W 저도 알아요. 그런데 그의 사무실에 전화했더니 고객을 만나러 시내에 나갔대요.

M 음, 인사부에 여름 고용 프로그램에 관한 정보가 모두 있을 거예요. 지원자들 이름만 알려 주세요. 제가 가서 파일을 찾아 올게요.

[어휘]

applicant 지원자 | position 직(책) | assistant 조수 | résumé 이력서 | folder 서류철 | phone 전화하다 | client 고객 | personnel 인사(부)의 | related to ~에 관련된

47

[번역]

여자는 무엇을 찾고 있는가?

(A) 메모

(B) 매뉴얼

(C) 송장

(D) 이력서

[해설]

여자의 첫 대화문 중 I can't find their résumés anywhere에 직접적으로 résumé(이력서)가 언급되었으므로, 정답은 (D)이다.

48

[번역]

머피 씨가 지금 만나고 있는 사람은 누구인가?

(A) 부서 관리자

(B) 새 영업팀

(C) 구직자

(D) 고객

[해설]

여자의 두 번째 대화문 중 he went across town to meet a client에서 '그(Mr. Murphy)가 고객을 만나러 시내에 갔다'고 했으므로, 정답은 (D)이다. 여기에서 (C) Job applicants는 남자가 오늘 오전에 만난 사람이므로 혼동하지 않도록 주의해야 한다.

49

[번역]

남자는 무엇을 하겠다고 제안하는가?

(A) 약속을 정한다.

(B) 파일을 찾는다.

(C) 비행기를 예약한다.

(D) 보고서를 이메일로 보낸다.

[해설]

남자의 두 번째 대화문 중 I'll go get their files for you에서 파일을 찾아 오겠다는 내용이 나온다. 따라서 정답은 (B)이다.

[어휘]

schedule 일정을 잡다 | locate 찾아 내다 | book 예약하다

Questions 50-52 refer to the following conversation.

> M Beverly? I wasn't expecting you to come in today. [50]Did you move into your new house all right?
>
> W [50][51]No, my contractor phoned last night to inform me of a problem. Apparently, the building supplier sent the wrong type of paneling, so they were unable to finish the basement yesterday.
>
> M Well, it's just another day. You can move in tomorrow morning.
>
> W Fortunately, no. [52]The contractor assured me that everything will be done by 1 P.M. today at the latest, so I'll be leaving the office at noon.

[번역]

M 비벌리? 오늘 당신이 오리라고는 생각 못했어요. 새 집으로 이사는 잘 했나요?

W 아니요, 어젯밤에 건설업자가 전화해서는 문제가 생겼다더군요. 건물 공급자가 엉뚱한 종류의 판자를 보내는 바람에 지하실 작업을 어제 못 끝냈대요.

M 음, 하루 더 걸리겠군요. 내일 아침에 들어갈 수 있겠네요.

W 다행히도, 그렇진 않아요. 건설업자가 책임지고 늦어도 오늘 오후 1시까지는 모든 것을 마치겠다고 해서, 전 정오에 퇴근할 거예요.

[어휘]

expect 기대하다, 예상하다 | move into 이사 가다, 옮겨 가다 | contractor 계약자, (건출 등의) 청부인, 도급자 | inform 알리다 | apparently 외관상으로는, 명백히 | supplier 공급자 | paneling 판자 | finish 마치다 | basement 지하실 | assure ~에게 보증하다, 안심시키다

50

[번역]

화자들은 무엇에 관해 얘기하고 있는가?

(A) 영화

(B) 뉴스 기사

(C) 일정 변경

(D) 자동차 문제

[해설]

대화 주제를 묻는 문제는 주로 전반부에 나오지만, 난이도가 있는 문제
는 대화내용 전체를 파악해야 한다. 여자가 이사하려는 집에 문제가 생
겨서 '일정'에 차질이 생겼지만, 오늘 오후면 해결되리라는 내용이다.
따라서 이 문제의 가장 적절한 답은 (C)이다.

51

[번역]

어젯밤에 여자에게 전화를 건 사람은 누구인가?

(A) 경찰관

(B) 주요 임원

(C) 치과의사 조수

(D) 건설업자

[해설]

여자의 첫 대화문 No, my contractor phoned last night에 건설업자가
전화했다는 내용이 나온다. 따라서 정답은 (D)이다.

52

[번역]

여자는 오늘 오후에 무슨 일을 하겠는가?

(A) 회의에 참석하러 간다.

(B) 취업 면접을 하러 간다.

(C) 새 집으로 이사한다.

(D) 자동차 수리를 맡긴다.

[해설]

대화 이후의 상황을 묻는 질문의 단서는 대체로 마지막 대화문에 나온
다. The contractor assured me that everything will be done by 1:00
P.M. today at the latest, so I'll be leaving the office at noon에서 정오
에 퇴근해 이사할 예정임을 유추할 수 있는 (C)가 정답이 된다.

Questions 53-55 refer to the following conversation.

M Hello. (53)I would like to talk to someone about
taking out a loan for a new house in the
downtown area.

W I'm sorry, sir, but none of our mortgage
professionals are available at the moment.
(54)You're welcome to take this application
form and (55)mail it later. After we review your
application, we will contact you about setting up
an appointment.

M Thank you, but is it not possible to submit an
application online?

W I'm sorry, but loan applications are not included
in our company's online service.

[번역]

M 안녕하세요. 시내에 새 집을 얻기 위한 대출 상담을 하고 싶습니
다.

W 죄송합니다. 고객님. 지금은 주택 담보 대출을 담당하는 분들과 상
담이 불가능합니다. 우선 이 신청서를 받으시고 나중에 우편으로
보내 주신다면 감사하겠습니다. 고객님의 신청서를 검토한 후 약
속 날짜를 정하기 위해 고객님께 연락드리겠습니다.

M 고맙습니다. 그런데 신청서를 온라인으로 제출할 수는 없나요?

W 죄송합니다만 대출 신청서는 저희 회사 온라인 서비스에 포함되어
있지 않습니다.

[어휘]

loan 대출, 융자 ｜ downtown 시내 ｜ mortgage 저당(권) ｜
application 신청 ｜ review 검토하다 ｜ contact 연락하다 ｜ submit
제출하다 ｜ include 포함하다

53

[번역]

이 대화는 어디에서 이루어지겠는가?

(A) 여행사

(B) 출판사

(C) 대출 회사

(D) 공공 도서관

[해설]

대화를 여는 남자의 첫 대화문 중 I would like to talk to someone
about taking out a loan for a new house에 대출을 상담하고 싶다는 내
용이 나온다. 따라서 정답은 (C)이다.

54

[번역]

여자가 남자에게 준 것은?

(A) 계산서

(B) 신청서

(C) 전화번호부

(D) 대여계약서

[해설]

여자의 행동을 묻는 질문이므로 여자의 말에 집중한다. 여자의 첫 번째
대화문에 You're welcome to take this application form이라는 내용이
나온다. 따라서 정답은 (B)이다.

[어휘]

billing statement 계산서, 청구서 ｜ rental 대여의

55

[번역]

여자는 남자에게 무엇을 하라고 제안하는가?

(A) 신청서를 우편으로 보내라.

(B) 신용카드로 온라인 결제를 하라.

(C) 웹사이트를 참고하라.

(D) 다른 회사를 방문하라.

[해설]

여자의 첫 번째 대화문의 You're welcome to take this application
form and mail it later에서 여자는 남자에게 일단 서류를 작성해서 신
청서를 우편으로 보내라고 했다. 따라서 (A)가 정답이다.

M (56)How are the preparations for the call center coming along?

W Excellent. The renovations are complete, all the computers and telephone headsets have been installed, and we've hired 120 operators and 10 supervisors.

M Fantastic. (57)Now we can open a month earlier than we had originally planned, and this facility will really help us manage the high volume of incoming calls.

W (58)But we still have to organize a two-week training orientation for the call center employees before the official opening.

[번역]

M 콜 센터 오픈 준비는 어떻게 되어 가나요?

W 아주 좋아요. 수리는 끝났고, 컴퓨터와 전화 헤드셋도 설치했고, 교환원 120명에 관리자 10명도 고용했어요.

M 환상적이군요. 원래 계획했던 것보다 한 달 정도 빨리 오픈할 수 있겠네요. 그리고 이 시설은 엄청나게 많이 걸려오는 전화를 관리하는 데 정말 도움이 될 거예요.

W 하지만 정식 오픈 전에 콜 센터 직원들을 교육할 2주 훈련 오리엔테이션을 마련할 필요는 여전히 있어요.

[어휘]

preparation 준비, 대비 | renovation 개축, 수리 | complete 끝내다 | install 설치하다 | hire 고용하다 | operator 교환원 | supervisor 관리자 | fantastic 환상적인 | originally 원래 | plan 계획하다 | facility 시설 | manage 관리하다 | the high volume of 엄청나게 많은 | incoming 들어오는 | organize 조직하다 | employee 직원 | official 공식적인

56

[번역]

화자들의 회사가 곧 오픈하는 것은 무엇인가?

(A) 지점

(B) 전시장

(C) 식당

(D) 콜 센터

[해설]

남자의 첫 번째 대화문 How are the preparations for the call center coming along?에서 call center가 직접적으로 언급되고 있으므로, (D)가 정답이다.

[어휘]

branch 지점의 | exhibition 전시 | restaurant 식당

57

[번역]

본 프로젝트는 계획보다 얼마나 빠르게 추진되고 있는가?

(A) 3일

(B) 2주

(C) 1개월

(D) 2개월

[해설]

남자의 두 번째 대화문 중 Now we can open a month earlier than we had originally planned에서 원래 계획했던 날짜보다 한 달 앞섰음을 알 수 있다. 따라서 정답은 (C)이다. (B) Two weeks는 여자의 두 번째 대화문에 나오는 We still have to organize a two-week training orientation을 이용해 오답을 유도하는 함정이니 주의하자.

58

[번역]

여자의 말에 따르면 앞으로 해야 할 일은 무엇인가?

(A) 컴퓨터 설치

(B) 실내 페인트칠

(C) 라디오 광고

(D) 훈련 오리엔테이션

[해설]

대화 후의 상황을 묻는 질문이므로 마지막 대화문에 집중하자. 여자의 두 번째 대화문 중 We still have to organize a two-week training orientation에 2주짜리 훈련과 관련된 내용이 나온다. 따라서 정답은 (D)이다.

[어휘]

installation 설치 | interior 실내(의) | advertisement 광고

Questions 59-61 refer to the following conversation.

M (59)The sign-up deadline for the market research workshop was yesterday. How many are attending?

W Let's see. 78 people have signed up. I didn't anticipate that many. We only have tables and chairs to accommodate 65 at the most.

M (60)Why don't you try Wilson's Rentals? We've rented from them before, and Jerry Wilson, the owner, always gives us a good deal. Plus, they're not too far from here.

W Okay. I'll drop by on my way back from lunch. (61) Can you give me the address?

[번역]

M 시장 조사 워크숍 신청 마감일이 어제였죠. 얼마나 참석하나요?

W 한 번 볼게요. 78명이 신청했어요. 이렇게 많으리라고 예상하지 못했는데. 우리 테이블과 의자로는 기껏해야 65명까지만 수용할 수 있어요.

M 윌슨 대여점에 연락하지 그래요? 우리는 전에 그곳에서 물품을 빌린 적이 있어요. 그곳 주인인 제리 윌슨은 늘 좋은 가격을 제시하죠. 게다가 여기서 그리 멀지 않아요.

W 좋아요. 점심 먹고 오는 길에 들러 봐야겠어요. 주소 좀 알려 주실래요?

[어휘]

sign-up 신청 | deadline 마감 | research 조사, 연구 | attend 참가하다 | anticipate 예상하다 | accommodate 수용하다 | at the most 기껏해야 | rent 대여하다 | deal 거래, 대우 | drop by 잠깐 들르다 | address 주소

59

[번역]

화자들은 무엇에 관해 얘기하고 있는가?
(A) 여행 세부 사항
(B) 신문 헤드라인
(C) 가게 할인 행사
(D) 워크숍 계획

[해설]

논의 내용을 묻는 문제는 주로 첫 번째 대화에서 답을 찾을 수 있다. 남자의 첫 번째 대화 The sign-up deadline for the market research workshop was yesterday에서 가장 적절한 답이 (D)임을 알 수 있다.

[어휘]

detail 세부(사항) | trip 여행 | newspaper 신문 | bargain 특가(품)

60

[번역]

남자가 제안한 내용은?
(A) 테이블과 의자를 빌려라.
(B) 약속을 다시 정하라.
(C) 회의실을 바꿔라.
(D) 복사기를 수리해라.

[해설]

남자의 말과 관련된 내용을 묻는 질문이므로 남자의 말에 집중해야 한다. Why don't you try Wilson's Rentals? ~ always gives us a good deal이라는 내용에서 물품을 임대할 것임을 알 수 있으므로 (A)가 정답이다.

[어휘]

rent 임대하다 | reschedule 일정을 다시 잡다 | repair 수리하다 | copier 복사기

61

[번역]

여자는 무엇을 요청하는가?
(A) 지하철 지도
(B) 능복 양식
(C) 팩스 번호
(D) 사업체 주소

[해설]

여자의 행동을 묻는 질문이므로 여자의 말에 집중하자. Can you give me the address?에서 address를 직접적으로 언급한다. 따라서 정답은 (D)이다.

[어휘]

subway 지하철 | registration 기재, 등록

Questions 62-64 refer to the following conversation.

M (62)Have you decided where to have the end-of-the-year party yet?

W No, I haven't really given it that much thought. I've been occupied with other things.

M But we're going to have it three weeks from today, and you're the person in charge of it.

W We still have plenty of time.

M I don't think so. At least 30 people will attend, so we need to reserve a large room at a restaurant or in a hotel. (63)And don't forget that many other law firms will be having special events around the same time.

W Oh, I hadn't thought of that. I'd better make some phone calls today.

M (64)Do you need a list of places that can accommodate us? I can give you one.

W That would be great. I'd really appreciate it.

[번역]

M 어디에서 송년회를 열지 결정했나요?

W 아니오, 그에 대해 그다지 많은 생각을 하지 못했어요. 다른 일들로 여념이 없었거든요.

M 하지만 오늘부터 3주 후에 송년회를 열어야 하고, 당신은 그 일의 담당자에요.

W 아직 시간이 많이 있잖아요.

M 저는 그렇게 생각하지 않아요. 최소한 30명의 사람들이 참석할 것이기 때문에, 식당이나 호텔의 대형 룸을 예약해야 해요. 그리고 다른 많은 법률 사무소들도 비슷한 시기에 특별 행사를 치르게 될 것이라는 점도 잊지 말아야 하고요.

W 오, 그 생각은 못했네요. 오늘 몇 군데에 전화를 해 보는 것이 좋겠어요.

M 우리를 수용할 수 있는 장소에 관한 목록이 필요한가요? 제가 한 부 드릴 수 있어요.

W 그렇게 해 주면 좋을 것 같아요. 정말 고마워요.

[어휘]

end-of-the-year party 송년회 | be occupied with ~에 몰두하다, ~으로 인해 여념이 없다 | in charge of ~을 책임지는, ~을 담당하는 | law firm 법률 사무소 | accommodate 수용하다

62

[번역]

화자들은 주로 무엇을 논의하고 있는가?
(A) 이전 송년회
(B) 회사 행사를 위해 계획을 세울 필요성
(C) 그들이 식사를 하게 될 식당
(D) 그들이 3주 후에 참석하게 될 세미나

[해설]

송년회의 준비를 빨리 해야 한다는 논의가 이루어지고 있다. 따라서 정답은 (B)이다.

[어휘]

previous 이전의

63

[번역]

화자들은 어디에서 일하는 것 같은가?
(A) 법률 사무소에서
(B) 식당에서
(C) 호텔에서

(D) 엔지니어링 회사에서

[해설]

남자의 말 중 And don't forget that many other law firms will be having special events around the same time.에서 정답의 단서를 찾을 수 있다. many other law firms라는 표현으로 미루어 볼 때 화자들 역시 법률 사무소에서 일한다고 추측할 수 있다.

64

[번역]

여자는 남자에게 무엇을 할 것을 부탁하는가?
(A) 그녀를 위해 전화를 몇 통 한다
(B) 인근 호텔에 전화를 한다
(C) 파티 전체를 기획한다
(D) 정보를 알려 준다

[해설]

남자가 '인원을 수용할 수 있는 장소 목록(a list of places that can accommodate us)'을 줄 수 있다고 말하자 여자가 이를 반기는 상황이다. 따라서 정답은 (D)이다.

Questions 65-67 refer to the following conversation with three speakers.

W   I'm pleased we finally wrapped up our work on the Harrison project.
M1 Did the clients say they were satisfied with everything we did?
W   (66)Yes, they did. (65)In fact, Mr. Steele called me this morning and asked me to thank everyone for doing a great job.
M1 I'm glad he's happy. We worked on that project for more than three months.
M2 So what will we be doing next?
W   (67)I'm meeting my boss ten minutes from now. He'll give me our newest assignment then.
M1 Do you have any guesses what it's going to be?
W   I'm not sure, but we might be collaborating with Mr. Jefferson's team. They're way behind schedule and have a hard deadline at the end of the month.
M1 That's fine. I know some of the people on his team.

[번역]

W   마침내 우리가 해리슨 프로젝트를 끝내다니 기쁘군요.
M1 고객들이 우리가 한 모든 일에 만족했다고 말했나요?
W   네, 그랬어요. 실제로, 스틸 씨는 오늘 아침 제게 전화를 해서 일을 잘 처리해 준 모든 분들께 감사를 표시해 달라고 저에게 부탁하셨죠.
M1 그가 만족해 했다니 저도 기쁘군요. 우리는 그 프로젝트에 관해 3개월 이상 일을 했어요.
M2 그러면 이다음으로 우리가 무엇을 하게 되나요?

W   지금부터 10분 후에 사장님과 회의가 있어요. 그때 사장님께서 저에게 우리의 새로운 업무를 부여해 주실 거예요.
M1 어떤 일이 될지 혹시 짐작이 가는 부분이 있나요?
W   확실하지는 않지만, 제퍼슨 씨 팀과 공동으로 작업을 하게 될 것 같아요. 그들의 일정이 한참 뒤쳐지고 있어서 이번 달 말인 마감 기한을 맞추기가 힘들게 되었거든요.
M1 괜찮군요. 저는 그의 팀 사람들을 몇 명 알고 있어요.

[어휘]

wrap up 마무리하다, 끝내다 | **be satisfied with** ~에 만족하다 | **in fact** 사실, 실은 | **assignment** 과제, 업무 | **collaborate** 협동하다, 공동으로 일하다 | **way behind schedule** 예정보다 한참 뒤쳐진

65

[번역]

스틸 씨는 누구인가?
(A) 여자의 상사
(B) 화자들의 동료
(C) 여자의 고객
(D) 해리슨 씨의 친구

[해설]

고객들의 만족 여부를 묻는 남자1의 질문에 여자는 그렇다고 답한 후, 실제로 스틸 씨가 전화로 고마움을 표시했다고 말한다. 이를 통해 스틸 씨는 여자의 고객임을 알 수 있다.

66

[번역]

해리슨 프로젝트에 관해 무엇이 언급되었는가?
(A) 완성시켜야 할 기한이 다가오고 있다.
(B) 고객들이 이루어진 일에 대해 만족해 한다.
(C) 그에 대한 작업은 예산을 초과했다.
(D) 한 달 정도 연기될 것이다.

[해설]

남자1이 '고객들이 만족했는지(they were satisfied with everything we did)'를 묻자 여자가 그렇다고 답변한다.

[어휘]

complete 완성하다, 완료하다 | **approach** 접근하다 | **go over budget** 예산을 초과하다

67

[번역]

여자는 다음에 무엇을 할 것인가?
(A) 스틸 씨에게 이메일을 보낸다
(B) 제퍼슨 씨와 직접 이야기한다
(C) 사장과의 회의에 참석한다
(D) 남자들에게 새로운 업무를 맡긴다

[해설]

여자는 '10분 후 사장과의 회의에 참석해야 한다(I'm meeting my boss ten minutes from now.)'고 언급한다.

Questions 68-70 refer to the following conversation and itinerary.

> W Hi, Jeff. I need to speak with you about your travel plans.
>
> M What exactly do you need to know?
>
> W You're scheduled to be in San Francisco on July 15, right?
>
> M Let me check . . . Yes, that's correct. I've got a meeting with Fred Powell there on the fifteenth. (69)And I have to go to Los Angeles to attend a seminar on the next day.
>
> W I think you might need to change your schedule.
>
> M Why do you say that?
>
> W (68)Mr. Powell just called to tell me that he's leaving the country on the fifteenth. (70)So he wants to meet you on the fourteenth instead.
>
> M Okay. I'll have to rearrange my schedule since I'm supposed to be in Seattle on that day.

[번역]

W 안녕하세요, 제프. 당신의 출장 일정에 관해 이야기를 나누어야 해서요.

M 정확히 무엇을 알아야 하나요?

W 당신은 7월 15일에 샌프란시스코에 있을 예정이죠, 그렇죠?

M 확인해 볼게요… 네, 맞아요. 그곳에서 15일에 프레드 파웰과 회의가 있어요. 그리고 그 다음날은 세미나 참석을 위해 로스앤젤레스로 가야 하고요.

W 당신 일정을 바꾸어야 할 수도 있다고 생각해요.

M 왜 그렇게 말하는 거죠?

W 파웰 씨께서 조금 전 제게 전화를 하셔서 15일에 출국을 할 것이라고 말씀해 주셨어요. 그래서 그 대신 당신을 14일에 만나고 싶어하세요.

M 알겠어요. 그날은 제가 시애틀에 있을 예정이기 때문에 일정을 다시 조정해야겠네요.

[어휘]

exactly 정확히 | rearrange 다시 배정하다, 재배치하다

68

[번역]

프레드 파웰은 왜 여자에게 전화를 했는가?

(A) 그녀를 초대해서 회의에 참석시키기 위해

(B) 남자와의 회의를 취소시키기 위해

(C) 여행을 떠날 것이라고 그녀에게 알리기 위해

(D) 남자와 밴쿠버에서 만나기 위해

[해설]

대화 후반부의 여자의 말 Mr. Powell just called to tell me that he's leaving the country on the fifteenth.에서 파웰 씨는 남자와 만나기로 약속한 날 출국을 하게 되어 이를 알리고자 전화를 걸었음을 알 수 있다. 따라서 정답은 (C)이다.

69

[번역]

남자는 세미나에 참석하기 위해 어디로 갈 것인가?

(A) 로스앤젤레스

(B) 시애틀

(C) 밴쿠버

(D) 샌프란시스코

[해설]

And I have to go to Los Angeles to attend a seminar on the next day. 라는 문장에서 남자는 세미나 참석을 위해 로스앤젤레스로 갈 것임을 알 수 있다.

70

[번역]

도표를 보아라. 남자는 어느 날 일정을 바꾸어야 하는가?

(A) 7월 13일

(B) 7월 14일

(C) 7월 15일

(D) 7월 16일

[해설]

파웰 씨가 남자와 14일에 만나고 싶어한다고 했으므로 남자는 7월 14일 일정을 변경해야 할 것이다.

PART 4

Questions 71-73 refer to the following announcement.

> Attention, customers, (72)Markey's will be closing in approximately half an hour. Before leaving, (71)(73)please browse our display of best-selling science fiction located in front of the cash registers beside the main entrance. All novels in this display have been marked down by 50 percent. And please come back tomorrow as Markey's will host a special signing. Well-known author Connie Lee will be autographing copies of *Reach High*, her new novel. Thank you for choosing Markey's.

[번역]

고객 여러분께 알려 드립니다. 마키스의 오늘 영업은 약 30분 후에 마칩니다. 나가시기 전에 중앙 출입구 방향 계산대 앞에 마련된 과학소설 베스트셀러 코너를 둘러 봐 주시기 바랍니다. 진열된 소설책 모두 50퍼센트까지 가격을 내렸습니다. 그리고 내일, 마키스가 준비한 특별 사인회가 있으니 다시 찾아 주시기를 바랍니다. 유명 작가 코니 리의 신작 *높이 나아가라*의 친필 사인회가 열립니다. 마키스를 찾아 주셔서 감사합니다.

[어휘]

attention 주의 | customer 고객 | approximately 대략 | browse ~을 마음 내키는 대로 읽다, (서점을) 이리저리 뒤지다 | display 전시, 진열 | science fiction 과학소설 | cash register 금전 등록기, 계산대 | novel 소설 | mark down 가격을 내리다 | host 주최하다 | well-known

유명한 | **author** 저자 | **autograph** 서명하다 | **copy** (책) 한 권 |
choose 선택하다

71

[번역]

마키스에서는 무엇을 파는가?

(A) 전자기기

(B) 식물

(C) 자동차

(D) 책

[해설]

지문이 들리는 장소와 관련된 질문은 전반부를 집중해서 들어야 한다.
please browse our display of best-selling science fiction이라는 내용
에서 Markey's가 파는 상품이 책이라는 것을 알 수 있다.

72

[번역]

마키스는 언제 닫을 예정인가?

(A) 15분 후

(B) 30분 후

(C) 1시간 후

(D) 2시간 후

[해설]

안내방송 전반부의 Markey's will be closing in approximately half an
hour에서 30분 후에 닫는다는 내용을 들을 수 있다. half an hour는 30
minutes로, an hour는 60 minutes로 바뀌어 출제되는 경우가 많으니
반드시 익혀두자.

73

[번역]

특별 진열대는 어디에서 찾을 수 있는가?

(A) 가게 입구 근처

(B) 엘리베이터 옆

(C) 꼭대기 층

(D) 주차장

[해설]

질문의 핵심 어구인 the special display가 언급되는 곳을 집중해서
들어야 하는 문제로, please browse our display ~ beside the main
entrance에서 정답을 찾을 수 있다.

[어휘]

entrance 입구 | **parking garage** 주차장

**Questions 74-76 refer to the following voice mail
message.**

Hello, Mr. Davidson. (74)(75)This is Michael Scoville
from Landscaping and Yard Care calling with regard
to the work on your garden. As soon as we arrive
on Monday morning, we will mow the lawn and trim
the hedges. You also asked us to remove the lower
branches from the big elm tree located on the west
side of your house. That will not be a problem, but to
avoid damaging any cars, please ensure that the

adjacent street nearest the elm is free of vehicles. If
you would like to change this appointment, please
call 503-1692. (76)If we do not hear from you, we will
be at your house at ten on Monday. Thank you.

[번역]

데이비슨 씨, 안녕하세요. 저는 랜드스케이핑 앤 야드 케어의 마이클 스
코빌이고, 귀하의 정원 일로 전화 드렸습니다. 저희가 월요일 오전에 귀
하의 집에 도착하는 대로, 잔디를 깎고 울타리 나무들을 손질할 예정입
니다. 귀하께서는 집 서쪽에 있는 큰 느릅나무의 아래쪽 가지들도 쳐달
라고 하셨습니다. 그렇게 하는 것이 어렵지는 않으나, 차량 손상을 피하
기 위해 느릅나무에 인접한 길에 차량이 세워져 있지 않도록 조치해 주
시기 바랍니다. 약속을 변경하고 싶으시면 503-1692로 전화 주시기
바랍니다. 연락이 없으면 저희는 월요일 10시에 찾아뵙겠습니다. 감사
합니다.

[어휘]

with regard to ~에 관해서 | **arrive** 도착하다 | **mow** 베다 | **lawn**
잔디 | **trim** 손질하다 | **hedge** 울타리 | **remove** 제거하다 | **branch**
가지 | **elm** 느릅나무 | **damage** 손상시키다 | **ensure** 확실하게 하다 |
adjacent 인접한 | **be free of** ~이 없는 | **appointment** 약속

74

[번역]

화자는 데이비슨 씨에게 왜 전화를 했는가?

(A) 서비스 내용을 광고하려고

(B) 배달 주소를 확인하려고

(C) 예정된 작업을 확인하려고

(D) 계획 변경을 요청하려고

[해설]

화자의 목적을 묻는 문제로, 전반부의 This is Michael Scoville from
Landscaping and Yard Care calling with regard to the work on your
garden에서 정원에 관련된 일 때문에 전화했다는 내용이 나온다. 이미
월요일 10시로 일정이 잡혀 있는 일이기 때문에 이를 scheduled work
라고 표현하고 이 내용을 확인/확정(confirm)하는 것이라고 한 (C)가
정답이다.

[어휘]

confirm 확인하다 | **request** 요청하다

75

[번역]

화자는 어디에서 일하겠는가?

(A) 자전거 가게

(B) 정원 손질 회사

(C) 운송 회사

(D) 부동산 중개업소

[해설]

화자의 직장을 묻는 문제로, 전반부의 This is Michael Scoville from
Landscaping and Yard Care에서 회사이름을 듣고 (B)가 정답임을 유
추할 수 있는데, 그 이후에 등장하는 the work on your garden이나,
we will mow the lawn and trim the hedges 등을 통해 그가 하는 일을
더욱 확실히 파악할 수 있다.

[어휘]

gardening 원예 | **real estate** 부동산

76

[번역]

화자는 몇 시에 데이비슨 씨를 방문하겠는가?

(A) 오전 8시

(B) 오전 10시

(C) 오후 2시

(D) 오후 4시

[해설]

미래의 일을 묻는 문제는 주로 후반부에서 답을 찾을 수 있다. If we do
not hear from you, we will be at your house at ten on Monday를 듣
고 (B)가 정답임을 알 수 있다.

Questions 77-79 refer to the following talk.

Ladies and gentlemen, (77)I have many people to
thank for this award, but, first of all, I would like
to say that I truly appreciate being honored for the
research I have completed on the benefits of using
computers in language education. This project was a
rewarding experience from beginning to end. Next, I
would like to thank my research assistants and office
staff for their continuous hard work and support.
I am also grateful to my esteemed colleagues (78)
at the University of Cornwall where, for just over
eight years, I have served as a faculty member in
the Linguistics Department. Finally, (79)I am deeply
indebted to the Learning Foundation for a generous
grant last year that allowed me to initiate this project.

[번역]

신사 숙녀 여러분, 제가 이 상을 받게 된 것에 감사 드려야 할 분들이 많
습니다. 그러나 우선, 제가 이번에 끝마친 '언어 교육에서 컴퓨터 사용
의 이점'에 관한 연구로 영광을 얻게 되어 너무나 감사하게 생각하고
있음을 말씀드리고 싶습니다. 이 프로젝트는 처음부터 끝까지 가치 있
는 경험이었습니다. 다음으로, 끊임없이 노력하고 지지해 준 연구 보조
원들과 사무실 직원들에게 감사합니다. 제가 언어학부 교수로 8년 이
상 재직하고 있는 콘월 대학의 훌륭한 동료들에게도 감사합니다. 마지
막으로, 제가 이 프로젝트를 시작할 수 있도록 작년에 큰 후원금을 주신
학문 재단에 깊은 감사를 드립니다.

[어휘]

award 상 | first of all 무엇보다도 먼저 | appreciate 감사하다 | honor
~에게 영광(명예)를 주다 | research 연구 | complete 끝내다 | benefit
이점 | language 언어 | rewarding 가치가 있는 | assistant 보조 |
continuous 끊임없는 | grateful 감사하는 | esteemed 존경 받는 |
colleague 동료 | faculty member 교직원 | indebted 빚이있는,
은혜를 입은 | foundation 재단 | generous 아낌없는 | grant 기부 |
allow 허락하다 | initiate 시작하다

77

[번역]

본 담화의 목적은 무엇인가?

(A) 수상소감을 발표하기 위해

(B) 새로 온 교수를 환영하기 위해

(C) 컴퓨터 프로그램을 설명하기 위해

(D) 사무실 직원을 소개하기 위해

[해설]

목적을 묻는 문제로, 전반부의 I have many people to thank for this
award에서 이 상에 대해 많은 사람들에게 감사하다는 내용이 나온다.
출제 빈도가 높은 appreciate(감사하다)와 appreciation(감사
=gratitude)을 꼭 익혀두자.

[어휘]

appreciation 감사 | welcome 환영하다 | faculty 직원

78

[번역]

담화에 따르면, 화자가 대학에서 일한 지는 얼마나 되었는가?

(A) 약 2년

(B) 약 4년

(C) 약 6년

(D) 약 8년

[해설]

후반부의 at the University of Cornwall where, for just over
eight years, I have served as a faculty member in the Linguistics
Department에서 8년 넘게 재직했다는 내용이 나온다.

79

[번역]

화자는 왜 학문 재단을 언급했는가?

(A) 교재 몇 권을 기증했기 때문에

(B) 교실 물품을 구매했기 때문에

(C) 프로젝트 기금을 제공했기 때문에

(D) 학생에게 상을 줬기 때문에

[해설]

질문의 핵심어구인 the Learning Foundation에 집중해서 들으면, 후반
부의 I am deeply indebted to the Learning Foundation for a generous
grant last year에서 답을 찾을 수 있다. grant는 '보조금, 기부금'이라는
뜻으로 (C)의 funds for the project를 의미한다.

[어휘]

mention 언급하다 | donate 기부하다 | fund 자금 | award 상

Questions 80-82 refer to the following introduction.

Good afternoon, everybody. Before starting, (80)please
let me take a minute to introduce Marie Perez, the
most recent addition to our company. Marie has
accepted a position as marketing analyst on the
home improvement team. Previously, Marie analyzed
data on consumer markets in northern Europe for
Thompson's Global Kitchen Products. She held that
position for five years before joining us. As you are
aware, we have recently committed ourselves to a
contract with many leading retailers in Finland and
Denmark. Under this agreement, (81)we will provide
those retailers with kitchen appliances. (83)Marie's
familiarity with this particular regional market will

assist us greatly in identifying which of our latest lines of blenders and microwaves will attract the highest number of consumers in both countries.

[번역]

좋은 오후입니다, 여러분. 시작하기 전에, 우리 회사에 가장 최근에 합류하신 마리 페레즈를 잠시 소개해 드릴까 합니다. 마리는 가정 개선용품 팀의 마케팅 분석가로 근무하기로 하셨습니다. 이전에는 톰슨 글로벌 키친 프로덕트 사에서 북유럽의 소비자 시장 데이터를 분석했습니다. 그곳에서 5년 동안 근무하시다가 이번에 우리와 일하게 되었습니다. 여러분도 아시다시피, 우리는 최근에 핀란드와 덴마크에 있는 많은 주요 소매업자들과 계약하기 위해 전념해 왔습니다. 이 계약 하에 우리는 그들에게 우리의 부엌 용품을 공급할 예정입니다. 이 지역 시장에 대한 마리의 전문성은 우리의 최신 믹서 및 전자 레인지 제품군들 중에서 어떤 제품이 이 두 나라에서 가장 많은 소비자들에게 어필할 것인지 파악하는데 큰 도움을 줄 것으로 기대됩니다.

[어휘]

addition 증원 인력 ｜ accept 수락하다 ｜ position 직(책) ｜ analyst 분석가 ｜ improvement 개선 ｜ analyze 분석하다 ｜ consumer 소비자 ｜ be aware 알다 ｜ recently 최근 ｜ commit 전념하다 ｜ contract 계약 ｜ leading 주요한 ｜ retailer 소매 상인 ｜ appliance 제품, 용품 ｜ familiarity 정통, 잘 앎 ｜ particular 특정의 ｜ regional 지역의 ｜ assist 돕다 ｜ identify 알아내다 ｜ line 제품군 ｜ blender 믹서 ｜ microwave 전자 레인지 ｜ attract 매혹하다

80

[번역]

본 담화의 목적은 무엇인가?

(A) 채용 절차 설명하기

(B) 직원 소개하기

(C) 마케팅 계획 바꾸기

(D) 새로운 부서를 만들기

[해설]

목적을 묻는 문제이므로, 전반부에 집중해서 들어 보자. please let me take a minute to introduce Marie Perez, the most recent addition to our company에서 가장 최근에 입사한 마리 페레즈를 소개하겠다는 내용이 나온다. introduce를 present로 바꾸어 표현한 (B)가 정답이다.

[어휘]

hiring process 채용 과정 ｜ present 보여주다 ｜ division 부서, 분과

81

[번역]

이 회사가 파는 제품은 무엇이겠는가?

(A) 자동차 부품

(B) 부엌 용품

(C) 아동복

(D) 야영 장비

[해설]

세부사항을 묻는 질문의 단서는 대체로 중반부에 나온다. we will provide those retailers with kitchen appliances에서 이 회사(we)가 판매하는 제품은 부엌 용품임을 알 수 있다.

[어휘]

equipment 장비

82

[번역]

담화에 따르면, 페레즈 씨가 이 회사에서 할 일은 무엇인가?

(A) 새로운 자동차 부품 디자인

(B) 유럽 지점 오픈

(C) 신상품 매뉴얼 초안 작성

(D) 구매자의 선호도 판단

[해설]

마지막 문장에서 그녀는 핀란드와 덴마크의 사정에 정통하고 있어 어떤 제품이 attract the highest number of consumers 할 것인지 identify (= determine)하는데 도움을 줄 것이라고 했으므로 (D)가 정답이다.

[어휘]

part 부품, 부분 ｜ draft 초안을 작성하다 ｜ manual 설명서 ｜ determine 알아내다, 밝히다 ｜ buyer 구매자, 바이어

Questions 83-85 refer to the following radio broadcast.

The National Weather Bureau has issued a heat warning for the south eastern region. This warning is in effect from early Saturday morning until Monday afternoon. (83)Temperatures will soar to 37 degrees Celsius, which is exceptionally high for this time of year. To prevent dehydration and heatstroke, (84)officials at the weather bureau suggest consuming lots of fluids and avoiding excessive physical activity. Officials also ask businesses to cut back on electricity. Relief from the burning heat will arrive on Monday evening in the form of showers. (85)On Tuesday, temperatures will drop to 25 degrees Celsius, so please wait until then before participating in any activities outside.

[번역]

국립 기상청은 남동부 지역에 폭염주의보를 발령했습니다. 이 주의보는 토요일 이른 오전부터 월요일 오후까지 유효합니다. 기온은 섭씨 37도까지 치솟을 것이며, 이는 연중 이맘때 날씨로는 대단히 높은 기온입니다. 탈수증과 열사병을 방지하기 위해 기상청 관계자들은 많은 수분을 섭취하고 과도한 신체 활동을 피할 것을 당부하고 있습니다. 관계자들은 또한 기업들이 전기 사용량을 줄일 것도 부탁했습니다. 폭염은 월요일 저녁에 내리는 소나기로 누그러질 것입니다. 화요일에는 기온이 섭씨 25도까지 떨어질 예정이니 외부에 나가서 활동하시려면 그때까지 기다려 주시기 바랍니다.

[어휘]

bureau (관청의) 국, 부 ｜ issue 공포하다, 발하다 ｜ warning 경고 ｜ region 지역 ｜ in effect 시행 중인 ｜ temperature 기온 ｜ soar 치솟다 ｜ Celsius 섭씨 ｜ exceptionally 유별나게, 대단히 ｜ this time of year 이맘때 ｜ prevent 방지하다 ｜ dehydration 탈수 ｜ heatstroke 열사병 ｜ suggest 제안하다 ｜ consume 소비하다 ｜ fluids 수분, 액체 ｜ avoid

피하다 | excessive 과도한 | physical 신체의 | activity 활동 | cut
back 줄이다 | electricity 전기 | relief 제거, 경감 | shower 소나기 |
drop 떨어지다 | participate in ~에 참여하다

83
[번역]

현재 기상 상태가 특이한 점은 무엇인가?
(A) 폭우
(B) 높은 기온
(C) 산발적 소나기
(D) 강풍

[해설]

문제의 unusual은 지문에서 exceptionally ~ for this time of year로 표
현되어 나타나고 있다. this time of year는 '이맘때'라는 뜻으로 여기에
'유별나게'란 의미의 exceptionally가 더해졌으니 결국 unusual이란 의
미가 되는 것이다. 기온이 섭씨 37도라고 한 후 high란 형용사로 기술
하고 있으므로 정답은 (B)이다.

[어휘]

scattered 산발적인

84
[번역]

기상청 관계자들의 조언은 무엇인가?
(A) 실내에 머무를 것
(B) 전기를 절약할 것
(C) 두꺼운 외투를 입을 것
(D) 물을 아껴 쓸 것

[해설]

질문의 핵심어인 official에 집중해 들으면 중반부의 officials at the
weather bureau suggest consuming lots of fluids and avoiding
excessive physical activity. Officials also ask businesses to cut back
on electricity에서 세부 사항을 찾을 수 있다. 문제의 보기에서 가장 적
합한 답은 cut back on을 conserve(보존하다, 아끼다)로 표현한 (B)이
다.

[어휘]

weather bureau 기상국 | conserve 아끼다, 아껴 쓰다 | save 절약하다

85
[번역]

언제 외부 활동하기에 좋은 날씨가 되겠는가?
(A) 월요일
(B) 화요일
(C) 수요일
(D) 목요일

[해설]

미래 상황을 묻는 질문이므로, 후반부에 집중해서 듣는다. On
Tuesday, temperatures will drop to 25 degrees Celsius, so please wait
until then before participating in any activities outside에서 화요일이
면 바깥 활동하기에 좋을 만큼 기온이 낮아진다는 내용이 나온다. 따라
서 답은 (B)이다.

[어휘]

outdoor 야외의, 외부의

Questions 86-88 refer to the following talk.

Good afternoon, everyone. (86)I would like to begin by
welcoming you to the historic Hamilton Residence.
(87)I'm Martin Drake, your guide. Please feel free
to ask questions during the tour. This magnificent
building was (88)the home of William Hamilton, who
accumulated great wealth in shipping from 1886
until his death in 1931. His eldest son continued
to reside here for an additional 20 years before the
house was officially named a tourist attraction. In
each room, you will notice eye-catching pieces of
furniture and art from every corner of the world. (88)
As president of the Great Shipping Company, Mr.
Hamilton frequently traveled abroad, which is how
he came to acquire these items.

[번역]

여러분, 안녕하세요. 역사적인 해밀턴 저택으로 여러분을 모시는 것으
로 시작하겠습니다. 저는 여러분의 가이드인 마틴 드레이크라고 합니
다. 관광하시면서 궁금한 점이 생기시면 언제든지 질문해 주시기 바랍
니다. 이 화려한 건물은 1886년부터 1931년 사망할 때까지 해운업으
로 엄청난 부를 쌓았던 윌리엄 해밀턴이 살았던 집입니다. 그의 장남은
이 집이 공식 관광 명소로 지정되기 전까지 여기에서 20년을 더 살았습
니다. 각 방마다 이색적인 가구와 세계 각지에서 들여 온 예술품이 눈에
띌 것입니다. 그레이트 쉬핑 컴퍼니 회장이었던 해밀턴은 해외여행을
자주 했는데, 그래서 그는 이런 물품들을 손에 넣을 수 있었던 것입니
다.

[어휘]

historic 역사적인 | residence 저택 | feel free to 편하게 ~하다 | tour
관광 | magnificent 화려한, 장대한 | accumulate 쌓아 올리다,
모으다 | shipping 해운업 | eldest 장남(장녀)의 | reside 살다, 거주하다
| additional 추가의 | officially 공식적으로 | name 명명하다, 지명하다
| tourist attraction 관광 명소 | eye-catching 이목을 끄는, 이색적인 |
furniture 가구 | president 회장 | frequently 자주 | abroad 해외 |
acquire 손에 넣다, 얻다

86
[번역]

청중은 어디에 있는가?
(A) 자동차 공장
(B) 민속촌
(C) 역사적인 저택
(D) 미술 전시장

[해설]

장소를 묻는 문제의 단서는 주로 담화의 전반부에 나온다. I would like
to begin by welcoming you to the historic Hamilton Residence에서
역사적인 해밀턴 저택이라는 내용에서 답을 찾을 수 있으며, residence
를 home으로 바꾸어 표현한 (C)가 정답이다.

[어휘]

folk village 민속 마을 | historic 역사적인

87

[번역]

마틴 드레이크는 누구인가?

(A) 여행 인솔자
(B) 예술품 수집가
(C) 건축가
(D) 화가

[해설]

전반부의 I'm Martin Drake, your guide에서 Martin은 본 담화의 화자이며, 그의 직업은 여행 인솔자임을 알 수 있다.

88

[번역]

윌리엄 해밀턴이 한 일은 무엇인가?

(A) 미술 박물관을 열었다.
(B) 교사였다.
(C) 여행사를 운영했다
(D) 해운업회사를 소유했다.

[해설]

문제의 핵심어인 Hamilton에 집중해서 들어 보자. 저택 소유주였던 해밀턴에 대한 부연 설명 부분인 the home of William Hamilton, who accumulated great wealth in shipping에서 shipping을 확인할 수 있으며, 후반부의 As president of the Great Shipping Company, Mr. Hamilton에서도 그가 한 일이 무엇인지 확인할 수 있다.

[어휘]

travel agency 여행사 | own 보유하다, 소유하다 | shipping company 운송회사, 택배회사

Questions 89-91 refer to the following talk.

> (89)Before conducting the interviews, we need to have a quick meeting. One candidate is Julie Park, who, according to her résumé, has been the assistant marketing director in our Jeju office since 2013. All of you most likely know the other candidate, Peter Mason, because he is our own assistant director of sales. Peter has held that position since 2014. The five interview questions are listed on your evaluation sheet. (90)As each applicant replies, please write down your impressions in the appropriate spaces, and don't forget to write a score from one to five in the rating box. (91)After comparing notes tomorrow morning, we must reach an agreement and select our new senior policy advisor of investor relations. If you have any questions, please ask them now.

[번역]

면접 시행에 앞서, 우리는 잠시 회의를 해야 합니다. 한 후보자는 줄리 박인데, 이력서를 보니 2013년부터 우리 회사 제주 지점에서 마케팅 부장으로 일해 왔습니다. 다른 후보자 피터 메이슨은 우리의 영업부 차장이므로 여러분 모두 알고 계실 것입니다. 그는 2014년부터 그 직책을 맡아 왔습니다. 면접에 다룰 다섯 가지 질문은 평가서에 적혀 있습니다. 각 지원자들의 답변에 따라, 여러분이 느낀 점을 해당 란에 적어 주

시고 평점 칸에는 1부터 5까지의 점수를 반드시 적어 주시기를 바랍니다. 내일 아침에 평가서를 비교하고 합의를 해서, 투자관계부서 새 선임 정책고문을 선출해야 합니다. 궁금하신 점이 있으면, 지금 질문해 주시기 바랍니다.

[어휘]

conduct 실시하다 | interview 면접 | quick 신속한 | candidate 후보자 | résumé 이력서 | listed 목록에 올라있는 | applicant 지원자 | reply 답변 | write down 적다 | impression 인상 | appropriate 적당한, 적합한 | rating 평점 | compare 비교하다 | reach an agreement 합의점에 도달하다 | investor relations 투자관계부서

89

[번역]

화자가 본 담화문을 말하는 까닭은?

(A) 판매 직원을 소개하기 위해
(B) 면접 절차를 설명하기 위해
(C) 주요 정책의 변경 사항을 알리기 위해
(D) 연구 결과를 검토하기 위해

[해설]

담화 주제(mainly about?)를 묻는 질문은 담화문 전체를 이해해야 한다. Before conducting the interviews에서 이어질 내용이 면접에 대한 내용임을 알 수 있다. 이어지는 내용이 '각 면접자에 대한 간략한 소개와 선정 절차 방법'이 설명되고 있기 때문에 정답은 (B)이다.

[어휘]

sales representative 판매 대리인 | interview 인터뷰, 면접 | key 주요한 | research study 조사 연구

90

[번역]

청자들이 해야 할 것은 무엇인가?

(A) 각 지원자들에 대한 인상 기록
(B) 지원서 작성
(C) 회담 세부 사항 제공
(D) 패널 토의 참가

[해설]

세부 사항을 묻는 질문의 단서는 대체로 중반부에 나온다. As each applicant replies, please write down your impressions in the appropriate spaces에서 write down을 note로 바꿔 표현한 (A)가 정답임을 알 수 있다.

[어휘]

note 적다, 기입하다 | impression 인상 | applicant 지원자 | fill out 작성하다 | provide 제공하다 | details 세부 사항 | panel discussion 패널 토론회, 공개 토론회

91

[번역]

청자들이 내일 아침에 할 일은 무엇인가?

(A) 외국인 고객 접대
(B) 근무 시간 변경
(C) 새 직원 고용
(D) 새 컴퓨터 설치

[해설]

미래의 일을 묻는 질문은 후반부에 집중하자. After comparing notes tomorrow morning, we must ~ select our new senior policy advisor of investor relations의 내용에 비추어 (C)가 정답임을 알 수 있다.

[어휘]

business hours 영업시간 ┆ install 설치하다

Questions 92-94 refer to the following excerpt from a speech.

It's my pleasure to be here in front of everyone today. (92)As the new head of Bedford Systems, it's my goal to lead us back down the road to success. (93)I realize that the situation here has been unsteady lately. And I'm aware that the company has lost money while high-level employees have defected to other companies. But all of you have remained. I have confidence in you, and I'm sure that, by working together, we can rebuild Bedford Systems. We were once the top electronics firm in the state. I intend to make us the biggest electronics firm in the country. I've been working with the department heads to come up with a plan for this coming year. (94)Let me provide you with a brief outline of it.

[번역]

오늘 여러분 앞에 서게 되어 기쁘게 생각합니다. 베드포드 시스템즈의 새로운 대표로서, 성공으로 가는 길로 우리를 이끄는 것이 저의 목표입니다. 저는 최근에 이곳 상황이 불안정하다는 점을 알게 되었습니다. 그리고 회사가 손실을 보고 있으며 우수한 직원들도 다른 회사로 떠나고 있다는 점도 알고 있습니다. 하지만 여러분 모두는 남아 있습니다. 저는 여러분들에 대한 신뢰를 가지고 있으며, 우리가 함께 일함으로써, 베드포드 시스템즈를 재건할 수 있다고 확신합니다. 우리는 한 때 주에서 제일가는 전자 제품 회사였습니다. 저는 우리를 전국에서 제일 큰 전자 제품 회사로 만들 생각입니다. 저는 올해의 계획을 세우기 위해 부서장들과 힘을 합치고 있습니다. 그에 대해 짧게 설명을 드리도록 하겠습니다.

[어휘]

goal 목표 ┆ realize 깨닫다, 알아채다 ┆ unsteady 불안정한 ┆ defect 떠나다 ┆ confidence 믿음, 신뢰 ┆ rebuild 다시 짓다 ┆ intend to ~할 의도이다 ┆ come up with ~을 떠올리다 ┆ brief 간략한 ┆ outline 개요

92

[번역]

화자는 누구인가?
(A) 바이어
(B) 엔지니어
(C) 이사
(D) 부서장

[해설]

서두에서 본인을 new head of Bedford Systems라고 소개하고 있고, 이후에도 한 회사의 대표로서 자신의 포부에 대해 이야기하고 있다. 따라서 정답은 '이사', '중역'이라는 의미의 (C)이다.

93

[번역]

화자는 베드포드 시스템즈에 관해 무엇을 말하는가?
(A) 예전만큼 잘 되고 있지 않다.
(B) 전국에서 가장 큰 전자 제품 회사이다.
(C) 신제품을 출시할 것이다.
(D) 우수한 신입 사원들을 고용했다.

[해설]

화자는 담화 중반에 회사가 수익을 내지 못하고 있으며 인재들이 빠져 나가고 있다고 언급한다. 또한 We were once the top electronics firm in the state.라는 말에서 현재 베드포드 시스템즈가 예전보다 실적이 좋지 못하다는 점을 추측할 수 있다.

94

[번역]

남자가 "Let me provide you with a brief outline of it"이라고 말했을 때, 그는 무엇을 의미하는가?
(A) 그는 회사의 과거에 대해 이야기할 것이다.
(B) 그는 회사에 대한 자신의 계획을 설명할 것이다.
(C) 그는 몇몇 부서장들을 소개할 것이다.
(D) 그는 최신 제품을 설명할 것이다.

[해설]

provide A with B가 'A에게 B를 제공하다'라는 뜻이고, 이 문장에서 it은 plan을 가리킨다는 점을 알고 있으면 쉽게 정답을 찾을 수 있다.

[어휘]

explain 설명하다 ┆ describe 묘사하다, 설명하다

Questions 95-97 refer to the following announcement and map.

Good afternoon and thank you for shopping at Red Terrace. We'd like to inform you of some special offers that are going to last for the rest of the day. (95)You can get a dozen apples for only $2 and half a dozen oranges for $3. Just head to the fruit and vegetable center and speak with a clerk there. And ground beef in the meat section is on sale for $1 a pound. We'd also like to remind you (97)that the information center next to the manager's office is going to be closed for the next two days. It's going to be renovated, so it will be even bigger and better when it reopens. If you have any questions, (96)send an e-mail to information@redterrace.com, and we'll answer it.

[번역]

안녕하세요, 레드 테라스에서 쇼핑을 해 주셔서 감사합니다. 여러분들께 오늘 나머지 시간 동안 진행될 예정인 특가 상품에 대해 알려 드리고자 합니다. 사과 12개를 단 2달러에, 그리고 오렌지 6개를 단 3달러에 구매하실 수 있습니다. 과일 및 야채 코너로 가셔서 그곳 점원에게 말씀만 하십시오. 그리고 육류 코너에서는 간 쇠고기를 파운드당 1달러에 판매하고 있습니다. 아울러 여러분들께 지점장 사무실 옆의 안내 데

스크가 이틀간 문을 닫을 것이라는 점도 알려 드리고자 합니다. 보수 공사를 할 것이기 때문에, 다시 문을 열면 훨씬 더 크고 좋아질 것입니다. 질문이 있으신 경우에는 information@redterrace.com으로 이메일을 보내 주시면 답변을 드리도록 하겠습니다.

[어휘]

inform A of B A에게 B에 대해 알리다 | special offer 특가 상품 | last 지속되다, 계속하다 | dozen 12개 | ground 빻은, (육류 등을) 간 | remind 상기시키다, 기억나게 하다 | renovate 혁신하다; 보수하다

95

[번역]

청자들이 세일 제품을 사기 위해서는 어디로 가야 하는가?

(A) 제빵 코너

(B) 조제 식품 코너

(C) 과일 야채 코너

(D) 전자 제품 코너

[해설]

세일 제품은 사과와 오렌지이고 이를 구입하기 위해서는 fruit and vegetable center로 가라고 말하고 있다. 따라서 정답은 (C)이다.

96

[번역]

화자는 청자들에게 무엇을 할 것을 제안하는가?

(A) 이메일을 보낸다

(B) 쿠폰을 사용한다

(C) 제안을 한다

(D) 계산대로 간다

[해설]

안내방송의 마지막 부분에서 안내 데스크가 폐쇄되었으니 문의 사항이 있는 경우에는 이메일을 이용할 것을 권장하고 있다.

97

[번역]

도표를 보아라. 매장의 어떤 코너가 일시적으로 문을 닫을 예정인가?

(A) 1

(B) 2

(C) 3

(D) 4

[해설]

문을 닫을 예정인 곳은 '지점장 사무실 옆(next to the manager's office)'에 위치해 있는 information center이다. 따라서 정답은 (D)이다.

Questions 98-100 refer to the following excerpt from a meeting and graph.

(98)Attendance at Wonder World during the past few months has been steadily increasing for the most part. We had fairly low numbers in both January and February, but that happens every year. The cold weather simply keeps too many people away from the amusement park. (100)In March, attendance rose by more than 100%. Basically, we got weather that was warmer than expected, and we opened a couple of new rides. The rollercoaster has proven to be especially popular, and we believe it's the main reason we've attracted so many visitors. In April, May, and June, attendance continued to rise, but it remained steady in July. (99)We got several thunderstorms, so we had to close some rides then. Fortunately, there were sunny skies in August, so attendance was the highest of the year last month.

[번역]

지난 몇 달 동안 원더 월드의 관람객수는 대체적으로 꾸준히 증가해 왔습니다. 1월과 2월에는 상당히 수치가 낮았지만, 이는 매년 나타나는 현상입니다. 추운 날씨로 인해 많은 사람들이 놀이 공원을 찾지 않습니다. 3월에는, 관람객수가 100% 이상 증가했습니다. 기본적으로, 예상보다 날씨가 따뜻했고, 두어 개의 새로운 놀이 기구가 신설되었습니다. 롤러코스터가 특히 인기가 많은 것으로 판명이 되었는데, 이것이 우리가 그처럼 많은 방문객들을 유치하게 된 주된 이유라고 생각됩니다. 4월, 5월, 그리고 6월 동안, 관람객 수는 계속해서 증가했지만, 7월에는 정체 상태였습니다. 몇 차례의 뇌우가 발생했기 때문에 몇몇 놀이 기구의 작동이 중단되어야 했습니다. 다행스럽게도, 8월에는 화창한 날씨가 이어져서 지난 달 관람객 수가 연중 최고치를 나타냈습니다.

[어휘]

attendance 출석률 | steadily 꾸준하게 | fairly 상당히, 꽤 | ride 탈 것, 놀이 기구 | attract 끌다, 유인하다 | thunderstorm 뇌우

98

[번역]

담화의 목적은 무엇인가?

(A) 앞으로의 계획을 설명하기 위해

(D) 더 많은 자금 지원을 요청하기 위해

(C) 최근의 관람객 수를 검토하기 위해

(D) 공원의 새로운 놀이에 대해 논의하기 위해

[해설]

월별로 놀이 공원의 관람객 수에 대해 이야기하고 있다.

[어휘]

funding 자금, 자금 지원 | go over 검토하다 | recent 최근의

99

[번역]

화자에 의하면, 7월에는 어떤 일이 일어났는가?

(A) 몇몇 놀이 기구의 운영이 일시적으로 중단되었다.

(B) 공원의 관람객 수가 증가했다.

(C) 주로 맑은 날씨가 이어졌다.

(D) 많은 새로운 방문객들이 공원을 찾았다.

[해설]

화자는 7월에 증가세가 둔화되었는데, 그 이유가 뇌우(thunderstorms)로 인해 몇몇 놀이 기구의 운영이 중단되었기 때문이라고 말한다.

100

[번역]

도표를 보아라. 새로운 롤러코스터는 몇 월에 운영되기 시작했는가?

(A) 3월
(B) 4월
(C) 6월
(D) 8월

[해설]

화자는 3월에 관람객 수가 100% 이상 증가했는데, 그 이유 중 하나가 롤러코스터의 신설 때문이라고 설명한다. 따라서 롤러코스터는 3월부터 운영되었다는 점을 알 수 있다.

Reading Comprehension

PART 5

[정답]

1 (C)	**2** (B)	**3** (A)	**4** (D)
5 (D)	**6** (D)	**7** (C)	**8** (A)

1

[번역]

배송물품들을 5일 이내에 받지 못하면, 운송부 부서장에게 즉시 연락해 주십시오.

[해설]

빈칸이 관사 the 뒤에 있고 문장에서 주어 자리이므로 '배송하다'는 뜻으로 쓰인 동사 (B) ship과 (D) shipped는 제외된다. 복수 동사 are not received 앞이므로 복수 주어가 필요하다. 따라서 정답은 복수 명사 (C) shipments(배송물품들)가 된다.

[어휘]

contact 연락하다 | immediately 즉시 | ship 운송하다, 선적하다 | shipment 선적물, 배송

2

[번역]

사고나 부상이 있을 경우 모든 고객들은 보상을 요청할 것이라고 예상된다.

[해설]

빈칸이 동사 will request 뒤에 있으므로 문장에서 목적어 자리이다. '보상하다'는 의미인 동사 (A) compensated, (C) compensate와 형용사 (D) compensatory(보상의)는 명사 자리에 올 수 없다. 따라서 정답은 명사 (B) compensation(보상)이 된다.

[어휘]

It is expected that ~ ~이 예상되다 | request 요청하다 | in the event of ~의 경우에 | injury 부상 | compensation 보상 | compensate 보상하다 | compensatory 보상의

3

[번역]

정평이 난 전자회사의 미국 확장은 그 지역 주민들 다수에 의해 환영받았다.

[해설]

빈칸이 소유격 company's 뒤에 있으므로 명사 자리이다. 따라서 정답은 명사 (A) expansion(확장)이다. (B) expand(확장하다)는 동사이고 (C) expansive(광범위한)는 형용사, (D) expansively(광대하게)는 부사이므로 명사 자리에 올 수 없다.

[어휘]

established 정평이 난; 설립된 | electronics company 전자회사 | expansion 확장 | expand 확장하다 | expansive 광범위한

4

[번역]

항공사는 불만이 접수되면 손상된 짐에 대해 승객들에게 보상할 것이다.

[해설]

빈칸이 동사 are received 앞에 있으므로 문장의 주어 자리이다. 따라서 정답은 명사 (D) complaints(불만)이다. '불평하다'는 뜻의 동사 (A) complain, (C) complains는 명사 자리에 올 수 없고, 동사가 복수이므로 단수 동사를 취하는 동명사 (B) complaining 역시 불가하다.

[어휘]

airline 항공사 | reimburse 상환하다, 변상하다 | damaged 손상된 | complain 불평하다 | complaint 불만

5

[번역]

그 유명한 레스토랑은 시설이 완전히 개조되도록 하기 위해 2달 동안 문을 닫을 것이다.

[해설]

빈칸이 관사 a와 형용사 complete 뒤에 있으므로 명사 자리이다. 따라서 정답은 명사 (D) renovation(개조)이다. '개조하다'는 뜻의 동사 (A) renovate, (B) renovated, (C) renovates는 주어 자리에 올 수 없다.

[어휘]

famous 유명한 | so that 절 ~하기 위해서 | facility 시설(물) | take place 일어나다, 발생하다 | renovate 개조[개선]하다 | renovation 개조

6

[번역]

보수 유지 부서 직원들은 전자기기의 다양한 문제들에 대해 통지받았다.

[해설]

빈칸이 관사 a와 형용사 wide 뒤에 있으므로 명사 자리이다. 따라서 정답은 명사 (D) variety이다. a variety of 는 '다양한'이라는 뜻이며 형용사 wide의 수식을 종종 받는다. '다양하다'는 뜻의 동사 형태인 (A) vary, (B) varies와 형용사 (C) various(다양한)는 명사 자리에 올 수 없다.

[어휘]

maintenance 보수, 유지 | inform A of B A에게 B에 대해 알리다 | a variety of 다양한 | device 기기, 장비

7

[번역]

이사회는 현재의 사무실 컴퓨터 시스템을 업그레이드할 가능성을 현재 고려하고 있다.

[해설]

빈칸이 전치사 of 뒤에 있고 its current office computer system을 목적어로 취하고 있으므로 동명사 자리이다. 따라서 정답은 동명사 (C) upgrading이다. 동사인 (A) upgrade, (D) upgraded와 to부정사 (B) to upgrade는 전치사 뒤에 올 수 없다.

[어휘]

board of directors 이사회 | consider 고려하다 | possibility 가능성 | current 현재의 | upgrade 업그레이드하다, (성능을) 높이다

8

[번역]

우리는 내일 저녁에 열릴 모금 만찬에 시장님이 참석하시기를 기대하고 있다.

[해설]

빈칸이 전치사 in 뒤에 있으므로 명사 자리이다 따라서 정답은 명사 (A) attendance(출석, 참석)이다. 동사 형태인 (B) attended, (C) attend는 명사자리에 올 수 없고, 동명사 (D) attending은 목적어가 필요한데 빈칸 뒤에 목적어가 없기 때문에 불가하다.

[어휘]

look forward to –ing ~하기를 기대하다, 고대하다 | mayor 시장 | fundraising 모금

PART 6

[정답]

1 (C) 2 (B) 3 (C) 4 (C)

1-4

[번역]

받는 사람: jasonsmith@westwood.com
보낸 사람: claudepeppers@westwood.com
제목: 일정 변경
날짜: 10월 12일

친애하는 스미스 씨께,

저는 최근에 10월 19일부터 23일까지의 주중 일정표를 받았습니다. 그에 따르면, 저는 매일 오전 9시부터 오후 6시까지 일을 하게 될 것입니다. 2주 전에, 저는 귀하에게 다음 주를 시작으로 추가 근무를 하고 싶다는 제 바람을 나타낸 이메일을 보냈습니다. 더 이상 센트럴 대학의 야간 수업을 듣지 않을 것이기 때문에, 저에게는 저녁에 더 오래 일을 할 수 있는 많은 시간이 있습니다. (하지만 안타깝게도 저는 추가 근무 시간을 받지 못했습니다.) 제게 몇 시간의 추가 근무를 배정해 주실 수 있으신가요?

몇 달 후 차를 구입할 정도의 돈이 모이기를 바라고 있기 때문에 그렇게 해 주시면 매우 감사하겠습니다. 제 부탁을 들어 주실 수 있는지 혹은 그러실 수 없는지를 제게 알려 주시기 바랍니다.

클로드 페퍼스 드림

[어휘]

desire 바람 | work overtime 초과 근무를 하다 | plenty of 많은 | assign 배정하다, 할당하다 | fulfill 이행하다, 수행하다

1

[해설]

바로 앞 문장을 통해서는 이메일 작성자인 클로드 페퍼스가 10월 19일부터 23일까지의 미래에 대해 이야기하고 있음을 알 수 있고, 해당 문장을 통해서는 그가 미래 중에서도 구체적인 기간, 즉 매일 오전 9시부터 오후 6시까지의 시간대를 가리키고 있음을 알 수 있다. 따라서 빈칸에 들어갈 알맞은 시제는 미래 진행형이다.

2

[해설]

빈칸에 들어갈 동사의 주어가 e-mail이라는 점과 목적어가 my desire라는 점을 감안하면 보기 중에서 빈칸에 들어가기에 가장 적합한 동사는 (B) expressed(표현하다)이다.

[어휘]

express 표현하다 | appoint 임명하다, 지명하다

3

[해설]

빈칸의 앞 문장에서는 작성자에게 일할 시간이 많다는 점을, 뒷문장에서는 그가 추가 근무 시간을 배정받고 싶다는 점을 알 수 있다. 따라서 보기들 중에서 이 두 문장을 가장 자연스럽게 연결시킬 수 있는 것은 (C)밖에 없으므로 정답은 (C)이다.

[어휘]

apparently 보아 하니, 듣자 하니 | in the past 과거에 | extra 추가의, 여분의 | hopefully 바라건대 | in person 직접, 몸소

4

[해설]

빈칸에는 동사인 appreciate를 수식할 수 있는 부사가 들어가야 한다. 따라서 정답은 (C) deeply이다.

DAY 02 형용사   p.134

PART 5

[정답]

1 (C) 2 (B) 3 (B) 4 (D)
5 (B) 6 (A) 7 (D) 8 (C)

1

[번역]

전력발전소의 모든 방문객들은 실험실에 들어갈 때 제공된 보호복을 착용해야 한다.

[해설]

명사 clothing(옷)앞에서 명사를 수식하는 것은 형용사이므로 정답은 (C) protective(보호하는)이다. 동사인 (A) protect(보호하다), 명사인 (B) protection(보호), 동명사 (D) protecting(보호하는 것)은 형용사 자리에 올 수 없다.

[어휘]

power plant 전력발전소 | wear 착용하다 | clothing 옷 | provided 제공된 | enter 들어가다 | laboratory 실험실 | protective 보호하는

2

[번역]

당신의 지원서가 여전히 불완전한 상태이기 때문에 당신의 서류작업을 제대로 처리할 수 없을 것입니다.

[해설]

빈칸이 be동사 상당어구 remain 뒤에 있으므로 형용사 보어 자리이다. 따라서 정답은 (B) incomplete(미완성의, 불완전한)이다. 부사 (A) incompletely(미완성으로), 명사 (C) incompletion(미완성), to부정사 (D) to complete는 형용사 자리에 올 수 없다.

[어휘]

application 응시(서), 신청(서) | remain + 형용사 ~인 상태이다 | be able to-V ~할 수 있다 | process 처리하다 | paperwork 서류작업 | properly 제대로, 적절하게

3

[번역]

지난 분기에 더 많은 자금이 추가되었기 때문에 심각한 재정 문제들이 처리하기 쉬워졌다.

[해설]

빈칸이 be동사 상당 어구 become 뒤에 있으므로 형용사 보어 자리이다 따라서 정답은 (B) manageable(처리하기 쉬운)이 된다. 동명사 (A) managing, 동사 (C) manage, 부사 (D) manageably는 형용사 자리에 올 수 없다.

[어휘]

serious 심각한 | financial 재정적인 | fund 자금 | add 더하다 | manageable 처리하기 쉬운

4

[번역]

환영회장에 들어오시기 전에 모든 양식을 정확하게 작성해주시기 바랍니다.

[해설]

빈칸이 be동사 is뒤에 있으므로 형용사 자리이다 따라서 정답은 (D) advisable(권할 만한, 현명한)이다. 명사인 (A) advice(충고), (B) advisor(고문)와 동사인 (C) advise(충고하다)는 형용사 자리에 올 수 없다.

[어휘]

form 서식, 양식서 | fill out 작성하다 | correctly 정확하게 | prior to -ing ~전에 | reception 연회, 리셉션 | advisable 권할 만한, 현명한

5

[번역]

새 경영진은 가까운 미래에 전략적인 성장 계획을 발표할 것으로 예상된다.

[해설]

빈칸은 소유격 its와 복합명사 growth plan 사이에 있으므로 형

용사 자리이다. 따라서 정답은 (B) strategic(전략적인)이다. 명사 (A) strategy(전략), 부사 (C) strategically(전략적으로), 동사 (D) strategize(전략화하다)는 형용사 자리에 올 수 없다.

[어휘]

management 경영(진) | be expected to-V ~할 예정이다 | announce 발표하다 | growth plan 성장 계획 | in the foreseeable future 곧, 가까운 미래에 | strategic 전략적인

6

[번역]

정부는 경제를 활성화시키기 위해 이자율을 낮출 준비가 되어 있다고 발표했다.

[해설]

빈칸이 be동사 was 뒤에 있으므로 형용사 자리이다. 따라서 정답은 (A) ready(준비가 된)이다. 비교급인 (B) readier는 뒤에 비교대상을 나타내는 than이 없기 때문에 불가하고 부사인 (C) readily(손쉽게, 즉시)와 명사 (D) readiness(준비되어 있음)는 형용사 자리에 올 수 없다.

[어휘]

government 정부 | announce 발표하다 | lower 내리다 | interest rate 이자율 | boost 촉진하다

7

[번역]

보고서에 따르면 잭타운 섬유회사는 지난 분기에 높은 수익을 기록했다.

[해설]

빈칸이 명사 profits(수익) 앞에 있기 때문에 형용사 자리이므로 동사인 (A) impress(감동을 주다)와 to부정사 (B) to impress는 불가하다. (C) impressed(감동받은)는 사람을 주어로 취하면서 서술적 용법에 쓰인다. 따라서 정답은 주로 사물을 수식하는 (D) impressive(인상적인)이다.

[어휘]

according to ~에 따르면 | post 공표하다, 게시하다 | profit 수익 | quarter 분기 | impressive 인상적인

8

[번역]

경영진은 최근의 판매 수치가 매우 실망스러워서 제품 품질을 향상시킬 계획이다.

[해설]

빈칸은 'find + 목적어 + ______' 형태이므로 목적 보어 즉 형용사 자리이다. 감정을 나타내는 형용사는 사람일 때 p.p.형 사물일 때는 -ing형을 취하므로 사물 명사 sales figures(판매 수치)를 수식하는 목적 보어 형용사 (C) disappointing(실망감을 주는)이 정답이 된다.

[어휘]

management 경영진 | recent 최근의 | sales 판매 | figures 수치 | improve 향상시키다 | quality 품질 | product 제품 | disappointing 실망스런

PART 7

[정답]

1 (C)　　**2** (B)　　**3** (D)

1-3
[번역]

> 직책명: 제품 개발 매니저
>
> 게재일: 8월 12일
>
> 기재 사항: 실버 도어 디자인스는 급속히 성장하는 국제적 명성을 지닌 인테리어 조명 제조업체로, 미시간 지사에 새롭게 마련된 제품 개발 매니저직을 맡으실 인재를 구하고 있습니다. 지원자는 뛰어난 조직력과 인테리어 조명 업계에서 최소 10년의 경험을 보유하신 활동적인 리더이셔야 합니다. 채용되시면 저희 회사의 디자이너팀, 엔지니어링팀, 제조팀과 함께 직접 근무하시게 되며 구체적인 시한 안에 새로운 조명제품을 시중에 공급할 책임을 맡게 됩니다. 석사 학위는 우대되나 필수 조건은 아닙니다. 채용되시면 급여는 경력에 따라 달라지며 완벽한 직원 복지 혜택이 제공될 것입니다.
>
> 커버레터와 이력서를 이메일 mlewis@silverdoordesigns.com 이나 우편번호 41085, 미시건주, 디트로이트, 나일즈 로드 200번지, 실버 도어 디자인스, 모니카 루이스 담당자 앞으로 우편으로 송부해 주십시오.
>
> 지원서 마감일은 9월 3일입니다. 서류가 선택되신 지원자 분들에 한해 연락이 갈 것입니다. 추가 질문은 모니카 루이스 씨에게 전화 (269) 456-8673이나 팩스 (269) 456-2245로 문의하십시오.

[어휘]

development 개발 ｜ post 게시하다 ｜ description 설명 ｜ rapidly 빠르게 ｜ growing 성장하는 ｜ internationally 국제적으로 ｜ renowned 유명한 ｜ lighting 조명 ｜ manufacturer 제조업자 ｜ fill 채우다 ｜ position 직책 ｜ -based ~에 본사를 가진 ｜ branch 지사 ｜ energetic 활동적인 ｜ exceptional 탁월한, 이례적인 ｜ organizational 조직의 ｜ skill 능력 ｜ minimum 최소 ｜ directly 직접 ｜ be responsible for ~에 대한 책임이 있다 ｜ specified 구체화된 ｜ time line (분·초까지 정밀하게 예정된) 시각표 ｜ master's degree 석사학위 ｜ preferred 선순위의, 우선의 ｜ required 필수의 ｜ depend on ~에 달려있다 ｜ benefit (보험회사·공제회·사회 보장제 따위에 의한) 급부금, 수당 ｜ package 일괄[종합] 대책[법안] ｜ candidate 후보자 ｜ cover letter 커버레터 ｜ résumé 이력서 ｜ mail 우편으로 보내다 ｜ Attn (attention의 준말) ~앞 ｜ deadline 마감일 ｜ submission 제출 ｜ application 지원, 신청 ｜ additional 추가의 ｜ inquiry 질문

1
[번역]

지원자의 필수 조건은 무엇인가?

(A) 석사학위
(B) 제 2외국어의 유창함
(C) 훌륭한 조직력
(D) 기술 자격증

[해설]

지문 중반부의 You will need to be an energetic leader with exceptional organizational skills에서 exceptional organizational skills가 단서이다. 훌륭한 조직력을 갖추어야 한다고 했으므로 이를 Excellent organizational ability로 paraphrasing한 (C)가 정답이다. 참고로 A master's degree is preferred but not required에서 석사학위는 우대조건에 속하는 것이지 필수 조건은 아니므로 (A)를 답으로 택하지 않도록 주의해야 한다.

[어휘]

fluency 능변, 달변 ｜ ability 능력 ｜ certification 증명, 자격증

2
[번역]

성공적인 지원자는 어떤 직무를 맡게 될 것인가?
(A) 회사의 신입 디자이너 교육
(B) 제한된 시간 내에 신제품 제작
(C) 해외 제조팀 지도
(D) 대기업 엔지니어링 사와 공동작업

[해설]

채용된 지원자의 직무는 You will work directly with our designers and our engineering and manufacturing teams, and will be responsible for bringing new lighting products to the market place within specified timelines에서 확인할 수 있다. 주어진 시간 안에 (within specified timelines = within a limited time) 새로운 조명 제품을 만들어야 한다고 했으므로 (B)가 정답이다.

[어휘]

train 교육하다 ｜ limited 한정된 ｜ overseas 해외의

3
[번역]

채용 과정에 관해 유추할 수 있는 것은?
(A) 2장의 추천서가 제출되어야 한다.
(B) 지원자는 짧은 프리젠테이션을 해야 한다.
(C) 필기 시험과 구두 시험이 모두 치러질 것이다.
(D) 실패한 지원자들에게는 연락이 가지 않을 것이다.

[해설]

채용 과정을 언급한 지문의 후반부 중 Only those candidates whose résumés are selected will be contacted에서 서류가 선택된 지원자들에게만 연락이 갈 것이라고 했으므로 이를 적절히 paraphrasing한 (D)가 정답이다.

[어휘]

hiring 채용 ｜ process 과정 ｜ reference 추천 ｜ brief 짧은 ｜ make a presentation 발표를 하다 ｜ oral 구두의

DAY 03 부사

PART 5

PART 5

[정답]

1 (B)	**2** (B)	**3** (D)	**4** (D)
5 (D)	**6** (A)	**7** (C)	**8** (D)

1

[번역]

최고경영자는 20년 이상 동안 근무해온 직원들에게 경의를 표하는 파티를 열기로 마침내 결정했다.

[해설]

빈칸이 동사 decided를 수식하는 자리이므로 부사 자리이다. 따라서 정답은 (B) finally(마침내)이다. 형용사인 (A) final(마지막인), 동사인 (C) finalize(마무리 짓다), 명사인 (D) finalist(결승전 출전자)는 부사 자리에 올 수 없다.

[어휘]

CEO(Chief Executive Officer) 최고경영자 | decide to-V ~하기로 결정하다 | hold 열다, 개최하다 | honor 경의를 표하다 | employee 직원

2

[번역]

직원들은 예상치 못한 긴급 상황에 그들의 상관에게 매우 의지하는 경향이 있다.

[해설]

빈칸이 자동사 rely와 전치사 on 사이에 있으므로 빈칸은 부사 자리이다. 따라서 정답은 (B) heavily(매우)이다. 형용사 (A) heavy(무거운), 명사 (C) heaviness(무거움), 형용사 비교급 (D) heavier(더 무거운)는 부사 자리에 올 수 없다.

[어휘]

tend to-V ~하는 경향이 있다 | rely on ~에 의지하다 | supervisor 상관, 감독관 | in case ~할 경우에 | unexpected 예상치 못한 | emergency 긴급 사태

3

[번역]

모든 세입자들은 새롭게 제정된 규정들을 지키도록 강력히 제안된다.

[해설]

빈칸이 be동사 is와 p.p.형 recommended 사이에 있으므로 빈칸은 부사 자리이다. 따라서 정답은 (D) strongly(강력하게)이다. 형용사 (A) strong(강력한), 명사 (B) strength(강점, 장점), 동사 (C) strengthen(강화하다)은 부사 자리에 올 수 없다.

[어휘]

recommend 추천하다, 제안하다 | tenant 세입자 | comply with 준수하다 | established 제정된 | regulations 규정

4

[번역]

그 신입사원은 긍정적인 자세와 헌신으로 그녀의 상사를 변함없이 감동시켰다.

[해설]

빈칸이 현재 완료 시제의 동사인 has와 been 사이에 있으므로 부사 자리이다. 따라서 정답은 (D) consistently(변함없이, 일관되게)이다. 동사인 (A) consist, (C) consisted와 형용사인 (B) consistent(일관된)는 부사 자리에 올 수 없다.

[어휘]

impress 감동시키다 | supervisor 상사 | positive 긍정적인 | attitude 태도 | commitment 전념, 헌신 | consistently 변함없이, 일관되게

5

[번역]

아덴 오디아는 그 지방에서 가장 편리하게 위치한 회의 장소 중 하나이다.

[해설]

빈칸은 형용사 located(위치한)를 수식하는 자리이므로 부사 자리이다. 따라서 정답은 (D) conveniently(편리하게)이다. 명사인 (A) convenience(편의), (C) conveniences와 형용사인 (B) convenient(편리한)는 부사 자리에 올 수 없다.

[어휘]

located 위치한 | site 장소 | province 지방

6

[번역]

매우 기대되는 새 영화를 위한 적극적인 광고 캠페인이 다음 주에 시작될 것으로 예상된다.

[해설]

빈칸은 형용사 anticipated(기대되는)를 수식하는 자리이므로 부사 자리이다. 따라서 정답은 (A) highly(매우)이다. 명사 (B) height(높이), 형용사 (C) high(높은), 동사 (D) heighten(높이다)은 부사 자리에 올 수 없다.

[어휘]

aggressive 적극적인 | advertising 광고 | anticipated 기대되는 | launch 시작하다

7

[번역]

인력 자원 부서장은 직원들의 제안에 대해 긍정적으로 반응했다.

[해설]

빈칸이 자동사 responded와 전치사 to 사이에 있으므로 부사 자리이다. 따라서 정답은 (C) positively(긍정적으로)이다. 명사인 (A) position(직책), (D) positioning(위치잡기)와 형용사인 (B) positive(긍정적인)는 부사 자리에 올 수 없다.

[어휘]

Human Resources Department 인력 자원 부서 | respond to ~에 응답하다 | suggestion 제안

8

[번역]

카슨 오가니제이션은 그들이 미국 경제 정책에 관한 가장 믿을만한 정보처라고 여러 차례 주장하고 있다.

[해설]

빈칸이 진행형(be 동사 + –ing)을 수식하는 자리이므로 부사 자리이다. 따라서 정답은 (D) repeatedly(여러 차례, 되풀이해서)가 된다. 동사인 (A) repeat(반복하다), 형용사인 (B) repeated(반복되는), (C) repetitive(반복적인)는 부사 자리에 올 수 없다.

[어휘]

claim 주장하다 | reliable 믿을 수 있는 | source 출처 | economic 경제의 | policy 정책

PART 6

[정답]

1 (D) **2** (B) **3** (D) **4** (A)

1-4

[번역]

> ### 파트리시오스에서 멋진 시간을 보내십시오
>
> 파트리시오스는 파인 산 주변에서 새로 문을 연 스키장입니다. 산자락에 위치한 파트리시오스는 여러분들이 다음 휴가 때에 방문할 만한 곳입니다. 저희는 120개의 객실을 보유하고 있으며, 전 객실이 호화롭게 장식되어 있습니다. 모든 객실에서는 멋진 지역 경치를 볼 수 있습니다. 산 정상으로 이어지는 스키 리프트가 정문으로부터 50미터도 안 떨어져 있기 때문에 파트리시오스는 스키를 타기에 완벽한 장소입니다. 그러니 하루 종일 스키를 타신 후, 파트리시오스로 돌아오셔서 4성 식당에서 저녁을 드십시오. 혹은 로비 바로 옆에 위치해 있는 바인 샌디스에서 음료를 한 두잔 마시면서 휴식을 취하십시오. 개장을 축하하기 위해, 다음 2달 동안은 모든 객실과 스키 강습 요금이 50% 할인될 것입니다. (보다 제세한 사항을 알기 위해서는 904-4344로 전화를 주십시오.) 파트리시오스에서 머무시면 최고의 휴가를 보내시게 될 것입니다.

[어휘]

ski resort 스키장 | foot of the mountain 산자락, 산기슭 | richly 부유하게, 호화롭게 | furnish (가구를) 비치하다 | spot 장소, 지점 | front entrance 정문, 현관 | celebrate 축하하다, 경축하다

1

[해설]

분사구문 문제이다. 문장의 주어가 스키장인 Patricio's이기 때문에 빈칸에는 과거분사 형태의 Located가 들어가야 한다.

2

[해설]

빈칸에는 120 rooms를 선행사로 삼을 수 있는 동시에 빈칸 다음의 are를 동사로 받을 수 있는 관계대명사가 들어가야 한다. 보기 중에서 이 두 가지 조건을 만족시키는 것은 which밖에 없으므로 (B)가 정답이다.

3

[해설]

문맥의 의미상 빈칸에는 '~하기 위해' 혹은 '~해서 (~하다)'라는 의미를 지닌 to부정사가 들어가야 한다. 이때 to부정사는 부사적 용법 중 목적이나 결과의 의미로 받아들일 수 있다.

4

[해설]

빈칸 앞 문장에서 간단하게 할인에 관한 안내를 하고 있다. 따라서 그 다음에 들어갈 말은 자세한 정보를 얻을 수 있는 내용이 이어져야 전체적인 문맥이 자연스럽게 연결된다. 따라서 정답은 (A)이다.

[어휘]

instructor 강사 | magnificent 장엄한, 웅장한

DAY 04 문장의 형식과 동사의 종류 p.144

PART 5

[정답]

1 (D) **2** (D) **3** (A) **4** (C)
5 (C) **6** (B) **7** (C) **8** (A)

1

[번역]

자연 재해와 같은 긴급 상황이 발생할 경우에는, 침착한 상태로 적절히 행동하는 게 현명하다.

[해설]

빈칸 뒤에 형용사 calm(침착한)과 어울리는 동사를 찾는 문제이다. 뒤에 형용사와 함께 사용하여 '~인 상태로 있다'는 의미를 갖는 remain이 자연스러우므로, (D) remain이 정답이다. 타동사인 (A) help(돕다), (B) find(찾다), (C) discuss(논의하다)는 목적어가 필요하다.

[어휘]

in case ~경우에 | such as ~와 같은 | calm 침착한 | natural disaster 자연 재해 | accordingly 적절히

2

[번역]

암스트롱 박사는 병을 효과적이고 쉽게 진단하는 방법에 대해 강의할 예정이다.

[해설]

illnesses를 목적어로 취하는 적절한 뜻의 동사를 찾는 문제이다. '병을 효과적이고 쉽게 진단하는 방법'이라고 해석하는 것이 자연스러우므로 '진단하다'라는 뜻의 (D)가 정답이 된다.

[어휘]

be expected to ~할 것으로 예상되다 | give a lecture 강의하다 | illness 병 | effectively 효과적으로 | easily 쉽게 | shift ~을 바꾸다 | respond to 응답하다, 대응하다 | acquaint oneself with ~을 알다 | diagnose (병을) 진단하다

3

[번역]

위원회는 부실 경영에 대해 즉각적인 조처를 취할 지 여부를 논의할 것이다.

[해설]

해석상 '~할지 안 할지를 논의하다'가 자연스러우므로 정답은 (A) discuss(논의하다)이다. (B) contribute는 'contribute to + 명사'(~에 기여하다)로, '알리다'는 뜻의 (C) notify와 (D) inform은 사람을 목적어로 취한다.

[어휘]

committee 위원회 | whether or not to-V ~할지 안 할지 | take action 조처를 취하다 | mismanagement 부실 경영 | discuss 논의하다

4

[번역]

그의 부하 직원인 애드윈 씨는 왜 정시에 회의에 도착할 수 없었는지를 설명했다.

[해설]

빈칸이 명사절 why she couldn't make it to the meeting(왜 정시에 회의에 도착할 수 없었는지)를 목적으로 취하는 동사가 와야 하므로 정답은 (C) explained(설명했다)이다. (A) told는 사람을 목적어로 취하고 (B) talked는 'talk to 사람'으로 (D) sent는 'send + 사람 + 사물=send + 사물 + to + 사람'으로 쓰인다.

[어휘]

subordinate 부하직원 | make it to ~에 도착하다 | explain 설명하다, 해명하다

5

[번역]

그 금융회사는 사업가들 사이에서 그들에게 창업자금을 대출해 주는 것으로 좋은 평판을 누리고 있다.

[해설]

해석상 'them(business people)에게 대출해주는 것으로 명성이 좋다'가 자연스러우므로 정답은 (C) loaning(대출해주다)이다. (A) borrowing(빌리다)은 'borrow + 사물 + from + 사람'으로, (B) emerging(나타나다)은 자동사이기 때문에 목적어를 취할 수 없고, (D) renting(임대하다)은 a house 따위를 목적으로 취한다.

[어휘]

finance company 금융회사 | reputation 명성 | start-up costs 창업 비용 | loan 대출해주다

6

[번역]

내 동료 한 명이 내가 지원 프로그램을 이용할 수 있도록 몇 가지 팁을 주겠다고 제안했다.

[해설]

빈칸 뒤에 사람 me, 사물 some tips가 나오므로 빈칸은 수여동사 자리이다. 따라서 정답은 (B) give(주다)이다. (A) proceed(진행되다)는 자동사이고 (C) feature(~을 특징으로 하다)와 (D) approve(허가하다)는 목적어 두 개를 취할 수 없다.

[어휘]

offer to-V ~할 것을 제안하다 | tip 충고 | so that ~할 수 있도록

7

[번역]

회사는 다음 달 초에 지오바 씨를 검사팀장으로 지명할 것이다.

[해설]

빈칸 뒤에 사람명과 직책이 나오므로 정답은 (C) name(name A B A를 B에 지명하다)이다. (A) express(표현하다)는 express my gratitude(고마음을 표하다)처럼 감정명사를 목적어로 취하고, (B) agree(동의하다)는 agree with 사람, (D) reserve(예약하다)는 문맥에 맞지 않다.

[어휘]

be going to -V ~할 것이다 | head 장, 우두머리 | inspection 검사 | at the beginning of ~초에

8

[번역]

테이블을 예약하려면 식당에 미리 전화하는 것이 좋다.

[해설]

해석상 '테이블을 예약하려면 식당에 미리 전화하는 것이 좋다'가 자연스러우므로 정답은 (A) reserve(예약하다)이다. (B) grant는 'grant + 사람 + 사물'('사람'에게 '사물'을 주다) 형태로 쓰이고, (C) connect(연결하다)와 (D) invest(투자하다)는 문맥에 어울리지 않는다.

[어휘]

had better V ~하는 게 낫다 | in advance 미리 | reserve 예약하다

PART 7

[정답]

1 (C)　2 (B)　3 (A)　4 (C)

1-4

[번역]

존슨, 에리카	5:04 P.M.
내일 오리엔테이션에서 누가 개회사를 할 것인지 알고 있나요?	
윌슨, 티나	5:05 P.M.
틀림없이 랄프 서머스일 거예요.	
존슨, 에리카	5:05 P.M.
말도 안 돼요. 그는 호주에서 세멕스 사람들과 회의를 하고 있는걸요.	
윌슨, 티나	5:06 P.M.
그 점은 제가 몰랐군요. 제 상사와 이야기를 해 볼게요.	
존슨, 에리카	5:06 P.M.
천천히 하세요.	
윌슨, 티나	5:11 P.M.
워터만 씨께서 줄리 젠킨스가 할 것이라고 말씀해 주셨어요. 그분의 말에 따르면, 그녀가 신입 연수생들에게 말하는 것은 이번이 처음이래요. 그래서 부탁을 하나 하셨고요.	
존슨, 에리카	5:11 P.M.
무엇을 원하시는데요?	
윌슨, 티나	5:13 P.M.
당신이 전에 여러 번 이러한 일을 했기 때문에 그녀를 만나서 그녀가 무엇을 이야기해야 할지 검토하기를 바라세요.	

존슨, 에리카   5:14 P.M.

농담이죠? 근무 시간이 거의 끝났고, 교육은 내일 오전 8시 30분에 시작되잖아요.

윌슨, 티나   5:16 P.M.

그것이 바로 제가 말씀드렸던 바였어요. 하지만 그분께서는 당신이 그녀를 도와 주기를 바라세요. 당신이 도움을 준다면 정말로 고마워할 것이라고 말씀하셨어요.

존슨, 에리카   5:17 P.M.

좋아요. 잠시 후에 그녀의 사무실에 들를게요. 하지만 저는 제 마감 시간을 맞추지 못하게 될 테니, 그분께서는 그러한 이유를 트래멜 씨에게 설명하셔야 해요.

[어휘]

opening speech 개회사 ｜ orientation session 오리엔테이션 ｜ be aware of ~에 대해 알다 ｜ trainee 훈련생, 연수생 ｜ make a request 부탁하다 ｜ go over ~을 검토하다 ｜ on a couple of occasions 여러 번, 여러 차례 ｜ workday 근무일, 근무 시간 ｜ lend a hand 돕다 ｜ drop by ~에 들르다 ｜ deadline 마감

1

[번역]

랄프 서머스는 누구인 것 같은가?
(A) 호주의 사업가
(B) 세멕스 직원
(C) 존슨 씨의 동료
(D) 윌슨 씨의 상사

[해설]

랄프 서머스가 연설을 할 것이라는 말을 듣고 에리카 존슨은 그가 현재 호주에서 미팅을 하고 있다며 그가 연설을 할 리가 없다고 말한다. 이를 통해 랄프 서머스는 화자들의 직장 동료임을 알 수 있다.

[어휘]

colleague 직장 동료

2

[번역]

워터만 씨는 존슨 씨에게 무엇을 하라고 요청하는가?
(A) 오리엔테이션에 참석한다
(B) 줄리 젠킨스에게 도움을 준다
(C) 근무 시간이 끝난 후에도 늦게까지 남아 있는다
(D) 자신이 한 일을 트래멜 씨에게 제출한다

[해설]

He'd like you to meet her to go over what she needs to discuss라는 부분에서 워터만 씨가 존슨 씨에게 요청한 것은 연설자인 줄리 젠킨스를 도와달라는 것임을 알 수 있다.

[어휘]

stay late 늦게까지 남아 있다. 야근하다 ｜ submit 제출하다

3

[번역]

오후 5시 16분에 윌슨 씨가 "That's what I told him"이라고 말한 의도는 무엇인가?

(A) 존슨 씨의 말에 동의한다.
(B) 이미 상사와 이야기를 했다.
(C) 발표를 혼자서 할 수 있다.
(D) 더 많은 도움이 필요하다.

[해설]

That's what I told him은 '그것이 바로 내가 말했던 바이다'란 뜻이다. 따라서 정답은 (A)이며, 이는 앞뒤 문맥을 통해서도 확인할 수 있다.

[어휘]

agree with ~에 동의하다

4

[번역]

존슨 씨는 무엇을 할 것이라고 말하는가?
(A) 상사에게 전화를 건다
(B) 마감 시간을 지킨다
(C) 동료를 찾아간다
(D) 트래멜 씨와 이야기한다

[해설]

메신저 마지막 부분의 I'll drop by her office in a bit이라는 말을 통해 존슨 씨는 그녀, 즉 줄리 젠킨스의 사무실로 찾아 갈 것이라는 점을 알 수 있으므로 정답은 (C)이다.

[어휘]

meet one's deadline 마감 기한을 지키다

DAY 05 명사 어휘 연습 / 복합 지문   p.150

PART 5

[정답]

1 (C)   2 (A)   3 (C)   4 (B)
5 (C)   6 (B)   7 (A)   8 (A)

1

[번역]

올해의 심한 독감 증상의 지속 기간이 추후 참조를 위해 기록되어야 한다.

[해설]

해석상 '독감의 지속 기간이 기록되어야 한다'가 자연스러우므로 정답은 (C) duration(기간)이다. (A) alternative(대안), (B) means(수단,방법), (D) clause(조항)은 문맥에 어울리지 않는다.

[어휘]

severe 심한 ｜ influenza 독감 ｜ symptom 증상 ｜ reference 참조 ｜ duration 지속 기간

2

[번역]

효과적인 시간 관리는 직장에서 가장 중요한 요소 중 하나로 간주된다.

[해설]

빈칸 앞의 time과 짝을 이루어 의미가 통하는 어휘를 선택해야 한다. 해석상 '효과적인 시간 관리'가 자연스러우므로 정답은 (A) management(관리)이다. 나머지 (B) comment(논평), (C) quality(품질), (D) specification(명세서)는 time과 어울리지 않는 어휘들이다.

[어휘]

effective 효과적인 | consider 간주하다 | factor 요소 | workplace 직장

3

[번역]

우리는 사전 통보 없이 건축 도면을 수정할 수 있는 권리를 보유하고 있다.

[해설]

해석상 동사 reserve(보유하다)의 목적어로 자연스러운 것은 (C) right(권리)이다. (A) trial(시도), (B) contact(접촉), (D) renewal(갱신)은 문맥에 어울리지 않는 어휘들이다.

[어휘]

reserve 보유하다 | modify 수정하다 | architectural 건축의 | plan 도면 | notice 통지

4

[번역]

몇 가지 장애에도 불구하고, 이사들은 만장일치로 그 프로젝트에 찬성했다.

[해설]

해석상 빈칸 앞의 동사 reached(도달했다)의 목적어이자 형용사 unanimous(만장일치의)의 수식을 자연스럽게 받을 수 있는 명사는 (B) consent(동의, 찬성동의)이다. (A) confidence(신용), (C) location(위치), (D) revision(수정)은 문맥에 어울리지 않는 어휘들이다.

[어휘]

despite ~에도 불구하고 | obstacle 장애 | reach 도달하다 | unanimous 만장일치의 | consent 동의, 찬성

5

[번역]

신용카드는 전 세계에서 고객들이 선호하는 지불 수단이 되었다.

[해설]

빈칸 다음의 of customer payment(고객 지불의)의 수식을 받으면서 빈칸 앞의 형용사 preferred(우선의, 선호되는)와 어울리는 명사는 (C) means(수단, 방법)이다. (A) sample(견본), (B) instrument(악기), (D) notice(통보, 통지)는 문맥에 어울리지 않는다.

[어휘]

credit card 신용카드 | preferred 우선의, 선호되는 | customer 고객 | payment 지불 | throughout the world 전 세계에서

6

[번역]

훨씬 더 많은 손님을 끌었기 때문에 레스토랑의 개조는 비용을 들일 가치가 있었다.

[해설]

관용어구 'be worth the expense(비용을 들일 가치가 있다)'를 알면 쉽게 찾을 수 있는 문제이다. (A) benefit(이점, 혜택), (C) donation(기부), (D) compensation(보상)은 문맥에 어울리지 않는 어휘들이다.

[어휘]

renovation 개조 | worth (금전 등의 면에서) 가치가 있는 | attract 끌다 | patron 손님 | expense 비용

7

[번역]

몇 가지 문제들로 인해, 회의는 추후 통지가 있을 때까지 연기될 것이다.

[해설]

관용어구 'until further notice(추후 통지가 있을 때까지)'를 알면 쉽게 찾을 수 있는 문제이다. (B) mark(표시), (C) commitment(헌신), (D) choice(선택)는 '~까지'란 뜻의 until과 어울리지 않는 어휘들이다.

[어휘]

due to ~ 때문에 | several 몇몇의 | postpone 연기하다 | further (미래로) 더 나아가 | notice 통지

8

[번역]

전자장비는 구매일로부터 3년간 품질 보증이 된다.

[해설]

해석상 '전자장비는 구매일로부터 3년간 품질 보증이 된다'가 자연스러우므로 '보증'이란 뜻의 (A) warranty가 정답이 되어 'under warranty(보증기간 중인)'란 숙어를 완성한다. (B) construction(공사), (C) renovation(개조), (D) stage(단계)는 문맥에 어울리지 않는 어휘들이다.

[어휘]

electronic 전자의 | equipment 장비 | under warranty 보증기간 중인 | purchase 구매

PART 7

[정답]

1 (A)	2 (B)	3 (B)	4 (C)	5 (C)
6 (B)	7 (B)	8 (A)	9 (C)	10 (C)

1-5

[번역]

8월 15일

머레이 홈즈 박사
기술 담당 최고 책임자
바벨 소프트웨어 시스템즈
230 스미손 드라이브, 스위트 340
일리노이주, 시카고 32353

홈즈 박사님 귀하,

11월 13-14일 캐나다 토론토의 런던 컨퍼런스 센터에서 개최될 SYM 개발 컨퍼런스에 귀하를 폐막 기조 연설자로 공식 초대하게 되어 기쁩니다.

귀하에게 참고가 되도록 글로벌 스탠더드 협회의 타라 래칫이 개막 기조 연설자이심을 알려드립니다. 그녀의 프리젠테이션 타이틀은 "새 천년 시대의 프로그래밍"입니다만 변경 가능성이 있기는 합니다. 특이사항으로는 귀하께서도 들으셨겠지만 캠브리지 대학의 국제적으로 저명한 교수이신 앨런 길러드가 최신 프로그래밍 언어에 대한 중대 논문을 발표하게 될 것입니다.

마지막으로, 귀하께서 SYM 개발 컨퍼런스의 폐막 연설자가 되어주시면 기쁘겠습니다. 동봉된 컨퍼런스 일정 초안을 참조하시어 조속한 시일 내에 귀하의 결정을 제게 알려주십시오.

레이첼 싱 드림
간부 이사
SYM 소프트웨어 재단

[어휘]

chief 수석의, 상임의 | officer 간부, 중역 | formally 정식으로, 공식적으로 | keynote speaker 기조 연설자 | upcoming 다가오는 | development 개발 | facility 시설 | for your information 당신에게 참고가 되도록 | association 협회 | renowned 유명한 | present 발표하다 | major 주요한 | latest 최신의 | delighted 기쁜 | consent 동의하다, 승낙하다 | refer 참조하다 | enclosed 첨부된, 동봉된 | tentative 실험적인, 임시의 | at your earliest convenience 형편이 닿는 대로 빨리 | foundation 재단

[번역]

SYM 개발 컨퍼런스 일정			
11월 13일 – 월요일		11월 14일 – 화요일	
8:15 – 8:45	등록 및 오전 조반 리셉션	8:30 – 9:00	오전 조반 리셉션
8:45 – 9:00	환영 인사 및 프로그램 소개	9:00 – 10:15	프리젠테이션 세션 2
9:00 – 10:15	개막 기조 연설	10:15 – 10:30	오전 휴식
10:15 – 10:30	오전 휴식	10:30 – 12:00	그룹 토론 2
10:30 – 12:00	프리젠테이션 세션 1	12:00 – 1:00	오찬
12:00 – 1:00	오찬	1:00 – 2:45	개괄 세션
1:00 – 2:45	그룹 토론 1	2:45 – 3:00	오후 휴식
2:45 – 3:00	오후 휴식	3:00 – 4:30	폐막 기조 연설
3:00 – 4:00	오픈 포럼 토론	4:00 – 6:00	자유시간
4:00 – 6:00	실험실 견학 및 실전 데모	6:00 – 9:00	작별 연회
6:00 – 8:00	와인 및 치즈 리셉션		

[어휘]

registration 등록 | reception 리셉션 | welcoming 환영의, 환영하는 | introduction 소개 | keynote address 기조 연설 | break 휴식 | session 회기 | luncheon 점심, 오찬 | discussion 토론 | forum 공개 토론, 포럼 | lab (laboratory의 준말) 실험실 | tour 견학 | practical 실용적인, 실제적으로 유용한 | demonstration 실물 설명, 실연 | summary 요약, 개요 | leisure 자유 | farewell 작별, 고별

1

[번역]

편지의 목적은 무엇인가?
(A) 행사에서 연설해 줄 것을 요청하기 위해
(B) 일정 변경을 통보하기 위해
(C) 새로운 모델을 홍보하기 위해
(D) 컨퍼런스에 대한 의견을 얻기 위해

[해설]

글의 목적이나 주제는 초반부에서 힌트를 얻을 수 있는 경우가 많음을 기억하자. 편지의 도입부 중 It is our pleasure to formally invite you to be the closing keynote speaker at the upcoming SYM Development Conference에서 폐막 기조 연설자가 되어 줄 것을 요청하고 있음을 알 수 있다. 따라서 이를 간략히 요약한 (A)가 정답이다.

[어휘]

announce 발표하다 | promote 홍보하다 | feedback 의견

2

[번역]

편지의 첫 단락 첫 줄에 있는 "formally"와 의미상 가장 가까운 단어는?
(A) 시험적으로
(B) 공식적으로
(C) 성심성의로
(D) 마지못해

[해설]

"formally"는 '형식적으로, 공식적으로'라는 뜻으로, 지문에서 〈귀하를 '정식으로' 초대합니다〉라는 내용을 완성하기 위해 사용되었다. 보기 중 이와 바꾸어 쓸 수 있는 단어는 (B) officially이다.

[어휘]

tentatively 시험[실험]적으로, 망설이며 | officially 공식적으로 | cordially 성심 성의로, 정성껏 | reluctantly 마지못해, 싫어하며

3

[번역]

타라 래칫에 대해 유추할 수 있는 것은?
(A) 컴퓨터 디자인 전문가이다.
(B) 월요일에 연설을 할 것이다.
(C) 컨퍼런스 기획 책임자이다.
(D) 화요일로 일정을 변경했다.

[해설]

질문의 키워드 Tara Ratchet이 언급되는 편지의 둘째 단락 중 For your information, Tara Ratchet of the Global Standards Association will be the opening keynote speaker에서 그녀는 개막 기조 연설자임을 알 수 있다. 컨퍼런스 일정에서 컨퍼런스 개막일은 November 13 - Monday임을 알 수 있으므로 이 두 내용을 종합한 (B)가 정답이다.

[어휘]

specialist 전문가 | make an address 강연(연설)을 하다 | be responsible for ~에 책임이 있다 | organize 조직하다, 편성(編成)하다 | appointment 약속

4

[번역]

편지에 의하면 올해 컨퍼런스의 특별한 점은 무엇인가?
(A) 영국에서 열리게 된다.
(B) 몇몇 정부 관리들이 참석한다.
(C) 유명 학자가 연설자가 될 것이다.
(D) 기금 모금 행사가 있을 것이다.

편지의 둘째 단락인 Of particular note, you may have heard that internationally renowned professor Alan Gillard from Cambridge University will be presenting a major paper on the latest programming languages에서 대학의 유명 교수가 컨퍼런스에서 논문을 발표할 것이라고 했으므로 정답은 (C)이다. 지문의 renowned와 보기의 famous는 같은 의미이다.

[어휘]

government 정부 | official 관리 | famous 유명한 | academic 학자, 교수 | fundraising 자금 조달(의), 모금(의)

5

[번역]

월요일 오후 7시에 예정된 것은?

(A) 그룹 토론
(B) 개괄 세션
(C) 와인 및 치즈 리셉션
(D) 작별 연회

[해설]

질문의 핵심어구 Monday at 7 P.M.이 해당되는 항목을 일정에서 찾으면 (C)와 일치함을 알 수 있다.

[어휘]

scheduled 예정된

6-10

[번역]

마리오스 케이터링
다음 번 파티에는 저희가 음식을 제공해 드리겠습니다

6월 1일부터 8월 31일까지:

- 여름 특별 패키지의 전 품목에 대해 25% 할인을 받으십시오. 여기에는 샌드위치 플래터, 바비큐 플레이트, 그리고 해산물 특별 요리가 포함됩니다.

- 한 번에 500달러 이상을 결제하실 때마다 무료 케이크를 받아 가십시오.

- 2개 이상의 메인 요리가 포함된 주문에 대해서는 사용하신 접시, 주방용품, 그리고 요리 기구들을 무료로 배달해 드리고 그 다음 날 무료로 찾아갑니다.

809-3033로 전화를 하시거나 저희의 웹사이트인 www.marioscatering.com를 방문하셔서 주문을 하십시오. 최소 1주일 전에 이루어진 주문은 보증을 해 드립니다. 48시간 이전에 이루어진 모든 주문에 대해서는 20%의 추가 금액을 내셔야 합니다.

[어휘]

platter 접시 | plate 접시, 판 | utensil 주방 기구 | place an order 주문하다 | in advance 미리 | prior to ~에 앞서

마리오스 케이터링
W. 메인 가 548번지
뉴욕, NY
809-3033

고객 성명: 나오미 워싱턴
주소: 18th 가 3423번지, 브루클린, NY
전화 번호: 833-2024
이메일 주소: nwashington@homemail.com

주문 일자: 6월 20일
주문 종류: [　] 직접 찾아 감
　　　　　[V] 배달 to 25ᵀᴹ 가 404번지, 브루클린
날짜: 7월 1일　　　　　시간: 오전 11시 30분

제품	수량	가격
비프 BBQ 플레이트	4	$320
서머 샌드위치 플래터	3	$210
디럭스 디저트 트레이	2	$120
아이스티 (5갤런)	2	$40
소계		$700
세금		$42
총액		$742

지시 사항: 무료 디저트로 바닐라 아이싱처리가 된 초콜릿 케이크를 선택. 7월 2일 오전 10시와 11시 사이에 사용된 제품을 모두 회수하러 갈 것.

[어휘]

icing 당의 | retrieve 회수하다

[번역]

7월 3일

페르미 씨께,

제 이름은 나오미 워싱턴입니다. 귀하의 업체는 7월 1일 올해 저희 회사의 야유회에 음식을 제공한 업체 중 한 곳이었습니다. 행사에 음식을 공급받기 위해 저희는 4년 연속으로 귀하를 고용했습니다. 안타깝지만, 그렇게 하는 것은 이번이 마지막이 될 것 같습니다.

음식은 여느 때와 마찬가지로 훌륭했습니다. 귀하의 종업원들이 보여 준 서비스에 대해서는 같은 말을 할 수 없을 것 같습니다. 우선, 우리가 받아야 할 무료 디저트가 결코 도착하지 않았습니다. 제가 칼에게, 그는 배달을 했던 사람인데, 전화를 했을 때, 청구서에 주문이 적혀져 있다는 사실에도 불구하고 그는 그에 대해 전혀 모른다고 주장했습니다. 게다가, 그 다음날, 오후 4가 되기 전까지 접시 및 기타 품목들을 수거하기 위해 귀하의 업체에서 온 사람은 없었습니다. 도착한 사람은 무례했고 그때 나타난 것에 대해 사과를 하지 않았습니다.

저는 그들의 행동에 크게 놀랐다는 점을 인정할 수 밖에 없습니다. 회사의 다른 사람들도 모두 마찬가지였습니다. 이와 같은 일이 다시는 발생하지 않을 것이라는 확답을 받기 전까지, 톰슨 플라스틱스는 더 이상 귀하의 업체와 거래를 하지 않을 것입니다.

그럼 이만 줄이겠습니다.
나오미 워싱턴

[어휘]

establishment 설립; 업체 | to begin with 우선 | claim 주장하다 | invoice 송장, 청구서 | rude 무례한 | admit 인정하다 | behavior 행동 | no longer 더 이상 ~않는

6

[번역]

다음 중 광고에서 언급되지 않은 것은 무엇인가?
(A) 주문은 온라인에서 혹은 전화로 이루어질 수 있다.
(B) 여름에 이루어진 모든 주문에 대해 무료로 배달을 해 준다.
(C) 일부 주문에 대해 고객들은 추가 요금을 내야 한다.
(D) 여름에 판매되는 제품들은 할인이 될 것이다.

[해설]

광고의 세 번째 항목에서 2개 이상의 메인 요리가 포함된 주문에만 무료 배달이 이루어진다는 사실을 알 수 있다. 즉 무료 배달은 조건부이다.

[어휘]

discount 할인하다

7

[번역]

주문은 언제 이루어졌는가?
(A) 6월 1일에
(B) 6월 20일에
(C) 7월 1일에
(D) 7월 3일에

[해설]

두 번째 주문서를 보면 주문 날짜란(Order Date)에 June 20로 적혀 있다.

8

[번역]

주문에 대해 사실인 것은 무엇인가?
(A) 무료 배달 서비스를 받을 수 있다.
(B) 전화로 이루어졌다.
(C) 워싱턴 씨가 찾아갈 것이다.
(D) 두 가지 종류의 음료가 포함되어 있다.

[해설]

두 번째 지문인 주문서에 메인 요리로 볼 수 있는 '비프 BBQ 플레이트(Beef BBQ Plate)'가 4개 적혀 있으므로, 두 번째 지문인 광고에 따라 무료 배달 서비스를 받을 수 있는 조건, 즉 메인 요리 2개 이상을 주문해야 한다는 조건을 충족시키고 있다.

[어휘]

qualify for ~에 대한 자격을 갖추다 | include 포함하다

9

[번역]

편지의 목적은 무엇인가?
(A) 환불을 요구하기 위해
(B) 사과를 요구하기 위해
(C) 불만을 표시하기 위해
(D) 할인을 요청하기 위해

[해설]

해당 업체 직원의 서비스에 대한 불만을 표현하고 있다. 따라서 정답은 (C)이다.

10

[번역]

워싱턴 씨가 받지 못한 것은 무엇인가?
(A) 여름 샌드위치 플래터
(B) 비프 BBQ 플레이트
(C) 케이크
(D) 요리 기구

[해설]

그녀는 '받기로 되어 있던 무료 디저트가 도착하지 않았다(the free dessert we should have received never arrived)'고 말한다.

DAY 06 조동사와 여러 가지 타동사 p.155

PART 5

[정답]

| 1 (B) | 2 (C) | 3 (A) | 4 (B) |
| 5 (A) | 6 (A) | 7 (C) | 8 (C) |

1

[번역]

우리 회사는 건설 프로젝트에 국제적인 투자를 받기 위해 애쓰고 있다.

[해설]

빈칸은 동사 is struggling의 목적어 자리인데 struggle은 to부정사를 목적어로 가지는 동사이므로 정답은 (B) to receive이다. 동명사 형태인 (A) receiving, 과거동사형인 (C) received, 3인칭 단수 현재동사형인 (D) receives는 정답이 될 수 없다.

[어휘]

struggle to-V ~하려 애쓰다 | international 국제적인 | investment 투자 | construction 건설

2

[번역]

비용 증가로 인해 우리는 더 싼 공급 계약 협상을 고려하도록 권고 받았다.

[해설]

빈칸은 동사 consider의 목적어 자리인데 consider은 동명사를 목적어로 가지는 동사이다. 따라서 동사원형인 (A) negotiate, 과거동사형인 (B) negotiated, to부정사인 (D) to negotiate는 불가하다. 정답은 (C) negotiating이다.

[어휘]

as a result of ~의 결과로,~ 때문에 | be advised to-V ~해야 한다 | consider 고려하다 | cheaper 더 싼 | supply 공급 | contract 계약 | negotiate 협상하다

3

[번역]

우리 회사는 기업 이미지 개선을 위해 더 엄격한 복장 규정을 제정해야 한다.

[해설]

빈칸이 조동사 must 뒤에 있으므로 빈칸은 동사원형 자리이다. 따라서 정답은 (A) establish(제정하다)이다. 동명사 형태인 (B) establishing, 3인칭 단수 현재동사형인 (C) establishes, to부정사인 (D) to establish 는 동사원형 자리에 올 수 없다.

[어휘]

strict 엄격한 | regulation 규정 | dress code 복장 규정 | corporate 기업의 | establish 제정하다

4

[번역]

그 데이터는 기밀사항이기 때문에 매니저들은 우리가 다른 이들에게 자료를 전송하는 것을 허락하지 않을 것이다.

[해설]

빈칸이 형용사 likely(가능성 있는) 뒤에 있기 때문에 to부정사 자리이므로 정답은 (B) to permit이다. 'be동사 + 형용사' 다음에 올 수 있는 형태는 '전치사 + 명사/to부정사/that 절'이므로 3인칭 단수 현재동사형인 (A) permits, 명사인 (C) permission, 동사원형인 (D) permit은 불가하다.

[어휘]

be likely to-V ~일 것 같다 | transfer 전송하다 | since ~ 때문에 | confidential 기밀의 | permit 허락하다 | permission 허락, 허가

5

[번역]

당신이 결근해야 하는 시기를 당신 상관에게 즉시 알리세요.

[해설]

사역동사 let은 '~하게 하다'란 뜻으로 목적어 다음에 동사원형을 쓰므로 정답은 (A) know이다. to부정사인 (B) to know, 과거분사형인 (C) known, 현재완료형인 (D) have known은 동사원형자리에 올 수 없다.

[어휘]

supervisor 상관 | immediately 즉시 | take a leave of absence 결근하다

6

[번역]

그 컨설턴트는 사람들이 가장 간단하고 효과적인 주거문제 해결책을 찾도록 돕고자 애썼다.

[해설]

준 사역동사 help는 목적 보어로 동사원형이나 to부정사를 취하므로 정답은 (A) find이다. 동명사 형태인 (B) finding, 과거분사형인 (C) found, '설립하다'는 뜻으로 쓰이는 동사원형 found의 과거분사형인 (D) founded는 불가하다.

[어휘]

simple 간단한 | effective 효과적인 | solution to ~에 대한 해결책 | housing 주거

7

[번역]

메이스 기업은 앞으로 더 싼 원료를 사용함으로써 수익을 늘릴 계획이다.

[해설]

빈칸은 동사 plans의 목적어 자리인데, plans는 to부정사를 목적어로 가지는 동사이다. 따라서 부사형인 (A) increasingly, 형용사형인 (B) increasing, 3인칭 단수 현재동사형인 (D) increases는 불가하다. 정답은 (C) to increase이다.

[어휘]

plan to-V ~할 계획이다 | profit 수익 | by –ing ~함으로써 | material 원료 | increase 증가시키다

8

[번역]

새 쇼핑 지역이 인접한 도시로부터 수천 명의 고객을 끌어들일 것으로 예상된다.

[해설]

빈칸이 수동태 is expected 뒤에 있으므로 문법상 '전치사 + 명사'나 'to부정사'가 와야 한다. 따라서 정답은 (C) to attract이다. 명사인 (A) attraction, 형용사인 (B) attractive, 동사원형인 (D) attract는 수동태 뒤에 올 수 없다.

[어휘]

district 지역 | be expected to –V 일 것으로 예상되다 | thousands of 수천의 | customer 고객 | neighboring 이웃한, 인접한 | attraction 끌림, 매력 | attractive 매력적인

PART 6

[정답]

1 (B)   2 (B)   3 (C)   3 (A)

1-4

[번역]

> 9월 9일
>
> 친애하는 윌킨슨 씨께,
>
> 여름에 도와 주셔서 정말 고마웠습니다. 당신 덕분에 맥그레거 인더스트리스에서 인턴으로 보낸 제 시간이 재미있기도 했고 유익하기도 했습니다. 제가 처음 일을 시작했을 때, 당신은 저의 마음을

편안하게 만들어 주었고 저에게 정말로 많은 것을 가르쳐 주었습니다. 저는 제가 모든 사람들을 위해 복사를 하느라 꼼짝하지 못할 것으로 걱정했습니다. (하지만 그럴 걱정은 할 필요가 없었습니다.) 당신은 저에게 제가 할 수 있는 많은 프로젝트를 주었습니다. 이번 여름 그곳에서 보낸 시간 덕분에, 저는 제가 로봇 산업에서 경력을 쌓기를 원한다는 점을 알게 되었습니다. 저는 학교에서의 마지막 해에 두어 개의 로봇 공학 수업에 등록했습니다. 저는 오로지 이들 수업에만 초점을 맞출 계획입니다. 그리고 다음 봄 제가 졸업을 한 후에는 아마도 맥그레거의 정규직에 지원할 것 같습니다. 다시 한 번, 모든 것에 대해 정말로 감사를 드립니다.

로이드 배니스터 드림

[어휘]

assistance 도움 | intern 인턴 | educational 교육적인, 유익한 | comfortable 편안한 | be stuck 꼼짝 못하다 | career 경력 robotics 로봇 공학 | enroll 등록하다 | intend to ~할 의도이다 | focus on ~에 집중하다 | intently 오로지

1

[해설]

'A와 B 양쪽 모두'라는 의미의 both A and B 구문을 알고 있으면 쉽게 풀 수 있는 문제이다. 정답은 (B)이다.

2

[해설]

빈칸 앞 문장의 '복사를 하느라 아무것도 할 수 없을 것이라고 걱정했다'라는 의미와 뒷문장의 '당신이 내게 많은 프로젝트를 주었다'라는 의미를 가장 자연스럽게 연결시킬 수 있는 문장이 정답이다. 따라서 '하지만 그럴 걱정을 할 필요가 없었다'는 의미인 (B)가 정답이다.

3

[해설]

'경력을 쌓다'라는 의미는 pursue a career로 나타낸다.

[어휘]

propose 제안하다; 프러포즈를 하다 | pursue 추구하나, 쫓다 | consider 고려하다, 생각하다

4

[해설]

'~에 지원하다'라는 의미는 apply for로 나타낸다. 따라서 정답은 (A)이다.

[어휘]

relate 관련시키다 | register 등록하다

PART 5

1 (C)　**2** (C)　**3** (D)　**4** (D)
5 (D)　**6** (A)　**7** (C)　**8** (B)

1

[번역]

지사를 확장하면서 회사는 매우 적극적인 사람들을 찾고 있었다.

[해설]

주절의 시제가 과거동사 was이므로 종속절 when절도 과거 시제여야 하므로 현재형인 (A) expands와 미래형인 (B) will expand는 우선 제외된다. 빈칸 다음에 목적어 its branch offices가 있기 때문에 수동태인 (D) was expanded역시 불가하다. 따라서 정답은 (C) expanded이다.

[어휘]

look for 찾다 | highly 매우 | motivated 적극적인 | branch office 지사 | expand 확장하다

2

[번역]

이사회는 공사의 진행과정을 감독하기 위한 건설사를 지난달에 선정했다.

[해설]

문장 끝에 과거 시제와 함께 쓰이는 부사 last month(지난달)가 있기 때문에 빈칸에는 과거 시제가 와야 한다. 따라서 정답은 (C) selected이다. 현재완료 시제인 (A) has selected와 미래 시제인 (B) will select와 (D) will be selected는 불가하다.

[어휘]

board of directors 이사회 | engineering company 건설사 | oversee 감독하다 | progress 진행 과정

3

[번역]

투자의 성공은 앞으로 몇 년 간의 부동산 시장의 안정성에 달려있을 것이다.

[해설]

문장 끝에 미래를 나타내는 over the next few years(앞으로 몇 년 간)가 있기 때문에 (D) will depend가 정답이다. 과거 시제인 (A) depended, 현재완료 시제인 (C) has depended가 우선 제외되고, 주어가 3인칭 단수 The investment's success이기 때문에 (B) depend 역시 불가하다.

[어휘]

investment 투자 | success 성공 | stability 안정성 | real estate 부동산 | depend on ~에 달려있다

4

[번역]

회사의 업적에 좀 더 초점을 맞출 수 있도록 우리의 프레젠테이션을 수정하는 것이 필요하다.

[해설]

빈칸이 주어 we 뒤에 있기 때문에 동사 자리이므로 동명사형인 (A)

modifying, to부정사인 (C) to modify는 제외된다. '필요성'을 나타내
는 형용사 necessary가 that절을 받을 때 that절의 동사는 인칭과 상관
없이 동사원형을 취하므로 정답은 (D) modify이다.

[어휘]

necessary 필요한 ｜ so that ~할 수 있도록 ｜ focus on 집중하다 ｜
achievement 업적 ｜ modify 수정하다

5

[번역]

시장 수요를 맞추기 위해 내년까지 생산량을 두 배로 만드는 것이 필요
할 것이다.

[해설]

미래 시점을 나타내는 시간부사구 by next year(내년까지)이 있으므로
미래 시제가 와야 한다. 따라서 정답은 (D) will be이다.

[어휘]

necessary 필요한 ｜ double 두 배로 하다 ｜ production 생산 ｜
quota 할당(량) ｜ keep up with 유지하다

6

[번역]

위원회 구성원들이 증거를 제시하기 전에 아마도 규정들이 제정될 것
이다.

[해설]

주절의 시제가 미래를 나타내는 will이기 때문에 시간 부사절(before
절)의 동사는 현재 시제가 와야 한다. '때'를 나타내는 시간부사절에서
는 현재 시제가 미래를 대신하기 때문이다. 따라서 정답은 현재 시제인
(A) present이다.

[어휘]

committee 위원회 ｜ evidence 증거 ｜ regulations 규정 ｜
establish 제정하다 ｜ present 제시하다

7

[번역]

지난 몇 년간 시장 점유율을 높이기 위한 회사의 많은 노력이 있어왔다.

[해설]

문장 끝에 현재완료시제와 함께 쓰이는 부사구 over the past few
years(지난 몇 년간)이 있기 때문에 빈칸에는 현재완료 시제가 와야 한
다. 따라서 정답은 (C) has been이다.

[어휘]

there is ~가 있다 ｜ enormous 막대한 ｜ effort 노력 ｜ share 점유율

8

[번역]

부서장으로 임명된 이래 벤슨 씨는 아무 것도 진전시키지 않았다.

[해설]

'~이래로 지금까지'를 뜻하는 접속사 since절의 동사가 과거 시제 was
named이기 때문에 주절은 현재완료 시제가 와야 한다. 따라서 정답은
(B) has made이다.

[어휘]

name A as B A를 B에 임명하다 ｜ make progress 진전시키다,
진행시키다

[정답]

1 (D)　**2** (B)　**3** (C)　**4** (B)

1-4
[번역]

웨스트 리치몬드 가든 센터

웨스트 리치몬드 가든 센터는 버지니아 주민들에게 반세기가 넘도
록 서비스를 제공해온 수상 경력이 있는 정원 조경 회사입니다. 버
지니아 지역 최대 규모의 가장 완벽한 가든 센터로서 웨스트 리치
몬드 가든 센터는 원예와 조경을 하기 위해 귀하가 필요한 모든 것
들이 있습니다.

웨스트 리치몬드 가든 센터는 가족 소유의 업체로 고객들에게 친
절한 서비스를 제공하는 데 헌신하는 200명 이상의 직원들을 보유
하고 있습니다. 게다가 귀하의 조경작업이 편이하고 성공적이실 수
있도록 도와드리기 위해 언제나 고객님을 도와드릴 수 있기에 행
복한 저희의 자격 있는 전문가 팀이 전문 조경 상담을 해 드립니다.

귀하의 식물, 나무, 꽃들을 최상으로 유지할 수 있도록 고객 맞춤
비료를 이번 주의 특별 20% 할인가로 이용해 보세요. 모든 식물은
비료의 도움을 받을 수 있지만 당신이 기르고 계신 식물의 필요에
특별히 맞도록 제작된 제품을 사용하는 것이 가장 좋습니다. 어떤
비료가 귀하의 필요에 맞으시는지 판단하시기 위해서 저희 직원과
상담하시는 것이 도움이 되실 것입니다.

페어팩스, 서덜랜드 애비뉴 120번지에 편리하게 위치해 있는 저
희 사무실에 내방하셔서 조경에 관한 많은 즐거움을 발견하십시
오.

영업 시간 (하절기):
월요일-토요일 오전 8:00 – 오후 9:00
일요일 오전 9:00 – 오후 2:00

영업 시간은 계절과 특정 공휴일에 따라 변경됩니다. 특정 공휴일
의 영업 시간은 703-523-6256으로 전화주세요.

[어휘]

award-winning 수상 경력이 있는 ｜ landscaping 경치, 조망 ｜ serve
봉사하다, 시중들다 ｜ resident 주민 ｜ complete 완벽한 ｜ entire
전체의 ｜ truly 진정으로 ｜ employee 직원 ｜ dedicated to ~ing
~하는 데 헌신하는 ｜ provide 제공하다 ｜ customer 고객 ｜ friendly
친절한 ｜ offer 제공하다 ｜ expert 숙달한, 노련한 ｜ qualified 자격 있는 ｜
professional 전문가 ｜ assist 돕다 ｜ take advantage of
~을 이용하다 ｜ customized 주문하여 만든, 고객 맞춤의 ｜ fertilizer
비료 ｜ plant 식물 ｜ benefit from ~에서 이익을 얻다 ｜ product
제품 ｜ intended 의도된 ｜ specially 특별히 ｜ unique 유일한, 특수한 ｜
feed 공급[제공]하다 ｜ consult 상담하다 ｜ determine 결정하다 ｜ suit
적합하게 하다, 적응시키다 ｜ stop by ~에 들르다 ｜ convenient
편리한 ｜ location 위치 ｜ pleasure 즐거움, 기쁨 ｜ operation 운영 ｜
seasonally 계절에 따라 ｜ certain 특정한 ｜ specific 구체적인

1

[번역]

웨스트 리치몬드 가든 센터에 대해 특별한 것은?
(A) 최첨단 기술을 사용한다.
(B) 유명한 화초 연구가들이 추천한다.
(C) 아이들에게 특별 수업을 제공한다.
(D) 50년 이상의 역사를 가지고 있다.

[해설]

광고의 첫 문장 West Richmond Garden Center is proud to be an award-winning garden and landscaping company that has been serving the residents of Virginia for over half a century에서 for over half a century를 이용해 more than 50 years of history로 풀어 쓴 (D)가 정답이다.

[어휘]

cutting-edge 최첨단의 ┃ technology 기술 ┃ recommend 추천하다 ┃ florist 화초 연구가 ┃ provide 제공하다

2

[번역]

웨스트 리치몬드 가든 센터에 대해 사실이 아닌 것은?
(A) 이 지역에서 가장 크다.
(B) 시 소유이다.
(C) 보통 일주일 내내 영업한다.
(D) 조경 전문가들을 보유하고 있다.

[해설]

NOT 질문은 지문과 보기를 꼼꼼히 대조하여 주의 깊게 정답을 찾아야 한다. As the largest ~ in the entire region, West Richmond Garden Center ~는 (A)와 조화를 이룬다. 하절기 영업 시간을 소개한 단락에서는 영업 시간은 다소 차이가 있지만 일주일 내내 영업함을 알 수 있으므로(Monday to Saturday from 8:00 A.M. to 9:00 P.M., Sunday from 9:00 A.M. to 2:00 P.M.) (C)도 사실이다. we offer expert gardening advice from a team of qualified professionals에서 (D) 역시 사실임을 확인할 수 있다. 그러나 West Richmond Garden Center is a family-owned business라고 했으므로 owned by the city라고 명시한 (B)가 잘못된 정보를 담아 정답임을 알 수 있다.

[어휘]

employ 채용하다

3

[번역]

비료에 대해 언급된 것은 무엇인가?
(A) 두 가지 다른 크기로 이용이 가능하다.
(B) 사용 전에 전문가와의 상담은 필수이다.
(C) 다른 식물은 다른 종류의 비료가 필요하다.
(D) 이번 주에만 정가에서 절반가이다.

[해설]

셋째 단락의 it is best to use a product intended specifically for the unique needs of the plant that you are feeding에서 자신이 기르고 있는 식물의 필요에 맞게 특수 제작된 비료를 쓰는 것이 가장 좋다고 하는 내용이 나오므로 (C)가 정답이다. 비료 사용에 대해 직원과 상담하는 것이 좋다고는 했지만(It might be helpful to consult with our staff to determine which fertilizer best suits your needs) 이것이 필수는 아니므로 (B)를 답으로 택하지 않도록 주의해야 한다. (A)는 언급된 바

없으며, 이번 주에 20%의 할인 행사를 한다고 했으므로 (D) 역시 지문의 사실을 바르지 못하게 서술하고 있는 오답임을 알 수 있다.

[어휘]

available 이용 가능한 ┃ necessary 필요한 ┃ regular price 정가

4

[번역]

광고에 의하면 왜 누군가 제시된 번호로 전화하겠는가?
(A) 특별 주문을 하기 위해
(B) 영업 시간에 대해 알기 위해
(C) 배송을 준비하기 위해
(D) 조경 조언을 받기 위해

[해설]

마지막 문장 Please call 703-523-6256 for specific holiday hours에서 특정 공휴일의 영업 시간을 파악하기 위해 제시된 번호로 전화할 것임을 알 수 있다.

[어휘]

place an order 주문하다 ┃ business hours 영업시간 ┃ arrange 준비하다 ┃ delivery 배송

DAY 08 수동태

p.166

PART 5

[정답]

| 1 (B) | 2 (B) | 3 (B) | 4 (C) |
| 5 (A) | 6 (B) | 7 (D) | 8 (D) |

1

[번역]

우리가 목표 달성을 위해 노력할 때마다 가장 어려운 문제들 중 하나가 발생한다.

[해설]

주어가 3인칭 단수 one이기 때문에 동사도 3인칭 단수 동사가 필요하므로 복수 동사형인 (A) arise와 (D) are arisen는 우선 제외된다. arise(발생하다)는 자동사이기 때문에 수동태를 만들 수 없으므로 (C) is arisen역시 불가하다. 따라서 정답은 (B) arises가 된다.

[어휘]

whenever ~할 때마다 ┃ achieve 달성하다 ┃ goal 목표 ┃ arise 발생하다, 일어나다

2

[번역]

하이 테크 주식회사는 같은 업계의 타사들보다 상대적으로 더 높은 수익을 내고 있다.

[해설]

빈칸 앞에 is가 있고 빈칸 뒤에 목적어 higher profits(더 높은 수익)가

있으므로 동사원형인 (A) generate와 빈칸 앞의 be동사 is와 함께 수동태를 만드는 p.p.형태인 (D) generated는 불가하다. to부정사가 오면 is to-V(~하는 것이다)구문을 만들어 의미가 해석상 어울리지 않는다. 따라서 정답은 (B) generating이다.

[어휘]

relatively 상대적으로 | profit 수익 | industry 업계, 산업 | generate 창출하다, 만들다

3

[번역]

출판권에 대한 3월 10일자 귀하의 편지는 즉각적인 조치를 위해서 적절한 부서로 전달되었습니다.

[해설]

타동사 forward(보내다)의 올바른 동사 형태를 찾는 문제인데 빈칸 뒤에 목적어가 없으므로 능동태는 불가하다. 따라서 능동형인 (A) forward, (C) has forwarded, (D) will forward는 제외되어 정답은 수동태인 (B) was forwarded가 된다.

[어휘]

regarding ~에 관하여 | publication 출판 | proper 적절한 | action 조치 | forward 보내다

4

[번역]

구 컴퓨터들은 회계 연도 말까지 새로운 컴퓨터로 교체될 것이라는 점을 알아두십시오.

[해설]

빈칸 앞에 조동사 will이 있으므로 동사원형 자리이다. 따라서 (A) replacing와 (B) replaces는 우선 제외된다. replace(교체하다)는 타동사인데 빈칸 뒤에 목적어가 없으므로 능동태는 불가하므로 (D) be replacing역시 제외되어 정답은 수동태인 (C) be replaced가 된다.

[어휘]

be aware that ~ ~을 인식하다 | fiscal year 회계 연도 | replace A with B A를 B로 교체하다

5

[번역]

대부분의 전문가들은 합병과 관련된 문제에 대해 잘 알고 있다.

[해설]

involve(관련시키다)는 타동사인데 빈칸 뒤에 목적어가 없으므로 수동태가 와야 한다. 따라서 현재완료 능동형인 (B) has involved와 (D) have involved는 제외되고, 관계대명사 that의 선행사가 3인칭 단수인 the issue(문제)이므로 복수 동사형인 (C) are involved도 불가하다. 따라서 정답은 (A) is involved이다.

[어휘]

expert 전문가 | be familiar with ~에 대해 잘 알다 | merger 합병 | be involved in ~와 관련되다

6

[번역]

분석가들은 기업들이 경제의 호전을 경험하게 될 것이라는 증거를 제시하게 되어 기뻐했다.

[해설]

타동사 please(기쁘게 하다) 뒤에 목적어가 없으므로 수동태 자리이기 때문에 정답은 (B) pleased(기쁜)이다. 원형인 (A) please는 수동태 자리에 올 수 없고, (C) pleasing과 (D) pleasant는 '(사물, 일 등이) 즐거운'이란 뜻이므로 주어가 사물이어야 한다.

[어휘]

analyst 분석가 | present 제시하다 | evidence 증거 | economic 경제의 | upturn 호전, 상승

7

[번역]

모든 파일들은 기록의 정확성을 향상시키기 위해 신속하게 제출되어야 한다.

[해설]

타동사 submit(제출하다)뒤에 목적어가 없으므로 수동태 자리이다. 빈칸 앞에 be동사가 있으므로 p.p.형인 (D) submitted가 정답이 된다. 능동형인 (A) submit, (B) submitting, (C) to submit는 수동태 자리에 올 수 없다.

[어휘]

promptly 신속히 | enhance 향상시키다, 강화하다 | accuracy 정확성 | submit 제출하다

8

[번역]

최근 더 많은 학생들이 더 나은 직업을 얻기 위해서 인턴쉽에 참여하는 추세이다.

[해설]

participate는 자동사이고 'participate in(~에 참여하다)'의 형태로 쓰이므로 수동태는 불가하다. 따라서 수동형인 (A) were participated와 (B) will be participated가 먼저 제외되고, 주어가 복수 more students이므로 3인칭 단수동사형인 (C) participates역시 불가하므로 정답은 (D) have been participating이다.

[어휘]

trend 경향, 유행 | recently 최근에 | obtain 얻다 | participate in ~에 참여하다

PART 6

[정답]

1 (C) 2 (C) 3 (A) 4 (D)

1-4

[번역]

받는 사람: 캐서린 존스 〈catherine_j@personalmail.com〉
보낸 사람: 고객 서비스 〈customerservice@weston.com〉
제목: 불만 사항

친애하는 존스 씨께,

저희는 8월 11일 귀하의 이메일을 받았으며 불만을 표현하신 문제에 대해 조사를 했습니다. 몇 가지 이유로, 귀하께서는 주문한 두 개의 별개 상품이 아니라 두 개의 동일한 제품을 받으셨습니다.

이러한 실수에 대해 사과를 드립니다. 저희는 조금 전에 귀하께서 받지 못하신 나머지 다른 제품(제품 번호 ER430A)을 발송했습니다. 특급 우편으로 보냈으며 영업일 기준으로 이틀 이내에 도착할 것입니다. 잘못 배송된 나머지 제품은 가지셔도 좋습니다. 그리고 다음 번 온라인 구매 시에 귀하께 20%의 할인 혜택을 드리고 싶습니다. 결제를 하실 때 쿠폰 코드인 "SUMMER SURPRISE"를 입력하시기만 하면 됩니다. (이번 일에 관한 저희의 대처 방식에 귀하께서 만족하시기를 바랍니다.)

웨스턴 주식회사 고객 서비스 담당
윈스턴 필립스 드림

[어휘]

look into ~을 조사하다 ┃ separate 별개의 ┃ express mail 특급 우편 ┃ be about to 막 ~하려고 하다 ┃ check out 계산하다, 결제하다

1

[해설]

rather than에 의해 연결되고 있는 부분의 의미를 살펴보면, 빈칸에는 separate(별개의)와 반대되는 의미의 단어가 들어가야 함을 알 수 있다. 따라서 정답은 (C) identical(동일한)이다.

[어휘]

damaged 파손된, 손상된 ┃ identical 동일한

2

[해설]

두 개의 물품을 받았는데, 둘 중 잘못 배송된 제품을 보내 주겠다는 의미이다. 따라서 빈칸에는 두 개 중의 다른 하나를 가리키는 (C)의 the other가 들어가야 한다.

3

[해설]

'잘못한' 혹은 '잘못해서'라는 의미는 in error로 나타낸다.

4

[해설]

사과 편지에서 끝인사로 가장 자연스럽게 들어갈 수 있는 문장을 고르도록 한다. 한편 빈칸 앞 문장에서 사과의 표시로 할인 쿠폰 코드를 알려 주고 있으므로 이러한 두 가지 조건을 감안하면 (D)가 빈칸에 들어가는 것이 가장 자연스럽다.

DAY 09 대명사

PART 5

[정답]

1 (B)	2 (B)	3 (A)	4 (D)
5 (B)	6 (A)	7 (B)	8 (D)

1

[번역]

상공회의소는 지역 사업체들이 쉽게 그들의 문제를 해결하도록 돕는다.

[해설]

인칭 대명사 중에서 명사 problems 앞에 오는 것은 소유격이다. 따라서 정답은 (B) their(그들의)이다.

[어휘]

chamber of commerce 상공회의소 ┃ local 지역의, 현지의 ┃ resolve 해결하다

2

[번역]

제품들에 만족하지 않으시면 30일 이내에 제품을 반환하여 전액 환불을 받으실 수 있습니다.

[해설]

빈칸이 동사 return(되돌려주다) 뒤에 있으므로 목적격이 필요한데, '되돌려주는 것'이 앞에 나온 'goods(제품들)'를 가리키므로 정답은 3인칭 복수 (B) them이 된다.

[어휘]

goods 상품, 제품 ┃ meet the satisfaction 만족시키다 ┃ return 반환하다 ┃ refund 환불

3

[번역]

그 두 매니저들은 그 기술적인 문제들을 그들 스스로 해결하겠다고 자원했다.

[해설]

by oneself는 관용어구로서 '혼자서'라는 뜻이다. 주어가 The two managers(그 두 매니저들) 즉, '그들'이기 때문에 they의 재귀대명사 (A) themselves가 정답이 된다.

[어휘]

volunteer 자원하다 ┃ deal with 다루다, 처리하다 ┃ technical 기술적인

4

[번역]

새로운 쇼핑 단지의 개장이 월요일에 있을 것이며 시장 자신도 역시 그 개장식에 참석할 것이다.

[해설]

빈칸 앞에 주어 the mayor(시장)가 있고 빈칸 뒤에 동사와 목적어(will attend the party)를 완벽히 갖춘 문장이므로 재귀대명사 강조용법 자리이다. 주어 the mayor를 강조하는 (D) himself가 정답이 된다.

[어휘]

complex 복합건물, 단지 | be held 개최되다, 열리다 | mayor 시장

5
[번역]

나는 이 씨와 수년간 함께 근무하고 있으며 그가 헌신적이고 부지런하다는 것을 알았다.

[해설]

빈칸이 동사 have found 뒤에 있으므로 목적격이 필요한데 주어가 I(나)이고 빈칸이 Mr. Lee를 가리키고 있으므로 he의 목적격인 (B) him이 정답이 된다.

[어휘]

find + 목적어 + to be + 형용사 ~라고 생각하다 | dedicated 헌신적인, 전념하는 | diligent 부지런한

6
[번역]

스테파니가 혼자서 퇴근 때까지 이 통계 분석을 마치는 것은 불가능하다.

[해설]

빈칸 앞이 완전한 문장이므로 해석상 빈칸은 '스테파니' 즉 she를 가리키는 강조용법 herself나 관용적 용법인 by herself 자리인데, 보기에 없으므로 by herself와 같은 의미의 (A) alone(혼자서)이 정답이 된다.

[어휘]

statistical 통계의 | analysis 분석 | by the end of the day 퇴근 때까지

7
[번역]

동봉된 조사서를 완성하신 후에 귀하의 응답을 저희에게 평일 기준 5일 이내로 보내 주세요.

[해설]

인칭 대명사 중에서 명사 responses(반응) 앞에 오는 것은 소유격이므로 정답은 (B) your(당신의)가 된다.

[어휘]

complete 기입하다, 완성하다 | survey (설문)조사(서) | enclosed 동봉된 | response 응답 | working days 평일

8
[번역]

품질에서의 발전이 인상적이었기 때문에 올해의 매출은 2014년 매출만큼 좋았다.

[해설]

빈칸은 this year's sales(올해의 매출)와 비교 대상이 되는 sales in the year 2014(2014년 매출)을 가리키는 지시대명사 자리이다. this year's sales의 동사가 were이므로 빈칸은 복수의 지시대명사가 와야 하므로 (D) those가 정답이 된다.

[어휘]

advances 진보, 발전 | quality 품질 | impressive 인상적인 | sales 매출, 판매

[정답]

1 (C) **2** (B) **3** (B)

1-3
[번역]

> 메리빌 (9월 10일) – 메리빌의 모든 해변이 공식적으로 폐장을 했다. 셸던 알링턴 시장에 따르면, 올해에는 보다 많은 방문객들이 네 곳의 해변을 찾았다. 이는 식당, 호텔, 여행사, 그리고 여행업과 관련된 기타 기업체들이 높은 수익을 거두는데 도움을 주었다.
>
> "우리는 지난 3년간 기반 시설을 정비하느라 막대한 돈을 썼습니다"라고 알링턴 시장은 말했다. "우리는 반경 100마일 이내에 최고의 시설을 갖추고 있다고 생각합니다. 저는 그러한 점이 올해 그처럼 많은 방문객들을 유치한 것과 큰 관련이 있다고 생각합니다."
>
> (시는 대부분의 여름 기간 동안 화창한 날씨를 얻을 정도로 운이 좋았다.) 보통 6월 1일부터 8월 31일까지 약 25일간 비가 내리지만, 이 기간 동안 메리빌에는 단 15일 동안만 비가 내렸다고 기록되었다. 따라서 화창한 날들이 더해지면서 시내 여행업계는 확실한 수익을 보장받았다.
>
> 알링턴 시장은 주 전체에서 가장 뛰어난 해변을 조성하는 것을 목표로 계속해서 시설을 개선시킬 계획을 가지고 있다고 말했다. 그는 다음 달에 몇몇 주차장이 확장될 것이며, 1월에는 신규 골프장 건설 공사도 시작될 것이라고 언급했다. 그러한 일들은 모두 시가 앞으로 보다 많은 방문객들을 유치하는데 도움을 줄 것이다.

[어휘]

officially 공식적으로 | involved in ~와 관련된 | profitable 수익성이 있는 | infrastructure 기반 시설 | comment 논평하다 | radius 반지름, 반경 | have a great deal to do with ~와 큰 관련이 있다 | normally 보통 | money in the bank 확실한 수익 | indicate 가리키다, 언급하다 | objective 목표 | premier 최고의 | in the future 미래에, 장차

1
[번역]

기사에 따르면, 메리빌은 더 많은 관광객을 유치하기 위해 무엇을 했는가?
(A) 보다 많은 식당이 문을 열도록 했다
(B) 기업들에게 세금 우대 조치를 해 주었다
(C) 기반 시설을 향상시켰다
(D) 해변을 크게 홍보했다

[해설]

두 번째 단락의 a great amount of money fixing our infrastructure라는 말을 통해 메리빌은 관광객 유치를 위하여 기반 시설에 막대한 투자를 했음을 알 수 있다.

[어휘]

tourist 관광객 | tax break 세금 우대 조치 | promote 홍보하다

2

[번역]

내년에 메리빌에는 어떤 일이 일어날 것인가?
(A) 시장 선거가 있을 것이다.
(B) 골프장이 건설될 것이다.
(C) 해변들이 청소될 것이다.
(D) 주차장이 확대될 것이다.

[해설]

마지막 단락에서 '1월에는 골프장이 건설될 것(construction on a new golf course will begin in January)'이라는 점을 알 수 있으므로 정답은 (B)이다. (D)의 주차장 확장은 '다음 달'에 이루어질 일이다.

[어휘]

election 선거

3

[번역]

[1], [2], [3], [4] 중에서 다음 문장이 들어갈 곳으로 가장 적합한 곳은 어디인가?
"시는 대부분의 여름 기간 동안 화창한 날씨를 얻을 정도로 운이 좋았다."
(A) [1]
(B) [2]
(C) [3]
(D) [4]

[해설]

주어진 문장은 날씨의 이점에 대해 소개하고 있으므로 주어진 문장이 들어갈 곳은 구체적인 날씨의 도움이 언급되고 있는 부분의 앞이 되어야 한다. 따라서 정답은 (B)이다.

DAY 10 형용사 어휘 연습 / 복합 지문 p.174

PART 5

[정답]

1 (A)　2 (D)　3 (C)　4 (A)
5 (D)　6 (B)　7 (B)　8 (D)

1

[번역]

당신의 회비가 나흘 연체되었으니 곧 지불해 주시기 바랍니다.

[해설]

'회비가 나흘 ______ 되었으니 곧 지불해 주시기 바랍니다'는 문맥에 적합한 어휘는 (A) overdue(연체된)이다. (B) permanent(영구적인), (C) ample(풍부한), (D) devoted(헌신적인)는 문맥에 어울리지 않는다.

[어휘]

membership fee 회비 ｜ be advised to-V ~해야 한다 ｜ pay 지불하다 ｜ overdue 연체된

2

[번역]

판매를 증가시키기 위해서 가치 있는 마케팅 방법을 개발하는 것이 중요하다.

[해설]

'______ 마케팅 방법을 개발하는 것이 중요하다'는 문맥에 적합한 어휘는 (D) valuable(가치 있는)이다. (A) official(공식적인), (B) interested(관심 있는), (C) unused(남은, 사용되지 않은)은 문맥에 어울리지 않는다.

[어휘]

develop 개발하다 ｜ marketing 마케팅 ｜ tool 방법 ｜ in order to-V ~하기 위해 ｜ increase 증가시키다

3

[번역]

디지털 코퍼레이션 사는 연말에 인상적인 수익을 발표했다.

[해설]

'______ 수익을 발표했다'는 문맥에 적합한 어휘는 (C) impressive(인상적인)이다. (A) intense(강렬한), (B) refundable(환불 가능한), (D) alternative(대안의)는 문맥에 어울리지 않는다.

[어휘]

announce 발표하다 ｜ profit 수익 ｜ at the end of ~의 말에 ｜ impressive 인상적인

4

[번역]

내년의 고용 전망은 올해보다 더 밝아 보인다.

[해설]

'내년의 고용 전망은 올해보다 더 ______ 보인다'는 문맥에 적합한 어휘는 (A) promising(전망이 밝은)이다. (B) applicable(적용할 수 있는), (C) obtained(획득된), (D) convenient(편리한)는 문맥에 어울리지 않는다.

[어휘]

employment 고용 ｜ prospect 전망, 예상 ｜ promising 전망이 밝은

5

[번역]

사람들은 건강한 식생활과 운동의 중요성을 인식해가고 있는 중이다.

[해설]

'건강한 식생활과 운동의 중요성을 ______ 있다'는 문맥에 적합한 어휘는 (D) aware(알고 있는, 인식하는)이다. (A) optimistic(낙관적인), (B) temporary(임시의), (C) courteous(예절 바른)는 문맥에 어울리지 않는다.

[어휘]

become + 형용사 ~하게 되다는 ｜ healthy 건강에 좋은 ｜ diet 식단 ｜ aware 알고 있는, 인식하

6

[번역]

직원들은 바쁜 일정 때문에 현재 증가하는 압박감에 시달리고 있다.

[해설]

'바쁜 일정 때문에 현재 _____ 압박감에 시달리고 있다'는 문맥에 적합한 어휘는 (B) mounting(증가하는)이다. (A) disappointing(실망스런), (C) declining(감소하고 있는), (D) delinquent(연체된)는 문맥에 어울리지 않는다.

[어휘]

under pressure 스트레스를 받고 있는 | because of ~ 때문에 | tight schedule 바쁜 일정

7

[번역]

당신의 차에 문제가 있으면 공인된 자동차 대리점을 방문하는 게 낫다.

[해설]

'차에 문제가 있으면 _____ 자동차 대리점을 방문하는 게 낫다'라는 문맥에 적합한 어휘는 (B) authorized(공인된, 허가 받은)이다. (A) unstable(불안정한), (C) final(마지막의), (D) lasting(지속적인)은 문맥에 어울리지 않는다.

[어휘]

had better + 동사원형 ~하는 게 낫다 | visit 방문하다 | dealership 대리점 | authorized 공인된, 허가 받은

8

[번역]

불필요한 일반경비를 없애는 것은 회사와 고객들에게 도움이 될 수 있다.

[해설]

'불필요한 일반경비를 없애는 것이 회사와 고객들에게 _____ 수 있다'는 문맥에 적합한 어휘는 (D) beneficial(도움이 되는)이다. (A) deliberate(고의적인), (B) financial(재정의), (C) possible(가능한) 은 문맥에 어울리지 않는다.

[어휘]

eliminate 없애다 | unnecessary 불필요한 | overhead (경비가) 일반의 | expense 지출 | beneficial 도움이 되는

PART 7

[정답]

| 1 (B) | 2 (C) | 3 (C) | 4 (B) | 5 (B) |
| 6 (B) | 7 (C) | 8 (D) | 9 (A) | 10 (B) |

1-5

[번역]

수신: customersvc@highseas.com
발신: 앤느 라이딩 ⟨aryding@techgear.com⟩
제목: 킹 오브 더 하이 시즈 크루즈

안녕하세요.

저는 최근 귀사의 킹 오브 더 하이 시즈 선박으로 크루즈 여행을 다녀왔습니다. 이 여행은 제 인생에서 가장 실망스런 경험 중의 하나였습니다.

먼저, 음식이 형편없었습니다. 한번은 스테이크를 주문했는데 음식으로 나온 스테이크는 마치 햄버거와 같더군요. 몇 번은 차갑게 식은 음식이 제공되기도 했습니다. 최악의 일은 제 남편이 첫날 식중독에 걸려 크루즈 기간의 첫 절반을 아무것도 즐기지 못했다는 것입니다.

제 남편의 상태가 마침내 괜찮아졌을 때 그는 몇 가지 편의시설을 이용하고자 했습니다. 그는 가장 윗층 갑판에서 즐길 수 있는 온욕을 정말 기대했는데요. 저희가 그것을 사용하려고 가니 "고장"이라는 팻말이 붙어 있더군요. 그는 대신 풀장을 이용하고자 했지만 어린이용이라는 말을 들었습니다. 저희 객실도 그다지 좋지는 않았습니다. 브로셔에서 보여지는 것보다 훨씬 작았고 이상한 냄새가 나기도 했습니다.

저는 귀사의 크루즈 여행을 다시는 이용하지 않을 것입니다.

앤느 라이딩

[어휘]

cruise 크루즈, 유람 여행 | recently 최근 | disappointing 실망시키는, 기대에 어긋나는 | experiences 경험 | terrible 심한, 지독한 | serve (음식 따위)를 내다[제공하다] | food poisoning 식중독 | facility 편의 시설, 설비 | look forward to ~을 기대하다 | hot tub 온수 욕조 | deck 갑판 | out of order 고장 난 | sign 표지판 | pool 풀장

[번역]

수신: 앤느 라이딩 ⟨aryding@techgear.com⟩
발신: customersvc@highseas.com
제목: 답장: 킹 오브 더 하이 시즈 크루즈

안녕하세요. 라이딩 씨,

저희에게 시간을 내어 킹 오브 더 하이 시즈 이용 경험에 대해 말씀해 주셔서 감사 드립니다. 저희 회사가 크루즈 월드 매거진에 의해 10년 연속 카리브해 최고 크루즈 회사로 평가 받아 왔다 해도 손님들이 좋지 못한 경험을 하시는 경우가 여전히 있기는 합니다. 저는 귀하의 경험에 대해 일부 직원들에게 직접 이야기했으며 그들은 매우 유감스러워하고 있습니다. 저희는 귀하께서 크루즈 여행에서 느끼신 문제들을 해결하기 위해 모든 조치를 취하겠습니다.

귀하의 경험에 대한 저희의 유감을 표하기 위해 향후 크루즈 여행에 이용하실 수 있는 50퍼센트 할인권을 제공해 드립니다. 귀하께서는 자동으로 일반 객실이 아닌 스위트룸을 이용할 수 있는 일등급 대우로 격상되실 것입니다. 이 할인권은 귀하께서 선택하시는 선박 여행에 대해 향후 1년간 유효할 것입니다. 귀하의 할인 코드인 5684509를 사용하시는 것을 반드시 기억하셔서 사진이 첨부된 신분증과 제출해 주십시오.

귀하의 경험에 대해 다시 한번 사과의 말씀을 드리며 향후의 크루즈는 좀 더 개선되었다고 느끼시기를 희망합니다.

다시 한번 감사 드립니다.

린 샨

[어휘]

rate 등급을 정하다 | in a row 잇따라, 연속적으로 | directly 직접 | apologetic 사과의, 사죄의 | fix 해결하다 | notice 알아차리다 |

automatically 자동으로 ｜ raise 올리다 ｜ first class 최고급의, 일류의
｜ treatment 대우 ｜ suite 특별실[스위트룸] ｜ valid 유효한, 효력 있는 ｜
present 제시하다

1

[번역]

라이딩 씨의 이메일 목적은 무엇인가?

(A) 여행 일정 변경을 요청하기 위해

(B) 서비스에 대한 불만을 제기하기 위해

(C) 크루즈 패키지에 대해 문의하기 위해

(D) 훌륭한 크루즈에 대해 린에게 감사하기 위해

[해설]

라이딩 씨는 이메일 서두에서 It was one of the most disappointing
experiences in my life라며 자신의 크루즈 여행이 실망스러웠다고 말
한다. 이메일 본문에는 실망스런 내용들을 나열하고 있으므로 이메일
의 목적은 (B)임을 알 수 있다.

[어휘]

itinerary 여행일정표 ｜ complain 불평하다 ｜ package 패키지 여행

2

[번역]

킹 오브 하이 시즈에 대해 사실인 것은?

(A) 전문 직원들은 모두 자격증을 보유하고 있다.

(B) 단골 고객들에게 할인가를 제시하고 있다.

(C) 어린이 전용 시설을 갖추고 있다.

(D) 배 위에서 과일과 야채를 재배한다.

[해설]

첫 이메일 셋째 단락 중 He wanted to use the pool instead, but he was
told that it was only for kids에서 어린이용 풀장이 있음을 알 수 있다.
지문의 only를 exclusively로 바꾼 (C)가 정답이다.

[어휘]

professional 전문적인 ｜ certified 공인된, 면허증을 가진 ｜ reduced
할인된 ｜ loyal 충성스러운 ｜ exclusively 독점적으로 ｜ grow 기르다,
재배하다 ｜ on board 배 안에, 배 위에

3

[번역]

린 샨은 사업체에 대해 뭐라고 언급하는가?

(A) 10년 전에 설립되었다.

(B) 더 많은 안전 요원을 채용할 것이다.

(C) 수년간 최고 회사로 선정되었다.

(D) 곧 해외 지역을 여행할 것이다.

[해설]

둘째 이메일 첫 단락 중 we have been rated the top cruise company
for the Caribbean ten years in a row by Cruise World magazine에
서 이 회사는 최고 크루즈 회사로 평가받고 있음을 알 수 있다. 지문의
rated를 selected로 표현한 (C)가 정답이다.

[어휘]

establish 설립하다 ｜ decade 10년 ｜ hire 채용하다 ｜ security 안전 ｜
guard 경호원 ｜ select 선발하다

4

[번역]

린 샨은 직원들에게 무슨 이야기를 했겠는가?

(A) 직원들은 일을 아주 잘 하고 있다.

(B) 손님에게 식은 음식이 제공되었다.

(C) 직원들은 종종 승선한 의사를 도와야 한다.

(D) 직원들은 앤느 라이딩에게 이메일을 보내야 한다.

[해설]

둘째 이메일 첫 단락 중 I have spoken directly with some of the staff
members about your experience and they were very apologetic에서
직원들에게 당신(앤느 라이딩)의 경험에 대해 이야기했다고 했다. 앤느
라이딩의 그녀의 이메일에서 다양한 불평사항을 나열하고 있는데 보기
(B)에 나와 있는 내용이 Several times the food we were served was
cold에 속함을 알 수 있다.

5

[번역]

린 샨은 어떠한 정보를 앤느 라이딩에게 주지 않았는가?

(A) 이용 가능한 객실 종류

(B) 자신의 전화번호

(C) 할인권 유효 기간

(D) 특별 코드

[해설]

둘째 이메일 둘째 단락에서 질문의 단서들을 찾을 수 있다. You will
automatically be raised to first class treatment with a suite rather than
a regular room은 (A)를, This offer is valid for the next year on any
ship that you choose는 (C)를, Please remember to use your discount
code, which is 5684509은 (D)에 대한 정보에 해당됨을 알 수 있다. (B)
에 대해서는 언급되지 않았으므로 (B)가 정답이다.

6-10

[번역]

9월 5일

커비 씨께,

저는 9월 30일자로 연구개발부의 상무직에서 물러나겠다는 계획
을 당신께 알려 드리기 위해 이 편지를 쓰고 있습니다. 당신도 잘
알고 있듯이, 저는 지난 2년 동안 은퇴를 생각해 왔습니다. 저는
마침내 남은 시간을 가족들과, 특히 제 손자들과 보내기 위해서 지
금이 떠나야 할 때라고 결정을 내렸습니다.

저는 지난 30년 동안 당신이 제게 해 준 모든 것에 대해 감사를 표
하고 싶습니다. 댄스비 화학에서 일한 것은 제게 영광이자 특권이
었습니다. 저는 우수한 팀의 일원이었고, 우리가 여러 가지 긍정적
인 기여를 해온 것으로 생각합니다.

저는 당신이 제 후임자를 찾아보기 시작할 것으로 알고 있습니다.
하지만, 저는 그 자리에 잭 와튼을 앉히는 것을 생각해 보아야 한
다고 강력히 주장합니다. 그가 여기에 온지는 불과 2년밖에 되지
않았지만, 그는 그 동안 일을 훌륭히 해냈습니다. 그는 우수한 과
학자일 뿐만 아니라, 탁월한 인간 관계 능력도 보유하고 있습니다.

웨인 로저스 드림

[어휘]

inform A of B A에게 B를 알리다 | intention 의도, 의향 | resign 물러나다, 사임하다 | senior director 상무 | as of ~일자로 | contemplate 숙고하다 | honor 명예 | privilege 특권 | outstanding 뛰어난 | contribution 기여 | initiate 시작하다 | replacement 대체(품) | urge 촉구하다, 재촉하다 | merely 단지 | possess 소유하다

[번역]

받는 사람: 멜라니 해밀턴 〈m_hamilton@atlanticindustrial.com〉
보낸 사람: 제시카 스틸 〈jessica@dansbychemicals.com〉
제목: 면접
날짜: 9월 15일

친애하는 해밀턴 씨께,

댄스비 화학의 채용 위원회는 귀하의 이력서를 검토해 보고 귀하께서 연구개발부 상무직의 유력한 후보자라는 점을 알게 되었습니다. 저희는 특히 귀하께서 7개의 특허를 보유하고 계시다는 사실에 관심이 있는데, 이는 귀하의 연구 능력 수준을 나타내 주는 것입니다.

저희는 채용 면접을 보기 위해 귀하께서 이곳으로 오시기를 바랍니다. 귀하께서 현재 직무로 바쁘다는 점은 저희도 이해하기 때문에, 9월 19일 토요일에 면접을 진행하는 것이 어떻겠습니까? 귀하께서 올버니에서 볼티모어까지 비행기로 이동하셔야 하기 때문에 이것이 촉박한 통보라는 것은 저희도 알고 있습니다. 저희는 실례를 무릅쓰고 귀하와 귀하의 남편을 위해 9월 18일 금요일 일등석 티켓을 예약해 두었습니다. 동봉된 여행 일정표를 봐 주십시오. 그곳에는 귀하의 여행 일정과 귀하가 숙박하게 될 호텔에 관한 정보가 포함되어 있습니다. 오시는데 동의를 하시면, 운전 기사가 귀하와 귀하의 남편을 마중하기 위해 공항으로 갈 것입니다.

시간이 촉박하므로, 저희가 귀하께서 올 것이라는 점을 확실히 알 수 있도록 가능한 빨리 이 이메일에 대한 답장을 보내 주시겠습니까? 채용 위원회의 모두가 귀하를 만나 뵙기를 고대하고 있습니다.

제시카 스틸 드림
댄스비 화학 부사장

[어휘]

candidate 후보 | particularly 특히 | patent 특허 | indicate 가리키다 | short notice 촉박한 통보 | take the liberty of 실례를 무릅쓰고 ~하다 | itinerary 여행 일정 | contain 포함하다 | confirm 확인하다 | look forward to ~을 고대하다, ~을 기대하다

[번역]

받는 사람: 데이비드 커비 〈davidk@dansbychemicals.com〉
보낸 사람: 제시카 스틸 〈jessica@dansbychemicals.com〉
제목: R&D 부서의 공석
날짜: 9월 21일

David,

당신이 지시했듯이, 멜라니 해밀턴은 매우 유력한 후보이기 때문에 그녀의 면접이 끝나는 대로 우리는 멜라니 해밀턴에게

직위를 제안했습니다. 그녀는 남편의 참석 없이 결정을 내리고 싶어하지 않았기 때문에 제안에 대해 생각해 볼 시간을 이틀 정도 달라고 요청했습니다.

그녀는 조금 전에 제게 이메일을 보냈고, 저는 나쁜 소식을 접했습니다. 그녀는 올버니 지역에 머무르기로 결심을 했습니다. 그녀는 정말로 이번 일자리를 얻고 싶어 했지만, 그녀의 두 아이들 모두가 고등학교에 다니고 있기 때문에, 그녀는 이사를 원하지 않았습니다. 하지만, 그녀의 딸이 대학에 다니기 시작하는 3년 후에는 기꺼이 이직을 할 것이라고 말했습니다.

해밀턴 씨가 우리와 함께 일을 하지 못하게 되었으므로, 웨인의 원래 제안을 따르는 것이 어떨까요? 그는 분명 그 직위에 대한 2순위 후보이며, 우리는 그가 어떤 일을 해낼 것인지 알고 있습니다. 어떻게 생각하나요?

멜라니

[어휘]

instruct 지시하다 | relocate 이전하다 | amenable 기꺼이 따르는 | original 원래의 | second-best 제2의

6

[번역]

로저스 씨는 왜 편지를 썼는가?
(A) 공석에 지원하기 위해
(B) 자신이 일을 그만 둘 것이라는 점을 알리기 위해
(C) 수상자로 동료를 지명하기 위해
(D) 자신이 하고 있는 새로운 프로젝트를 홍보하기 위해

[해설]

첫 편지의 첫 문장에서 그는 '직위에서 물러날 생각(my intention to resign from my position)'을 알리기 위해 편지를 쓰고 있다고 했다.

[어휘]

quit 그만두다 | nominate 지명하다

7

[번역]

첫 번째 이메일에 따르면, 해밀턴 씨에 관해 사실인 것은 무엇인가?
(A) 그녀는 볼티모어 지역에 산다.
(B) 그녀는 회사의 연구개발부에서 일한다.
(C) 그녀는 댄스비 화학의 공석에 대한 충분한 자격을 갖추고 있다.
(D) 그녀는 발명품 중 하나에 대한 특허를 받았다.

[해설]

이메일에서 그녀는 '연구부서의 상무직에 유력한 후보자(the leading candidate for the position of senior director of the R&D Department)'라고 언급되고 있다. 따라서 정답은 (C)이다. 참고로 (A)의 볼티모어는 댄스비 화학이 위치해 있는 곳이며, (B)의 경우, 그녀가 현재 연구개발부에서 근무하는지는 확인할 수 없는 사항이다.

8

[번역]

스틸 씨는 해밀턴 씨에게 무엇을 할 것을 요청하는가?
(A) 일과가 끝날 무렵에 그녀에게 전화를 한다
(B) 그녀만의 여행 일정을 정한다

(C) 이번 주말에 볼티모어로 차를 몰고 온다
(D) 그녀의 이메일에 신속히 답한다

[해설]

이메일의 마지막 부분에서 '가능한 빨리 답신을 해 줄 것(would you please respond to this e-mail as soon as possible)'을 요청하고 있으므로 정답은 (D)이다.

9

[번역]

두 번째 이메일에서, 두 번째 단락의 "relocate"라는 단어와 의미가 가장 비슷한 것은?

(A) 이사하다
(B) 조사하다
(C) 바꾸다
(D) 시도하다

[해설]

relocate는 '이전하다'라는 뜻으로 보기 중에서는 move와 그 의미가 가장 비슷하다.

10

[번역]

스틸 씨는 커비 씨에게 무엇을 할 것을 제안하는가?

(A) 로저스 씨에게 직위에 계속 남아 있으라고 권한다
(B) 공석에 와튼 씨를 앉힌다
(C) 해밀턴 씨에게 너 높은 초봉을 제안한다
(D) 해밀턴 씨와 개인적으로 이야기하기 위해 비행기를 타고 올버니로 간다

[해설]

세 번째 지문의 마지막 단락에서 스틸 씨는 '웨인의 원래 제안(Wayne's original suggestion)'을 따르자고 말하는데, 이 제안은 첫 번째 지문인 편지를 통해, 아튼 씨를 자신의 후임으로 삼자는 것임을 알 수 있다.

[어휘]

encourage 격려하다. 고무시키다 ｜ starting salary 초봉 ｜ personally 개인적으로

PART 5

[정답]

1 (B)	2 (C)	3 (C)	4 (D)
5 (B)	6 (C)	7 (B)	8 (A)

1

[번역]

상사가 요청했기 때문에 나는 그를 대신해서 워크숍에 참가할 것이다.

[해설]

빈칸 뒤에 절이 있으므로 전치사 (A) because of와 (D) despite가 제외

된다. 해석상 '상사가 요청했기 때문에 나는 그를 대신해서 워크숍에 참가할 것이다'가 되어야하므로 정답은 (B) because(~ 때문에)이다. (C) although(~에도 불구하고)는 문맥에 맞지 않다.

[어휘]

participate in ~에 참여하다 ｜ on behalf of ~을 대신하여 ｜ boss 상사 ｜ ask 요청하다

2

[번역]

건물 내 전력보수공사 때문에 금요일 3시부터 5시까지 전력 서비스가 중단될 것이다.

[해설]

해석상 '건물 내 전력보수공사 때문에 전력 서비스가 중단될 것이다'가 되어야하므로 정답은 (C) Due to(~때문에)이다. (A) Not only는 but also가 필요하며, (B) Despite(~에도 불구하고)는 문맥에 어울리지 않고, (D) If 뒤에는 절이 와야 한다.

[어휘]

power 전력 ｜ maintenance 보수, 유지 ｜ interrupt 중단시키다

3

[번역]

중앙은행은 현행 정책이 이자율을 높이고 수많은 파산을 야기하는데도 불구하고 현행 정책을 유지할 것이다.

[해설]

빈칸 뒤에 절이 있기 때문에 전치사인 (A) in spite of(~에도 불구하고)와 (D) in case of(~인 경우에)는 우선 제외된다. (B) both(둘 다)는 절을 받을 수 없으므로, 정답은 절을 받는 양보대조의 접속사 (C) even if(~에도 불구하고)이다.

[어휘]

maintain 유지하다 ｜ existing 현행의 ｜ policy 정책 ｜ cause 야기하다 ｜ Interest rates 이자율 ｜ a number of 수많은 ｜ bankruptcy 파산

4

[번역]

불충분한 지원과 헌신의 부족 어느 것도 판매 하락의 요소는 아니라고 발표되었다.

[해설]

빈칸 앞에 상관접속사 neither가 있으므로 정답은 (D) nor가 되어 상관접속사 neither A nor B(A도 B도 아니다)를 완성한다. (A) so(그래서), (B) but(그러나), (C) yet(그러나)는 불가하다.

[어휘]

insufficient 불충분한 ｜ support 지원 ｜ a lack of ~의 부족 ｜ commitment 헌신 ｜ factor 요소 ｜ declining 하락하고 있는

5

[번역]

조치가 취해지지 않으면 곧 교통 체증이 훨씬 악화될 것이다.

[해설]

빈칸 뒤에 절이 오므로 정답은 (B) Unless(~하지 않으면)이다. (A) Also(역시), (C) Therefore(그래서), (D) Nevertheless(그러나)는 절을 받을 수 없는 부사들이다.

[어휘]

take measures 조치를 취하다 | traffic 교통 | congestion 체증 |
even 훨씬 | worse 악화된 | in no time 곧

6
[번역]

논란의 여지가 있는 그 보고서는 엄중한 개혁과 임시 직원들의 해고 둘
다를 포함하고 있었다.

[해설]

빈칸 앞에 상관접속사 both가 있으므로 정답은 (C) and가 되어 상관접
속사 both A and B(A와 B 둘 다)를 완성한다. 따라서 (A) or(또는), (B)
but(그러나), (D) nor(~도 아니다)는 불가하다.

[어휘]

controversial 논란의 여지가 있는 | include 포함하다 | strict 엄중한 |
reform 개혁 | layoff 해고

7
[번역]

그 지역의 심각한 홍수 피해로 인한 손실들에도 불구하고 상당한 수익
이 얻어졌다.

[해설]

빈칸 뒤가 절이 아니므로 (C) but(그러나)과 (D) although(~에도 불구
하고)가 우선 제외된다. 해석상 '심각한 홍수 피해로 인한 손실에도 불
구하고 상당한 수익이 얻어졌다'가 자연스러우므로 정답은 전치사인
(B) despite(~에도 불구하고)이다. 전치사인 (A) regarding은 '~에 관
해서'란 뜻이다.

[어휘]

considerable 상당한 | profit 수익 | obtain 얻다 | loss 손실 |
serious 심각한 | flood 홍수 | damage 손실, 손상 | region 지역

8
[번역]

더 낮은 가격 덕택에 더 많은 잠재고객이 그 부동산을 매입할 수 있을
것이다.

[해설]

빈칸 뒤가 절이 아니므로 절을 받는 (C) Whether(~인지 아닌지), (D)
In case(~한 경우에)는 우선 제외된다. 해석상 '더 낮은 가격 덕택에 더
많은 잠재고객이 그 부동산을 매입할 수 있을 것이다'가 자연스러우므
로 정답은 (A) Owing to(~ 덕택에, ~ 때문에)이다. (B) As much as(~
만큼 많이)는 문맥상 어색하다.

[어휘]

potential 잠재적인 | be able to-V ~할 수 있다 | property 부동산,
재산 | owing to ~덕택에, ~때문에

PART 6

[정답]

1 (C)   2 (C)   3 (A)   4 (C)

1-4
[번역]

카슨 시 (4월 11일) – 4월 10일 기자회견에서, 지역 기업인 피터
슨 실버의 대변인이 놀라운 소식을 전했다. 한 달 전, 피터슨 실버
가 네바다에서 새로운 은광을 발견했다. 현재, 광산의 위치는 비
밀에 부쳐져 있다. 대변인에 따르면, 그곳은 전국에서 발견된 은
광 중 가장 규모가 큰 은광일 수도 있다. 피터슨 실버는 해당 지역
에 최소한 5억 온스의 은이 매장되어 있다고 추산 중이다. (회사는
현재 그처럼 대형 광산을 개발하기 위해 필요한 장비를 구하고 있
다.) 또한 200명 이상의 신규 직원을 고용할 계획이다. 카슨 시는
지난 몇 년 간 경제적으로 어려움을 겪고 있었다. 대부분의 일자리
는 카슨 시의 주민들에게 돌아갈 것으로 예상되고 있는데, 이는 지
역 경제에 보탬이 될 것이다.

[어휘]

press conference 기자 회견 | spokesman 대변인 | stunning 놀라
운 | mine 광산 keep a secret 비밀에 부치다 | estimate 추산하다, 추
정하다 | contain 포함하다 | suffer 고생하다 | economically 경제적으
로 | resident 주민

1
[해설]

빈칸에는 made의 목적어 역할을 하면서 stunning의 수식을 받을 수
있는 명사가 들어가야 한다. 따라서 정답은 (C) announcement이다.
make an announcement(발표하다)라는 표현을 알고 있으면 보다 쉽게
정답을 찾을 수 있다.

[어휘]

announcer 아나운서 | announcement 발표

2
[해설]

'근원', '원천', '수원' 등의 의미는 source로 나타낸다.

[어휘]

foundation 기초 | source 근원, 원천

3
[해설]

빈칸 다음 문장의 also에 유의하면 정답을 쉽게 찾을 수 있다. 빈칸 다
음 문장에서 일할 사람이 더 필요하다고 했다. 따라서 그 앞의 문장에
도 은광을 채굴하기 위해 필요한 것이 언급되어 있어야 한다. 보기 중
이러한 조건을 만족시키는 것은 '회사는 현재 그처럼 대형 광산을 개발
하기 위해 필요한 장비를 구하고 있다'라는 의미의 (A)뿐이므로 (A)가
정답이다.

[어휘]

acquire 얻다, 획득하다 | equipment 장비, 시설 | run 운영하다 | head
to ~으로 향하다 | deposit 매장, 매장층 | appoint 지명하다

4
[해설]

주어가 most of the jobs이므로 빈칸에 expect(기대하다)가 들어가기
위해서는 수동형으로 바뀌어야 한다. 보기 중에서 수동태 형식은 (C)
are expected뿐이다.

PART 5

[정답]

1 (B)	**2** (D)	**3** (C)	**4** (D)
5 (C)	**6** (B)	**7** (D)	**8** (D)

1

[번역]

컴퓨터를 구입할 때 가격과 제품 품질을 비교해 주세요.

[해설]

'컴퓨터를 구입할 때, 가격과 제품 품질을 비교해 주세요'라는 문맥이 자연스러우므로 정답은 (B) When(~할 때)가 된다. When you are buying a computer에서 you are가 생략된 구문이다. (A) Whether와 (C) That은 분사구문과 함께 쓰지 않으며, (D) Unless는 문맥상 어울리지 않는다.

[어휘]

be encouraged to-V ~하도록 권장되다 ｜ compare 비교하다 ｜ price 가격 ｜ quality 품질

2

[번역]

아이들은 어른과 동행하지 않으면 연회장 입장이 허용되지 않는다.

[해설]

'어른과 동행하지 않으면 허용되지 않는다'라는 문맥이 자연스러우므로 정답은 (D) unless(~하지 않으면)이다. unless they are accompanied by adults에서 they are가 생략된 구문이다. (A) although(~에도 불구하고)는 문맥상 어울리지 않고, 전치사인 (B) before(~하기 전에)와 (C) without(~없이)뒤에 p.p.형은 올 수 없다.

[어휘]

allow 허용하다 ｜ enter 들어가다 ｜ reception hall 연회장 ｜ accompanied by ~와 동행한 ｜ adult 어른

3

[번역]

많은 잠재적인 일꾼들이 있다는 것을 고려해 볼 때, 우리는 몇 년 동안 걱정할 필요가 없다.

[해설]

쉼표 뒤에 주어 we와 동사 do not need to worry를 갖춘 완전한 절이 있으므로, 쉼표 앞은 분사 구문이 와야 할 자리이고, 분사 구문 관용어구 'considering that 절(~을 고려해 볼 때)'를 알면 보다 쉽게 풀 수 있는 문제이다.

[어휘]

there are ~들이 있다 ｜ potential 잠재적인 ｜ worry 걱정하다 ｜ considering that 절 ~을 고려해 볼 때

4

[번역]

관광 명소 근처에 위치해있기 때문에 에이스 호텔은 관광객들에게 매우 매력적이다.

[해설]

두 문장을 연결할 때 중복되는 부분을 생략해 보다 간단하게 표현할 때 분사구문(주어 + be동사 생략)을 쓴다. 해석이 명확하면 접속사까지 생략되므로 As it is located near the tourist attraction에서 As it is가 생략된 구문이다. 따라서 정답은 (D) Located(위치한)이다.

[어휘]

located 위치한 ｜ near ~근처에 ｜ tourist attraction 관광 명소 ｜ attractive 매력적인 ｜ tourist 관광객

5

[번역]

지원서들을 검토할 때, 인사 관리자가 중점적으로 본 것은 지원자들의 소프트웨어 디자인 경험이었다.

[해설]

접속사 when 뒤에는 절이 와야 하는데 빈칸은 동사 꼴을 묻는 문제이므로 분사구문임을 알아채야 한다. 즉, When the personnel manager is reviewing the applications에서 the personnel manager is가 생략된 것이므로 정답은 (C) reviewing이다.

[어휘]

application 지원서 ｜ personnel 인사과 ｜ main 주요한 ｜ focus 중점 ｜ candidate 지원자 ｜ review 검토하다

6

[번역]

모든 참석자들은 지시받은 대로 안전 규정을 준수해야한다.

[해설]

접속사 when 뒤에는 절이 와야 하는데 빈칸은 동사의 형태를 묻는 문제이므로 분사구문임을 알아채야 한다. 즉, as they were directed에서 they were가 생략된 것이므로 정답은 (B) directed(지시받은)이다. 빈출 관용어구 'as + p.p.: ~대로'를 알면 보다 쉽게 해결할 수 있다.

[어휘]

participant 참석자 ｜ require 요구하다 ｜ follow 준수하다 ｜ safety 안전 ｜ regulation 규정 ｜ as directed 지시받은 대로

7

[번역]

지금까지 최상의 서비스를 제공하면서, 우리는 가장 유명한 여행사 중 하나가 되었다.

[해설]

빈칸 앞이 완전한 문장이므로 빈칸 이하는 분사구문이 올 자리이다. 빈칸 뒤에 목적어 the best service ever가 있으므로 p.p.형인 (C) provided는 불가하다. 따라서 정답은 (D) providing이다. 분사가 올 자리에 (A) provide, (B) provides는 올 수 없다.

[어휘]

the most 가장 ｜ famous 유명한 ｜ travel 여행 ｜ ever (최상급 뒤에서) 지금까지 ｜ provide 제공하다

8

[번역]

해외 연수를 받은 이후에 우리는 다른 문화를 수용하는 법을 배웠다.

[해설]

쉼표 뒤가 완전한 문장이므로 쉼표 앞은 분사구문이 올 자리이다. 분

사구문의 시제(After we had received the overseas training)가 주절 (we learned)보다 앞서기 때문에 having p.p.를 써야하므로 정답은 (D) Having이다.

[어휘]

overseas 해외 | training 훈련, 연수 | learn 배우다 | how to ~하는 방법 | accommodate 수용하다 | different 다른 | culture 문화

PART 7

[정답]

1 (C)　**2** (A)

1-2

[번역]

수신: 데릭 젠틀리 〈derek_gently@virginia.edu〉
발신: 더그 애덤스 〈d.adams@soluspharm.net〉
날짜: 6월 11일
제목: 비즈니스 고문단 초빙

젠틀리 교수 귀하,

제약업계에서 귀하와 같은 경험과 식견을 가지신 분이라면 저를 도와 저희 솔루스 제약회사의 미래를 이끄실 수 있는 적임자가 되실 수 있습니다. 따라서 저는 기꺼이 귀하께서 저희 회사의 비즈니스 고문단 회원이 되어 주십사 요청합니다.

비즈니스 고문단은 분기별로 모임을 가지며 각 모임은 2시간의 토론과 오찬으로 이어집니다. 물론 고문단 회의에 참가하시기 위해 쓰셔야 하는 비용은 제가 부담해 드리며 추가로 귀하께 직접 또는 귀하께서 선택하시는 자선 단체로 2,500달러를 드릴 것입니다.
시간을 내어 솔루스 제약회사 비즈니스 고문단의 일원이 되어 주시는 일을 고려해 주셔서 감사합니다. 귀하께서 질문이 있으시면 언제든지 답변해 드리겠습니다. 제게 전화 (416) 545-3256으로 연락하실 수 있습니다. 귀하의 답신을 기다리겠습니다.

CEO 더그 애덤스 드림
솔루스 제약 주식회사

[어휘]

advisory board 자문 위원회, 고문단 | invitation 초대 | individual 사람, 개인 | experience 경험 | insight 식견, 안식 | pharmaceutical 제약(의) | perfect 완벽한 | determine 결정하다 | direction 방향 | quarterly 연(年) 4회의 | consist of ~으로 구성되다 | discussion 토론 | followed by 뒤이어, 잇달아 | luncheon 오찬 | cover 부담하다 | expense 비용 | attend 참석하다 | directly 직접 | charity 자선단체 | consider 고려하다 | available 만날[말할] 수 있는 | look forward to ~을 기대하다 | reply 답신

1

[번역]

이메일의 목적은 무엇인가?
(A) 신약을 소개하기 위해
(B) 견적가를 요청하기 위해
(C) 고문 직책을 제안하기 위해
(D) 이사회 회의를 마련하기 위해

[해설]

이메일의 첫 단락 마지막 문장 Therefore, I'm pleased to invite you to become a member of my company's Business Advisory Board에서 비즈니스 고문단의 일원이 되어 주시기를 요청한다는 내용이 나온다. 마지막 단락의 Thank you for taking the time to consider being a part of Solus Pharmaceuticals Business Advisory Board에서도 이에 대해 다시 한번 언급하고 있으므로 member of my company's Business Advisory Board를 advisory position으로 요약한 (C)가 이메일의 목적으로 적절하다.

[어휘]

medicine 약 | estimate 견적 | position 직책 | arrange 준비하다 | board 위원회

2

[번역]

비즈니스 고문단에 대해 유추할 수 있는 것은?
(A) 일년에 4차례 정기적으로 만난다.
(B) 연간 회원비는 2,500달러이다.
(C) 제품 가격 인상에 동의한다.
(D) 회원들은 경력이 필요 없다.

[해설]

고문단에 대해 소개하는 둘째 단락 중 The Business Advisory Board will meet quarterly ~에서 분기별(quarterly) 모임을 갖는다고 했으므로 이를 four times a year로 표현한 (A)가 정답이다. annually(일 년에 한 번), biannually(2년에 한 번) 등의 단어도 함께 참고로 알아두도록 하자.

[어휘]

regularly 정기적으로 | annual 연간의 | membership 회원 | agree 동의하다

DAY **13** 관계대명사　　　　p.188

PART 5

[정답]

1 (A)　**2** (A)　**3** (D)　**4** (A)
5 (D)　**6** (B)　**7** (C)　**8** (D)

1

[번역]

시간이 있는 매니저들이 아픈 직원을 대신 일해 준다면 존경받을 것이다.

[해설]

주어 managers, 동사구 fill in for, 목적어 sick employees를 갖춘 완벽한 절이므로 '______ have time'은 앞의 명사 managers를 수식하는 형용사절, 즉 관계대명사 자리이다. 따라서 정답은 fill의 주격인 (A) who 이다. (B) whoever(누구라도)는 선행사와 함께 쓰이지 않고 (C) whose 는 소유격이고 (D) which는 선행사가 사물일 때 쓴다.

[어휘]

fill in for ~을 대신하다 | sick 아픈 | employee 직원 | respect 존경하다

2

[번역]

우리는 문제들을 처리하기 위해 현장에서 매일 전문가들을 교육하는 몇 명의 사람들을 보유하고 있다.

[해설]

빈칸 앞이 주어 동사 목적어를 갖춘 완벽한 절이므로 빈칸 이하는 형용사 절이다. 빈칸 다음에 동사 train(훈련시키다)이 있으므로 정답은 주격인 (A) who이다. (B) whether(~인지 아닌지)는 관계대명사 자리에 올 수 없고 (C) which는 선행사가 사물일 때 쓰이며 (D) what은 선행사와 함께 쓰질 않는다.

[어휘]

several 몇 몇의 | train 훈련시키다 | professional 전문가 | on site 현장에서 | deal with 다루다

3

[번역]

결함이 있는 상품은 구매 1주일 이내에 반환해야 합니다.

[해설]

빈칸 앞이 주어 동사 목적어를 갖춘 완벽한 절이므로 '_____ has defects'가 앞의 사물명사 merchandise(상품)를 수식하는 관계대명사 절이므로 정답은 (D) that이다. 부사인 (A) there(거기에), 선행사가 사람일 때 쓰는 (B) who, 절을 받는 (C) when(~할 때)은 불가하다.

[어휘]

ensure 확실히 하다 | have to ~ 해야 한다 | return 반환하다 | merchandise 상품 | defect 결함 | purchase 구매

4

[번역]

대부분의 지원자들은 그들이 신청한 직책의 대기자 명단에 올려져 있었다.

[해설]

빈칸이 사물 명사 positions를 선행사로 취하는 관계대명사 자리이므로 전치사의 목적격인 (A) which가 정답이다. 관계대명사 (B) that은 전치사 뒤에 쓸 수 없고, (C) who는 선행사가 사람일 때 쓰고, (D) what은 선행사와 함께 쓰이지 않는다.

[어휘]

put ~ on the waiting list 대기자 명단에 올리다 | position 직책 | sign up for 신청하다

5

[번역]

그 일에 적합한 자격을 지닌 후보자들의 이름이 내일 게시될 것이다.

[해설]

문장 구조를 살펴보면, 주어가 The names of the candidates이고 동사가 will be posted이므로 '_____ qualifications are suitable for the job'이 선행사 candidates를 수식하는 형용사절임을 알 수 있다. 따라서 정답은 관계대명사 소유격 (D) whose이다. (A) that, (B) which, (C) who는 소유격 자리에 올 수 없다.

[어휘]

candidate 후보자 | qualification 자격 | be suitable for ~에 적합하다 | post 게시하다

6

[번역]

불필요한 경비를 줄이고 싶은 사람들은 파커 씨의 최근 저서를 읽어 주세요.

[해설]

관계대명사 who의 동사가 3인칭 복수동사 want이므로 단수인 (A) That, (C) Everyone, (D) Anybody는 불가하다. 따라서 정답은 (B) Those가 되어 관계 대명사 관용어구 'those who ~(~하는 사람들)'를 완성한다.

[어휘]

reduce 감소하다 | unnecessary 불필요한 | expense 경비 | be advised to-V ~해 주세요 | recent 최근의

7

[번역]

임시 직원들은 주마다 봉급을 받는데, 이는 대다수 직장에서 공통적인 현상이다.

[해설]

빈칸이 is common의 주어 자리이므로 부사인 (B) where가 우선 제외되고, 빈칸 앞에 쉼표가 있으므로 (D) that도 제외된다. (A) who는 선행사가 사람일 때 쓰이므로 불가하다. 따라서 정답은 앞 문장 전체를 선행사로 받는 (C) which이다.

[어휘]

temporary 임시의 | get paid 지불받다 | on a weekly basis 주에 한 번씩 | common 공통의 | work place 일터

8

[번역]

타잔 나레이션 주식회사는 7명의 직원들로 구성되어 있으며, 그들은 모두 30세 이하이다.

[해설]

빈칸 앞에 선행사가 있으므로 선행사를 포함하고 있는 (A) what은 제외되고, 쉼표 앞 문장과 쉼표 뒤의 문장을 연결하는 접속사가 없으므로 일반 대명사 (B) them도 불가하고, 빈칸 다음의 동사가 are이므로 단수인 (C) this도 불가하다. 따라서 정답은 (D) whom이다.

[어휘]

consist of ~로 구성되다 | employee 직원 | under the age of ~ 나이가 ~ 아래인

PART 6

[정답]

1 (B)   **2** (A)   **3** (D)   **4** (C)

1-4

[번역]

받는 사람: 린다 추 〈lindachu@perryfinancial.com〉
보낸 사람: 톰 로저스 〈t_rogers@davisconsulting.com〉
제목: 강연 날짜

친애하는 추 씨께,

귀사를 방문해서 귀사의 직원들에게 강연을 해 달라고 요청해 주셔서 감사를 드립니다. 저는 귀사에서 귀금속 시장에 관해 사람들과 이야기를 나누게 되면 더할 나위 없이 기쁠 것 같습니다. 안타깝게도, 저는 귀하께서 요청하신 날짜에는 시간이 되지 않습니다. 저는 11월 6일부터 10일까지 해외에 있을 것입니다. 귀국을 하면, 11일에는 하루 종일 약속이 있습니다. (하지만, 현재 제 달력상 그 다음 이틀은 비어 있습니다.) 귀하께서는 제게 7일 오전 11시부터 12시까지 강연을 부탁하셨습니다. 그 대신 12일이나 13일 중 하루에 같은 시간대에 귀사를 방문하는 것은 어떨까요? 그 시간을 받아드릴 수 없는 경우, 제가 언제 그곳에 가는 것이 좋을지 알려 주시기 바랍니다.

그럼 이만 줄이겠습니다.

톰 로저스, 데이비드 컨설팅

[어휘]

give a presentation 발표를 하다 | precious metal 귀금속 |
request 요청하다, 요구하다 | appointment 약속 | either A or B A와
B 중 둘 중 하나 | unacceptable 받아들일 수 없는 | inform 알리다

1

[해설]

you가 강연을 부탁한 회사의 직원이라는 것을 파악하면 정답은 (B)
colleagues(직장 동료)임을 쉽게 알 수 있다.

[어휘]

client 고객 | colleague 동료

2

[해설]

빈칸 앞 문장에서 강연을 한다면 기쁘겠다고 말한 후, 빈칸 뒷문장에서는 해당 기간에 해외에 나가 있을 것이라고 말한다. 따라서 빈칸에는 일정상 강연이 불가능하다는 의미가 들어가야 자연스러운 문맥이 완성되므로 정답은 '이용할 수 없는' 혹은 '만날 수 없는'이라는 의미를 가진 unavailable이다.

[어휘]

unavailable 이용할 수 없는, 만날 수 없는 | approved 승인된 |
unapproachable 접근할 수 없는

3

[해설]

빈칸 앞 문장에서 11일에는 약속이 있다는 소식을 전하고 있지만, 그 이후의 문장에서는 강연이 가능한 다른 날짜를 언급하고 있다. 따라서 빈칸에 들어갈 문장은 '하지만, 현재 제 달력상 그 다음 이틀은 비어 있다'라는 의미의 (D)이다.

[어휘]

moreover 게다가, 또한 | be unaware of ~을 모르다 |
consequently 따라서 | precisely 정확히 | empty 빈

4

[해설]

'~이 ~하기를 원하다'라는 표현은 'would like + 목적어 + to'로 나타낸다.

PART 5

[정답]

| 1 (C) | 2 (D) | 3 (B) | 4 (D) |
| 5 (C) | 6 (C) | 7 (C) | 8 (B) |

1

[번역]

직장에서 전자기기 사용을 금지하는 회사 정책이 발표되었다.

[해설]

주어가 The company policy이고 동사가 has been announced이므로 '_____ the use of electronic devices at work'가 The company policy를 수식하는 관계대명사 절이다. '주격 관계대명사 + be동사'가 생략된 문장으로, 빈칸 다음에 목적어 the use of electronic devices가 있으므로 현재분사 형태인 (C) prohibiting이 정답이다.

[어휘]

policy 정책 | use 사용 | electronic device 전자 기기 | announce
발표하다 | prohibit 금지하다

2

[번역]

우리 집에서 걸어갈 수 있는 거리에 위치한 사람들이 가장 많이 찾는 그 박물관은 광범위한 소장품으로 잘 알려져 있다.

[해설]

주어가 The most visited museum이고 본동사가 is이므로, The most visited museum that is located within walking distance of my place (우리 집에서 걸어갈 수 있는 거리에 위치한 박물관)에서 that is가 생략된 것이다. 따라서 정답은 (D) located(~에 위치한)이다.

[어휘]

the most visited 사람 방문이 가장 많은 | museum 박물관 | within
walking distance 걸어갈 수 있는 거리에 | known for ~로 유명한 |
extensive 광범위한 | collection 소장

3

[번역]

매달 마지막 주에 출판되는 회사 사보는 유익한 정보를 담고 있다.

[해설]

주어가 The company newsletter이고 본동사가 contains이므로, The company newsletter that is published on the last week of every month(매달 마지막 주에 출판되는 회사 사보)에서 that is가 생략된 것이다. 따라서 정답은 (B) published(출판되는)이다.

[어휘]

newsletter 사보 | contain 담다 | useful 유익한 | publish 출판하다

4

[번역]

포드 씨는 교육 개혁 프로젝트에 대한 일을 하고 있는 위원회를 이끌도록 임명되었다.

[해설]

빈칸 앞이 완전한 문장이므로 '_____ on the educational reform project'는 선행사 the committee를 수식하는 형용사 절이다. 즉 ~ the committee that is working on the educational reform project(교육 개혁 프로젝트에 대한 일을 하고 있는 위원회)에서 that is가 생략된 것이므로 정답은 (D) working이다.

[어휘]

appoint 임명하다 | head ~의 장이 되다, 지휘하다 | committee 위원회 | reform 개혁 | work on ~에 대해 일하다 | educational 교육의

5

[번역]

사업차 동남아시아를 여행할 일정이었던 부사장은 항공사들의 파업으로 여행을 취소해야 했다.

[해설]

주어가 The vice president이고 동사가 had to cancel이므로 '_____ to travel to Southeast Asia on business'는 선행사 The vice president를 수식하는 형용사절이다. 즉 The vice president who was scheduled to travel to Southeast Asia on business(사업차 동남아시아를 여행할 예정이었던 부사장)에서 who was가 생략된 것이므로 정답은 (C) scheduled(예정인)이다.

[어휘]

vice president 부사장 | travel 여행하다 | on business 사업차 | cancel 취소하다 | strike 파업 | airline 항공사 | be scheduled to-V ~할 예정이다

6

[번역]

부실한 서비스와 직원 부주의로 야기된 불편에 대해 진심으로 사과드립니다.

[해설]

빈칸 앞이 완전한 문장이므로 '_____ by poor service and employee negligence'는 선행사 inconvenience를 수식하는 형용사 절이다. 즉, ~ inconvenience that is caused by poor service and employee negligence(부실한 서비스와 직원 부주의로 야기된 불편)에서 that is가 생략된 것이므로 정답은 (C) caused(야기된)이다.

[어휘]

apologize for ~에 사과하다 | inconvenience 불편 | poor 부실한 | negligence 부주의 | cause 야기하다

7

[번역]

그 자선 활동에 참여한 모든 사람은 옷과 약간의 돈을 가난한 사람들에게 기부했다.

[해설]

주어가 Everyone이고 본동사가 donated이므로 '_____ in the charity activity'는 선행사 Everyone을 수식하는 형용사 절이다. 즉 Everyone who is involved in the charity activity(그 자선 활동에 참여한 모든 사람)에서 who is가 생략된 것이므로 정답은 (C) involved(참여한)이다.

[어휘]

charity activity 자선 활동 | donate 기부하다 | people in need 가난한 사람들 | be involved in ~에 참여하다, 관여하다

8

[번역]

기술적인 문제에 직면하는 경험을 겪으면, 즉시 우리에게 연락해서 도움을 청하세요.

[해설]

빈칸 앞이 완전한 문장이므로 '_____ any technical problem'은 선행사 experience를 수식하는 형용사 절이다. 즉 ~ experience that is encountering any technical problem(기술적인 문제에 직면하는 경험)에서 that is가 생략된 것이므로 정답은 (B) encountering(마주치는)이다.

[어휘]

technical 기술적인 | contact 연락하다 | promptly 즉시 | assistance 도움 | encounter 마주치다

PART 7

[정답]

1 (C) 2 (B) 3 (B)

1-3

[번역]

3월 21일

사장님께,

제 이름은 헤더 마이어스입니다. 저는 2005년부터 귀하의 식당에서 식사를 했으며 최소한 한 달에 한 번은 남편과 함께 그곳을 찾고 있습니다. 3월 18일, 저희는 6시 30분경에 그곳에서 저녁 식사를 했습니다.

저녁 식사는, 저희가 골든 타임즈에서 먹었던 여느 때의 식사와 마찬가지로, 훌륭했습니다. 하지만 웨이터 중 한 명인 존이 제공한 서비스는 훨씬 더 좋았습니다. 존은 전에 저희가 그곳을 방문했다는 점에서 저희를 기억하고 있었습니다. (그 결과, 그는 우리가 원하는 음료가 무엇인지 정확하게 알고 있었습니다.) 그는 또한 저희의 주문을, 그 주문은 다소 복잡한 것이었는데, 완벽하게 받아주었고, 그래서 저희는 저희가 정확히 원하는 음식을 받았습니다. 존은 항상 우리가 저녁 식사를 즐기고 있는지, 그리고 우리에게 필요한 것이 없는지를 확인했습니다.

하지만 가장 좋은 점은 저희가 주차장에 있을 때였습니다. 귀가를 하려고 막 차에 오르려고 하던 때에 존이 달려 나왔습니다. 보아하니, 제 남편이 지갑을 잊고 나왔습니다. 존은 그것을 발견해서 남편에게 돌려 주었습니다. 그는 남편이 주려고 한 20달러도 받지 않으려고 했습니다.

저는 귀하께서 존이 얼마나 훌륭한 직원인지 아시고 싶어할 것 같다고 생각했습니다. 저는 그가 귀하의 식당에서 오래 머무르기를 바라며, 저희가 그곳에서 식사를 할 때에는 항상 그가 우리의 웨이터가 될 수 있도록 부탁을 드리겠습니다.

헤더 마이어스 드림

1

[번역]

편지의 목적은 무엇인가?
(A) 불쾌한 일을 설명하기 위해
(B) 사과를 요청하기 위해
(C) 직원을 칭찬하기 위해
(D) 식사를 높이 평가하기 위해

[해설]

편지 전반에 걸쳐 골든 타임즈(Golden Times)라는 식당의 존이라는 종업원의 서비스에 대해 칭찬을 하고 있다. 따라서 정답은 (C)이다.

[어휘]

unpleasant 불쾌한 | compliment 칭찬하다

2

[번역]

마이어스 씨에 의해 무엇이 암시되는가?
(A) 그녀는 집에서 저녁 식사를 하는 것을 좋아하지 않는다.
(B) 그녀는 앞으로도 골든 타임즈를 방문할 생각이다.
(C) 여러 차례 존이 그녀의 웨이터였다.
(D) 그녀는 골든 타임즈의 낮은 가격을 좋아한다.

[해설]

편지의 마지막 부분, I definitely will request that he be our server whenever we dine there에서 마이어스 씨는 앞으로도 골든 타임즈를 방문할 의사가 있음을 내비치고 있다. 따라서 정답은 (B)이다.

[어휘]

intend to ~할 의도이다, ~할 의향이 있다

3

[번역]

[1], [2], [3], [4] 중에서 다음 문장이 들어갈 곳으로 가장 적합한 곳은 어디인가?
"그 결과, 그는 우리가 원하는 음료가 무엇인지 정확하게 알고 있었습니다."
(A) [1]
(B) [2]
(C) [3]
(D) [4]

[해설]

주어진 문장의 as a result는 원인과 결과를 연결시킬 때 주로 사용되는 표현이다. 따라서 주어진 문장은 자신들이 원하는 음료를 가져다 줄 수 있었던 이유 혹은 원인이 될 수 있는 John remembered us from the previous time we visited라는 문장 뒤에 오는 것이 가장 자연스럽다.

DAY 15 타동사 어휘 연습 / 복합 지문 p.197

PART 5

[정답]

> **1** (A) **2** (B) **3** (B) **4** (D)
> **5** (B) **6** (A) **7** (C) **8** (B)

1

[번역]

직원들은 모든 여행 경비를 확인해서 재무부서에 보고해야 한다.

[해설]

'모든 여행 경비를 ______ 해서 보고해야 한다'라는 문맥에 적합한 어휘는 (A) verify(확인하다)이다. (B) renew(갱신하다), (C) display(전시하다), (D) compile(편집하다)은 문맥에 어울리지 않는다.

[어휘]

expense 경비 | report to ~에게 보고하다 | Financial Department 재무부서 | verify 확인하다

2

[번역]

그 확장은 우리가 더 많은 고객들에게 훨씬 더 나은 서비스를 제공 가능하게 할 것입니다.

[해설]

'그 확장은 고객들에게 더 나은 서비스를 제공 ______ 할 것이다'라는 문맥에 적합한 어휘는 (B) enable(가능하게 하다)이다. (A) demonstrate(시연하다), (C) prohibit(금지시키다), (D) compare(비교하다)는 문맥에 어울리지 않는다.

[어휘]

expansion 확장 | offer 제공하다 | customer 고객 | even 훨씬

3

[번역]

이스턴 건설사는 그 계획된 건설 프로젝트의 진척상황을 감독하기를 원한다.

[해설]

'그 계획된 건설 프로젝트의 진척상황을 ______ 하기를 원한다'라는 문맥에 적합한 어휘는 (B) oversee(감독하다)이다. (A) implement(시행하다)와 (D) surpass(초과하다)는 문맥에 어울리지 않는다. (C) assist는 사람을 목적어로 취하며, 사물을 받을 때는 'assist with 사물'로 쓰인다.

[어휘]

progress 진척상황 | planned 계획된 | construction 건설 | oversee 감독하다

4

[번역]

우리는 야외에서 잃어버린 귀중품에 대해 어떠한 책임도 지지 않습니다.

[해설]

'야외에서 잃어버린 귀중품에 대해 어떠한 책임도 ______지 않습

니다'라는 문맥에 적합한 어휘는 '책임이 있음을 받아들이다'는 뜻인 (D) accept이다. (A) leave(놔두다), (B) remind(상기시키다), (C) resume(재개하다)는 문맥에 어울리지 않는다.

[어휘]

responsibility 책임 | valuables 귀중품 | lost 잃어버린 | outdoors 야외

5

[번역]

이 세미나는 합작투자에 대한 우려를 완화시키기 위해 만들어진 것이다.

[해설]

'세미나는 우려를 ＿＿＿ 시키기 위해 만들어진 것이다'라는 문맥에 적합한 어휘는 (B) alleviate(완화시키다)이다. (A) hesitate(주저하다), (C) deteriorate(나빠지다), (D) exceed(초과하다, 능가하다)는 문맥에 어울리지 않는다.

[어휘]

designed 고안된 | concerns 걱정, 우려 | joint venture 합작투자 | alleviate 완화시키다

6

[번역]

냉장 컨테이너로 야채를 운송하는 것은 신선도를 유지하는 데 도움이 된다.

[해설]

'냉장 컨테이너로 야채를 운송하는 것은 신선도를 ＿＿＿ 하는 데 도움이 된다'라는 문맥에 적합한 어휘는 (A) retain(유지하다)이다. (B) purchase(구매하다), (C) undergo(겪다), (D) diversify(다양화하다)는 문맥에 어울리지 않는다.

[어휘]

ship 운송하다 | vegetables 야채 | refrigerated 냉장된 | container 컨테이너 | freshness 신선함 | retain 유지하다

7

[번역]

그 보고서는 도로 공사가 경제의 전반적인 발전에 영향을 준다는 것을 보여준다.

[해설]

'도로 공사가 전반적인 발전에 ＿＿＿ 한다'라는 문맥에 적합한 어휘는 (C) influence(영향을 주다)이다. (A) relocate(이전하다), (B) respond(응답하다), (D) dilute(희석하다)는 문맥에 어울리지 않는다.

[어휘]

report 보고서 | show 보여주다 | extensive 전반적인 | development 발전 | economy 경제

8

[번역]

대부분의 조직들은 연구 사업을 위한 자금을 마련하기 위해 일련의 행사들을 개최했다.

[해설]

'자금을 ＿＿＿ 하기 위해 일련의 행사들을 개최했다'라는 문맥에 적합한 어휘는 (B) raise(마련하다)이다. (A) adopt(채택하다), (C)

inform(알리다), (D) attribute(~탓으로 여기다)는 문맥에 어울리지 않는다.

[어휘]

organization 조직 | hold 열다 | a series of 일련의 | event 행사 | fund 기금 | research 연구

[정답]

1 (D)	**2** (B)	**3** (B)	**4** (B)	**5** (A)
6 (A)	**7** (D)	**8** (B)	**9** (B)	**10** (A)

1-5

[번역]

수신: 조셉 콘 〈josephcohn@northstarfood.com〉
발신: 캘빈 매스터즈 〈cmasters@sdaa-con.com〉
제목: 캘리포니아 농업 컨퍼런스 후원

콘 씨 귀하,

샌디에이고 농업 협회(SDAA)를 대표해 올해 10월 10일부터 12일까지 개최될 캘리포니아 농업 컨퍼런스에 등록해 주신 노스 스타 푸드 사에 진심으로 감사를 드립니다.

노스 스타 푸드 사의 수석 마케팅 이사인 귀하께서는 캘리포니아 농업 컨퍼런스가 캘리포니아의 선두 농업 생산자와 소매자들을 한 곳에 불러 모은다는 것을 알고 계실 것입니다. 또한 참석하는 회사들이 컨퍼런스의 다른 부분들을 후원할 수 있는 완벽한 기회이기도 합니다.

따라서 SDAA는 귀사가 올해 킨퍼런스의 후원사가 되기를 부탁드리는 바입니다. 귀사의 참여를 다음의 후원금 레벨과 혜택은 위해 알려드립니다.

브론즈 스폰서 – $1,000
- 컨퍼런스 프로그램에 브론즈 후원사로 등록됨
- 마지막 날 연회에 참석 가능

실버 스폰서 – $1,500
- 브론즈 스폰서와 동등한 혜택
- 컨퍼런스 패키지에 자사 브로셔 첨부 가능

골드 스폰서 – $2,500
- 실버 스폰서와 동등한 혜택
- 모든 프리젠테이션 룸 사용 가능

추가 세부사항 문의나 후원 계약을 위해서는 전화 (914) 324-5353이나 이메일 cmasters@sdaa-con.com으로 제게 연락 주십시오.

올해 캘리포니아 농업 컨퍼런스에 참여해 주셔서 다시 한 번 감사 드립니다.

캘빈 매스터즈 드림
컨퍼런스 책임자
캘리포니아 농업 컨퍼런스

[어휘]

agricultural 농업의 | sponsorship 보증인[스폰서]임, 후원 |
on behalf of 남을 대신[대표]해서 | association 협회 | express
표현하다, 말로 나타내다 | sincere 성실한, 진심에서 우러난 | gratitude
감사 | registration 등록 | chief 최고의, 제1위의 | executive 임원,
이사 | leading 인도하는, 선행하는 | producer 생산자 | retailer
소매상인 | location 위치, 장소 | ideal 이상적인 | opportunity 기회 |
participate 참여하다 | element 요소, 부분 | accordingly 따라서,
그래서 | invite 부탁하다[요구하다] | following 다음의, 다음에 오는 |
benefit 혜택 | acknowledgement 인정, 승인 | banquet 연회 |
allow 허락하다, 허가하다 | insert 삽입하다, 끼워[집어] 넣다 | contact
연락하다 | additional 추가의 | detail 세부사항 | arrange (일을)
처리하다, 조처하다 | coordinator 책임자, 코디네이터

[번역]

> 수신: 캘빈 매스터즈 〈cmasters@sdaa-con.com〉
> 발신: 조셉 콘 〈josephcohn@northstarfood.com〉
> 제목: 답장: 캘리포니아 농업 컨퍼런스 후원
>
> 매스터즈 씨 귀하,
>
> 저희 노스 스타 푸드는 신중히 생각한 끝에 캘리포니아 농업 컨퍼
> 런스의 실버 스폰서가 되기로 결정하였으며 이를 귀하께 알려 드
> 리게 되어 기쁩니다. 귀하의 이메일에서 언급된 바와 같이 이는 노
> 스 스타의 브랜드명을 참석한 업체들에게 널리 홍보할 수 있는 이
> 상적인 기회로 저희는 이를 놓치고 싶지 않습니다.
>
> 후원금 지불 내역에 관한 세부사항을 제공해 주시면 감사하겠
> 습니다. 저는 다음주 내내 사무실에 있지 않을 것이므로 제 비서
> 데이비드 애덤스 (전화: 914-252-8329, 이메일: dadams@
> northstarfood.com)에게 이 내용을 알려주십시오.
>
> 조셉 콘 드림

[어휘]

careful 주의 깊은, 조심성 있는 | consideration 고려, 고찰 | mention
언급하다 | promote 홍보하다 | brand 상표, 브랜드 | miss 놓치다 |
provide 제공하다 | payment 지불 금액 | grateful 고맙게 생각하는,
감사하는 | forward 보내다, 발송하다 | assistant 보조, 비서

1
[번역]

캘빈 매스터즈는 왜 조셉 콘에게 이메일을 썼는가?
(A) 스폰서 등록을 확인하기 위해
(B) 최고의 스폰서 회사를 알리기 위해
(C) 기업들에게 소기업 지원을 권장하기 위해
(D) 스폰서 기회를 소개하기 위해

[해설]

캘빈 매스터즈가 조셉 콘에게 쓴 첫 번째 이메일을 확인해야 한다. 글
의 목적을 내용을 파악한 뒤에 찾을 수 있으므로 다소 주의가 필요하
다. 이메일 전반부에서는 컨퍼런스에 등록해 준 회사에 감사의 말을 전
하고 있으며, 중반부에서는 컨퍼런스에서 제공하는 후원제도를 소개
하며 참여 회사가 이 후원사가 될 것을 권유(Accordingly, the SDAA
would like to invite your company to become a sponsor of this year's
conference)하고 있으므로 이메일의 목적은 (D)가 적절하다.

[어휘]

confirm 확인하다 | announce 발표하다, 알리다 | encourage 권장하다

2
[번역]

캘빈 매스터즈는 컨퍼런스에 대해 무엇을 암시하는가?
(A) 참석률이 과거 몇 년 동안 높아지고 있다.
(B) 주요 업계 대표들이 참석한다.
(C) 컨퍼런스 운영 비용이 매우 높다.
(D) 몇몇 유명 초대 연사들이 참석할 것이다.

[해설]

캘빈 매스터즈가 쓴 첫 번째의 이메일의 둘째 단락 중 you know the
Californian Agricultural Conference brings together California's
leading agricultural producers and retailers in one location에서
이 컨퍼런스에는 선두 농업계 종사자들이 참석한다고 했으므로
leading agricultural producers and retailers를 important industry
representatives로 바꾼 (B)가 정답이다.

[어휘]

representative 대표 | operate 운영하다 | guest speaker 초대 연사

3
[번역]

브론즈 스폰서가 갖지 않는 어떤 혜택을 실버 스폰서는 갖는가?
(A) 주요 컨퍼런스 프로그램에 등록된다.
(B) 컨퍼런스 참석자들에게 브로셔를 배포할 수 있다.
(C) 모든 프리젠테이션 룸을 이용할 수 있다.
(D) 마지막 날 연회에서 연설을 할 수 있다.

[해설]

각각의 스폰서에 대한 설명이 있는 첫 번째 이메일에서 Silver
Sponsor와 Bronze Sponsor를 지문에서 주의 깊게 대조하며 정답을 찾
아야 한다. 브론즈 스폰서는 컨퍼런스 프로그램에 등록되며 (You will
be listed as a Bronze Sponsor in the conference program) 마지막 날
연회에 참석할 수 있다(Acknowledgement during the final banquet)
고 했는데, 실버 스폰서는 브론즈 스폰서의 모든 혜택을 받을 수 있다
(All the benefits of a Bronze Sponsor)고 했으므로 (A)와 (D)는 차이
점이라고 할 수 없다. 실버 스폰서는 컨퍼런스 패키지에 자사 브로셔
를 첨부할 수 있다(Allowed to insert your company's brochures in the
conference packages)고 했으므로 이를 적절히 paraphrase한 (B)가 정
답이다. (C)는 골드 스폰서에 관한 내용이므로 오답이다.

[어휘]

distribute 분배하다, 나누어 주다 | deliver an address 연설하다

4
[번역]

노스 스타 푸드는 얼마의 후원금을 지불할 것인가?
(A) 1,000달러
(B) 1,500달러
(C) 2,000달러
(D) 2,500달러

[해설]

두 번째 이메일 도입부 중 it is a pleasure to inform you that North
Star Food has decided to become a Silver Sponsor of the Californian
Agricultural Conference에서 노스 스타 푸드는 실버 스폰서가 되기로
결정했다는 내용이 나온다. 앞선 이메일에서 실버 스폰서는 1,500달러

를 지불할 것(Silver Sponsor - $1,500)이라고 했으므로 이 두 가지 내용을 종합하여 (B)를 정답으로 찾을 수 있다.

5

[번역]

데이비드 애덤스는 어떤 정보를 매스터즈 씨에게서 받을 것인가?
(A) 후원금 지불 방법에 관한 세부내역
(B) 컨퍼런스 센터에 가는 길 안내
(C) 이용 가능한 숙박시설 목록
(D) 예정된 초대 연사들의 프로필

[해설]

조셉 콘은 매스터즈 씨에게 후원금 지불에 관한 세부사항을 제공해 줄 것(If you could provide payment details for sponsorship)을 요청한다. 다음 문장에서 이를 자신의 비서인 데이비드 애덤스에게 보내달라고 (please forward this information to my assistant, David Adams) 말하므로 정답은 (A)임을 알 수 있다.

[어휘]

directions 길 안내 | available 이용 가능한 | accommodations 숙박시설 | profile 인물 소개, 프로필

6-10

[번역]

기계 공학자 협회가 미니애폴리스에서 컨퍼런스를 개최합니다

최근 회의에서, 기계 공학자 협회(SME)는 투표를 통해 연례 컨퍼런스를 미네소타의 미니애폴리스에서 개최하기로 결정했습니다. 컨퍼런스는 3월 10일부터 12일까지 진행될 것입니다. 평소와 마찬가지로, 여러 행사들이 진행될 것인데, 여기에는 세미나, 연설, 워크숍, 그리고 국제 취업 박람회가 포함됩니다. 또한 개인들이 자신의 연구 논문을 발표할 수 있는 기회도 많이 있을 것입니다. 컨퍼런스에 관해 그리고 어떻게 참여하는지에 관한 정보가 더 필요하시면, 저희 웹사이트인 www.sme.org를 방문해 주십시오. 두어 곳외 국적 항공사뿐만 아니라 몇몇 지역 호텔과 렌터카 회사들도 참석자들에게 최대 40%의 할인을 제공하기로 동의해 주었습니다. 이러한 기업에 관한 전체 리스트는 웹사이트에서 얻으실 수 있습니다. 컨퍼런스의 참가비는 SME 회원인 경우 50달러이며, 비회원인 경우에는 120달러입니다. 티켓은 정문에서 구입이 가능하기 때문에 사전 등록은 필요하지 않습니다. 저희는 다가오는 행사에서 모든 회원분들을 - 그리고 다른 분들도 - 뵐 수 있기를 기대합니다.

[어휘]

vote 투표하다 | as usual 평소대로 | job fair 채용 박람회 | numerous 많은 | opportunity 기회 | research paper 연구 논문 | national airline 국적 항공사 | up to ~까지 | preregistration 사전 등록

[번역]

기계 공학자 협회
연례 컨퍼런스
등록 양식

성명: 피터 도슨
이메일 주소: petedawson@arlingtonconstruction.com
전화번호: (205) 402-5648

SME 자격: [V] 회원　　[ ] 비회원
회원 번호: 59430

등록비: [V] 지불　　[ ] 미지불
결제 수단: [ ] 현금　　[V] 수표　　[ ] 신용 카드

참석 예정일: [V] 3월 10일　　[V] 3월 11일　　[V] 3월 12일

호텔 예약에 도움이 필요하신가요? [ ] yes　　[V] no

차량 예약에 도움이 필요하신가요? [ ] yes　　[V] no

[번역]

받는 사람: 비공개 수신인
보낸 사람: haroldsmith@sme.org
제목: SME 콘퍼런스
날짜: 3월 5일

친애하는 SME 회원님께,

여러분 모두에게 다음 주 컨퍼런스가 취소되었다는 점을 알리게 되어 대단히 송구스럽게 생각합니다. 최근 미니애폴리스 지역의 궂은 날씨로 미니애폴리스 시민 회관에 큰 피해가 발생했는데, 이곳은 컨퍼런스 장소로 예정되어 있던 곳이었습니다. 어제, 시의 엔지니어들이 건물을 조사했고, 그곳의 구조적 안정성이 손상을 입었다는 점을 밝혀냈습니다. 따라서, 수리가 이루어지기 전까지는 그 건물에서 더 이상 행사가 허락되지 않습니다.

저희는 이와 같은 일이 일어날 수도 있다고 예상을 했기 때문에, 미니애폴리스와 인근 세인트폴 모두에서 대체를 할만한 장소를 물색해 보았습니다. 안타깝게도, 저희가 살펴본 장소는 모두 예약이 차 있습니다.

킨퍼런스 등록비를 지불하신 모든 분들께서는 늦어도 3월 15일까지 환불을 받으실 것입니다. 호텔, 차량, 혹은 항공기 예약에 관한 환불을 받는데 도움이 필요하신 경우에는, 저희에게 연락을 주십시오.

충분한 수의 회원님들께서 여름의 또 한 번의 행사에 기꺼이 참석하시겠다고 의견을 주시는 경우, 저희는 그때 일정을 잡도록 하겠습니다. 이 이메일에 답신을 하셔서 여름에 시간이 되시는지 그리고 언제 시간이 되시는지 저희에게 알려 주시기 바랍니다.

다시 한 번 말씀을 드리지만, 저희 SME는 이번 불상사에 대해 사과를 드리고자 합니다.

SME 회장 해럴드 스미스 드림

[어휘]

regret 후회, 유감 | inclement 궂은 | examine 검사하다 | structural integrity 구조적 안정성 | permit 허락하다, 허가하다 | anticipate 예상하다 | venue 장소 | reimburse 보상하다, 변제하다 | willingness 기꺼이 하고자 함

6

[번역]

컨퍼런스에 대해 무엇이 암시되고 있는가?
(A) 작년에도 개최되었다.

(B) SME 회원이 아닌 사람은 거의 참석하지 않는다.
(C) SME를 위한 수익 사업이다.
(D) 매년 미니애폴리스에서 열린다.

[해설]

첫 번째 지문에서 이번 행사를 annual conference라고 소개하고 있으므로 컨퍼런스는 매년 열리는 행사임을 알 수 있다.

[어휘]

previous 이전의 | profitable 수익성이 있는

7

[번역]

컨퍼런스에서 진행되지 않는 것은 무엇인가?
(A) 워크숍
(B) 채용 박람회
(C) 세미나
(D) 무역 박람회

[해설]

첫 번째 지문에서 다양한 행사에 대해 이야기하고 있는 부분(including seminars, speeches, workshops, and an international job fair)을 주의해서 살펴본다. 여기에서 '무역 박람회'에 관한 행사는 언급되지 않고 있다.

8

[번역]

도슨 씨는 컨퍼런스 등록을 위해 얼마를 지불했는가?
(A) 40달러
(B) 50달러
(C) 100달러
(D) 120달러

[해설]

첫 번째 지문에서 입장료는 회원인 경우 50달러, 비회원인 경우는 120달러라고 말했다. 두 번째 지문인 신청서를 보면, 이를 작성한 피터 도슨이 회원 여부란에 '회원'이라고 표시했으므로 그가 낸 금액은 50달러일 것으로 생각할 수 있다.

9

[번역]

이메일의 목적은 무엇인가?
(A) 컨퍼런스 장소가 다른 도시로 바뀌는 이유를 설명하기 위해
(B) 컨퍼런스의 취소를 알리기 위해
(C) 컨퍼런스가 연기되었다고 말하기 위해
(D) 환불은 되지 않을 것이라고 언급하기 위해

[해설]

이메일의 첫 문장, It is with great regret that I must inform you all that next week's conference has been canceled.에서 편지의 목적이 행사의 취소 통보임을 명확히 밝히고 있다.

10

[번역]

스미스 씨는 사람들이 무엇을 할 것을 요청하는가?
(A) 올해 중 추후에 컨퍼런스에 올 수 있는지 말한다
(B) 컨퍼런스 장소를 대체할 수 있는 곳을 제안한다

(C) 등록비에 대해 환불을 요청한다
(D) 세인트폴에서 열리는 행사에 간다

[해설]

이메일 후반부의 Please respond to this e-mail and inform us if and when you have time in the summer.라는 문장에서 스미스 씨는 회원들에게 여름에 컨퍼런스를 개최하면 참가를 할 수 있는지를 자신에게 알려 달라고 부탁하고 있다.

DAY 16 수량형용사와 수 일치 p.202

PART 5

[정답]

| 1 (C) | 2 (A) | 3 (D) | 4 (C) |
| 5 (B) | 6 (B) | 7 (C) | 8 (C) |

1

[번역]

그 사무실로 이전한 이후에, 컴퓨터에 몇 가지 이상을 경험하기 시작했다.

[해설]

빈칸 다음이 복수 명사 malfunctions(고장)이므로 복수 명사와 함께 쓰는 수량형용사 (C) a few(몇몇의)가 정답이다. (A) a little(약간의)과 (B) much(많은)는 불가산 명사 앞에 쓰고 (D) every(모든)는 단수 명사 앞에 쓴다.

[어휘]

move to ~로 이사 가다 | experience 경험하다 | a few 몇 몇의 | malfunction 고장

2

[번역]

있을 수 있는 결함을 막기 위해 모든 조치들이 취해져야 한다는 것을 알고 있어야 합니다.

[해설]

빈칸 다음이 복수 명사 measures(조치)이므로 복수 명사와 함께 쓰는 수량형용사 (A) all(모든)이 정답이다. (B) every(모든)는 단수 명사 앞에, (C) much(많은)는 불가산 명사 앞에 쓴다. (D) almost(거의)는 부사이므로 명사 앞에 쓸 수 없다.

[어휘]

aware 인식하는 | measures 조치 | implement 시행하다 | in order to ~하기 위해서 | prevent 막다 | possible 있을 수 있는 | defect 결함

3

[번역]

몇몇의 연구가들이 회사의 필요성에 맞추기 위해 새 컴퓨터 시스템을 고안했다.

[해설]

빈칸 앞에 복수 명사와 함께 쓰는 수량 형용사 several(몇몇의)이 있으

므로 정답은 복수 명사인 (D) researchers(연구가들)이다. 단수형인 (A) research, 동명사인 (B) researching, 단수형인 (C) researcher는 불가하다.

[어휘]

several 몇몇의 | suit 맞다, 적합하게 하다 | need 필요(성) | research 연구, 조사; 연구하다

4

[번역]

몇몇의 판매 직원들이 제품 시연을 보기 위해 로비에 모였다.

[해설]

빈칸 앞의 주어가 복수인 A few sales representatives(몇몇의 영업사원들)이므로 복수 동사가 필요하다. 따라서 정답은 (C) have이다. 3인칭 단수 동사형인 (A) has, (B) is, (D) was는 불가하다

[어휘]

a few 몇 몇의 | sales 판매 | representative 직원 | gather 모이다 | product 제품 | demonstration 시연

5

[번역]

많은 직원들이 회사가 제공하는 집중적인 트레이닝에 참여했다.

[해설]

빈칸 앞의 주어가 복수인 A number of employees(많은 직원들)이므로 복수 동사가 필요하다. 따라서 정답은 (B) have taken이다. 3인칭 단수 동사형인 (A) has taken, (C) takes, (D) is taken은 불가하다.

[어휘]

a number of 많은 | employee 직원 | take part in 참여하다 | intensive 집중적인 | session (특정 활동을 위한) 시간, 강습 | provide 제공하다

6

[번역]

그 절차에 대한 싱사의 지식은 직원들이 심각한 기술적인 문제를 해결하는 것을 도울 수 있게 한다.

[해설]

빈칸의 주어가 단수 The supervisor's knowledge이므로 빈칸은 3인칭 단수 동사 자리이다. 따라서 정답은 (B) enables(가능하게 하다)이다. 3인칭 단수 동사 자리에 (A) enable, (C) enabling, (D) to enable는 불가하다

[어휘]

supervisor 상사 | knowledge of ~에 대한 지식 | procedure 절차 | resolve 해결하다 | serious 심각한 | technical 기술적인

7

[번역]

윌리엄 씨의 연구 결과들이 지난주에 마침내 출판되었을 때 그는 매우 기쁜 것처럼 보였다.

[해설]

빈칸 뒤에 동사가 복수 동사인 were이므로 빈칸은 복수 주어가 올 자리이다. 따라서 정답은 복수인 (C) results(결과들)이다. 복수 명사가 올 자리에 (A) result, (B) resulting, (D) resulted는 불가하다.

[어휘]

several 몇몇의 | suit 맞다, 적합하게 하다

8

[번역]

그 직책의 고려 대상이 되기 위해서는 관련 분야에 높은 수준의 전문지식을 보여주는 것이 요구된다.

[해설]

동사가 3인칭 단수인 is required(요구되다)이므로 '______ a high level of expertise in related fields'를 주어로 만들어야 한다. 주어 자리에 올 수 있는 동사 형태는 동명사이므로 정답은 (C) Demonstrating(보여주는 것)이다.

[어휘]

expertise 전문지식 | related 연관된 | field 분야 | in order to-V ~하기 위해 | considered 고려되는, 중히 여겨지는 | position 직책 | demonstrate 보여주다

PART 6

[정답]

1 (B)　　**2** (B)　　**3** (C)　　**4** (A)

1-4

[번역]

> ### 보수 공사로 인해 리딩 교가 폐쇄됩니다
>
> (리딩 교가 폐쇄되었습니다.) 이 다리는 바지선이 다리에 충돌한 10월 8일에 피해를 입었습니다. 다리의 일부 부분이, 교량 하나를 포함하여, 광범위한 피해를 입었습니다. 이 다리는 교통에 안전하지 않은 것으로 발표되었습니다. 다리의 보수 공사는 10월 12일에 시작될 예정입니다. 공사가 끝나기까지는 최소한 한 달이 걸릴 것으로 예상됩니다. 이 기간 동안, 웨스트 강을 건너기 위해서는 운전자들이 우회 도로를 찾아야 합니다. 햄프턴 교와 실버 교 모두가 인근에 위치해 있습니다. 리딩 교가 다시 개통될 때까지, 운전자들은 이러한 다리나 기타 다리를 이용할 것이 권장됩니다. 리딩 교와 관련된 질문이 있으신 경우에는, 근무 시간 중에 423-3030으로 전화를 주십시오.

[어휘]

barge 바지선 | collide with ~와 충돌하다 | extensive 광범위한, 넓은 | seek 찾다, 추구하다 | nearby 인근의, 근처의 | regular 정규의

1

[해설]

다리 폐쇄에 관한 소식을 전하고 있다. 따라서 첫 문장으로 들어가기에 가장 알맞은 문장이면서 빈칸 이후의 The bridge가 가리키는 대상을 언급하고 있는 문장이 정답이다. 보기 중에서는 '리딩 교가 폐쇄되었다'고 언급한 (B)가 정답으로서 가장 적절하다.

[어휘]

steadily 꾸준하게 | toll 통행료 | charge 부과하다

2

[해설]

'통행에 안전하지 않다고 발표되다'라는 의미를 전하기 위해서는 빈칸에 declared가 들어가야 한다. announce도 '발표하다'라는 의미를 가지고 있지만, 공중을·대상으로 하는 공식적인 발표의 의미는 주로 declare를 이용하여 나타낸다.

[어휘]

declare 선언하다, 공포하다 | state 진술하다, 주장하다 | announce 발표하다

3

[해설]

빈칸에는 명사 ways를 수식할 수 있는 형용사가 들어가야 하는데, '우회 도로'라는 의미는 alternate way로 나타낼 수 있다. 따라서 정답은 (C)이다.

[어휘]

alternately 번갈아, 교대로 | alternate 교대의, 교체의; 우회의

4

[해설]

내용상 '다른 다리들을 이용할 것이 권장된다'는 의미가 완성되어야 한다. 보기 중 그러한 의미를 완성시키는 것은 '재촉하다' 혹은 '권장하다'라는 의미를 지닌 (A) urged이다.

[어휘]

urge 재촉하다, 촉구하다; 권하다 | approve 승인하다 | inform 알리다

DAY **17** 비교급과 최상급   p.207

PART 5

[정답]

1 (B)	2 (C)	3 (C)	4 (D)
5 (B)	6 (D)	7 (C)	8 (D)

1

[번역]

이 새 컴퓨터는 우리가 몇 년 전 구매했던 예전 컴퓨터보다 더 효율적이다.

[해설]

빈칸 뒤에 비교급과 함께 쓰이는 than이 있으므로 정답은 비교급인 (B) more efficient(더 효율적인)이다.

[어휘]

efficient 효율적인 | purchase 구매하다

2

[번역]

우리 제품이 시판되고 있는 제품들 가운데 가장 뛰어나서 자랑스럽다.

[해설]

빈칸 앞에 정관사 the가 있고 빈칸 뒤의 of any available products(이용가능한 모든 제품 중에서)도 셋 이상을 나타내므로 정답은 최상급인 (C) best(가장 좋은)이다.

[어휘]

proud 자랑스러운 | product 제품 | available 이용할 수 있는 | on the market 시판되고 있는

3

[번역]

이 프로젝트는 우리 부서가 맡아왔던 것 중에서 가장 도전 의식을 북돋는 일이다.

[해설]

뒤에 assignment(일)를 꾸미는 관계사절에 최상급과 함께 쓰는 ever(이때까지 ~한 중에서)이 있으므로 정답은 최상급인 (C) the most challenging(가장 도전 의식을 북돋는)이다.

[어휘]

challenging 도전 의식을 북돋는, 도전적인 | assignment 일, 업무 | department 부서 | undertake (일 따위를) 맡다

4

[번역]

상환하기가 힘들면 힘들수록 더 많은 은행들이 심각한 손실을 입는다.

[해설]

앞에 'the + 비교급(The harder)'가 있으므로 뒤에도 'the + 비교급'인 (D) more가 와야 한다.

[어휘]

hard 힘든 | repay 상환하다 | suffer 겪다 | loss 손실

5

[번역]

나는 김 씨가 일주일 전에 한 제안이 단연코 가장 좋다고 생각한다.

[해설]

빈칸 앞에 최상급을 강조할 때 쓰는 by far(단연코)가 있으므로 정답은 최상급인 (B) the best(가장 좋은)이다.

[어휘]

suggestion 제안 | give 주다 | by far 단연코

6

[번역]

챈 씨는 부서 예산을 감시하는데 있어 가장 탁월한 직원들 중 한명이었다.

[해설]

앞에 one of the가 있으므로 빈칸은 최상급 자리이다. 따라서 정답은 (D) most이다.

[어휘]

outstanding 탁월한 | employee 직원 | monitor 감시하다 | in -ing ~할 때 | budget 예산

7

[번역]

비난을 피하기 위해 가능하면 빨리 배상금이 지불될 것이다.

[해설]

빈칸 앞이 완전한 수동태 문장이므로 빈칸에는 부사가 올 자리이다. 따라서 정답은 (C) quickly(빨리)이다.

[어휘]

reimbursement 상환(금), 배상(금) | pay 지불하다 | in order to-V ~하기 위해서 | avoid 피하다 | criticism 비판, 비난

8

[번역]

위험한 도로 상황이 운전이 훨씬 더 쉬워지는 것을 막는 것 같다.

[해설]

빈칸 뒤에 비교급 easier(더 쉬운)이 있으므로 비교급 강조 부사 (D) far(훨씬)이다. '매우'라는 뜻으로 쓰이는 부사인 (A) very, (B) so, (C) too는 원급과 함께 쓴다.

[어휘]

likely 가능성 있는 | hazardous 위험한 | road conditions 도로 상황 | prevent A from -ing A가 – 하는 것을 막다 | driving 운전

PART 7

[정답]

1 (A)　**2** (B)　**3** (D)

1-3

[번역]

LZR-테크, 창사 이래 최대 규모의 리콜 시행

LZR-테크가 인기 높은 잔디깎기기계 모델들 중 하나에 대해 전국적인 리콜을 발표했다. 회사 직원들은 올해 5월부터 8월 사이에 판매된 LZR-테크 A32 잔디깎기기계 구입품 전량을 회수하고 있다.

회사에서 발표한 보도 자료에 따르면, 이 A32 모델은 미승인 부품으로 제조되었다. 디트로이트에 있는 LZR-테크 공장에 국한된 것으로 여겨지는 이 실수는 부품에 라벨을 잘못 붙인 탓으로 벌어진 일이다. 이 공장에서는 여러 해외 상품도 제조하고 있기에, 5월부터 8월 사이에 제조된 A32 모델에 필요보다 큰 규모의 연료 탱크가 들어가는 실수가 생긴 것이다.

회사 측에서는 A32 모델이 대중의 안전에 아무런 위협도 없지만, 고객 서비스를 개선하려는 차원에서, 해당 모델을 회수한다고 주장한다. 상기 언급된 기간에 A32 모델을 구입한 고객은 회사 웹사이트를 방문해 기기 시리얼 번호와 청구서를 제출하면 된다. 현재 소유 중인 결함 제품의 상태에 무관하게 LZR-테크는 새 제품을 보낼 것이며, 신청일로부터 7일 정도 걸린다고 추정하고 있다.

[어휘]

issue 선언[공포]하다 | recall (결함 상품 따위의)회수/회수하다 | country-wide 전국적인, 전국에 걸친 | lawn mower 잔디 깎는 기계 | representative 직원 | obtain 획득하다 | according to ~에 따르면 | press release 보도 자료 | manufacture 제조하다 | unapproved 허가되지 않은 | component 부품 | confine 국한시키다 | occur 일어나다, 발생하다 | as a result of ~의 결과로서 | mislabel 라벨을 잘못 붙이다 | part 부품 | oversight 실수 | be fitted with 설비가 갖추어 지다 | claim 주장하다; 주장, 청구, 신청 | risk 위험(요소) | in an effort to ~하려는 노력으로 | time frame 기간 | along with ~와 함께 | replacement 교체(품) | regardless of ~에 상관없이 | condition 상태 | defective 결함이 있는 | estimate 추산[추정]하다 | approximately 거의, 대략

1

[번역]

LZR-테크 A32에 대해 뭐라고 언급되는가?

(A) 디트로이트에서 제조되었다.

(B) 최근 개발된 제품이다.

(C) 더 이상 구입하지 못할 것이다.

(D) 구입 시기와 무관하게 회수될 것이다.

[해설]

본 지문이 핵심 어구 'LZR-Tech A32'의 회수 문제에 대한 기사임을 파악하고 살펴 보면, 둘째 문단의 believed to be confined to the Detroit LZR-Tech factory를 통해 정답 (A)를 찾을 수 있다. 참고로, (D)는 time of purchase 대신 condition이어야 적절한 설명이 된다.

[어휘]

no longer 더 이상 ~않는

2

[번역]

A32 모델은 왜 회수될 것인가?

(A) 색이 잘못 되어서

(B) 틀린 부품으로 만들어져서

(C) 사용하기 위험해서

(D) 유해 화학물질이 포함되어서

[해설]

'회수 요인'이 포인트이다. 둘째 문단에서 the A32 models were manufactured with unapproved components라며 미승인 부품으로 제조되었다고 보도 자료를 인용하므로 unapproved components를 incorrect parts로 paraphrasing한 (B)가 정답이다.

[어휘]

incorrect 부정확한, 맞지 않는 | contain 포함하다 | harmful 해로운, 유해한 | chemical 화학물질

3

[번역]

고객들은 무엇을 준비해야 하는가?

(A) 모델 번호

(B) 구입 증빙서

(C) 설명 매뉴얼

(D) 시리얼 번호

[해설]

셋째 문단에서 해당 고객들은 웹사이트에 방문해 시리얼 번호와 청구서를 제출하라(Customers who have purchased an A32 model during the above mentioned time frame are asked to visit the company's website and submit a claim along with the machine's serial number)

고 한다. 따라서 정답은 (D)이다.

[어휘]

proof 증거, 증명 | instruction 설명, 지시

DAY **19-20** **Actual Test**　　　　　p.214

[정답]

101 (C)	102 (D)	103 (D)	104 (D)	105 (D)
106 (D)	107 (C)	108 (C)	109 (D)	110 (B)
111 (A)	112 (D)	113 (C)	114 (A)	115 (B)
116 (B)	117 (A)	118 (D)	119 (B)	120 (A)
121 (C)	122 (B)	123 (D)	124 (D)	125 (C)
126 (A)	127 (D)	128 (B)	129 (D)	130 (A)
131 (D)	132 (D)	133 (B)	134 (A)	135 (D)
136 (B)	137 (D)	138 (D)	139 (D)	140 (A)
141 (A)	142 (D)	143 (D)	144 (C)	145 (D)
146 (C)	147 (D)	148 (B)	149 (D)	150 (A)
151 (D)	152 (B)	153 (A)	154 (C)	155 (B)
156 (C)	157 (D)	158 (B)	159 (A)	160 (C)
161 (D)	162 (C)	163 (A)	164 (C)	165 (B)
166 (D)	167 (D)	168 (C)	169 (A)	170 (A)
171 (A)	172 (C)	173 (C)	174 (C)	175 (B)
176 (C)	177 (A)	178 (A)	179 (C)	180 (C)
181 (B)	182 (B)	183 (A)	184 (D)	185 (B)
186 (C)	187 (A)	188 (C)	189 (D)	190 (A)
191 (C)	192 (D)	193 (D)	194 (A)	195 (C)
196 (D)	197 (A)	198 (C)	199 (A)	200 (A)

PART 5

101

[번역]

10에서 20퍼센트의 비용을 절약할 수 있게 해주는 할인권이 제공될 것이다.

[해설]

문맥에 맞는 동사어휘를 찾는 문제이다. 본 문장에서 that은 discount coupons를 선행사로 하는 주격 관계대명사이고, that절 이하는 '할인 쿠폰은 당신이(목적어) 10에서 20퍼센트의 비용을 절약할 수 있도록 해 준다'라고 해석되므로 (C) allow(~을 가능하게 해주다)가 정답이다.

[어휘]

discount coupon 할인권 | provide 제공하다 | ranging from A to B A에서 B의 범위에 이르는 | promote 승진시키다 | accept 받아들이다 | give 주다

102

[번역]

레논 씨는 지난 달 말쯤 '직원들에게 동기를 부여하는 방법'이라는 제목의 세미나에 참가할 것을 부탁받았다.

[해설]

the end of last month 앞에 쓸 수 있는 전치사를 찾는 문제이다. toward 는 '~무렵'이라는 뜻으로 시간과 함께 쓰이며, toward the end of last month는 '지난 달 말쯤'이라고 해석된다.

[어휘]

be asked to ~을 부탁 받다, 요청 받다 | participate in ~에 참가하다 | seminar 세미나 | entitled ~라는 제목의 | regarding ~에 관해서 | against ~에 반대하여 | above ~보다 위에 | toward ~무렵

103

[번역]

모든 방문객과 배송 직원들은 어느 부서에 방문할지에 대해 먼저 경비 데스크에 알려야 한다.

[해설]

우선 department와 they 사이에는 목적격 관계대명사 that이 생략되었음을 파악할 수 있어야 한다. 그러므로 빈칸에는 department를 목적어로 취하는 동사가 필요하다. 방문객과 배송 직원들이 department에 대해 취할 수 있는 행동으로 (D) visiting(방문하다)가 가장 적합하다.

[어휘]

delivery 배송 | first 우선 | inform 알리다 | security 보안 | department 부(서) | accept 받아들이다 | request 요청하다 | count 세다

104

[번역]

금융산업 전문가들은 현재 투자 활동 감소에 관한 문제를 해결하고 있다.

[해설]

concerns(우려, 걱정거리)를 목적어로 받을 수 있는 동사어휘를 찾는 문제이다. '금융산업 전문가들이 현재 문제에 대처하고 있다'라는 해석이 자연스러우므로 (D)가 정답이 된다. 우리말로 보면 '~을 말하다'라는 뜻의 (C)도 답이 될 것 같지만 remark는 보통 'remark + that절' 또는 'remark + on/about+명사'의 형태로 쓰이므로 본 문장에서는 적절치 않다.

[어휘]

expert 전문가 | financial industry 금융 산업 | concern 근심, 걱정 | decline 감소 | investment 투자 | activity 활동 | exclaim ~이라고 외치다 | comment on ~에 대해 논평하다

105

[번역]

베어링 인더스트리즈는 업계의 가장 숙련되고 재능 있는 기술자들을 끌어들이는 가장 경쟁력 있는 급료를 현재 제시하고 있다.

[해설]

명사 salary를 수식하는 형용사를 묻는 문제이므로 '경쟁력 있는'이란 뜻의 형용사 (D) competitive가 정답이다. (A) competition(경쟁, 대회), (B) compete(경쟁하다), (C) competitors(경쟁 상대)는 정답으로 부적절하다.

[어휘]

currently 현재 | offer 제공하다 | salary 급료 | attract 끌다 |
industry 업계 | skilled 숙련된 | talented 재능 있는

106

[번역]

브라이언과 그의 팀이 베스트 디자인 상을 받아 기쁘기는 하지만, 우리는 아직도 그 상을 우리가 받았어야 한다고 생각한다.

[해설]

대명사의 알맞은 격을 찾는 문제이다. 콤마 다음의 that절의 구조를 보면 '주어(the award) + 동사(should have been) + 주격보어(_____)'의 문장이므로 the award와 빈칸은 'A=B'의 관계를 형성할 수 있는 단어가 필요하다. 내용상 '그 상이 우리 것이었어야 했다'가 되어야 타당하므로 소유대명사 (D)가 정답이다.

[어휘]

win the award for ~때문에 상을 받다 | believe 믿다, 생각하다

107

[번역]

정책 입안자들은 제한된 주택공급이 가격을 급격히 상승시키지 않게 하기 위해 대체 수단을 마련하고 있다.

[해설]

빈칸 앞뒤로 절이 있으므로 이를 연결하는 접속사가 들어가야 한다. 앞부분이 대안을 마련하고 있다는 내용이므로 뒷부분은 수단을 마련하는 이유나 목적을 제시하는 것이 자연스럽다. 그러므로 목적의 부사절을 이끄는 (C) so that(할 수 있도록)이 정답이다. (A) in order to 뒤에는 동사원형이 와야 하기 때문에 불가하다.

[어휘]

policy 정책 | come up with ~을 고안해 내다 | alternative 대안
| limited 제한된 | supply 공급 | drive up (가격, 값을) 끌어 올리다 |
sharply 급격히 | in order to ~하기 위하여 | because of ~ 때문에 |
so that ~할 수 있도록 | just as ~와 같이

108

[번역]

캠핑 무스는 훌륭한 야외 레저 서비스로 오랫동안 인정을 받아오고 있다.

[해설]

services를 수식하는 적절한 뜻의 형용사를 찾는 문제이므로 정답은 (C)가 된다. 참고로 여기서의 outstanding은 '훌륭한, 뛰어난' 이란 뜻이지만, '미지급된'이라는 뜻도 있어서 outstanding debts는 '미지급 채무'로 해석된다.

[어휘]

be recognized for ~로 인정받다 | outdoor 야외의 | leisure 여가,
레저 | approving 찬성하는 | magnified 확대된 | outstanding
뛰어난, 우수한; 미지급된 | hopeful 희망에 찬

109

[번역]

행운의 고객 단 한 명만 이번 주 경품인 일본 여행권 2매의 수혜자가 될 것입니다.

[해설]

정관사 the 뒤는 명사 자리이므로 형용사 (A) beneficial (유익한)은 바

로 제외된다. 나머지 보기 중 '혜택'이란 뜻의 (B)와 (C)도 해석상 적절치 않으므로 제외시킨다. 문맥상 '이번 주 상의 수령인이 될 것이다'가 자연스러우므로 정답은 (D) beneficiary(수령인)이다.

[어휘]

lucky 운이 좋은 | customer 고객 | prize 상, 경품

110

[번역]

연구과제를 받은 연구원들은 새 프로젝트를 논의하기 위해 회의에 참석할 것이다.

[해설]

빈칸 앞에 있는 선행사 researchers를 수식하면서 전치사 to의 목적어 역할을 해야 하므로 정답은 (B)이다. 참고로 which는 선행사가 사물일 때, whom은 선행사가 사람일 때 전치사의 목적격으로 쓰이며, whose는 소유격 관계대명사이기 때문에 '명사 whose 명사'의 형태로 쓰이며, who는 주격 관계대명사이다. who가 목적격 대신 사용되기도 하지만 전치사의 목적어가 될 때는 whom을 쓴다.

[어휘]

researcher 연구원 | assignment 과제 | discuss 논의하다

111

[번역]

12세 미만의 어린이는 누구나 자신과 가족에 대한 훌륭한 에세이를 제출함으로써 대회에 참가할 수 있다.

[해설]

빈칸 앞에 '방법 · 수단'을 나타내는 전치사 by가 있으므로 명사나 동명사가 필요하다. 그래서 (B) submitted(제출된)와 (D) submits(제출하다)는 제외된다. 빈칸 뒤에 목적어(a well written essay)가 있기 때문에 명사 (C) submission(제출)도 제외되어 정답은 'by V-ing (~함으로써)'의 형태를 이루는 (A) submitting이 된다.

[어휘]

under the age of ~세 미만인 | enter the competition 대회에 참가하다

112

[번역]

다른 판매점들과의 계약 조건에 따라, 모든 배송 요금은 앞으로 3개월 동안 청구되지 않을 것이다.

[해설]

in accordance with(~에 따라)를 알고 있으면 문제를 수월하게 풀 수 있다. 문법적으로도 전치사 사이에 들어갈 수 있는 품사는 명사이므로 정답은 (D)가 된다. according은 to와 함께 쓰여 '~에 따르면'이라는 뜻이다.

[어휘]

terms 조건, 조항 | agreement 계약, 협약 | distributor 유통업체[자],
판매 대리점 | shipping 선적, 배송 | fee 요금 | charge (대가, 요금을)
청구하다 | accordingly 그것에 따라서 | accord 일치하다, 조화하다 |
accordance 일치, 조화

113

[번역]

이 쿠폰들은, 10월 한 달 동안만 이 매장에 전시된 특정 상품을 구입하는 데 사용될 수 있습니다.

[해설]

문맥에 맞는 동사 형태를 찾는 문제이다. These coupons can be used
_____ any particular item은 '이 쿠폰들은 특정 상품 구입하기 위해 사
용될 수 있다'라는 의미가 되어야 자연스럽다. 따라서 보기에서 '~하기
위해'라는 의미를 형성하는 것은 to부정사인 (C)이다. 'be used to 동사
원형'은 '~하는 데 사용된다'라고 해석된다. be used to V-ing(~에 익숙
하다)와 구분해서 외워둬야 실수하지 않는다.

[어휘]

particular 특정한 | item 물건 | display 전시하다 | purchase
~을 사다; 구매

114

[번역]

지역 관광 협회들은 음식점들은 휴가철에 앞서 광고 예산을 증가시킬
것을 계획해야 한다고 제안했다.

[해설]

동사 increase의 목적어가 되며 advertising과 함께 복합명사를 형성
할 수 있는 명사를 찾아야 한다. increase는 크기, 수, 양을 증가시키는
것을 의미하므로 돈의 의미가 들어간 (A)와 (C)가 목적어가 될 수 있
는데, fees는 '요금, 수수료'를 의미하므로 문맥상 '예산'이라는 의미의
(A)가 가장 적절하다.

[어휘]

local 지역의, 현지의 | tourism 관광 | association 협회 | suggest
제안하다, 권하다 | plan 계획하다 | increase 증가시키다 | advertising
광고 | viewer 시청자 | fee 요금 | scene 장면

115

[번역]

잠재 고객들에게 귀사의 서비스를 홍보할 수 있는 몇 가지 방법이 있음
을 자신있게 말씀드리고자 합니다.

[해설]

빈칸은 명사 services를 수식하는 형용사가 들어갈 자리이다. 대명사의
소유격은 명사를 수식하는 형용사의 역할을 하므로 정답은 (B)가 된다.

[어휘]

assure ~에게 보증하다, 안심시키다 | promote 촉진하다, 증진하다 |
prospective customer 잠정 고객

116

[번역]

뛰어난 업무 성과를 가진 사람들만이 승진 대상으로 고려될 것이다.

[해설]

빈칸은 '사람들'이란 의미의 대명사 those 앞에 놓여 있는데, 대명사
를 수식할 수 있는 품사는 형용사이므로 부사로만 사용되는 (A)와 (C)
는 가장 먼저 소거될 수 있다. (D)의 neither는 '(둘 중의) 어느 쪽도 아
닌'이란 의미이므로 본 문장과는 어울리지 않는다. 본 문장에서 those
with(~를 가진 사람들)는 those (who are) with를 의미함을 알아야 문
제를 푸는데 도움이 될 것이다. only는 이 문장에서 '뛰어난 업무 성과
를 가진 사람만'이라는 승진 대상자를 한정하는 역할을 하게 된다. 따
라서 특정 대상을 한정하는 (B)가 정답이 된다.

[어휘]

outstanding 뛰어난 | performance 성과 | consider 고려하다 |
promotion 승진 | almost 거의 | only 오직, ~만이 | entirely 완전히
| neither ~도 또한 ~않다

117

[번역]

대부분의 회사들은 연간 광고 비용으로 얼마를 지출할 지를 정하는 규
정을 가지고 있다.

[해설]

문맥에 적합한 동사 형태를 찾는 문제이다. 본 문장에서 that은
regulations를 선행사로 하는 주격 관계대명사이며 that 이하에서 how
much they should spend on advertising for a year(연간 광고 비용으로
얼마를 지출할 지)가 목적어가 된다. 따라서 빈칸은 관계대명사의 서술
어가 되며 목적어를 취할 수 있는 품사인 동사가 들어가야 하는데 선행
사가 복수(regulations)이므로 정답은 (A)가 된다.

[어휘]

regulations 규정, 규제 | spend on ~에 돈을 쓰다, 지출하다 |
advertising 광고 | determine ~을 정하다 | determiner 결정하는
사람[것]

118

[번역]

브랜트 씨는 공급업체로부터 예상되는 새 컴퓨터들의 배송 및 설치 날
짜에 대해서 최근 결정된 내용을 기다리는 중이다.

[해설]

브랜트 씨가 공급업체로부터 무엇인가를 기다리고 있는 상황인데,
about 이하에 나오는 delivery, date와 자연스럽게 연결될 수 있는 어휘
는 (A) invoice(송장, 청구서), (B) analyst(분석가), (C) expectation(예
상), (D) update(갱신, 최신 정보) 중 (D)가 가장 적절하다.

[어휘]

supplier 공급업자 | estimated 예상되는 | delivery 배달, 납품 |
installation 설치

119

[번역]

모든 이력서들을 살펴본 후에, 우리는 그 직책에 필요한 모든 요건에 부
응하지 못하는 지원자들과 가능성을 가진 지원자들을 신중하게 분류했
다.

[해설]

문맥에 적합한 부사어휘를 찾는 문제이다. '분류하다'라는 뜻의 동사
separated를 자연스럽게 수식하는 부사는 '(A) apparently(명백히), (B)
carefully(신중히), (C) cordially(정중하게), (D) aggressively(공격적으
로) 중에서 (B)이다. (A)의 apparently는 우리말로 보면 정답으로 느껴
질 수도 있는데, 이때 '명백히'란 'The man was apparently a doctor.'와
같은 문장에서 '겉보기에 분명히 그렇게 보인다'라는 의미로 사용되는
부사이기 때문에 본 문장에는 적절하지 않다.

[어휘]

look through 살펴 보다 | résumé 이력서 | separate A from B A를
B로부터 분류하다, 나누다 | potential 가능성 | requirement 필수 요건

120

[번역]

대부분의 직원들은 컨퍼런스를 계획하는 데 다른 대행사를 이용하는
것에 찬성하는 친 씨의 주장이 매우 설득력이 있다고 생각했다.

[해설]

문장을 살펴보면, 주어(Ms. Chin's argument) + 동사(was) + 주격보어
(very _____)의 구조로 형용사가 필요한 자리이므로 (C)와 (D)는 바로

제외된다. 형용사인 (A) persuasive(설득력 있는)와 (D) persuaded(설득 받는)를 답으로 고려해 볼 수 있는데, 해석상 '주장이 설득력이 있었다'가 적합하므로 정답은 (A)이다.

[어휘]

argument 주장 | in favor of ~에 찬성하는 | agency 대행사 |
persuasive 설득력 있는

121

[번역]

이 매뉴얼은 귀하의 새 전자레인지를 올바르게 작동시키는 방법에 관한 설명을 제공합니다.

[해설]

빈칸은 타동사 provides의 목적어인 명사가 들어갈 자리이다. 보기에서 명사는 (B)와 (C)인데 매뉴얼에서 제공되는 것은 제품 사용에 관한 '설명'이므로 정답은 (C)가 된다.

[어휘]

manual 매뉴얼, 안내서 | provide 제공하다 | operate 작동하다 |
microwave oven 전자레인지 | properly 올바르게, 정확히 | instruct
~을 가르치다, 교육하다 | instructor 강사, 교사 | instruction 설명, 교육 |
instructional 교육적인, 도움이 되는

122

[번역]

우리는 상황이 위급해지기 전에 새 회계사를 가능한 한 빨리 고용해야 한다.

[해설]

동사 becomes에서 단서를 잡아 품사를 찾는 문제이다. 보어로 올 수 없는 (D)는 바로 소거되며, 내용상 '상황이 악화되기 전에'가 타당하므로 '아슬아슬한, 위기의'라는 뜻을 지닌 (B)가 정답이다.

[어휘]

employ 고용하다 | accountant 회계사 | as soon as possible
가능한 한 빨리 | situation 상황 | criticism 비평, 비난 | critical 비평의,
위험한, 위기의 | critic 비평가 | critically 비판적으로

123

[번역]

이 여행 안내소의 직원들은 지역 관광지에 대한 그들의 지식에 대해 방문객들로부터 종종 칭송을 받는다.

[해설]

여행 안내소의 이용자들이 좋게 평가하는 것은 그곳 직원들의 지역 관광지에 대한 '지식(knowledge)'이라고 할 수 있다.

[어휘]

tourism center 여행 안내소 | compliment 칭찬 | local 지역의 |
attraction 관광지, 유인물 | familiarity 친밀, 친근 | exhibition 전시 |
agreement 계약, 협정 | knowledge 지식

124

[번역]

능력 있고 유능했기 때문에, 매기 브라운은 마크의 은퇴 후 그를 대신할 위원회의 차기 의장으로 확실한 선택이었다.

[해설]

등위접속사 and는 같은 '품사[구조]'를 연결하므로 앞서 나온 형용사

competent를 보고 형용사를 찾는 문제이므로 정답은 (D) efficient(유능한, 효율적인)이다.

[어휘]

competent 능력 있는 | obvious 명백한 | choice 선택 | replace
대신하다, 후임으로 오다 | chairperson 의장 | committee 위원회 |
retirement 은퇴, 퇴직 | efficiency 효율성 | efficiently 능률적으로 |

125

[번역]

예상치 못한 문제들 때문에 이번 주 남은 기간 내내 그 소프트웨어 회사의 기술 서비스를 이용할 수 없을 것이다.

[해설]

문맥에 적합한 형용사 어휘를 찾는 문제이다. 예상치 못한 문제들 때문이라는 이유가 나와 있으므로 그것으로 인한 사실이나 결과가 언급되어야 자연스럽다. 따라서 '예상치 못한 문제들 때문에 기술 서비스를 이용할 수 없다'라는 문장이 형성되어야 하므로 정답은 (C)가 된다. refrain은 보통 'refrain 목적어 from V-ing'의 형태로 쓰여 '~가 …하는 것을 못하게 하다, 억제하다'라고 해석된다.

[어휘]

technical 기술의 | throughout ~동안 내내 | remainder 나머지
| due to ~때문에 | unexpected 예기치 않은 | refrained 억제된 |
understood 이해된 | unavailable 이용할 수 없는 | affordable 저렴한

126

[번역]

우리가 식당에서 음식 서빙하는 속도를 빠르게 하려고 애쓰는데도, 계속해서 손님들의 불평을 듣는다.

[해설]

타동사 receive의 목적어 자리에는 명사가 들어가야 한다. 따라서 (B)와 (D)는 바로 소거된다. '불평, 불만사항'을 뜻하는 (A)와 (C)가 남는데, complaint는 가산명사이므로 부정관사 없이 단수형으로 사용될 수 없으며, 의미상으로도 여러 손님들의 '불만사항들'이 타당하므로 정답은 (A) complaints이다.

[어휘]

improve 개선하다 | speed 속도 | serve 시중들다 | receive 받다 |
customer 고객

127

[번역]

이 상품권은 귀하의 자동차용 새 CD플레이어를 구입하는 용도로만 사용되어야 합니다.

[해설]

적절한 품사를 찾는 문제이다. 수동태(be + p.p.) 뒤는 부사 자리이므로 정답은 (D) solely(단지)이다. 해석상으로도 '단지 _____할 목적으로 사용되다'가 자연스럽다.

[어휘]

voucher 상품권, 할인권 | be to ~하는 것이다 | for the purpose of
~의 목적으로

128

[번역]

그 버스회사는 지난 월요일 저녁 대로변에서 발생한 사고에 대해 일부 책임이 있다는 사실을 부인하고 있다.

[해설]

문맥에 맞는 적절한 동사어휘를 찾는 문제이다. '사고에 대해 책임이 있음을 _____ 하고 있다'에 들어가 의미를 가장 자연스럽게 완성해 주는 것은 (A) split(나누다), (B) deny(부인하다), (C) plead(탄원하다), (D) grant(수여하다) 중에 (B)이다.

[어휘]

share 나누다, 공유하다 | responsibility 책임 | accident 사고

129
[번역]

당신이 이달의 낮은 판매실적에 대해 이야기하기를 아무리 피한다 할지라도, 오늘 오후에 판매부 부장과 미팅하면서는 설명해야 할 것이다.

[해설]

두 개의 절(주어+동사)을 연결시킬 수 있는 알맞은 단어를 찾아야 하는데, 빈칸 뒤에 부사 much가 나와 있음을 파악해야 한다. 보기에 제시된 단어들 중에서 뒤에 형용사나 부사를 동반할 수 있는 단어는 (D) However 밖에 없으며 '아무리 ~해도, ~라 해도'라는 뜻을 완성한다.

[어휘]

avoid 피하다 | sales figures 판매실적 | explanation 설명 | moreover 게다가 | because ~이기 때문에 | still 여전히 | however 아무리~해도, 그러나

130
[번역]

샤론은 혼자 일하는 것을 더 좋아하는 것 같지만, 안타깝게도 이 프로젝트는 팀원들 각자가 저마다의 역할을 완수해야만 성공할 수 있을 것이다.

[해설]

by oneself는 '홀로, 혼자서'라는 뜻으로 alone, on one's own과 같은 의미이다. 따라서 빈칸에는 (A) by가 필요하다.

[어휘]

prefer 좋아하다 | unfortunately 불행하게도 | succeed 성공하다 | fulfill 완수하다, 이행하다 | role 역할

PART 6

131-134
[번역]

홀리스 플라워즈를 찾아 주십시오

홀리스 플라워즈는, 서던 가 59번지에 위치해 있으며, 시내에서 가장 우수하고 신선한 꽃을 판매합니다. 저희는 장미, 카네이션, 백합부터 원산지가 해외인 이국적인 난초에 이르기까지, 온갖 종류의 꽃을 구비하고 있습니다. 저희는 꽃을 송이 단위로도 그리고 다발로도 판매합니다. 저희 판매 직원에게 꽃을 구입하시는 이유를 말씀해 주시면, 그들이 여러분들께 어떤 종류의 꽃이 가장 적절한지 알려 드릴 것입니다. 저희는 꽃을 꽃병과 함께 판매하며, 화환과 기타 꽃꽂이 상품 역시 제공해 드릴 수 있습니다.

봄이 왔으므로, 많은 분들의 삶 속에 졸업식과 결혼식과 같은 여러 가지 특별한 행사들이 발생하고 있습니다. 단지 싸다는 이유로 시

들고 품질이 떨어지는 꽃을 구입함으로써 이러한 기회를 망치지 마십시오. (대신, 홀리스 플라워즈에서 약간은 비싸지만 품질은 최고인 제품을 구입하십시오.)

[어휘]

exotic 외래의, 이국적인 | orchid 난 | individually 개별적으로 | bunch 다발, 묶음 | along with ~와 함께 | wreath 화환 | floral arrangement 꽃꽂이 | ruin 망치다 | wilted 시든 | bargain price 할인 가격, 염가

131
[해설]

빈칸에는 부대 상황 혹은 동시 상황의 의미를 나타내는 분사 구문이 들어가야 한다. 따라서 정답은 all kinds of flowers를 의미상 주어로 삼을 수 있는 (D) ranging이다.

[어휘]

range from A to B 범위가 A에서 B까지 이르다

132
[해설]

꽃을 구입하는 이유를 알려 주면, 그에 '적합한' 꽃을 찾아 주겠다는 내용이다. 따라서 정답은 (D) appropriate이다.

[어휘]

comparable 비교할 만한, 비슷한 | disposable 일회용의 | viable 실행 가능한, 현실적인 | appropriate 적절한, 적합한

133
[해설]

빈칸에는 지시 형용사 these의 수식을 받으면서 ruin의 목적어가 될 수 있는 명사가 들어가야 한다. 보기에서 명사는 (B) occasions뿐이므로 정답은 (B)이다.

[어휘]

occasional 가끔의 | occasion 경우 | occasionally 가끔, 때때로

134
[해설]

빈칸 앞 문장에서 '싸다고 품질이 떨어지는 꽃은 사지 말라'는 메시지를 전하고 있으므로 빈칸에는 '조금 비싸더라도 품질이 우수한 꽃을 사라'는 내용이 언급되는 것이 가장 자연스럽다. 따라서 정답은 (A)이다.

135-138
[번역]

월튼 부사장 사임

오늘 오전, 제시카 월튼이 스탠턴 대표 이사에게 이번 달 말에 사임을 하겠다는 의사를 밝혔습니다. 월튼 씨는 잭슨 매뉴팩처링의 사장직을 수락했는데, 이곳은 영국의 맨체스터에 위치해 있습니다. 우리는 월튼 씨가 인생의 새로운 장을 열기 위해 바다를 건널 것이므로 그녀에게 행운이 있기를 바랍니다. 또한 이곳 더블톤에서의 23년간 근무에 대해 감사를 드리고 싶습니다. 그녀는 회사의 소중한 자산이었으며, 우리는 그녀를 매우 그리워할 것입니다. 월튼 씨를 위해서 그녀가 떠나기 전에 송별회가 열릴 것입니다.

(이번 행사의 세부 사항은 차후에 게시될 것입니다.) 한편, 새로운 부사장을 찾기 위한 조사 위원회도 결성될 것입니다. 이 일에 지원하고자 하시는 분께서는 내선번호 506으로 로버트 펜스케에게 연락을 하셔야 합니다.

[어휘]

inform 알리다, 통지하다 | wish ~ all the best ~에게 행운을 빌어 주다 | valuable 귀중한, 소중한 | depart 떠나다, 출발하다 | get in touch with ~와 연락하다

135

[해설]

월튼 씨가 기존의 부사장 자리에서 물러나서 타사의 사장직으로 가게 되었다는 내용이다. 따라서 빈칸에는 새로운 회사의 사장직을 '수락했다'는 의미의 동사가 들어가야 한다. 따라서 정답은 (D) '수락하다'이다.

[어휘]

apply 지원하다 | transfer 전근하다, 전근시키다 | accept 수락하다, 받아들이다

136

[해설]

빈칸에는 '~하기 위하여'라는 의미의 to부정사가 들어가야 가장 자연스러운 의미가 완성된다. 따라서 정답은 (B)이다.

137

[해설]

'회사의 소중한 자산'이라는 의미가 완성되기 위해서는 (A) asset이 들어가야 한다.

[어휘]

asset 자산 | equipment 장비, 시설 | talent 재능, 재주

138

[해설]

빈칸의 바로 앞 문장에서 '송별회(farewell party)'를 소개하고 있다. 따라서 빈칸에는 그에 관한 부연 설명이 들어가는 것이 가장 자연스럽다. 따라서 정답은 '세부 사항은 추후에 게시될 것이다'라는 의미의 (D)이다.

139-142

[번역]

보낸 사람: 엔리코 로마노
받는 사람: 회계부 전 직원
제목: 오타
날짜: 2월 10일

저는 지난 달에 회계 직원들에 의해 많은 오타들이 발생했다는 점에 주목하게 되었습니다. 여기에는 급여 명세서의 오타와 함께 다른 회사와 체결한 계약서 상의 오타들도 포함됩니다.

이러한 오타들은 받아들일 수 없는 것이며 근절되어야만 합니다. 지금부터, 모든 수치들은 확정될 때까지 관리자들에 의해 이중으로 확인되어야 합니다. 이러한 일은 추가적인 근무 시간을 요하게 될 것이지만, 우리가 모든 일을 제대로 처리하고 있다는 점을 확인하기 위해서는 반드시 실시되어야 할 일입니다. (하지만 저는 모든 업무가 제 시간 내에 완성될 수 있기를 기대합니다.) 초과 근무를 해야 한다면, 여러분들은 그렇게 해야 할 것입니다. 또한 여러분 각자가 2월 21일에 개설되는 회계 보충 수업에 참석해야 합니다. 이 수업은 의무적인 것이며 수강을 하지 않으면 고용 계약이 종료되는 결과를 가져올 것입니다.

[어휘]

error 실수, 오타 | attention 주의, 주목 | a large number of 많은, 다수의 | accountant 회계사, 회계 직원 | paycheck 급여, 급여 명세서 | contract 계약서 | unacceptable 받아들일 수 없는, 수용할 수 없는 | from now on 지금부터 | double-check 이중으로 확인하다, 재확인하다 | ensure 확실히 하다 | remedial 보충의 | failure 실패 | result in 결과로서 ~이 되다 | terminate 끝내다, 종료하다

139

[해설]

contracts(계약서)를 목적으로 삼을 수 있는 동사가 들어가야 한다. 보기 중에서 이러한 조건에 부합되는 것은 (D) signed(체결하다)이다.

[어휘]

hire 고용하다 | register 등록하다 | sign 서명하다, (계약을) 체결하다

140

[해설]

문맥상 '앞으로 추가 근무를 하게 될 것이다'는 미래의 의미가 완성되어야 하므로 빈칸에는 미래 시제인 (A) will require가 들어가야 한다.

141

[해설]

빈칸 앞 문장에서는 초과 근무를 하게 될 수도 있다고 했고, 빈칸 다음 문장에서는 필요한 경우에는 초과 근무를 반드시 해야 한다는 내용이 담겨 있다. 따라서 이 두 문장 사이에 들어갈 가장 적절한 표현은 '가급적 초과 근무를 하는 경우가 없기를 바란다'는 취지의 문장이 들어가야 가장 자연스러운 문맥이 완성된다. 따라서 정답은 '모든 업무가 제 시간 내에 완성될 수 있기를 기대한다'는 의미인 (A)이다.

[어휘]

assignment 과제, 업무 | on time 제 시간에, 제때에 | perform 수행하다, 이행하다; 공연하다

142

[해설]

접속사 and에 유의하면 쉽게 정답을 찾을 수 있다. 보기 중 '수업에 참석하지 않으면 해고될 것이다'라는 의미와 일맥 상통하는 표현은 (B) mandatory(강제적인, 의무적인) 뿐이므로 정답은 (B)이다.

[어휘]

immediate 즉각적인 | mandatory 강제적인, 의무의 | extensive 넓은, 광범위한 | elective 선택에 의한; 선거로 뽑힌

[번역]

> 받는 사람: 〈customerservice@deluxecard.com〉
> 보낸 사람: 〈geraldsellers@mymail.com〉
> 제목: 부정 사용으로 인한 대금 청구
> 날짜: 4월 26일
>
> 담당자님께,
>
> 제 이름은 제럴드 셀러스입니다. 저는 최근에 디럭스 카드의 4월 분 명세서를 받았는데 개봉해 보고 크게 놀랐습니다. 4월 2일과 4월 5일, 저는 각 일자로 현금 서비스 요금을 부과받았습니다. 저는 결코 제 신용 카드로 현금 서비스를 받아 본 적이 없기 때문에 이 요금이 무엇인지 전혀 모르겠습니다.
>
> 제가 이의를 제기하는 요금에 동그라미를 쳐 둔 청구서 사본을 첨부합니다. 저에게는 그에 대한 책임이 없기 때문에 귀사가 청구서에서 그 부분을 삭제해 주시기를 요청드립니다. (또한, 그 신용 카드는 즉시 해지시켜 주십시오.) 누군가가 제 신용카드 번호를 알게 되어 제가 모르는 사이에 사용한 것처럼 보입니다. 가능한 빨리 제게 새 카드를 발급해 주시면 고맙겠습니다.
>
> 제럴드 셀러스 드림

[어휘]

statement 성명, 진술; 입출금 내역서 ｜ incredibly 믿을 수 없을 정도로, 매우 ｜ charge 부과하다 ｜ cash advance 현금 서비스 ｜ attach 붙이다, 첨부하다 ｜ bill 청구서 ｜ contest 이의를 제기하다 ｜ be responsible for ~에 대해 책임지다 ｜ as if 마치 ~처럼 ｜ obtain 얻다, 획득하다

143
[해설]

사용하지 않은 현금 서비스 요금이 부과되었을 때의 감정이 어떨지 생각해 보면 쉽게 정답을 찾을 수 있다.

[어휘]

shocked 놀란, 충격을 받은 ｜ impressed 감명을 받은

144
[해설]

빈칸에는 간접 의문문을 이끌 수 있는 의문사 what이 들어가야 한다. 참고로 have no idea는 do not know와 쓰임이 같다.

145
[해설]

바로 뒷문장에서 누군가가 카드 번호를 도용한 것 같다고 주장하고 있다. 따라서 카드를 해지해야 한다는 내용이 앞서야 자연스러운 문맥이 완성된다.

[어휘]

cancel 취소하다 ｜ payment 지급 ｜ intend to ~할 의도이다 ｜ issue 발급하다 ｜ credit limit 신용 한도

146
[해설]

appreciate는 바로 목적어를 취하는 타동사로 주로 사용되나, 현대 영어에서는 'appreciate + 목적어 + -ing' 형태도 많이 사용된다.

PART 7

147-148
[번역]

> **전 직원에게 알림**
>
> 모든 직원들은 일을 시작하기 전과 화장실에 다녀 온 후에는 손과 팔을 반드시 씻어야 합니다. 이 사항은 음식을 준비하는 사람, 접시를 닦는 사람, 음식을 나르는 사람 등 음식이나 음식관련 도구 및 장비를 만지는 사람이면 누구에게나 해당합니다. 일반적인 경우 모든 직원은 조리가 다 된 음식(샌드위치, 샐러드, 과일, 빵 등)을 맨손으로 만지는 일은 피해야 합니다. 음식을 만질 때는 집게·티슈·포크·국자·장갑 등과 같은 도구를 사용해야 합니다. 음식을 준비하는 사람은 손 씻는 규칙을 엄밀히 지킨다는 전제 하에, 필요하다면 조리가 다 된 음식을 맨손으로 만질 수도 있습니다. 음식을 나르는 사람들은 특히 맨손으로 조리된 음식을 만져서는 안 됩니다. 우리 일터를 깨끗하고 안전하게 지켜 나갑시다!

[어휘]

employee 직원 ｜ wash 씻다 ｜ toilet 화장실 ｜ begin work 일을 시작하다 ｜ include 포함하다 ｜ preparer 준비하는 사람 ｜ dishwasher 접시 닦는 사람 ｜ server 시중드는 사람 ｜ have contact with ~와 접촉하다 ｜ utensil 기구 ｜ equipment 장비 ｜ as a general rule 대체로 ｜ bare 노출된, 나체의 ｜ ready-to-eat 조리가 다 된, 먹을 수 있는 ｜ avoid 피하다 ｜ tong 집게 ｜ tissue 티슈 ｜ fork 포크 ｜ scoop 국자, 주걱 ｜ glove 장갑 ｜ necessary 필요한 ｜ provided 만약 ~ 이라면 ｜ strictly 엄격히 ｜ adhere to ~을 준수하다 ｜ requirement 필수요건 ｜ specifically 특히 ｜ prohibit 금지하다 ｜ workplace 직장, 일터

147
[번역]

이 공고는 어디에서 볼 수 있겠는가?
(A) 헬스 클럽
(B) 슈퍼마켓
(C) 병원
(D) 식당

[해설]

전반부에서 단서를 찾을 수 있다. 글의 main idea는 첫 번째 문장 All employees must wash their hands and arms before beginning work and after using the toilet인데, 바로 뒤의 문장에서 All employees에 해당하는 사람들로 '음식을 준비하는 사람, 접시를 닦는 사람, 음식을 나르는 사람(food preparers, dishwashers, servers)'을 열거하고 있다. 따라서 정답은 (D)이다.

[어휘]

supermarket 슈퍼마켓 ｜ hospital 병원 ｜ restaurant 식당

148
[번역]

음식을 나르는 사람이 하면 안 되는 일은 무엇인가?
(A) 7시 이후에 세면장에 들어가는 것
(B) 음식에 손 대는 것
(C) 향이 없는 비누를 사용하는 것
(D) 비번일 때 직장에 나오는 것

질문의 키워드 servers에 집중하여 지문을 파악해야 한다. 후반부의 Servers are specifically prohibited from touching ready-to-eat food with their bare hands에 음식을 맨손으로 만지지 말라는 내용이 나온다. 여기서 be prohibited from은 '~이 금지되다'는 뜻으로 질문의 'not allowed to do'와 일맥상통한다.

[어휘]

washroom 세면장 | fragrance-free 무향의, 향기가 없는 | soap 비누 | off-duty 근무 외의, 비번인

149-150

[번역]

> 머레이, 아론 2:55 P.M.
> 안녕하세요, 캐롤. 어디에 있나요? 면접이 5분 후에 시작되는 것으로 예정되어 있어요.
>
> 채프먼, 캐롤 2:55 P.M.
> 여전히 제퍼슨 씨 사무실 밖에서 기다리고 있는 중이에요. 그분과 제가 이야기할 기회가 아직 없었어요.
>
> 머레이, 아론 2:56 P.M.
> 그분과의 약속은 2시 30분이 아니었나요? 무슨 일이 있는 거죠?
>
> 채프먼, 캐롤 2:56 P.M.
> 그분께서는 러시아의 새 고객과 화상 화의를 하고 있다고 비서가 말해 주었어요. 그녀는 언제 끝날지 모르고 있고요.
>
> 머레이, 아론 2:57 P.M.
> 그 회의의 일정을 조정해서 나중에 그분과 이야기할 수 있나요?
>
> 채프먼, 캐롤 2:58 P.M.
> 미안하지만, 즉시 그분과 이야기를 나누는 것이 중요해서요. 저 없이 진행하는 것이 낫겠어요.
>
> 머레이, 아론 2:59 P.M.
> 좋아요. 하지만 가능한 빨리 오세요. 오늘 오후에 면접을 볼 사람들이 여러 명 있어요.

[어휘]

have a chance to ~할 기회를 갖다 | secretary 비서 | teleconference 화상 회의 | crucial 중요한, 중대한

149

[번역]

머레이 씨는 채프먼 씨에게 무엇을 할 것을 요청하는가?
(A) 러시아 고객과 이야기한다
(B) 제퍼슨 씨와 만날 약속을 한다
(C) 면접을 위해 그의 사무실을 방문한다
(D) 이후에 제퍼슨 씨와 만난다

[해설]

메신저의 마지막 부분에서 머레이 씨는 채프먼 씨에게 가능한 빨리 오라고 말한 후, 오후에 면접을 볼 사람들이 여러 명 있다는 점을 상기시킨다. 이를 통해 정답이 (D)임을 알 수 있다.

[어휘]

make an appointment 만날 약속을 하다

150

[번역]

오후 2시 58분에 채프먼 씨가 "You'd better go ahead without me" 라고 쓴 의도는 무엇인가?
(A) 머레이 씨는 그녀 없이 면접을 시작해야 한다.
(B) 머레이 씨는 혼자서 제퍼슨 씨와 이야기를 나누어야 한다.
(C) 머레이 씨는 홀로 준비를 해야 한다.
(D) 머레이 씨는 그 밖의 다른 사람들과 점심을 먹으러 가야 한다.

[해설]

You'd better go ahead without me는 '나 없이 진행하는 것이 낫겠다'라는 뜻으로 이를 통해 채프먼 씨는 머레이 씨에게 혼자서 면접을 진행할 것을 제안하고 있다. 따라서 정답은 (A)이다.

[어휘]

by oneself 혼자서 | alone 홀로 | arrangement 준비; 배열, 배치

151-153

[번역]

> ### 협상에 성공하려면
> 뛰어난 협상 기술을 습득하세요.
>
> 협상은 쌍방 모두를 위한 가치를 최대화하기 위해 여러분이(그리고 우리 회사가) 오랫동안 지속되는 우호적인 관계를 형성하고자 노력하고 있음을 보여 줄 수 있는 기회입니다. 협상 기술이 좋으면 여러분이 고객과 나누는 신뢰와 진실성을 높일 수 있습니다. 다음은 여러분이 다음 협상에 앞서 대비해야 할 검토사항입니다.
>
> ✓ 당신의 제안을 충분히 고객에게 설명할 기회가 없다면 협상을 시작하지 마십시오.
> ✓ 대화 상대자가 협상 및 결정권이 있는지 확인하십시오.
> ✓ 당신과 우리 회사에게 유리한 합의점이 어디까지인지 미리 파악하고, 그 합의점 이하에서는 협상을 중단하십시오.
> ✓ 협상 동안 참을성을 가지십시오.
>
> 물론, 위 사항은 지극히 기본적인 것입니다. 우리가 준비한 무료 교육 세미나에 등록하시면 협상 기술에 대해 더 많은 부분을 배울 수 있을 것입니다. 지금 바로 인사부의 팀에게 전화해서(내선 5646) 예약하십시오.

[어휘]

negotiate 협상하다 | ensure 확실하게 하다 | top-notch 최고의, 일류의 | negotiation 협상 | opportunity 기회 | demonstrate 보여주다, 증명하다 | commitment 의무, 헌신 | long-term 장기의 | relationship 관계 | maximize 최대로 하다 | value 가치 | both parties 양측 | increase 늘리다 | level 단계 | trust 신뢰 | credibility 진실성, 확실성 | checklist 검토사항 | provide 제공하다 | key 중요한 | preparation 준비 | proposition 건의, 발의 | fully 완전히 | certain 확신하는 | authority 권한 | in advance 미리 | no longer 더 이상~가 아니다 | beneficial 유리한 | be prepared to ~에 대비하다 | walk away 떠나다 | patient 참을성이 있는 | basic 기본, 기초 | sign up for 등록하다 | educational 교육적인 | art 기술, 기교 | Human Resources 인사부 | reserve 예약하다

151

[번역]

공고에 따르면, 협상 기술이 좋을 때 얻는 혜택은 무엇인가?

(A) 더 빠른 문제 해결책을 찾는다.

(B) 원료를 저렴하게 구입한다.

(C) 더 넓은 지역에 제품을 유통한다.

(D) 고객들로부터 더 많은 신뢰를 얻는다.

[해설]

공고의 주제를 묻는 전반부형 문제이다. 질문의 핵심어구 benefit of good negotiation skills에 집중해서 지문을 살펴 보면, 두 번째 문장 Good negotiation skills can increase the level of trust and credibility you have with your customers에 고객과의 만남에서 신용을 높일 수 있다는 내용이 나온다. 따라서 답은 (D)이다.

[어휘]

quicker 더 빠른 ｜ solution 해결책, 솔루션 ｜ purchase 구입하다 ｜ raw material 원료 ｜ inexpensively 저렴하게 ｜ distribute 분배하다 ｜ earn 벌다, 얻다

152

[번역]

협상 준비 단계로 언급되지 않은 것은 무엇인가?

(A) 적합한 사람과 협상하는지 확인하라.

(B) 협상 장소에 반드시 일찍 도착하라.

(C) 협상을 끝내야 할 때를 알아라.

(D) 과정을 급히 끌어 가지 마라.

[해설]

언급하지 '않은' 내용을 찾는 경우에는 보기와 지문을 대조하여 오답을 소거하면서 답을 찾는 것이 바람직하다. 지문에서 The following checklist ~ for your next negotiation에 이어지는 내용과 각각의 보기를 비교하면, (A)는 Be certain you're dealing with a person ~ make decisions와, (C)는 Know in advance ~ be prepared to walk away와, (D)는 Be prepared to be patient와 맞닿는다. 따라서 정답은 (B)이다.

[어휘]

rush 돌진하다, 급히 하다

153

[번역]

더 많은 내용을 알고 싶은 사람은 어떻게 해야 하는가?

(A) 직원에게 전화한다.

(B) 학원을 방문한다.

(C) 웹사이트를 방문한다.

(D) 안내책자를 읽는다.

[해설]

앞으로 발생할 일이나 해야 할 일에 대한 질문의 단서는 주로 후반부에 있다. Call Tim in Human Resources (ext. 5646) and reserve your space now에 인사부 직원 팀에게 전화하라는 내용이 나온다.

[어휘]

academy 학원 ｜ brochure 브로셔, 소책자

154-156

[번역]

받는 사람: 전 부서장

보낸 사람: 리사 어빙턴, 인사부

제목: 인사 고과

날짜: 10월 4일

직원들의 인사 고과가 늦어도 이번 주 금요일인 10월 8일 오후 5시까지 제출되어야 한다는 점을 모든 분들께 상기시켜 드리고자 합니다. 모든 고과는 올해 3/4분기 동안 직원들이 했던 업무와만 관련이 있어야 합니다.

두어 분께서는 이번 일을 처음으로 하시기 때문에, 제가 짧게 절차를 설명드리겠습니다. 이미 직원들에 관한 양식은 받으셨을 것입니다. 각각의 양식의 빈칸에 내용을 채워 주셔야 합니다. 타이핑을 하시기보다는 손으로 써 주셔야 합니다. 각 개인들이 7월, 8월, 그리고 9월 동안 자신의 업무를 어떻게 했는지에 관해서 솔직한 의견을 주시면 됩니다. 어떤 사람이 주목할 만한 일을 했다면, 하단의 논평란에 반드시 내용을 포함시켜 주십시오. 마지막으로, 이번 양식에는 새로운 질문이 들어 있습니다. 해당 직원을 계속 고용해야 할지 아니면 방출시켜야 할지에 대해 묻고 있습니다. (후자를 선택하시는 경우에는, 반드시 본인의 입장을 글로서 설명하셔야 합니다.)

양식에 관해 질문이 있으신 경우, 제 사무실 문은 항상 열려 있습니다. 혹은 내선 번호 34로 전화를 주시면 제가 최선을 다해 여러분의 질문에 답변을 드리도록 하겠습니다. 하지만 제가 금요일에는 하루 종일 회의가 있어서 질문에 즉각적인 답변을 할 수 없을 것이므로 막판까지 기다리지는 마시기 바랍니다.

[어휘]

performance review 인사 고과, 업무 평가 ｜ remind 기억나게 하다, 상기시키다 ｜ refer to ~와 관련이 있다 ｜ for the first time 처음으로 ｜ process 과정, 절차 ｜ fill out 내용을 채우다 ｜ handwrite 손으로 쓰다 ｜ opinion 의견 ｜ duty 임무, 업무 ｜ notable 주목할 만한 ｜ include 포함하다 ｜ retain 보유하다 ｜ let go 내보내다, 방출하다 ｜ regarding ~에 관하여 ｜ inquiry 질문 ｜ all day 하루 종일

154

[번역]

업무 평가에 관해 언급되지 않은 것은 무엇인가?

(A) 한 해의 일정 기간에만 해당되는 것이다.

(B) 손으로 작성되어야 한다.

(C) 직원들의 급여를 인상시켜야 하는지에 관해 언급해야 한다.

(D) 작성을 하는 사람들은 논평을 해야 한다.

[해설]

(A), (B), 그리고 (D)의 내용은 지문에 언급되어 있으나 급여 인상에 관한 작성 지침은 찾아볼 수 없으므로 정답은 (C)이다.

[어휘]

indicate 가리키다, 나타내다 ｜ raise (급여) 인상

155

[번역]

회람에 따르면, 어빙턴 씨는 10월 8일에 무엇을 할 것인가?

(A) 양식을 배포한다

(B) 회의에 참석한다

(C) 고과를 제출한다

(D) 양식들을 처리한다

[해설]

마지막 문장의 I'm going to be in meetings all day on Friday에서 어빙턴 씨는 고과 제출일인 금요일에 하루 종일 회의가 잡혀 있다고 했으므로 그가 10월 8일에 할 일은 회의에 참석하는 것이다.

[어휘]

pass out 나누어 주다, 배포하다 | process 처리하다

156

[번역]

[1], [2], [3], [4] 중에서 다음 문장이 들어갈 곳으로 가장 적합한 곳은 어디인가?

"후자를 선택하시는 경우에는, 반드시 본인의 입장을 글로서 설명하셔야 합니다."

(A) [1]

(B) [2]

(C) [3]

(D) [4]

[해설]

the latter option이 가리키는 것이 무엇인지 생각해 보면 정답을 쉽게 찾을 수 있다. 회람에서 언급되는 옵션은 '고용 유지'와 '퇴출'이므로 주어진 문장에서의 the latter option은 '퇴출'을 가리킨다. 따라서 (C)가 정답이다.

[어휘]

latter 후자의 | position 지위, 직위; 입장

157-159

[번역]

2015 국제 뉴스 미디어 컨퍼런스 이벤트 프로그램

9월 15일자 발표 일정

발표 주제	발표자	약력	장소
중동 지역의 언론의 자유	사-이드 알바자즈	아자만 데일리 신문 편집장 겸 발행인, 이라크	다이아몬드 홀 (2층)
뉴 디지털 미디어의 기회	테리 피더슨	VG 멀티미디어 전무이사, 노르웨이	루비 홀 (3층)
타블로이드 열광, 기회인가 위협인가	에이크 룬드	베를링스케 티덴데 선임 편집자, 덴마크	에메랄드 룸 (2층)
포토저널리즘과 새로운 시각 전략	장 무니에	AFP 프랑스 통신사 연합, 수석사진기자, 프랑스	사파이어 룸 (1층)

[어휘]

conference 협의회, 컨퍼런스 | presentation 발표 | topic 주제 | presenter 발표자 | biographical 전기의 | venue 개최지 | freedom 자유 | press 언론 | tabloid 타블로이드판 신문 | boom 벼락 경기, 붐 | threat 위협 | visual 시각의 | strategy 전략

157

[번역]

이 정보가 게재되기에 가장 적합한 곳은 어디이겠는가?

(A) 신문사 웹사이트

(B) 대학 교재

(C) 학교 게시판

(D) 컨퍼런스 정보지

[해설]

2015 International News Media Conference Event Program에서 컨퍼런스 행사 편성표임을 알 수 있으므로, 정답은 (D)이다.

[어휘]

textbook 교재 | bulletin board 게시판

158

[번역]

사진 관련 일을 하는 발표자는 누구인가?

(A) 사-이드 알바자즈

(B) 장 무니에

(C) 테리 피더슨

(D) 에이크 룬드

[해설]

질문의 키워드 photographs에 유념해 지문의 '약력'란을 살펴 보면, Head of Photography인 (B) Jean Mounier가 정답이다.

159

[번역]

테리 피더슨이 발표할 장소는 어디인가?

(A) 루비 홀

(B) 사파이어 룸

(C) 다이아몬드 홀

(D) 에메랄드 룸

[해설]

질문의 키워드 Terry Pedersen에 집중해서 지문의 '장소'를 살펴보면, Ruby Hall (3rd Floor)이다. 따라서 정답은 (A)이다.

160-161

[번역]

골드버그, 제너렉스 선임 부사장으로 다시 합류

허버트 골드버그는 12월 14일 제너렉스 비디오의 선임 부사장으로 합류할 예정입니다. 그는 제너렉스 비디오의 모든 활동을 책임짐과 동시에, 제너렉스 엔터테인트먼트 주식회사의 CEO인 랜스 브라운을 직속상관으로 모시게 됩니다. 그는 로스앤젤레스에서 근무할 예정입니다.

골드버그는 1997년 제너렉스 비디오에 입사하여, VIP 엔터테인트먼트 그룹의 국제판매부 부사장으로 옮기기 전까지 판매이사로 근무했습니다. 그는 제너렉스 비디오로 돌아오면서, 홈 비디오 분야를 책임지게 되었고 또한 12월 10일에 퇴사하는 조지 세인필드 선임 판매 부사장의 책무까지 위임 받을 예정입니다.

마케팅 부사장 수잔 휴잇과 투자관계 부사장 다니엘 림을 포함한
제너렉스의 몇몇 임원도 최근의 구조 조정 기간 동안 퇴사를 결정
했습니다.

[어휘]

rejoin 재결합하다, 다시 합류하다 | senior 선임의 | position 직(책) |
vice president(VP) 부사장 | effective 유효한, 효력 있는 |
responsibility 책임 | activity 활동 | report to ~의 직속이 되다, ~에게
보고하다 | be based in ~을 본거지로 삼다 | originally 원래 | serve
근무하다 | take over ~을 떠맡다 | inherit 상속하다 | depart 떠나다 |
several 몇몇 | executive 임원 | leave 떠나다 | restructuring
구조 조정

160

[번역]

허버트 골드버그에 대한 내용으로 짐작할 수 있는 것은 무엇인가?

(A) 그는 회사의 최연소 최고 경영자이다.

(B) 그는 새 부서를 책임진다.

(C) 그는 이전에 제너렉스에서 근무했었다.

(D) 그는 몇몇 산업 분야 상을 수상했다.

[해설]

제목인 Goldberg rejoins Generex as senior VP와 중반부의 Goldberg
originally joined Generex Video in 1997 and served as director of
sales before moving to the VIP Entertainment Group, where he was
the VP of International Sales에서 골드버그가 제너렉스에서 근무한 적
이 있음을 알 수 있다. 따라서 정답은 (C)이다.

[어휘]

youngest 가장 젊은 | division 부문 | industry 산업

161

[번역]

회사를 곧 떠난다고 알려지지 않은 사람은?

(A) 다니엘 림

(B) 수잔 휴잇

(C) 조지 세인필드

(D) 랜스 브라운

[해설]

보기와 지문 내용을 비교하며 '떠날 사람'을 소거해 나가야 한다.
George Seinfeld, who departs the company on December 10와
Several other Generex executives have chosen to leave the company
during the recent period of restructuring, including Marketing VP
Susan Hewitt and Investor Relations VP Daniel Lim을 보기와 비교하
면 (A), (B), (C)는 떠날 사람이다. 따라서 정답은 (D)이다.

162-164

[번역]

모든 환자분께 알립니다.
여러분의 건강 정보를 보호해 주는 연방법 상의 권리가 있습니다.

- 여러분은 여러분의 의료 기록 복사본을 요청할 수 있습니다.
  대체로 복사본은 15일 이내에 수령되어야 합니다. 복사본 요
  청 시 복사 비용이나 발송 비용을 여러분이 지불해야 할 수도
  있습니다.

- 여러분은 여러분의 의료 정보를 정정할 수 있습니다.
  여러분은 파일의 잘못된 정보를 바꾸거나 불충분한 정보를 채
  워 달라고 요청할 수 있습니다. 대부분의 경우 여러분의 요구
  가 있은 지 30일 이내에 변경되어야 합니다.

- 여러분은 여러분의 건강 정보가 어떻게 이용되는지 통제할 수
  있습니다.
  일반적으로 여러분이 특별 신청서에 서명하여 허가하지 않으
  면 누구도 귀하의 건강 정보를 사용한다거나 제 3자와 공유할
  수 없습니다.

이상은 연방 건강법으로 규정된 보호조항을 간단히 요약한 내용입
니다. www.hhs.gov/privacyinfo에 방문하시면 여러분의 권리
에 대해 더 많은 것을 알 수 있습니다.

[어휘]

notice 통지 | patient 환자 | right 권리 | federal law 연방법 |
ensure 확실하게 하다 | protection 보호 | medical record 의료 기록
| pay for 지불하다 | cost 비용 | request 요구 | correction 정정 |
wrong 잘못된 | add A to B A를 B에 추가하다 | incomplete 불완전한
| control 통제하다 | third parties 3자들 | permission 허가
| specific 특별한, 일정한 | authorization 허가 | brief 짧은 |
summary 요약

162

[번역]

이 공고의 목적은 무엇인가?

(A) 보험 조건에 대해 환자들을 상기시키기 위해

(B) 의료 기록의 복사본을 요청하기 위해

(C) 사람들에게 그들의 권리를 알려 주기 위해

(D) 정부 정책의 변경 내용을 알리기 위해

[해설]

지문의 목적을 묻는 문제는 대체로 전반부에 그 단서가 있다. You have
rights under federal laws that ensure the protection of your health
information에 '연방법에 의거 의료 정보를 보호하는 권리가 있다'는 내
용으로 보아 정답은 (C)이다.

[어휘]

remind 생각나게 하다, 상기시키다 | insurance requirements 보험 조건
| inform 알리다 | announce 알리다, 발표하다

163

[번역]

다른 사람이 여러분의 개인정보에 접근할 수 있는 방법은 무엇인가?

(A) 서식에 여러분의 서명을 요청해야 한다.

(B) 여러분의 고용인과 연락을 해야 한다.

(C) 관청을 방문해야 한다.

(D) 편지를 써야 한다.

[해설]

세부 내용을 묻는 문제는 보기와 지문 전체를 비교해야 답을 찾을 수
있다. 마지막 조항에 you give your permission by signing a specific
authorization form에 '일정 양식에 서명해서 허가해야만' 제 3자와 정
보를 공유할 수 있다는 내용이 나온다. 따라서 정답은 (A)이다.

164

[번역]

공고에 따르면, 추가 정보는 어디에서 받을 수 있는가?
(A) 안내책자에서
(B) 상담을 통해서
(C) 웹사이트에서
(D) 세미나에서

[해설]

추가 내용이나 보다 상세한 정보를 묻는 문제는 보통 후반부에서 답을 찾을 수 있다. You can learn more about your rights by visiting www. hhs.gov/privacyinfo에 'www.hhs.gov/privacyinfo를 방문하면 더 많은 권리를 알 수 있다'는 내용이 나온다.

[어휘]

brochure 안내책자 | consultation 상담

165-167

[번역]

> 받는 사람: 제리 암스트롱 〈jerrya@castawaytours.com〉
> 보낸 사람: 헬렌 앰블러 〈helenambler@homemail.com〉
> 제목: 감사합니다
> 날짜: 8월 23일
>
> 친애하는 암스트롱 씨께,
>
> 제 남편과 저는 지난 달에 귀하께서 예약해 주신 여행을 마치고 얼마 전 집으로 돌아왔습니다. 해 주신 모든 일에 큰 감사를 드립니다. 저희는 여행에서 일생 일대의 시간을 보냈으며, 이는 귀하와 캐스트어웨이 여행사의 직원 덕분이었습니다.
>
> 우리가 차를 대여해서 이탈리아 각지를 돌아다녀야 한다고 처음에 귀하가 제안을 했을 때, 저는 그것이 말도 안 되는 아이디어라고 생각했습니다. 하지만, 제 남편은 귀하가 이야기하는 것에 대해 귀하가 분명히 잘 알고 있을 것이라고 저를 설득시켰고, 그래서 저는 동의를 했습니다. 저는 두 분 모두가 옳았다는 것을 인정해야만 합니다; 믿을 수 없었습니다. 베니스에서 플로렌스와 로마로 비행을 하는 것보다, 운전을 함으로써, 우리는 그 나라의 많은 곳을 보게 되었습니다. 각 도시를 방문할 때마다 우리는 몇몇 작은 도시와 덜 알려진 역사적 장소를 돌아다닐 기회를 얻게 되었습니다. 심지어는 로마에서 북쪽으로 70킬로미터 정도 떨어진 작은 마을에서는 이제껏 먹어본 것 중 최고의 음식을 맛보기도 했습니다.
>
> 이번에 그처럼 멋진 시간을 보냈으므로 저희는 또 다른 유럽 여행에 대해 생각해 보고 있습니다. 스페인과 헝가리 중에서 결정을 내리지 못하고 있습니다. (저는 귀하께서 각각의 지역에 가 보셨다고 알고 있기 때문에, 어느 쪽을 더 선호하시나요?) 12월 말과 1월 초에 2주 동안 여행할 시간이 있을 것입니다. 기회가 되신다면, 저에게 전화를 주시면 제 남편과 제가 그러한 문제에 대해 논의할 수 있도록 귀하의 사무실을 방문하도록 하겠습니다.
>
> 헬렌 앰블러

[어휘]

book 예약하다 | time of one's life 일생 일대의 시간 | terrible 끔찍한 | convince 설득시키다 | go along with ~에 동의하다 | admit 인정하다 | incredible 믿을 수 없는, 멋진 | opportunity 기회 | explore 탐험하다 | historical site 역사적 장소 | tiny 작은

165

[번역]

앰블러 씨는 왜 이메일을 썼는가?
(A) 이전 행동에 대해 사과하기 위해
(B) 암스트롱 씨의 노고에 감사를 하기 위해
(C) 최근 여행에 대한 환불을 요구하기 위해
(D) 그녀의 납부액에 대해 논의하기 위해

[해설]

이메일의 첫 번째 단락에서 앰블러 씨는 암스트롱 씨 덕분에 여행이 즐거웠다는 점을 밝히고 그에게 감사의 인사를 건네고 있다. 따라서 정답은 (B)이다.

[어휘]

previous 이전의 | behavior 행동 | contribution 기여, 이바지

166

[번역]

엠블러 씨에 의하면, 그녀의 여행에 관해 사실인 것은 무엇인가?
(A) 그녀는 1개국 이상을 방문했다.
(B) 그녀는 가족 전체와 함께 여행을 했다.
(C) 그녀는 작은 마을의 호텔에 묵었다.
(D) 그녀는 여행 기간 동안 여행을 즐겼다.

[해설]

이메일의 두 번째 단락에서 앰블러 씨는 차로 이동함으로써 느낄 수 있었던 즐거움에 대해 이야기하고 있다. 따라서 정답은 (D)이다. 그녀가 작은 마을에 방문했다는 이야기는 찾을 수 있지만 그곳에서 숙박을 했다는 내용은 찾아볼 수 없으므로 (C)는 정답이 될 수 없다.

167

[번역]

[1], [2], [3], [4] 중에서 다음 문장이 들어갈 곳으로 가장 적합한 곳은 어디인가?
"저는 귀하께서 각각의 지역에 가 보셨다고 알고 있기 때문에, 어느 쪽을 더 선호하시나요?"
(A) [1]
(B) [2]
(C) [3]
(D) [4]

[해설]

each place가 스페인과 헝가리를 가리키고 있다는 점을 파악하면 정답은 (D)임을 쉽게 알 수 있다.

168-171

[번역]

수신: 헬렌 스파크스 〈h.sparks@freemail.com〉
발신: 마거릿 풀 〈clarkalbert@caresociety.com〉
제목: 회원제 정보
날짜: 3월 15일

스파크스 씨 귀하

암 연구 학회의 회원제에 대한 귀하의 질문에 감사 드립니다. 귀하께 암 연구 학회 회원 신청서를 보내드리게 되어 기쁩니다.

암 치료 및 완치 연구에 헌신하고 있는 과학자들로 구성된 세계 최대 규모 단체인 암 연구 학회에 가입하시기에 지금만큼 좋은 때도 없습니다. 회원이 되시면 최신 연구 소식과 최첨단 기술 관련 특집 기사를 제공하는 분기별 암 연구지 및 온라인 건강 저널 구독에 자동으로 등록됩니다. 또한 암 연구 학회의 각종 기금과 상을 받을 자격도 갖게 되며, 여러 과학 잡지 구독료도 할인해 드립니다.

저희 학회의 프로그램과 서비스에 대한 추가 정보를 신청서 양식 및 회원비 납부 양식과 함께 첨부해 드립니다. 회원 종류와 각종 혜택에 관한 보다 자세한 사항은 첨부한 정보지를 참고하시기 바랍니다. 신청서를 보내실 때 귀하의 이력서를 반드시 같이 넣어 주시기 바랍니다. 학생 회원을 신청하시는 경우에는, 학위 수여 기관의 재학 증명서도 필요합니다.

암 연구 학회에 대한 귀하의 관심에 다시 한 번 감사 드립니다.

마거릿 풀 드림
회원관리 담당자

[어휘]

Inquiry 질문, 문의 | regarding ~에 대한 | be pleased to ~하게 되어 기쁘다 | application 신청서 | organization 조직 | dedicated to ~에 헌신한 | treatment 치료, 취급 | ultimate 궁극적인 | cure 치유 | include 포함하다 | automatic 자동의 | subscription 구독 | quarterly 분기마다의 | provider 공급자 | state-of-the-art 최첨단의, 최신식의 | feature 주안점, 특집 | provide 공급하다, 제공하다 | eligibility for ~에 적격 | various 다양한 | grant 보조금 | award 상 | additional 추가의 | attached 첨부된 | along with ~와 함께 | payment 지불, 납부 | refer to ~을 참조하다 | fact sheet 개황 (정보) 보고서 | category 범주 | advantage 이점 | curriculum vitae 이력서 | accompany 동반하다, 동봉하다 | apply for ~을 신청하다 | proof 증거 | enrollment 입학 | degree-granting 학위를 수여하는 | institution 기관 | interest 관심

168

[번역]

스파크스 씨에게 본 이메일이 발송된 이유는?
(A) 그녀가 의학단체에 가입했다.
(B) 그녀가 온라인 잡지를 신청했다.
(C) 그녀가 어떤 정보를 요청했다.
(D) 그녀가 신청서를 제출했다.

[해설]

글의 목적을 묻는 Why 의문문이다. 전반부의 Thank you for your inquiry를 보면 이 이메일은 스파크스 씨(you, your)가 무엇인가 문의

했기 때문에 보내는 것임을 알 수 있다. 따라서 정답은 (C)이다.

[어휘]

organization 단체 | subscribe to 구독하다 | request 요청하다 | submit 제출하다

169

[번역]

암 연구 학회에 가입 시 생기는 혜택이 아닌 것은?
(A) 명예 학위 획득
(B) 과학 잡지 구독료 할인
(C) 인터넷 잡지 무료 이용
(D) 재정 혜택 수혜자로 고려

[해설]

'NOT'이 들어간 질문은 보기와 지문을 대조하며 답을 찾아야 한다. 중반부의 Your membership includes an automatic subscription to Cancer Research Quarterly and The Journal of Health Online은 Free access to an Internet journal로, Membership also provides eligibility for various grants는 Consideration for financial benefits로 바꿔 표현되었다. discounts on additional scientific journal subscriptions도 나와 있으므로 회원 가입 시 생기는 혜택이 '아닌' 것은 (A)이다.

[어휘]

obtainment 획득 | honorary 명예의 | access 이용 | consideration 고려(대상)

170

[번역]

정보지에 포함된 내용은 무엇인가?
(A) 회원 종류와 혜택
(B) 최신 의학 연구 결과
(C) 국제 컨퍼런스에 대한 세부 사항
(D) 주요 의학 출판물 목록

[해설]

질문의 키워드 fact sheet에 집중해서 지문을 살펴 보면, 후반부의 Please refer to the attached fact sheet for further details on membership categories and advantages에서 categories를 types로, advantages를 benefits로 달리 표현한 (A)가 정답이다.

[어휘]

type 종류 | benefit 혜택, 이익 | publication 출판

171

[번역]

스파크스 씨가 제출해야 하는 추가 서류는 무엇인가?
(A) 이력서
(B) 학위
(C) 연구 기사
(D) 의학 보고서

[해설]

글쓴이가 수신인(you → 스파크스 씨)에게 당부하는 내용을 찾아야 풀 수 있는 문제이다. 후반부의 Remember that your curriculum vitae must accompany your application에 '신청서를 제출할 때 이력서를 함께 보내라'는 내용이 있다. 따라서 정답은 (A)이다. curriculum vitae가 résumé와 같은 뜻임을 알아야 한다.

172-175

[번역]

> 모리스, 크리스   11:22 A.M.
> 수잔, 오늘 오찬 준비는 어떻게 되어가고 있나요?
>
> 앤더슨, 수잔   11:23 A.M.
> 매우 잘 되고 있어요. 밥과 조지가 모두 도착을 했고, 그들이 의자와 테이블을 준비하는 것을 도와 주고 있죠.
>
> 모리스, 크리스   11:25 A.M.
> 잘 되었군요. 당신에게 도움이 필요한지 그들에게 확인해 보라고 제가 말을 해 두었거든요. 그들이 당신에게 도움이 된다니 기쁘네요.
>
> 앤더슨, 수잔   11:25 A.M.
> 예, 모든 것이 앞으로 10분 이내에 준비가 될 거에요.
>
> 모리스, 크리스   11:26 A.M.
> 음식은 어떤가요? 모든 것이 그곳에 도착했나요?
>
> 앤더슨, 수잔   11:28 A.M.
> 줄리스 케이터링 사람들이 방금 전에 들어왔어요. 지금은 룸으로 음식을 나르고 있죠. 테이블 위에 음식을 차려야 하나요?
>
> 모리스, 크리스   11:30 A.M.
> 그렇게 하는 것이 낫겠어요. 점심 시간이 가까워졌으니까요. 케이크는 도착했나요?
>
> 앤더슨, 수잔   11:30 A.M.
> 무슨 케이크요?
>
> 모리스, 크리스   11:31 A.M.
> 베이크드 딜라이츠에서 주문한 것이요. 늦어도 11시 전에 누군가가 가져다 주기로 예정되어 있었는데요. 룸 안의 어딘가에 있을 거에요.
>
> 앤더슨, 수잔   11:34 A.M.
> 미안하지만, 크리스, 어디에도 케이크는 없어요. 그에 관해서는 제가 전혀 모르고 있군요. 딩신이 ㄱ 일을 맡는 것이 어때요?
>
> 모리스, 크리스   11:36 A.M.
> 그 편이 나을 것 같군요. 연락처를 퍼시에게 물어봐야겠어요. 그가 주문을 한 사람이니까요.

[어휘]

preparation 준비 ┃ luncheon 오찬, 점심 ┃ set up 설치하다, 준비하다 ┃ be of use 쓸모가 있다, 도움이 되다 ┃ might as well ~하는 편이 낫다 ┃ be supposed to ~하기로 되어 있다 ┃ drop off ~을 놓고 가다 ┃ no later than 늦어도 ~까지 ┃ take care of ~을 처리하다; ~을 돌보다 ┃ contact information 연락처

172

[번역]

모리스 씨는 왜 앤더슨 씨에게 연락을 했는가?
(A) 그녀에게 조언을 구하기 위해
(B) 도움을 부탁하기 위해
(C) 진행 상황을 보고받기 위해
(D) 그녀에게 주문을 하라고 말하기 위해

[해설]

모리스 씨는 앤더슨 씨에게 오찬 행사의 준비가 어떻게 되고 있는지, 음식은 어떤지, 케이크가 도착했는지 등에 관해 묻고 있다. 따라서 그가 연락을 취한 이유는 (C)로 볼 수 있다.

[어휘]

progress report 진행 상황 보고, 경과 보고

173

[번역]

모리스 씨는 밥과 조지에 대해 무엇을 암시하는가?
(A) 그 둘은 신입 직원이다.
(B) 그들 모두 케이터링 업체에서 일을 한다.
(C) 그는 그들에게 도움을 줄 것을 요청했다.
(D) 그들은 베이크드 딜라이츠에 고용되어 있다.

[해설]

I told them to see if you needed any assistance라는 말을 통해 모리스 씨가 두 사람에게 앤더슨 씨를 도우라고 지시했음을 알 수 있다. 따라서 정답은 (C)이다.

[어휘]

catering company 케이터링 업체, 음식 공급업체 ┃ provide 제공하다

174

[번역]

오전 11시 34분에 앤더슨 씨가 "Why don't you take care of it"이라고 쓴 의도는 무엇인가?
(A) 그녀에게는 모리스 씨의 요청을 들어 줄 시간이 없다.
(B) 모리스 씨는 그녀를 즉시 방문해야 한다.
(C) 모리스 씨는 베이크드 딜라이츠에게 전화를 걸어야 한다.
(D) 그녀는 오찬 행사 준비를 계속할 것이다.

[해설]

take care of는 '~을 처리하다' 혹은 '~을 담당하다'라는 뜻이다. 앤더슨 씨는 케이크에 관한 이야기를 듣지 못했다면서, 케이크와 관련된 업무를 모리스 씨에게 넘기고 있다.

[어휘]

fulfill 이행하다, 수행하다

175

[번역]

모리스 씨는 이다음에 아마도 무엇을 할 것인가?
(A) 케이크를 구입한다
(B) 동료와 이야기한다
(C) 줄리스 케이터링에 전화를 한다
(D) 밥과 조지에게 연락한다

[해설]

메신저의 마지막 부분에서 모리스 씨는 I'll have to ask Percy for the contact information이라고 말한다. 이를 통해 그는 퍼시라는 직원에게 케이크 업체의 연락처를 물어볼 것이라는 점이 예상되므로 정답은 (B)이다.

176-180

[번역]

> 다니엘 베이츠
> 타코마 애비뉴 502번지
> 워싱턴 시애틀 98104
>
> 베이츠 씨 귀하,
>
> 귀하의 5월 2일 예매에 감사 드립니다. 5월 27일자 백조의 호수 공연의 좌석예약이 확정되었음을 알려 드리며, 입장권 2매(B1 구역)를 동봉합니다. 입장권 내용이 귀하의 예매 내역과 맞는지 확인해 주시기 바랍니다.
>
> 아시다시피, 내셔널 시애틀 댄스 씨어터가 생긴 지 올해로 50년째입니다. 저희는 수십 년 동안 발레와 현대 무용 두 분야에서 세계 유명 댄스단의 수준과 맞먹는 우수한 공연을 보여드리는 데 초점을 맞추어 왔습니다. 이번 시즌에는 고전 발레와 현대 작품을 자랑스럽게 선보입니다. 저희는 삭제 없는 신데렐라, 호두까기 인형, 에스메랄다를 포함한 발레 총 34편을 개발했습니다. 이와 같이 다양한 경험을 제공함으로써, 저희는 관람객들의 광범위한 요구에 부응하는 풍성한 프로그램을 만들고 있습니다.
>
> 예매사항을 변경하고 싶으시면 555-3853번으로 제게 전화주시거나 dschulenberg@ndts.com으로 이메일을 보내주시고, 아니면 극장 메인 층에 있는 매표소를 방문해 주시기 바랍니다.
>
> 저희 공연에 대한 귀하의 관심에 다시 한 번 감사 드립니다. 내셔널 시애틀 댄스 씨어터에서 뵙겠습니다.
>
> 다이앤 슐렌버그 그림

[어휘]

pleasure 기쁨 | inform 알리다 | performance 공연 | confirmed 확인된 | enclosed 동봉된 | ensure 확실하게 하다 | in line with ~에 일치한, ~에 따른 | celebrate 축하하다 | anniversary 기념(일) | over the decades 수십 년간 | focus on ~에 초점을 맞추다 | offer 제공하다 | superior 우수한, 뛰어난 | on a par ~와 동등한, 같은 수준의 | troupe 극단 | ballet 발레 | contemporary dance 현대 무용 | proud 자랑스러운 | works 작품들 | develop 개발하다 | including ~을 포함해서 | full-length 삭제 없는 | diverse 다양한 | create 창작하다, 만들다 | enriching 풍부한 | audience 청중 | meet 만족시키다 | wide 광범위한 | range 범위

[번역]

> 수신: 다이앤 슐렌버그 〈dschulenberg@ndts.com〉
> 발신: 다니엘 베이츠 〈dbather88@freshmail.com〉
> 제목: 입장권 교환
> 날짜: 5월 9일
>
> 슐렌버그 씨 귀하
>
> 입장권을 보내 주셔서 감사합니다. 가능하다면 같은 공연의 5월 25일자 입장권으로 바꿀 수 있을까요? 그리고 한 장 더 예약하고 싶습니다. 그날 시외에 사는 제 친구 한 명이 저를 만나러 오기로

했는데, 그 친구가 그 발레를 상당히 좋아해서요. 입장권 교환이 가능한지 알려 주시기를 부탁 드립니다. 답변 기다리겠습니다.

> 다니엘 베이츠 드림

[어휘]

exchange A for B A를 B로 교환하다 | additional 추가의 | particular 특정한, 바로 그 | favorite 가장 좋아하는 것 | reply 회신, 답변

176

[번역]

편지의 목적은 무엇인가?
(A) 입장권을 예약하기 위해서
(B) 새로운 발레를 설명하기 위해서
(C) 요청에 응답하기 위해서
(D) 프로그램 변경을 알려주기 위해서

[해설]

글의 목적을 묻는 전반부형 질문이다. Thank you for your reservation request of May 2에서 수신인(you)이 요청했던 내용에 대한 답변임을 알 수 있다. 따라서 정답은 (C)이다.

[어휘]

reservation 예약 | describe 설명하다 | respond to 답하다

177

[번역]

예약을 변경하는 방법으로 언급된 내용이 아닌 것은 무엇인가?
(A) 팩스 보내기
(B) 담당자에게 이메일 보내기
(C) 사무실에 찾아가기
(D) 담당자에게 전화하기

[해설]

'NOT mentioned'는 보기와 지문을 대조하며 언급된 내용을 소거해 가면서 답을 찾는다. 첫 번째 지문 후반부의 please call me at 555-3853, e-mail me at dschulenberg@ndts.com, or visit our ticket office on the main level of the theater building에서 언급된 내용은 (D), (B), (C)이다. 따라서 정답은 (A)이다.

[어휘]

send 보내다 | representative 대표자, 대리인

178

[번역]

편지의 두 번째 단락 두 번째 줄의 "focused"와 의미상 가장 가까운 단어는?
(A) 집중했다
(B) 강화했다
(C) 반영했다
(D) 보았다

[해설]

각각의 보기를 focused 자리에 넣었을 때 앞뒤 맥락과 더불어 의미가 가장 적절한 단어는 '집중하다'라는 의미의 (A) concentrated이다.

[어휘]

concentrate on 집중하다 | enhance 향상시키다 | reflect 반사하다, 반
영하다 | view 보다

179

[번역]

다니엘 베이츠의 친구가 가장 좋아하는 발레는 무엇인가?

(A) 신데렐라
(B) 호두까기 인형
(C) 백조의 호수
(D) 에스메랄다

[해설]

이 문제는 두 개의 지문 내용을 연계해서 파악해야 해결할 수 있는 문
제이다. 첫 번째 지문은 극단 측에서 다니엘의 '백조의 호수' 입장권 예
매를 확인하고(your seat reservations for the May 27 performance of
Swan Lake have been confirmed) 입장권을 동봉한 내용이고, 두 번째
지문은 다니엘이 표를 한 장 더 구매하겠다는 내용인데 그 이유는 바
로 그 발레를 좋아하는 친구가 방문하기 때문이다(I have a friend who
will be visiting me that day from out of town, and that particular
ballet is her favorite). 이 맥락에서 보면, 다니엘의 친구가 특히 좋아하
는 발레는 (C) Swan Lake이다.

180

[번역]

베이츠 씨가 발레를 보려는 날짜는 언제인가?

(A) 5월 2일
(B) 5월 9일
(C) 5월 25일
(D) 5월 27일

[해설]

베이츠 씨가 쓴 이메일(두 번째 지문) 전반부의 If possible, would I be
able to exchange these tickets for the same performance on May 25?
에 '5월 25일자 공연 입장권으로 바꿀 수 있느냐'는 내용이 나온다. 따
라서 정답은 (C)이다. (A)는 예매한 날짜이고, (D)는 처음에 공연을 보
려 했던 날짜이다.

181-185

[번역]

스팍 주식회사에서 기술 담당 최고 책임자로 오랜 기간 근무해 온
알버트 영이 이번 7월에 은퇴할 예정이다. 현재 61세인 영은 스팍
에서 30년을 보낸 베테랑이다. 가장 최근에 영은 스팍이 아시아
시장으로 성공적인 진입을 하는 데 선두주자 역할을 했다.

이 다국적 컴퓨터 칩 생산 회사에서의 30년 근무 기간 중 18년 동
안 영은 최첨단 기술 개발에 전념했다. 스팍의 기술과 디자인 부서
수장으로서 영은 스팍의 최근 작품인 인테그라 시리즈 외에도 여
러 새로운 칩 디자인의 개발을 감독했다. 업계 전문가들은 현재 전
세계 칩 시장을 지배하는 스팍의 든든한 기반 마련을 영 덕택이라
생각하며 세계 컴퓨터 산업 발전에 대한 그의 공로는 5월 4일 샌
디에이고에서 열릴 시상식에서 인정받게 될 예정이다.

"알버트는 수년간 스팍의 성공에 힘쓴 주요 공헌자이며, 우리는 그
가 편안한 은퇴생활을 즐기길 바란다"고 스팍 CEO 리차드 베레타
는 발표했다. 영의 마지막 근무 일자는 7월 5일이다.

[어휘]

longtime 오랫동안의 | chief technology officer(CTO) 기술 담당
최고 책임자 | retire 은퇴하다 | veteran 베테랑 | recently 최근에 |
expansion 확장 | multinational 다국적의 | be devoted to 전념하다,
바치다 | cutting-edge 최첨단의 | division 부서 | oversee 감독하다 |
expert 전문가 | attribute A to B A를 B 덕택이라 여기다 | foundation
토대 | dominate 지배하다, 좌우하다 | global 전 세계의 | dedication
헌신 | advancement 발전, 진보 | industry 산업 | recognized
인정받는 | award ceremony 시상식 | contributor to ~의 공헌자 |
success 성공 | retirement 은퇴 | statement 진술, 성명(서)

[번역]

샌디에이고 상공회의소에서 진심으로 초대합니다

테렌스 켄트, 토마스 건축회사 CEO 님

주목할 만한 성과를 이룬 국제적인 기업인 및 선구자를 시상하는
제23회 연례 세계 기업인 시상식이
샌디에이고 웨스트 하버 드라이브 333번지
마르키스 호텔에서 5월 4일 오후 7시 30분에 개최됩니다.

정장 차림의 행사이며, 칵테일과 저녁을 제공합니다.
참가하실 분은 래리 갠더스에게 l.ganders@sdcc.org로
회답 바랍니다.

[어휘]

Chamber of Commerce 상공회의소 | cordially 정성껏 | annual
연간의 | honor 축하하다 | remarkable 두드러진 | accomplishment
성과, 업적 | international 국제의 | pioneer 개척자, 선구자 |
dress code 옷 규정 | formal 정장 차림의 | RSVP 회답 바람

181

[번역]

기사의 목적은 무엇인가?

(A) 사람들에게 신상품을 알리기 위해서
(B) 은퇴를 발표하기 위해서
(C) 마케팅 계획을 설명하기 위해서
(D) 직원 성과를 검토하기 위해서

[해설]

목적을 묻는 질문의 단서는 주로 전반부에 있다. 첫 번째 지문의 첫 문
장 Albert Young, Sparc Incorporated's longtime chief technology
officer, will retire this July에 장기간 근무했던 알버트 영이 7월에 은
퇴할 예정이라는 내용이 나오므로, 정답은 (B)이다.

[어휘]

inform 알리다 | product 제품 | announce 발표하다 | retirement
은퇴 | describe 설명하다 | employee 직원 | performance 업무,
성과 | review 검토하다

182

[번역]

영 씨가 경력을 통틀어서 가장 많은 시간을 할애했던 일은 무엇인가?

(A) 시장 확대
(B) 개발
(C) 생산
(D) 회계

186-190

[번역]

평가서
제럴즈 버거

저희 제럴즈 버거에서는 고객님들께 가능한 최고의 음식과 서비스를 제공해 드리기 위해 노력하고 있습니다. 잠시 시간을 내 주셔서 이 설문지의 질문에 답해 주시기 바랍니다. 완성하시면, 근무 중인 매니저에게 제출해 주십시오. 다음 제럴즈 버거 방문 때 사용이 가능한, 레귤러 사이즈의 감자 튀김이나 어니언 링의 무료 쿠폰을 받게 되실 것입니다.

Gerald's Burgers에서는…	매우 우수	우수	나쁨	매우 나쁨
음식의 맛		V		
음식의 신선도	V			
음식의 가격	V			
서비스의 질				V
서비스의 속도			V	

의견란: 저는 제럴즈 버거에 일주일에 한 번 가족들과 함께 오고 있습니다. 이곳 가격을 내릴 수는 없을 것입니다. 음식 또한 나쁘지 않습니다. 하지만 요새 서비스가 나빠지고 있습니다. 또한 저희가 평소에 방문하는 지점은 그다지 깨끗하지 않습니다. 저희는 조만간 해피 버거로 가기 시작할지도 모릅니다. 티나 웨덜리

[어휘]

strive to ~하려고 노력하다 | survey 설문 조사 | valid 유효한 | freshness 신선함 | these days 요즘, 최근에

[번역]

받는 사람: 팀 베일즈 〈timbales@geraldsburgers.com〉
보낸 사람: 리사 켄트웰 〈lisac@geraldsburgers.com〉
제목: 고객 평가
날짜: 8월 12일

팀,

7월 동안 진행된 설문 조사의 결과를 보았나요? 쥬디가 10분 전에 제게 수치를 보냈는데, 놀랍더군요. 우리는 예상과 달리 잘 하고 있지를 못해요. 그리고 우리 수익이 왜 올해 1분기와 2분기에 모두 하락했는지 제가 그 이유를 찾은 것 같아요.

전체적으로, 우리는 음식 가격에 대해서는 높은 점수를 받았어요. 하지만 우리는 우리가 전국에서 가장 저렴한 햄버거를 팔고 있다는 점은 이미 알고 있죠. 그러나 우리가 지점을 보유하고 있는 모든 주의 지점들마다, 우리가 제공하고 있는 서비스에 대해서는 형편없는 평가를 받았어요. 많은 의견들은 우리 직원들이 고객들을 얼마나 무례하게 대접하고 있는지, 그리고 그들이 얼마나 느리게 일을 하고 있는지에 초점을 맞추고 있었죠. 그리고 우리 지점들이 얼마나 더러운지에 관해서도 자발적으로 제시한 의견들이 많았고요.

[해설]

첫 번째 지문의 세 번째 문장인 For 18 of his 30 years at the multinational computer chip maker, Young was devoted to the development of cutting-edge technologies에 '30년 중에 18년을 최첨단 기술 개발에 전념했다'는 내용이 나온다. 따라서 정답은 (B)이다.

[어휘]

expansion 확대, 확산 | production 생산 | accounting 회계, 경리

183

[번역]

기사의 첫 번째 단락 여섯 번째 줄의 "oversaw"와 의미상 가장 가까운 단어는?

(A) 감독했다

(B) 훑어봤다

(C) 검토했다

(D) 간과했다

[해설]

oversaw는 '감독하다'라는 의미인데 the development of several new chip designs를 목적어로 취해 유사한 의미를 형성할 수 있는 것은 (A) supervised이다.

[어휘]

supervise 감독하다 | glance 힐끗 보다, 훑어보다 | review 검토하다, 조사하다 | overlook 간과하다

184

[번역]

영 씨는 마르키스 호텔에서 무엇을 할 것으로 보이는가?

(A) 발표를 한다.

(B) 신상품을 소개한다.

(C) 저녁 행사의 사회를 본다.

(D) 상을 받는다.

[해설]

두 지문의 내용을 모두 이해해야 풀 수 있는 문제이다. 첫 번째 지문, 첫 번째 단락 마지막의 his dedication to the advancement of global computer industry will be recognized at an award ceremony to be held in San Diego on May 4는 '샌디에이고에서 5월 4일에 열릴 시상식에서 영의 업적이 인정받을 것'이라는 내용이고, 두 번째 지문은 그 시상식(개최지: 마르키스 호텔)의 초대장임을 알 수 있다. 따라서 문제의 정답은 (D)이다.

[어휘]

deliver a presentation 발표하다 | host 주최하다 | receive 받다 | award 상

185

[번역]

테렌스 켄트는 누구인가?

(A) 회의소 대표

(B) 회사 최고 경영자

(C) 호텔 매니저

(D) 칩 디자이너

[해설]

테렌스 켄트는 초대장을 받는 사람이다. 두 번째 지문 전반부의

저는 우리 매장을 위한 새로운 가이드라인를 만들기 위해 당신에게 위원회의 책임을 맡길게요. 가맹점주들이 우리에게 곧 연락을 취할 것이고, 우리는 지금 당장 그들을 위한 해답을 가지고 있어야 해요. 늦어도 이번 주 금요일까지는 당신으로부터 무언가가 나와야 해요.

리사

[어휘]

stunning 놀라운 ┃ revenue 수입 ┃ decline 쇠퇴하다 ┃ focus upon ~에 초점을 맞추다 ┃ treat 대접하다; 취급하다 ┃ unsolicited 원치 않는; 자발적인

[번역]

받는 사람: 제럴즈 버거의 전 가맹점주
보낸 사람: 부사장 리사 캔트웰
제목: 새로운 가이드라인
날짜: 8월 20일

최신 설문 조사의 결과를 검토한 후, 저희 Gerald's Burgers는 사업 방식에 있어서 몇 가지 변화를 주기로 결정했습니다. 아래 규칙들은 즉시 효력을 갖습니다:

* 모든 종업원들은 근무시간 한 시간마다 10분간 매장을 청소해야 한다. 여기에는 화장실과 식음 공간 청소가 포함된다.

* 모든 종업원들은 화장실 사용 후 1분간 온수와 비누로 손을 씻어야 한다. 그렇게 하지 않은 종업원은 그 즉시 해고될 것이다.

* 모든 종업원들은 고객 서비스에 관한 3시간짜리 유급 수업을 들어야 한다.

* 모든 매니저들은 고객 관리에 관한 2시간짜리 유급 수업을 들어야 한다.

이들은 몇 가지 변화 중 첫 번째가 될 것입니다. 저희는 앞으로 며칠 후에 회람을 더 보내 드릴 것입니다. 또한 본사에서 나온 직원들이 늦어도 8월 31일까지 어러분과 만날 약속을 잡을 것입니다. 제럴즈 버거를 다시 한 번 국내 제일의 햄버거 매장으로 만드는 것이 저희의 목표입니다.

[어휘]

institute 도입하다, (방침 등을) 세우다 ┃ in effect 효력이 있는 ┃ representative 대표; 직원 ┃ arrange to meet 만날 약속을 정하다

186

[번역]

평가서에 따르면, 고객에 대해 암시되어 있는 것은 무엇인가?
(A) 그녀는 제럴즈 버거의 가격이 높다고 생각한다.
(B) 그녀는 매주 해피 버거를 방문한다.
(C) 그녀는 제럴즈 버거의 서비스에 만족하지 못하고 있다.
(D) 그녀는 해피 버거의 지점이 더럽다고 생각한다.

[해설]

첫 번째 지문의 의견란(Comments)를 살펴보면 정답을 찾을 수 있다. 그녀는 서비스가 좋지 못하고 매장이 청결하지 못하다고 불만을 표시하고 있다.

187

[번역]

이메일에서, 두 번째 단락 세 번째 줄의 "marks"라는 단어의 의미와 가장 가까운 것은?
(A) 결과
(B) 제안
(C) 논평
(D) 반응

[해설]

mark는 원래 '표시'라는 뜻이지만 여기서는 서비스에 대한 평가 결과를 나타내기 위해 사용되었다. 따라서 mark의 의미는 (A) results와 가장 가깝다고 볼 수 있다.

188

[번역]

캔트웰 씨는 베일즈 씨에게 무엇을 할 것을 요청하는가?
(A) 중요한 가맹점주들에게 연락한다
(B) 매장의 고객들과 이야기를 나눈다
(C) 문제를 해결하기 위한 그룹을 이끈다
(D) 금요일에 그녀의 사무실에서 그녀와 만난다

[해설]

이메일 마지막 단락의 I'm putting you in charge of a committee to come up with some new guidelines for our stores.라는 말에서 캔트웰 씨는 베일즈 씨에게 가이드라인 작성을 위한 위원회의 책임을 맡기고 있다.

[어휘]

leading 선도적인, 가장 중요한 ┃ dedicate 헌신하다

189

[번역]

새 규정들은 제럴즈 버거에 관한 어떤 불만 사항을 다루지 않고 있는가?
(A) 매장의 청결도
(B) 직원들이 제공하는 서비스
(C) 고객과 직원과의 관계
(D) 고객들이 일하는 속도

[해설]

가이드라인 중 (A)는 첫 번째와 두 번째 항목에서, (B)는 세 번째 항목에서, 그리고 (C)는 네 번째 항목에서 다루어지고 있으나 (D)를 언급하고 있는 항목은 찾아볼 수 없다.

[어휘]

cleanliness 청결 ┃ relation 관계

190

[번역]

캔트웰 씨는 회람에서 무엇을 언급하는가?
(A) 종업원들은 규칙을 따르지 않았다는 이유로 일자리를 잃을 수 있다.
(B) 그녀는 8월 31일에 본사에서 회의를 개최할 것이다.
(C) 회사에서 더 이상의 변화는 없을 것이다.
(D) 제럴즈 버거는 곧 새로운 지점을 개설할 것이다.

회람의 두 번째 항목 중 '손을 씻지 않은 직원은 즉시 해고될 것이다 (Those who do not will be fired immediately.)'라는 문구를 통해 종업원들이 해고될 수 있음을 경고하고 있다.

191-195

[번역]

> 리치몬드 (4월 17일) – 리치몬드 시장인 스탠리 로렌스는 기자 회견에서 기업들을 시내로 유치할 수 있기를 바란다고 발표했다. 그는 리치몬드 시가 10명 이상의 지역 주민을 정규직으로 고용하고 있는 기업에게 세금 혜택을 제공할 것이라고 말했다. 리치몬드의 세금은 주의 대다수 도시에서보다 높다. 하지만 로렌스 시장은 앞으로 그러한 점을 변화시키겠다는 목표를 가지고 있다.
>
> 로렌스 시장은 또한 리치몬드에서 매장을 개설하려는 기업들이 관료적 형식주의에 대처할 필요가 없을 것이라고 언급했다. 그는 사업체 설립 절차와 필요한 라이선스 취득 및 용도 승인 절차도 간소화시킬 생각이다. 이는 최근 몇 년 동안 많은 기업들과 개인들이 소리 높여 불만을 제기해왔던 사항이다.
>
> 마지막으로, 시장은 시 소유의 토지를 리치몬드에서 매장이나 사업체를 개설하겠다는 협정에 서명한 기업들에게 시세 보다 낮은 금액으로 매각할 것이라고 말했다. 시는 시내 중심가에 막대한 양의 토지를 소유하고 있으며, 그중 일부는 매우 좋은 입지에 위치해 있다. 현재, 그러한 토지는 사용되고 있지 않지만, 로렌스 시장이 자신의 생각을 관철시킨다면, 조만간 매각되어 건물이 들어설 것이다.

[어휘]

mayor 시장 | press conference 기자 회견 | encourage 격려하다. 고무시키다 | tax incentive 세금 혜택, 감세 조치 | full-time position 정규직 | aim to ~을 목표로 삼다 | bureaucratic red tape 관료적 형식주의 | streamline 간소화하다 | license 면허, 라이선스 | zoning permit (건물 등의) 용도 승인 | desirable 바람직한; 가치 있는 | have one's way 자신의 뜻대로 하다, 자기의 뜻을 관철시키다

[번역]

> ### 리치몬드 최고의 건설사인 윌슨 건설에 입사 지원을 하십시오,
>
> 최근 리치몬드 시에서 건설 붐이 일어나고 있으며, 여러분은 그 일부가 될 수 있습니다. 윌슨 건설이 현재 직원을 채용하고 있습니다. 지원이 가능한 직종의 몇 가지 예를 알려 드립니다.
>
> **건설 인부**: 2년 경력 필요. 지시 사항을 따르고 팀과 어울려 일을 할 수 있어야 함. 시급으로 계산. 초과 수당 지급. 경력에 따라 급여 결정
>
> **접수 직원**: 경력 무관. 직업 교육을 받을 수 있음. 상냥한 성격을 가지고 있어야 함. 업무에는 방문객을 맞이하고, 전화를 받고, 메시지를 남기는 일이 포함됨. 인간 관계 능력이 우수해야 함. 정규직.
>
> **목수**: 5년 경력 필요. 면접에서 기본적인 테스트에 통과해야 함. 세세한 점에 대한 날카로운 안목이 필요. 정규직. 기본급 이외에 초과 수당 및 성과급이 지급될 수 있음.

> **트럭 기사**: 상용차 운전 면허증을 보유하고 있어야 함. 운전 경력에 사고 기록이 없어야 함. 정규직. 18세 이상이어야 함. 경력 무관.
>
> 저희 웹사이트(www.wilsonconstruction.com)를 방문하셔서 위와 같은 직종이나 기타 직종에 지원하십시오. 건설업에서 귀하의 경력을 쌓으십시오.

[어휘]

boom 호황, 붐 | opportunity 기회 | performance bonus 성과금 | commercial 상업의

[번역]

> 5월 24일
>
> 친애하는 코린스 씨께,
>
> 로버트슨 씨와 저는 5월 22일 면접에서 귀하에게 매우 깊은 인상을 받았습니다. 저희는 귀하께서 모든 입사 지원자 중 가장 높은 점수로서 실기 테스트를 합격하셨다는 점을 아셨으면 합니다. 그 결과, 저희는 귀하에게 윌슨 건설에서의 취업을 제안하고자 합니다.
>
> 저희 제안을 받아드리시면, 귀하께서는 내일부터라도 일을 시작하실 수 있습니다. 실제로, 저는 그렇게 되기를 바랍니다. 현재 진행 중인 프로젝트가 많아서, 저희는 구할 수 있는 인력이 모두 필요합니다. 근무 시간 중 405-6586으로 제게 전화를 하셔서 회신을 하시면 됩니다.
>
> 급여에 대해 말씀을 드리면, 귀하께서는 초봉으로 55,000달러를 받게 되실 것입니다. 시간당 34달러의 비율로 초과 근무 수당도 받게 되실 것입니다. 보너스를 받으시는 경우에는, 귀하께서 하신 업무의 질과 프로젝트가 완성된 속도에 근거하여 금액이 결정될 것입니다.
>
> 귀하로부터 긍정적인 대답을 듣기를 고대하고 있겠습니다.
>
> 제프리 윌슨 드림
> 윌슨 건설 대표

[어휘]

numerous 많은 | manpower 인력 | response 대답, 회신 | as for ~에 대해 말하자면 | at the rate of ~의 비율로 | depend upon ~에 좌우되다

191

[번역]

기사에 의하면, 로렌스 씨에 대해 사실인 것은 무엇인가?
(A) 그는 얼마 전에 리치몬드 시장으로 선출되었다.
(B) 그는 리치몬드의 기업가이다.
(C) 그는 기업들을 리치몬드에 유치하기를 바란다.
(D) 그는 평생 리치몬드에서 살고 있다.

[해설]

기사 초반부에 '그가 기업 유치를 희망한다(he hopes to encourage businesses to come to the city)'는 내용을 찾아볼 수 있으므로 정답은 (C)이다.

192

[번역]

기사에서, 두 번째 단락 세 번째 줄의 "streamline"이라는 단어의 의미와 가장 가까운 것은?

(A) 줄이다

(B) 검사하다

(C) 고려하다

(D) 단순화하다

[해설]

streamline은 '간소화하다' 또는 '효율화하다'라는 의미이다. 따라서 보기 중 이 단어와 가장 의미가 가까운 것은 '단순화하다'라는 의미의 (D) simplify이다.

[어휘]

reduce 줄이다, 감소시키다 ┃ simplify 단순화하다, 간소화하다

193

[번역]

접수 직원에 대해 언급되지 않은 것은 무엇인가?

(A) 근무 중에 전화 통화를 하게 될 것이다.

(B) 정규직 업무를 수반할 것이다.

(C) 경력이 필요하지 않다.

(D) 외국어 능력이 우대된다.

[해설]

광고에서 접수 직원(receptionist position) 항목을 살피면 정답을 쉽게 찾을 수 있다. (D)의 '외국어 능력'에 대해서는 전혀 언급된 바가 없기 때문에 정답은 (D)이다.

194

[번역]

코린스 씨는 어떤 직종에 지원했는가?

(A) 목수

(B) 트럭 기사

(C) 접수 직원

(D) 건설 인부

[해설]

이메일 초반부에 '코린스 씨가 실기 테스트에 통과했다(you passed the skills test)'는 내용이 나오는데, 채용 공고에서 테스트를 언급하고 있는 직종은 Carpenter 뿐이므로 정답은 (A)이다.

195

[번역]

윌슨 씨는 코린스 씨가 언제 일을 시작하기를 바라는가?

(A) 4월 17일

(B) 5월 24일

(C) 5월 25일

(D) 6월 1일

[해설]

이메일에서 윌슨 씨는 '코린스 씨가 내일부터라도 일을 시작할 수 있다(you can start working as soon as tomorrow)'고 말한 후, 본인은 그렇게 되기를 희망한다고 언급한다. 편지가 작성된 날짜가 5월 24일이므로, 두 가지 사항을 종합하면 윌슨 씨가 원하는 날짜는 (C) '5월 25일'임을 알 수 있다.

196-200

[번역]

머레이 학회
글로벌 마케팅에 관한 일일 세미나
10월 12일, 토요일

시간	강사	제목
오전 9시 – 오전 10시 40분	로저 잭슨	글로벌 마케팅의 법적인 측면
오전 11시 – 오후 12시	제이슨 로렐	해외 지점을 마케팅하는 법
오후 1시 – 오후 2시 20분	안드레아 카터	소셜 미디어와 글로벌 마케팅
오후 2시 30분 – 오후 4시 20분	마커스 리우	해외에서의 TV 광고
오후 4시 30분 – 오후 6시	케이트 맥도웰	해외에서 수익 내기

모든 강사들은 해당 분야에서 저명하고 존경을 받는 분들입니다. 이용하실 수 있는 좌석이 150석뿐이므로, 오늘 예약을 하십시오. 더 많은 정보를 알고 싶으시면 www.murrayinstitute.com을 방문하시거나 609-4400으로 전화를 주십시오. 수강료는 250달러입니다. 죄송하지만 환불은 되지 않습니다.

[어휘]

institute 학회 ┃ legal 법적인 ┃ profit 이윤, 이익 ┃ field 들판; 분야 ┃ fee 요금

[번역]

받는 사람: 마케팅부 전 직원
보낸 사람: 글로리아 마이어스
제목: 머레이 학회 세미나
날짜: 9월 29일

저는 머레이 학회에서 지금부터 2주 후에 글로벌 마케팅에 관한 세미나를 개최할 것이라는 점을 최근에 알게 되었습니다. 우리가 올해 첫 번째 해외 매장을 개설했기 때문에, 저는 우리가 이번 세미나에 참석함으로써 많은 것을 배울 수 있을 것이라고 생각합니다. 제가 이 회람에 첨부해 둔 시간표를 살펴 보십시오. 강의들 중 흥미가 가는 것이 있다면, 저는 여러분들이 세미나에 참석할 것을 강력히 추천합니다.

저는 총무부의 로드 그로버와 이야기를 나누었는데, 그는 참석을 원하는 모든 마케팅부 직원에게 등록비를 지원해 줄 것이라고 말했습니다. 하지만, 제가 머레이 학회에 전화를 걸어보니, 그곳 담당자는 남아 있는 자리가 20석밖에 없다고 제게 말해 주었습니다.

그러니 참석에 흥미가 있다면, 늦어도 오늘 오후 5시까지 제게 알려 주십시오. 그러면 제가 전화를 걸어서 예약을 하겠습니다. 저는 참석할 계획이며, 이탈리아, 인도, 그리고 러시아의 벤처 사업과 관련된 분들께서도 참석하시기를 바랍니다.

[어휘]

lecture 강연, 강의 ┃ administration office 총무국, 총무부 ┃ involved in ~과 관련이 있는 ┃ venture 벤처 사업

[번역]

받는 사람: 글로리아 마이어스 〈gmyers@htd.com〉
보낸 사람: 스튜어트 모리스 〈stewart_m@htd.com〉
제목: 글로벌 마케팅 세미나
날짜: 9월 29일

친애하는 마이어스 씨께,

저는 마케팅부의 스튜어트 모리스입니다. 머레이 학회가 후원하는, 곧 있을 세미나에 대해 제게 알려 주셔서 매우 감사합니다. 저는 예전에 그들의 특별 행사에 3번 참석한 적이 있지만, 이번 행사에 대해서는 모르고 있었습니다. 저는 시간표를 보고 참석에 흥미를 갖게 되었습니다. 저는 안드레아 카터가 연설하는 것을 정말로 듣고 싶습니다.

저는 당신이 저를 위해 예약을 해 주셨으면 합니다. 하지만, 제가 마지막 강연에는 참석하지 못할 것이라는 점을 알려 드려야 할 것 같습니다. 저는 오후 8시에 러시아의 모스크바로 떠날 예정이어서, 늦어도 5시까지는 공항으로 출발해야 합니다. 제가 맥도웰 씨의 강연을 듣지 못하는 것이 문제가 될까요? 그것이 문제가 되지 않는다면, 이번 행사에 저를 위해 예약을 해 주시기 바랍니다.

스튜어트 모리스 드림

[어휘]

upcoming 다가 오는, 곧 있을 | sponsor 후원하다 | be unaware of ~에 대해 모르다 | be scheduled to ~하기로 예정되어 있다 | fail to ~하지 못하다 | issue 문제; 화제

196

[번역]

세미나에 대해 사실이 아닌 것은 무엇인가?
(A) 다른 사람들에게 알려진 연사들을 내세운다.
(B) 하루 동안 진행될 것이다.
(C) 좌석 수가 제한되어 있다.
(D) 온라인으로만 등록할 수 있다.

[해설]

첫 번째 지문을 살펴보면 정답을 쉽게 찾을 수 있다. 연사들이 유명한 사람들이라고 했으므로 (A)는 사실인 내용이며, One-Day Seminar라는 타이틀을 통해 (B) 또한 맞는 내용임을 알 수 있다. 좌석이 150개뿐이라고 했으므로 (C) 역시 언급된 사항이다. 하지만 등록 방법에 대해서는 언급된 바가 없으므로 정답은 (D)이다.

[어휘]

feature ~을 특징으로 삼다

197

[번역]

회람의 목적은 무엇인가?
(A) 직원들에게 세미나를 알리기 위해
(B) 직원들이 행사에 참여한다고 주장하기 위해
(C) 다가 올 회사의 세미나를 홍보하기 위해
(D) 직원들이 마케팅에 집중하도록 격려하기 위해

[해설]

회람은 직원들에게 머레이 학회의 세미나를 알리고 참여를 독려하고 있다. 따라서 정답은 (A)이다. 세미나 참석은 장려 사항일 뿐 강제 사항은 아니므로 (B)를 정답으로 보기에는 무리가 있다.

[어휘]

insist 주장하다   focus on ~에 집중하다, ~에 초점을 맞추다

198

[번역]

마이어스 씨는 사람들에게 무엇을 할 것을 요청하는가?
(A) 그녀의 사무실에서 브로셔를 가지고 간다
(B) 그녀에게 신청서를 준다
(C) 행사 참여에 관해 그녀에게 연락을 한다
(D) 등록비를 미리 지불한다

[해설]

두 번째 지문인 회람에서 Myers 씨는 남아 있는 좌석이 몇 개 없으므로 5시까지 참석 여부를 알려 주면 자신이 대신 예약을 하겠다고 말한다. 따라서 정답은 (C)이다.

199

[번역]

모리스 씨는 어떤 제목의 강연에 참석하고 싶어하는가?
(A) 소셜 미디어와 글로벌 마케팅
(B) 해외 지점을 마케팅하는 법
(C) 해외에서 수익 내기
(D) 해외에서의 TV 광고

[해설]

세 번째 지문인 이메일에서 모리스 씨는 I would love to hear Andrea Carter speak.라고 말한다. 따라서 그가 듣고 싶어하는 Andrea Carter의 강연을 첫 번째 지문의 표에서 찾아보면, 그녀의 강연 타이틀이 Social Media and Global Marketing임을 알 수 있다.

200

[번역]

모리스 씨에 대해 암시되는 것은 무엇인가?
(A) 그는 회사 업무 때문에 러시아에 갈 것이다.
(B) 그는 때로로 마케팅에 관한 강연을 한다.
(C) 그는 예전에 맥도웰 씨를 만난 적이 있다.
(D) 그는 종종 해외로 여행을 떠난다.

[해설]

이메일에서 모리스 씨는 세미나의 마지막 강연은 듣지 못할 것이라고 말한 후, I am scheduled to fly to Moscow, Russia, at 8:00 P.M., so I have to leave for the airport no later than 5:00.라고 그 이유를 밝히고 있다.

단기간에 실전 적응력 배양

LC와 RC를 20일 만에 학습할 수 있도록 구성되어 있어서
단기간의 학습을 통해 실제 시험에 대비할 수 있습니다.

문제 유형에 따른 집중 훈련

LC의 경우 매일 Part 1에서 Part 4까지의 모든 유형의 문제를 풀어 보고
RC의 경우 시험에 꼭 나오는 문법 사항들과 연습 문제들을 학습하면서
단기간의 집중 훈련을 통해 빠른 실력 향상을 기대할 수 있습니다.

최신 경향이 반영된 적중 예상 문제 수록

기출 문제를 분석하여 엄선한 연습 문제와 LC와 RC에 각각 포함되어 있는
1회분의 모의고사를 풀어 보면서 실제 시험에 대한 자신감을 얻을 수 있습니다.